The *Stage*

and the *School*

Ninth Edition

Harry H. Schanker
Katharine Anne Ommanney

Mc Graw Hill **Glencoe**

New York, New York   Columbus, Ohio   Chicago, Illinois   Peoria, Illinois   Woodland Hills, California

 **Glencoe**

The *McGraw·Hill* Companies

Copyright © 2005 by The McGraw-Hill Companies, Inc.
All rights reserved. Copyright © 1999, 1989, 1982, 1972, 1960, 1950, 1939, 1932 by
the McGraw-Hill Companies, Inc. All rights reserved. Printed in the United States of
America. Except as permitted under the United States Copyright Act of 1976, no part
of this publication may be reproduced or distributed in any form or by any means, or
stored in a database or retrieval system, without the prior written permission of the
publisher.

Send all inquiries to
Glencoe/McGraw-Hill
8787 Orion Place
Columbus, OH 43240

ISBN 0-07-861627-1

9 10 11 12 110/043 12 11 10 09

About the Author

HARRY H. SCHANKER is an award-winning teacher-director of high school drama with extensive training and experience in all its phases, from the classroom to mainstage production. He taught English, speech, drama, and stagecraft in the Denver Public Schools for almost four decades, including twenty-nine years at Thomas Jefferson High School. Upon his retirement, the auditorium at Thomas Jefferson High School was renamed in his honor. During his career Mr. Schanker served as producer, director, and technical director for more than two hundred productions.

A devoted student of the theater, Mr. Schanker earned a B.S. degree in language arts from the University of Kansas and an M.S. degree in secondary education from the University of Colorado. His achievements as an educator are widely recognized. He has received the Distinguished Teacher Award and twice received honorable mention as Colorado Teacher of the Year. In 1992 he received the "A+ for Teachers" award from KCNC-TV and in 1994 was named Colorado Theatre Educator of the Year. He is listed in *Who's Who in American Education.*

As the originator of the summer theater program in Denver schools, Mr. Schanker served as director and technical director for many of the summer high school theater productions as well as the middle school and elementary school programs. He served as state director of the International Thespian Society for two years. Since 1975 Mr. Schanker has served on the Board of Directors of Colorado Youth Citizenship Awards and is currently on the board of the Town Hall Arts Center.

Mr. Schanker is also the author of *Dramatic Comedy,* an anthology of classic comedies and a part of the McGraw-Hill Patterns in Literary Arts series, and *The Spoken Word,* a McGraw-Hill speech text. Since retiring from public school teaching, Mr. Schanker has continued to direct high school productions, lead workshops, and teach in a private acting school.

Dedication

KATHARINE ANNE OMMANNEY, to whom this edition is dedicated, died in 1983. She was a pioneer in educational dramatics, writing the first edition of *The Stage and the School* in 1932. In addition to teaching high school dramatics for a quarter of a century, she taught and lectured at the university level, acted on the stage and in radio, and directed all types of professional productions. Her credentials include an M.A. from Stanford University as well as study at the Royal Academy of Dramatic Art in England and the American Academy of Dramatic Art.

Ms. Ommanney received numerous honors during her lifetime, including The Founders' Award from the SSTA Secondary Division of ATA and listings in *Who's Who of American Women* and *Leaders in Education.* During her retirement she was active in the theater of Hawaii. The Maui Community Theater's annual Kitty Awards were established in her honor.

Teacher Reviewers

We gratefully acknowledge the contributions of the theater educators throughout the United States who have consulted with us in the development of *The Stage and the School.*

Beatrice Bush
English and Drama Teacher
Thomas Jefferson High School
Richmond City Public Shools
Richmond, Virginia

Clifford H. Langford
Theatre Department Chair
Hall High School
Little Rock School District
Little Rock, Arkansas

Howard McMillan
Associate Professor of English
Indiana State University
Terre Haute, Indiana

Karen C. Paisley
Theatre Arts Department Chair
Bandys High School
Catawba County Schools
Catawba, North Carolina

H. Thomas Prill
Teacher of Drama, Speech, English,
  and Radio-TV
Jefferson High School
Lafayette School Corporation
Lafayette, Indiana

Robert M. Singleton
Theatre Coordinator
High School for the Performing and
  Visual Arts
Houston Independent School District
Houston, Texas

Karen Smith-Meyer
Associate Professor, Drama/Theatre
  for the Young Program
Eastern Michigan University
Ypsilanti, Michigan

Billie Stultz
Drama Teacher and Drama Department
  Head
Jenks High School
Jenks Public Schools
Jenks, Oklahoma

John Sullivan
Drama Coach and Animation Teacher
Barnstable High School
Hyannis, Massachusetts

JoAnn H. Taylor
Theatre Teacher
Avery County High School
Avery County
Newland, North Carolina

Martin W. Walsh, Ph.D. Cantab
Professor, Department of Theater and
  Drama, Residential College
University of Michigan
Ann Arbor, Michigan

Stephen A. Wolf
Design and Technical Theater Coordinator
High School for the Performing and
  Visual Arts
Houston Independent School District
Houston, Texas

Susan L. Wurster
Director of Drama/Speech
The Calhoun School
New York, New York

iv

Table of Contents

Table of Contents

PART TWO
A Treasury of Scenes and Monologues

Table of Contents

ELIZABETHAN THEATER

Table of Contents

Table of Contents

How to Use This Book

The notes and features in *The Stage and the School* are your entryway to the world of the theater. As you use these notes and features, you'll learn about aspects of the theater that you've grown to love. You'll also practice and master the skills that theater professionals use in their work.

Get Ready to Learn

Chapter Opener pages use engaging photos and informative captions to introduce you to the chapter topic.

5 The Structure of Drama

In this scene early in Shakespeare's *Romeo and Juliet*, the two main characters, children from feuding families, meet and fall in love. The situations that arise from this initial incident provide the action in this classic tragedy.

Drama is life with the dull bits cut out.

—ALFRED HITCHCOCK, DIRECTOR

SETTING THE SCENE

Focus Questions

What are the narrative essentials of a written play?
What influence has Aristotle had on drama?
How does modern drama differ from traditional drama?
What does the exposition of a play reveal?
How is a plot divided into parts?
How do playwrights create characters?
What is the theme of a play?
How do playwrights use dialogue, action, and situation?

Vocabulary

protagonist	mood	plot	soliloquy	dialogue
exposition	preliminary	antagonist	theme	action
atmosphere	situation	denouement	moral	situation

The play is the central element of the art of theater. It is brought to life by the actors; expressed through the media of color, light, and movement against a background of stage and scenery; and unified by the creative vision of the director.

A play has four narrative essentials: exposition, plot, characters, and theme. These four elements are communicated through the dialogue and action of a drama. The way the playwright arranges and presents these four narrative essentials is the structure of the play.

Whatever the future structure of drama may be, the plays that will survive will be those that reveal the heights and depths of human experience and serve as an uplifting and creative force in civilization.

252

Vocabulary introduces you to key terms defined in the chapter. As you read, be on the lookout for discussion of these terms.

Focus Questions prepare you for the key themes and ideas in the chapter. They help you set your purpose for reading.

Read, Respond, Perform

Exercise — Posture

Repeat the following exercise several times daily.

1. Stand erect with your feet parallel.
2. Bend forward from the hips, completely relaxed, with your loosely hanging arms almost touching the floor.
3. Place your right hand on your chest where the chest and abdomen meet and your left hand at the small of your back.
4. Slowly raise your body to an upright position, expanding the diaphragm so

that you feel your hands being pushed apart. (See page 68 in Voice and Diction.)
5. Bring your head to an upright position. Hold your chin perpendicular to your throat.
6. Drop your arms to your sides. Shift your weight to the ball of one foot and move forward. Keep your chest high, your head erect, and the small of your back flat.

WALKING AND SITTING

The following guidelines will help you move confidently onstage. Va[...] them only when your roles demand it.

Walking   Most of us walk without giving much consideration to what w[...] are doing. Onstage, however, the manner in which actors walk is observ[...] very carefully. The following guidelines will help you walk confident[...] onstage.

HOW TO WALK ONSTAGE
Maintain good posture.
Keep your shoulders square and your chest high.
Keep the axis of your body directly over your feet.
Think "tall."
Move straight ahead with your weight on the balls of your feet[...]
Movement should be easy, poised, and rhythmical.
Walk in a straight line (to keep your silhouette narrow).
Let your body swing easily from your hips.
Let your arms swing in easy opposition to your legs.
Turn by rotating on the balls of your feet, shifting y[...] weight from one foot to the other.
Turn your entire body, including your head.
Do not turn on your heels.
As you turn, do not cross one foot over the other.
Avoid plodding or long strides or tip[...] steps.
Do not habitually look at the gro[...] as you walk.

CUE ▼
Walking up and down stairs is excellent exercise. Rest your hand lightly on the handrail. Try not to look at the stairs, regardless of the kind of costume you are wearing.

30 ▧ Interpreting the Drama

> **Exercises** and **Application Activities** provide you with the chance to discuss, practice, and apply new skills.

Application ACTIVITIES

Read aloud the following selections, concentrating mainly on the vowel sounds. Try to make each vowel in an accented syllable as full and rich as possible. Sound these vowels alone many times and then put them back into the words.

1. from *Romeo and Juliet*
   by William Shakespeare

JULIET   The clock struck nine when I did
   send the Nurse;
In half an hour she promised to return.
Perchance she cannot meet him: that's not so.
O, she is lame! love's heralds should be thoughts,
Which ten times faster glide than the sun's
   beams,
Driving back shadows over louring hills: . . .

2. from "The Raven"
   by Edgar Allan Poe

Once upon a midnight dreary, while I pondered, weak and weary,
Over many a quaint and curious volume of forgotten lore—
While I nodded, nearly napping, suddenly there came a tapping,
As of someone gently rapping, rapping at my chamber door—
"'Tis some visitor," I muttered, "tapping at my chamber door—
Only this and nothing more."

CUE ▼
Before reading any excerpt or passage, read the complete work, if possible. This will help you understand fully the mood and meaning of the selection.

> **Cue** notes give you practical tips and fascinating information about the theater.

[...] in creating a role. [...] come so involved [...]mmunicate to the audience. Their speech is often slovenly and their actions overdone. They make the mistake of believing that emotional identification with a character is more important than learning the lines as written or responding alertly to others onstage.

Stanislavski's so-called "magic *if*" should be most helpful to you in creating a character. Stanislavski advised that actors should use their full powers of concentration to ask what they would do *if* the events in the play were actually happening and they were intimately involved in these events. For example, ask yourself, "If I were Abigail in the courtroom scene in *The Crucible*, how would I feel as Proctor accused me of being a witch? How would I react? What would I do to stop him?" In answering questions such as these, actors analyze both their inner natures and their characters' inner natures. Only then can an actor use the technical resources of voice and body movement to accurately interpret the likely reactions of the character. This analysis can also lead to a deeper understanding of the play itself.

In approaching a role, it is helpful to consider the types of roles typically employed by a playwright. The main characters in a play are referred

FROM THE PROS
"Imagination, industry, and intelligence—'the three I's'—are all indispensable to the actor, but of these three the greatest is, without doubt, imagination."

—ELLEN TERRY, ACTOR

[...] highness or lowness of the voice at any given time is called [...] person's voice has a characteristic pitch level from which it [...]nd down. Women's voices are pitched on a higher level than [...] children's voices are higher still. Pitch is determined by the [...]h which the vocal folds vibrate.

[...]ersons use only four or five notes in ordinary speaking, but a [...]r can use two octaves or more. Many girls and women pitch [...]t at too high a level, not realizing that a low voice is far more [...] easily heard. As a rule, therefore, girls and women should do [...]xercises on the lower pitch levels.

In an early rehearsal, these students work with few props in order to more fully concentrate on developing their characters.

> **From the Pros** notes let actors, directors, and other theater professionals share their insights.

Acting ▧ **103**

▧   **1**

Read, Respond, Perform

Chapter Review pages include a variety of activities to help you explore what you've learned.

Summary and Key Ideas focuses your attention on the key points of the chapter.

Discussing Ideas lets you examine and apply the ideas of the chapter in exciting ways.

CHAPTER **5** REVIEW

Summary and Key Ideas

Summarize the chapter by answering the following questions.

1. Name and define the four narrative essentials of a p these narrative essentials communicated by the d
2. Who first expressed the principles of traditional dra identify as the key elements of a play?
3. How does some modern drama differ from tradition
4. How does mood differ from atmosphere?
5. What are the five major parts of plot structure that follow the liminary situation?
6. Describe three methods of characterization available to playwrights
7. How does a theme differ from a moral?

Discussing Ideas

1. Select a movie or a television play. Identify the four narrative ess tials. Discuss how the dramatist presents each element.
2. Twentieth- and twenty-first-century playwrights often break the rules of traditional drama. Read either Samuel Beckett's *Waiting Godot* or Eugène Ionesco's *The Chairs*. Describe some of the ru these dramatists break.
3. Describe a play or a movie that made you think about its them

FOCUS ON Community Theater

Would you like to give support to a resource that strengthens your community and lets people of all ages participate? Then community theater might be for you. Community theaters throughout the country provide a great venue for performing and viewing drama. Community theaters give burgeoning actors and directors the opportunity to practice and improve their skills.

Directing Community Theater The director is the link between the playwright and the actors. He or she must have strong skills in analyzing plays and working with people. Directors must also be familiar with

all the arts and crafts that contribu duction. With your teacher's perm some research using Internet sites as the Community Theater Gree (www.communitytheater.org) to more about what directing com theater involves. In a brief essay your findings.

Volunteering With a partn out more about community th town or state. Are they curre volunteers? Share your volu tion with the rest of the clas

Focus on... helps you make connections to real-world theater issues.

REVIEW WORKSHOP
THE STRUCTURE OF DRAMA

INDEPENDENT ACTIVITY

A Day in the Life The first dramas people experience are in their own lives. Choose a day from your life and explain how you would use your day as the basis for a play. It can be an exciting or frustrating day or just a typical twenty-four-hour period—every day holds drama of one kind or another. As you construct the plan for your drama, incorporate the four narrative essentials.

Consider the following points:

- Decide whether you are the protagonist, the antagonist, or both.
- Make sure your exposition describes the *where, when, why,* and *who* of your drama and establishes the atmosphere and mood of your play.
- Plan your plot so that it follows the plot-structure diagram.
- Choose interesting characters, and plan to develop them well.
- Decide on a theme or a moral.

Cooperative Learning Activity

Analyzing a Nontraditional Play With a group of classmates, read a modern play that has abandoned traditional dramatic structure, such as Edward Albee's *The Sandbox.* Use the plot-structure diagram on page 259 to trace the action. Then use the following questions to discuss why and how the playwright departed from traditional form.

- How does the playwright communicate the *where, when, why,* and *who* of the play?
- How does the playwright use dia-   ation to
- art from the

- What is the theme or the moral of the play?
- Is the play more or less effective because it does not follow the traditional structure?

Compare your group's conclusions with those of other groups.

Across the CURRICULUM Activity

Literature Choose a short story you like. How would you translate the story into a play? Identify the four narrative essentials. Analyze the plot according to the plot-structure diagram. Describe the characters, and evaluate their development in the story. Are they interesting? Do the dialogue, action, and situations adequately develop the characters? Can you infer a theme or moral from the story? How does a drama differ from a short story?

The following activities provide you with projects to help you assess and improve your skills:

- **Independent Activity** offers appealing do-it-yourself projects.
- **Cooperative Learning Activity** lets you work in a team.
- **Across the Curriculum Activity** lets you apply what you've learned to math, history, art, and other subject areas.

Enrich Your Understanding

To enrich your understanding of key theater topics, be sure to check out these Special Features at the end of each part:

- **Theater Etiquette** (Part One)
- **Readers Theater** (Part Two)
- **Puppet Theater** (Part Three)
- **How to Judge a Play** (Part Four)
- **Media and Culture** (Part Five)

Theater Etiquette

Successful performances are possible only if everyone—the actors, the director, the stage crew, and even the audience—shows proper respect for everyone involved. Achieving the best results is possible only in an environment of personal responsibility and mutual respect.

Often theater etiquette is nothing more than showing common courtesy. However, theater presents some unique situations, ones where the ground rules for interacting with others might not always be clear. The following guidelines to behavior will make it possible for everyone involved in a performance to enjoy the theater experience.

THE ACTORS

- Arrive at rehearsals and makeup calls on time.
- Learn lines, business, and blocking on schedule.
- Never peek through the curtains before (when the audience is present) or during a performance.
- Do not remove your makeup until after the curtain call. Never mingle with members of the audience or leave the theater while in costume or makeup.
- Do not change lines or stage business or tell others to do so unless the change has been approved by the director.
- Subordinate yourself to the performance by accepting your role and the costume, hairstyle, and makeup that go with it.
- Never knowingly upstage other performers. Be careful n~~ot~~ dentally, either.
- Be attentive~~...~~

EVERYONE ASSOCIATED WITH THE PRODUCTION

- Respect and encourage the contributions of each member of the cast and crew by complimenting good rehearsals, effective lighting, skillful costuming, and creative construction and design.
- Unless you are on the props crew, do not handle the props or sets.
- Know emergency procedures and the locations of firefighting equipment, the exits, and the fire alarms.
- Respect those who want to carry on theater traditions even though these traditions might seem like superstitions to you.
- After the show, make any presentations or recognitions for outstanding contributions at a time when everyone associated with the performance can be present.
- Post-performance cast parties should involve only those who worked on the show.

A successful production depends on cooperation among the cast, the crews, and the director.

159

158

SCENES for Mixed Groups

The Diary of Anne Frank

dramatized by Frances Goodrich and Albert Hackett (1954) from the book *Anne Frank: Diary of a Young Girl*

Characters: ANNE FRANK—Anne is a fourteen-year-old. She is lively, polite, optimistic, and compassionate.
MR. FRANK—He is a gentle, cultured, middle-aged man with a trace of a German accent.
MARGOT FRANK—She is an eighteen-year-old who is quiet and shy.
MR. VAN DAAN—He is a tall, dignified man in his late forties.
MRS. VAN DAAN—She is a woman in her early forties.
MRS. FRANK—She is genteel and reserved. She has a slight German accent.
PETER VAN DAAN—He is a shy and awkward sixteen-year-old.

Situation: This play is based on historical fact and was inspired by Anne's diary, which was published after her death. It is the first night of the Jewish holiday of Hanukkah, the Festival of Lights. World War II is in progress, and the Frank and the Van Daan families are hiding from the Nazis on the top floor of a warehouse in Amsterdam, Holland. Mr. Frank is at the head of the table and has lit the shammes, or servant candle. All are dressed in their best; the men wear hats, and Peter wears his cap.

ANNE *(Singing)* "Oh, Hanukkah! Oh, Hanukkah! The sweet celebration."

MR. FRANK *(Rising)* I think we should first blow out the candle; then we'll have something for tomorrow night.

MARGOT But, Father, you're supposed to let it burn itself out.

MR. FRANK I'm sure that God understands shortages. *(Before blowing it out)* "Praised be Thou, oh Lord our God, who hath sustained us and permitted us to celebrate this joyous festival."

(He is about to blow out the candle when suddenly there is a crash of something falling below. They all freeze in horror, motionless. For a few seconds there is complete silence. MR. FRANK slips off his shoes. The others noiselessly follow his example. MR. FRANK turns out a light near him. He motions to PETER to turn off the center lamp. PETER tries to reach it, realizes he cannot and gets up on a chair. Just as he is touching the lamp he loses his balance. The chair goes out from under him. He falls. The iron lamp shade crashes to the floor. There is a sound of feet below, running down the stairs.)

MR. VAN DAAN *(Under his breath)* God Almighty! *(The only light left comes from the Hanukkah candle. . . . MR. FRANK creeps over to the stairwell and stands listening. The dog is heard barking excitedly.)* Do you hear anything!

MR. FRANK *(In a whisper)* No. I think they've gone.

MRS. VAN DAAN It's the Green Police. They've found us.

Scenes for Mixed Groups 219

A Treasury of Scenes and Monologues gives you the chance to perform a wealth of scenes from classic and contemporary plays.

Enrich Your Understanding

☒ How to Produce a Play

The Production Process

The following guide will take you and your class stage-by-stage through the production process—your key to building an effective public performance. To aid your understanding, you will begin by producing a specific work, *The Importance of Being Earnest*, First Act. However, you can adapt the process outlined here to any script that you and your classmates select.

During your preparation time, maintain an encouraging, positive spirit with your classmates and work together to accomplish your best with each stage of the process. The rewards will be tremendous.

The Stages of the Process

The most essential stages of the production process are shown below.

> Select and read the script
> ⇩
> Analyze and evaluate the script
> ⇩
> Find a place to stage the play
> ⇩
> Cast the play
> ⇩
> Conduct rehearsals
> ⇩
> Create set designs, props, and costumes
> ⇩
> Present a public performance

The stages of production often overlap, and their order can vary according to your needs and goals. There will be times when you and your classmates will need to work on several stages simultaneously. At each stage, you should consider how your decisions will affect other areas of production. As you proceed, use what you've learned about the production process in earlier chapters. **Review Part Four, pages 332–529, for detailed descriptions of job responsibilities and production procedures.**

Objectives

• To collaborate to present unified productions for public performance

• To practice and master acting, stagecraft, and directing skills

• To analyze dramatic texts for structure, genre, and historical context

How to Produce a Play ☒ **R1**

Reference Section gives you the following opportunities to write, produce, and perform like the pros:

• **How to Produce a Play** takes you start-to-finish through the production of a scene. It will be a valuable resource for all of your performances.

• **How to Write a Dramatic Script** takes you through the process of creating your own script.

Be an active reader. Use the following strategies to help you stay focused and involved as you read.

Reading Dos

- Set a purpose for reading.
- Think about how your own experiences relate to the topic.
- Jot down questions or comments as you read.

Reading Don'ts

- Ignore how the book is organized.
- Overlook the visuals—photos, diagrams, forms, and charts.
- Rush to finish the material.

Interpreting the Drama

The actors' skills, developed and polished through dedication and hard work, bring a play to life. (Play: *Grease*)

CHAPTER

1 Improvisation

Mirroring each other's actions, these two actors perform an exercise in improvisation. Improvisation can be fun and help you gain confidence as an actor.

General improvisations often give actors an insight beyond their words by helping them to "see the word" and achieve a reality for the scene.

—Viola Spolin, Author

SETTING THE SCENE

Focus Questions

What is improvisation?

What makes improvisation a foundation for interpretation?

How do character-centered and situation-centered storytelling differ?

What are the important factors in creating a successful improvisation?

Vocabulary

improvisation	scene-stealing	situation-centered approach
spontaneity	character-centered approach	motivated sequence
"illusion of the first time"		

Are you ready to act? A technique that will help you gain confidence is called improvisation. **Improvisation** is the portrayal of a character or a scene without rehearsal or preparation. You will make up the character, the lines, and the action as you go along, without a formal script. You will enjoy yourself as you learn some of the fundamentals of acting and become better acquainted with your classmates. Imagination is the key to improvisation. You must learn to say the most with the least; that is, you must convey personality and physical traits, conflicts and desires, and age and dress with a minimum of aids. Sometimes you may be allowed to use a few props, but your character must be conveyed primarily by voice, body language, and movement.

Spontaneity, credibility, and freshness in each performance are the goals of the director of a play, the challenge to the cast, and the pleasure of the audience. After weeks of rehearsals or after many performances, however, making the audience feel that each performance is the first—the **"illusion of the first time"**—is sometimes difficult; then the play becomes stale. Improvisations are enjoyable in their you-never-know-what's-coming-next freshness. They should help you to recognize the sparkle that comes with a first-time performance. Through improvisation you will learn to appreciate the most important factor in the execution of lines or actions—timing. Play casts may rehearse for weeks to achieve the kind of fresh, natural timing that can come as you improvise.

About Improvisation

CUE ▼

Drama began as descriptive action expressed only by facial expressions and body movement (pantomime). It then became stylized dance. Finally, it developed into formal dramas.

Improvisation is one of the foundations of interpretation, emphasizing creativity and imagination. The beginning performer, however, often wants to experience the actual emotion rather than to portray it. The student must always bear in mind that a person may go only so far and still be acting. Beyond that point, the actor *is* rather than *is pretending to be.*

What is happening now is the keynote of improvisation. Improvisation focuses your attention on natural actions and reactions and should force you to concentrate on immediate responses. All action should be motivated by what you already know about the characters and situation and by what is brought forth as you improvise. You do not have the advantage—or disadvantage—of knowing what lines come next in a script. You must play the role as it develops. You will learn how a scene may change direction as the result of a single line or action. You may even find it necessary to meet one of the toughest challenges that faces an actor: to "do nothing"

Part of improvisation is not knowing what anyone else will say or do. Notice how attentive everyone in this scene is to the central character.

effectively—that is, to be visible onstage but not to play an active part in the scene. In such cases, you must get the audience to accept your presence without being distracted by you. To call attention to your presence would be **scene-stealing,** or diverting attention from the other actors. You will learn to appreciate the interrelationships of the characters and how essential it is that an actor be a member of a team.

🌿 *Character-Centered and Situation-Centered Approaches*

The two basic approaches to telling a story are through character-centered action and through situation-centered action. The **character-centered** approach focuses on a character or a group of characters who experience different situations one after another. This approach emphasizes each character's response to those situations as they occur. *Man of La Mancha* and *Big River* are examples of this approach.

The **situation-centered** approach typically takes a single situation and places a number of characters in the situation to demon-

Little Shop of Horrors, a situation-centered play, demonstrates how different personalities respond to a single situation.

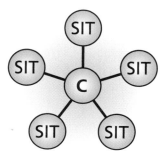

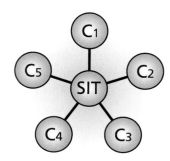

Every stage happening is based on one of two conditions: (1) a single character facing multiple situations, or (2) multiple characters facing a single situation.

strate how different personalities will respond to the same event. Many improvisations are set up as situation centered. Many television programs are situation centered. This is why they are referred to as "sitcoms," or situation comedies. Plays such as *Arsenic and Old Lace* and *Little Shop of Horrors* are situation centered.

Exercises — Improvisation

1. **The Mirror** Face a partner. One person is the activator; the other is the responder. The activator moves the hands, the head, and eventually any part of the body while pretending to look into a mirror. The responder matches the actions of the activator without making physical contact. The goals are to develop concentration skills, to learn to work smoothly with a partner, and to feel the single impulse of an action. Keep your movements steady and fluid. Do not try to trick your partner, but work together.

2. **The Machine** This is a group improvisation that puts your imagination to the test. One person starts the machine by performing a physical action, such as pumping an arm or lifting a knee. Another person joins the first piece of the machine by linking a different physical action to the first. Other actors join in until as many members of the group as possible become part of the machine.

Variation 1: Make the machine perform a manufacturing process in which raw materials are turned into a finished product.

Variation 2: Add sounds to the actions. Each new action must be accompanied by its own new sound.

🌀 *Improvising Scenes*

As a beginning actor, you can perform successful improvisations by learning some basic techniques. Remember to work out your stage setting carefully, knowing just where the entrances will be. You probably will have nothing more than a table and a few chairs to work around. Use actions to suggest entrances and major props. You may carry small articles you need. In turning the classroom into a street, a ballroom, a theater dressing room, an office, or whatever you choose, you are developing your own imagination along with the imaginations of the rest of the class. They will see whatever you make clear through your explanation and your performance.

Visualize your character in detail, and try to feel his or her emotions. Before you enter, take on the physical attitude of your character as dictated by the character's age, size, and mood. Walk in character as you enter, staying aware of your audience at all times.

A few pieces of furniture may be all the staging you need for improvising a scene. Since improvisation involves fewer props, the ones that are used tend to be more noticeable.

As you practice improvising scenes, you will begin to learn some of the subtleties of acting. You will find that you can stand still without fidgeting and that you can make definite gestures when you feel the need, avoiding the little, aimless ones. When you must move to a chair or toward another person, learn to go straight there without rambling. If you are to pick up an article, actually look at it before you touch it. By observation you will learn that your head usually reacts first (sometimes just your eyes), then your torso, and finally the rest of your body.

Reminders for Successful Improvisation

- Speak loudly enough to be heard throughout the theater or auditorium.

- Do not hide behind pieces of furniture or other people.

- Move about freely. Try not to stand beside other characters all the time.

- Take plenty of time to speak and to move so that you can create a definite impression.

- Stay in character *all* the time. Listen and speak as your character would in every situation. Always exhibit actions and reactions that are appropriate for your character.

---

1. Choose a familiar action to perform, and gather whatever simple props you need. In performing this action, there must be a sense of urgency motivating you to perform the action and to complete the task *now*. After completing the action, explain the reason behind the need to rush. Some sample actions are listed below.

   Hemming a skirt
   Photographing a subject
   Changing a bicycle tire
   Applying makeup
   Writing a letter
   Hiding a valuable

2. As you perform the action in exercise 1, a second student comes into the scene. This second student also has an action to perform. Neither of you, however, must be distracted by the other's behavior.

3. Add conversation to the scene. Both of you continue to perform your actions. However, you now talk to each other or mutter to yourselves. Continue to concentrate on the actions in spite of the complication of talking.

THE MOTIVATED SEQUENCE

Skilled actors mirror people's natural responses to internal or external stimuli—thoughts, actions, or what they hear, see, taste, feel, or smell. The steps in this **motivated sequence** are described below.

The Motivated Sequence

1. You experience the stimulus.
2. You respond instinctively to the stimulus. (primary response)
3. The idea "connects." Your brain registers the stimulus—this usually takes only a fraction of a second. (idea connection)
4. If the stimulus is the kind that causes a reflex action, you might jerk back your head, or you might make a sound. Your eyes look in that direction. Then your body reacts; your chest moves in the direction of the stimulus. (secondary response)
5. You react vocally and/or physically with your main response.

This whole sequence may be completed in less than a second, but all of the steps must be present if the reaction is to be believable. For example, it is early morning on a school day. You are asleep in bed. The alarm goes off (stimulus). You awaken (primary response); your brain tells you that the alarm is going off (idea connection). You think, "It's

Tuesday—school today!" (idea connection), and you glare at the clock (secondary response). "Yes, it really is 6:00 A.M." (idea connection). You reach out and shut off the alarm (main response).

If you follow a motivated sequence onstage, your actions will be believable to the audience. When you have a script in your hand, however, you will discover how easy it is to jump to a response without following the sequence. Your audience might not see your performance as believable.

Exercises

Motivated Sequence

Apply the motivated sequence to an improvisation of one of the following situations:

1. You are preparing to enjoy a meal in a fine restaurant. As you pick up your fork, you see a fly in your food.

2. The principal enters your classroom and in a serious voice asks you to accompany her to her office.

3. You pick up the morning newspaper and read that a close friend has been selected for a prestigious award.

4. Your history teacher announces a pop quiz on a chapter you have not read.

ESTABLISHING A CHARACTER

It is very demanding for inexperienced actors to build a character, work out a situation, formulate actions, and create effective dialogue all at the same time. Therefore, if you establish a character beforehand, the words and the action will come much more easily. Ask questions and, if possible, do research to help define your character. You will soon learn that a raised eyebrow, a silent stare, a one-word response, or a groan might convey more information about your character than a dozen sentences.

Questions to Ask About Your Character

- Who am I?

- What kind of person am I?

- How am I different from the other characters?

- What are the fewest things I can do to convey the most information about my character?

- What does my character want?

Reenact some event, real or imaginary, such as the following:

1. At lunch someone rushes in with news that a spaceship has just landed in a nearby park. Speculate on the ship, its occupants, its origin, and so forth.

2. You are a member of the Roman Senate; Julius Caesar has just been stabbed to death. Recall something Caesar did to you that makes you support or reject the conspirators.

3. After having just been given an engagement ring, announce it to the world—including your former admirers and your fiancé's former admirers.

In your characterization, do not yield to the common impulse to "play the character down." Shallow characterizations are weak characterizations. Italian playwright Luigi Pirandello said that a person plays a "game of masks" in life, putting on a different mask for each person or occasion faced. Seldom does a person want anyone to see what is really behind the mask. The convincing actor not only lets the audience see the various masks of a character but also allows them to see what is behind the masks, even if only for brief moments. When these glimpses into the character are carefully worked out, the audience sees a well-rounded, thoroughly developed personality.

▼ **CUE**

Most directors encourage improvising while the actor is working toward the development of a character. A combination of inner-developed improvisations and suggestions from the director, however, usually results in the best theater.

When improvising strong emotions, an actor must be completely focused. Any wavering or indecision will be perceived by the audience.

IMPROVISATIONS WITH A PARTNER OR A GROUP

Before you begin working with a partner or a group on an improvised scene, there are a few *do*s and *don't*s to keep in mind. Following the simple rules in the chart below will free your imagination and keep your improvisation moving.

Do . . .	Don't . . .
1. Do quickly establish your character in your mind (age, occupation, physical and mental traits, and so on).	1. Don't deny anything your scene partners say about you or the situation. If your partners say you have lovely yellow eyes, accept the statement as true, and use your imagination as you respond.
2. Do identify the problem and your goal by asking what your character wants or needs.	2. Don't ask questions. Questions turn an improvisation into a question-and-answer routine. Especially avoid "terminal questions"—those that can be answered with a *yes* or a *no* or with a response that shuts down the flow of the dialogue.
3. Do keep focused on meeting your need or goal.	
4. Do let the situation provide the basis for how your character attempts to reach the goal.	
5. Do react spontaneously to what is said or done.	3. Don't use simple statements of information. Use descriptive language to make active statements about your feelings, observations, needs, and goals.
6. Do see things through the eyes of your character.	
7. Do listen to and observe what others are saying and doing.	4. Don't explain situations and feelings. If you are happy, show it. If you are afraid of the dark, show it. Telling is storytelling, not acting. Acting is doing.
8. Do take your cues from your scene partner or partners.	
9. Do play your scene from moment to moment.	
10. Do say or do things that demand a definite response.	

Group improvisations, such as this skit in which Conehead tourists photograph restaurant patrons, require coordination as well as spontaneity.

Group Improvisations

1. With a partner, act out a scene of your own choosing. You might get ideas from the photographs in this book, newspaper clippings, cartoons, anecdotes from magazines, events in the lives of people you know, or historical and literary sources. Choose any type of scene—comic or sad, fanciful or realistic. Decide on the mood and the general idea you want to convey. Select the character you will play. Each character should have a distinct personality. The greater the difference in age, personality, and type between the characters, the more contrast your scene will contain.

2. Form a group consisting of three females and two males to improvise the following scene:

   It is 4:30 P.M. There are five people on an elevator: a film star on her way to a 4:40 audition; a courier delivering an urgent legal brief; a professional athlete who is to be interviewed on the 5:00 P.M. sportscast; a window washer headed for the twelfth floor to finish the last task of the day before leaving work to catch the 5:12 uptown bus; a thirteen-year-old going to see a parent on the sixth floor. Just as the elevator leaves the third floor where the window washer got on, there is a power failure, stranding the passengers between floors. IMPROVISE!

3. The teacher will assign you and your partner a simple location and a relationship. For example, the relationship could be between brother and sister, and the location could be the family's garage. One person is already in the garage engaged in an activity, such as pumping up a bike tire. That person is in a certain mood. The second person arrives from a specific location and is in a specific mood. Act out your scene, building around your two moods, the relationship, and the location of the present action.

INDIVIDUAL IMPROVISATIONS

After working with a partner or a group, you might also want to try to develop individual characters in definite situations, reacting to imaginary persons or crowds, or showing particular moods. It is harder to work by yourself than with other people, but by yourself you can take more time to create a personality and to show your character's feelings in more depth. In these improvisations, keep relaxed and have fun. Do not allow yourself to feel embarrassed by the reactions of others.

If you practice all sorts of characterizations on the spur of the moment at home, you will find doing improvisations in class much easier. Feel free to experiment, using motivation as your driving force. Imagination will be the key to characterization, so make every look, every line, and every action count. Try being all sorts of people—Joan of Arc at her trial, a star during a television interview, an Olympic champion after a big event, and so on. Get yourself into all sorts of emotional states, laughing out loud and even crying if you can. With no one around, you will be more relaxed and less inhibited. The practice will show in your classwork because you will be more responsive and sensitive to changing moods and situations. You will find your voice and body becoming more flexible and expressive. Remember: IMPROVISE!

Individual improvisations, such as the one shown here, allow for greater individual imagination and deeper characterization than group improvisations.

1. Choose a prop, such as a cane, an umbrella, a fan, a pair of glasses, or a book. After thirty seconds of preparation time before a full-length mirror, present a thirty-second characterization built around the prop you chose. It is recommended that the mirror be located away from the class's view so that you can concentrate alone. While one person performs, another can be preparing.

   Variation: Use the prop you have chosen for something other than its normal function. Improvise a character using the prop's new function. For example, you could change a cane into a laser beam, a magic wand, or a golf club.

2. Bring a mask to class. It can be a Halloween mask, another commercial mask, or a mask you have made for yourself. Use the mirror for preparation. Present the character that the mask suggests for thirty seconds. You may then add sounds or speech.

   Variation 1: Add nonverbal sounds to the improvisation: a grunt, a hum, clearing the throat, or a chuckle.
   Variation 2: Add words to the action.

3. Individual improvisations provide an excellent opportunity to present monologues. Choose a character and a situation, then decide what or who you want to address in the monologue. Practice in front of a mirror for a few minutes, focusing on conveying emotion and motivation in your voice, facial expressions, and gestures. After you have refined your monologue, present it to the class.

Application
ACTIVITIES

The following suggestions for improvisations provide a step-by-step progression from simple emotional responses to the improvised writing of a play.

Emotional Responses

1. React to the following sentences with one gesture or bodily stance.

Your face is red!
You have pretty eyes.
I love you.

Do you always look like that?
I think you're frightened.
You're standing on my toe.

(continued)

2. Your teacher will place different items in individual paper sacks and distribute the sacks to the class. In turn, reach into your sack, feel the object that is in it, say "one thousand one" silently, and then convey your reaction to the item by a facial expression and one sentence. The following list contains possible items to be placed in the sacks.

sandpaper	cold cream	raisins
cooked spaghetti	feathers	knitting yarn
a cotton ball	a flower petal	cracker crumbs
rough tree bark	a piece of lettuce	a marble
a pickle	crumpled cellophane	

3. Express the following feelings with a facial response, and then combine the facial response with a bodily reaction. Try to recall a personal experience that caused you to experience these feelings. One to five participants may do this exercise at a time. Compare the responses. What are their similarities and differences?

love	greed	embarrassment	shock
hope	jealousy	understanding	sympathy
fear	joy	anger	patience
bitterness	rebuke	disbelief	fickleness
doubt	happiness	pleading	courage
longing	grief	sadness	surprise

Vocal Responses

1. Make up a list of statements similar to the examples below. Exchange lists with a classmate, and react to one statement as five different people.

STATEMENT "I don't like asparagus!"
RESPOND AS Your parent, your doctor, your server, your host, your child

STATEMENT "I've been asked to the prom!"
RESPOND AS Your best friend, a jealous rival, the teacher whose class you have interrupted, your father, your sister

(continued)

2. Two to five persons will begin improvising a scene based on a simple situation. Either your teacher or a member of your class will act as the director. As the scene develops, the director will call out an emotion to the performer who is speaking at that moment. That person must immediately assume the emotion mentioned.

3. This is a two-person activity that develops a sense of conflict within a scene. Each person wants to fulfill a specific objective. One person might want the other's shoe, while the other person might want to leave the room. The object of the improvisation is to get what you want without asking for it.

4. Line up side by side with two friends—A-B-C. The person in the center (B) begins telling about something strange that happened recently. The person on the right (A) interrupts and begins a conversation with B. A few seconds later, C starts a conversation with B while A continues talking. B must try to maintain both conversations.

Scripts

1. As you develop scripts for the following situations, make sure you include dialogue that sets up the action and advances the plot. You must also pay attention to the characters' emotions and motivations.

   - Two salesclerks are discussing a department manager they dislike. The manager appears and accuses one of them of having stolen a necklace that has disappeared.
   - A father meets his teenage daughter at midnight on her return from a party that ended at 10:30 P.M. Show what happens.

2. People from varied walks of life are sometimes thrown together by chance. Work out your characters, reactions, and a conclusion for each of these situations:

   - People in a boat or in an aircraft that is having engine trouble
   - People in a traffic jam or on a subway train during a power failure

Creating the Improvised Play

In groups of five to eight persons, work out a script that can be made into a simple, improvised play. Decide on the theme of the play, the characters, their motivations, and the basic conflicts. After improvising the script several times to establish some actions, dialogue, and workable scenes, fill in the outline until you have a skeletal script. Improvise two or three more times, and you will be able to produce a written script.

1 REVIEW

Summary and Key Ideas

Summarize the chapter by answering the following questions.

1. What is improvisation?
2. What is "the illusion of the first time"? Why is it sometimes difficult to capture?
3. Why is to "do nothing" effectively a challenge? What is the connection between this challenge and scene-stealing?
4. Identify the two basic approaches to telling a story. Explain each.
5. List the steps of the motivated sequence.
6. What are some questions to ask when establishing a character?
7. What are some essential things to keep in mind as you improvise?

Discussing Ideas

1. Discuss how character is conveyed through voice, body language, and movement. Is one of these methods more effective than the others?
2. Discuss the role that imagination plays in improvisation.
3. Discuss the difference between experiencing an emotion and portraying an emotion.
4. Discuss the benefits and drawbacks of the improvised approach to acting. Discuss how a combination of this approach with suggestions from a director might result in a better performance.

FOCUS ON   Scripts

Why should acting students try their hand at scriptwriting?   The answer is simple: Going through the process of creating a script is a great way to learn about dramatic structure. When you work to present exposition, plot, characters, and theme in your own way, you move to a higher level of thinking. Scriptwriting will help you to become a wiser reader—and it may lead you to discover new powers of communication as an actor.

Creating a Script   Outline and create a short script about a situation of your choice. Your script should be easily adaptable for theater, film, or television. Make sure to include motivated characters, unique dialogue, and convincing conflict and resolution. For help with the scriptwriting process, see the Reference Section. When you're finished, exchange scripts with a partner.

Analyzing Scripts   Locate scripts for a stage play, a television show, and a movie. Compare and contrast the three scripts. Then write a short report answering these questions: What conventions, or practices, do all three forms seem to share? What conventions differ? What similarities and differences do you see in the scripts' dramatic structure?

IMPROVISATION

INDEPENDENT ACTIVITIES

Using a Prop   Choose an unusual object, such as an old toy, a photograph album, a microscope, or a small kitchen appliance. Spend four or five minutes thinking about how this object came to be the prized possession of a particular person. Present a three-minute monologue about the object, revealing your character's emotional attachment to it.

Masking Physical Irritation   You have just been introduced to an important person, such as the President of the United States, your future employer, or the director of admissions at the college you want to attend. Unfortunately, just at the moment of introduction, you experience a physical irritation, such as a runny nose, a piece of food caught between your teeth, an itchy mosquito bite, or a collar that is too tight. Improvise your part of the conversation while trying to remedy the physical irritation unobtrusively.

Cooperative Learning Activity

Conflict and Fantasy   With a partner, choose one of the imaginary situations below. Plan the conflict and its resolution, but do not discuss the characterization of the people involved. Then improvise the scene.

After discussing character motivation, repeat the scene. Then discuss these questions: What types of characters were portrayed? How did the characters change? Which scene was more effective?

- A genie grants ten wishes to a person who would prefer to have only two.
- An impostor impersonates a dentist, a ballet instructor, or a museum guide.

Across the CURRICULUM Activity

Art   Choose a painting, such as Edward Hopper's *Soir Bleu,* Sandro Botticelli's *La Primavera,* or Edgar Degas's *The Rehearsal.* By yourself, with a partner, or with a small group, visualize the situation and the emotional context that prompted the painting. Improvise character roles (you may include the painter or one of the subjects in the painting), and present your "picture window" for the class. Show the class a picture of the painting so that they can visualize your role better.

2 *Pantomime and Mime*

Marcel Marceau (left), appearing here with other mimes, is one of the best-known mimes in the history of the art.

y technique is the outcome of thinking for myself, of my own logic and approach; it is not borrowed from what others are doing.

—CHARLIE CHAPLIN, ACTOR IN SILENT FILMS

SETTING THE SCENE

Focus Questions

What are the basic principles of pantomime?

What can you do to relax?

How do you walk onstage?

How do you take a stage fall?

How do you gesture effectively onstage?

What are the differences between pantomime and mime?

Vocabulary

pantomime	gesture	inclination
nonverbal communication	kinesthesis	rotation
cross	mime	isolation

*P*antomime is the art of acting without words. It is often called the art of silence. The art of pantomime is basic to your training as an actor, because a character is portrayed through gestures, facial expressions, and movement—the first things an audience notices. Pantomime goes hand in hand with dance and was the forerunner of classical ballet.

Pantomime has delighted audiences for centuries. Indeed, pantomime was the first form of acting. Silent film stars such as Charlie Chaplin were masters of the art of pantomime. However, it was the French mime Marcel Marceau who reawakened America to the power of silent acting. His expressions and movements are outstanding examples of the original art.

〰 *Basic Pantomime Movements*

Much of our daily communication is **nonverbal communication**—communicating without words. We use facial expressions, gestures, and body language constantly. Yet when inexperienced actors perform onstage, they tend to rely mainly on their voices to communicate with the audience. Pantomime is valuable because it encourages meaningful movements, significant gestures, and animated facial expressions in actors. Because physical actions, not words, are the basis of most characterizations, the art of acting without speaking is the first phase of your training as an actor.

For most people, physical coordination and poise are more a matter of training than of heredity. Through a program of exercises, you can learn to keep your muscles flexible and to develop coordination and body control.

Any exercise that develops physical coordination is valuable in preparing to perform. Fencing and dance are required courses in most drama schools. Tennis, golf, swimming, and skiing will all help develop coordination. Jogging and other aerobic and isometric exercises also develop coordination. Whenever possible, do not take a car, an elevator, or a bus—walk. Walking and climbing stairs are still two of the best forms of exercise.

The actors in Japanese Kabuki theater must have perfect control of their facial expressions and bodies. They incorporate pantomime into their performances to tell classic Japanese tales.

One benefit of proper conditioning is developing a talent for moving your body as a whole, an important ingredient of pantomime. From the top of your head to the tips of your fingers and toes, your body should be expressive. As a matter of fact, it is *always* expressive, but not always in the way you might desire. For example, a slovenly walk, a rigid or slouching posture, aimless gestures, or a wooden face reveals your personality just as clearly as purposeful, strong movements and a radiant face. Usually, the world will take you at your "face value." You are judged first by your appearance and manner and later by what you say and how you say it.

Your body is therefore your tool for expressing a character's personality. Consider the differences between the actions of people who are confident and strong-willed and those of people who are shy and retiring.

PERSONALITY	ACTIONS
strong-willed and confident	<ul><li>stands tall</li><li>uses broad, emphatic gestures</li><li>moves with authority and self-assurance</li><li>makes quick, definite movements</li><li>directs actions away from the body</li></ul>
shy and retiring	<ul><li>stands timidly, drawn in as if for protection</li><li>uses small, weak gestures</li><li>moves slowly, with limited motion</li><li>directs actions down and toward the body</li></ul>

RELAXATION

Behind bodily poise and skill in action is relaxation. This is a matter of inner composure and mental awareness as well as of physical flexibility. Successful actors, like successful athletes, must not be emotionally or physically tense. You should learn right away to consciously let go all over, from the top of your head to the soles of your feet, whenever you feel a sense of strain onstage or in real life. Taking a few deep breaths and loosening all your muscles can help you relax.

The following exercises will help you relax. Repeat each exercise four times. These relaxation techniques are particularly useful for preparing for physical activities or exercises.

1. Raise, lower, and rotate your head without moving your shoulders. Let it roll freely, without the slightest tension. Turn your head to the left as if looking over your shoulder. Then, turn your head to the right in a similar manner. Lower your head so that your chin touches your chest. Rotate your head to the left, trying to touch your shoulder without straining. Roll your head back, then around to your right shoulder, continuing to the front starting position.

2. Rotate your shoulders forward, then backward.

3. Move your arms in wide circles, using a forward motion, first close to your body and then at shoulder height. Repeat, using a backward motion.

4. Holding your arms straight down and slightly away from your body, rotate your lower arms from the elbow, clockwise and then counterclockwise.

5. Rotate your hands from the wrists moving in a clockwise direction and then in a counterclockwise direction.

6. Lift your arms with wrists leading, first to the side, and then to the front.

7. Shake your hands vigorously, keeping them completely relaxed at your sides.

8. Open and close your fists, stretching the fingers apart and then drawing them together.

9. Do the "five-finger exercise." Hold your hands out in front of you. Place the heels of your hands side by side with the open palms facing you. Make each hand into a fist. Roll back each finger one at a time—little, ring, middle, index, and thumb. Alternate one finger of your right hand with one finger of your left hand. Return hands to fists, closing one finger at a time. Try to make a smooth, wavelike action, beginning with the left thumb and then releasing one finger at a time all the way to the right thumb. Reverse the action.

10. Bend your body forward at the waist, then backward, then to each side.

11. Clasping your hands together, push your arms above your head. Then rotate your body to the left and to the right, keeping your head within your arms.

12. Rotate each leg in circles, first to the right and then to the left. Kick as high as possible.

13. Rise on your toes. Slowly sink as you bend your knees until you are sitting on your heels. Very slowly reverse the process.

14. Rotate each foot at the ankle.

15. Pick up marbles with your toes.

Relaxation is essential for bodily poise and control onstage. Here student actors are doing some of the exercises from the previous page.

POSTURE

Your posture is fundamental to your health and to your personal appearance. Often good posture carries an air of confidence, maturity, and success, while poor posture suggests weakness, lack of poise, and insecurity. Therefore, the next step in training your body deals with normal posture and movement.

To stand properly, hold your body erect with chest high, chin up, back flat, arms slightly bent, and legs straight. Keep one foot slightly in front of the other, with your weight on the balls of your feet.

Repeat the following exercise several times daily.

1. Stand erect with your feet parallel.

2. Bend forward from the hips, completely relaxed, with your loosely hanging arms almost touching the floor.

3. Place your right hand on your chest where the chest and abdomen meet and your left hand at the small of your back.

4. Slowly raise your body to an upright position, expanding the diaphragm so that you feel your hands being pushed apart. (See page 68 in Voice and Diction.)

5. Bring your head to an upright position. Hold your chin perpendicular to your throat.

6. Drop your arms to your sides. Shift your weight to the ball of one foot and move forward. Keep your chest high, your head erect, and the small of your back flat.

WALKING AND SITTING

The following guidelines will help you move confidently onstage. Vary them only when your roles demand it.

Walking   Most of us walk without giving much consideration to what we are doing. Onstage, however, the manner in which actors walk is observed very carefully. The following guidelines will help you walk confidently onstage.

HOW TO WALK ONSTAGE
Maintain good posture.
Keep your shoulders square and your chest high.
Keep the axis of your body directly over your feet.
Think "tall."
Move straight ahead with your weight on the balls of your feet.
Movement should be easy, poised, and rhythmical.
Walk in a straight line (to keep your silhouette narrow).
Let your body swing easily from your hips.
Let your arms swing in easy opposition to your legs.
Turn by rotating on the balls of your feet, shifting your weight from one foot to the other.
Turn your entire body, including your head.
Do not turn on your heels.
As you turn, do not cross one foot over the other.
Avoid plodding or long strides or tiny steps.
Do not habitually look at the ground as you walk.

CUE ▼

Walking up and down stairs is excellent exercise. Rest your hand lightly on the handrail. Try not to look at the stairs, regardless of the kind of costume you are wearing.

These exercises are designed to help you walk correctly.

Imagine you are walking

- on a sandy beach on a hot afternoon with a fresh wind blowing
- in a large city, looking up at a tall building

- in a dark forest of tall trees with the wind howling
- across a platform to receive an award
- onto a stage, to audition for a part
- off a stage, disappointed by your audition

Sitting   Sitting is often a problem for inexperienced actors. Follow these steps to make sitting appear natural.

HOW TO SIT ONSTAGE

1. Without being obvious, locate out of the corner of your eye the chair in which you will sit.
2. Decide the best route to the chair that you will occupy. Normally you will walk there directly, but sometimes you will have to get around people and obstacles.
3. When you arrive, turn so that the calf of your leg touches the chair. Then place the calf of the other leg against the chair, and sit.
4. When sitting, keep the back of your spine at a ninety-degree angle to the seat. Onstage you will usually sit forward in a chair, particularly if it is padded or if you are playing an older person. However, if the chair is firm and your character would do so, you may lean back easily.
5. Your hands will ordinarily rest in your lap or on the arms of the chair. Crossing your arms on your chest or folding them restricts your breathing and causes you to look tense.
6. Your feet may be crossed at the ankles, or one foot may be placed slightly in front of the other. Do not cross your legs, spread your feet apart, or rest your hands or elbows on your knees unless you want to convey specific moods or characteristics by these actions.
7. In rising, let your chest lead, not your head. Keep your weight balanced on the balls of your feet, placing one foot slightly forward and using the rear one as a lever in pushing yourself up, once again keeping the axis straight. Never hold on to the arms of the chair or push yourself up from them unless your character is elderly or weak. Take a deep breath while rising. This relaxes your throat, gives a sense of control, keeps your chest high, and leads into a good standing position.

▼ CUE

Common Habits to Avoid

- Holding one shoulder higher than the other
- Dragging your feet
- Walking on your heels
- Keeping your feet apart
- Tensing parts of your body

The way a character sits can reveal information about his or her personality. For example, the actor sitting on the couch is meant to appear engaging and intelligent, while the actor sitting with her knees together in the top photo appears anxious.

CROSSING, TURNING, AND FALLING

Moving from one place onstage to another is called **crossing**. On entering the stage, lead with the foot farther from the audience. By leading with this upstage foot, you enter with your body facing the audience. So, if you enter from stage right as you face the audience, you start on your left foot. If you enter from stage left, you start on your right foot. When you stop, stop with the upstage foot forward; when you move again, start with the forward foot. Normally, all turns are made to the front, rotating on the balls of your feet.

To be both safe and believable, stage fighting, shown here from *The Pirates of Penzance*, requires training in crossing, turning, and falling.

Some roles will require you to fall onstage. The following are keys to safe and effective stage falls.

HOW TO FALL ONSTAGE

- Divide your body into segments—head, torso and arms, hips, thighs, and legs—and lower each segment to the floor.
- Control your body; you should be very close to the floor before you actually "fall."
- Absorb the fall with the soft parts of the body—the forearms, thighs, legs—rather than the bony projections—elbows, hipbones, knees.

1. Crossing and Turning

- Enter stage right to speak at a microphone downstage center. Start with your left foot. Cross to center, and turn downstage. Stand with one foot slightly advanced with your weight forward. To leave, turn right, start with your right foot, and exit stage right. Reverse the movement by starting from stage left.

- Enter stage right, and cross to center. Remember that you have forgotten something and turn front, rotating on the balls of your feet. Start on your right foot and exit. Again, do the same movement, entering from stage left.

- Enter left and walk diagonally upstage to up center, where there is an imaginary bookcase. Get a book, and exit right, starting on your right foot.

- Enter stage right as if to meet a friend. Cross to a chair at left center. Without looking at the chair, turn front, touching the chair with the calf of your right leg. Move your left leg so the calf touches the chair. Lower your body into the chair, keeping your head and chest high. Place one foot slightly in front of the other. See your friend approaching stage left. Rise, pushing with the leg closest to the chair. Move to front center. Meet your friend and exit.

2. Falling
- Relax, and sway or stagger backward.
- Sway forward, dropping the hands and arms.
- Relax from the ankles, and bend the knees.
- Pivot slowly and, as you do, go closer and closer to the floor. Lower the shoulder that is closer to the floor and sink down.
- Land on the side of your leg. Roll on your hip. Catch your weight on your forearm.
- Lower your head to the ground, letting it land on your arm.

GESTURES

The movement of any part of your body to help express an idea or an emotion is called a **gesture**. There are two types of gestures: facial expressions and hand and arm movements.

Facial expressions occur so quickly that they appear to take place all at once, but when analyzed closely, facial expressions follow a certain, natural sequence. This sequence begins with the eyes, followed by the mouth and other facial muscles. The following chart describes some typical facial expressions.

IDEA OR EMOTION	FACIAL EXPRESSION
Surprise	Eyes widen. Brows lift. Mouth opens into an *O*.
Happiness	Eyes squint. Brows lift. Mouth curves up, sometimes with lips parting.
Sadness	Eyes narrow and lids drop. Outer brow turns downward. Mouth turns down. Facial muscles sag.
Anger	Eyes narrow considerably. Brows furrow. Mouth twists downward. Lips sometimes curl out and down into a sneer. Jaw drops and sets firmly.

Good facial expressions take practice. Pay attention to how your face feels when you make certain expressions. This way, when you're onstage and can't see yourself, you'll still know what you look like.

A few practical suggestions regarding the use of your arms and hands will help you develop controlled gestures. Remember, however, that all technical practice must eventually become second nature if your gestures are to appear natural. Use relaxation exercises to loosen tight muscles and to establish habits of graceful coordination.

Almost every body movement begins with the chest. An arm movement passes from your chest through your shoulder, your elbow, and your wrist and "slips off" the ends of your fingers. It is important that every arm gesture finish at the fingertips. An arm movement in which the fingers are curled weakly at the ends or are stiff like paddles is ineffective. Your wrists should lead your hand gestures as if marionette strings were attached to the backs of them.

The key to a smooth gesture is getting your elbows away from your body slightly before making the gesture. Every gesture must have a definite purpose. If there is no purpose, there should be no gesture. Since the sole purpose of a gesture is to emphasize or clarify a thought or feeling, it is better to do nothing at all than to make meaningless movements. Try to cultivate definite, clear gestures.

Exercises — Gestures

When doing the following exercises, use your entire body, but focus your attention on the objects mentioned. See the object, touch it, react to it mentally, and finally take action. Let your face show your reactions. The shape, weight, and size of any object you pick up should be evident to the audience. After you have picked it up, be sure to hold it or put it down definitely.

1. You are walking in a garden. Pick a flower, and smell it. Show whether the smell is pleasing using facial expressions. Select fruit from a tree, taste it, and throw it away, expressing your dislike.

2. Suggest, by facial expression, the following situations:

   - A chef cracking open a rotten egg
   - A small child taking a nasty-tasting medicine
   - A person catching a whiff of his or her favorite food

3. You arrive at an airport shortly before take-off time. You are carrying a suitcase, an umbrella, and magazines. You drop your suitcase, and everything spills out. As you try to recover the contents of your suitcase, express agitation with both your facial expressions and body gestures.

4. You are wearing new shoes when you encounter a muddy patch of ground. You must walk among the puddles and mud, carefully choosing each step so as not to soil your shoes. Show hesitation in your body gestures and facial expressions.

❧ *Principles of Pantomime*

The techniques of pantomime are based on what human beings do physically in response to emotional stimulation, other people, and the objects around them. The richest source of authentic material for pantomime is careful observation of people in daily life, individually or in crowds. Pay attention to the different facial expressions, mannerisms, gestures, and ways of walking of people around you. You may find it profitable to analyze the movements of television, movie, and stage actors. Also note how your own physical responses reflect your feelings.

There are two phases of your work with pantomime. You have studied the first—exercises to relax your muscles and free your body for quick expression of feeling. The second phase is the creation of characterizations in which feeling prompts a bodily response. Both activities demand concentration of thought and focus on detail. You will find it takes a great deal of time and practice to achieve the exact effect you desire.

The following are a few established principles that affect acting. They are based on how people actually communicate feelings or ideas. Try to apply these principles as you work out your pantomimes.

> ## *F*ROM THE PROS
>
> "Although I was gifted, I was surprised at rehearsals to find how much I had to learn about technique."
>
> —CHARLIE CHAPLIN
> (1889–1977),
> ACTOR IN SILENT FILMS

BASIC PRINCIPLES OF BODY LANGUAGE

1. Your chest is the key to all bodily action.
2. Your wrists lead most hand gestures.
3. Move your elbows away from your body when making arm or hand gestures.
4. Except on specific occasions when it is necessary for communication purposes, do not gesture above your head or below your waist.
5. Opposite action emphasizes physical movement. Pulling your arm back before delivering a blow makes the punch more emphatic.
6. Arms and hands should move in curves, not in straight lines, unless you are deliberately trying to give the impression of awkwardness, uneasiness, force, or strength.
7. Positive emotions, such as love, honor, courage, and sympathy, are evidenced by a high chest and head, free movements, broad gestures, and animated facial expressions.
8. Negative emotions, such as hate, greed, fear, and suffering, contract and twist the body and are evidenced by a sunken chest, tense movement, restricted gestures, and drawn features.

9. Facial expressions—the use of the eyes, eyebrows, and mouth—usually precede other physical actions.
10. Whenever possible, make all gestures with your upstage arm, the one away from the audience, and avoid covering your face.
11. Some exaggeration of movement is often essential.
12. Always keep the audience in mind, and direct your actions to them.
13. All actions must be definite in concept and execution, and all movements must be clearly motivated.

STANDARD PANTOMIME EXPRESSIONS

Below are a number of standard pantomime techniques to express different situations. Keep in mind the principles you have just studied to achieve a convincing characterization.

BODY AS A WHOLE

1. A stance with heels together, weight on both feet, and chest and head slightly lifted suggests confidence, aloofness, indifference, or restrained self-control.
2. A stance with weight shifted to the front foot, with the head and body leaning slightly forward, represents interest, persuasion, sympathy, enthusiasm, or other positive emotions.
3. A stance with weight shifted to the rear foot, with the head and chest pulled back and turned away, represents hesitation, deep thought, amazement, fear, or other negative emotions.
4. A stance with sunken chest and bowed head, with shoulders forward and down, represents old age, envy, greed, pain, sorrow, or other negative emotions.

Even the most natural gesture or stance may be choreographed to achieve a certain effect. For example, as the actors stand in line for an audition in *A Chorus Line*, the way they stand reveals something about the attitudes and personalities of their characters.

FEET AND LEGS

1. A stance with feet apart and legs straight denotes arrogance, strong confidence, or defiance.
2. A stance with feet apart and legs bent denotes lack of bodily control, old age, great fatigue, or intoxication.
3. Tapping a foot depicts irritation, impatience, or nervousness; stomping a foot shows anger, frustration, or peevishness; twisting a foot denotes embarrassment.
4. A stance with feet apart, head high, and hands or fists on hips represents conceit, scorn, contempt, self-assertiveness, or challenge.

HEAD AND FACE

1. An expression with head raised, eyebrows lifted, eyes wide, and mouth open represents fear, horror, joy, or surprise.
2. An expression with head raised, eyebrows lifted, and mouth drawn down depicts comic bewilderment or inquisitiveness.
3. An expression with head down, eyebrows down, and mouth set or twisted by biting lips shows worry, meditation, or suffering.
4. An expression with raised eyebrows, wide eyes, and smiling or open lips depicts innocence, stupidity, or flirtatiousness.

FINGERS AND HANDS

1. A pointed finger commands, directs, or indicates an idea or the number *one*.
2. A clenched fist emphasizes an idea, threatens, shows anger, or demonstrates forced self-control.
3. Placing palms down indicates refusal, denial, condemnation, fear, rejection, horror, resistance, or other negative ideas.
4. Placing palms up indicates giving, pleading, receiving, requesting, presenting ideas, offering sympathy. A palms-up shrug means "I don't know" or "What's the use?"

After you have familiarized yourself with the standard pantomime techniques, try the following exercises.

1. Using only facial expressions, see how many different emotions you can display.

2. Combine one pantomime stance or expression from each category to portray an excited teenager receiving his or her first car.

3. Create a situation in which a character expresses varied emotions by incorporating as many pantomime stances and expressions as possible.

CUE ▼

Emotion affects your body in various ways. Practice feeling the emotion first. Then let your face and body respond.

CHARACTERIZATION

Characterization in pantomime involves placing a character in a situation and showing that character's thoughts through nonverbal expression. This entails two mental processes: imitation and imagination. You must develop a memory bank of emotions by carefully observing other people. When you see a person involved in a highly emotional situation, observe facial expressions, gestures, and body language. Draw on your observations when creating parts to make your characterization true to life. This is only the beginning, however, for you must use your imagination to place and maintain yourself in the part you are playing.

In pantomime, meaning usually conveyed with words must be conveyed by nonverbal expression. This means that your movements must be clear and recognizable to the audience.

Put on some comfortable clothes that allow you to move freely. Run through the relaxation and other practice exercises earlier in this chapter. Then imagine yourself in the following situations:

1. You are alone in your home watching the climax of a horror film on TV. Suddenly you hear a sound at the window. The window slowly opens, and a hand appears. You seize a book and hurl it at the hand, which promptly disappears. You tiptoe to the window, shut it, lock it, close the curtains, and fall into a chair, relieved but frightened.

2. Practice falling several times (see pages 33 and 34). Then imagine yourself in the following situations:

   - You receive a wound in the shoulder and then fall from the pain.
   - You step on roller skates. Fall, get up, and put the skates in a closet, limping from a sprained ankle.
   - You suddenly feel faint and fall. Then you recover, get up, and stagger to a chair, sitting down weakly.
   - You are walking downstairs. You slip and fall down several steps.

3. You have quarreled with your girlfriend or boyfriend. You are standing by a window, looking out, frowning, and biting your lip. Your chest is sunken; your body is slumped. The phone rings. Your face lights up. You run to the phone and lift the receiver. Let your face reflect the conversation. When you hang up, you show by your movements whether or not the quarrel is resolved.

4. You are a feeble man or woman going out to sit on the porch. You walk with short, uncertain steps, your feet six to eight inches apart. Your head is down, and your face is drawn. You sit down slowly with great effort and gradually relax as the sun warms you. Someone calls you, and you express your irritation by frowning and shaking your head. Then you rise, pushing yourself up from the chair. Hurry away as fast as your stiff limbs will allow. Your face should express a mixture of worry and agitation.

❧ *Individual Pantomimes*

Preparing for a pantomime, whether it involves people you know or imaginary characters, involves careful planning and rehearsing. Your pantomime will probably also include certain imaginary objects.

PANTOMIME AND OBJECTS

Portraying the size, shape, weight, resistance, texture, placement, and condition of objects is an important part of pantomime. Whenever possible, make evident to your audience the exact size of an object; consider its

Whiteface circus clowns like Emmett Kelly's mournful tramp, "Weary Willie," use the art of pantomime to entertain crowds that are much too large to be able to hear dialogue. The props used by circus clowns traditionally contain surprises; for instance, what seemed to be a heavy trunk when it was being pulled into the ring with sweat and toil might open to reveal nothing heavier than a flock of doves.

height, length, and width. Small objects, such as cups, books, and food, can be outlined with your hands. Large objects, such as furniture or shrubbery, require the involvement of your whole body. Extremely large objects, such as trees or houses, need to be outlined through eye and head movements. Some objects, such as a balloon that is being filled with air, may change in size during your pantomime.

Objects have different shapes. Some common shapes are circles, squares, ovals, triangles, and rectangles. Convey shape as you do size, through the use of your eyes, hands, and whole body.

Every item you handle has weight. A sack of popped popcorn does not weigh the same as a sack of sugar of the same size. A cement brick weighs more than a feather but far less than a car. Your pantomimed muscular tension conveys an object's weight. Never let the audience have a vague notion of weight. For example, the idea that something is being carried is not specific enough. You must show that a small, square box is being carried, picked up, or put down. You must show that the box is empty or contains clothes weighing ten pounds or books weighing forty pounds.

Objects also have a quality called resistance. Resistance is the firmness or solidity of an object. A balloon gives under the pressure of your fingers and changes when it bursts in your hands. A down-filled pillow gives far more when it is grasped in your hands than does a basketball. Squeezing a sponge demonstrates much less resistance than squeezing a rock. Resistance also involves the object's response to your actions. If you pull a rope, does something go up or come toward you? If you pull a rose petal, does it come off easily or must you yank it? One major principle of pantomime applies when you push against something that moves very little or not at all, such as an automobile or a wall. When pushing on such objects, it is you that moves the most, and you move in the opposite direction.

The surfaces of objects have definite textures. Before you pantomime, determine the texture of the object you will use. Is it rough or smooth? Jagged or rounded? Is the surface sandy? Pebbly? Prickly? Concentrate on that texture as you touch the object. Allow your senses to respond to what you are touching. The more sensory involvement you have with the object, the more expressive your reactions will be. You will convey through your facial expressions and body language your sensory experience of the object. Touching a velvet cushion causes a very different reaction than touching a cactus does.

One of the major challenges in pantomime is placement, the location of things. It is very important that a table top, a shelf, or the spot where you picked a flower remain the same. Many actors remember locations by **kinesthesis**, the neuromuscular awareness the body feels in a particular physical position. Placement can also be determined by relating things to your own body: eye level, shoulder height, tiptoe height, and so on.

Exercises — Objects in Pantomime

1. Place one round object at a time out of sight behind a small screen or in a box. Have another person pick up the object without looking at it and describe it in terms of size, weight, shape, texture, and resistance, using specific terms. Some possible objects include the following:

golf ball	cotton ball
baseball	orange
soccer ball	olive
marble	jawbreaker

2. Place your hands on an imaginary car while keeping your elbows bent, your back arched forward with one foot in advance of the other, and your weight on the forward foot. Then, as you push the car, allow the resistance to force your body backward. As you step forward with the back foot, slowly straighten your arms.

3. Blow up an imaginary balloon, showing its changing size.

4. Pantomime preparing chili, gradually adding spices until it's too spicy.

5. Go into an imaginary movie theater, and purchase popcorn and a soft drink. Crawl over five people to get to your seat. Do not spill your popcorn or soda on them.

6. Pantomime walking through the park. You realize that someone has left a purse by a bench. You pick it up, sit down, and examine its contents, looking for the owner's identification.

7. Walk an imaginary dog. Determine the size, weight, and temperament of the dog. As you walk along, the dog stops, and you attempt to move it.

CUE ▼

Practice your pantomime in front of a mirror to see if your actions will be clear to an audience.

Many imaginary props that you use in your pantomimes will be in a particular condition or state that must be expressed through your actions. Conditions include such things as temperature (hot, cold, lukewarm) and states of matter (solid, liquid, gas). Conditions also apply to the senses (taste—sweet, sour, bitter, salty; sight—bright, dim, dark, clear, misty; and sound—loud, soft, melodious, discordant, distant, close). Motion is a condition essential to pantomime. Are you still or moving? Is someone or something else still or moving? How do age, fatigue, and state of mind affect motion?

HOW TO DEVELOP A PANTOMIME

1. Decide if you will begin your pantomime onstage in a neutral position—head down or looking straight ahead (upstage or downstage), arms down, hands folded in front—or if you will enter from the wings.

2. Set your mental image in detail. Know exactly how much space you will use, the location of the furniture, and the shape, weight, and position of every imaginary prop you will be using. You must remember not to break the illusion by shifting an object without clear motivation and action.

3. Visualize the appearance and emotional state of your character in minute detail.

4. Imagine yourself dressed in the clothes of your character. Make your audience see the weight, shape, and material of each garment.

5. Remember that in all dramatic work, the thought comes first; think, see, and feel before you move. Let your eyes respond first, then your face and head, your chest, and finally, the rest of your body. This is a motivated sequence.

6. Keep your actions simple and clear.

7. Always have a key action early in the pantomime that establishes who you are and what you are doing. Pantomime should not be a guessing game.

8. Keep every movement and expression visible to your entire audience at all times. Place as many imaginary tables, shelves, and props as you can in front of you, and face the audience.

9. Never make a movement or gesture without a reason. Ask yourself, "Does this movement or gesture clarify who my character is, how he or she feels, or why he or she feels that way?"

10. Practice and analyze every movement and gesture until you are satisfied that it is the most truthful, effective, and direct means of expressing your idea or feeling.

11. Make only one gesture or movement at a time, but coordinate your entire body with it, and focus the attention of the audience on it.

12. Rehearse until you are sure that you have created a clear characterization and that the action began definitely, remained clear throughout, and came to a conclusion.

13. Plan your introduction carefully. It may be humorous or serious, but it must arouse interest in your character and in the situation in which your character is placed. It must also establish all of the essential details of the setting.

14. Plan the ending carefully. Leave the stage in character.

Exercises Pantomiming Imaginary People

Start to prepare your pantomime by running through each of the following exercises in rapid succession. Then select one and work it out in detail, elaborating on mannerisms and concentrating on details. After practicing a single study, build up a sequence of events that bring about a change of mood and situation. Finally, build up to a definite emotional climax and conclusion.

1. Standing erect, with your feet close together, suggest the following:

   - A butler or a housekeeper
   - A model displaying the latest fashions
   - A traffic officer

2. With legs wide apart and in a comfortable posture, represent the following:

   - A warm-hearted host standing in front of a fireplace beaming at guests
   - A political candidate addressing a friendly meeting

   - A quiz show participant confidently awaiting the next question

3. Walk across the room, and bow or curtsy in the manner of the following characters:

   - A colonial woman at a formal party, wearing a full-skirted gown and a towering headdress
   - A famous performer taking a bow
   - A diplomat greeting a foreign representative

(continued)

4. With alert posture, one foot somewhat ahead of the other and your weight definitely placed on the ball of the forward foot, represent the following:

- A high school student intently watching a football game
- A clerk handing a package to a customer
- A politician campaigning for votes

5. In a similar posture, with your weight definitely shifted to the rear foot, impersonate the following:

- A person afraid to cross the street
- A teenager opening the gym bag she or he has forgotten in the locker for a month
- A hiker who has stirred up a rattlesnake

6. Cross the room, sit in a chair, and rise as the following characters:

- A guilty person in the witness box at a trial

- A miser counting money and listening for eavesdroppers
- A parent at the bedside of a sick child
- A king or queen dismissing his or her court

7. Suggest, by smiling, the following characters:

- A seasick traveler trying to appear sociable
- A teacher greeting new students
- A salesperson dealing with an unpleasant customer

8. Present the following characters as completely as you can. Sit or walk, as you choose, and include enough actions to show each one in a real situation.

- An egotistical, self-confident businessperson
- A conceited musician
- A child pretending to be sick so that he or she can stay home from school
- A distinguished society leader
- A teacher teaching for the first time

PANTOMIME OF A REAL PERSON AND A REAL EVENT

When you prepare a pantomime of a real person and a real event, you have a model after which to fashion your pantomime. You do not have to imagine how that person performs that particular activity because you know what that person looks like and how he or she moves and behaves. To begin pantomiming a real person and a real event, choose an action that you do frequently, perhaps every day. Pantomime something such as getting ready for school, eating breakfast, or starting a car. For this pantomime, you should have the following three goals:

1. Make what you are doing clear to the audience.
2. Enable the audience to identify each object you use.
3. Strive for exactness and detail.

Pantomime an activity you do often, following these steps.

1. Choose an activity that you can pantomime in two to five minutes.

2. Practice the activity as you normally would do it, using the actual objects, furnishings, and materials.

3. Break the activity into steps, analyzing each one.

4. Record the sequence of actions. Take note of small details that are likely to be overlooked.

5. Rehearse with the specific objects you use—*your* hairbrush, for example, not an imaginary brush.

6. After rehearsing with real objects, try pantomiming several times. Check your pantomime against your outline. You might want to use real objects again to confirm the exactness of your pantomime.

PANTOMIME OF A REAL PERSON AND AN IMAGINARY EVENT

Next, plan a pantomime placing a real person other than yourself in an imaginary situation. Review the three goals as you plan your pantomime. Choose a person whose chief characteristics and habits you know very well. Observe the person as you consider what action you will pantomime and how you will convey the uniqueness of that person. Think about the situation you will use and the environment of the situation, including any props you will need. You need not have actually seen your character in such a situation, but you must be able to imagine how that person would react in it.

THE GREATS
★ ★ ★ ★ ★

You can almost "see" the telephone in Marcel Marceau's right hand. What kind of telephone is he using? Explain your answer. With what movement will he hang up when his pantomimed conversation is completed?

Pantomiming a Real Person

Choose a person to pantomime. Decide what makes that person different from anyone else. Then place your character in a situation.

1. Determine the person's chief characteristics. Is he or she friendly? Timid? Boisterous? Suspicious? Glamorous? Strong? Discontented?

2. Mentally note the details of the person's habitual facial expressions, especially the eyes and mouth.

3. Observe how that person holds his or her head, moves his or her hands, and walks.

4. Be sure that you know the exact position of the doors, windows, furniture, and props you will use. Make the location of props clear to your audience.

5. Have your character enter a definite environment in a definite state of mind.

6. Invent something that will change your character's mood.

7. Imitate what you have imagined your character would do.

The actors in Thornton Wilder's *The Happy Journey to Trenton and Camden* pantomime taking a trip in an automobile. Group pantomimes are challenging because they require that the actors cooperate to tell a unified story while at the same time maintaining the uniqueness of their own roles.

✣ *Group Pantomimes*

Group pantomimes should follow your individual ones and eventually lead into the acting of a short play. They will demand even more careful planning and rehearsal time than you have devoted to your individual pantomimes. Group pantomimes may be based on plays, novels, stories, poems, or such secondary sources as photographic magazines, newscasts, or films. Feel free, also, to draw on the things you observe around you daily.

Plan a group pantomime as carefully as you would a short play. Focus on a single, interesting situation with a conflict, a climax, and a clear resolution. Use five or six characters with distinctive personalities. Be sure all action is motivated and that you present a balanced stage picture free of bunching or huddling behind furniture. Rehearse until you have a unified presentation. Do not rush the action. The audience must be able to follow the development. Remember, you are limited to a visual presentation of your ideas, so be original and imaginative.

Exercises — Group Pantomimes

Try these group pantomimes, concentrating on cooperating with others to create the best effect.

1. A first-grade class is at the zoo. Pantomime the actions of the children, the teachers, the vendors, and the animals.

2. Two athletic teams are playing a game. After a hard-fought game, one team scores the winning run, basket, or goal. Pantomime the actions of the athletes, the coaches, and the fans.

3. Act out the poem "Casey at the Bat," pantomiming the ball players, the umpire, and the fans.

4. Pantomime the actions of several persons applying to a personnel director for a job.

5. A baby-sitter is trying to take charge of two unruly children. Pantomime the actions of the baby-sitter and the children.

6. A photographer is taking a family picture of four generations. Pantomime the actions of the photographer and the family members.

7. A customer service representative is trying to handle the complaints of several customers. Each customer pantomimes the object being returned and what is wrong with it. The employee pantomimes how the object should have been cared for or operated.

Application
ACTIVITIES

1. Write on separate pieces of paper five suggestions for pantomimes that can be presented by a single person. Your five pantomimes should reflect the following types:

   - a pantomime showing a single mood
   - a pantomime revealing a transition from one mood to another
   - a pantomime requiring a definite entrance and exit
   - a pantomime necessitating sitting and rising
   - a pantomime that includes falling and getting up

   Bring these suggestions to class, and mix them together in a paper bag. Let each class member draw one and present it in class. Go around the class as many times as you wish.

2. Present as many individual and group pantomimes as possible in front of the class. Analyze each performance to see whether it has convincing characterization, clarity, reality, and effectiveness. The following questions, among others, should be discussed.

   - Has the pantomime been carefully prepared?
   - Are the characters interesting, lifelike, and vivid? Do you become emotionally involved with them?
   - Do the gestures and movements seem sincere, convincing, clear, and properly motivated?
   - Do all the actions help flesh out and clearly represent the characters and their situations?
   - Are the actions clear, realistic, sufficiently prolonged, and exaggerated enough to be seen by the whole audience?
   - Can you visualize the setting, the props, and the clothing of the characters?
   - Does the pantomime have a definite beginning and ending?

CUE ▼

When preparing and presenting a group pantomime, keep the following guidelines in mind:

- Plan the entrances and exits carefully.
- Keep the action clear and unhurried.
- Make sure each character is a distinct personality.
- Make sure the stage picture is well balanced at all times.
- Do not rush the action.
- Be original and imaginative.

Mime

Although many performers make no distinction between mime and pantomime, **mime** is a special art form, an offspring of pantomime. Both the performer and the performance are called mime. Mime is abstract and highly stylized. Because it is abstract, mime does not imitate physical action as it occurs in life. Rather, it gives an illusion of that action. In fact, it is through that lack of exactness and the exaggeration of actions and facial expressions that its greater meaning is conveyed. Mime replaces exactness with conventions, abstractions that communicate symbolic or literal meanings. For example, mimes do not walk as we ordinarily do. None of the mime walks—and there are several—look like normal walking. The mime walk is an illusory walk, giving only the idea of walking. In addition, mimes work from just five basic facial expressions: happy, sad, surprised, angry, and afraid. Because mimes must rely so much on facial expressions to communicate emotions, these expressions must be easily seen and interpreted by the audience. Mimes traditionally emphasize their eyes and mouths with makeup to exaggerate their facial expressions and make them more visible.

THE GREATS
★ ★ ★ ★ ★

In "The Mask Maker," Marcel Marceau combines his mime makeup with exaggerated expression to emphasize his character's sadness.

MIME VERSUS PANTOMIME

There are several distinctions between mime and pantomime. Recall the principles of pantomime as you consider the special characteristics of mime.

PANTOMIME	MIME
The action conveys only action; for example, flying a kite.	The action conveys the theme; for example, snagging a kite on a tree after struggling to get it soaring in the sky might be a mime's way of saying, "Our aspirations often become entangled with the things of this world."
The artist works with imaginary objects.	The artist works with imaginary objects but may also use part or all of the body to become an object or express an idea.
No sounds are used.	Nonverbal sounds, such as escaping air, a telephone busy signal, or the screech of tires, may be used.
All pantomimes are based on reality.	Mimes go beyond reality; they are not limited to the real world.
The main goal is the exact pantomime of a specific action.	The main goal is the expression of an idea; themes can often be expressed in simple terms: *loneliness, young dreams*, or *forgiveness*.

Each primary mime action is preceded by a preparatory action. This preparatory action is usually a movement opposite to the action the mime wishes the audience to follow. It is much like the windup of a baseball pitcher prior to delivering a ball. For instance, the mime, before reaching out for an object, would first draw the arm back somewhat.

Everything in mime must be exaggerated. This exaggeration lifts mime above simple imitation of an action. For example, if you were to take an imaginary drinking glass, at the moment at which the glass is grasped, your fingers should snap around the glass. This snap establishes the glass's shape, size, and resistance in one action. This setting up of an action with definite hand movements is referred to as the "click." The setting up of the action is seen quite readily when a mime suggests the presence of a wall. Each hand snaps into place from the wrist as contact with the wall is made. The snap shows the wall, its flatness, and its resistance.

CONVENTIONAL MIME ACTIONS

Mime is made up of many traditional conventions. One of the most basic mime conventions is that of the illusory walk. There are several mime walks that are commonly used.

MIME WALKS

1. The simplest illusory walk is done in the following manner:

   Stand with your feet pointed out at a forty-five-degree angle. Place your weight on your right foot. Lift your left heel so that you are on the ball of your left foot. Then, shift your weight to your left foot by dropping the left heel and at the same time raising the right heel. Once you have your feet shifting rhythmically, add an arm swing. Swing your arms in an exaggerated but not overdone manner, crossing in front of your body. The illusion of walking appears when you move opposite arms and feet. Swing your right arm forward when you lift your left foot and your left arm forward when you lift your right foot.

THE GREATS
★ ★ ★ ★ ★

Marcel Marceau never speaks when he's onstage in character, of course, but in this Maître Mime he is seen instructing students in the art he revitalized for the twentieth century. In his own words, mime is "the art of expressing feelings by attitudes and not a means of expressing words through gestures."

2. A second illusory walk begins with the same starting position. Your left foot is lifted and stretched out away from you at a forty-five-degree angle and then brought back toward you in a sliding motion, ending on the ball of the sliding foot. As the heel is lowered to the floor, the other foot is extended.

3. The third illusory walk is much like the second, except that when the heel of your left foot reaches the instep of your right foot, shift your weight. At the same time, lift your left heel to the back and pivot your body slightly to the right. This puts you in position to start the step with the right foot. The weight is always on the stepping foot. Although this illusory walk is difficult to master, the illusion is quite effective. It is the walk used by many famous mimes.

In all the mime walks, there should be a lifting of the body just as the weight is shifted from one foot to the other. This is very important to the illusion. The exaggerated arm movement is also important. Speeding up the walk, leaning the body forward, and swinging the arms across in front of the body (much as in ice skating) will create the illusion of running.

Other mime conventions are the rope pull, the ladder climb, and climbing up and down stairs. In the rope pull, an artist creates the illusion of pulling a large rope. In the ladder climb, the rungs of a ladder form a sort of picture frame that helps create the illusion as the audience sees the mime's face move from frame to frame. In climbing up and down stairs, a mime uses the first illusory walk and presents an imaginary rail.

ROPE PULL

1. Stand with your left foot forward, knee bent, and your weight on it.

2. Reach out as far as you can with your left hand, and grasp a one-inch rope. Take the rope with your right hand just in front of your left hip. Now pull. Your weight shifts to your right foot, and your left hand follows your right hand until your left hand is in front of your right hip. The rope should be straight through your hands, which are parallel to the floor. The rope should maintain its diameter throughout the pull.

3. Let go with your right hand, reach over your left, and grasp the rope about one foot in front of your left hip. Then, with a quick movement, shift your weight back onto your left foot as you reach out as far as you can with your left hand to take the rope for another pull. It is the quick one-two of the right hand-left hand switch that creates the illusion of pulling a large rope.

LADDER CLIMB

1. Bend the elbows slightly, raise your arms above your head, and grasp the rung of the ladder with both hands.
2. Lift your right foot, and then lower it.
3. Lift your left foot; as you lower it, bring your left arm straight down. Your left hand still appears to be grasping the rung of the ladder.
4. Look up, see the next rung, take it with your right hand, lift your right foot, and bring hand and foot down together, watching the rung as it passes before your eyes.
5. Coming down is a little more challenging because there is more illusion to create. Place your hands on the ladder rungs as before. Lift your left foot and suspend it on the rung. Look down (about shoulder level) at the rung you are going to grasp.
6. Let go with your left hand, and take the rung below as you step down. As your left hand comes down, your right hand must go up to the rung above position, and your right foot must be lifted, ready to step down. Obviously, your hands are passing each other, but the illusion is that of descending.

CLIMBING UP AND DOWN STAIRS

1. Go up the stairs, using the first mime walk.
2. Grasp the handrail about eye level with your right hand. If you are not sure about the size of the rail, take hold of your left wrist, get the feel of that size, and use that for the rail.
3. Now, as you walk, usually taking three steps, bring your hand down past your body at the angle of the rail until your hand is just past your hip. Then reach up and take the rail again. Remember the click before each new action starts. Continue up the stairs.
4. To come down the stairs, reach down in front of you at a comfortable distance (about midthigh), grasp the rail lightly with your right hand, and move your hand up beside you to about the midchest level. As you bring your arm up, extend your elbow out. This will enable you to keep the rail straight.

CONVENTIONAL MIME MAKEUP AND COSTUME

The classic mime tries to neutralize the face by painting it with a white mask that stops at the jawline, the hairline, and in front of the ears. The detailed makeup is individualized by each mime, but most mimes make up their eyes and mouths, the two most expressive parts of the face. Some

The classic mime neutralizes the face by making it a white mask but adds emphasis to the mouth and eyes, the most expressive features.

mimes draw in brows; some add a tear, a flower, a star, or other characteristic feature somewhere on their faces. Most classic mimes still use the conventional makeup, but many mimes perform without the white mask. The choice is yours.

There are many kinds of mime dress. The most important item of clothing is a flexible shoe, such as a ballet shoe or a sneaker. Some mimes perform in a leotard and tights or dance pants. Others wear jumpsuits. Some wear bib overalls and striped knit shirts. Professional mimes often use specially made costumes consisting of fairly tight stretch pants and a matching short-waisted jacket worn over a knit shirt. Marcel Marceau is one of the few to use a character costume.

The Swiss-trained mime troupe Mummenschanz opened the doors of mime to the use of special props and nontraditional subjects. Many of their props, such as stretch sacks, were really costumes. The troupe's imaginative style and inventive mimes, however, challenged other mimes to expand the art beyond the costumeless, propless tradition of classic mime.

MIME EXERCISES

There are three types of mime exercises: inclinations, rotations, and isolations (separations). An **inclination** is the bending of the body to the front, the side, or the rear. A **rotation** is the turning or pivoting of a part of the body, such as the head or the chest. An **isolation** separates parts of the body for individual development and expression. Isolations are usually the most challenging exercises for inexperienced mimes because beginners tend to respond with the whole body rather than with isolated parts.

Mime exercises begin with the heels close together and the toes pointing out at a forty-five-degree angle. Mimes divide the body into six major parts: head, neck, shoulders, chest, waist, and hips. These may be further subdivided for more refined exercises. Complete each movement before moving to the next. Do not rush.

INCLINATIONS (MOVE EACH BODY PART ONE AT A TIME.)

1. Incline your head, your neck, your shoulders, your chest, your waist, and then your hips to the right. As your hip inclines right, slide your left foot along the floor away from your body. Straighten up one body part at a time. Then repeat the action to the left. Remember to slide your right foot out for the hip inclination.

2. Do a vertical inclination, keeping your body relaxed. Drop your head forward and then your neck. Your chin should be resting lightly on your chest. Now drop your shoulders. (You will look round-shouldered.) Now drop your chest forward. Imagine that your chest has

THE GREATS
★ ★ ★ ★ ★
Here Marcel Marceau incorporates movements from mime exercises into his movement onstage. He is bending his body to the front (an inclination) and pivoting his right leg (a rotation).

caved in just above your stomach. Now drop at your waist. This should put your back in a position parallel to the floor with your arms dangling perpendicular to the floor. Finally, drop from your hips. Depending on your flexibility, you should be touching your toes or the floor; perhaps you can even place your hands flat on the floor.

Now go back to your standing position by doing your inclinations slowly in reverse order.

ROTATIONS (MOVE EACH BODY PART IN SMOOTH CIRCLES.)

1. To rotate your head and neck, start by dropping your chin onto your chest. Rotate your head and neck to the right, back, left, and front. Raise your head.

2. To rotate your shoulder, lift it, and move it in a circle forward, down, and back to the original position.

3. To rotate your chest laterally, lift it, and move it in a clockwise fashion. You may also rotate your chest forward and back.

4. To rotate your waist, move it in a circle clockwise.

5. Following the same procedure, rotate your hips clockwise.

6. Now repeat these five rotations, but reverse directions. Follow each step as described above.

ISOLATIONS

1. Isolate your head by moving it straight forward, returning it to center, then moving it straight back. Next, move your head to the left, back to the center, and then to the right. Keep your head level; do not incline it. Now rotate your head to the right, then to the left, without moving your shoulders.

2. Isolate your right shoulder. Raise it; lower it; move it forward; move it back. Rotate your shoulder forward. Rotate it to the rear. Repeat with your left shoulder.

3. Try isolating each leg from the hip. Then isolate your lower leg, and after that isolate your foot. For each part, raise it; lower it; move it forward; move it back. Rotate it clockwise, then counterclockwise.

Mummenschanz, a mime company based in Switzerland, has brought modern technology to the traditional art. Its performances, while innovative, nonetheless bear a resemblance to ancient Roman pantomime, in which the actors wore various masks. (*Mumme* is German for "mask"; *Schanze* is archaic German for "chance.")

Application

1. Line up as two teams facing each other for a rope pull. Your teacher will call out which team pulls. Remember, when one team pulls, the other team must give by leaning forward.

2. You are in a box. Show the size and shape of the box.

3. Get a kite into the air. Tug on the string to get it higher and higher. The string breaks, and the kite drifts away. Watch it and then walk offstage sadly.

4. You are caught in a fierce storm with extremely high winds. You are attempting to walk against the wind to reach the safety of a building. Open the door, close it behind you, and slowly collapse from exhaustion.

5. You are standing on the bow of a small boat as it plows through rough water. You sway gently as each wave moves the boat from side to side. Gradually you become seasick.

6. Design a mime. Give it a title. Write your title on a large piece of paper or cardboard, and set it up before the class. Turn in the description of your mime to your teacher before you begin. Then present your mime to the class. You may enter from the wings, or you may begin from a neutral standing position.

7. A **combination** is the putting together of inclinations, rotations, and isolations. Try this combination. Isolate your right arm by lifting it from your body slightly. Raise it from your elbow until your arm is at shoulder level. Your forearm should hang down toward the floor with your hand relaxed. Imagine that a string is attached to your wrist, and raise the isolated forearm perpendicular with your body until it is parallel to your shoulder. Your hand should still be hanging limply. Next, lift your left foot and place it toe down across your right foot. Now, incline your head to the right and let your weight sag on your right arm. You should appear to be leaning on a wall, a mantel, or a shelf.

CHAPTER 2 REVIEW

Summary and Key Ideas

Summarize the chapter by answering the following questions.

1. Why should pantomime be the first stage in an actor's training?
2. Identify three forms of nonverbal communication that people use daily.
3. What are some rules for walking, sitting, and falling onstage?
4. What qualities of objects are portrayed in pantomime?
5. Explain how mime differs from pantomime.
6. What features of the face are most important in expressing ideas and emotions? How do mimes emphasize these features?
7. Why do mimes use gestures?
8. Name and explain some typical mime actions.

Discussing Ideas

1. Why is a responsive, expressive body important to an actor?
2. Discuss the importance of gestures onstage. Explain why it is sometimes better to make no gesture at all.
3. Characterization in pantomime demands both imitation and imagination. Discuss the importance of each in character portrayal.
4. Mime does not imitate physical action as it occurs in real life. Instead it gives an illusion of that action. Discuss why this key feature of mime appeals to audiences.

FOCUS ON Choreography

Choreographers create the dances, or choreography, in a production. These dance professionals need to understand human movements just as mimes do. After all, they create the body language that dancers use to communicate theme, mood, and plot. Next time you're watching a movie and come upon a dance scene, fight scene, or stunt sequence, remember there's a good chance that it was designed by a choreographer.

Analyzing Dance and Theater With a partner, discuss what you know about dance and how it communicates themes, motivations, and emotions. Then make a chart comparing and contrasting the ways that dance and theater communicate meaning to an audience. Share your chart with the class.

Creating a Dance In a small group, write a script for a short scene that includes a dance sequence. Work together to create a dance that will enhance the meaning of the scene. Practice the scene, and then present it to the class. After your performance, discuss with your group the artistic discipline required for choreography and dance, whether pursued as a career or an avocation.

PANTOMIME AND MIME

INDEPENDENT ACTIVITIES

Emergence   Create a mime for a store mannequin that comes to life. Keep your actions simple, but indicate a change in mood or feeling, such as the movement from wonderment to fear.

Emotion   Create a pantomime or mime that expresses an emotion, such as anger, pain, joy, frustration, or resignation. When you present it to your class, tie a scarf around your face to mask your expression. This will make your presentation and your audience's interpretation dependent on your body's movement and position.

Extreme Temperatures   Imagine you are in one of the following situations. Show extreme heat or extreme cold in your posture, gestures, actions, and facial expressions.

- Building a snowman
- Ice skating or cross-country skiing
- Relaxing at the beach
- Taking a hot, relaxing bath (or sauna)

Cooperative Learning Activity

Moving Day
Imagine that you and a partner have an enormous box to move. Although the box is not exceptionally heavy, it is cumbersome, and its contents keep shifting. Plan a pantomime that illustrates the conflict and its resolution. Create two distinct characters who handle the situation differently but learn to compromise in order to get the task accomplished.

The Sculptor and the Block of Wood
Working with a partner, plan a pantomime that shows what happens when a sculptor starts with an enormous block of wood and creates a piece of art. Visualize the sculptor working on one part of the block at a time with a hammer and chisel, allowing the figure to emerge gradually.

Across the CURRICULUM Activities

Physical Education
Choose a favorite sport, such as boxing, tennis, or basketball. Working independently, with a partner, or with a small group, develop a slow-motion form of a meet, a match, or a game. Remember that each action and facial expression should be exaggerated and slow. Take plenty of time to prepare the exact reactions you will have to your imaginary situation, and then present your sport to the class.

History   With a group of your classmates, choose a historical event, such as the signing of the Declaration of Independence or the first use of the telephone. Gather enough factual details to help you re-create the characters and the situation. Have your classmates guess what event you are pantomiming.

CHAPTER

3

Voice and Diction

As Shylock in Shakespeare's *The Merchant of Venice*, Dustin Hoffman must speak persuasively to Portia, played by Geraldine Jones, as well as project his voice in order to be heard from the last row of seats in the theater.

peak the speech, I pray you, as I pronounced it to you, trippingly on the tongue.

—from *Hamlet* by William Shakespeare

62

SETTING THE SCENE

Focus Questions

What are the keys to a good speaking voice?

Why is breath control so important?

How can you develop a rich, strong, and interesting stage voice?

Vocabulary

quality	pitch	volume	schwa	pronunciation
resonance	inflection	rate	voiceless	
nasality	monotone	diction	voiced	

An expressive voice and clear, correct speech are not only indispensable tools for the actor, they are also assets in almost everyone's life. Personnel directors list them among the qualities needed for any position that requires working with others.

This chapter will show you how to meet the speaking requirements that plays, roles, directors—and employers—demand. It presents fundamental principles that you must understand and apply, along with simple and practical exercises that are designed to improve and polish your speaking ability. If you understand these principles and practice the exercises regularly, you can dramatically improve the effectiveness of your voice.

🎕 Developing an Effective Voice

There is nothing mysterious or complicated about developing an effective voice. It depends primarily on bodily relaxation, proper breathing, and good posture. Few people realize the close relationship between the voice, the emotions, and the body. The voice of a person who is ill, tired, worried, angry, nervous, hurried, or tense reflects those feelings. The voice becomes high-pitched, monotonous, or colorless. On the other hand, a person who is poised, self-confident, and healthy is more likely to have a pleasing voice. Consequently, your first efforts should be directed toward building both a vigorous, well-controlled body and a confident, healthy attitude.

Voice is produced by the air from the lungs passing over the vocal folds, which are thin curtains of muscles with delicate edges. These folds set up vibrations, or waves. The vibrations become sounds and are amplified when they strike the resonating chambers of the throat, head, nose, and mouth. Exactly what sounds are produced depends on the shape of these chambers, and this shape is determined by the position of the tongue, soft palate, lips, and lower jaw. For correct speech and voice production, it

THE GREATS
★ ★ ★ ★ ★

Orson Welles's rumbling, resonant voice communicated conviction and authority. Even in the medium of radio, his power and presence could be felt.

THE VOCAL TRACT

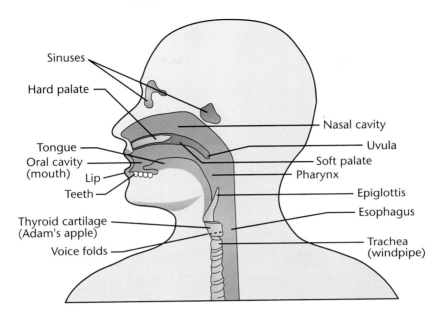

- Sinuses
- Hard palate
- Tongue
- Oral cavity (mouth)
- Lip
- Teeth
- Thyroid cartilage (Adam's apple)
- Voice folds
- Nasal cavity
- Uvula
- Soft palate
- Pharynx
- Epiglottis
- Esophagus
- Trachea (windpipe)

Knowing where the resonating chambers of the mouth, nose, head, and throat are and knowing how to change the shape of those chambers to produce different sounds can be helpful as you are developing your voice.

is necessary for you to have an open, relaxed throat; a flexible tongue and lips; and a relaxed lower jaw. It is also necessary to practice deep central breathing.

For an actor, exercising the voice is as important as exercising and conditioning the body. Every student of the theater should begin a program of voice training as soon as possible. Poor vocal habits can be eliminated within an amazingly short period of time by regular exercise and deliberate concentration.

RELAXATION

The degree of relaxation determines the carrying power of the vowel sounds. Proper vowel sounds are the key to a powerful and beautiful voice, and vowel sounds are made with an open, relaxed throat, a relaxed jaw, and flexible lips. Therefore, before attempting any voice exercises, you must relax, consciously doing so both mentally and physically. A tense or tight throat will cause hoarseness when you try to project your voice in practice or in performance.

With practice, you can learn to run through the following process when you are waiting to make a speech or standing in the wings before an entrance onto the stage. You will also find it an excellent cure for stage fright.

You should spend about fifteen minutes a day doing the exercises in this chapter. It is best to choose a time when you are feeling fresh and relaxed.

1. Stretch your whole body as an animal does after a nap. (Incidentally, watching a cat relax and move is an excellent exercise in itself.) Feel the big muscles of your back, legs, and arms ease first.

2. Imagine that a warm, relaxing shower is falling over your head. Imagine it passing over your forehead and wiping out the frown lines. Imagine it releasing the tension of the little muscles around your eyes, nose, mouth, and especially your cheeks. Roll your head first to the left, then to the right, keeping the neck muscles relaxed.

3. Imagine the shower pouring over your whole body, relaxing your arms and fingertips, your chest, lungs, diaphragm, and even your toes. You should be yawning by this time, and that is one of the best voice exercises.

Before you begin vocal work, run through the posture exercises on page 30. (You may also want to do the breathing exercises on pages 68 and 69.) The importance of an erect, easily relaxed body should not be underestimated. The following exercises demand careful use of your vocal apparatus. Refer to the pronunciation key on page 85 for examples of the vowel sounds.

In order for your vocal apparatus to function powerfully and flexibly, it must be relaxed and not constricted by muscular tension.

1. For Relaxed Jaw

- Let your head fall forward onto your chest. Lift it up and back, letting your jaw remain loose. Drop it again and slowly roll your head over your right shoulder, back, over your left shoulder, and forward.
- Drop your head forward again. Place your hands lightly on your cheeks and lift your head with your hands, keeping the jaw relaxed and being careful to avoid using the jaw muscles. When your head is lifted, the jaw should hang open. Make your face as expressionless as possible.

2. For Open Throat

- Yawn freely, getting the feeling of an open, relaxed throat.
- Take in a deep breath, relax your jaw, and exhale slowly.
- Say, "I can talk as if I were going to yawn. Hear me talk as if I were going to yawn."

3. For Flexible Lips

- Say ōō-ō-ô-ŏ-ä, opening your lips from a small circle to a large one. Then reverse, saying ä-ŏ-ô-ō-ōō. These sounds may be sung, keeping to one note. Keep the tongue flat with the tip at the lower teeth. Keep your throat open and your jaw relaxed.
- Say mē-mō-mē-mō-mē-mō-mē-mō. Then sing these sounds.

4. For Flexible Tongue

- Say these sounds rapidly: *fŭd-dŭd-dŭd-dŭd-däh-fŭd-dŭd-dŭd-dŭd-däh-fŭd-dŭd-dŭd-dŭd-däh-frĭl*. Trill the *r* in *frĭl*.
- Keeping your jaw relaxed, repeat the following sounds, watching with a hand mirror to see that your tongue is slowly arched as you go from one position to the next: *ä-ŭ-ûr-ä-ă-ĕ-ā-ĭ-ē*.
- Babble like a baby, saying *dä-dä-dä-dä lä-lä-lä-lä-lä* moving only the tip of the tongue.

BREATH CONTROL

Breath control determines the carrying power and loudness of your voice. It also enables you to rehearse and perform over long periods of time with less strain or damage to your voice.

No one needs to teach you how to breathe; you have been breathing successfully since birth. There is some difference, however, between regular breathing and breathing for speech. In regular breathing, the inhalation (breathing in) and exhalation (breathing out) periods are of equal length. Breathing for speech requires a very brief inhalation period and a slow, controlled exhalation period. This is true because, for all practical purposes, speech is produced only when the breath is exhaled. In breathing for speech, therefore, you should inhale through the mouth, since this allows

Shakespearean dialogue, because of its complex sentences full of interrelated images, demands carefully planned and practiced breath control. Here Kevin Kline delivers Hamlet's "Alas, poor Yorick. I knew him, Horatio" speech in the New York Shakespeare Festival.

for more rapid intake of breath than does inhalation through the nose. You should work for a prolonged and controlled exhalation so that the outgoing breath will match your needs for sustained vocal tone. Controlled breathing is more important to an actor than deep breathing.

The following exercises will focus the breathing process in the center of your body and strengthen and control the breath stream. Practice these exercises every night and morning until central breathing gradually becomes automatic.

Exercises — Breath Control

1. Place your hands on either side of the lower part of your rib cage. Now pant rapidly, laugh silently, and sniff in the air in tiny whiffs. Lie on your back and breathe deeply and regularly. Keep your hands in the same position.

2. With your hands in the same position as for Exercise 1, stand straight with an easy, well-balanced posture. Inhale slowly, making sure from the feeling under your hands that the whole rib cage is expanding. Hold your breath without straining for a count of six. Then exhale slowly and evenly while you mentally count, first to fifteen and then to twenty, twenty-five, and thirty. Be particularly careful to avoid muscular tension.

3. Repeat Exercise 2, gauging the evenness of your exhalation either by whistling or by making a soft sound as you breathe out, such as the sound of *s* or *ah*. If the sound is jerky or irregular or fades at the end, repeat the exercise until you can keep the sound smooth and regular.

(continued)

4. Breathe in, relaxing your throat and lower jaw. Count "one" as you exhale. Repeat and count "one, two." Continue until you can count to twenty using just one breath. Be careful not to tighten up. It may take several weeks before you can reach twenty, but take time so that you can do it without straining. Any tension is bad.

5. Breathe in. Relax your throat and lower jaw. Say "Hear the tolling of the bells— iron bells" as you exhale, prolonging the vowels and the *ng* and *n* sounds.

6. Breathe in. Relax your throat and lower jaw. Say "Hong Kong" as you exhale, prolonging the vowel and *ng* sounds.

7. Breathe in. Relax your throat and lower jaw. Without straining, try to retain the position of your diaphragm as you exhale, saying slowly, "Roll on, thou deep and dark blue ocean, roll."

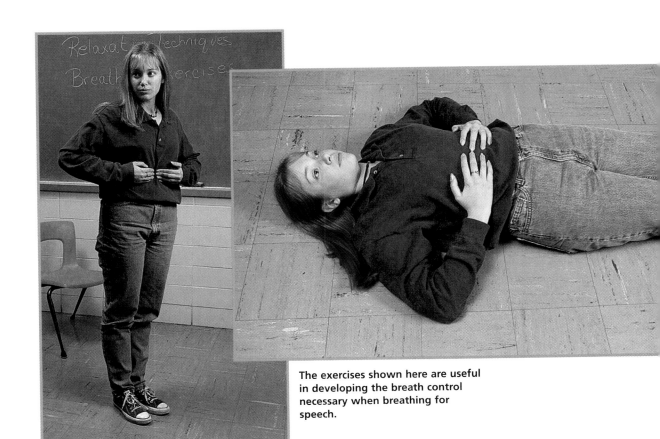

The exercises shown here are useful in developing the breath control necessary when breathing for speech.

❧ Using Your Voice Effectively

Four characteristics of the voice must be used correctly if you are to become an effective and expressive speaker. These characteristics are quality, pitch, volume, and rate. Developing and controlling them constitutes voice training.

QUALITY

The individual sound of your particular voice is called its **quality**. The quality of your voice depends, for the most part, upon resonance and the correct formation of vowel sounds by the speech organs.

    Resonance is the vibrant tone produced when sound waves strike the chambers of the throat, head, nose, and mouth. The best practice for resonance is humming with an open, relaxed throat. The cavities of the head will vibrate automatically if you hum while throwing the voice forward through the facial mask. In English, only *m, n,* and *ng* should be sounded through the nose. All other sounds should come from the mouth alone. If the nasal passages are closed by a cold or by a raised soft palate, the sound becomes dull and blocked. The much-criticized **nasality** of many American voices occurs when vowel sounds are diverted from the oral cavity into the nasal cavities, cutting down resonance and leaving the voice flat.

Emotions such as fear affect the quality of your voice. Frightened people, who tend to draw themselves inward physically, also draw in their voices. The voice of a frightened person usually sounds timid and hesitant.

The vowel sounds, so important in the quality of your tone, are all made with the lower jaw relaxed. The position of the lips and tongue determines the sound.

Voice quality may also be affected by emotion. The voice might quiver with fear, sweeten with sympathy, or harden with anger. In addition, the age of a character will affect the quality of the voice. With age, the vocal apparatus usually becomes less flexible, and the outlook on life has been affected for better or worse by life's experiences. These things must be made apparent in an actor's characterizations.

Exercises — Voice Quality

1. To locate your larynx and feel the vibration of the vocal folds, place your fingers lightly on your thyroid cartilage, or Adam's apple. Pronounce the consonant sounds *bŭh* and *pŭh*, and notice which pronunciation makes the vocal folds vibrate. Repeat the test with the consonant-sound pairs *dŭh* and *tŭh*, then *vŭh* and *fŭh*, and then *zŭh* and *sŭh*.

2. To feel the effect of obstructing the resonators, sing the word *hum* and then repeat it while you pinch your nose closed. Say "good morning," opening your mouth and your throat. Say it as if you were on the verge of tears and were swallowing them. Say it holding your nose closed. Say it with your teeth tightly set. Say it while drawing back your tongue in your mouth.

3. Repeat a single word—*no, yes, dear, really*—conveying the following emotions: surprise, scorn, irritation, sarcasm, boredom, suspicion, eagerness, love, doubt, weariness, determination, horror, pain, despair, and joy. Notice how the quality of your voice changes with different emotions.

4. Assume the character of a happy child, a cross adult, a dictatorial employer, a discouraged job-seeker, a political candidate, a distinguished actor, a plotting criminal, and a hysterical survivor of an earthquake. Speak the following sentences as each of these characters would.

   - Now is the time to make your choice.
   - Yes, I see the light!
   - Whatever will be will be.
   - Stop! Think it over before you do anything you might regret!

5. Say the following words, recalling personal experiences to give them "color," the special tone quality resulting from feeling and imagination:

home	icy
ocean	roar
sunset	welcome
jingle	magnificent
dog	star

Application
ACTIVITIES

Read aloud the following selections, concentrating mainly on the vowel sounds. Try to make each vowel in an accented syllable as full and rich as possible. Sound these vowels alone many times and then put them back into the words.

1. from *Romeo and Juliet*
   by William Shakespeare

JULIET   The clock struck nine when I did
    send the Nurse;
  In half an hour she promised to return.
  Perchance she cannot meet him: that's not so.
  O, she is lame! love's heralds should be thoughts,
  Which ten times faster glide than the sun's
    beams,
  Driving back shadows over louring hills: . . .

2. from "The Raven"
   by Edgar Allan Poe

Once upon a midnight dreary, while I pondered, weak and weary,
Over many a quaint and curious volume of forgotten lore—
While I nodded, nearly napping, suddenly there came a tapping,
As of someone gently rapping, rapping at my chamber door—
"'Tis some visitor," I muttered, "tapping at my chamber door—
Only this and nothing more."

CUE ▼

Before reading any excerpt or passage, read the complete work, if possible. This will help you understand fully the mood and meaning of the selection.

PITCH

The relative highness or lowness of the voice at any given time is called **pitch**. Each person's voice has a characteristic pitch level from which it moves up and down. Women's voices are pitched on a higher level than men's, and children's voices are higher still. Pitch is determined by the rapidity with which the vocal folds vibrate.

Most persons use only four or five notes in ordinary speaking, but a good speaker can use two octaves or more. Many girls and women pitch their voices at too high a level, not realizing that a low voice is far more musical and easily heard. As a rule, therefore, girls and women should do their vocal exercises on the lower pitch levels.

The pitch of the voice gives meaning to speech. When speakers are excited, interested, and enthusiastic in conversation, they unconsciously lift the pitch on important words to emphasize them and lower the pitch on unimportant words to subordinate them. In the exchange of lines in a play or in a long speech by a single character, the pitch rises as conflict increases, excitement stirs, or comedy builds. This rise in pitch adds to the interest of a scene. However, the actor's voice cannot continue to rise until it squeaks or cracks. Knowing how and when to bring the voice down is one of the skills an actor must develop.

Variety in pitch, called **inflection**, makes the voice musical and interesting. Speaking in a **monotone** results from speaking continuously on one level. Monotony is a flaw in speaking. Without variety in pitch, speakers are unable to hold the attention of their audiences. Public speakers, teachers, and lawyers sometimes fall unconsciously into pitch patterns and speak in monotones. Monotony in pitch can usually be overcome by practice and conscious attention. It is due largely to lack of vitality and enthusiasm in thought and feeling or in vocal and bodily response.

As a student of dramatics, you must learn to control the number, length, and direction of pitch changes. Try to notice your own and other people's changes in pitch in normal conversation and how these changes affect the communication of thoughts and feelings. Notice what anger, exhaustion, irritation, worry, joy, and excitement do to the pitch of people's voices. You will find that the pitch is usually higher when a person is angry, that dominant people use falling inflections for the most part, and that timid people use brief, rising inflections. Sneering and sarcasm are often shown by rising-falling inflections, which convey subtle meanings.

If you play a lively character who delivers an angry speech, the pitch of your voice will probably rise. When characters who are more subdued become angry, they often lower their tone of voice and become immersed in a mood of sullen brooding.

1. Find your range and optimum (ideal) pitch by matching tones with a piano. Begin by reading a selection in your normal voice. As a friend plays up the scale, match each note. Record the highest note you can reach without strain. Then go down the scale and record the lowest note you can reach comfortably. This is your range. Now find the middle of your range. This is your optimum pitch. Your optimum pitch will often be two or three notes lower than your normal speaking voice.

2. Count from one to ten, beginning as low as you can and going as high as you can without strain. Then reverse the count and come down. Be sure that it is pitch and not loudness that makes the difference in each count.

3. Count slowly from one to ten, giving the vowel in each number a long falling inflection. Repeat with a long rising inflection on each. Then alternate the two exercises.

4. Select a nursery rhyme and recite it as a comforting parent, a Shakespearean actor, a bored teenager, and a frightened child.

5. Read the following sentences aloud with the widest possible range. Put emphasis on the important words and syllables by raising the pitch. Drop the pitch noticeably on unimportant words.

   - What a great idea!
   - To speak effectively, you must raise your voice on the important words.
   - In direct conversation, we constantly change the pitch of the voice.
   - Did you hear what I said? Then go!
   - No, I will not go!

6. Stand out of sight of your listeners, and give the following lines. Have someone note your variations in pitch.

   - No, never. Well, hardly ever.
   - To be, or not to be: that is the question.
   - Do unto others as you would have them do unto you.
   - Give me liberty or give me death!

Once you find your range, you can do vocal exercises to help you increase it. A greater vocal range gives you more emotional range as an actor.

Application
ACTIVITIES

Analyze the following selections and decide what inflections will bring out the predominant mood and inner meaning of each. Read each selection aloud. If possible, use a tape recorder to study the pitch of your voice. Reread each selection aloud, concentrating on improving your inflection and voice quality.

1. from *The Taming of the Shrew*
   by William Shakespeare

   PETRUCHIO   Good morrow, Kate, for that's your name, I hear.
   KATHERINE   Well have you heard, but something hard of hearing:
       They call me Katherine that do talk of me.
   PETRUCHIO   You lie, in faith, for you are called plain Kate,
       and bonny Kate, and sometimes Kate the curst;
       But Kate, the prettiest Kate in Christendom.

2. from *The Rime of the Ancient Mariner*
   by Samuel Taylor Coleridge

   All in a hot and copper sky,
   The bloody Sun at noon,
   Right up above the mast did stand
   No bigger than the Moon.

VOLUME

The relative strength, force, or intensity with which sound is made is called **volume**. You must not confuse volume with mere loudness. You can utter a stage whisper with great intensity, or you can call across a room with little intensity. Volume depends upon the pressure with which the air from the lungs strikes the vocal folds. While a certain amount of tension is required to retain the increased breath pressure, this tension should be minimal. If your throat is as relaxed as possible, you will not become hoarse when speaking with increased volume or even when shouting, and your words will be resonant and forceful.

There are two types of force: explosive and expulsive. A sudden, sharp breath pressure creates explosive force, which is useful in commands, shouts, loud laughter, and screams. When the

> ### ▼ CUE
>
> To be heard in a large auditorium without forcing the words from your throat, you must breathe deeply and centrally. Imagine that you are talking to a person in the last row of the theater.

breath pressure is held steady and the breath is released gradually, the force is said to be expulsive. This type of force is necessary in reading long passages without loss of breath and in building to a dramatic climax.

Like the other voice characteristics, volume is closely related to the expression of ideas and emotions. Fear, excitement, anger, hatred, defiance, and other strong emotions are usually accompanied by an explosive intensity. On the other hand, quiet, calm thoughts call for a minimal amount of force.

CUE ▼

When using a microphone, remember that increasing your volume beyond that used in ordinary conversation is not necessary, no matter how large the auditorium.

Volume is used in combination with other voice characteristics to suggest various feelings. For example, a quiet voice accompanied by a flat quality suggests dullness, indifference, or weariness. A quiet voice with a full tonal quality may express disappointment, shock, despair, bewilderment, and sometimes even great joy.

When you are onstage, it is important to remember that you must use more energy to convey impressions of all kinds than is necessary offstage. Thus, if you are merely chatting comfortably at home with a friend, your voice will have relatively little intensity. Put that identical scene on the stage, try to make it equally informal, and you will have to increase your vocal intensity considerably; otherwise, the scene will fall flat. You will find that if you think about where your voice is to go and keep your throat relaxed, your projection will improve without vocal strain.

Using greater force to emphasize the important words in a sentence is the most common means of clarifying a thought. You can change the meaning of a sentence by shifting the force from one word to another, thus expressing innocence, surprise, anger, or other emotions. In acting, the entire thought of a line can be clarified or obscured by emphasizing a word or phrase. Key words brought out forcibly can make a character's personality understandable to the audience.

Patti LuPone and Robert Gutman as Juan and Eva Perón in the rock opera *Evita* must use precise enunciation to portray the Argentinean president and his wife. The voice and diction demands are especially great in *Evita* because all the dialogue is sung rather than spoken.

Whether speaking or singing, an actor must eventually rehearse at the energy level needed for the performance. It takes considerable practice to learn to control vocal intensity. Here an actor rehearsing for *Evita* judges how much volume is needed to fill the room.

Exercises

Volume

1. Pant like a dog. While you do so, feel the movement of your diaphragm with your hands. Then say "ha-ha" as you pant.

2. Take a full breath and call out "one" as if you were throwing a ball against a wall at some distance. Exhale, relax, inhale, and call out "one, two" in the same manner. Count up to ten in this way, but be careful to relax between each effort. Get your power from a quick "kick" of the rib cage rather than from tightening the throat. In the same way, use the words *no, bell, on, never,* and *yes.*

3. Say the letters of the alphabet, increasing your energy whenever you come to a vowel. Keep all the sounds on the same pitch.

4. Say the sentence "I am going home" as though you were saying it to the following people:

   • A friend sitting next to you
   • A person ten feet away
   • Someone across the room
   • Someone in the back row of an auditorium

5. Change the meaning of the following sentences in as many ways as you can by using force to emphasize different words. Explain your exact meaning.

   • I didn't say that to her.
   • You don't think I ate the cake, do you?
   • Nothing is too good for you.
   • You gave the money to him.

Application
ACTIVITIES

Read these passages aloud, making the mood and meaning clear by the amount of force you use and the words you emphasize. Do this while standing, keeping your weight balanced and your chin lifted slightly. Speak "through your eyes."

1. "The Rebel"
   by Mari Evans

   When I   coming to see
   die   if I
   I'm sure   am really
   I will have a   Dead
   Big Funeral   or just
   Curiosity   trying to make
   seekers . . .   Trouble

2. "The Rhinoceros"
   by Ogden Nash

   The rhino is a homely beast,
   For human eyes he's not a feast,
   But you and I will never know
   Why nature chose to make him so,
   Farewell, farewell, you old rhinoceros,
   I'll stare at something less prepoceros!

3. from *Macbeth*
   by William Shakespeare

   To-morrow, and to-morrow, and to-morrow,
   Creeps in this petty pace from day to day,
   To the last syllable of recorded time;
   And all our yesterdays have lighted fools
   The way to dusty death. Out, out, brief candle!
   Life's but a walking shadow, a poor player,
   That struts and frets his hour upon the stage,
   And then is heard no more. It is a tale
   Told by an idiot, full of sound and fury,
   Signifying nothing.

Even low-key speeches, such as the one shown here from Shakespeare's *All's Well That Ends Well*, must be projected from the inner energy an actor builds through the internalization of a role.

PAUSE AND RATE

Practically all our sentences in both speaking and reading aloud are divided into groups of words separated by pauses of varying lengths. The breathing pause is a necessity because we must have breath in order to speak. One of the worst faults a beginner can have is breaking the thought of a sentence by gasping for breath. You must train yourself to get your breath between thought groups. You undoubtedly manage it properly in normal conversation, unconsciously putting words that belong together into groups before you catch your breath. You will find it harder to do this on the stage. The number of words in a group necessarily varies with the thought. A single word may be important enough to stand alone, or there may be twelve or more words in a group; ordinarily there are four or five. Too many breath groups tend to create choppy speech. Punctuation can be of great assistance, for it often clarifies meaning as well as grammatical relationships.

The secret of interpretative power is the ability to realize an idea—to visualize, emotionalize, and vitalize it for yourself—and then give the audience an opportunity to do the same thing. Logical and dramatic pauses demand thought and feeling on your part, or you will not have your audience thinking and feeling with you. Therefore, work out your thought groups carefully. After the pattern is set, approach each group as if for the first time every time you speak or read aloud. The **"illusion of the first time"** is one of the secrets of giving a sense of spontaneity and freshness to every performance.

The speed at which words are spoken is called **rate**. Each person has a characteristic rate of speech, which is usually more rapid in informal conversation than in public speaking or in dramatics. Like quality, pitch, and volume, rate is an important means of suggesting ideas and emotional states. A steadily increasing speed creates a feeling of tension and excitement, while the slow, deliberate delivery of important passages impresses the hearer with their significance. Light, comic, happy, and lyric passages are usually spoken rapidly. Calm, serene, reverent, tragic, and awesome passages are delivered more slowly.

▼ CUE

On the stage a half-second pause is significant; a full-second pause is emphatic; a two-second pause is dramatic; and, a three-second pause is usually catastrophic!

Application ACTIVITIES

1. The internal punctuation has been removed from the following passages. Read each passage aloud, experimenting with pauses and rate to see how many different meanings you can convey. Read one version to the class.

from *Macbeth*
by William Shakespeare

The queen my lord is dead.

from *Romeo and Juliet*
by William Shakespeare

What's in a name that which we call a rose
By any other name would smell as sweet
So Romeo would were he not Romeo call'd
Retain that dear perfection which he owes
Without that title.

2. Go back over the passages you have read aloud in this chapter and decide where the thought groups divide. Then read the passages aloud again, watching your pauses and rate. Hold the important words longer than others, and slip rapidly over the unimportant ones. Let the idea speed you up or slow you down, and take time to feel the emotions and moods.

CUE

Some punctuation marks in written material do not signal a pause, while others indicate a definite break in the flow of ideas. Don't rely entirely on punctuation for your pauses.

COMBINING TECHNIQUES IN INTERPRETATION

Emphasis and subordination are the light and shadow of interpretation in acting. The key words of every passage must be highlighted to be heard and understood by everyone in the audience. To emphasize such words, you must first feel their emotional context to give them color.

Words can be emphasized in the following ways: by delivering them with greater force; by holding them for a longer period of time; by lifting or lowering them in pitch; and by giving the vowels a rich resonant quality and the consonants a strong, crisp attack and finish.

Emphasis (also called stress) involves tone placement and projection. There are two rather different but not conflicting ideas regarding the placement of tone. One is that tone should be placed in the mask of the face, the area of the face where you feel vibrations when you hum. This is done by forming sounds with the lips, lower jaw, and tongue. The second is that the

for colored girls who have considered suicide/when the rainbow is enuf, by Ntozake Shange, is classified as a choreopoem. In this contemporary verse play, the audience feels the emotional intensity of the poetry because the performers are masterful vocal inter- preters. In this scene, their jobs are the harder because the performers are seated. When you sit, kneel, or lie down, your rib cage is constricted, making it harder to get enough breath to project your voice throughout the theater.

voice should be thrown as far as the size of the auditorium requires. This is accomplished by breathing deeply, opening the mouth, and forming the sounds accurately, while consciously focusing on the people farthest away. The throat should remain relaxed and open. The term *swallowing words* refers to what happens when the throat is closed by tension or by careless- ness in controlling the breath. As a result, an insufficient amount of air passes over the vocal folds, and the sound never reaches the resonating chambers of the head.

An actor must also have a good sense of timing and rate in order to interpret a passage effectively. (A climactic passage must, of course, be well written by the author before it can be effectively spoken by the speaker.) In such a passage, the emotional intensity of the lines increases to a high point of feeling at the end. Naturally, to reach a high point, it is necessary to start at a relatively low one. In a strong emotional passage, begin with a relatively slow rate, delib- erate utterance, low pitch, and little or medium vocal energy. Gradually raise the pitch and increase the energy, rate, and emphasis as you reach the highest point of interest or feeling.

▼ CUE

A timely pause is often more effective in con- veying meaning than the words it separates.

Voice Interpretation

1. Say "oh" to suggest keen interest, sudden pain, deep sympathy, delight, irritation, anger, sarcasm, hesitation, embarrassment, good-natured banter, polite indifference, horror, and surprise.

2. Address the following sentences first to someone five feet away and then to someone twenty-five, one hundred, and three hundred feet away. Keep an open throat; control your breath from the diaphragm. Focus on the vowel sounds.

   - Run for your life!
   - Fire! Help!
   - Are you all right?
   - Come here at once!
   - Can you hear me?

Application ACTIVITIES

1. Study the following passages. Decide what type of person is speaking, what exactly is being said, what mood that person is in, and why that person is saying these lines. Read them aloud, trying to convey the exact meaning and mood.

   from the play *The Diary of Anne Frank*
   by Frances Goodrich and Albert Hackett

   ANNE'S VOICE   I expect I should be describing what it feels like to go into hiding. But I really don't know yet myself. I only know it's funny never to be able to go outdoors . . . never to breathe fresh air . . . never to run and shout and jump. It's the silence in the nights that frightens me most. Every time I hear a creak in the house, or a step on the street outside, I'm sure they're coming for us.

   from *Julius Caesar*
   by William Shakespeare

   JULIUS CAESAR   Cowards die many times before their deaths;
   The valiant never taste of death but once.

   from "Sea Fever"
   by John Masefield

   I must down to the seas again, to the lonely sea and the sky,
   And all I ask is a tall ship and a star to steer her by,
   And the wheel's kick and the wind's song and the white sail's shaking,
   And a grey mist on the sea's face and a grey dawn breaking.

2. Read the following passages aloud. First, carefully analyze their meanings. Then determine the mood, the situation, and the emotion portrayed. Finally, decide what quality, energy, change of pitch, and rate will best suit your interpretation.

from *The Pirates of Penzance*
by W. S. Gilbert

I am the very model of a modern Major-General,
I've information vegetable, animal, and mineral,
I know the kings of England, and I quote the fights historical,
From Marathon to Waterloo, in order categorical;
I'm very well acquainted too with matters mathematical,
I understand equations, both the simple and quadratical,
About binomial theorem I'm teeming with a lot o' news—
With many cheerful facts about the square of the hypotenuse.

from "The Fall of the House of Usher"
by Edgar Allan Poe

During the whole of a dull, dark, and soundless day in the autumn of the year, when the clouds hung oppressively low in the heavens, I had been passing alone, on horseback, through a singularly dreary tract of country, and at length found myself, as the shades of the evening drew on, within view of the melancholy House of Usher.

from *The Merchant of Venice*
by William Shakespeare

THE PRINCE OF MOROCCO [reading]
All that glitters is not gold,
Often have you heard that told;
Many a man his life has sold
But my outside to behold.
Gilded tombs do worms infold.
Had you been as wise as bold,
Young in limbs, in judgment old,
Your answer had not been inscroll'd.
Fare you well, your suit is cold.

⁂ *Improving Your Diction*

There are various definitions of **diction**, but for all practical purposes, diction refers to the selection and pronunciation of words and their combination in speech. If your speech is to be an asset in your daily usage, you must choose your words carefully and utter them distinctly. Your aim should be clear, correct, pleasing speech that carries well. Practice reading aloud every day, using your own best speaking techniques, and then relax and speak naturally. You will find your vocal habits improving.

Ear training is almost as important as speech training. Recording and analyzing your speech and the speech of others in a variety of situations can be extremely helpful.

Application
ACTIVITIES

1. Record an informal speaking situation such as a class discussion or a casual conversation. As you replay the recording, listen for the strong and weak points of pronunciation and word choice.

2. Record yourself reading some of the selections in this book. At the end of the term, record a new reading of the same selections and note your improvement.

3. Obtain a recording of a poem, play, or prose piece done by a professional. Try to find one that includes the use of dialect, such as the poems of Robert Burns or the musical *My Fair Lady*. Study the diction of these professionals.

4. Listen to the speech of public speakers or news commentators on television. Note the use of what is called General American Dialect by speakers in mass media.

VOWEL SOUNDS

All vowel sounds pass unobstructed through the mouth, but the position of the lips, tongue, jaw, and soft palate differ for each vowel sound. Vowel sounds are classified as front vowels, middle vowels, or back vowels, according to the position of the tongue as the vowel is formed. When studying vowels, it is important to remember the distinction between sounds and letters. There are just six vowel letters in English—*a, e, i, o, u,* and sometimes *y*. However, there are many vowel sounds. As a result, the same vowel letter can represent more than one vowel sound. For example, the letter *a* is pronounced differently in *father, cat,* and *came.* The vowel sound in an unstressed syllable is often pronounced as a soft "uh." This vowel sound, called **schwa** (ə), might be spelled by any vowel letter or combination of letters. Thus, spelling is not a reliable guide to pronunciation.

Speech sounds are represented by special phonetic alphabets. You see them most often in the pronunciations provided by dictionaries. Because the languages of the world do not share a common way to spell each sound, an International Phonetic Alphabet (IPA) was created to represent the sounds found in all languages. Knowing the IPA can be a great help to actors working with dialects. The chart below lists the vowel sounds of English and their phonetic respellings.

PRONUNCIATION KEY		
Dictionary Respelling	**IPA Symbol**	**Examples**
ă	[æ]	pat, plaid
ā	[eɪ]	pay, paid
âr	[ɛə]	care, pear
ä	[ɑ]	father
ĕ	[ɛ]	pet, head
ē	[i]	be, sea
ĭ	[ɪ]	pit
ī	[aɪ]	pie, line
îr	[ɪə]	pier
ŏ	[ɒ]	pot
ō	[oʊ]	toe, blow
ô	[ɔ]	paw
oi	[ɔɪ]	boy, boil
ou	[aʊ]	out, cow
o͝o	[ʊ]	took, put
o͞o	[u]	boot, blue
ŭ	[ʌ]	cut
ûr	[ʊə]	urge
ə	[ə]	about, item mobile, lemon circus

Because of their many variations, certain vowels present a challenge. The problem often is the result of substituting one vowel sound for another vowel sound.

VOWEL SOUNDS THAT ARE OFTEN CONFUSED

1. The ô sound in words like *audience, daughter, because, automobile,* and *thought* is sometimes confused with the ŏ sound heard in *hot* and *mop.*

2. The ŏ sound in words like *hot, stop, John,* and *cot* is sometimes confused with the ä sound heard in *father.*

3. The ē sound in words like *sleek, creek, sheep,* and *peek* is sometimes confused with the ĭ sound heard in *print* and *pin.*

4. The ă sound in words like *have, man, began, shall, and, than,* and *glad* is sometimes confused with the ä sound heard in *father.*

5. The ûr sound in words like *perfect, purple, world, girl, learn,* and *nerve* is sometimes confused with the ŭ sound heard in *must* or the oi sound heard in *boil.*

6. The ĕ sound in words like *men, engine,* and *get* is sometimes confused with the ĭ sound heard in *pin* and *fit.*

Exercises — Vowel Sounds

Read the words in the following lists. Practice distinguishing among the vowel sounds in each group.

1.	2.	3.	4.
feel	teen	eat	peak
fell	ten	at	peck
fail	ton	ate	puck
foil	tune	it	park
fill	tin	ought	pork
fall	tan		pike
file	turn		pick
foul	torn		pack
	town		perk
			pock
			poke

Application
ACTIVITIES

Read the following lines aloud clearly, pronouncing the vowel sounds carefully.

1. from *The Rime of the Ancient Mariner*
   by Samuel Taylor Coleridge

   Water, water, everywhere,
   And all the boards did shrink.
   Water, water, everywhere,
   Nor any drop to drink.

2. "How to Eat a Poem"
   by Eve Merriam

   Don't be polite.
   Bite in.
   Pick it up with your fingers and lick the juice that may run down
      your chin.
   It is ready and ripe now, whenever you are.
   You do not need a knife or fork or spoon
   or plate or napkin or tablecloth.
   For there is no core
   or stem
   or rind
   or pit
   or seed
   or skin
   to throw away.

3. from "The Windhover"
   by Gerard Manley Hopkins

   I caught this morning morning's minion, king-
      dom of daylight's dauphin, dapple-dawn-drawn Falcon, in his
         riding
      Of the rolling level underneath him steady air, and striding
   High there, how he rung upon the rein of a wimpling wing
   In his ecstasy! then off, off forth on swing,
      As a skate's heel sweeps smooth on a bow-bend: the hurl and
         gliding
      Rebuffed the big wind. My heart in hiding
   Stirred for a bird,—the achieve of, the mastery of the thing!

CONSONANT SOUNDS

The consonant sounds are made by deliberately blocking the air passage at some point with the tongue, soft palate, or lips. If there is no vibration of the vocal folds, the consonant is **voiceless**. If there is a vibration of the vocal folds, the consonant sound is **voiced**. You can tell whether a consonant sound is voiced or voiceless by placing your finger lightly on your throat and feeling whether there is any vibration. Practice by alternately pronouncing these word pairs: *sue–zoo, fail–vail, thin–then.*

The following chart lists three types of consonants. When pronouncing plosive consonants, air is stopped and suddenly released. With the fricative consonants, the air passage is narrowed at some point and a slight friction results. When pronouncing the nasal consonants, the mouth is completely closed at some point and the soft palate is lowered. As a result, the air is forced to pass through the nose.

Plosive Consonants

VOICELESS	VOICED	AIR STOPPED BY
p as in *pop*	*b* as in *bob*	Lip against lip
t as in *tame*	*d* as in *dame*	Tip of tongue against upper gum ridge
k as in *kick*	*g* as in *game*	Back of tongue against soft palate

Fricative Consonants

VOICELESS	VOICED	AIR PASSAGE NARROWED BY
f as in *fan*	*v* as in *van*	Upper teeth on lower lip
s as in *bus*	*z* as in *buzz*	Front of tongue against upper and lower teeth, which are almost closed
sh as in *sure*	*zh* as in *azure*	Tip of tongue turned toward hard palate; teeth almost closed
th as in *breath*	*th* as in *breathe*	Tip of tongue against upper teeth

Nasal Consonants

m as in *mommy*	Mouth closed by lip on lip
ng as in *sing*	Mouth closed by back of tongue on soft palate
n as in *nine*	Mouth closed by tip of tongue on upper gum

How you form your consonants will tell the audience much about the character you are portraying. Strong, crisp consonants usually indicate an intelligent character.

Like vowels, certain consonants present a challenge to speakers and actors. Three common problems are outlined below.

DIFFICULT CONSONANTS

1. The *r* before a vowel as in *red, grumble, three,* and *breeze* or in such expressions as *bread and butter* and *as far as you go* (The tip of the tongue should be held at the base of the lower teeth and not permitted to turn back to form what is called the rolled *r*.)

2. The *l* in words like *elm* and *fool* (The tip of the tongue is pressed against the upper gum with air passing over the side of the body of the tongue. Do not turn the tip of the tongue back in the mouth or follow the *l* with a *u* or put an *e* before the *l*.)

3. Combinations of words such as "Didn't you?", "Wouldn't you?", and "Did you?" (The words should be separated to avoid saying "Didncha?", "Wouldnja?", and "Didja?")

Exercises — Consonant Sounds

Practice distinguishing among the consonant sounds as you pronounce the words in these lists.

1. smack, span, scan, trap, dram, prank, bran, frank, crab, grab, thrash, shrapnel

2. have, cat, gap, quack, land, nag, tap, dash, rat, map, pat, bat, fat, vat, thank

3. than, sad, sham, chap, jam, plaid, black, flat, slack, clan, glad, snack, stand

4. pen, Ben, ten, den, ken, fen, when, wen

5. strap, sprat, scrap, splash, swam, twang, wag, yap

6. hood, could, good, look, nook, put, book, foot, soot, should, brook, crook, wood

Application

Read the following selections aloud, carefully pronouncing the consonant sounds.

1. "Thumbprint"
   by Eve Merriam

On the pad of my thumb
are whorls, whirls, wheels
in a unique design:
mine alone.
What a treasure to own!
My own flesh, my own feelings.

No other, however grand or base,
can ever contain the same.
My signature,
thumbing the pages of my time.
My universe key,
my singularity.
Impress, implant,
I am myself,
of all my atom parts I am the sum.
And out of my blood and my brain
I make my own interior weather,
my own sun and rain.
Imprint my mark upon the world,
whatever I shall become.

2. from "The Highwayman"
   by Alfred Noyes

Over the cobbles he clattered and clashed in the dark innyard
And he tapped with his whip on the shutters, but all was locked and barred;
He whistled a tune to the window, and who should be waiting there
But the landlord's black-eyed daughter,
    Bess, the landlord's daughter,
Plaiting a dark red love knot into her long black hair.
. . . .
"Then look for me by moonlight,
    Watch for me by moonlight,
I'll come to thee by moonlight, though hell should bar the way."

PRONUNCIATION

Good **pronunciation** requires using the correct vowel and consonant sounds in words. Some words might be mispronounced because they contain letters that should not be pronounced.

cor**p**s **h**eir su**b**tlety indi**c**tment de**b**t

The pronunciation of words also depends on which syllable is accented. Some words have pronunciations that vary with the placement of the accent.

mis´ chie vous	(mis chie´ vous)	ad dress´	(ad´ dress)
in´ flu ence	(in flu´ ence)	in quir´ y	(in´ quir y)
the´ a ter	(the a´ ter)	en tire´	(en´ tire)
a dult´	(a´ dult)		

> **▼ CUE**
>
> Avoid these common habits of sloppy speech:
>
> - Mumbling, muttering, or dropping words at the end of sentences and letters at the ends of words
> - Using the vocal apparatus, especially the tongue, in a lazy manner, resulting in indistinctness
> - Being too meticulous, artificial, or theatrical

Exercises — Pronunciation

1. Very carefully read these sentences aloud.

- The speech of the children over the radio was scarcely intelligible and entirely lacking in spirit and enthusiasm.
- Some sparks from the largest of the rockets burned holes in her scarlet jacket.
- The President of the United States of America delivered the dedicatory address.
- Her thought that remaining in the automobile would allow them to see over the audience placed them in an awkward position.
- They quarreled as to whether or not to take the spotted dog onto the yacht.
- Aunt Blanche answered the demand by advancing with her passport.
- We hope next year to hear that she has started her career as an engineer rather than as a cashier.

2. Read the following aloud as rapidly as you can, keeping the sounds clear.

- The perfectly purple bird unfurled its curled wings and whirled over the world.
- Amidst the mists and coldest frosts
  With stoutest wrists and sternest boasts,
  He thrusts his fists against the posts
  And still insists he sees the ghosts.
- The weary wanderer wondered wistfully whether winsome Winifred would weep.
- When and where will you go and why?
- They know not whence, nor whither, where, nor why.
- Judge not that ye be not judged, for with what judgment ye judge ye shall be judged.
- The clumsy kitchen clock click-clacked.
- The very merry Mary crossed the ferry in a furry coat.

❧ *Voice and Diction in Acting*

A play comes to life by means of the voices and words of the actors. It is their ability to arouse emotion through the playwright's lines that creates the illusion of reality for the audience. Actors must make the meaning of every passage clear to all listeners by the proper projection of the words. It is their responsibility to avoid spoiling lines by blurring pronunciation, muffling enunciation, or speaking with a nervous rhythm. The inner soul of the characters they are creating must be expressed through clear patterns of voice quality, pitch, and tempo.

Conscientious actors should be guided by these five principles:

1. Vowels are the sounds actors can work with in interpretation. Vowels can be lengthened, shortened, and inflected.

2. Verbs are the strongest words in the language. Except for forms of *be*, verbs should be stressed.

3. Look for "color words"—those that are vividly descriptive. Look especially for those words whose sounds suggest their meaning (onomatopoeia), such as *crash, stab, grunt, splash.*

4. Rarely stress negatives, pronouns, and articles.

5. When a word or phrase is repeated, stress each repetition more than the preceding repetition.

Exercise Warm-up

These tongue twisters are often used by actors for practice or warm-ups before a performance. Recite each one slowly, articulating each word clearly. Then repeat it several times, gradually increasing your rate until you can say it quite rapidly.

- Rubber baby buggy bumpers
- To make the bitter batter better, Betty bought better butter, beating the better butter into the batter to make the batter better.
- The dedicated doctor diagnosed the dreaded disease as December dithers.
- Fickle fortune framed a fine finale for a fancy finish.
- Could creeping cat keep crafty claws clear of kitchen curtains?

- Many mortals miss mighty moments more from meager minds than major mistakes.
- Some people say I lisp when I say *soup, soft soap,* or something similar, but I don't perceive it myself.
- Round and round the ragged rock the rugged rascal ran.
- Which is the witch that wished the wicked wishes?

Application
ACTIVITIES

Read the following poem aloud rapidly, carefully articulating the consonants and conveying the sound of the water with the vowels.

from "The Cataract of Lodore"
by Robert Southey

The Cataract strong
Then plunges along,
Striking and raging,
As if a war raging
Its caverns and rocks among;
Rising and leaping,
Sinking and creeping,
Swelling and sweeping,
Showering and springing,
Flying and flinging,
Writhing and ringing,
Eddying and whisking,
Spouting and frisking,
Turning and twisting,
Around and around,
With endless rebound!
Smiting and fighting,
A sight to delight in;
Confounding, astounding,
Dizzying and deafening the ear
with its sound.

Collecting, projecting,
Receding and speeding,
And shocking and rocking,
And darting and parting,
And threading and spreading,
And whizzing and hissing,
And dripping and skipping,
And hitting and splitting,
And shining and twining,
And rattling and battling,
And shaking and quaking,

And pouring and roaring,
And waving and raving,
And tossing and crossing,
And flowing and going,
And running and stunning,
And foaming and roaming,
And dinning and spinning,
And dropping and hopping,
And working and jerking,
And guggling and struggling,
And heaving and cleaving,
And moaning and groaning; . . .

And glittering and frittering,
And gathering and feathering,
And whitening and brightening,
And quivering and shivering,
And hurrying and skurrying,
And thundering and floundering;

Dividing and gliding and sliding,
And falling and brawling and
sprawling,
And driving and riving and striving,
And sprinkling and twinkling
and wrinkling,
And sounding and bounding and
rounding,
And bubbling and troubling and
doubling,
And grumbling and rumbling
and tumbling,
And clattering and battering and
shattering.

3 REVIEW

Summary and Key Ideas

Summarize the chapter by answering the following questions.

1. What three things form the keys to a good speaking voice?
2. What is resonance? Tell several ways it can be practiced.
3. Explain how nasality occurs.
4. Name and describe four characteristics of the voice that an effective speaker must use correctly.
5. What is the most valuable asset an actor or speaker can have? Why?
6. What is diction? What habits must be avoided for good diction?
7. Why are vowels so important to a good voice and diction?

Discussing Ideas

1. Discuss the importance of improving diction. What benefits can improved diction bring to you both on and off the stage?
2. Discuss the differences between the voice and diction of ordinary conversation and the voice and diction required onstage.
3. Think about your own speaking quality. Discuss the individual improvement exercises that would be of most help to you.

FOCUS ON   Radio

To hear voices of quality and versatility, turn on your radio. Radio announcers and performers have strong, clear, flexible voices.

Acting on the Radio In the 1930s and 1940s, Americans listened to comedies and dramas and followed tales of horror and suspense presented on the radio. To learn more about radio and its history, do research in books and on the Internet about the most celebrated broadcast in radio history, the Mercury Theatre's 1938 "War of the Worlds" broadcast. If you have access to RealAudio, also listen to the broadcast on the Internet with your teacher's permission. Then write a short report summarizing your research.

Include your responses to these questions: Which conventions, or practices, of radio seem to be similar to the conventions of theater? Which seem different? From what you've learned, how would you describe radio's importance to American society at the time of the broadcast? How would you describe radio's importance today?

Exploring Careers Do some research on the training, skills, and discipline needed to build a career as a radio announcer or performer. You may want to investigate whether there are opportunities to learn more by volunteering at your local public-service station. Share your findings with the class.

VOICE AND DICTION

INDEPENDENT ACTIVITIES

Projecting Your Voice   Imagine that you are a climbing instructor at the bottom of a thirty-foot rock wall. One of your beginning pupils is frozen midway up the rock face, unable to find a satisfactory ledge to get a hand- or foothold. You have a better perspective from the bottom and can see several alternative paths. Create a scene in which you give detailed instructions, moral support, and encouragement to your nervous student so that he or she does not miss a word.

Communicating   Imagine that you are trying to explain how to check a book out of a library. Explain it first to a young child, then to a person with a hearing impairment, and finally to someone who speaks little English.

Cooperative Learning Activity

Choral Reading   Working with a group of five or six classmates, select a narrative poem, such as Henry Wadsworth Longfellow's "Paul Revere's Ride," John Stone's "Double Header," Anne Sexton's "Cinderella," or one you choose. Analyze the mood, theme, imagery, rhyme scheme, and tonal qualities (including alliteration and onomatopoeia) of the poem. Aim for an understanding of the relationship between form and meaning. Decide which lines will be read by a single person and which will be read by the group. Mark a copy of the poem to indicate rate, emphasis, inflection, modulation, and volume. Practice reading the poem in unison. Present your choral reading to the class.

Across the CURRICULUM Activity

History   Choose a historical drama, such as William Shakespeare's *Julius Caesar*, Robert Sherwood's *Abe Lincoln in Illinois*, or Maxwell Anderson's *Elizabeth the Queen*. Select a monologue or extended speech from the play and modernize it, transporting the character to a contemporary setting and situation. Read your revised speech for the class, expressing the emotions of your character through your voice quality, pitch, and tempo. Then read the original aloud, asking your classmates to compare and contrast the two versions. You might ask them to respond to questions like these: Which version did you prefer and why? Which one was more effective in terms of voice and diction? In which version was there a better blend of content and delivery?

4 Acting

No role is too small. In this scene from *Julius Caesar,* the varied responses of the crowd members to Caesar's death give the scene more depth. One can see Mark Antony, played by Al Pacino, judging the crowd's mood and planning how to manipulate it.

Acting is a question of absorbing other people's personalities and adding some of our own experience.

—PAUL NEWMAN, ACTOR

SETTING THE SCENE

Focus Questions

What special terminology is used in acting?

What are the different types of roles?

How do you create a character?

What does it mean to act?

Vocabulary

emotional *or* subjective acting	straight parts	master gesture
technical *or* objective acting	character parts	inflection
leading roles	characterization	subtext
protagonist	primary source	substitution
antagonist	secondary sources	improvisation
supporting roles	body language	paraphrasing

*S*o now you're ready to act! For most students of drama, this is the moment you have been waiting for. You probably share the dream of every actor to create a role so convincing that the audience totally accepts your character as real, forgetting that you are only an actor playing a part.

You must work hard to be an effective actor, but acting should never be so real that the audience loses the theatrical *illusion* of reality. Theater is *not* life, and acting is *not* life. Both are illusions that are larger than life. If both theater and acting are too real, the illusion is destroyed and replaced by what is normal. Onstage, the normal can be boring.

Restraint can sometimes be the best method for conveying strong emotion. Notice how John Malkovich in *True West* uses his arms, back, and facial expression to create a sense of restraint.

🐾 *Shakespeare's Advice to Actors*

Some classic lessons in dramatic art come from one of the world's most famous actor-dramatists, William Shakespeare. They were given as advice to actors in Act III, Scene 2, of *Hamlet*.

IN SHAKESPEARE'S WORDS

Speak the speech, I pray you, as I pronounced it to you, trippingly on the tongue: but if you mouth it, as many of your players do, I had as lief the town-crier spoke my lines. Nor do not saw the air too much with your hand, thus, but use all gently; for in the very torrent, tempest, and, as I may say, the whirlwind of passion, you must acquire and beget a temperance that may give it smoothness. O, it offends me to the soul to hear a robustious periwig-pated fellow tear a passion to tatters, to very rags, to split the ears of the groundlings, who for the most part are capable of nothing but inexplicable dumb-shows and noise: I would have such a fellow whipped for o'erdoing Termagant; it outherods Herod: pray you, avoid it.

IN MODERN WORDS

Speak the lines of the author as written, distinctly and fluently, with an understanding of their meaning.

Do not use elaborate and artificial gestures. Keep energy in reserve in order to build to an emotional climax smoothly and effectively.

Do not resort to farfetched action or noise simply to please unintelligent and unappreciative onlookers.

The Special Language of Acting

Very early in the rehearsal process, you will also begin hearing a number of theater expressions. To work comfortably and efficiently onstage, you must become familiar with these expressions. Those most often used in connection with acting are listed and defined in the following chart.

ad-lib	to improvise stage business or conversation
at rise	who and what are onstage when the curtain opens
back or *backstage*	the area behind the set or that part of the stage that is not visible to the audience, including dressing rooms, shops, and offices
bit part	an acting role with very few lines
blocking yourself	getting behind furniture or other actors so that you cannot be seen by the audience
building a scene	using dramatic devices, such as increased tempo, volume, and emphasis, to bring a scene to a climax
business	any specific action (other than changing location) performed on the stage, such as picking up a book or turning on a television set
C	the symbol used to identify the center of the stage
countercross	a movement in a direction opposite to a cross to balance the stage picture
cover	to obstruct the view of the audience; use of ad-lib to cover an unexpected, unwanted event during a performance
cross	the movement by an actor from one location onstage to another
cue	the last words, action, or technical effect that immediately precedes any line or business; a stage signal
curtain	the curtain or drapery that shuts off the stage from the audience; when written in all capital letters in a script, it indicates that the curtain is to be closed
cut	to stop action; to omit
cut in	to break into the speech of another character
down or *downstage*	the part of the stage toward the audience
dressing the stage	as a technical term, placing furnishings, pictures, and similar items to complete and balance a set; keeping the stage picture balanced during the action
enter	to move onto the stage
exit or *exeunt*	to leave the stage
feeding	giving lines and action in such a way that another actor can make a point or get a laugh

foil	an acting role that is used for personality comparison, usually with the main character
hand props	items (properties) such as tools, weapons, or luggage carried onstage by an individual player
hit	to emphasize a word or line with extra force
holding for laughs	waiting for the audience to quiet down after a funny line or scene
leading center	the body part or feature used by an actor to lead movements; often used to reflect a character's major personality trait
left and *right*	terms used to refer to the stage from an actor's point of view, not from that of the audience
master gesture	a distinctive action that serves as a clue to a character's personality
milk	to draw the maximum response from the audience from comic lines or action
off or *offstage*	off the visible stage
on or *onstage*	on the visible stage
overlap	to speak when someone else is speaking
pace	the movement or sweep of the play as it progresses
personal props	small props that are usually carried in an actor's costume, such as money, matches, a pipe, or a pen
places	the stage command for actors to take their positions at the opening of an act or scene
plot	to plan stage business, as to plot the action; to plan a speech by working out the phrasing, emphasis, and inflections
pointing lines	emphasizing an idea
principals	the main characters in a play or the named characters in a musical
properties or *props*	all the stage furnishings, including furniture and those items brought onstage by the actors
ring up	to raise the curtain
role scoring	the analysis of a character
script scoring or *scripting*	the marking of a script for one character, indicating interpretation, pauses, phrasing, stress, and so on
set	the scenery for an act or a scene
set props	properties placed onstage for the use of actors
sides	half-sheet pages of a script that contain the lines, cues, and business for one character
stealing a scene	attracting attention from the person to whom the audience's interest legitimately belongs
subtext	the unstated or "between the lines" meaning that an actor must draw from the script
tag line	the last speech in an act or a play, usually humorous or clever

taking the stage	giving an actor the freedom to move over the entire stage area, usually during a lengthy speech
tempo	the speed at which the action of a play moves along
timing	the execution of a line or a piece of business at a specific moment to achieve the most telling effect
top	to make a line stronger than the line or lines preceding it by speaking at a higher pitch, at a faster rate, or with greater volume and emphasis
up or *upstage*	the area toward the rear of the stage—away from the audience
upstaging	improperly taking attention from an actor who should be the focus of interest
walk-on	a small acting part that has no lines
warn cue	notification of an upcoming action or cue; usually indicated in the promptbook

Application
ACTIVITIES

1. Choose a scene from Part 2, and analyze the setting and stage directions. With a partner or small group, act out the scene, focusing on the movements onstage. Decide when you should use the different techniques, such as the cross and countercross. Have the audience evaluate your stage movements and tell how the movements affect the meaning of your presentation. Also, the audience should note if anyone stole the scene or upstaged another actor.

2. In a small group, create a comic script that contains motivated characters, conflict, and a resolution. Include the different techniques used in comedy. Make sure you include a character with a humorous master gesture.

3. With a partner, choose one of the monologues from Part 2. Decide who will be the director and who will be the actor. The director will need to inform the actor, using the terminology given, of the different things he or she needs to do.

⚹ *Approaches to Acting*

CUE ▼

Aim for a balanced approach to a role. If you lose yourself in the character you portray, an uneven and uncontrolled performance could result. If your approach to characterization is too technical, an artificial, shallow, and unconvincing portrayal could result.

There are two major approaches to acting. In the first, **emotional** or **subjective acting**, actors play their parts in such a way that they actually weep, suffer, or struggle emotionally in front of the audience. As nearly as they can, they *become* the parts they play and experience all that their characters experience. In the second, **technical** or **objective acting**, performance is based on acting technique. In this approach, an actor analyzes the play's structure and the personalities of the characters. The actor then uses the learned skills of acting, movement, speech, and interpretation to create the role. Emotional response is not allowed to interfere with the creation of the role. Instead, conscious technical control is responsible for the results. The actor does not actually live the part but acts it so well that the illusion of living the part is created. In the emotional approach, personal inner reactions form the actor's emotional response. In the technical approach, the process of study, analysis, and creative imagination forms the assumed personality.

There is much to be said for both approaches to acting. Today, however, most actors use a combination of the two. It is therefore best to identify yourself with your part so that you can interpret it naturally, simply, and spontaneously. At the same time, use your technical training to achieve a clear-cut, convincing, and consistent characterization.

"The Method" is the most discussed and influential acting theory today. It was formulated by Russian actor and director Konstantin Stanislavski. He explained his theories on the art of acting and offered practical exercises in the techniques of vocal and bodily expression in his books *My Life in Art, An Actor Prepares, Building a Character,* and *Creating a Role.* His ideas greatly influenced the theater in the twentieth century.

Many people have misinterpreted Stanislavski's theories by placing too much emphasis on the actor's use of

⦂THEATER HISTORY⦂

Method actors tap their own emotions and channel them through their characters. Konstantin Stanislavski was the father of Method acting.

self-analysis and personal emotional experience in creating a role. As a result, many so-called "Method" actors become so involved with their inner resources that they fail to communicate to the audience. Their speech is often slovenly and their actions overdone. They make the mistake of believing that emotional identification with a character is more important than learning the lines as written or responding alertly to others onstage.

Stanislavski's so-called "magic *if*" should be most helpful to you in creating a character. Stanislavski advised that actors should use their full powers of concentration to ask what they would do *if* the events in the play were actually happening and they were intimately involved in these events. For example, ask yourself, "If I were Abigail in the courtroom scene in *The Crucible*, how would I feel as Proctor accused me of being a witch? How would I react? What would I do to stop him?" In answering questions such as these, actors analyze both their inner natures and their characters' inner natures. Only then can an actor use the technical resources of voice and body movement to accurately interpret the likely reactions of the character. This analysis can also lead to a deeper understanding of the play itself.

In approaching a role, it is helpful to consider the types of roles typically employed by a playwright. The main characters in a play are referred

ℱROM THE PROS

"Imagination, industry, and intelligence—'the three I's'—are all indispensable to the actor, but of these three the greatest is, without doubt, imagination."

—ELLEN TERRY, ACTOR

In an early rehearsal, these students work with few props in order to more fully concentrate on developing their characters.

to as the **leading roles.** They include the **protagonist**, who must solve the problem that arises in the play or be defeated in the conflict. There is often an **antagonist**, who opposes the goals of the protagonist. Other leading roles are the **juvenile,** the term for a young male lead between the ages of sixteen and thirty, and the **ingenue** (än•jə•noo′), a young female lead. The leads are referred to as the **principals.** While many inexperienced actors are often disappointed if they are not cast in leading roles, **supporting roles** are often more challenging and demanding. The challenge of a role lies in the type of person to be portrayed, not in how long or short the part might be. One of the most important supporting roles is that of the **foil,** a character with whom another character, usually the protagonist, is compared. There can be more than one foil in a play.

Both leading and supporting roles can be either straight or character parts. The actors chosen for **straight parts** usually resemble in appearance and personality the characters the playwright had in mind. Actors chosen for roles that match their own voices, personalities, and appearances are said to be cast by type. **Character parts** will almost always include some distinguishing trait, idiosyncrasy, or personality type. This distinguishing feature might be either physical or psychological. These parts demand a high degree of acting ability. Such roles rarely resemble their actors in either appearance or personality.

An actor who is cast by type brings a sturdy realism to his or her role. George Rose's whiskers, physical appearance, and natural poise make him perfect for his role as the eccentric Major-General Stanley in Gilbert and Sullivan's *The Pirates of Penzance.*

Some actors become identified with a certain personality—the girl next door, the business tycoon, the confused fool, or the faithful companion. Casting someone over and over again in the same kind of role is called **typecasting.** There is a difference between typecasting and casting by type. If a role calls for a man with a Santa-Claus-like build and the actor chosen happens to be a portly, white-bearded gentleman in his late sixties, the director has probably cast by type. However, if a similarly built man with dark hair and beard has been cast in his last twenty roles as a "heavy," this actor has very likely been typecast as a villain.

An actor who has only a few lines is said to have a bit part. An actor who appears briefly onstage with no lines at all has a walk-on part. These minor roles demand as much careful attention to detail as supporting roles. The difference lies only in the number of lines and scenes involved.

Application
ACTIVITY

Recall a serious movie or play you have seen recently. List the leading roles and identify the protagonist, antagonist, supporting roles, and other types of roles you recognize. Analyze the actors chosen for these roles and decide if they are straight parts or character parts.

Characterization

For you as an actor, the creative process of **characterization** should occur in two stages. First, you attempt to grasp the fundamental personality of a part. Then, you project that personality to the audience in such a way that your character becomes a living, convincing human being.

Characterization is the substance of acting. Therefore, it is your responsibility as an actor to increase your knowledge of the lives and emotions of real people in order to understand how they respond and behave. The constant study of human beings both in real life and in literature is one of your major responsibilities as an actor. It is an unending source of material and inspiration upon which to draw.

Successful projection of character depends on the skillful use of techniques. It also depends on insights into a character's behavior and the ability to express those insights in interpreting the character. The successful blending of technique and interpretation comes only with continued analysis of character and script and with the rehearsing and portrayal of varied roles.

Experience will teach you to use and to master some of the characteristics of acting. You will learn the use of **pause**—a lull, or stop, in dialogue or action—in order to sustain emotion while the voice and body are still. You will learn how to communicate originality, a freshness of acting style that colors and characterizes the work of every distinguished dramatic artist. You will learn to apply **versatility**—the ability to change style or character with ease—which always surprises and delights. These are some of the means that experienced actors use as they interpret the characters they portray.

STUDYING THE PLAY

Before you can understand and interpret a role faithfully, you must study the play closely. Usually the entire script is read through at the first rehearsal. Some directors choose to read the entire play to the cast. Others prefer to have the actors read their assigned parts, although the director might also participate in the reading. This reading should bring out the author's purpose and theme. It should also identify the protagonist's main problems and the structure of the plot, especially how it builds to a climax and holds interest to the end. Pay close attention not only to your own lines but also to those lines about your character that are spoken by others. Note the shifting of moods throughout the play and how your character is affected by them.

Actors must develop their characters in relation to their setting so that props like antique telephones feel as natural as what they really own. These actors seem strikingly at home in this scene from the 1940s.

You will obviously want to know what kind of person you are in the play and why you behave as you do. You will also want to understand what your character wants and what stands in the way of getting it. Pay particular attention to what your character does; characters reveal themselves in what they do as well as in what they say. Note any changes that take place in your character during the play.

If the setting of a play is unfamiliar, study the place and the historical period. Learn all you can from books and pictures and, if possible, from people who have visited the place. Try to enter into the atmosphere of the location. If your character speaks a local dialect, try to talk to people from the locality or listen to recordings of speakers from the area. Notice their pronunciation and their inflections. You might also want to read other plays by the same playwright or by other playwrights of the same era or geographical region. Look up historical references and check the meanings of unfamiliar words.

DEVELOPING A CHARACTER SKETCH

You will find it helpful to write a character sketch or brief biography of your character to supply information not provided in the script. Go through the play thoroughly and look for clues to the character you are to portray.

You can summarize your character sketch by listing the traits, behaviors, and motivations under several headings, such as the following:

▼ **CUE**

When studying your character, ask the following questions:

- What does the author say about your character in the stage directions?

- What do your character's lines reveal?

- What do other characters say about your character?

- How do other characters respond to your character?

PLAY: *The Miracle Worker*
CHARACTER: **Annie Sullivan**

MENTAL TRAITS	EMOTIONAL TRAITS	BEHAVIOR	MOTIVATIONS	PHYSICAL TRAITS
Intelligent Not well educated	A strange mix of patience and impatience Strong-willed Outspoken	Willing to confront her employer Tried to separate "teaching" from "feeling"	Determined to get through to Helen Believed one "connection" was all it would take	Eyes sensitive to light Strong enough to carry Helen Hands very communicative

Ask and answer some basic questions about your character: What is my character's purpose? What is my character's function in the play? Am I playing a protagonist, an antagonist, or a foil? Is my character there for comic relief? What does my character want to do? What does my character want to be? What is my character's goal in the play as a whole and in each particular scene? State the answers to the last question in the form of a verb, such as *get even, deceive, trap, vindicate,* or *liberate.*

As you complete your character sketch and become better acquainted with your part, ask yourself more questions:

- How well adjusted to others is my character?
- Is my character shy or uninhibited?
- How intelligent is my character?
- In what ways has environment influenced my character?

Actors who performed in *Our Country's Good* had to understand how both upper and lower class British during Australia's colonization dressed, thought, and spoke. Such mastery requires intensive rehearsal so that the actors' appearance, behavior, and speech do not seem artificial.

- What are my character's particular problems?
- Is my character meeting or avoiding responsibilities? How and why?
- How does my character react to all of the other characters in the play?
- Does my character unknowingly avoid the main issues in situations?
- Is my character cynical, talkative, rowdy, tense, aggressive, charming, friendly, fearful, envious, courageous, or idealistic? Why?

The answers to questions such as these will allow you to understand more fully your character's personal and social background.

Application
ACTIVITY

Watch a first-class actor at work on the stage, in a motion picture, or on television. Then do the following:

1. Write a character sketch similar to one an actor might have written when preparing for this role.

2. What elements of the performance indicate the actor has researched the place and period in which the play takes place?

SCORING A ROLE

Role scoring is a helpful process in character analysis. The process consists of answering a series of questions. If you take the time to answer these questions, you will unlock important information about your character.

ROLE SCORING QUESTIONS

1. How does the title of the play relate to your character?

2. What is your character's main sense of urgency? What strong impulse motivates your character to act?

3. If your character has a secret, what is it?

4. What rhythm might you associate with your character?

5. What sound might you associate with your character? (Sighing, wheezing, and grunting are sounds that might be associated with a character.)

6. What is your character's master gesture?

7. What is your character's leading center? (The head? The heart? The stomach?)

8. What color might you associate with your character? Why?

9. What object might you associate with your character? Why?

10. What animal might you associate with your character? Why?

11. What are your character's two primary senses?

12. Does your character "mask," or cover up, feelings and behaviors? If so, what does your character mask?

13. Does your character have a sense of humor? Is this sense of humor used in a positive or negative way?

14. In real life, would you be your character's friend? Why or why not?

15. What is your character's most positive trait?

16. What is your character's status in the world? Does your character have money and power?

17. What are your character's major wants and desires?

18. What is your character's major objective for each scene in which he or she appears?

19. How does your character go about achieving those major objectives?

20. What is your character's life objective?

21. How does your character go about achieving his or her life objective?

22. Has your character changed by the end of the play? If so, in what ways?

Here two actors in *Julius Caesar* hold a pause, building the scene's suspense and adding impact to the words that will follow.

SCORING A SCRIPT

You score a script by marking the pauses, pitch levels, emphasis, speed of delivery, phrasing, pronunciation, character revelation, movement, stage business, and any special function a given line or direction might have within the context of the play. Scoring a script is another useful tool in character analysis. The term comes from a musical score, which has similar markings to indicate tempo, rhythm, pauses, style, and interpretation. In its simplest form, a scored script may be marked to show only pronunciation, pauses, emphasized words and phrases, movement, and stage business.

There are no hard-and-fast rules for script scoring, nor is there any agreement about what symbols or marks should be used to score a script. Actors are free to use any personal marking system that will be of help to them.

Marullus

Wherefore rejoice? / What conquest brings he home? //

What tributaries follow him to Rome,

To grace in captive bonds his chariot-wheels?

You blocks, you stones, / you worse than senseless things! //

O you hard hearts, you cruel men of Rome,

Knew you not Pompey? // Many a time and oft

Have you climb'd up to walls and battlements, +

To towers and windows, yea, to chimney-tops,

Your infants in your arms, and there have sat

The live-long day with patient expectation,

To see great Pompey pass the streets of Rome

from: *Julius Caesar*

Motivation: Self-interest and revenge. Marullus and Flavius were tribunes of the slain Pompey. They fear the loss of democracy in Rome.

Pointing to decorated statues
PP "Why are you celebrating?"
"What is Caesar's conquest – victories over Rome's enemies or over Pompey, Rome's friend?"
tributaries = captives

Irony: Common people will react in a similar manner after Caesar's death.

chimney tops (Shakespeare's London, not Rome)

Symbol Key

+	slight pause	∿⌐	speed up reading
/	1-second pause	∿∿⌐	slow down
//	2-second pause	⌐	rising inflection
⌒	phrase	⌐	falling inflection
—	simple stress	L	laugh line
═	greater stress	C	character line
≡	greatest stress	P	plot line
⌐	pitch level rising	T	theme line
⌐	pitch level falling	PP	paraphrase

Script Scoring

Work with a partner to do the following:

1. Prepare two copies of the script on page 111, but do not include the scoring symbols on one copy. One of you reads the script without the scoring; the other studies the scoring and then reads the script, using the notations.

2. Trade roles and read the script again.

3. Discuss which reading sounded more interesting and believable. Discuss how reading a scored script differs from reading an unmarked script.

4. Study the scored copy and discuss any variations that might be made and any other symbols that might be used to mark the pauses, pitch levels, and emphasis. Using your personalized set of symbols, use the unmarked copy of the script to create your own scoring.

Application
ACTIVITY

Working with a partner, choose one of the monologues on pages 232 through 245. Study the background situation provided for the monologue. Individually score the script, using the symbols on page 111 or your own set of marks. Pay particular attention to pauses, emphasis, and speed of delivery. When both you and your partner have finished, present your monologues to each other. Discuss the differences in delivery and how those differences affected the meaning conveyed.

🪷 Building Up Your Part

There are two stages in building up your part. The first stage begins when the director gives the cast his or her own view of the play, its characters and their relationships, its theme, and its style. Then, as you study the play and the characters, you develop your own concept of the part.

It is often best not to see a motion picture or stage production of a play in which you are preparing to appear. If you do, you are likely to find yourself copying another actor's mannerisms rather than developing your own understanding of the role and the play. To build a characterization, choose a person you know who is similar to the character you are playing.

The faces of Kevin Kline as Hamlet and Dana Ivey as Gertrude reflect the depth to which they have internalized their roles in this production of *Hamlet*. A deep understanding of how a character thinks and feels allows an actor to respond believably to any situation in a play.

This individual becomes your **primary source**. Study and adopt this person's posture, movements, habits, and voice inflections. In many situations, you might choose more than one primary source and combine characteristics from all. The books that you read to help shed light on your character are your **secondary sources**. They are helpful, but good actors must always refer to life itself for appropriate models.

The second stage begins as you go to rehearsals with the entire cast under the director's guidance. It is during these rehearsals, as you react to others and incorporate the principles of acting, that your character develops into a living person. To avoid conflicts, differences in interpretations should be discussed with the director as soon as possible.

Once you have settled on the general interpretation of your part, you must then grow into it physically, intellectually, and emotionally. Your character's actions and speech are your means of making that character real to your audience. Voice, movements, and imagination are the tools you will use to make your character come alive on the stage.

SIXTEEN KEYS TO CHARACTERIZATION

Each of these keys should help you as you learn to develop the characters you play.

1. **Internalizing**   When actors internalize a character, they develop a deep personal understanding of what the character is really like. The actor has already studied the play carefully, answered the questions *Who?* *What?* and *Why?* about the character, written a character sketch, and scored the role. Having done all these things, the actor knows how the character thinks and feels.

    Once the character has been internalized, an actor develops the ability to respond in character to any given situation. An actor's interpretation of a line and the reaction to the words or actions of other characters are all in a state of readiness. In the event of a dropped line or

Phyllis Frelich as Sarah Norman and John Rubinstein as James Leeds in *Children of a Lesser God* appear to be completely absorbed by their conversation. This level of concentration holds the audience's interest and makes the story come alive.

other unplanned mistake, an actor who is deeply in character will improvise a response in character.

2. **Externalizing**   Externalization is the process by which the true personality of a character is made visible to an audience. This is done through careful interpretation, nonverbal expression, voice quality, pitch, rate, and physical action. For example, in *The Caine Mutiny Court Martial*, Captain Queeg's conviction that he is being persecuted is externalized through the ball bearings that he carries in his pocket. Whenever the captain becomes nervous and panicky, he removes the ball bearings from his pocket and begins fidgeting with them in his hand. As a result, the audience can see evidence of the inner man breaking down.

3. **Concentrating**   Concentration is the ability to direct all your thoughts, energies, and skills into what you are doing at any single moment. It often helps to remember that every line comes from the middle of some larger thought. Lines are not isolated and independent from other thoughts and actions. As an actor, you must learn how to concentrate simultaneously on character, lines, and action. You must sustain that concentration through each performance and over the length of the production's run.

4. **Observing**   The fourth key to characterization is observation. Observe people carefully, noting how they communicate fine shades of emotions. Notice in particular how they use their small facial muscles. Notice also their distinguishing physical characteristics and their unique voice and diction patterns. Do what most professional actors do: begin an actor's notebook and record your observations. Also, include pictures of real people that you might want to use as makeup models in the future. Record comments and suggestions made by directors and other actors. As you become more skilled in observation, you will begin to see the many subtle things people do that reveal their inner thoughts and feelings.

5. **Emotional Memory**   Emotional memory is the recalling of specific emotions that you have experienced or observed. You have directly or indirectly experienced fear, joy, jealousy, timidity, anger, love, and many more emotions. However, emotions may need to be adjusted to fit your character, situation, time, and environment. As an actor, you draw on those emotional memories to give life to the characters that you play. Keep in mind, however, that people can experience more than one level of emotion at a time. A person, for example, is sometimes happy and sad at the same time. The expression of conflicting emotions is challenging. When a part calls for the expression of conflicting emotions, you must reach into your emotional memory bank to determine how to show the audience the tug-of-war between the two feelings.

6. **Projecting**   Once inner feelings are externalized, they must then be projected to the audience. Projection is the sixth key to characterization. Strong volume is a part of projecting, but projection is more than loudness. Projection is "reaching out" to the last person in the last row of a distant balcony. You project your character through dialogue and focused action that seems larger than life. This projection of character "across the footlights" generates the empathy between actor and audience that is the heart of theater.

Projection is as much about drawing your audience to you as it is about extending yourself to your audience. This actor in *FOB*, a play written by David Henry Hwang, uses his hands and facial expression to reach everyone in the theater.

7. **Motivating**   Motivation is the *why* of characterization. To be believable your character's behavior must be driven by an inner force. The inner force is intent. Intent is *what* the character wants to do. Motivation is *why* the character wants to do it. Motivations impelling a character to act are influenced by personal convictions, mind-set, self-interest, past experience, situation, environment, friends, and loved ones. Good acting always makes a character's motivation clear to an audience.

8. **Stretching a Character**   Ordinary personalities onstage are very limited and rather boring. Stretching a character is the eighth key to characterization. Stretching a character is the process of making a role unique, individual, and interesting. The process should result in a character who is noticeably different from the other characters in a play. In stretching a character, an actor's aim is not to create an unbelievable exaggeration but to identify the character's primary personality trait and then to emphasize it. If the actor is portraying a villain, for example, he or she might develop and emphasize the cruelty that is the character's primary personality trait. Even if a character is stretched only slightly, the result can be a characterization that the audience will long remember. There is an old saying in theater: "A tenth of an inch makes a difference."

9. **The Consistent Inconsistency**   The ninth key to characterization is called the consistent inconsistency. This key has to do with a special personality trait of a character that the actor chooses to emphasize. That trait is the character's *inconsistency*, the thing that makes him or her different from others. It might be a dialect, a limp, an arrogance, or a cackling laugh. Once it is chosen, it must not be dropped, even for a line or two. If the dialect slips away, if the limp shifts to the other leg, if the arrogance is mellowed, or if the cackle loses its fiendish quality, the characterization is bound to suffer. Actors, especially beginning actors, must strive to be consistent with their characters' inconsistencies.

10. **Playing the Conditions**   The tenth key to characterization is playing the conditions. The conditions are the elements of time, place, weather, objects, and the state of the individual. These conditions affect the manner in which characters meet their objectives and deal with obstacles. Time can be the hour of the day, the day itself, the month, year, or season. The place can be indoors or outdoors, familiar or unfamiliar, threatening or comforting. The weather may be hot or cold, sunny or rainy, calm or blustery. Objects may be familiar or unfamiliar, in adequate supply or scarce, in working order or broken. The state of the individual may be extremely fatigued or well rested, wounded or healed, freezing or sweltering, healthy or ill. Actors must

keep all of these conditions in mind as they interpret their characters, for each of these conditions can influence the way a character responds.

11. **Playing the Objectives**   The eleventh key to characterization is playing the objectives. This includes all of the ways and means that a character uses to reach a goal. The method used to attain a goal might be a physical act, such as a slap, a kick, or a kiss. It might be a mental act, such as a decision, a deliberate strategy, or an assumption. The method used might also be an object, such as a gun, a key, or a secret code. It might also be an action, such as writing a letter, making a phone call, or planting an explosive device. An actor must be completely familiar with a character's objectives and must be totally aware of all the means that the character uses to reach them. An actor must also know how the character will respond if the objectives are achieved or if they are not.

12. **Playing the Obstacles**   The twelfth key to characterization is playing the obstacles or, in other words, facing each crisis or obstacle that stands in the way of an objective as the character would face it. An actor must note carefully how the personality of the character deals with these situations. For example, an actor must notice whether a character tackles an obstacle head on by considering it thoughtfully or whether the character ignores it, denies that it exists, transfers it to someone else, loses control, becomes rattled, or runs away from it. Each personality approaches a similar obstacle differently. You must know your character's response so that it can be forcefully communicated to an audience.

13. **Playing the Object**   Not to be confused with "playing the objective," playing the object has to do with how an actor uses objects onstage to project character. These objects may be costume accessories, general props, furniture, tools, or weapons. We learn much from the way a character holds a phone, uses a knife and fork, or flutters a fan. Objects can be used to "set" or emphasize a line in the script. This can be accomplished through *preceding action, interrupted action,* or *concluding action.* An actor using preceding action might jab a log with a poker before delivering a line. With interrupted action, an actor having a cup of tea might lift the cup as if to take a sip, but just before the cup reaches the lips, hesitate, lower the cup, and deliver a line. The interruption of the flow of action causes the audience to focus on the line. A judge who bangs a gavel after saying, "Case dismissed," is using concluding action.

When an actor seems in control of his or her character, using no more energy than each scene requires, the audience is more deeply moved when the climax finally comes.

14. **Energy** Energy is the fuel that drives acting, both individual performance and group performance. Energy enlivens a performance, makes forceful character portrayal possible, and creates greater empathy between the actor and the audience. Physical energy produces the freshness, sparkle, and spontaneity on which theater depends. The finest actors learn how to control energy and how to conserve it. Because most plays build steadily to a major climax, the key scenes of most characters occur well along in the play. Every performer must therefore control the use of energy and save some for important scenes.

15. **Focus** Focus directs the actor's attention, action, emotion, or line delivery to a definite target. There are many forms of focus. Internal focus on character includes focus on thought. Focus on scene concentrates on the central idea toward which a scene moves. Focus on stage position turns a scene in and concentrates audience attention on the key player in a scene. Visual focus that an actor creates with the eyes leads the audience to concentrate on the object of the actor's gaze. Vocal focus projects the voice to the members of the audience farthest

from the stage or bounces a line off another player and then out to the audience. Focus of feeling exists when an actor concentrates on a physical or emotional pain. This focus of feeling is called the point of pain. If the character has a physical pain in the chest, the actor focuses on the specific spot where the pain exists—the chest. If the character is suffering from a broken heart, the hurt is focused on the heart.

The playwright's writing, the director's staging, and the actor's delivery of lines can all create focus. The main responsibility for focusing attention, however, is the actor's. By stressing particular lines, gestures, mannerisms, facial expressions, or behaviors, the actor focuses audience attention on the key ideas of theme, plot, or characterization.

16. **Uniqueness**   The final key to characterization is uniqueness. Every actor who plays a character should be unique in that role, not merely a close copy of someone else. Each actor and each director will have a different picture of the play and its characters. The director envisions each character as part of the total production. Within the director's image of a character, the actor must shape a personality that is special unto itself.

Elements of characterization, such as character stretching and focus, are often inseparable. The intense focus of Cleavon Little and Judd Hirsch in this scene from *I'm Not Rappaport* helps them stretch their characters.

The father in *Fences,* played by John Amos, shares a quiet moment with his son. Sometimes subtlety produces the best dramatic effect, especially when an actor has fully built up a character.

Application
ACTIVITY

Choose a familiar character from a well-known play you have studied but have never seen performed. It might be a tragic figure from Shakespeare or another play you have read in a literature class. Decide on a primary source, a person you know who you feel is similar to the character in this play. Make a list of traits from your primary source that you could adapt to the character. You might list them under the following headings: posture, movements, habits, vocal inflections.

Physical Acting

According to the experts, the majority of our daily communication occurs through physical action. This nonverbal communication is often called **body language**. Physical acting relies on body language. It allows actors to communicate far more than the words of a script alone can convey. Beginning actors generally rely too heavily on the voice; most new actors need to work on and improve their physical acting.

GESTURE

To get some idea of how people use their bodies, it is helpful to imagine that each of us operates within a bubble. This bubble is an imaginary circle that people establish around themselves. Imagine that each character portrayed on the stage is surrounded by a personal bubble in which he or she "lives." The size of each bubble is determined by the personality of the character. Shy, withdrawn, and frail personalities have small bubbles. Swaggering, bold, and daring personalities have large bubbles. Since customary gestures are made within the bubble, less forceful characters do not really need much room for their uncertain movements. More forceful characters, on the other hand, often need bubbles that are large enough to contain the arms fully extended. Audiences are very much aware of the bubble space. They realize at once that when two personal bubbles overlap, there is likely to be either a confrontation or an embrace.

As you work on your physical acting, you will want to develop a **master gesture**, a distinctive action that serves as a clue to a character's personality. The master gesture might be a peculiar walk or laugh or some other recognizable form of behavior. Even the position of your feet while you are standing, walking, or sitting can be a master gesture.

Almost every character onstage begins movement or "leads" with a part of the body that is appropriate for the character's personality. A lead looks as if a string attached to a part of the body is pulling that part away from the other parts. The movement of the **leading center** can be either slight or exaggerated, depending on the character and the style of the play. The body part that a character leads with is determined by the character's major personality trait. For example, if you are playing an intelligent person, lead with the forehead. If you are playing a haughty character, lead with the chin, face slightly tilted upward. Brave characters might lead with the chest, and well-fed characters might lead with the stomach.

▼ CUE

The size of the imaginary bubbles that surround us is cultural as well as individual. Americans tend to define their space like this:

- Six feet or more is "formal."
- Three to five feet is "friendly."
- Less than two feet is "intimate."

Without being aware of it, people guard their bubbles. (This is often apparent in crowded elevators and buses.)

COMMON ONSTAGE MOVEMENTS

Certain movements onstage are so common that all actors must master them. Among these are entering, exiting, crossing, sitting, and standing.

Because entrances introduce your character into a scene, you must prepare for them long before you come onstage. Plan exactly how you wish to appear. Pay particular attention to your posture. Remember that posture will be determined by your character's age, mood, and attitude toward the

Entrances can be tricky, particularly when they involve many actors. Each actor must have his or her own sense of purpose and at the same time be able to coordinate the entrance with others.

CUE ▼

Be sure that hand props are where they are supposed to be so you will not be worrying about them onstage. As you wait for your entrance, do not stand in front of a backstage light, or you will cast your shadow onstage. Also, be sure that you do not block the exit for other actors.

other characters onstage. Be sure that every detail of your costume and makeup is exactly as it should be and that you have all necessary hand props.

You must always plan your entrance so that you have enough time to come onstage and speak exactly on cue. If the set has steps that you must climb or walk down when making your appearance, be sure to walk up or down them carefully. Think about where your character was and what your character was doing before your entrance. Know exactly why you are entering. If you have a line to say upon entering and if the action of the play permits it, pause in the doorway and deliver the line. Such a pause can be very effective. If several characters enter together and one of them is speaking, the character who is speaking should enter last so that he or she does not have to turn to talk to the others.

Exits are as important as entrances. Plan ahead for them. Always leave the stage in a definite state of mind and with a definite place to go. If you have an exit line or a reason to turn back, turn on the balls of your feet and deliver the line or glance pointedly, still holding the doorknob.

Application
ACTIVITIES

1. Imagine the personal bubbles around the characters described below. Then act out a scene in which they board a crowded, standing-room-only bus.

   - A boisterous salesperson who enjoys being around people on the way home from a very successful day selling appliances
   - A shy librarian on the way to a lecture on bird watching who wants to read a book while riding the bus
   - A high school football star known for his bone-crushing tackles and all-around rough play
   - A wealthy business owner who usually rides a chauffeured limousine to her office and is not used to standing and having all types of people bump against her

2. Decide on an appropriate "lead" for each of the following characters. Then act out that character as he or she begins to cross an intersection as the "Don't Walk" sign changes to "Walk."

   - A highly respected literary scholar from a prestigious university
   - The star dancer from a professional ballet troupe
   - An overweight accountant
   - The lead guitarist for a popular rock group

Frankenstein's monster leads with his bent arm, suggesting a defensive attitude. His facial expression and posture suggest that despite his size, he is mentally incapable of dealing with his predicament.

Onstage movement sends messages to the audience. You will recall that a movement from one stage position to another is called a **cross.** In general, actors usually move in gently curving patterns that resemble an S unless the movement is agitated or urgent. The curved pattern allows actors to open up or face the audience more easily. It also suggests that the stage space, which in reality is about one and a half times as large as the actual space being represented, is more similar to the actual space. It is always more forceful to move toward the audience or other characters than to move away. Standing is more forceful than sitting. Therefore, seated characters must expend more energy to build a scene.

The movement of two characters requires special consideration. Such scenes must be carefully rehearsed to be sure that one actor does not cover the other and also to be sure that both do not hold the same position for too long or use similar gestures. When one character moves, the stage picture loses its balance. Therefore, for each cross onstage, there is usually a movement in the opposite direction by another character. This is called a **countercross.** It does not have to cover a distance equal to the first movement. Crossing and countercrossing are important parts of rehearsing, and they must be carefully worked out so they look natural onstage. It is always best not to move on important lines, either your own or those of another character, because movement distracts the audience from the words spoken. Try to cross between speeches on a definite piece of business. Countercross easily and naturally when giving way to someone else.

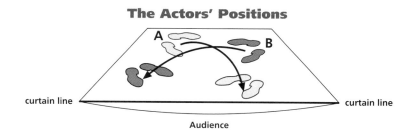

The Actors' Positions

curtain line

curtain line

Audience

COUNTERCROSS
When character A crosses from the UR position to DL, character B will move from UL to DR to balance the stage, to offset the movement of A, and to avoid being blocked by A's new position.

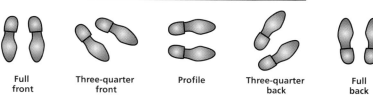

Full
front

Three-quarter
front

Profile

Three-quarter
back

Full
back

Decreasing Emphasis

Rules of Stage Movement

DO . . .	DON'T . . .
Do open a door using the hand nearest the hinges, and close it with the other hand.	**Don't** block an exit while waiting to enter the stage or stand in front of a backstage light that might cast your shadow onstage.
Do enter the stage with your upstage foot first, so your body is turned downstage.	
Do cross downstage of furniture or characters who are standing.	**Don't** move during important lines, a laugh line, or while the audience is laughing.
Do cross upstage of seated characters.	**Don't** cover your face with your hands or with a prop.
Do make gestures with the upstage arm, and make turns toward the front.	**Don't** cross your knees or feet or spread your feet apart with the knees together unless your character would do so.
Do move forward on the upstage foot, and kneel on the downstage knee.	
Do sit with your feet and knees together unless you are playing a character who would sit otherwise, such as a child.	**Don't** grab the arms of a chair to push yourself up unless your character would do so.
Do stay in character when leaving the stage until you are out of sight of the audience.	

The movements associated with sitting and rising must be done naturally and effectively. Continually practice crossing to a chair or a sofa and sitting down in character until it feels comfortable and becomes natural. Avoid looking back for the chair or the sofa before you sit. Locate the edge of the chair or the sofa with the back of the calf of your leg. Then sit down, remaining in character as you do so. When rising, put one foot slightly in front of the other and push yourself up with the back foot, letting the chest lead. To make rising easier, sit on the front half of a chair or a sofa.

Exercises   Entrances and Exits or Movement

Practice these stage movements with a partner.

1. Actor A enters from stage left and stands at center stage. Then Actor B enters from stage right and stands slightly upstage of Actor A. Actor A crosses to stage right. Then Actor B countercrosses. Both actors turn and look offstage right. While exiting stage left, the actors ad-lib a conversation.

2. Practice sitting and rising from different types of chairs and in different characters. As one of you practices, the other can critique the performance.

STAGE POSITIONS AND GROUPING

The positions and grouping of actors onstage are very important because they convey the spirit of a situation without any lines being spoken. There are four basic staging techniques:

1. An actor is said to **"cheat out"** when he or she pivots the torso and turns the face toward the audience. Two actors may "cheat out" when they "share a scene." You **"share a scene"** equally with another actor when you stand or sit parallel to each other. A shared scene should be played three-quarter front or in profile. A profile is rather weak, however, because it does not allow the audience to see your face. Also, a profile scene is a confrontation-type scene. It can be played for only a short time before the audience expects a strong emotional reaction, such as a fight or an embrace.

2. An actor is **"giving the scene"** when he or she crosses downstage and then turns slightly upstage toward the other actor. This shifts the audience's attention to the upstage actor.

3. Actors who are not the key characters in a scene are said to be **"turning the scene in"** when they shift the angle of their bodies upstage and look directly at the scene's key character. This focuses the attention of the audience on the center of the action.

4. An actor who turns away from the audience into a three-quarter back or full back position draws attention away from himself or herself. This is called **"taking yourself out of a scene."**

Peter O'Toole and Joyce Redman, playing Professor Higgins and his mother in *Pygmalion*, demonstrate cheating out. The way they lean toward each other, with his arm behind her, indicates a bond between the characters.

An actor can be emphasized simply by his or her position onstage. One technique that works well is to position the important character at the highest point of a triangle formed by actors, furniture, or other set pieces at the downstage "corners." Frames, such as doorways and archways, also set off an actor. Similarly, elevations such as platforms, steps, and landings give a character dominance over other actors onstage. Because people in Western societies are conditioned to move their eyes from left to right, down right is a stronger stage position in Western theater than down left.

A character who is upstage of another is usually dominant. Therefore, the term **upstaging** is used for scene-stealing when an actor intentionally moves upstage drawing attention away from the focus of the scene. Actors who keep the stage picture in mind allow the audience to see the performance clearly. They will not cover other actors, huddle in tight groups, stand in straight lines, or take an emphasized position at an inappropriate time.

Application
ACTIVITIES

Work in groups to deliver the following lines, using the staging technique indicated.

1. Move downstage and cheat out saying, "I knew I should never have trusted him."

2. As Actor A gives the scene, Actor B upstage says, "I have come to an important decision."

3. Several actors turn the scene in as an upstage actor says, "Who among you will challenge my claim?"

STAGE BUSINESS

Stage business is an essential part of acting and involves the use of hand props, costume props, stage props, other actors, and even parts of the set (doors, windows, lighting fixtures, and so forth). How you handle a cup and saucer, a pair of glasses, or a handkerchief will, of course, vary from characterization to characterization. It takes training and a lot of practice to handle props well. This is especially true of such historical props as swords, fans, parasols, canes, and swagger sticks. If such items are not

Stage Positions

Sharing
A and B are on even line.
Both three-quarter front.

Taking
A moves into position
upstage of B.

Giving
A turns three-quarter upstage to B.

Taking out of Scene
A turns full back.

Dominant Stage Positions

handled properly, their use will appear awkward and distracting and the audience will focus on the props instead of on the actor using them. Stage business, such as writing a letter, drinking from a cup, or stirring a fire, demands concentration and much practice before it looks natural. Good stage business aids a characterization and enhances an entire production. Too much stage business, however, especially that which is out of character and nonmotivated, is meaningless and even distracting.

Eating and drinking onstage present special problems. Real food is rarely used onstage, so an actor needs imagination to convince an audience that the food or drink is real. When you drink onstage, think about what the real drink is like. If you are supposed to be drinking a cup of cocoa, think about how hot it is. If it is really hot, you will sip it carefully. If it is lukewarm, you might gulp it down before it gets colder. Does it have a marshmallow on top? How full is the cup? When you eat onstage and dark bread has been substituted for steak, imagine what kind of steak it is, how it has been cooked, and whether it is tender and juicy or tough and dry.

▼ CUE

When You Eat Onstage

- To avoid choking, do not eat or drink any more than is necessary and do not deliver lines with food in your mouth.
- Cups, utensils, and foods that have been in contact with your mouth must be disposed of properly.

Live props can be either impressive if handled well or unintentionally comic if handled poorly. Here, Carol Channing successfully works with pigeons in a scene from *Sugar Babies*.

SPECIAL STAGE TECHNIQUES

Two areas of stage technique deserve particular attention: combat and romance. The former includes delivering blows, pulling hair, and choking. The latter focuses primarily on the stage kiss.

Stage Combat   Stage combat requires considerable training and practice. Only a few general principles will be given here. Most important, most stage combat is noncontact. If the combat is executed properly, the audience responds as if actual physical contact had taken place. Combat should never be treated as a game, and participants should always take care of their partners.

There are three stages to most combat:

1. The Preparation—usually an action opposite to the direction of the blow, such as the drawing back of the fist
2. The Blow—the execution of the blow, jab, or pull
3. The Reaction—a combination of sound, physical response, and freeze

Both actors should take in air before a blow is delivered so that both can respond vocally to the assault. Immediately following and timed to coincide with the landing of the blow is a second sound called a **knap,** a sliding, slapping sound or clap. The knap is usually made by the deliverer of the blow, who may hit his or her own chest with the free hand. It is not the sound of a closed fist hitting the palm. The knap should not be seen by the audience, except in commedia dell'arte, where seeing the knap is part of the comedy. There must be a slight pause after each hit of combat registers with the audience. The actor who receives the blow reacts immediately with both facial expression and body movement, freezes, and then lets air out with a pained sound.

Pulling the hair and choking are also used in stage combat. To create the illusion of pulling hair, an actor holds a closed fist against the back of the victim's head. The actor whose hair is being pulled distorts the face in anguish, twists the body in pain, and produces a sound of suffering. This is all that is necessary to convince the audience that the hair has been pulled. Choking, whether with two hands from the front or with the arm from the back, can be very dangerous if not done properly. It is best done by placing the hands or forearm on the collarbone instead of on the neck itself. The victim then reaches up and pulls the hands or forearm of the attacker toward him or her, thereby controlling the pressure. At the same time, the actor doing the choking pulls the hands or forearm away from the victim as the victim grimaces in pain.

Romantic Scenes Romantic scenes require careful rehearsal. They should be rehearsed privately with the director before they are attempted in rehearsals with the entire cast.

There are four key parts to a successful stage kiss: (1) proper foot position; (2) correct body position; (3) exact time count; and (4) a smooth break. The script or the director will tell you what kind of kiss is needed in the scene—a motherly peck or a romantic embrace. The first part is getting into the embrace. The woman usually faces the audience with her feet about six inches apart. The man then steps toward the woman on the foot closest to her, puts that foot between her feet and swings around so that they end up facing each other.

Body position is the second part of a stage kiss. For most romantic kisses little or no light should be seen between the couple. The woman should be facing the audience, and the man should be facing her, his back squarely toward the audience. The couple should decide ahead of time which way they will tilt their heads—to the right or to the left. The couple does not have to make any actual physical contact at all; many professional actors do not. Correct foot and body position give the illusion of a real kiss.

The third and most important part of the kiss is the count. A sweet romantic kiss lasts one second; a reasonably romantic kiss lasts two seconds; and a very romantic kiss lasts from three to five seconds. Anything over five seconds will usually cause the wrong audience response.

Perhaps the most difficult part of the stage embrace is the parting or separation of the couple. First, it must be done with the same emotional value as the kiss established, usually a smooth slow release. Second, it is important for the couple to maintain physical contact with the hands until the "break"—the actual separation. To do this, the couple slowly pulls apart while sliding their hands down each other's arms. The break may occur at the forearms, or the couple may continue until they are holding hands. Then they may step away from each other, gently releasing their hands.

Kissing scenes are often altogether silent, with just two actors onstage. Try to imagine beforehand how this will be, so that when the moment actually comes you won't seem surprised.

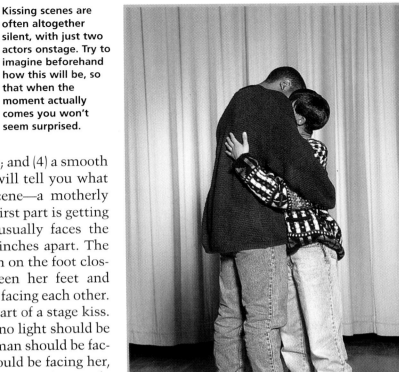

▼ **CUE**

One of the most expressive parts of a stage kiss is the woman's hands embracing the man's back. Because the man has his back to the audience, this is what the audience sees.

for colored girls who have considered suicide/when the rainbow is enuf is a choreo-poem—a dramatic performance that blends poetry, dance, and stories. Actors communicate to the audience using a combination of vocal tone, word meanings, and movement.

❧ *Vocal Acting*

Your voice is one of the strongest instruments you have for creating a character. In addition to the principles of voice and diction that you studied in the previous chapter, certain principles of vocal behavior affect characterization.

PITCH AND INFLECTION

Most characters can be classified as either "pitch up" or "pitch down" personalities. Pitch-down characters are self-assured, dominating, authoritative, and overbearing, whereas pitch-up characters lack confidence and tend to be fearful, intimidated, seeking, or confused.

Closely related to the general rising and falling pitch patterns are the four **inflections**—rising, falling, sustained, and circumflex. **Rising inflection** is used to indicate questioning, surprise, or shock. **Falling inflection** usually signals the end of a statement. It is also used to express depression, finality, or firmness. **Sustained inflection**—staying on the same note—suggests calmness, decisiveness, or steadiness of purpose. **Circumflex inflec-**

tion is the intonation of two or more vowel sounds for what ordinarily is a single vowel sound. This inflection allows an actor to suggest a change in meaning of a word or to stress a particular meaning. This twisting of sound can alter the literal meaning of a word and even reverse the meaning entirely. One of the best known examples of the circumflex inflection is found in Marc Antony's funeral oration in *Julius Caesar*. Each time Antony says the word *honorable*, he inflects the vowel sounds more and more until the word suggests the meaning "dishonorable."

Exercises — Inflection

1. Say the following lines, using the inflection indicated in parentheses.

- It was you! (rising inflection)
- What's the use? (falling inflection)
- I have made up my mind. This is how we're going to do it. (sustained inflection)
- Surely, you're not going to go out in this weather. (rising inflection)
- I'm sorry, but I just can't allow you to copy my notes. (falling inflection)

2. Say the following lines. Inflect the underlined vowels with a circumflex.

- She is s<u>o</u> grateful.
- It h<u>u</u>rts a lot.
- It's s<u>o</u> str<u>a</u>nge.
- L<u>oo</u>k at those fl<u>a</u>mes!
- S<u>ee</u>, I t<u>o</u>ld you she was surpr<u>i</u>sed.

VOCAL RESPONSE

CUE

Never become so locked into how you deliver certain lines that you are unable to respond to the lines given by other actors.

When you rehearse alone, you may guess how lines will be delivered by other actors. But when you go into rehearsal, you may find that your planned delivery does not match up with that of the other actors. For example, if someone shouts at you, you instinctively want to shout back. As a scene builds, the volume levels usually become louder and louder. If the pace of a conversation quickens, you naturally tend to speak more rapidly. As an actor, you must respond to the emotion, pitch, and volume levels of the other actors onstage. However, you must always do so within the personality and mind-set of the character you are playing. Some personalities will respond to a given situation in a manner that is almost directly opposite to the way in which most people respond. While most characters will raise the volume of their voices in response to shouting, a particular character might whimper in response. You must not allow the flow of emotion from other characters to pull you out of your own characterization.

❧ *Getting Onstage*

You have been given a part. Now it is time to put all you have learned to work in the day-to-day business of preparing for opening night. There are lines to be memorized, characters to be analyzed, and techniques to be refined.

MEMORIZING YOUR LINES

A chief responsibility that follows getting a part is memorizing your lines. Lines must be learned according to the director's schedule. Directors realize that an actor is severely limited as long as the script is still in hand. Therefore, the sooner the lines are memorized, the sooner the actor is free to concentrate on the action and to respond naturally to the other actors.

There are two approaches to memorizing. Whole-part memorization requires the actor to read through the whole play several times. The actor then reads a complete act several times, followed by several readings of those scenes in which the actor appears. The actor focuses on individual lines only after whole units of the play are firmly in mind. This method develops an internal feel for the entire play and for the other characters.

The second method is called part-whole memorization. In this approach the actor studies the script line-by-line until it is memorized. This method has a number of disadvantages. First, since each line is learned by itself, the risk of forgetting exists with each line. Second, the play may seem very fragmented in the early rehearsals, since the differences between memorized lines and still-to-be-memorized lines are rather dramatic. Finally, actors who have memorized line by line tend to focus more on cues for their lines than on the meaning of the other characters' lines.

CUE ▼

Unless the director says otherwise, lines should always be memorized exactly as written. Sometimes beginning actors complain that they don't like a line or that a line doesn't sound right. With few exceptions, the problem is with the actor. The line or lines that the actor is complaining about will sound right once the actor gets more into character.

READING BETWEEN THE LINES

The author supplies the character's words in the text of the script. You, the actor, must supply the **subtext.** The subtext is the "meaning between the lines"—what is implied but not directly stated. The subtext is what your character thinks but does not say.

Actors should know what their characters are thinking when they are onstage and even what they are thinking off-stage. Many actors write out a complete subtext. They then think as their character would think while other actors are delivering their lines.

A play, of course, is not a real-life situation. It is the illusion of real life. "Forgetting what you know" helps you maintain this illusion. After studying and rehearsing a play over and over, you get to know things your character really wouldn't know. For example, you know how things are going to turn out, you know the content of conversations that your character did not participate in, and you know what takes place when your character is not onstage. To create the illusion of reality in a convincing manner, you must "remember to forget" all of these things.

Another way of putting it is to say you are "playing the moment." Playing the moment means that you respond to each line, each action, and each character in the permanent present time that theater demands. The theater lives in the permanent "now," and you must not anticipate what is about to happen. An actor who plays the moment never turns to a phone before it actually rings and never opens a door before the knock. Beginning actors must remember not to shift emotions before the onstage action makes the emotional shift understandable. Maintain the "illusion of the first time" and the air of suspense that keeps the audience wondering what will happen next.

Although actors must play the moment, "working backwards" is a helpful technique. This means that although you will not give away a

An actor can say much while remaining silent. In this scene from *King Lear*, the facial expressions of the two men and Lear's outstretched arm reveal a powerful subtext.

character's future actions, you will find ways of making those actions believable when they do occur. You must know where a character is headed and then work backwards to prepare an audience. If a somewhat villainous character will undergo a change of heart and show mercy instead of pure vengeance, disclose the possibility of this change early by emphasizing certain lines, by actions, or by tone of voice. Such a character, for example, might show an obvious compassionate side to an acquaintance or loved one early in the play. Audiences enjoy surprises but will not accept dramatic character changes for which they are not prepared.

Application
ACTIVITIES

1. Working with a partner, choose one of the scenes in Part 2 and read it aloud before studying it. Then review the scene and write the subtext for your respective character. Present the scene again, paying particular attention to the increased meaning this performance contains.

2. Practice delivering each of these lines, using the subtext stated in parentheses:

   - "Thanks a lot!" (That was absolutely no help!)
   - "I'm so happy you were able to come tonight." (I thought you'd never get here.)
   - "There is no cause for alarm. Everything is under control." (I hope that keeps everyone calm until I figure out what to do.)
   - "Sure, now you want me to be your friend." (You weren't very friendly to me before I won the lottery.)
   - "Oh! What a lovely outfit. It must have cost you a great deal of money." (You certainly spend your money foolishly!)
   - "Oh! What a lovely outfit. It must have cost you a great deal of money." (I wish I could afford to spend such an amount on clothes.)
   - "Oh! What a lovely outfit. It must have cost you a great deal of money." (That is one of the ugliest outfits I have ever seen, regardless of how much you paid for it.)
   - "Oh! What a lovely outfit. It must have cost you a great deal of money." (You are such a show-off. You can't afford such things.)

𒀀 Acting Techniques

No actor could possibly have experienced every emotion demanded by the roles he or she assumes. Most actors, however, have developed certain techniques for portraying such emotions. One such technique is called **substitution**. An actor might be faced with the challenge of playing the role of a parent who has to watch his or her own child die. The actor may never have been a parent and may never have experienced the death of any loved one. However, the actor might have experienced the death of a beloved pet. In playing the scene, the actor recalls the death of the pet and therefore uses a similar experience to help capture and project the emotional response called for in the scene.

Another useful technique is **improvisation,** the impromptu portrayal of a character without preparation or rehearsal. This technique is particularly useful when you are working on a period play or any play that has lines or actions far removed from your personal experience.

You can improvise once you know your character rather well, understand the general content of the lines and the reasons for the actions, and grasp the objectives and obstacles of a scene. If you are working alone, you can carry on a one-sided conversation that parallels the script. In a cast improvisation, you can play the whole scene. Under these circumstances, improvisation often allows you to understand more clearly how your character feels and what the other characters are feeling. It frequently enables you to see how the scene should be built when you return to the script.

Raul Julia portrays Othello, a character whose own jealousy destroys his happiness. For the performance to work, the audience must feel Othello's bewildered suspicion and all-consuming rage.

In *Cats* the actors crouch on their haunches and use their hands like paws. The right mixture of human and animal characteristics in roles such as these can be most effective.

Sometimes it is helpful to play certain roles as animal personalities. A particular mannerism associated with an animal's physical or vocal characteristics can sometimes be carried over to an actor's portrayal of a role. Various animals have physical actions and produce vocal sounds that can be worked into roles. This technique works especially well for children's theater. Some animal types that especially lend themselves to certain roles include the lion, bear, wolf, fox, rabbit, dog, cat, donkey, elephant, monkey, gorilla, turtle, alligator, snake, owl, vulture, chicken, duck, parrot, fly, and butterfly. Ben Jonson's *Volpone* is an example of a play written with animal personalities in mind. This same technique can be extended to other nonhuman types, such as androids, the Tin Woodsman and Scarecrow of Oz, robots, and other inanimate objects.

Scripts often include incomplete lines or one-sided telephone conversations. These must be practiced carefully, for to handle them correctly demands precise timing. There are two types of incomplete lines—**cut-off lines** and **fade-off lines**. Cut-off lines are lines that are interrupted by another speaker. In most scripts, cut-off lines are indicated by a dash (—). An actor who has a cut-off line should imagine what the rest of the line would be if it weren't cut off and should finish the line mentally. The actor who creates the cut-off line by interrupting must decide on a cue word ahead of the cut-off in order to interrupt at the right time.

cue word   cut-off   imagined finish

MARY   I don't care if — (she does leave.)
JANE   What do you mean you don't care!

In a fade-off line, the speaker trails off rather than finishing the line. Sometimes the speaker expects an interruption that does not come. Sometimes the meaning is so obvious that it is pointless to express it. In most scripts, a fade-off line is indicated by a series of dots (. . . .).

MARY   I knew it was wrong all along, but . . . .
JANE   *(after an awkward pause)* It's all right, Mary. It's all over now.

Phone conversations are common onstage. To make them believable, you should include legitimate pauses during the other party's words. If your part includes a phone conversation, it is always best to write out the conversation that occurs on the other end of the line. You can then memorize it and repeat it silently in between your spoken lines.

MIKE   Hello? [Hello, Mike?] Yeah, this is Mike. Who's this? [Mike, this is Bill—you know, Mary's fiancé?] Oh, yeah—Bill. What can I do for you? [Well, I just wanted you to know that it's off. It's all over between us—Mary and me—you understand?] What? Oh, yeah, sure. It's over. I understand.

To have natural-seeming telephone conversations onstage, listening is as important as talking. By portraying a good listener, you make not only your own character but also the character you are talking to real for the audience.

1. Explain one or more techniques you might use to prepare for one of these roles:

   - An astronaut attempting to return to Earth discovering that the rockets are inoperable
   - A foreign visitor who is unable to speak or write English arriving at Kennedy International Airport
   - A convicted murderer being led to the electric chair
   - A fourteenth-century physician treating a patient
   - An unscrupulous poker player dealing crooked hands to three unsuspecting players

2. Write a script for the other voice in the following telephone conversation. Then practice reading just the original script. Compare several interpretations of these lines and assess the effect of the other voice on the interpretation.

   Hello?
   Yeah, this is the Smiths'.
   No, she is away at the moment.
   Really! I had no idea.
   Of course, I'll give her a message.
   You want her to report at eight o'clock Monday morning.
   Sure thing! Thanks for calling. Bye.

✺ *Communicating Onstage*

The lines spoken in a play combine with the action to communicate a playwright's meaning and style as well as to reveal the characters and their emotions. Lines must coordinate with actions in order to tell the complete story. Speech, however, must never be lost or blurred by movements or it will lose its impact and meaning.

KEY LINES

Significant lines must be heard by each person in the audience no matter where that person is seated. You should mark the significant lines plainly on your script as soon as you have studied every situation carefully. Recheck them after the first rehearsals, when movements will be determined. Avoid practicing inflections until action is set, for after they become automatic, it is difficult to change them.

A rapid picking up of cues must be established as early in rehearsals as possible. The cues should be memorized along with the lines. Many beginning actors wait for their cue before they show any facial or bodily reaction. Your face should respond *during* the other person's lines. You will then be ready to speak on cue. A good technique is to take a breath during the cue. Failure to pick up cues quickly causes many amateur performances to drag in spite of painstaking rehearsals. The loss of only a fraction of a second before each speech slows the action dramatically.

The ad-lib is an emergency measure that should be used only to avoid a dead silence. If it is necessary to ad-lib, the lines must be spoken as though they were a part of the script without any change in volume or inflection. If one actor forgets lines or begins a speech ahead of the appropriate point in the action and skips important information, the other actors have to ad-lib the missing information while carrying on the conversation naturally.

Pointing lines means placing the emphasis on exactly the right word and timing the rate and pauses so that the audience gets the full emotional impact. A useful technique to use when you are uncertain how a line should be delivered is **paraphrasing**. Paraphrasing is simply figuring out the meaning of the line and stating it in your own words. Since the vocal patterns for similar thoughts are almost identical, the vocal pattern of your paraphrasing and that of the line will be very much alike. This exercise gives you a very good idea of how the line should be delivered.

Pointing lines is particularly essential in comedy; getting laughs in the right places makes or breaks a scene. Actors must work together to build up to the laugh line, so feeding cues properly is essential. Unless the preceding line or word leads to the point of the joke, the joke will fall flat. You can watch people in comic sketches on television leading into laughs. Notice how they combine pausing in the right place with facial expressions to help get laughs. They do this without stealing the

▼ **CUE**

In crowd scenes or scenes that portray a large social gathering, entire background conversations are often improvised. These must never drown out the lines of the speaker who is carrying the scene. Frequently, reciting the alphabet quietly, with appropriate inflections, can be used in background groupings to suggest conversation.

Raul Julia dresses as a woman in *Where's Charlie?* For comic dialogue, timing and rate are everything. Unless they are nearly perfect, the punch lines become predictable and go flat.

scene from the actor who should have it. In a play on the stage, it is inexcusable for the actor feeding the line or the actor making the point to laugh, although this is often done on television.

Key lines frequently include a person's name. How a person's name is spoken shows how the speaker feels about another character at a given moment. A name can be uttered with love, hatred, envy, flirtatiousness, or in any of countless ways that express how the speaker feels about the person. One reason playwrights use names so frequently in dialogue is to clarify a speaker's feelings. The position of a name in a line determines whether the pitch will rise or fall. (That is why actors should not change the position of a name in a line.) Playwrights also have reasons for placing *oh's* or *well's* or similar "sound words" at the beginning of lines and sentences. These terms serve as vocal transitions that allow an actor to raise or lower the pitch level of the lines without interfering with the meaning of key words.

Exercises — Delivering Lines

1. Read these lines. Note how the pitch changes with the position of the name.

"Tom, I can't understand how you could have done such a thing."

"I can't understand how you could have done such a thing, Tom."

"I can't understand, Tom, how you could have done such a thing."

2. Study the following speech from Shakespeare's *Romeo and Juliet*. Then paraphrase it and practice reading both your paraphrase and the original speech.

JULIET   'Tis but thy name that is my enemy;
Thou art thyself, though, not a Montague.
What's Montague? It is nor hand nor foot,
Nor arm, nor face, [nor any other part]
Belonging to a man. O, be some other name!
What's in a name? That which we call a rose
By any other name would smell as sweet;

So Romeo would, were he not Romeo call'd,
Retain that dear perfection which he owes
Without that title: Romeo, doff thy name,
And for that name, which is no part of thee,
Take all myself.

3. Read these sentences. Note how the use of the sound word allows you to change the pitch level while keeping the meaning of the key words.

(In shock) Oh, how awful for you!
(In disgust) Well, I always said he'd turn out bad.
(In admiration) My, that's a gorgeous jacket!
(In polite agreement) Yes, I would like another cup of tea.
(In reserved dismay) Oh, dear, did I do something wrong?
(In mild denial) Well, no, I wouldn't say that.

PLAYING COMEDY

Much of the success of comedy depends on the comic mood that the cast establishes. The cast must always communicate enjoyment as they maintain the fast pace that comedy requires. Individual actors must keep in mind a few techniques for playing comedy successfully.

- Lift the end of a punch line and leave it hanging, or play it "flat," or deadpan, in order to say to the audience, "Laugh now."
- Clinch the punch line with a facial or bodily reaction. It is helpful to develop an air of innocence; comic characters are often naive.

Learn to feed a line to a fellow performer so that the other actor can catch it in midair and clinch the laugh on the following line. Remember that laugh lines are usually short and that their length is determined by sounds as much as by words. A line too long or too short will kill a laugh. This is one major reason actors are told over and over again to deliver comic lines exactly as they are written. Adding or omitting one word can lose the laugh that the line is designed to get.

Topping becomes a particularly important factor in comedy. Actors top each other through increased volume, higher pitch, faster tempo, or greater emphasis. When a comic actor breaks a topping sequence, however, he or she may get a laugh through a sudden change of pitch, by saying the line in an almost expressionless manner, or with a look or gesture that seems inconsistent with the character or the situation. Remember, timing must be perfect or the laugh can easily be killed. Comedians even learn how to "milk" audiences for laughs by adding some exaggerated bits of business to their punch lines.

Beginning actors often fail to hold for laughs. Even after weeks of rehearsal during which many hours are spent picking up cues, beginning performers may rush from line to line without giving the audience an opportunity to react by laughing. An audience will naturally silence itself to hear lines. An actor must anticipate where the audience is likely to laugh and then be prepared to freeze until the laughter dies naturally. The actor must listen for the **laugh curve**. This begins with the laughter of those members of the audience who catch on more quickly. The laughter then swells more rapidly as others join in, for laughter is contagious, until a peak is reached. Just after the peak, the laughter will start to fade. At this instant the actor with the "cut-in" line must kill the laughter. Usually the first part of the cut-in line is not all that important to the play. Its main

CUE

Theater people often say, "No two audiences are alike!" This is probably most true of comedy audiences. One night a line might get a faint chuckle, and the next night the same line is greeted with a roar of laughter. Some audiences will laugh at almost nothing, while others seem never to stop laughing.

Laugh Curve

Peak of Laughter

"Shaking" Sound

Laughter Builds

Cut-in Line or Movement

Normal Audience Sound Level

Actors freeze; Laughter Begins

purpose is to silence the audience. It is important that an audience not be allowed to "laugh itself out." If it did, its members would then sit back relaxed, satisfied, and willing to wait a while before being entertained again. The pace of the comedy would then be seriously slowed.

LAUGHTER AND TEARS

Comedies as well as other forms of drama sometimes require the actors themselves to laugh. The best approach is to observe laughter closely, both in real life and on stage and television. Pay particular attention to unusual laughs. There are many kinds, including uproarious guffaws, artificial simperings, musical ripples, hysterical gurgles, and sinister snorts. The first step in learning to laugh is to pant like a dog. Tighten your abdominal muscles as you exhale and relax them as you inhale. On your first try, you might only make faces, because you will probably try to say "ha" when

Laughter is a good way to encourage audience empathy with your character. Characters who laugh often seem more likable and more wellrounded than those who do not.

To appear natural, an actor's level of grief must be appropriate for the situation. Death scenes, such as this one from *Amadeus,* require the greatest display of grief.

you are drawing in the breath instead of when you are expelling it in sharp, quick spurts. As you practice, literally "laugh until your sides ache."

In order to master the laugh, you must first relax and then let yourself go. Take the vowel combinations heard in laughter—"ha-ha-ha, ho-ho-ho, he-he-he, heh-heh-heh"—and say them in rapid succession with sharp contractions of the abdominal area. Do not stop or become self-conscious.

Crying onstage is much easier than laughing. The breathing technique for crying is much the same as that for laughing. Gasp for breath, flexing the abdominal muscles in short, sharp movements. Words are often spoken on the gasping breath, so you must be careful to keep the meaning clear by not obscuring the key words. In sobbing without words, try using different vowel sounds through the gasps. Intensify and prolong the sounds to avoid monotony. Occasional indrawn and audible breaths for the "catch in the throat" are effective. "Swallowing tears" is simulated by tightening the throat muscles and really swallowing. In uncontrolled or hysterical crying, the vowel sounds will be stronger. If words are needed, they will be greatly intensified. When you are crying, your entire body should react. Your shoulders will shake and heave. Facial expression is most important. An appropriate expression can be created by puckering the eyebrows, biting the lips, and twisting the features to obtain the necessary effect.

Application
ACTIVITIES

1. Practice laughing like the following people: a giggling child on the telephone; a rude actor in a comic television show; a very polite woman reacting to a joke she has heard many times; a villain who has at last captured the hero; a miser gloating over a box of money; an elementary school student seeing a friend trip over a brick.

2. Say the lines below, accompanying each with laughter as (a) a five-year-old child; (b) a teenager; (c) a middle-aged conservative person; (d) an elderly, wealthy person.

   "That's the silliest thing I've ever heard."
   "Look at that crazy monkey!"
   "But that's so embarrassing!"

3. Read the following passages from Shakespeare, accompanying the lines with appropriate laughter.

   a. FROM *As You Like It*
   JAQUES   A fool, a fool!—I met a fool i' the forest,
       A motley fool; a miserable world!

   b. FROM *As You Like It*
   CELIA   O wonderful, wonderful, and most wonderful, wonderful, and yet again wonderful!

   c. FROM *The Merchant of Venice*
   GRATIANO   Let me play the fool,
       With mirth and laughter let old wrinkles come.

4. Practice sobbing like each of the following: a young child who has lost his or her only stuffed animal; a husband at the bed of his sick wife, who is asleep; a spoiled child having a tantrum; a hysterical driver after a serious automobile accident; an elderly person alone on a holiday.

5. Read the following passage. Cry through the words, but be careful to keep the meaning clear.

   FROM *Pearls* by Dan Totheroh
   (A young girl has just learned that her brother is a thief.)
   POLLY   I can't believe it. I can't—I can't—He's only a little boy—just a kid.

🌿 *Accents and Dialects*

National and regional speech differences are evident in the pronunciation and selection of words and in the inflection of sentences. Train your ears to catch changes in quality, pitch, timing, stress, and rhythm and the occasional substitutions and omissions of sounds.

When you are beginning work with a role involving a dialect shift in English, nothing can take the place of listening to people who use the dialect until you catch the inflections, omissions, and patterns of sounds. You might find recordings helpful, however, because you can play them again and again. There are also a few good books that will help you with dialects, idioms, and colloquial speech. A dialect that is too precise, however, can be very distracting to an audience. Dialects used onstage are rarely authentic but are accepted stage versions of dialects.

When you speak in a dialect, it is important to make the words recognizable. Sometimes it helps to face the audience so they can watch your mouth form the words. These actors in *Fiddler on the Roof* must enunciate all the more carefully because their beards and mustaches interfere with lip-reading by audience members.

ENGLISH

British English is the basis for so-called stage diction. It can be heard in BBC dramas on television or on recordings made by such actors as Laurence Olivier, John Gielgud, or Edith Evans.

The British use a higher tonal pitch and a much wider range than Americans. There are also a number of important differences in pronunciation. Here are five such differences. Refer to the chart on page 85 for help with pronunciations.

1. The *a* in words like *basket, aunt, banana,* and *laugh* is pronounced ä instead of ă as in American English.

2. The final vowel in words like *Tuesday, nobody,* and *certainly* is pronounced ĭ.

3. The vowel sound in the word *been* is ĭ; the vowel sound in *either* and *neither* is ī, while the vowel in the second syllable of *again* is pronounced ĕ.

4. The first syllable is stressed in many words, such as *secretary, library,* and *necessary* (sĕk•rŭ•trĭ; lī•brĭ; nĕ•sŭ•srĭ). Note that in such words as *secretary* and *necessary,* the last two syllables are run together in their pronunciation.

5. The *r* sound is dropped after a vowel or when it is the final sound. So *father* becomes fä′ thə; *never* becomes nĕ′ və; and *park* becomes päk. An *r* between vowels or a doubled *r* is trilled. You hear this in such words as *very, orange, marry,* and *courage.*

Cockney, a distinct version of British English, is difficult to master, yet it is one of the most common stage dialects. Note the unusual pronunciations used in Cockney. The Cockney dialect commonly drops initial and final consonants from words.

Word	Standard Pronunciation	Cockney Dialect
place	plās	plīs
ice	īs	ois
know	nō	nou
right	rīt	rŏ(t)
habit	hăb′ ĭt	ăbĭ(t)
home	hōm	ōm

The Irish dialect, on the other hand, is a lilting one, marked by much variety in pitch and inflection and a pace that is a little faster than American speech.

Note the vowel changes in these Irish pronunciations:

Word	Standard Pronunciation	Irish Dialect
fine	fīn	foin
when	hwĕn	hwĭn
one	wŭn	wo͞on
love	lŭv	lo͞ov
deal	dēl	dāl
you	yo͞o	yŭh

American English dialects vary in practically every state in the United States, but there are a few distinguishing characteristics that apply to whole areas. As a general rule, the farther a person is from an urban area, the slower and more nasal the speech. Southern and Western accents are known for their drawl—speaking slowly and inflecting the vowels (changing the tone or pitch of the voice). The various Southern accents have vowels that are rich and round. The long *i* often becomes ä in words like *I, my,* and *like,* and a final *er* nearly disappears. So "I like that view over yonder" might become "Äh läk that vēo͞o ovä yŏndə." Other commonly used American stage dialects are those from Brooklyn, New Jersey, and Boston.

EUROPEAN ACCENTS

European accents are too difficult to imitate without listening to people who use them habitually. A few suggestions may be helpful.

Italian is exceedingly musical and patterned with many inflections. The occasional *ŭh* sound added to consonant sounds is most pleasing, as in *soft-uh-ting* (soft thing) or *fruit-uh-stand,* and *I gottuh* as in T. A. Daly's delightful poem, "I gotta love for Angela, I love Carlotta, too." All of Daly's poems offer excellent phrasing and pronunciations; he uses *dä* for *the,* *ā* for *ē,* and adds *uh*'s between words.

The German accent is definitely gutteral; many of the sounds are made with the back of the tongue. *V* takes the place of *w,* *d* is used for *t,* and *p* is used for *b.*

Swedish is inclined to be high in pitch with recurring rising inflections and a flat tone that is not nasal. The o͝o is pronounced o͞o, so *good* rhymes with *food.* The voiced *th* becomes *d,* so *that* is pronounced *dăt.* A *w* becomes *v,* so *wet* is pronounced *vĕt,* and *j* becomes *y* as in *yŭst* for *just.*

All the European accents are based on the inflections, rhythms, and word order of the original language. These frequently differ very much from those of the English language. Authors can give some help in writing passages, but listening to people and recordings is essential to an actor learning the accents.

The popularity of *Fiddler on the Roof* and Neil Simon's comedies have increased the popularity of Yiddish, which is a mixture of High German and Hebrew. It is the American stage Yiddish that actors should know. The pitch is much higher than American speech, often rising into a falsetto and seldom dropping to low pitch levels. Most sentences end with a rising pitch. The quality is quite nasal, and the pace is fairly slow.

In general, accents are difficult to master. However, there are often many roles for actors who can handle accents well. Stage accents are seldom authentic. Many authentic accents would be too difficult to understand. Some stage accents are more a theatrical convention than an imitation of the real thing.

Exercises — Dialect

Read the following lines in the dialect indicated.

1. My aunt will arrive at the library on Tuesday. (British English)

2. My love for you will never die. (Irish)

3. I figure we'll see your father tomorrow. (Southern United States)

4. I have a place close to home. (Cockney)

🕸 *Rehearsing*

Rehearsals are essential for full development of a play's unity, timing, and characterization. Rehearsals allow the director to shape the play, and the actors to develop their characters by interacting with one another.

PREPARING FOR A PRODUCTION

Actors should come to rehearsals prepared to rehearse by using the methods that the director prefers. Directors are different. Some directors will block one movement at a time. Other directors will have the actors write down the blocking for a page or scene and then have them walk through the scene. Still other directors will have actors move as they feel motivated to move and then correct awkward moves. Always bring a script to rehearsal so you can write the blocking, the stage business, and the director's comments on the script *in pencil*.

In early rehearsals, when the script is still being memorized, an actor can request a prompt for a forgotten line by saying "line" or "prompt" or by snapping a finger. The director may specify the method before the first rehearsal.

Actors should clearly mark all of their lines in the script. If rented scripts are used, the markings should be made only with a soft lead pencil. If the scripts have been purchased, underlining the character's name or highlighting the lines are the preferred methods. Underlining all of a character's lines makes a script too difficult to read. A different color can be used to mark movement or stage business or to note interpretation. Many directors prefer to number each speech on the page consecutively so that page and line numbers can easily be referred to in critiques and written notes.

Actors should always be prepared for frequent interruptions by the director during rehearsals. This is especially true of the early

These actors are having an early rehearsal with only a few props. At this point the relationships and habits are formed that will later shape the production.

rehearsals. As rehearsals progress, lines should be so well memorized that a director can say, "Start with 'and furthermore.'" The actor should be able to pick up the line at just that point.

It is during rehearsals that the tempo of a play is set. The rapid pick-up of cues determines the play's tempo. If the tempo is slower than it should be, the delay is probably caused by slight pauses between speeches. During rehearsals actors must learn to come in on another actor's final word without a pause.

At rehearsals it makes sense to wear clothing that is generally related to your character's personality. Avoid styles that are entirely out of keeping with your character. Wear clothes that are like those your character might choose. They will help to put you in the right mood for a scene. Shoes are very important, for your movements are greatly affected by footwear. Men should wear suit jackets if their characters would wear them. This will allow them to get the feel of wearing a coat. Too often an actor who starts wearing a jacket at dress rehearsal will jam his hands into the coat pockets or grab awkwardly at the lapels. Women should wear appropriate rehearsal jewelry but should remove any bracelets, necklaces, or watches that are entirely out of character. A long necklace might tempt them to fidget. It is helpful to wear a skirt of the same length the costume will be or even a hoop if a hoop skirt will be worn.

If a cast works closely together at rehearsals, the members will experience the joy that real teamwork brings. As lines are tossed back and forth appropriately, the members will feel the different personalities reacting to one another and begin to understand that acting is a cooperative experience. Discovering how personality plays upon personality in a scene is what makes rehearsing worthwhile.

Stage techniques must become automatic and subconscious during rehearsals and performances. If you follow a daily practice schedule for as long as you are involved in dramatics, you will establish stage techniques and keep your body and voice at their best. The following chart outlines a series of exercises recommended for daily use. The instructions for these exercises are found in chapters 2 and 3.

DAILY PRACTICE	
BODY EXERCISES	**VOCAL EXERCISES**
Deep breathing	Relaxing the entire body
Loosening up: stretching, bending, twisting	Yawning to relax throat
Pantomime exercises	Jaw exercises
Posture exercises	Lip exercises
Shaking hands vigorously	Babbling
Opening and closing fists	Humming
Moving fingers as in five-finger exercises	Breathing and counting
Rotating hands in circles from the wrists	Tongue twisters
Moving arms from elbow in circles	Chanting lines of poetry
Moving entire arms in circles	Reading stories aloud
Using body and arm gestures to show pleading, fear, and commanding	

As you study theater more deeply, audition for all kinds of parts, and spend a number of weeks at rehearsals, it is easy to focus exclusively on yourself and on what progress you are making. You must remember, however, that actors perform for an audience and gain empathy from an audience. Actors must always keep the interests, needs, and enjoyment of the audience uppermost in their minds.

The individuals who make up your audience are auditory, visual, and kinesthetic people. Some will respond more to what they hear. Others will respond more to what they see, and still others will respond more to the kinds of physical action with which they identify. Therefore, in order to appeal as strongly as you can to all of the members of your audience, your acting must be a blending of sound, sight, and action.

🐾 Adapting to the Arena and Thrust Stages

Everything an actor says or does onstage must be done with an awareness of the physical dimensions of the stage itself. The position of an actor in relation to the audience profoundly affects his or her speech, movement, exits, entrances, and even the lighting. In order to achieve the best productions possible, actors involved in productions on arena and thrust stages need to rehearse diligently. Because of the special conditions imposed by these two types of stages, the acting and staging differ from those required by the more traditional proscenium stage. The experience gained through rehearsing becomes crucial.

When a play is acted in the round, the audience is very close to the performers. This scene from a stage adaptation of Voltaire's *Candide* shows audience interaction with arena staging.

Learning to act on an arena or stage "in the round" is now becoming a necessary part of dramatic training. The open stage, surrounded on four sides by seats, results in close contact between actors and spectators. Arena staging demands careful planning and rehearsing. The director cannot depend heavily on a set for effects, and the audience is so close that every detail of costumes, furniture, and lighting must be right. The acting area must be lighted by spotlights that do not hit any member of the audience in the eyes. Acts can be ended by blacking out the lights or by incorporating exits into the play's action. Either will take the place of the usual stage curtain. The furniture must not block the action from any side, and scenes must be arranged so that they can be seen from all angles.

The director must plan to keep the actors moving and speaking as they cross and countercross rather than have them seated for long periods of time. Keeping the actors in motion allows their faces and voices to carry the meaning of the play to everyone. The actors often face each other offset by at least two feet so that the audience can always see the face of one actor. If possible, the director must plan the action so that it can be seen from all sides at once.

The arena stage places more demands on the actors than the proscenium stage does. Each actor must be continually conscious of being surrounded by spectators who must see and hear everything. Actors must speak very clearly and project their words so that everyone in the audience can hear even when the actors turn away. Very accurate pointing of lines and accenting of key words must combine with a few clear-cut gestures that are effective from every angle. With the audience so close, artificiality or exaggeration becomes so apparent that all sense of reality is lost. Also, fidgeting and aimless gestures are far more irritating at close range.

Plays for an arena production must be carefully selected. Entrances and exits are sometimes difficult in arena staging because actors can be seen long before they reach the acting area and for some time after they exit from the stage. Entrances must permit effective approaches for actors before they speak, and exits must allow for convenient departures. Actions and lines must be suitable for the close attention of the audience. Sofas, benches, and low-backed chairs must be appropriate as a background for the actors since there is minimal scenery. A suitable play in the round can move spectators deeply when it is well done. A production that might be acceptable on the regular stage might be a failure in the round.

Thrust staging offers some of the advantages of both the proscenium stage and the arena. The thrust, sometimes called horseshoe staging, uses a low platform surrounded on three sides by the audience.

Since the thrust has a back wall, many plays requiring scenery that would be difficult, if not impossible, on an arena stage can be presented. Entrances can come from the back wall as well as from the three sides of the thrust. Much of the action needs to take place mid-stage; otherwise, the audience sitting on the sides will see only the backs of the actors. When there is a large cast, as in a musical, the chorus members must be placed in a curved *V*—the opposite of proscenium blocking.

The flexibility and intimacy of the thrust have made it a very popular type of staging. It works well in a large classroom, and if the audience does not exceed two hundred, a thrust arrangement can be set up on the stage, in a gym, or in a lunchroom.

This scene from *Where's Charlie?* shows successfully blocked thrust staging. At least one actor faces each side of the stage, thus drawing the audience into the action.

4 REVIEW

Summary and Key Ideas

Summarize the chapter by answering the following questions.

1. What advice do directors often give to beginning actors?
2. Who was Konstantin Stanislavski? What is his "magic *if*"?
3. What information should be in a character sketch?
4. What are role scoring and script scoring? How does each help an actor?
5. Describe at least five keys to characterization.
6. What is a cross? Why is a cross usually followed by a countercross?
7. Name at least three *Do*s and three *Don't*s of stage movement.
8. What are three rules for eating onstage?
9. What are some techniques for playing comedy?

Discussing Ideas

1. Compare the emotional, subjective approach to acting to the technical, objective approach. How would an actor use each approach to prepare for the part of a mother whose child is missing?
2. Discuss the different types of roles and why each type of role is important in a play.
3. Choose a role you have played or would like to play. Explain how you would use any or all of the sixteen keys to characterization to build your role.
4. What demands do arena and thrust stages place on actors?

FOCUS ON   Evaluating Theater

Learning to evaluate, or judge, live theater, film, and television will make your viewing more enjoyable and will help you develop as a cast member. Get in the habit of making precise, specific observations about the productions you view. Think about the play itself, the set design, the direction, and the acting.

Judging a Play With a partner, view a live theater, film, or television production. Then evaluate the play itself as well as the set design, direction, and acting. Were the play and its various elements effective? Why or

why not? With your partner, discuss your response. Then summarize your evaluation in a short paper. Try to repeat this process any time you view a student or professional production.

Learning from the Critics Critics—those who review and analyze drama—open readers' minds to creative and lively interpretations. Find two pieces of criticism about a live theater, film, or television production that you've seen. Then give the class a short presentation comparing and contrasting the pieces of criticism.

ACTING

INDEPENDENT ACTIVITIES

Observation While watching television, observe an actor very closely. Pay attention to the way he or she walks, talks, moves, smiles, laughs, sits down, stands up, and so forth. Imitate the person for the class and ask class members whom you are imitating.

Externalization Choose an action verb, such as *fight, confess, attack,* or *collide,* and create a scene around it. Think of a master leading gesture and a leading center that will provide clues to your character's personality and situation. For example, if you chose the action verb *defend*, you might fend off a slavering pit bull with an arm outstretched to protect the face and body. Act out the scene for your classmates and see if they can figure out what is happening.

Cooperative Learning Activities

Concentration The Mirror is a classic comedy routine. Working with a partner, improvise a character watching his or her moving image in a mirror. Move together as though you are one person. After receiving feedback from your classmates, try the scene again to improve both your concentration and synchronicity.

Stage Position and Movement With two or three classmates, develop a scene in which the characters have a conflict: a parent and children, a supervisor and employees, a coach and players or a similar relationship. Work out the conflict and its resolution onstage, making sure that every player is visible to the audience at all times. You will need to make some decisions about sharing the scene or giving the scene.

Across the CURRICULUM Activities

History Choose your favorite historical character and prepare to portray that person in a play. Using the questions on page 109, write a description of your characterization of the person. Include a character sketch (refer to pages 107–108.)

Foreign Language Imagine that you are a brash, self-confident, somewhat obnoxious tourist in a foreign country. You are intent on communicating with the residents regardless of your ignorance of the language. Ask a classmate to play the role of the resident of the country. Then act out a scene in which you attempt to communicate with the native resident by speaking English with a foreign accent mixed with an occasional foreign word.

Theater Etiquette

Successful performances are possible only if everyone—the actors, the director, the stage crew, and even the audience—shows proper respect for everyone involved. Achieving the best results is possible only in an environment of personal responsibility and mutual respect.

Often theater etiquette is nothing more than showing common courtesy. However, theater presents some unique situations, ones where the ground rules for interacting with others might not always be clear. The following guidelines to behavior will make it possible for everyone involved in a performance to enjoy the theater experience.

THE ACTORS

- Arrive at rehearsals and makeup calls on time.
- Learn lines, business, and blocking on schedule.
- Never peek through the curtains before (when the audience is present) or during a performance.
- Do not remove your makeup until after the curtain call. Never mingle with members of the audience or leave the theater while in costume or makeup.
- Do not change lines or stage business or tell others to do so unless the change has been approved by the director.
- Subordinate yourself to the performance by accepting your role and the costume, hairstyle, and makeup that go with it.
- Never knowingly upstage other performers. Be careful not to do it accidentally, either.
- Be attentive and receptive to the director's comments, and make an honest effort to make requested adjustments.
- Do not borrow another actor's makeup.
- Promptly report any damage to costumes or props before leaving the theater after each performance.

- Join the audience in applauding the musicians at the end of a musical's curtain call.
- Always show your appreciation to the director, the crews, and any other staff members associated with the production.
- Offer to assist the stage crew whenever possible.

EVERYONE ASSOCIATED WITH THE PRODUCTION

- Respect and encourage the contributions of each member of the cast and crew by complimenting good rehearsals, effective lighting, skillful costuming, and creative construction and design.
- Unless you are on the props crew, do not handle the props or sets.
- Know emergency procedures and the locations of firefighting equipment, the exits, and the fire alarms.
- Respect those who want to carry on theater traditions even though these traditions might seem like superstitions to you.
- After the show, make any presentations or recognitions for outstanding contributions at a time when everyone associated with the performance can be present.
- Post-performance cast parties should involve only those who worked on the show.

A successful production depends on cooperation among the cast, the crews, and the director.

THE AUDIENCE

- Arrive early enough to be seated before the lights dim.
- At a musical, it is customary to applaud as the conductor approaches the podium.
- When the curtain goes up, if the set pleases you, compliment the designer and crew by applauding.
- Do not talk or make noises with food or drink items.
- Silence any phones, pagers, or watches before the performance begins.
- Leave the theater during a performance only out of necessity.
- Applaud an especially fine scene or individual performance only in cases of rare "show stoppers," and reserve standing ovations for truly outstanding performances.
- Presentations of flowers, gifts, or similar recognitions are usually made offstage; exceptions should have the approval of the director or the stage manager.
- Never be openly critical of a performance.

An appreciative, courteous audience contributes to the success of a production.

A Treasury of Scenes and Monologues

Gaining experience by reading scenes and monologues helps aspiring actors develop poise and acting skills.
(Play: *Oh, Coward*)

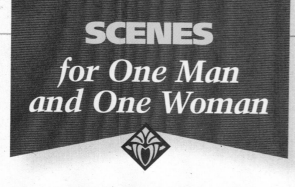

SCENES
for One Man and One Woman

Romeo and Juliet
by William Shakespeare (1594–5)

Characters: ROMEO—A Montague, he is an impulsive young aristocrat who has fallen in love with the daughter of the Capulets, a family despised by the Montagues.
JULIET—A Capulet, she is a romantic and somewhat headstrong aristocrat.

Situation: The action takes place in Verona, Italy. Young Romeo and Juliet have fallen in love at a masked ball, only to discover that they are members of two families that despise each other. In this scene, Romeo hides in the orchard below Juliet's bedroom window. Romeo expresses his love for Juliet, and then he overhears Juliet expressing her love for him.

[Capulet's orchard. ROMEO *advances from the wall.]*

ROMEO   He jests at scars that never felt a wound.
(Juliet appears above at her window.)
But soft! What light through yonder window breaks?
It is the east, and Juliet is the sun!
Arise, fair sun, and kill the envious moon,
Who is already sick and pale with grief
That thou, her maid, art far more fair than she.
Be not her maid, since she is envious;
Her vestal livery is but sick and green,
And none but fools do wear it; cast it off.
It is my lady, O, it is my love!

Oh, that she knew she were!
She speaks, yet she says nothing; what of that?
Her eye discourses. I will answer it.—
I am too bold, 'tis not to me she speaks.
Two of the fairest stars in all the heaven,
Having some business, do entreat her eyes
To twinkle in their spheres till they return.
What if her eyes were there, they in her head?
The brightness of her cheek would shame those stars,
As daylight doth a lamp; her eyes in heaven
Would through the airy region stream so bright
That birds would sing and think it were not night.
See, how she leans her cheek upon her hand!
O, that I were a glove upon that hand,
That I might touch that cheek!

JULIET   Ay me!

ROMEO   She speaks!
O, speak again, bright angel! For thou art
As glorious to this night, being o'er my head,
As is a winged messenger of heaven
Unto the white-upturned wond'ring eyes
Of mortals that fall back to gaze on him
When he bestrides the lazy-pacing clouds
And sails upon the bosom of the air.

JULIET   O Romeo, Romeo, wherefore art thou Romeo?
Deny thy father and refuse thy name,
Or, if thou wilt not, be but sworn my love
And I'll no longer be a Capulet.

ROMEO   *(Aside)* Shall I hear more, or shall I speak at this?

JULIET   'Tis but thy name that is my enemy.
Thou art thyself, though not a Montague.
What's a Montague? It is nor hand, nor foot,
Nor arm, nor face, nor any other part
Belonging to a man. Oh, be some other name!

What's in a name? That which we call a rose
By any other name would smell as sweet;
So Romeo would, were he not Romeo call'd,
Retain that dear perfection which he owes
Without that title. Romeo, doff thy name,
And for thy name, which is no part of thee,
Take all myself.

The Importance of Being Earnest

by Oscar Wilde (1895)

Characters: LADY BRACKNELL—She is an elderly English woman who is neither deep nor subtle. Her ideas about what makes a suitable husband are extremely rigid.
JACK—Jack Worthing is superficial, flippant, flirtatious, dishonest, witty, charming, and entirely self-serving.

Situation: In this satirical farce, Wilde ridicules the social attitudes of nineteenth-century England. The action takes place in a fashionable apartment in London. Lady Bracknell interviews Jack for the position of son-in-law.

LADY BRACKNELL *(Sitting down)* You can take a seat, Mr. Worthing. *(Looks in her pocket for a notebook and pencil)*

JACK Thank you, Lady Bracknell, I prefer standing.

LADY BRACKNELL *(Pencil and notebook in hand)* I feel bound to tell you that you are not down on my list of eligible young men, although I have the same list as the dear Duchess of Bolton has. We work together, in fact. However, I am quite ready to enter your name, should your answers be what a really affectionate mother requires. Do you smoke?

JACK Well, yes, I must admit I smoke.

LADY BRACKNELL I am glad to hear it. A man should always have an occupation of some kind. There are far too many idle men in London as it is. How old are you?

JACK Twenty-nine.

LADY BRACKNELL A very good age to be married at. I have always been of opinion that a man who desires to get married should know either everything or nothing. Which do you know?

JACK *(After some hesitation)* I know nothing, Lady Bracknell.

LADY BRACKNELL I am pleased to hear it. I do not approve of anything that tampers with natural ignorance. Ignorance is like a delicate exotic fruit; touch it and the bloom is gone. The whole theory of modern education is radically unsound. Fortunately in England, at any rate, education produces no effect whatsoever. If it did, it would prove a serious danger to the upper classes, and probably lead to acts of violence in Grosvenor Square. What is your income?

JACK Between seven and eight thousand a year.

LADY BRACKNELL *(Makes a note in her book)* In land, or in investments?

JACK In investments, chiefly.

LADY BRACKNELL That is satisfactory. What between the duties expected of one during one's lifetime, and the duties exacted from one after one's death, land has ceased to be either a profit or a pleasure. It gives one position, and prevents one from keeping it up. That's all that can be said about land.

JACK   I have a country house with some land, of course, attached to it, about fifteen hundred acres, I believe; but I don't depend on that for my real income. In fact, as far as I can make out, the poachers are the only people who make anything out of it.

LADY BRACKNELL   A country house! How many bedrooms? Well, that point can be cleared up afterwards. You have a town house, I hope? A girl with a simple, unspoiled nature, like Gwendolen, could hardly be expected to reside in the country.

JACK   Well, I own a house in Belgrave Square, but it is let by the year to Lady Bloxham. Of course, I can get it back whenever I like, at six months' notice.

LADY BRACKNELL   Lady Bloxham? I don't know her.

JACK   Oh, she goes about very little. She is a lady considerably advanced in years.

LADY BRACKNELL   Ah, now-a-days that is no guarantee of respectability of character. What number in Belgrave Square?

JACK   149.

LADY BRACKNELL   (Shaking her head) The unfashionable side. I thought there was something. However, that could be easily altered.

JACK   Do you mean the fashion, or the side?

LADY BRACKNELL   (Sternly) Both, if necessary, I presume. What are your politics?

JACK   Well, I am afraid I really have none. I am a Liberal Unionist.

LADY BRACKNELL   Oh, they count as Tories. They dine with us. Or come in the evening, at any rate. Now to minor matters. Are your parents living?

JACK   I have lost both my parents.

LADY BRACKNELL   To lose one parent, Mr. Worthing, may be regarded as a misfortune; to lose both looks like carelessness. Who was your father? He was evidently a man of some wealth. Was he born in what the Radical papers call the purple of commerce, or did he rise from the ranks of the aristocracy?

JACK   I am afraid I really don't know. The fact is, Lady Bracknell, I said I had lost my parents. It would be nearer the truth to say that my parents seem to have lost me . . . I don't actually know who I am by birth. I was . . . well, I was found.

LADY BRACKNELL   Found!

JACK   The late Mr. Thomas Cardew, an old gentleman of a very charitable and kindly disposition, found me, and gave me the name Worthing, because he happened to have a first-class ticket for Worthing in his pocket at the time. Worthing is a place in Sussex. It is a seaside resort.

LADY BRACKNELL   Where did the charitable gentleman who had a first-class ticket for this seaside resort find you?

JACK   (Gravely) In a hand-bag.

LADY BRACKNELL   A hand-bag?

JACK   (Very seriously) Yes, Lady Bracknell. I was in a hand-bag—a somewhat large, black leather hand-bag, with handles to it—an ordinary hand-bag, in fact.

LADY BRACKNELL   In what locality did this Mr. James, or Thomas, Cardew come across this ordinary hand-bag?

JACK   In the cloak-room at Victoria Station. It was given to him in mistake for his own.

LADY BRACKNELL   The cloak-room at Victoria Station?

JACK   Yes. The Brighton line.

LADY BRACKNELL   The line is immaterial. Mr. Worthing, I confess I feel somewhat bewildered by what you have just told me. To be born, or at any rate bred, in a hand-bag, whether it had handles or not, seems to me to display a contempt for the ordinary decencies of family life that remind one of the worst excesses of the French Revolution. And I presume you know what that unfortunate movement led to? As for the particular locality in which the hand-bag was found, a cloak-room at a railway station might serve to conceal a social indiscretion—has probably, indeed, been used for that purpose before now—but it could hardly be regarded as an assured basis for a recognized position in good society.

JACK   May I ask you then what you would advise me to do? I need hardly say I would do anything in the world to ensure Gwendolen's happiness.

LADY BRACKNELL   I would strongly advise you, Mr. Worthing, to try and acquire some relations as soon as possible, and make a definite effort to produce at any rate one parent, of either sex, before the season is quite over.

JACK   Well, I don't see how I could possibly manage to do that. I can produce the hand-bag at any moment. It is in my dressing-room at home. I really think that should satisfy you, Lady Bracknell.

LADY BRACKNELL   Me, sir! What has it to do with me? You can hardly imagine that I and Lord Bracknell would dream of allowing our daughter—a girl brought up with the utmost care—to marry into a cloak-room, and form an alliance with a parcel? Good morning, Mr. Worthing!
(LADY BRACKNELL *sweeps out in majestic indignation.*)

JACK   Good morning!

Whose Life Is It Anyway?
by Brian Clark (1978)

Characters: MRS. BOYLE—A social worker, she tries to do her job in a caring but professional way.
KEN HARRISON—A car accident has left him paralyzed from the neck down. Depressed and bitter, he wants to be allowed to die.

Situation: The scene takes place in a private hospital room.

MRS. BOYLE   Why don't you want any more treatment?

KEN   I'd rather not go on living like this.

MRS. BOYLE   Why not?

KEN   Isn't it obvious?

MRS. BOYLE   Not to me. I've seen many patients like you.

KEN   And they all want to live?

MRS. BOYLE   Usually.

KEN   Why?

MRS. BOYLE   They find a new way of life.

KEN   How?

MRS. BOYLE   You'll be surprised how many things you will be able to do with training and a little patience.

KEN   Such as?

MRS. BOYLE   We can't be sure yet. But I should think that you will be able to operate reading machines and perhaps an adapted typewriter.

KEN   Reading and writing. What about arithmetic?

MRS. BOYLE   *(Smiling)* I dare say we could fit you up with a comptometer if you really wanted one.

KEN   Mrs. Boyle, even educationalists have realized that the three r's do not make a full life.

MRS. BOYLE   What did you do before the accident?

KEN   I taught in an art school. I was a sculptor.

MRS. BOYLE   I see.

KEN   Difficult, isn't it? How about an electrically operated hammer and chisel? No, well. Or a cybernetic lump of clay?

MRS. BOYLE   I wouldn't laugh if I were you. It's amazing what can be done. Our scientists are wonderful.

KEN   They are. But it's not good enough, you see, Mrs. Boyle. I really have absolutely no desire at all to be the object of scientific virtuosity. I have thought things over very carefully. I do have plenty of time for thinking and I have decided that I do not want to go on living with so much effort for so little result.

MRS. BOYLE   Yes, well, we shall have to see about that.

KEN   What is there to see?

MRS. BOYLE   We can't just stop treatment, just like that.

KEN   Why not?

MRS. BOYLE   It's the job of the hospital to save life, not to lose it.

KEN   The hospital's done all it can, but it wasn't enough. It wasn't the hospital's fault; the original injury was too big.

MRS. BOYLE   We have to make the best of the situation.

KEN   No. "We" don't have to do anything. I have to do what is to be done and that is to cash in the chips.

MRS. BOYLE   It's not unusual, you know, for people injured as you have been, to suffer with this depression for a considerable time before they begin to see that a life is possible.

KEN   How long?

MRS. BOYLE   It varies.

KEN   Don't hedge.

MRS. BOYLE   It could be a year or so.

KEN   And it could last for the rest of my life.

MRS. BOYLE   That would be most unlikely.

KEN   I'm sorry, but I cannot settle for that.

MRS. BOYLE   Try not to dwell on it. I'll see what I can do to get you started on some occupational therapy. Perhaps we could make a start on the reading machines.

KEN   Do you have many books for those machines?

MRS. BOYLE   Quite a few.

KEN   Can I make a request for the first one?

MRS. BOYLE   If you like.

KEN   "How to be a sculptor with no hands."

MRS. BOYLE   I'll be back tomorrow with the machine.

KEN   It's marvelous, you know.

MRS. BOYLE   What is?

KEN   All you people have the same technique. When I say something really awkward you just pretend I haven't said anything at all. You're all the bloody same . . . Well, there's another outburst. That should be your cue to comment on the light-shade or the color of the walls.

MRS. BOYLE   I'm sorry if I have upset you.

KEN   Of course you have upset me. You and the doctors with your appalling so-called professionalism, which is nothing more than a series of verbal tricks to prevent you relating to your patients as human beings.

MRS. BOYLE   You must understand; we have to remain relatively detached in order to help . . .

KEN   That's all right with me. Detach yourself. Tear yourself off on the dotted line that divides the woman from the social worker, and post yourself off to another patient.

The Rainmaker
by N. Richard Nash (1954)

Characters: STARBUCK—Bill Starbuck is big, but lithe and agile. He is a mixture of loud braggart and gentle dreamer. He carries a short hickory stick, which is his weapon, his magic wand.

LIZZIE—Lizzie Curry is a strong yet incomplete woman. She is twenty-seven years old and has never loved or been loved. She yearns for romance but feels she must conceal her longings, given her situation, under the guise of being a good-natured tomboy.

Situation: The following exchange takes place on a summer day in a western state suffering from drought. Starbuck has arrived out of the blue claiming he could bring rain for a fee. He is presently boarding with the Curry family. Lizzie has brought bed linens out to the bunkhouse.

STARBUCK   What are you scared of?

LIZZIE   You! I don't trust you!

STARBUCK   Why? What don't you trust about me?

LIZZIE   Everything! The way you talk, the way you brag—why, even your name.

STARBUCK   What's wrong with my name?

LIZZIE   It sounds fake! It sounds like you made it up!

STARBUCK   You're darn right! I did make it up.

LIZZIE   There! Of course!

STARBUCK   Why not? You know what name I was born with? Smith! Smith, for the love of Mike, *Smith!* Now what kind of handle is that for a fella like me? I needed a name that had the whole sky in it! And the power of a man! Star-buck! Now there's a name— and it's mine.

LIZZIE   No, it's not. You were born Smith— and that's your name.

STARBUCK   You're wrong, Lizzie. The name you choose for yourself is more your own than the name you were born with. And if I was you I'd choose another name than Lizzie.

LIZZIE   Thank you—I'm very pleased with it.

STARBUCK   Oh, no you ain't. You ain't pleased with anything about yourself. And I'm sure you ain't pleased with "Lizzie."

LIZZIE   I don't ask *you* to be pleased with it, Starbuck. I *am*.

STARBUCK   Lizzie? Why, it don't *stand* for anything.

LIZZIE   It stands for me! *Me!* I'm not the Queen of Sheba—I'm not Lady Godiva—I'm not Cinderella at the Ball.

STARBUCK   Would you like to be?

LIZZIE   Starbuck, you're ridiculous!

STARBUCK   What's ridiculous about it? Dream you're somebody—*be* somebody! But Lizzie? That's nobody! So many millions of wonderful women with wonderful names! *(In an orgy of delight)* Leonora, Desdemona, Carolina, Paulina! Annabella, Florinda, Natasha, Diane! *(Then, with a pathetic little lift of his shoulders)* Lizzie.

The Diary of Anne Frank

dramatized by Frances Goodrich and Albert Hackett (1954) from the book *Anne Frank: Diary of a Young Girl*

Characters: ANNE—Anne Frank is a fourteen-year-old. She is self-controlled, lively, polite, optimistic, curious, creative, and compassionate.

PETER—Peter Van Daan is an awkward sixteen-year-old. He is angry and frustrated with the powerlessness and injustice of his situation.

Situation: This play, based on historical fact, was inspired by Anne's diary, which was published after her death. Anne was in fact eventually taken to a German concentration camp where she died at age fifteen. Only her father survived. This excerpt occurs at almost the end of the play. It is February 1944, World War II is in progress, and the Frank and the Van Daan families are hiding from the Nazis on the top floor of a warehouse in Amsterdam, Holland. The three rooms and a small attic are sparsely furnished, and all of the windows have blackout curtains. There is immense tension. Anne tries to comfort Peter.

ANNE   *(Looking up through skylight)* Look, Peter, the sky. What a lovely day. Aren't the clouds beautiful? You know what I do when it seems as if I couldn't stand being cooped up for one more minute? I *think* myself out. I think myself on a walk in the park where I used to go with Pim. Where the daffodils and the crocus and the violets grow down the slopes. You know the most wonderful thing about *thinking* yourself out? You can have it any way you like. You can have roses and violets and chrysanthemums all blooming at the same time. . . . It's funny. . . . I used to take it all for granted . . . and now I've gone crazy about everything to do with nature. Haven't you?

PETER   *(Barely lifting his face)* I've just gone crazy. I think if something doesn't happen soon . . . if we don't get out of here . . . I can't stand much more of it!

ANNE   *(Softly)* I wish you had a religion, Peter.

PETER *(Bitterly)* No, thanks. Not me.

ANNE Oh. I don't mean you have to be Orthodox . . . or believe in heaven and hell and purgatory and things. . . . I just mean some religion . . . it doesn't matter what. Just to believe in something! When I think of all that's out there . . . the trees . . . and flowers . . . and seagulls . . . when I think of the dearness of you, Peter . . . and the goodness of the people we know . . . Mr. Kraler, Miep, Dirk, the vegetable man, all risking their lives for us every day. . . . When I think of these good things, I'm not afraid any more. . . . I find myself, and God, and I . . .

PETER *(Impatiently, as he gets to his feet)* That's fine! But when I begin to think, I get mad! Look at us, hiding out for two years. Not able to move! Caught here like . . . waiting for them to come and get us . . . and all for what?

ANNE We're not the only people that've had to suffer. There've always been people that've had to . . . sometimes one race . . . sometimes another . . . and yet . . .

PETER *(Sitting on upstage end of bed)* That doesn't make me feel any better!

ANNE I know it's terrible, trying to have any faith . . . when people are doing such horrible . . . *(Gently lifting his face)* but you know what I sometimes think? I think the world may be going through a phase, the way I was with Mother. It'll pass, maybe not for hundreds of years, but some day. . . . I still believe, in spite of everything, that people are really good at heart.

Barefoot in the Park
by Neil Simon (1963)

Characters: CORIE—She is young and optimistic.
PAUL—He is a conservatively dressed, serious young lawyer.

Situation: Paul and Corie are newlyweds. The scene occurs in a large, unfurnished, one-room apartment on the top floor of an old brownstone in Manhattan. It is a cold February afternoon, and Paul has just climbed five flights of stairs to the apartment Corie rented for them.

CORIE The furniture will be here by five. They promised.

PAUL *(Dropping affidavits into case, looks at his watch)* Five? . . . It's five-thirty. *(Crosses to bedroom stairs)* What do we do, sleep in Bloomingdale's tonight?

CORIE They'll be here, Paul. They're probably stuck in traffic.

PAUL *(Crossing up to bedroom)* And what about tonight? I've got a case in court tomorrow. Maybe we should check into a hotel? *(Looks into bedroom)*

CORIE *(Rises and moves towards PAUL)* We just checked *out* of a hotel. I don't care if the furniture *doesn't* come. I'm sleeping in my apartment *tonight*.

PAUL Where? Where? *(Looks into bathroom, closes door, and starts to come back down the steps)* There's only room for one in the bathtub. *(He suddenly turns, goes back up steps and opens door to the bathroom.)* Where's the bathtub?

CORIE *(Hesitantly)* There is no bathtub.

PAUL   No bathtub?

CORIE   There's a shower . . .

PAUL   How am I going to take a bath?

CORIE   You won't take a bath. You'll take a shower.

PAUL   I don't like showers. I like baths. Corie, how am I going to take a bath?

CORIE   You'll lie down in the shower and hang your feet over the sink. . . . I'm sorry there's no bathtub, Paul.

PAUL   *(Closes door, and crosses down into the room)* Hmmmm . . . Boy, of all the nights . . . *(He suddenly shivers.)* It's freezing in here. *(He rubs his hands.)* Isn't there any heat?

CORIE   Of course there's heat. We have a radiator.

PAUL   *(Gets up on steps and feels radiator)* The *radiator's* the coldest thing in the room.

CORIE   It's probably the boiler. It's probably off in the whole building.

PAUL   *(Putting on gloves)* No, it was warm coming up the stairs. *(Goes out door into hall)* See . . . It's nice and warm out here.

CORIE   Maybe it's because the apartment is empty.

PAUL   The *hall* is empty too but it's warm out here.

CORIE   *(Moves to the stove)* It'll be all right once I get a fire going.

PAUL   *(Goes to phone)* A fire? You'd have to keep the flame going night and day. . . . I'll call the landlord.

CORIE   *(Putting log into stove)* He's not home.

PAUL   Where is he?

CORIE   In Florida! . . . There's a handy man that comes Mondays, Wednesdays, and Fridays.

PAUL   You mean we freeze on Tuesdays, Thursdays, and Saturdays?

CORIE   He'll be here in the morning.

PAUL   *(Moving R.)* And what'll we do tonight? I've got a case in court in the morning.

CORIE   *(Moves to PAUL)* Will you stop saying it like you always have a case in court in the morning. This is your first one.

PAUL   Well, what'll we do?

CORIE   The furniture will be here. In the meantime I can light the stove and you can sit over the fire with your law books and a shawl like Abraham Lincoln. *(Crosses to the Franklin Stove and gets matches from the top of the stove)*

PAUL   Is that supposed to be funny? *(Begins to investigate small windows)*

CORIE   No. It was supposed to be nasty. It just came out funny. *(She strikes match and attempts to light the log in stove. PAUL tries the windows.)* What are you doing? *(Gives up attempting to light log)*

PAUL   I'm checking to see if the windows are closed.

CORIE   They're closed. I looked.

PAUL   Then why is it windy in here?

CORIE   *(Moves R. to PAUL)* I don't feel a draft.

PAUL   *(Moves away from windows)* I didn't say draft. I said wind . . . There's a brisk, northeasterly wind blowing in this room.

CORIE You don't have to get sarcastic.

PAUL *(Moving up into the kitchen area)* I'm not getting sarcastic, I'm getting chapped lips. *(Looking up, he glimpses the hole in the skylight.)*

CORIE How could there be wind in a closed room?

PAUL How's this for an answer? There's a hole in the skylight. *(He points up.)*

CORIE *(She looks up, sees it and is obviously embarrassed by it.)* Gee, I didn't see that before. Did you?

PAUL *(Moves to ladder)* I didn't see the *apartment* before.

CORIE *(Defensively. Crosses to the railing and gets her coat)* All right, Paul, don't get upset. I'm sure it'll be fixed. We could plug it up with something for tonight.

PAUL *(Gets up on ladder)* How? How? That's twenty feet high. You'd have to fly over in a plane and *drop* something in.

CORIE *(Putting on coat)* It's only for one night. And it's not that cold.

PAUL In February? Do you know what it's like at three o'clock in the morning? In February? Ice-cold freezing.

CORIE It's not going to be freezing. I called the weather bureau. It's going to be cloudy with light s—*(She catches herself and looks up.)*

PAUL What? *(CORIE turns away.)* What? . . . A light what?

CORIE Snow!

PAUL *(Coming down ladder)* Snow?? . . . It's going to snow tonight? . . . In here?

CORIE They're wrong as often as they're right.

PAUL I'm going to be shoveling snow in my own living room.

CORIE It's a little hole.

PAUL With that wind it could blow six-foot drifts in the bathroom. Honestly, Corie, I don't see how you can be so calm about all this.

CORIE Well, what is it you want me to do?

PAUL Go to pieces, like me. It's only natural.

Harvey
by Mary Chase (1943)

Characters: VETA—Veta Simmons is overwrought. She wants Dr. Sanderson to commit her brother, Elwood, to a mental hospital so that she can entertain her friends without being embarrassed by him.
SANDERSON—A psychiatrist, he believes Veta is having a nervous breakdown.

Situation: The scene takes place in Dr. Sanderson's office.

VETA Doctor—everything I say to you is confidential? Isn't it?

SANDERSON That's understood.

VETA Because it's a slap in the face to everything we've stood for in this community the way Elwood is acting now.

SANDERSON I am not a gossip, Mrs. Simmons. I am a psychiatrist.

VETA   Well—for one thing—he drinks.

SANDERSON   To excess?

VETA   To excess? Well—don't you call it excess when a man never lets a day go by without stepping into one of those cheap taverns, sitting around with riffraff and people you never heard of? Inviting them to the house—playing cards with them—giving them food and money. And here I am trying to get Myrtle Mae started with a nice group of young people. If that isn't excess I'm sure I don't know what excess is.

SANDERSON   I didn't doubt your statement, Mrs. Simmons. I merely asked if your brother drinks.

VETA   Well, yes, I say definitely Elwood drinks and I want him committed out here permanently, because I cannot stand another day of that Harvey. Myrtle and I have to set a place at the table for Harvey. We have to move over on the sofa and make room for Harvey. We have to answer the telephone when Elwood calls and asks to speak to Harvey. Then at the party this afternoon with Mrs. Chauvenet there—We didn't even know anything about Harvey until we came back here. Doctor, don't you think it would have been a little bit kinder of Mother to have written and told me about Harvey? Be honest, now—don't you?

SANDERSON   I really couldn't answer that question, because I—

VETA   I can. Yes—it certainly would have.

SANDERSON   This person you call Harvey—who is he?

VETA   He's a rabbit.

SANDERSON   Perhaps—but just who is he? Some companion—someone your brother has picked up in these bars, of whom you disapprove?

VETA   (Patiently) Doctor—I've been telling you. Harvey is a rabbit—a big white rabbit—six feet high—or is it six feet and a half? Heavens knows I ought to know. He's been around the house long enough.

SANDERSON   (Regarding her narrowly) Now, Mrs. Simmons, let me understand this—you say—

VETA   (Impatient) Doctor—do I have to keep repeating myself? My brother insists that his closest friend is this big white rabbit. This rabbit is named Harvey. Harvey lives at our house. Don't you understand? He and Elwood go every place together. Elwood buys railroad tickets, theater tickets, for both of them. As I told Myrtle Mae—if your uncle was so lonesome he had to bring something home—why couldn't he bring home something human? He has me, doesn't he? He has Myrtle Mae, doesn't he? (She leans forward.) Doctor—(She rises to him. He inclines toward her.) I'm going to tell you something I've never told anybody in the world before. (Puts her hand on his shoulder) Every once in a while I see that big white rabbit myself. Now isn't that terrible? I've never even told that to Myrtle Mae.

SANDERSON   (Now convinced. Starts to rise) Mrs. Simmons—

VETA   (Straightening)And what's more— he's every bit as big as Elwood says he is. Now don't ever tell that to anybody, Doctor. I'm ashamed of it. (Crosses to C., to chair R. of desk)

SANDERSON   (Crosses to VETA) I can see that you have been under a great nervous strain recently.

VETA   Well—I certainly have.

SANDERSON   Grief over your mother's death depressed you considerably?

VETA   *(Sits chair R. of desk)* Nobody knows how much.

SANDERSON   Been losing sleep?

VETA   How could anybody sleep with that going on?

SANDERSON   *(Crosses to back of desk)* Short-tempered over trifles?

VETA   You just try living with those two and see how your temper holds up.

SANDERSON   *(Presses buzzer)* Loss of appetite?

VETA   No one could eat at a table with my brother and a big white rabbit. Well, I'm finished with it. I'll sell the house—be appointed conservator of Elwood's estate, and Myrtle Mae and I will be able to entertain our friends in peace. It's too much, Doctor. I just can't stand it.

The Dining Room
by A. R. Gurney Jr. (1982)

Characters: ARTHUR—With his father dead and his mother now living in Florida, Arthur needs to divide his parents' belongings between himself and his sister.
SALLY—Arthur's sister, Sally has adult children but still reverts to childish behavior in her brother's presence. She wants the dining room furnishings partly because they remind her of her happy, secure childhood and partly because her brother wants them.

Situation: This play has just one set, a dining room. The playwright portrays dining rooms as symbolic of the changing lifestyle of the American upper middle class. In this play the dining room was once the center of family life but is now neglected and cluttered.

ARTHUR   The dining room.

SALLY   Yes. . . .

ARTHUR   Notice how we gravitate right to this room.

SALLY   I know it.

ARTHUR   You sure mother doesn't want this stuff in Florida?

SALLY   She hardly has room for what she's got. She wants us to take turns. Without fighting.

ARTHUR   We'll just have to draw lots then.

SALLY   Unless one of us wants something, and one of us doesn't.

ARTHUR   We have to do it today.

SALLY   Do you think that's enough time to divide up a whole house?

ARTHUR   I have to get back, Sal. *(He looks in the sideboard.)* We'll draw lots and then go through the rooms taking turns. *(He brings out a silver spoon.)* Here. We'll use this salt spoon. *(He shifts it from hand to hand behind his back, then holds out two fists.)* Take your pick. You get the spoon, you get the dining room.

SALLY   You mean you want to start here?

ARTHUR   Got to start somewhere. *(SALLY looks at his fists.)*

SALLY   *(Not choosing)* You mean you want the dining room?

ARTHUR Yeah.

SALLY What happened to the stuff you had?

ARTHUR Jane took it. It was part of the settlement.

SALLY If you win, where will you put it?

ARTHUR That's my problem, Sal.

SALLY I thought you had a tiny apartment.

ARTHUR I'll find a place.

SALLY I mean your children won't want it.

ARTHUR Probably not.

SALLY Then where on earth? . . .

ARTHUR Come on, Sal. Choose.*(He holds out his fists again. She starts to choose.)* You don't want it.

SALLY Of course I want it.

ARTHUR I mean you already have a perfectly good dining room.

SALLY Not as good as this.

ARTHUR You mean you want two dining rooms?

SALLY I'd give our old stuff to Debbie.

ARTHUR To Debbie?

SALLY She's our oldest child.

ARTHUR Does Debbie want a dining room?

SALLY She might.

ARTHUR In a condominium?

SALLY She might.

ARTHUR In Denver?

SALLY She just might, Arthur.

ARTHUR *(Shuffling the spoon behind his*

back again; then holding out his fists) I don't want to fight. Which hand? *(SALLY starts to choose, then stops.)*

SALLY Are you planning to put it in storage?

ARTHUR I might.

SALLY I checked on that. That costs an arm and a leg.

ARTHUR So does shipping it to Denver. *(He holds out his fists.)*

SALLY *(Almost picking a hand, then stopping)* I know what will happen if you win.

ARTHUR What?

SALLY You'll end up selling it.

ARTHUR Selling it?

SALLY That's what will happen. It will kick around for a while, and you'll end up calling a furniture dealer.

ARTHUR I am absolutely amazed you'd say that.

SALLY I don't want to fight, Arthur.

ARTHUR Neither do I. Maybe we should defer the dining room. *(He starts for door, stage right.)*

SALLY *(Following him)* Maybe we should.

ARTHUR Selling the dining room? Is that what you told mother I'd do?

SALLY *(Following him out)* I told her I'd give you the piano if I can have the dining room. . . .

ARTHUR I'll be lucky if I keep this spoon.

SALLY I'll give you the piano and the coffee table if I can have the dining room.

The Breakfast Special
by Matthew Calhoun (1984)

Characters: WAITRESS—She is in her early twenties and has little interest in being a waitress.
CUSTOMER—He is a well-dressed young man in his late twenties.

Situation: The characters are in a dingy diner on the Lower East Side in New York City.

WAITRESS   Menu, sir?

CUSTOMER   No thanks. I know just what I want.

WAITRESS   Uh huh?

CUSTOMER   A robin egg omelette topped with coriander made French style—*red* caviar in that, and a licorice liqueur, please.

WAITRESS   Huh?

CUSTOMER   Yes, all that and some Wonder Bread toast with wild gooseberry preserves. Shave the crusts, please.

WAITRESS   We don't have that . . . here.

CUSTOMER   No Wonder Bread? You should try it. That cheap, synthetic texture provides a delightful contrast to some of the more docile of the wild preserves. Wild raspberry needs more of a . . .

WAITRESS   We don't have those.

CUSTOMER   You mentioned that. Make it wild blackberry then, and put it on Arnold brick oven white. Broil it, though, please. It makes a subtler taste, broiled.

WAITRESS   We don't have that stuff. We have scrambled or fried, or we could poach it

for you, and it comes with home fries and coffee. Or French toast, if you want.

CUSTOMER   What?

WAITRESS   This is a diner, not a French cookbook place. We don't have robin eggs. You can get a Denver omelette, if you want.

CUSTOMER   This is a diner, as you said. I'd like to dine. I don't understand your attitude.

WAITRESS   We don't have liqueurs. We got O.J. or grapefruit juice.

CUSTOMER   This is New York City, lady. Can't I get breakfast?

WAITRESS   Pancakes? Tomato juice? Cold cereal? We got that.

CUSTOMER   Where am I, in primitive colonial New England where all they know how to fix is turkey and succotash?

WAITRESS   It's summer. We don't have a Thanksgiving menu till November.

CUSTOMER   Don't you have *anything* here?

WAITRESS   *(Shrugging)* Yankee bean soup.

CUSTOMER   OK, OK, bring me a menu. I'll eat that.

WAITRESS   There are some nice more exotic restaurants in Midtown. You can get the D train right over . . .

CUSTOMER   I don't want to take a subway to get a little breakfast. I'm not on a safari here. I don't want to have to hunt lion to get a bite to eat.

WAITRESS   Lion?

CUSTOMER   I suppose next you'll be telling me I can't get a little fresh squeezed tangerine juice here.

WAITRESS   The restaurant two doors north'll give you fresh squeezed O.J. if you want.

CUSTOMER   I'm sure they could give me bubble gum freshly garnered from under their tables, too, but I don't *want* that.

WAITRESS   You are being entirely unreasonable. A small, unassuming, lower East Side diner and you come in here and expect Julia Child to cater to your every whim. You get eggs here. You get toast. You get home fries. You can have a donut if you want. Glazed or plain. That's what you get. If you don't like it, then go hire a cook and a butler and live in a mansion on a hill somewhere. OK?

CUSTOMER   *(Momentarily stunned)* You're right. I expect too much out of life. I always have. I'm a bit neurotic that way. I just want things right, that's all. But I have no right to force my outlandish expectations on others. *(Stands, hugs her)* Thanks for the outburst. A fella has to be put in his place sometimes. *(Sits)* Bring me the breakfast special. Whatever it is. Thanks.

WAITRESS   You can't have the special because it's 11:02. You can only get it before 11. You should have ordered it when you sat down.

CUSTOMER   You're right. My fault. Two fried eggs, then. That'll be fine.

WAITRESS   White, whole wheat or rye?

CUSTOMER   You have whole wheat eggs?

WAITRESS   *(Irritated)* Toast.

CUSTOMER   Oh, I see. Anything's fine. Anything that's easiest.

WAITRESS   White?

CUSTOMER   Rye. *(Beat; worriedly)* If I'm not imposing.

WAITRESS   Rye. Coffee?

CUSTOMER   Sure.

WAITRESS   OK, then. *(She starts to exit.)*

CUSTOMER   Oh!

WAITRESS   What?

CUSTOMER   Could I maybe have a table here, to eat off of?

WAITRESS   A table, sir?

CUSTOMER   Well there's two chairs here, but no table. I hate to eat off my lap.

WAITRESS   Couldn't you just pull up the other chair?

CUSTOMER   Well . . . *(Short pause)*

WAITRESS   Maybe we should just come to your house and serve you breakfast in bed, huh?

CUSTOMER   *(Embarrassed)* OK. Sorry. *(He pulls up the chair.)* Chair will be fine.

WAITRESS   You can pick up breakfast in the kitchen in about twenty minutes.

CUSTOMER   Twenty minutes? For eggs?

WAITRESS   Whadaya think, sir, we're gonna have a foreman whip the cook to work at superhuman speed to kill himself on your eggs? You've *got* a chair, sir. You think *we* get to sit down?

CUSTOMER   But there's no customers here!

WAITRESS   Cook's a freelance writer. He writes comedy skits as he works. Slows him down a little. What are you, anti-art?

CUSTOMER And what did you mean pick it up in the kitchen?

WAITRESS In twenty minutes. Kitchen's over there, right past the communal bathroom.

CUSTOMER Aren't you going to bring it to me?

WAITRESS What am I, your slave? Would you show a little initiative around here?

CUSTOMER *(Getting up)* I'm leaving.

WAITRESS It's about time. Robin egg omelette.

CUSTOMER Eat off chairs.

WAITRESS Wild gooseberry jam.

CUSTOMER Twenty minutes so the moron can write comedy skits.

(The following dialog is spoken simultaneously.)

WAITRESS *Red* caviar. Licorice liqueur. Shave the crusts. Cook it French style. Wants a table. Expects me to *wait* on him.

CUSTOMER Pick it up myself in the kitchen past the communal bathroom. Don't even have Wonder Bread toast. Wants me to take a subway for breakfast. Don't even have tangerine juice! *(Lights fade to end scene)*

The Sound of a Voice
by David Henry Hwang (1984)

Characters: WOMAN—In a remote corner of a forest lives a Japanese woman in a small hut. With no neighbors nearer than two days' journey, she is lonely. Many of the distant villagers think she is a witch and believe she turns her visitors into flowers that she keeps in a vase. MAN—Wearing a sword, the man seems to be a soldier but has no mission, no assignment.

Situation: Chinese American playwright David Henry Hwang has modeled this short play on Japanese ghost stories. As in those traditional tales, his play lets the audience decide whether the characters are humans or spirits. In this scene, the man happens upon the woman's hut. He is puzzled by her solitary life, but stays on as her guest.

[Evening. Woman warms tea for man. Man rubs himself, trying to get warm.]

MAN You are very kind to take me in.

WOMAN This is a remote corner of the world. Guests are rare.

MAN The tea—you pour it well.

WOMAN No.

MAN The sound it makes—in the cup—very soothing.

WOMAN That is the tea's skill, not mine. *(She hands the cup to him.)* May I get you something else? Rice, perhaps?

MAN No.

WOMAN And some vegetables?

MAN No, thank you.

WOMAN Fish? *(Pause)* It is at least two days walk to the nearest village. I saw no horse. You must be very hungry. You would do a great honor to dine with me. Guests are rare.

MAN Thank you.

(Woman gets up, leaves. Man gets up, walks to the kitchen door, listens. The room is

sparsely furnished, except for one shelf on which stands a vase of brightly colored flowers. The flowers stand out in sharp contrast to the starkness of the room. He crosses to the vase of flowers. He touches them. Quickly, he takes one of the flowers, hides it in his clothes. The woman re-enters. She carries a tray with food.)

WOMAN   Please. Eat. It will give me great pleasure.

MAN   This—this is magnificent.

WOMAN   Eat.

MAN   Thank you. *(He motions for the woman to join him.)*

WOMAN   No, thank you.

MAN   This is wonderful. The best I've tasted.

WOMAN   You are reckless in your flattery, sir. But anything you say, I will enjoy hearing. It's not even the words. It's the sound of a voice, the way it moves through the air.

MAN   How long has it been since you last had a visitor?

(Pause)

WOMAN   I don't know.

MAN   Oh?

WOMAN   I lose track. Perhaps five months ago, perhaps ten years, perhaps yesterday. I don't consider time when there is no voice in the air. It's pointless. Time begins with the entrance of a visitor, and ends with his exit.

MAN   And in between? You don't keep track of the days? You can't help but notice—

WOMAN   Of course I notice.

MAN   Oh.

WOMAN   I notice, but I don't keep track. *(Pause)* May I bring out more?

MAN   More? No. No. This was wonderful.

WOMAN   I have more.

MAN   Really—the best I've had.

WOMAN   You must be tired. Did you sleep in the forest last night?

MAN   Yes.

WOMAN   Or did you not sleep at all?

MAN   I slept.

WOMAN   Where?

MAN   By a waterfall. The sound of the water put me to sleep. It rumbled like the sounds of a city. You see, I can't sleep in too much silence. It scares me. It makes me feel that I have no control over what is about to happen.

WOMAN   I feel the same way.

MAN   But you live here—alone?

WOMAN   Yes.

MAN   It's so quiet here. How can you sleep?

WOMAN   Tonight, I'll sleep. I'll lie down in the next room, and hear your breathing through the wall, and fall asleep shamelessly. There will be no silence.

MAN   You're very kind to let me stay here.

WOMAN   This is yours. *(She unrolls a mat.)*

MAN   Did you make it yourself?

WOMAN   Yes. There is a place to wash outside.

MAN   Thank you.

WOMAN   Good night.

MAN   Good night. *(He starts to leave.)*

WOMAN   May I know your name?

MAN   No. I mean, I would rather not say. If I gave you a name, it would only be made up. Why should I deceive you? You are too kind for that.

WOMAN   Then what should I call you? Perhaps—"Man Who Fears Silence"?

MAN   How about, "Man Who Fears Women"?

WOMAN   That name is much too common.

MAN   And you?

WOMAN   Hanako.

MAN   That's your name?

WOMAN   It's what you may call me.

MAN   Good night, Hanako. You are very kind.

WOMAN   You are very smart. Good night.

Green Grow the Lilacs
by Lynn Riggs (1930)

Characters: LAUREY—An orphan who lives on her aunt's farm, Laurey dreams of pretty, elegant surroundings but knows firsthand the hardships of farm living.
CURLY—A rowdy cowhand who claims to be the best bronco buster and bulldogger in seventeen counties, Curly finds himself attracted to Laurey.

Situation: This play by Cherokee playwright Lynn Riggs is set in 1900 in Indian Territory, which will become part of the state of Oklahoma in just seven years. Rodgers and Hammerstein based their popular musical *Oklahoma!* (1943) on *Green Grow the Lilacs.* Curly and Laurey are on opposite sides of the cowhand-farmer feud that divides Indian Territory, but politics won't keep him from pursuing her. In the scene below, Curly has already rented a fancy surrey to take Laurey to a dance, but he hasn't yet asked her if she'll go with him.

[The door slides back, and LAUREY *comes out. She is a fair, spoiled, lovely young girl about eighteen in a long white dress with many ruffles. She sees* CURLY.*]*

LAUREY   Oh! Thought you was somebody. *(To* AUNT ELLER*)* Is this all that's come a-callin' and it a'ready ten o'clock of a Satiddy mornin'?

CURLY   *(Sullenly)* You knowed it was me 'fore you opened the door.

LAUREY   No sich of a thing.

CURLY   You did, too! You heared my voice and knowed it was me.

LAUREY   I did not, I tell you! Heared a voice a-talkin' rumbly along with Aunt Eller. And heared someone a-singin' like a bull-frog in a pond—

CURLY   I don't talk rumbly. And I don't sing like no bull-frog—

LAUREY   Bull-frog in a pond, I told you. But how'd I know it was you, Mr. Curly McClain? You ain't so special. All men sounds alike to me.

CURLY (*Doggedly*) You knowed it was me, so you set in there a-thinkin' up sump'n mean to say. I'm a good mind not to tell you nuthin' about the play-party now. You c'n jist stay at home, for yer tongue. Don't you tell her whur it is, Aunt Eller. Me'n you'll go and leave her at home.

LAUREY If you *did* ast me, I wouldn't go with you. Besides, how'd you take me? You ain't bought a new buggy with red wheels onto it, have you?

CURLY No, I ain't.

LAUREY And a spankin' team with their bridles all jinglin'?

CURLY No.

LAUREY 'Spect me to ride on behind ole Dun, I guess. You better ast that ole Cummins girl you've tuck sich a shine to, over acrost the river.

CURLY If I was to ast you, they'd be a way to take you, Miss Laurey Smarty.

LAUREY Oh, they would?

CURLY A bran' new surrey with fringe on the top four inches long—and *yeller!* And two white horses a-rarin' and faunchin' to go! You'd shore ride like a queen settin' up in *that* carriage! Feel like you had a gold crown set on yer head, 'th diamonds in it big as goose eggs.

LAUREY Look out, you'll be astin' me in a minute!

CURLY I ain't astin' you, I'm *tellin'* you. And this yere rig has got four fine side-curtains, case of a rain. And isinglass winders to look out of! And a red and green lamp set on the dashboard, winkin' like a lightnin' bug!

LAUREY Whur'd you git sich a rig at? (*With explosive laughter*) Anh, I bet he's went and h'ard it over to Claremore, thinkin' I'd go with him!

CURLY 'S all you know about it—

LAUREY (*Jeering*) Went and h'ard it! Spent all his money h'arin' a rig, and now ain't got nobody to ride in it.

CURLY Have, too! Did *not* h'ar it. Made the whole thing up outa my head—

LAUREY What! Made it up?

CURLY Dashboard and all!

LAUREY (*Flying at him*) Oh! Git outa the house, you! Aunt Eller, make him git hisself outa here 'fore I take a stove arn to him! Tellin' me lies—!

CURLY (*Dodging her*) Makin' up a few— Look out, now! Makin' up a few purties ain't agin no law 'at I know of. Don't you wish they *was* sich a rig, though? Nen you could go to the party and do a hoe-down till mornin' 'f you was a mind to. Nen drive home 'th the sun a-peekin' at you over the ridge, purty and fine.

LAUREY I ain't wantin' to do no hoe-down till mornin'. And whut would I want to see the sun come up fer, a-peekin' purty and fine—alongside of you, anyhow?

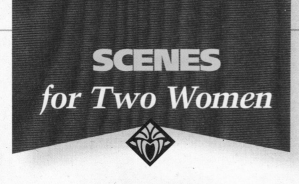

SCENES
for Two Women

Antigone
translated from the French play
written by Jean Anouilh in 1943

Characters: ISMENE—(pronounced ĭz•mā´•nē)
The older sister of Antigone, she is trying to
keep Antigone from an action that would mean
certain death.
ANTIGONE—(pronounced ăn•tĭg´•ə•nē) She is a
passionate young woman who will not compromise her principles, even if she must die for
them.

Situation: At the time this was written and
first produced, France was under German occupation. Although this text could not be explicit
since it had to be approved by German censors,
a French audience would identify with
Antigone; the French, too, were being promised
happiness if they surrendered their consciences
and sold their souls. Anouilh's play is based on
the Sophocles tragedy of the same name.
Antigone's two brothers, Eteocles and Polynices,
competed for power after the death of their
father, Oedipus, the king of Thebes. The struggle resulted in the brothers killing each other.
The current king of Thebes, Creon, has ruled
that only Eteocles shall be given a burial, while
Polynices will be left to rot where he lies.
Antigone has decided to disobey Creon's law.

ISMENE   Antigone, I've thought about it
a lot.

ANTIGONE   Have you?

ISMENE   I thought about it all night long.
Antigone, you're mad.

ANTIGONE   Am I?

ISMENE   We cannot do it.

ANTIGONE   Why not?

ISMENE   Creon will have us put to death.

ANTIGONE   Of course he will. That's what
he's here for. He will do what he has to do,
and we will do what we have to do. He is
bound to put us to death. We are bound to go
out and bury our brother. That's the way it is.
What do you think we can do to change it?

ISMENE   *(Releases* ANTIGONE'S *hand;
draws back a step)* I don't want to die.

ANTIGONE   I'd prefer not to die, myself.

ISMENE   Listen to me, Antigone. I thought
about it all night. I'm older than you are. I
always think things over and you don't. You
are impulsive. You get a notion in your head
and you jump up and do the thing straight off.
And if it's silly, well, so much the worse for
you. Whereas, I think things out.

ANTIGONE   Sometimes it is better not to
think too much.

ISMENE   I don't agree with you! Oh, I know
it's horrible. And I pity Polynices just as much
as you do. But all the same, I sort of see what
Uncle Creon means.

ANTIGONE   I don't want to "sort of see"
anything.

ISMENE   Uncle Creon is the king. He has to
set an example!

ANTIGONE   But I am not the king; and I
don't have to set people examples. Little
Antigone gets a notion in her head—the nasty

brat, the wilful, wicked girl; and they put her in a corner all day, or they lock her up in the cellar. And she deserves it. She shouldn't have disobeyed!

ISMENE   There you go, frowning, glowering, wanting your own stubborn way in everything. Listen to me. I'm right oftener than you are.

ANTIGONE   I don't want to be right!

ISMENE   At least you can try to understand.

ANTIGONE   Understand! The first word I ever heard out of any of you was that word "understand." Why didn't I "understand" that I must not play with water—cold, black, beautiful flowing water—because I'd spill it on the palace tiles. Or with earth, because earth dirties a little girl's frock. Why didn't I "understand" that nice children don't eat out of every dish at once; or give everything in their pockets to beggars; or run in the wind so fast that they fall down; or ask for a drink when they're perspiring; or want to go swimming when it's either too early or too late, merely because they happen to feel like swimming. Understand! I don't want to understand. There'll be time enough to understand when I'm old. . . . If I ever *am* old. But not now.

The Glass Menagerie
by Tennessee Williams (1945)

Characters: LAURA—Laura has grown up to be a very shy young woman largely as a result of her embarrassment over a deformed foot. Her escape from her handicap is a collection of delicate glass animals that she tends lovingly. A loner, Laura is as fragile as her glass menagerie.

AMANDA—Amanda Wingfield raised her children, Tom and Laura, alone. She is a woman of great but confused vitality. Unintentionally cruel at times, Amanda means well.

Situation: The Wingfield apartment is at the back of a lower-middle-class tenement. This is a memory play, so the scene should be dimly lit, sentimental, and not realistic.

LAURA   Hello, Mother, I was—

(*She makes a nervous gesture toward the chart on the wall.* AMANDA *leans against the shut door and stares at* LAURA *with a martyred look.*)

AMANDA   Deception? Deception?

(*She slowly removes her hat and gloves, continuing the sweet suffering stare. She lets the hat and gloves fall on the floor—a bit of acting.*)

LAURA   (*Shakily*) How was the D.A.R. meeting? (AMANDA *slowly opens her purse and removes a dainty white handkerchief which she shakes out delicately and delicately touches to her lips and nostrils.*) Didn't you go to the D.A.R. meeting, Mother?

AMANDA   (*Faintly, almost inaudibly*)— No—No. (*Then more forcibly*) I did not have the strength—to go to the D.A.R. In fact, I did not have the courage! I wanted to find a hole in the ground and hide myself in it forever!

(*She crosses slowly to the wall and removes the diagram of the typewriter keyboard. She holds it in front of her for a second, staring at it sweetly and sorrowfully—then bites her lips and tears it in two pieces.*)

LAURA   (*Faintly*) Why did you do that, Mother? (AMANDA *repeats the same proce-*

dure with the chart of the Gregg Alphabet.) Why are you—

AMANDA   Why? Why? How old are you, Laura?

LAURA   Mother, you know my age.

AMANDA   I thought that you were an adult; it seems that I was mistaken.

(She crosses slowly to the sofa and sinks down and stares at LAURA.)

LAURA   Please don't stare at me, Mother.

(AMANDA closes her eyes and lowers her head. Count ten.)

AMANDA   What are we going to do, what is going to become of us, what is the future?

(Count ten.)

LAURA   Has something happened, Mother? *(AMANDA draws a long breath and takes out the handkerchief again. Dabbing process)* Mother, has—something happened?

AMANDA   I'll be all right in a minute, I'm just bewildered—*(Count five.)*—by life. . . .

LAURA   Mother, I wish that you would tell me what's happened.

AMANDA   As you know, I was supposed to be inducted into my office at the D.A.R. this afternoon. But I stopped off at Rubicam's Business College to speak to your teachers about your having a cold and ask them what progress they thought you were making down there.

LAURA   Oh . . .

AMANDA   I went to the typing instructor and introduced myself as your mother. She didn't know who you were. Wingfield, she said. We don't have any such student enrolled at the school!

I assured her she did, that you have been going to classes since early in January.

"I wonder," she said, "if you could be talking about the terribly shy little girl who dropped out of school after only a few days' attendance?" "No," I said, "Laura, my daughter, has been going to school every day for the past six weeks!"

"Excuse me," she said. She took the attendance book out and there was your name, unmistakably printed, and all the dates you were absent until they decided that you had dropped out of school.

I still said, "No, there must have been some mistake! There must have been some mix-up in the records?"

And she said, "No—I remember her perfectly now. Her hands shook so that she couldn't hit the right keys! The first time we had a speed-test, she broke down completely—was sick at the stomach and almost had to be carried into the wash-room! After that morning she never showed up any more. We phoned the house but never got any answer"—while I was working at Famous and Barr, I suppose, demonstrating those—Oh!

I felt so weak I could barely keep on my feet!

I had to sit down while they got me a glass of water!

Fifty dollars' tuition, all of our plans—my hopes and ambitions for you—just gone up the spout, just gone up the spout like that. *(LAURA draws a long breath and gets awkwardly to her feet. She crosses to the victrola and winds it up.)* What are you doing?

LAURA   Oh! *(She releases the handle and returns to her seat.)*

AMANDA Laura, where have you been going when you've gone out pretending that you were going to business college?

LAURA I've just been going out walking.

AMANDA That's not true.

LAURA It is. I just went walking.

AMANDA Walking? Walking? In winter? Deliberately courting pneumonia in that light coat? Where did you walk to, Laura?

LAURA All sorts of places—mostly in the park.

AMANDA Even after you'd started catching that cold?

LAURA It was the lesser of two evils, Mother. I couldn't go back up. I—threw up—on the floor!

AMANDA From half past seven till after five every day you mean to tell me you walked around in the park, because you wanted me to think that you were still going to Rubicam's Business College?

LAURA It wasn't as bad as it sounds. I went inside places to get warmed up.

AMANDA Inside where?

LAURA I went in the art museum and the birdhouses at the Zoo. I visited the penguins every day! Sometimes I did without lunch and went to the movies. Lately I've been spending most of my afternoons in the Jewel-box, that big glass house where they raise the tropical flowers.

AMANDA You did all this to deceive me, just for deception? (LAURA *looks down.*) Why?

LAURA Mother, when you're disappointed, you get that awful suffering look on your face, like the picture of Jesus' mother in the museum!

AMANDA Hush!

LAURA I couldn't face it!

(Pause. A whisper of strings)

AMANDA (Hopelessly fingering the huge pocketbook) So what are we going to do the rest of our lives? Stay home and watch the parades go by? Amuse ourselves with the glass menagerie, darling? Eternally play those worn-out phonograph records your father left as a painful reminder of him.

We won't have a business career—we've given that up because it gave us nervous indigestion! (Laughs wearily) What is there left but dependency all our lives? I know so well what becomes of unmarried women who aren't prepared to occupy a position. I've seen such pitiful cases in the South—barely tolerated spinsters living upon the grudging patronage of sister's husband or brother's wife!—stuck away in some little mouse-trap of a room—encouraged by one in-law to visit another—little birdlike women without any nest—eating the crust of humility all their life!

Is that the future that we've mapped out for ourselves? I swear it's the only alternative I can think of! It isn't a very pleasant alternative, is it? Of course—some girls *do marry.* (LAURA *twists her hands nervously.*) Haven't you ever liked some boy?

LAURA Yes. I liked one once. (Rises) I came across his picture a while ago.

AMANDA (With some interest) He gave you his picture?

LAURA No, it's in the year-book.

AMANDA *(Disappointed)* Oh—a high-school boy.

LAURA Yes. His name was Jim. *(LAURA lifts the heavy annual from the claw-foot table.)* Here he is in *The Pirates of Penzance*.

AMANDA *(Absently)* The what?

LAURA The operetta the senior class put on. He had a wonderful voice and we sat across the aisle from each other Mondays, Wednesdays and Fridays in the Aud. Here he is with the silver cup for debating! See his grin?

AMANDA *(Absently)* He must have had a jolly disposition.

LAURA He used to call me—Blue Roses.

AMANDA Why did he call you such a name as that?

LAURA When I had that attack of pleurosis—he asked me what was the matter when I came back. I said pleurosis—he thought I said Blue Roses! So that's what he always called me after that. Whenever he saw me, he'd holler, "Hello, Blue Roses!" I didn't care for the girl that he went out with. Emily Meisenbach. Emily was the best-dressed girl at Soldan. She never struck me, though, as being sincere. . . . It says in the Personal Section—they're engaged. That's—six years ago! They must be married by now.

AMANDA Girls that aren't cut out for business careers usually wind up married to some nice man. *(Gets up with a spark of revival)* Sister, that's what you'll do!

(LAURA utters a startled, doubtful laugh. She reaches quickly for a piece of glass.)

LAURA But, Mother—

AMANDA Yes? *(Crossing to photograph)*

LAURA *(In a tone of frightened apology)* I'm—crippled!

AMANDA Nonsense! Laura, I've told you never, never to use that word. Why, you're not crippled, you just have a little defect—hardly noticeable, even! When people have some slight disadvantage like that, they cultivate other things to make up for it—develop charm—and vivacity—and—*charm!* That's all you have to do! *(She turns again to the photograph.)* One thing your father had *plenty of*—was *charm!*

Wine in the Wilderness
by Alice Childress (1969)

Characters: CYNTHIA—She is a college-educated social worker in her early twenties who has befriended Tommy.
TOMMY—She is a factory worker with an eighth-grade education. She wears artistically mismatched clothes.

Situation: This comedy-drama is set in a one-room apartment in a Harlem tenement building. The room is in a state of artistic disorder, decorated with pictures and ornaments from a variety of cultures. Bill Jameson, an artist friend of Cynthia's, is looking for an African American woman to model for him. Tommy has just the look he needs. Cynthia wants to protect Tommy from getting emotionally involved with Bill, knowing that he is interested in Tommy as a model, not as a woman.

CYNTHIA *(A bit uncomfortable)* Oh, Honey, . . . Tommy, you don't want a poor artist.

TOMMY Tommy's not lookin' for a meal ticket. I been doin' for myself all my life. It takes two to make it in this high-price world. A black man see a hard way to go. The both of you gotta pull together. That way you accomplish.

CYNTHIA I'm a social worker . . . and I see so many broken homes. Some of these men! Tommy, don't be in a rush about the marriage thing.

TOMMY Keep it to yourself, . . . but I was thirty my last birthday and haven't even been married. I coulda been. Oh, yes, indeed, coulda been. But I don't want any and every-body. What I want with a no-good piece-a nothin'? I'll never forget what the Reverend Martin Luther King said . . . "I have a dream." I like him sayin' it 'cause truer words have never been spoke. *(Straightening the room)* I have a dream, too. Mine is to find a man who'll treat me just half-way decent . . . just to meet me half-way is all I ask, to smile, be kind to me. Somebody in my corner. Not to wake up by myself in the mornin' and face this world all alone.

CYNTHIA About Bill, it's best not to ever count on anything, anything at all, Tommy.

TOMMY *(This remark bothers her for a split second but she shakes it off.)* Of course, Cynthia, that's one of the foremost rules of life. Don't count on *nothin'!*

CYNTHIA Right, don't be too quick to put your trust in these men.

TOMMY You put your trust in one and got yourself a husband.

CYNTHIA Well, yes, but what I mean is . . . Oh, you know. A man is a man and Bill is also an artist and his work comes before all else and there are other factors . . .

TOMMY *(Sits facing CYNTHIA)* What's wrong with me?

CYNTHIA I don't know what you mean.

TOMMY Yes you do. You tryin' to tell me I'm aimin' too high by lookin' at Bill.

CYNTHIA Oh, no my dear.

TOMMY Out there in the street, in the bar, you and your husband were so sure that he'd *like* me and want to paint my picture.

CYNTHIA But he does want to paint you, he's very eager to . . .

TOMMY But why? Somethin' don't fit right.

CYNTHIA *(Feeling sorry for TOMMY)* If you don't want to do it, just leave and that'll be that.

TOMMY Walk out while he's buyin' me what I ask for, spendin' his money on me? That'd be too dirty. *(Looks at books. Takes one from shelf)* Books, books, books every-where. "Afro-American History." I like that. What's wrong with me, Cynthia? Tell me, I won't get mad with you, I swear. If there's somethin' wrong that I can change, I'm ready to do it. Eighth grade, that's all I had of school. You a social worker, I know that mean college. I come from poor people. *(Examining the book in her hand)* Talkin' 'bout poverty this and poverty that and studyin' it. When you in it you don't be studyin' 'bout it. Cynthia, I remember my mother tyin' up her stockin's with strips-a rag 'cause she didn't have no garters. When I get home from school she'd say, . . . "Nothin' much here to eat." Nothin' much might be grits, or bread and coffee. I got sick-a all that, got me a job. Later for school.

CYNTHIA   The Matriarchal Society.

TOMMY   What's that?

CYNTHIA   A Matriarchal Society is one in which the women rule . . . the women have the power . . . the women head the house.

TOMMY   We didn't have nothin' to rule over, not a pot nor a window. And my papa picked hisself up and run off with some finger-poppin' woman and we never hear another word 'til ten, twelve years later when a undertaker call up and ask if Mama wants come claim his body. And don'cha know, mama went on over and claim it. A woman need a man to claim, even if it's a dead one. What's wrong with me? Be honest.

CYNTHIA   You're a fine person . . .

TOMMY   Go on, I can take it.

CYNTHIA   You're too brash. You're too used to looking out for yourself. It makes us lose our femininity . . . It makes us hard . . . it makes us seem very hard. We do for ourselves too much.

TOMMY   If I don't, who's gonna do for me?

CYNTHIA   You have to let the black man have his manhood again. You have to give it back, Tommy.

TOMMY   I didn't take it from him, how I'm gonna give it back?

Butterflies Are Free
by Leonard Gershe (1969)

Characters: MRS. BAKER—She is a well-dressed, attractive woman who is highly protective of her adult son, Don, who is blind. JILL—Jill is nineteen years old, a would-be actress with a delicate, little-girl quality and long hair. She is always hungry. Jill and Don are neighbors who have become very close.

Situation: The scene is set in 1969 in Don Baker's apartment. Don has not lived on his own for very long.

MRS. BAKER   *(Mumbling to herself)* Mrs. Benson!!!

JILL   *(Opening her door)* Yes?

MRS. BAKER   *(Is startled for a moment, but recovers, quickly. In friendly tones)* Could you come in for a moment, Mrs. Benson?

JILL   *(Uneasily)* Well, I have my audition. I should leave in about fifteen minutes. I don't know New York and I get lost all the time.

MRS. BAKER   *(Ingratiatingly. Steps toward JILL a bit)* Don't you worry. I'll see that you get off in time. (JILL *enters, reluctantly, stands behind table)* I thought you and I might have a little talk. You know—just girls together. Please sit down. (JILL *remains standing, avoiding too close contact with* MRS. BAKER.) Would you like a cup of coffee? Tea?

JILL   No, thank you . . . *(Crosses off platform to L. of sofa)* but if that apple is still there.

MRS. BAKER   *(Crosses to refrigerator, gets apple and lettuce on plate, crosses to sink)* I'm sure it is.

JILL *(Crosses between sofa and coffee table to ladder, sits on step)* Where's Don?

MRS. BAKER Shopping. *(Washes apple and polishes it with dish towel)* You must be so careful to wash fruits and vegetables, you know. They spray all those insecticides on everything now. I'm not at all sure the bugs aren't less harmful. *(Crosses to JILL with apple)* I like apples to be nice and shiny. *(Holds the apple out to JILL, who looks at it and then at MRS. BAKER oddly)*

JILL This reminds me of something. What is it?

MRS. BAKER I have no idea.

JILL You . . . handing me the apple . . . nice and shiny. . . . Oh, I know! Snow White. Remember when the witch brought her the poisoned apple? Oh, Mrs. Baker, I'm sorry. I didn't mean that the way it sounded. I know you're not a witch.

MRS. BAKER Of course not. And I know you're not Snow White.

JILL *(Takes the apple, rises, crosses below MRS. BAKER, through kitchen to D.L. post)* I may have to wait hours before I read. I'll probably starve to death before their eyes.

MRS. BAKER *(Crosses to kitchen, takes lettuce, picks off a few pieces, washes them, puts them on plate)* You're going to get that part, you know.

JILL What makes you so sure?

MRS. BAKER Well, you're a very pretty girl and that's what they want in the theatre, isn't it?

JILL *(Crosses below to D.R. post, away from MRS. BAKER)* Today you have to have more than a pretty face. Anyway, I'm not really pretty. I think I'm interesting-looking and in certain lights I can look sort of . . . lovely . . . but I'm not pretty.

MRS. BAKER *(Crosses with lettuce, sits C. sofa)* Nonsense! You're extremely pretty.

JILL *(Laugh)* No, I'm not.

MRS. BAKER Yes, you are.

JILL *(Turns, leans on post)* No, I'm not. I've got beady little eyes like a bird and a figure like a pogo stick. *(Waits for a reaction from MRS. BAKER. There isn't one.)* Well? Aren't you going to deny you said that?

MRS. BAKER *(Unperturbed)* How can I, dear? Obviously, you heard it.

JILL *(Crosses above director's chair)* There are plenty of true things you can put me down with. You don't have to put me down with lies.

MRS. BAKER You know what I like about you?

JILL Uh-huh. Nothing.

MRS. BAKER Oh yes. I like your honesty . . . your candor. You're really quite a worldly young woman, aren't you, Mrs. Benson?

JILL I suppose I am. *(Crosses above "picnic," away from MRS. BAKER)* I wish you wouldn't call me Mrs. Benson.

MRS. BAKER Isn't that your name . . . Mrs. Benson?

JILL But you don't say it as though you mean it.

MRS. BAKER I'm sorry. Why don't I call you Jill? That's more friendly . . . and I'll try to say it as though I mean it. Now, Jill. *(JILL— R. turn, back to audience)* . . .

MRS. BAKER   I was interested in seeing what you and Donny might have in common. He likes you very much.

JILL   *(Crosses U. end of coffee table)* And I like him very much. He may very well be the most beautiful person I've ever met. Just imagine going through life never seeing anything . . . not a painting . . . or a flower . . . or even a Christmas card. I'd want to die, but Don wants to live. I mean really live . . . *(Crosses onto platform to above table)* and he can even kid about it. He's fantastic.

MRS. BAKER   Then you would want what's best for him, wouldn't you?

JILL   *(Crosses U.S. end of coffee table)* Now, we're getting to it, aren't we? Like maybe I should tell him to go home with you. Is that it?

MRS. BAKER   Donny was happy at home until Linda Fletcher filled him with ideas about a place of his own.

JILL   *(Crosses through kitchen to above table)* Maybe you just want to believe that he can only be happy with you, Mrs. Baker. Well, there are none so blind as those who will not see. *(Crosses D.L. post)* There. I can quote Dylan Thomas AND Little Donny Dark.

MRS. BAKER   *(Rises, takes lettuce to counter)* You constantly astonish me.

JILL   Well . . . we women of the world do that.

MRS. BAKER   *(Crosses to "picnic," picks up pillows and cloth, folds cloth)* Funny how like Linda you are. Donny is certainly consistent with his girls.

JILL   Why do you call him Donny?

MRS. BAKER   It's his name. Don't I say it as

though I mean it?

JILL   He hates being called Donny.

MRS. BAKER   *(Crosses to sofa, pillows at each end, crosses to counter, puts cloth on it)* He's never mentioned it.

JILL   Of course, he has. *(Crosses off platform to D. end of sofa)* You just didn't listen. There are none so deaf as those who will not hear. You could make up a lot of those, couldn't you? There are none so lame as those who will not walk. None so thin as those who will not eat . . .

MRS. BAKER   *(Crosses off platform to U.C.)* Do you think it's a good idea for Donny to live down here alone?

JILL   I think it's a good idea for *Don* to live wherever he wants to . . . and he's not alone. I'm here.

MRS. BAKER   *(Crosses U. end of coffee table)* For how long? Have you got a lease on that apartment?

JILL   No.

MRS. BAKER   So, you can leave tomorrow if you felt like it.

JILL   That's right.

MRS. BAKER   You couldn't sustain a marriage for more than six days, could you?

JILL   *(Upset. Crosses D.R.)* My marriage doesn't concern you.

MRS. BAKER   It didn't concern you much, either, did it?

JILL   Yes, it did!

MRS. BAKER   *(Crosses above director's chair)* Have you thought about what marriage to a blind boy might be like? . . . You've seen

Donny at his best—in this room, which he's memorized . . . and he's memorized how many steps to the drugstore and to the delicatessen . . . but take him out of this room or off this street and he's lost . . . he panics. Donny needs someone who will stay with him—and not just for six days.

JILL   You can stop worrying, Mrs. Baker. Nothing serious will develop between Don and me. I'm not built that way.

MRS. BAKER   But Donny *is* built that way.

JILL   Oh, please—we're just having kicks.

MRS. BAKER   Kicks! That's how it started with Linda—just kicks . . . but Donny fell in love with her . . . and he'll fall in love with you. Then what happens?

JILL   (*Crosses below to D. end of sofa*) I don't know!!

MRS. BAKER   (*Crosses U. end of sofa*) Then don't let it go that far. Stop now before you hurt him.

JILL   What about you? Aren't you hurting him?

MRS. BAKER   I can't. I can only irritate him. You can hurt him. The longer you stay the harder it will be for him when you leave. Let him come with me and you go have your kicks with someone who won't feel them after you've gone!!

JILL   I'm not so sure you can't hurt him. Maybe more than anybody. (*Crosses above table*) I think you deserve all the credit you can get for turning out a pretty marvelous guy—but bringing up a son—even a blind one—isn't a lifetime occupation. (*MRS. BAKER turns U., away from JILL.*) Now the more you help him, the more you hurt him. It

was Linda Fletcher—not you— (*MRS. BAKER turns and looks at JILL slowly.*) who gave him the thing he needed most—confidence in himself. (*Crossing away L.*) You're always dwelling on the negative—always what he needs, never what he wants . . . always what he can't do, never what he can. (*Crosses D. end of sofa*) What about his music? Have you ever heard the song he wrote? I'll bet you didn't even know he could write songs! (*Crosses above table*) You're probably dead right about me. I'm not the ideal girl for Don, but I know one thing—neither are you!! And if I'm going to tell anyone to go home, it'll be you, Mrs. Baker. YOU go home!! (*Turns and exits into her apartment, closing door behind her. MRS. BAKER watches her go.*)

Romeo and Juliet
by William Shakespeare (1595–6)

Characters: JULIET—Juliet is a young aristocrat who is romantic, stubborn, and independent. She and Romeo have just been secretly married by Friar Laurence, and she is waiting to hear when Romeo will arrive.
NURSE—An elderly woman, the nurse is a cross between Juliet's nanny and a doting grandparent.

Situation: In this scene, the nurse arrives with the rope that Romeo was to use to climb to Juliet's room, but Romeo has just killed Juliet's cousin Tybalt and has been banished from the city. The nurse is upset, and Juliet has trouble understanding what has happened.

JULIET   O, here comes my nurse,
And she brings news; and every tongue that speaks

But Romeo's name speaks heavenly eloquence.
(NURSE *enters with cords.*)

JULIET Now, nurse what news? What has thou there? the cords
That Romeo bid thee fetch?

NURSE *(Throwing them down)* Ay, ay, the cords.

JULIET Ay me! what news? why dost thou wring thy hands?

NURSE Ay, well-a-day! he's dead, he's dead, he's dead.
We are undone, lady, we are undone!
Alack the day! he's gone, he's kill'd, he's dead!

JULIET Can heaven be so envious?

NURSE Romeo can,
Though heaven cannot: O Romeo, Romeo!
Who ever would have thought it? Romeo!

JULIET What devil art thou, that dost torment me thus?
This torture should be roar'd in dismal hell.
Hath Romeo slain himself? say thou but 'I,'
And that bare vowel 'I' shall poison more
Than the death-darting eye of cockatrice:
I am not I, if there be such an I;
Or those eyes shut, that make thee answer 'I.'
If he be slain, say 'I'; or if not, no:
Brief sounds determine of my weal or woe.

NURSE I saw the wound, I saw it with mine eyes,—
God save the mark!—here on his manly breast:
A piteous corse, a bloody piteous corse;
Pale, pale as ashes, all bedaub'd in blood,
All in gore-blood: I swounded at the sight.

JULIET O, break, my heart! poor bankrupt, break at once!
To prison, eyes, ne'er look on liberty!

Vile earth, to earth resign; end motion here;
And thou and Romeo press one heavy bier!

NURSE O Tybalt! Tybalt, the best friend I had!
O courteous Tybalt! honest gentleman!
That ever I should live to see thee dead!

JULIET What storm is this that blows so contrary?
Is Romeo slaughter'd, and is Tybalt dead?
My dear-loved cousin, and my dearer lord?
Then, dreadful trumpet, sound the general doom!
For who is living, if those two are gone?

NURSE Tybalt is gone, and Romeo banished;
Romeo that kill'd him, he is banished.

JULIET O God! did Romeo's hand shed Tybalt's blood?

NURSE It did, it did; alas the day, it did!

JULIET O serpent heart, hid with a flowering face!
Did ever dragon keep so fair a cave?
Beautiful tyrant! fiend angelical!
Dove-feather'd raven! wolvish-ravening lamb!
Despised substance of divinest show!
Just opposite to what thou justly seem'st,
A damned saint, an honourable villain!
O nature, what hadst thou to do in hell,
When thou didst bower the spirit of a fiend
In mortal paradise of such sweet flesh?
Was ever book containing such vile matter
So fairly bound? O, that deceit should dwell
In such a gorgeous palace!

NURSE There's no trust,
No faith, no honesty in men; all perjured,
All forsworn, all naught, all dissemblers.
Ah, where's my man? give me some aqua vitae:

These griefs, these woes, these sorrows make
    me old.
Shame come to Romeo!

JULIET   Blister'd be thy tongue
For such a wish! he was not born to shame:
Upon his brow shame is ashamed to sit;
For 'tis a throne where honour may be
    crown'd
Sole monarch of the universal earth.
O, what a beast was I to chide at him!

NURSE   Will you speak well of him that
    kill'd your cousin?

JULIET   Shall I speak ill of him that is my
    husband?
Ah, poor my lord, what tongue shall smooth
    thy name,
When I, thy three-hours wife, have
    mangled it?
But, wherefore, villain, didst thou kill my
    cousin?
That villain cousin would have kill'd my
    husband:
Back, foolish tears, back to your native spring;
Your tributary drops belong to woe,
Which you, mistaking, offer up to joy.
My husband lives, that Tybalt would have
    slain;
And Tybalt's dead, that would have slain my
    husband:
All this is comfort; wherefore weep I then?
Some word there was, worser than Tybalt's
    death,
That murder'd me: I would forget it fain;
But, O, it presses to my memory,
Like damned guilty deeds to sinners' minds:
'Tybalt is dead, and Romeo—banished;'
That 'banished,' that one word 'banished'
Hath slain ten thousand Tybalts. Tybalt's
    death

Was woe enough, if it had ended there:
Or, if sour woe delights in fellowship
And needly will be rank'd with other griefs,
Why follow'd not, when she said 'Tybalt's
    dead,'
Thy father, or thy mother, nay, or both,
Which modern lamentation might have
    moved?
But with a rearward following Tybalt's death,
'Romeo is banished,' to speak that word,
If father, mother, Tybalt, Romeo, Juliet,
All slain, all dead. 'Romeo is banished!'
There is no end, no limit, measure, bound,
In that word's death; not words can that woe
    sound.
Where is my father, and my mother, nurse?

NURSE   Weeping and wailing over Tybalt's
    corse:
Will you go to them? I will bring you thither.

JULIET   Wash they his wounds with tears:
    mine shall be spent
When theirs are dry, for Romeo's banishment.
Take up those cords: poor ropes, you are
    beguiled,
Both you and I; for Romeo is exiled:
He made you for a highway to my bed;
But I, a maid, die maiden-widowed.
Come, cords, come, nurse: I'll to my wedding-
    bed;
And death, not Romeo, take my maidenhead!

NURSE   Hie to your chamber: I'll find
    Romeo
To comfort you: I wot well where he is.
Hark ye, your Romeo will be here at night:
I'll to him; he is hid at Laurence' cell.

JULIET   O, find him! give this ring to my
    true knight,
And bid him come to take his last farewell.

Brighton Beach Memoirs
by Neil Simon (1982)

Characters: KATE—Kate is about forty. She is a very generous woman who is also outspoken on occasion. She has few friends.
BLANCHE—She is a thirty-eight-year-old widow and Kate's sister. She and her two daughters live with Kate and her family.

Situation: The play is set in September 1937 in a house close to Brighton Beach in Brooklyn, New York. It is an ethnically diverse, lower-middle-class area. Kate and Blanche have had an argument over household expenses, and Blanche has decided to move elsewhere with her girls. This scene takes place a couple of hours after their argument.

KATE Is she alright?

BLANCHE Yes.

KATE She's not angry anymore?

BLANCHE No, Kate. No one's angry anymore. I just explained everything to Nora. The girls will help you with all the housework while I'm gone. Laurie's strong enough to do her share. I've kept her being a baby long enough.

KATE They've never been any trouble to me, those girls. Never.

BLANCHE I'll try to take them on the weekends if I can . . . It's late. We could both use a good night's sleep. *(She starts out of the room.)*

KATE Blanche! . . . Don't go! *(BLANCHE stops.)* I feel badly enough for what I said. Don't make me feel any worse.

BLANCHE Everything you said to me tonight was true, Kate. I wish to God you said it years ago.

KATE What would I do without you? Who else do I have to talk to all day? What friends do I have in this neighborhood? Even the Murphys across the street are leaving.

BLANCHE You and I never had any troubles before tonight, Kate. . . . It's the girls I'm thinking of now. We have to be together. The three of us. It's what they want as much as I do.

KATE Alright. I'm not saying you shouldn't have it. But you're not going to find a job overnight. Apartments are expensive. While you're looking, why do you have to live with strangers in Manhattan Beach?

BLANCHE Louise isn't a stranger. She's a good friend.

KATE To me good friends are strangers. But sisters are sisters.

BLANCHE I'm afraid of becoming comfortable here. I don't get out now, when will I ever do it?

KATE The door is open. Go whenever you want. When you got the job, when you find the apartment, I'll help you move. I can look with you. I know how to bargain with these landlords.

BLANCHE *(Smiles)* You wouldn't mind doing that?

KATE They see a woman all alone, they take advantage of you . . . I'll find out what they're asking for the Murphy place. It couldn't be expensive, she never cleaned it.

BLANCHE How independent can I become if I live right across the street from you?

KATE Far enough away for you to close your own door, and close enough for me not to feel so lonely. *(BLANCHE looks at her with great warmth, crosses to KATE and embraces her. They hold on dearly.)*

BLANCHE If I lived on the moon, you would still be close to me, Kate.

KATE I'll tell Jack. He wouldn't go to sleep until I promised to come up with some good news.

BLANCHE I suddenly feel so hungry.

KATE Of course. You haven't had dinner. Come on. I'll fix you some scrambled eggs.

BLANCHE I'll make them. I'm an independent woman now.

KATE With your eyes, you'll never get the eggs in the pan.

I Love You, I Love You Not
by Wendy Kesselman (1988)

Characters: DAISY—Daisy is a typical adolescent who is on a roller coaster of emotions. She is insecure, and Nana is the one person with whom she feels she can freely express herself. NANA—(pronounced Nahnah) Daisy's grandmother, Nana is a survivor of the Holocaust. She understands the mood swings Daisy is going through, and she always provides a listening ear and unconditional love.

Situation: This play is set in the present in a country house, where Daisy is visiting Nana for the weekend. Daisy's parents will be picking her up shortly. It has been an emotional visit. In this scene, the conversation turns more reflective as

Daisy enters a contemplative mood.

DAISY I feel so ugly, Nana.

NANA *(Sitting down beside her)* What are you talking about? You're a beautiful girl.

DAISY I know what I look like.

NANA Silly Daisy.

DAISY Don't call me that. I hate that name.

NANA It's a beautiful name. A beautiful flower. A flower that grows in the wild.

DAISY He loves me, he loves me not, he loves me, he loves me not. And all that's left is that horrible little thing in the middle. It's ugly—a daisy with all its petals gone.

NANA It's a survivor. That's what I always felt. A yellow sun. A yellow star. *(There is a long pause.)*

DAISY *(Quietly)* Nana, let me see. *(Very soft)* Let me see it, Nana. Show it to me. *(Slowly, NANA pulls back her sleeve, holds out her arm.)* Remember when I was little and I asked you?

NANA You were so tiny. Not even three. "What's that?" you said. *(Imitating DAISY at three)* "What's that, Nana?" *(She laughs softly.)* And month after month, year after year went by, and it was always, "Nana, what is that? Why do you wear that? Why do you have that on your arm?" *(She pauses.)* And then one day, I was putting some dishes up on the shelf, when I felt those huge eyes staring at me. And I heard, "Nana—"

DAISY *(Breaking in. Slowly)* "Are you sure you didn't do anything wrong to make them do that to you?" *(She leans closer and touches NANA'S arm. Quietly reading the number out loud.)* A. A is for Auschwitz.

Riders to the Sea
by John M. Synge (1904)

Characters: MAURYA—An old woman of the Irish peasant class whose family have always been fishers, Maurya lives in a cottage on an island off the west coast of Ireland.
NORA—Maurya's daughter, she is a teenager. To play her takes a focus on silent but eloquent sorrow and sympathy, for she has but one speech.

Situation: Maurya's son Michael has recently died at sea, as have all of the men in Maurya's life. Now Bartley, her only surviving son, has insisted on sailing to the mainland in bad weather to sell two horses. Pursuing Bartley to the shore, Maurya sees the image of Michael riding one of the horses. Upset, she returns to the house, fearing the worst for Bartley.

MAURYA *(In a low voice, but clearly)* . . . Bartley will be lost now, and let you call in Eamon and make me a good coffin out of the white boards, for I won't live after them. I've had a husband, and a husband's father, and six sons in this house—six fine men, though it was a hard birth I had with every one of them and they coming to the world—and some of them were found and some of them were not found, but they're gone now the lot of them. . . . There were Stephen, and Shawn, were lost in the great wind, and found after in the Bay of Gregory of the Golden Mouth, and carried up the two of them on the one plank, and in by that door. . . . There was Sheamus and his father, and his own father again, were lost in a dark night, and not a stick or sign was seen of them when the sun went up. There was Patch after was drowned out of a curagh that turned over. I was sitting here with Bartley, and he a baby, lying on my two knees, and I seen two women, and three women, and four women coming in, and they crossing themselves, and not saying a word. I looked out then, and there were men coming after them, and they holding a thing in the half of a red sail, and water dripping out of it—it was a dry day, Nora—and leaving a track to the door. . . . (. . . *men carry in the body of Bartley, laid on a plank, with a bit of sail over it, and lay it on the table.*) . . . They're all gone now, and there isn't anything more the sea can do to me . . . I'll have no call now to be up crying and praying when the wind breaks from the south, and you can hear the surf is in the east, and the surf is in the west, making a great stir with the two noises, and they hitting one on the other. I'll have no call now to be going down and getting Holy Water in the dark nights after Samhain, and I won't care what way the sea is when the other women will be keening. Give me the Holy Water, Nora, there's a small sup still on the dresser. *(Nora gives it to her.)*

MAURYA *(Drops Michael's clothes across Bartley's feet, and sprinkles the Holy Water over him)* It isn't that I haven't prayed for you, Bartley, to the Almighty God. It isn't that I haven't said prayers in the dark night till you wouldn't know what I'd be saying; but it's a great rest I'll have now, and it's time surely. It's a great rest I'll have now, and great sleeping in the long nights after Samhain, if it's only a bit of wet flour we do have to eat, and maybe a fish that would be stinking. *(She kneels down again, crossing herself and saying prayers under her breath.)* . . .

NORA *(In a whisper . . .)* She's quiet now and easy; but the day Michael was drowned you could hear her crying out from this to the spring well. It's fonder she was of Michael, and would anyone have thought that? . . .

MAURYA *(Puts the empty cup mouth downwards on the table, and lays her hands together on Bartley's feet)* They're all together this time, and the end is come. May the Almighty God have mercy on Bartley's soul, and on Michael's soul, and on the souls of Sheamus and Patch, and Stephen and Shawn *(Bending her head)*; and may He have mercy on my soul, Nora, and on the soul of every one left living in the world. . . . Michael has a clean burial in the far north, by the grace of the Almighty God. Bartley will have a fine coffin out of the white boards, and a deep grave surely. What more can we want than that? No man at all can be living for ever, and we must be satisfied. *(She kneels down again and the curtain falls slowly.)*

Haiku
by Katherine Snodgrass (1988)

Characters: NELL—In her fifties, Nell is a widow with two daughters, Billie (the older) and Louise (the younger). She is losing her eyesight. LOUISE—Louise, in her twenties, lives at home with her mother, because of a serious mental condition that makes her incapable of coping with reality. Her behavior is violent and destructive when not controlled by medicine. However, the medicine hinders her ability to think. She often communicates by haiku—a verse form that requires seventeen syllables.

Situation: The scene takes place in the living room. Nell has a noticeable bruise on her wrist, and Louise has a bandage on her forehead, both injuries apparently caused by one of Louise's violent rages. Louise is wearing a football helmet for her own protection. Nell is allowing Louise's medicine to wear off a little so that Louise will be able to communicate with Billie, who is coming to visit. As the numbing effects of the medicine diminish, Louise responds to Nell's reminiscence with haiku, which Nell records.

NELL You were born in early winter. John and I planned it that way. I couldn't imagine having a baby in the summertime. It gets so sticky in August, humid. A breech baby. You tried to back into the world. I remember, the doctor had to pull you out. It was night when they finally brought you to me.

LOUISE November evening.
Blackbirds scull across the moon.
My breath warms my hands.

(Nell writes haiku, then checks what she has written, holding the paper two inches from her eyes.)

NELL John said you were too beautiful to live. It was true. You and Bebe together, you were like china dolls. Delicate, perfect. And then . . . I sensed it that day when I saw you through the window. Billie was on the swingset, and you were there. Outside. She was in red, and you had on that blue jumpsuit, the corduroy one with the zipper. The ball lay beside you and that Mama doll that winked. You were so quiet. You'd stared before, of course, when something fascinated you, as all children do when they . . . as all children do. But this time, you were . . . different. I called for you to come inside. *Lulu, come inside and have some lunch!* But you didn't hear me. *Bebe, bring Lulu and come inside!* I went out then. I had to get down on my knees beside you. I touched your hair and then your face. I held up that Mama-doll, but you stared through it in a way that . . . Funny, I don't remember being afraid. I remember the look on Bebe's face.

LOUISE   Chainmetal swings clanging
In the empty school yard.
Silent summer rain.

(Nell writes haiku. She goes through same process as before.)

NELL   Do you know, I used to cry when school ended? It's true! I used to cry on the last day of school every year. My mother thought I was crazy. I'd come dragging my book bag over the fields, my face all wet. And my momma! . . . Nellie, she'd say . . .

LOUISE   Nellie, she'd say . . . *(Nell looks sharply at Louise.)* You're the strangest girl I ever did see!

NELL   Yes, that's what she said. Are you tired?

LOUISE   No, no. Tell me again about John.

NELL   You look tired.

LOUISE   Please. You haven't talked about John in a long time.

NELL   John. All right then. John was tall and thin like Icabod Crane, only not so scared.

LOUISE   John wasn't scared of anything.

NELL   He wasn't scared of anything, not John. He had a big, strong jaw and a tuft of yellow hair that stood up on his head, as yellow . . .

LOUISE   . . . as Mr. Turner's daffodils.

NELL   At least. And he would take you on his knee. Do you remember the song he used to sing? *(Nell clears her throat and sings.)* "Here come a Lulu! Here come a Lulu to the

Indian dance." *(Louise joins in.)* "All of them Indians, all of them Indians dance around Lulu's tent." *(Like a drum)* "Here come a Lulu! Here come a Lulu! Here come a Lulu!" *(They laugh, remembering.)*

LOUISE   Icy branches bend,
Breaking over stones.
I hear my dead father laugh.

On Golden Pond
by Ernest Thompson (1979)

Characters: ETHEL—Ethel Thayer, Chelsea's mother, is an intelligent, sixty-nine-year-old, middle-class American.
CHELSEA—Chelsea is forty-two, athletic-looking, and tanned. She is a nervous type with a dark sense of humor. She has had an unhappy childhood and is divorced.

Situation: It is early morning in August at the Thayers' summer lakeside home in Maine. Chelsea's friend Bill has a thirteen-year-old son, Billy, who has been staying with Chelsea's parents while she and Bill traveled to Europe. Chelsea has come to take Billy home.

ETHEL   How'd you get here?

CHELSEA   I rented a car. A Volare. It's made by Plymouth. I got it from Avis. *(She walks to ETHEL. They embrace.)* They *do* try hard.

ETHEL   You're not supposed to come till the fifteenth.

CHELSEA   Today's the fifteenth.

ETHEL   No!

CHELSEA   'Fraid so.

ETHEL   Well. No wonder you're here.

CHELSEA   Still have the kid or did you drown him?

ETHEL   Still have him.

CHELSEA   Are he and Norman asleep?

ETHEL   You must be joking. They're out on the lake already, antagonizing the fish. Still have Bill or did you drown him?

CHELSEA   Still got him. But he's not with me. He went back to the coast. He had a mouth that needed looking into.

ETHEL   Oh. You must have left Boston at the crack of dawn.

CHELSEA   I left Boston in the middle of the night. I felt like driving. I didn't feel like getting lost, but it worked out that way.

ETHEL   If you'd come more often, you wouldn't get lost.

CHELSEA   You're right. If I promise to come more often will you give me a cup of coffee?

ETHEL   All right. I could do that. Yes. You must have had a lovely time in Europe. You look wonderful.

(She exits to the kitchen.)

CHELSEA   I do? I did. I had a lovely time. *(Peers out at the lake)*

ETHEL   *(Offstage)* I always thought Norman and I should travel, but we never got to it somehow. I'm not sure Norman would like Europe.

CHELSEA   He wouldn't like Italy.

ETHEL   *(Offstage)* No?

CHELSEA   Too many Italians.

ETHEL   *(Enters)* I've got the perker going. See the boys?

CHELSEA   Yes. What are they doing out there? It's starting to rain.

ETHEL   Ah, well. I told Norman not to go. The loons have been calling for it. I'm afraid Norman doesn't give them much credence.

CHELSEA   They're going to get drenched.

ETHEL   I think between the two of them they have sense enough to come in out of the rain. At least I hope they do.*(A moment passes as they look out at the lake.)* Isn't it beautiful?

CHELSEA   *(She nods and looks at* ETHEL.*)* Look at you. You've had that robe for as long as I can remember.

ETHEL   *(She tries to arrange it.)* It looks like it, doesn't it?

CHELSEA   It looks great.

(She stares at ETHEL. *She steps to her and hugs her emphatically.)*

ETHEL   You're in a huggy mood today. What's the matter?

CHELSEA   You seem different.

ETHEL   You mean old.

CHELSEA   I don't know.

ETHEL   Well, that's what happens if you live long enough. You end up being old. It's one of the disadvantages of a long life. I still prefer it to the alternative.

CHELSEA   How does it really make you feel?

ETHEL   Not much different. A little more aware of the sunrises, I guess. And the sunsets.

CHELSEA   It makes *me* mad.

ETHEL   Ah, well, it doesn't exactly make me want to jump up and down.
(CHELSEA *hugs* ETHEL *again.*)
Oh, dear. They're not digging the grave yet. Come sit down. You must be exhausted.

(ETHEL *sits.* CHELSEA *wanders.*)

CHELSEA   Have Billy and Norman gotten along all right?

ETHEL   Billy is the happiest thing that's happened to Norman since Roosevelt. I should have rented him a thirteen-year-old boy years ago.

CHELSEA   You could have traded me in.
(ETHEL *laughs.*) Billy reminds me of myself out there, way back when. Except I think he makes a better son than I did.

ETHEL   Well, you made a very nice daughter.

CHELSEA   Does Billy put the worm on the hook by himself?

ETHEL   I'm really not sure.

CHELSEA   I hope so. You lose points if you throw up, I remember that. I always apologized to those nice worms before I impaled them. Well, they'll get even with me someday, won't they?

ETHEL   You're beginning to sound an awful lot like your father.

CHELSEA   Uh oh. (*Changing direction*) Thank you for taking care of Billy.

ETHEL   Thank *you.* I'm glad it gives us another chance to see you. Plus, it's been a tremendous education. Norman's vocabulary will never be the same but that's all right.

SCENES
for Two Men

You Can't Take It with You
by Moss Hart and George S. Kaufman (1936)

Characters: HENDERSON—Mr. Henderson is employed by the Internal Revenue Service to collect past-due taxes.
GRANDPA—This is a man at peace with himself. Physically, he is a wiry little man of about seventy-five years with a youthful face.

Situation: The action takes place in the Vanderhof home on the Upper West Side of Manhattan. It is a house filled with family where anything goes. Grandpa Vanderhof has never filed an income tax return, and Henderson calls on Grandpa to collect the past-due taxes.

HENDERSON   *(Pulling a sheaf of papers from his pocket)* Now, Mr. Vanderhof, *(A quick look toward hall)* we've written you several letters about this, but have not had any reply.

GRANDPA   Oh, that's what those letters were.

[ESSIE *(Sitting on couch R.)* I told you they were from the government.]

HENDERSON   According to our records, Mr. Vanderhof, you have never paid an income tax.

GRANDPA   That's right.

HENDERSON   Why not?

GRANDPA   I don't believe in it.

HENDERSON   Well—you own property, don't you?

GRANDPA   Yes, sir.

HENDERSON   And you receive a yearly income from it?

GRANDPA   I do.

HENDERSON   Of—*(He consults his records.)*—between three and four thousand dollars.

GRANDPA   About that.

HENDERSON   You've been receiving it for years.

GRANDPA   I have. 1901, if you want the exact date.

HENDERSON   Well, the Government is only concerned from 1914 on. That's when the income tax started. *(Pause)*

GRANDPA   Well?

HENDERSON   Well—it seems, Mr. Vanderhof, that you owe the Government twenty-four years' back income tax. Now, Mr. Vanderhof, you know there's quite a penalty for not filing an income tax return.

GRANDPA   Look, Mr. Henderson, let me ask you something.

HENDERSON   Well?

GRANDPA   Suppose I pay you this money—mind you, I don't say I'm going to pay it—but just for the sake of argument—what's the Government going to do with it?

HENDERSON   How do you mean?

GRANDPA   Well, what do I get for my money? If I go to Macy's and buy something, there it *is*—I see it. What's the Government give me?

HENDERSON Why, the Government gives you everything. It protects you.

GRANDPA What from?

HENDERSON Well—invasion. Foreigners that might come over here and take everything you've got.

GRANDPA Oh, I don't think they're going to do that.

HENDERSON If you didn't pay an income tax, they would. How do you think the Government keeps up the Army and Navy? All those battleships . . .

GRANDPA Last time we used battleships was in the Spanish-American War, and what did we get out of it? Cuba—and we gave that back. I wouldn't mind paying if it were something sensible.

HENDERSON Sensible? Well, what about Congress, and the Supreme Court, and the President? We've got to pay *them*, don't we?

GRANDPA Not with my money—no, sir.

HENDERSON (*Furious. Rises, picks up papers*) Now wait a minute! I'm not here to argue with you. (*Crossing L.*) All I know is that you haven't paid an income tax and you've got to pay it!

GRANDPA They've got to show me.

HENDERSON (*Yelling*) We *don't* have to show you! I just told you! All those buildings down in Washington, and Interstate Commerce, and the Constitution!

GRANDPA The Constitution was paid for a long time ago. And Interstate Commerce—what *is* Interstate Commerce, anyhow?

HENDERSON (*Business of a look at* GRANDPA. *With murderous calm, crosses and places his hands on table*) There are forty-eight states—see? And if there weren't Interstate Commerce, nothing could go from one state to another. See?

GRANDPA Why not? They got fences?

HENDERSON (*To* GRANDPA) No, they haven't got fences. They've got *laws!* (*Crossing up to arch L.*) My . . . , I never came across anything like *this* before!

GRANDPA Well, I might pay about seventy-five dollars, but that's all it's worth.

HENDERSON You'll pay every cent of it, like everybody else! And let me tell you something else! You'll go to jail if you don't pay, do you hear that? That's the law, and if you think you're bigger than the law, you've got another think coming. You're no better than anybody else, and the sooner you get that through your head, the better . . . you'll hear from the United States Government, that's all I can say. . . (*The music has stopped. He is backing out of the room.*)

GRANDPA (*Quietly*) Look out for those snakes.

(HENDERSON, *jumping, off L.*)

No Time for Sergeants
by Ira Levin and Mac Hyman (1955)

Characters: WILL STOCKDALE—He is a private in the United States Army who has no idea that his observations are funny and perceptive. He is naive, forthright, and sensible. PSYCHIATRIST—He is a somewhat cartoonish army psychiatrist who is too easily frustrated and too quick to diagnose.

Situation: The action takes place on a U.S. Army base in 1955. Will's unusual behavior has disrupted Army routine, so his sergeant has sent him to the base psychiatrist with the hope that grounds can be found for transferring Will elsewhere.

[PSYCHIATRIST, *a major, signs and stamps a paper before him, then takes form from* WILL, *seated next to desk.* PSYCHIATRIST *looks at form, looks at* WILL. *A moment of silence*]

WILL   I never have no dreams at all.

PSYCHIATRIST   (*A pause. He looks carefully at* WILL, *looks at form.*) Where you from, Stockdale?

WILL   Georgia.

PSYCHIATRIST   That's . . . not much of a state, is it?

WILL   Well . . . I don't live all over the state. I just live in this one little place in it.

PSYCHIATRIST   That's where "Tobacco Road" is, Georgia.

WILL   Not around my section. (*Pause*) Maybe you're from a different part than me?

PSYCHIATRIST   I've never been there. What's more I don't think I would ever *want* to go there. What's your reaction to that?

WILL   Well, I don't know.

PSYCHIATRIST   I think I would sooner live in the rottenest pigsty in Alabama or Tennessee than in the fanciest mansion in all of Georgia. What about that?

WILL   Well, sir, I think where you want to live is your business.

PSYCHIATRIST   (*Pause, staring*) You don't mind if someone says something bad about Georgia?

WILL   I ain't heared nobody say nothin' bad about Georgia.

PSYCHIATRIST   What do you think I've been saying?

WILL   Well, to tell you the truth, I ain't been able to get too much sense out of it. Don't you know?

PSYCHIATRIST   Watch your step, young man. (*Pause*) We psychiatrists call this attitude of yours "resistance."

WILL   You do?

PSYCHIATRIST   You sense that this interview is a threat to your security. You feel yourself in danger.

WILL   Well, kind of I do. If'n I don't get classified Sergeant King won't give me the wrist watch. (PSYCHIATRIST *stares at* WILL *uncomprehendingly.*) He *won't!* He said I only gets it if I'm classified inside a week.

PSYCHIATRIST   (*Turns forlornly to papers on desk. A bit subdued*) You get along all right with your mother?

WILL   No, sir, I can't hardly say that I do—

PSYCHIATRIST   (*Cutting in*) She's very strict? Always hovering over you?

WILL   No, sir, just the opposite—

PSYCHIATRIST   She's never there.

WILL   That's right.

PSYCHIATRIST   You resent this neglect, don't you?

WILL   No, I don't resent nothin'.

PSYCHIATRIST   (*Leaning forward paternally*) There's nothing to be ashamed of, son. It's a common situation. Does she ever beat you?

WILL   No!

PSYCHIATRIST   (*Silkily*) So defensive. It's not easy to talk about your mother, is it.

WILL   No, sir. She died when I was borned.

PSYCHIATRIST   (*A long, sick pause*) You . . . could have told me that sooner . . .

WILL   (*Looks hang-dog. PSYCHIATRIST returns to papers. WILL glances up at him.*) Do you hate *your* mama? (*PSYCHIATRIST'S head snaps up, glaring.*) I figgered as how you said it was so common . . .

PSYCHIATRIST   I do not hate my mother.

WILL   I should hope not! (*Pause*) What, does she beat you or somethin'?

PSYCHIATRIST   (*Glares again, drums his fingers briefly on table. Steeling himself, more to self than* WILL) This is a transference. You're taking all your stored up antagonisms and loosing them in my direction. Transference. It happens every day . . . .

WILL   (*Excited*) It does? To the Infantry?

PSYCHIATRIST   (*Aghast*) The Infantry?

WILL   You give Ben a transfer, I wish you'd give me one too. I'd sure love to go along with him.

PSYCHIATRIST   Stop! (*The pause is a long one this time. Finally* PSYCHIATRIST *points at papers.*) There are a few more topics we have to cover. We will not talk about transfers, we will not talk about my mother. We

will only talk about what *I* want to talk about, do you understand?

WILL   Yes, sir.

PSYCHIATRIST   Now then—your father. (*Quickly*) Living?

WILL   Yes, sir.

PSYCHIATRIST   Do you get along with him okay?

WILL   Yes, sir.

PSYCHIATRIST   Does he ever beat you?

WILL   You bet!

PSYCHIATRIST   Hard?

WILL   And how! Boy, there ain't nobody can beat like my Pa can!

PSYCHIATRIST   (*Beaming*) So *this* is where the antagonism comes from! (*Pause*) You hate your father, don't you?

WILL   No . . . I got an uncle I hate! Every time he comes out to the house he's always wantin' to rassle with the mule, and the mule gets all wore out, and *he* gets all wore out . . . Well, I don't really *hate* him; I just ain't exactly partial to him.

PSYCHIATRIST   (*Pause*) Did I ask you about your uncle?

WILL   I thought you wanted to talk about hatin' people.

PSYCHIATRIST   (*Glares, drums his fingers, retreats to form. Barely audible*) Now—girls. How do you like girls?

WILL   What girls is that, sir?

PSYCHIATRIST   Just girls. Just any girls.

WILL   Well, I don't like just any girls.

There's one old girl back home that ain't got hair no longer than a hounddog's and she's always—

PSYCHIATRIST No! Look, when I say girls I don't mean any one specific girl. I mean girls in general; women, sex! Didn't that father of yours ever sit down and have a talk with you?

WILL Sure he did.

PSYCHIATRIST Well?

WILL Well what?

PSYCHIATRIST What did he say?

WILL *(With a snicker)* Well, there was this one about these two travelin' salesmen that their car breaks down in the middle of this terrible storm—

PSYCHIATRIST Stop!

WILL —so they stop at this farmhouse where the farmer has fourteen daughters who was—

PSYCHIATRIST *Stop!*

WILL You heared it already?

PSYCHIATRIST *(Writing furiously on form)* No, I did not hear it already . . .

WILL Well, what did you stop me for? It's a real knee-slapper. You see, the fourteen daughters is all studyin' to be trombone players and—

PSYCHIATRIST *(Shoving form at* WILL*)* Here. Go. Good-by. You're through. You're normal. Good-by. Go. Go.

WILL *(Takes the form and stands, a bit confused by it all)* Sir, if girls is what you want to talk about, you ought to come down to the barracks some night. The younger fellows there is always tellin' spicy stories and all like that.

Dial M for Murder
by Frederick Knott (1952)

Characters: MAX—Max is a friend of Tony's wife, Margot. He is a writer of mysteries and has a vivid imagination.
TONY—Tony is a former professional tennis player who married Margot for her money.

Situation: Tony wanted to inherit his wife's money, so he persuaded an old college friend, Swann, to murder her. Instead, Margot killed Swann in self-defense. She was convicted of Swann's murder and sentenced to death. Max has a plan to free Margot, but it requires Tony's help.

MAX Tony, I take it you'd do anything—to save her life?

TONY *(Surprised)* Of course.

MAX Even if it meant going to prison for several years?

TONY *(After a pause)* I'd do absolutely anything.

MAX I think you can—I'm certain. *(Slowly)* If you tell the police *exactly* the right story.

TONY The right story?

MAX Listen, Tony. I've been working this out for weeks. Just in case it came to this. It may be her only chance.

TONY Let's have it.

MAX You'll have to tell the police that you hired Swann to murder her. (*Long pause.* TONY *can only stare at* MAX.)

TONY (*Rises*) What are you talking about?

MAX It's all right, Tony—I've been writing this stuff for years. I know what I'm doing. Margot was convicted because no one would believe her story. Prosecution made out that she was telling one lie after another—and the jury believed him. But what did this case amount to? Only three things. My letter—her stocking, and the idea that, because no key was found on Swann, she must have let him in herself. (*Pause*) Now Swann is dead. You can tell any story you like about him. You can say that you did know him. That you'd met him, and worked out the whole thing together. Now the blackmail. Swann was only suspected of blackmail for two reasons. Because my letter was found in his pocket and because you saw him the day Margot's bag was stolen.

TONY Well?

MAX You can now tell the police that you never saw him at Victoria. That the whole thing was an invention of yours to try and connect him with the letter.

TONY But the letter was found in his pocket.

MAX Because you put it there.

TONY (*Pause*) You mean I should pretend that I stole her handbag?

MAX Sure. You could have.

TONY But why?

MAX Because you wanted to find out who was writing to her. When you read my letter you were so mad you decided to teach her a lesson.

TONY But I can't say that I wrote those blackmail notes.

MAX Why not? No one can prove that you didn't. (TONY *thinks it over.*)

TONY All right. I stole her bag and black-mailed her. What else?

MAX You kept my letter and planted it on Swann after he'd been killed.

TONY Wait a minute—when could I have done that?

MAX After you got back from the party and before the police arrived. At the same time you took one of Margot's stockings from the mending basket and substituted it for whatever Swann had used. (TONY *thinks it over.*)

TONY Max, I know you're trying to help but—can you imagine anyone believing this?

MAX You've got to make them believe it.

TONY But I wouldn't know what to say. You'd have to come with me.

MAX No. I couldn't do that. They know the sort of stuff I write. If they suspected we'd talked this out they wouldn't even listen. They mustn't know I've been here.

TONY Max! It's ridiculous. Why should I want anyone to murder Margot?

MAX Oh, one of the stock motives. Had Margot made a will? (*Pause*)

TONY I—yes, I believe she had.

MAX Are you the main beneficiary?

TONY I suppose so.

MAX Well, there you are.

TONY But thousands of husbands and wives leave money to each other, without murdering each other. The police wouldn't believe a word of it! They'd take it for exactly what it is. A husband desperately trying to save his wife.

MAX Well, it's worth a try. They can't hang you for planning a murder that never came off. Face it. The most you'd get would be a few years in prison.

TONY Thanks very much.

MAX . . . And you'd have saved her life. That doesn't seem too big a price.

The Importance of Being Earnest
by Oscar Wilde (1895)

Characters: ALGERNON—A fashionable member of the British upper class, Algernon occupies himself dining with friends, attending plays and operas, and avoiding his tailor and hatter, whose bills he never pays. JACK—Known to Algernon as Ernest, Jack is unable to keep his private affairs to himself in the face of Algernon's probing curiosity.

Situation: This play, Oscar Wilde's masterpiece, is partly high comedy and partly farce. To satirize the shallow attitudes of the British aristocracy during the reign of Queen Victoria, Wilde created characters who take themselves seriously even though the audience sees how trivial their interests are. In this scene Algernon begins to unravel Jack's secret: he has been maintaining two identities.

ALGERNON My dear fellow, Gwendolen is my first cousin; and before I allow you to marry her, you will have to clear up the whole question of Cecily.

JACK Cecily! What on earth do you mean? What do you mean, Algy, by Cecily! I don't know anyone by the name of Cecily.

ALGERNON *(To butler)* Bring me that cigarette case Mr. Worthing left in the smoking-room the last time he dined here.

JACK Do you mean to say you have had my cigarette case all this time? I wish to goodness you had let me know. I have been writing frantic letters to Scotland Yard about it. I was very nearly offering a large reward.

ALGERNON Well, I wish you would offer one. I happen to be more than usually hard up.

JACK There is no good offering a large reward now that the thing is found.

ALGERNON *(Taking case from butler)* I think it rather mean of you, Ernest, I must say. However, it makes no matter, for now that I look at the inscription inside, I find that the thing isn't yours after all.

JACK Of course it is mine. You have seen me with it a hundred times, and you have no right whatsoever to read what is written inside. It is a very ungentlemanly thing to read a private cigarette case.

ALGERNON Yes, but this is not your cigarette case. This cigarette case is a present from someone of the name of Cecily, and you said you didn't know anyone of that name.

JACK Well, if you want to know, Cecily happens to be my aunt.

ALGERNON Your aunt!

JACK Yes. Charming old lady she is, too. Lives at Tunbridge Wells. Just give it back to me, Algy.

ALGERNON But why does she call herself little Cecily if she is your aunt and lives at Tunbridge Wells? "From *little* Cecily with her fondest love."

JACK My dear fellow, what on earth is there in *that*? Some aunts are tall, some aunts are not tall. That is a matter that surely an aunt may be allowed to decide for herself. *You* seem to think that every aunt should be exactly like your aunt! That is absurd! For Heaven's sake give me back my cigarette case.

ALGERNON Yes. But why does your aunt call you her uncle? "From little Cecily, with her fondest love to her dear Uncle Jack." There is no objection, I admit, to an aunt being a small aunt, but why an aunt, no matter what her size may be, should call her own nephew her uncle, I can't quite make out. Besides, your name isn't Jack at all; it is Ernest.

JACK It isn't Ernest; it's Jack.

ALGERNON You have always told me it was Ernest. I have introduced you to everyone as Ernest. You answer to the name of Ernest. You look as if your name was Ernest. You are the most earnest-looking person I ever saw in my life. It is perfectly absurd your saying that your name isn't Ernest. It's on your cards. Here is one of them. "Mr. Ernest Worthing, B.4, The Albany." I'll keep this as a proof that your name is Ernest if ever you attempt to deny it to me, or to Gwendolen or to anyone else.

JACK Well, my name is Ernest in town and Jack in the country, and the cigarette case was given to me in the country.

ALGERNON Yes, but that does not account for the fact that your small Aunt Cecily, who lives in Tunbridge Wells, calls you her dear uncle. Come, old boy, you had much better have the thing out at once.

JACK My dear Algy, you talk exactly as if you were a dentist. It is very vulgar to talk like a dentist when one isn't a dentist. It produces a false impression.

ALGERNON Well, that is exactly what dentists always do. Now, go on! Tell me the whole thing.

JACK —Well, old Mr. Thomas Cardew, who adopted me when I was a little boy, made me, in his will, guardian to his granddaughter, Miss Cecily Cardew. Cecily, who addresses me as her uncle, from motives of respect that you could not possibly appreciate, lives at my place in the country, under the charge of her admirable governess, Miss Prism.

ALGERNON Where is that place in the country, by the way?

JACK That is nothing to you, dear boy. You are not going to be invited. I may tell you candidly that the place is not in Shropshire.

ALGERNON I suspected that, my dear fellow.—Now go on. Why are you Ernest in town and Jack in the country?

JACK My dear Algy, when one is placed in the position of guardian, one has to adopt a very high moral tone on all subjects. It's one's duty to do so. And as a high moral tone can hardly be said to conduce very much to either one's health or happiness, in order to get up to town I have always pretended to have a younger brother of the name of Ernest, who lives at the Albany, and gets into the most dreadful scrapes. There, my dear Algy, is the whole truth, pure and simple.

ALGERNON   The truth is rarely pure and never simple.

Brighton Beach Memoirs
by Neil Simon (1982)

Characters: EUGENE—Almost fifteen years old, he is innocent, generous, and sentimental. STAN—Stan, Eugene's older brother, is eighteen years old. He has been working to help support the family, and he is much more mature and hardened than Eugene.

Situation: The play is set in September 1937 in a house close to Brighton Beach in Brooklyn, New York. It is an ethnically diverse, lower-middle-class area. Stan has decided to leave home because he is ashamed of losing his week's pay—$17.00—in a poker game.

EUGENE   Aunt Blanche is leaving.

STAN   *(Sits up)* For where?

EUGENE   *(Sits on his own bed)* To stay with some woman in Manhattan Beach. She and Mom just had a big fight. She's going to send for Laurie and Nora when she gets a job.

STAN   What did they fight about?

EUGENE   I couldn't hear it all. I think Mom sorta blames Aunt Blanche for Pop having to

work so hard.

STAN   *(Hits his pillow with his fist)* Oh, God! . . . Did Mom say anything about me? About how I lost my salary?

EUGENE   You told her? Why did you tell her? I came up with twelve terrific lies for you. *(STANLEY opens up his drawer, puts on a sweater.)*

STAN   How much money do you have?

EUGENE   Me? I don't have any money.

STAN   *(Puts another sweater over the first one)* The hell you don't. You've got money in your cigar box. How much do you have?

EUGENE   I got a dollar twelve. It's my life's savings.

STAN   Let me have it. I'll pay it back, don't worry. *(He puts a jacket over sweaters, then gets a fedora from closet and puts it on. EUGENE takes cigar box from under his bed, opens it.)*

EUGENE   What are you putting on all those things for?

STAN   In case I have to sleep out tonight. I'm leaving, Gene. I don't know where I'm going yet, but I'll write to you when I get there.

EUGENE   You're leaving home?

STAN   When I'm gone, you tell Aunt Blanche what happened to my salary. Then she'll know why Mom was so angry. Tell her please not to leave because it was all my fault, not Mom's. Will you do that? *(He takes coins out of cigar box.)*

EUGENE   I have eight cents worth of stamps, if you want that too.

STAN   Thanks. *(Picks up a small medal)* What's this?

EUGENE   The medal you won for the hundred yard dash two years ago.

STAN   From the Police Athletic League. I didn't know you still had this.

EUGENE   You gave it to me. You can have it back if you want it.

STAN   It's not worth anything.

EUGENE   It is to me.

STAN   Sure. You can keep it.

EUGENE   Thanks . . . Where will you go?

STAN   I don't know. I've been thinking about joining . . . the army. Pop says we'll be at war in a couple of years anyway. I could be a sergeant or something by the time it starts.

EUGENE   If it lasts long enough, I could join too. Maybe we can get in the same outfit.

STAN   You don't go in the army unless they come and get you. You go to college. You hear me? Promise me you'll go to college.

EUGENE   I'll probably have to stay home and work, if you leave. We'll need the money.

STAN   I'll send home my paycheck every month. A sergeant in the army makes real good dough . . . Well, I better get going.

EUGENE   *(On the verge of tears)* What do you have to leave for?

STAN   Don't start crying. They'll hear you.

EUGENE   They'll get over it. They won't stay mad at you forever. I was mad at you and *I* got over it.

STAN   Because of me, the whole family is breaking up. Do you want Nora to end up like one of those cheap boardwalk girls?

EUGENE   I don't care. I'm not in love with Nora anymore.

STAN   Well, you *should* care. She's your cousin. Don't turn out to be like me.

EUGENE   I don't see what's so bad about you.

STAN   *(Looks at him)*. . . Take care of yourself, Eug. *(They embrace. He opens the door, looks around, then back to* EUGENE.*)* If you ever write a story about me, call me Hank. I always liked the name Hank. *(He goes, closing the door behind him.)*

Fences
by August Wilson (1985)

Characters: CORY—Cory Maxson is an aspiring football player hoping to win a college scholarship. A typical teenager, he is ambitious and optimistic, but not always sensible or reliable. TROY—Born to a sharecropper who was an angry failure of a man, Troy Maxson tries hard to be a responsible family man and a good father to Cory. He is large, has big hands, and is fifty-three years old.

Situation: Written by an African American playwright, this play is set in 1957 and concerns the Maxsons, who live in an ancient two-story brick house set off a small alley in a big-city neighborhood. Cory is helping his dad make a fence for their yard but gets sidetracked, a habit of his, as he tries to convince Troy that they should buy a television set.

[CORY *takes the saw and begins cutting the boards.* TROY *continues working. There is a long pause.*]

CORY   Hey, Pop . . . why don't you buy a TV?

TROY   What I want with a TV? What I want one of them for?

CORY   Everybody got one. Earl, Ba Bra . . . Jesse!

TROY   I ain't asked you who had one. I say what I want with one?

CORY   So you can watch it. They got lots of things on TV. Baseball games and everything. We could watch the World Series.

TROY   Yeah . . . and how much this TV cost?

CORY   I don't know. They got them on sale for around two hundred dollars.

TROY   Two hundred dollars, huh?

CORY   That ain't that much, Pop.

TROY   Naw, it's just two hundred dollars. See that roof you got over your head at night? Let me tell you something about that roof. It's been over ten years since that roof was last tarred. See now . . . the snow come this winter and sit up there on that roof like it is . . . and it's gonna seep inside. It's just gonna be a little bit . . . ain't gonna hardly notice it. Then the next thing you know, it's gonna be leaking all over the house. Then the wood rot from all that water and you gonna need a whole new roof. Now, how much you think it cost to get that roof tarred?

CORY   I don't know.

TROY   Two hundred and sixty-four dollars. . . cash money. While you thinking about a TV, I got to be thinking about the roof . . . and whatever else go wrong around here. Now if you had two hundred dollars, what would you do . . . fix the roof or buy a TV?

CORY   I'd buy a TV. Then when the roof started to leak . . . when it needed fixing . . . I'd fix it.

TROY   Where you gonna get the money from? You done spent it for a TV. You gonna sit up and watch the water run all over your brand new TV.

CORY   Aw, Pop. You got money. I know you do.

TROY   Where I got it at, huh?

CORY   You got it in the bank.

TROY   You wanna see my bankbook? You wanna see that seventy-three dollars and twenty-two cents I got sitting up in there.

CORY   You ain't got to pay for it all at one time. You can put a down payment on it and carry it on home with you.

TROY   Not me. I ain't gonna owe nobody nothing if I can help it. Miss a payment and they come and snatch it right out your house. Then what you got? Now, soon as I get two hundred dollars clear, then I'll buy a TV. Right now, as soon as I get two hundred and sixty-four dollars, I'm gonna have this roof tarred.

CORY   Aw . . . Pop!

TROY   You go on and get you two hundred dollars and buy one if ya want it. I got better things to do with my money.

CORY   I can't get no two hundred dollars. I ain't never seen two hundred dollars.

TROY I'll tell you what . . . you get you a hundred dollars and I'll put the other hundred with it.

CORY Alright, I'm gonna show you.

TROY You gonna show me how you can cut them boards right now.

How I Got That Story
by Amlin Gray (1979)

Characters: GUERRILLA—He is an information officer in a guerrilla uprising fighting for political power. Cold and direct, he has known nothing but war his entire life.
REPORTER—In his late twenties, he is a former journalist who has been taken hostage by the guerrilla insurgents. Afraid for his life, he tries to persuade the guerrilla that he poses no threat.

Situation: This play is set in a fictional southeast Asian country called Am-Bo Land, where the United States is supporting the government in a war against guerrilla insurgents.

[*A small, bare hut. The* REPORTER *is sleeping on the floor. His head is covered by a black hood and his hands are tied behind his back. A* GUERRILLA *Information Officer comes in carrying a bowl of rice.*]

GUERRILLA Stand up, please.

REPORTER (*Coming awake*) What?

GUERRILLA Please stand up.

REPORTER It's hard with hands behind the back.

GUERRILLA I will untie them.

REPORTER That's all right. I'll make it. (*With some clumsiness, he gets to his feet.*) There I am.

GUERRILLA I offered to untie your hands.

REPORTER I'd just as soon you didn't. When you know that you can trust me, then untie my hands. I'd let you take the hood off.

GUERRILLA (*Takes the hood off*) Tell me why you think that we should trust you.

REPORTER I'm no threat to you. I've never done you any harm.

GUERRILLA No harm?

REPORTER I guess I've wasted your munitions. Part of one of your grenades wound up imbedded in my derriere—my backside.

GUERRILLA I speak French as well as English. You forget—the French were here before you.

REPORTER Yes.

GUERRILLA You told us that you came here as a newsman.

REPORTER Right.

GUERRILLA You worked within the system of our enemies and subject to their interests.

REPORTER Partly subject.

GUERRILLA Yet you say that you have never done us any harm.

REPORTER All I found out as a reporter was I'd never find out anything.

GUERRILLA Do we pardon an enemy sniper if his marksmanship is poor?

REPORTER Yes, if he's quit the army.

GUERRILLA   Ah, yes. You are not a news-man now.

REPORTER   That's right.

GUERRILLA   What are you?

REPORTER   What am I? *(The* GUERRILLA *is silent.)* I'm what you see.

GUERRILLA   What do you do?

REPORTER   I live.

GUERRILLA   You live?

REPORTER   That's all.

GUERRILLA   You live in Am-Bo Land.

REPORTER   I'm here right now.

GUERRILLA   Why?

REPORTER   Why? You've got me prisoner.

GUERRILLA   If you were not a prisoner, you would not be here?

REPORTER   No.

GUERRILLA   Where would you be?

REPORTER   By this time, I'd be back in East Dubuque.

GUERRILLA   You were not leaving when we captured you.

REPORTER   I was, though. I was leaving soon.

GUERRILLA   Soon?

REPORTER   Yes.

GUERRILLA   When?

REPORTER   I don't know exactly. Sometime.

GUERRILLA   Sometime.

REPORTER   Yes.

GUERRILLA   You have no right to be here even for a minute. Not to draw one breath.

REPORTER   You have no right to tell me that. I'm here. It's where I am.

GUERRILLA   We are a spectacle to you. A land in turmoil.

REPORTER   I don't have to lie to you. Yes, that attracts me.

GUERRILLA   Yes. You love to see us kill each other.

REPORTER   No. I don't.

GUERRILLA   You said you didn't have to lie.

REPORTER   I'm not. It does—excite me that the stakes are life and death here. It makes everything—intense.

GUERRILLA   The stakes cannot be life and death unless some people die.

REPORTER   That's true. But I don't make them die. They're dying anyway.

GUERRILLA   You just watch.

REPORTER   That's right.

GUERRILLA   Your standpoint is aesthetic.

REPORTER   Yes, all right, yes.

GUERRILLA   You enjoy our situation here.

REPORTER   I'm filled with pain by things I see.

GUERRILLA   And yet you stay.

REPORTER   I'm here.

GUERRILLA   You are addicted.

REPORTER   Say I am, then! I'm addicted! Yes! I've said it! I'm addicted!

GUERRILLA Your position in my country is morbid and decadent. It is corrupt, reactionary, and bourgeois. You have no right to live here.

REPORTER This is where I live. You can't pass judgment.

GUERRILLA I have not passed judgment. You are useless here. A man must give something in return for the food he eats and the living space he occupies. This is not a moral obligation but a practical necessity in a society where no one is to be exploited.

REPORTER Am-Bo Land isn't such a society, is it?

GUERRILLA Not yet.

REPORTER Well, I'm here right now. If you don't like that then I guess you'll have to kill me.

GUERRILLA We would kill you as we pick the insects from the skin of a valuable animal.

REPORTER Go ahead, then. If you're going to kill me, kill me.

GUERRILLA We are not going to kill you.

REPORTER Why not?

GUERRILLA For a reason.

REPORTER What's the reason?

GUERRILLA We have told the leadership of TransPanGlobal Wire Service when and where to leave one hundred thousand dollars for your ransom.

REPORTER Ransom? TransPanGlobal?

GUERRILLA Yes.

REPORTER But that's no good. I told you, I don't work there anymore.

GUERRILLA Your former employers have not made the separation public. We have made our offer public. You will not be abandoned in the public view. It would not be good business.

REPORTER *(Truly frightened for the first time in the scene)* Wait. You have to think this out. A hundred thousand dollars is too much. It's much too much. You might get ten.

GUERRILLA We have demanded one hundred.

REPORTER They won't pay that. Take ten thousand. That's a lot to you.

GUERRILLA It is. But we have made our offer.

REPORTER Change it. You're just throwing away money. Tell them ten. They'll never pay a hundred thousand.

GUERRILLA We never change a bargaining position we have once set down. This is worth much more than ten thousand dollars or a hundred thousand dollars.

REPORTER Please—

GUERRILLA Sit down.

REPORTER *(Obeys, then, quietly)* Please don't kill me.

GUERRILLA Do not beg your life from me. The circumstances grant your life. Your employers will pay. You will live.

REPORTER You sound so sure.

GUERRILLA If we were not sure we would not waste this food on you. *(He pushes the bowl of rice towards the* REPORTER.*)*

REPORTER How soon will I know?

GUERRILLA   Soon. Ten days.

REPORTER   That's not soon.

GUERRILLA   This war has lasted all my life. Ten days is soon. *(Untying the* REPORTER'S *hands)* You will be fed on what our soldiers eat. You will think that we are starving you, but these are the rations on which we march toward our inevitable victory. Eat your rice. In three minutes I will tie you again.

Man with Bags
by Eugène Ionesco (1977)

Characters: VOICE—This is an offstage mystery voice.
FIRST MAN—He is an innocent traveler who is trying to obtain a guide to lead him out of the country.
YOUNG MAN—He is an armed and demanding aggressor.
SPHINX—He is an absurd creature who demands answers to riddle-type questions. [*N.B.* Voice, Young Man, and Sphinx may all be played by one actor.] (*N.B.* stands for *nota bene,* which in Latin means "note well.")

Situation: The First Man is traveling through the country of his birth, which has a dreamlike quality. Things happen for no reason. He is harassed by people who take their questions very seriously. It is as though he were trapped in a silly version of the game *Jeopardy!* in which losers die. In this scene, he is questioned first by a young man, apparently a guard, and next by a sphinx.

[Male VOICE *calls to* FIRST MAN *from Offstage Right]*

VOICE   Who's out there?

FIRST MAN   *(Turns from audience, moves Upstage Right)* Me! *(*YOUNG MAN *enters, Stage Right. He holds M-1 rifle trained on* FIRST MAN*)*

YOUNG MAN   Hold it there!

FIRST MAN   *(Drops suitcases, raises arms overhead)* Hey, c'mon. Nothin' in those but the usual junk . . .

YOUNG MAN   Password?

FIRST MAN   The password? What password?

YOUNG MAN   If you don't know the password, you're a goner . . .

FIRST MAN   *(False amusement)* Oh, well, of course . . the password! Wow! What's the matter with my brain, huh? I just keep forgetting everything! Les'see now . . . You're gonna' hav'ta' give me a clue . . . OK? Is the password a phrase or actually just a word? I can't quite remember.

YOUNG MAN   Phrase.

FIRST MAN   *(Screams)* A fool and his money are soon parted!

YOUNG MAN   As quickly as water to a duck's back. *(Drops rifle down to his side; smiles)* Very good. *(Pauses)* What's up?

FIRST MAN   You mean I got it?! The password?

YOUNG MAN   What're'ya' looking for here?

FIRST MAN   Here? Oh! Here! A guide. I'd like a guide.

YOUNG MAN   Girl guide or boy guide? Or a whole troop of both?

FIRST MAN   Cancel the order and send up a prune Danish!

YOUNG MAN   Excuse me?

FIRST MAN   Look, I'd like to hire a guide.

YOUNG MAN   What are you looking for?

FIRST MAN   Out. That's what I'm looking for: out. That's what I want: out. I'd like a guide, OK? I'll pay.

YOUNG MAN   You're gonna have a lot of trouble finding a guide around these parts . . . especially for what you want one for . . . Ya' know what I mean? Out is not easy. Not here. *(Pauses)* Anyway, you haven't finished your quiz.

FIRST MAN   My what?

YOUNG MAN   Quiz. There's a pop quiz given at this point. Have you met the Sphinx yet?

FIRST MAN   If this is s'pose'ta' be funny, it isn't, ya' know! I mean, I'm not exactly tickled by you, your gun, any of it . . . *(YOUNG MAN exits, Stage Right)* Where'ya' goin'? Hey, wait up! *(From the same point, a SPHINX enters.)*
[N.B. Possible that SPHINX is YOUNG MAN *wearing wings and insect-head mask]*

SPHINX   Answer my question and answer it quickly. A true genius keeps what for last?

FIRST MAN   That's a question?

SPHINX   Answer!

FIRST MAN   I don't feel like it. This is ridiculous!

SPHINX   It's your life.

FIRST MAN   My life? I see. What was the question again?

SPHINX   A true genius keeps what for last?

FIRST MAN   The last word . . . for last: the word.

SPHINX   Upper regions of space?

FIRST MAN   . . . Ummm . . . Ether.

SPHINX   Musical ending?

FIRST MAN   Coda.

SPHINX   Tabula-what?

FIRST MAN   Rasa?

SPHINX   Land of Saint Patrick . . . four letters.

FIRST MAN   Eire.

SPHINX   Brainchild.

FIRST MAN   Thank you.

SPHINX   No, that's a question!

FIRST MAN   Whether I am?

SPHINX   Don't answer a question with a question!

FIRST MAN   Gim'me an answer then. I'll give you a question.

SPHINX   Who's the Sphinx here anyway?

FIRST MAN   You are. You are.

SPHINX   Brainchild. Four letters . . .

FIRST MAN   I've got an idea . . .

SPHINX   Idea?

FIRST MAN   Right.

SPHINX   Right!

FIRST MAN   Huh?

SPHINX   Disturb. Four letters.

FIRST MAN   What is it with you and these four-letter words? So far, this play has been clean enough for children!

SPHINX   Hurry! Disturb!

FIRST MAN   Roil. Roil.

SPHINX   That's eight letters!

FIRST MAN   OK. OK. Roil.

SPHINX   Now that's twelve letters!

FIRST MAN   Roil.

SPHINX   Good.

FIRST MAN   This is ridiculous. And that's sixteen letters!

SPHINX   OK, here it is: the penultimate question. A true genius keeps what for last.

FIRST MAN   I told you that already! The last word. OK, I'm in, right? I passed.

SPHINX   Out of the question. Failed! That's precisely the point, ducky. A true genius keeps the last word for last. You didn't. You blew it right off the bat!

Othello
by William Shakespeare

Characters: OTHELLO—An African Moor, he is a general on whom the city-state of Venice depends. He is respected, courageous, and happily married. He trusts too easily in his adviser Iago.
IAGO—Iago is an ensign, an honorable but not prestigious rank. He resents Cassio's recent promotion to lieutenant, a post Iago himself had

desired. A brilliant but evil tactician, he is a supreme egotist dedicated to revenge.

Situation: This pivotal scene takes place in the garden of Othello's castle headquarters in Cyprus. Desdemona, Othello's Caucasian wife, is speaking with Cassio as Othello and Iago enter the garden. Cassio leaves suddenly, and Iago seizes on this apparently suspicious behavior to trap the unsuspecting Othello. After Desdemona leaves, Iago fills Othello's head with the false idea that Desdemona has betrayed him with Cassio.

OTHELLO   Excellent wretch[1]! Perdition catch my soul
But I do love thee! and when I love thee not,
Chaos is come again.

IAGO   My noble lord,—

OTHELLO   What dost thou say, Iago?

IAGO   Did Michael Cassio, when you woo'd my lady,
Know of your love?

OTHELLO   He did, from first to last. Why dost thou ask?

IAGO   But for a satisfaction of my thought.
No further harm.

OTHELLO   Why of thy thought, Iago?

IAGO   I did not think he had been acquainted with her.

OTHELLO   O yes; and went between us very oft.

IAGO   Indeed?

OTHELLO   Indeed? ay, indeed. Discern'st thou aught in that?
Is he not honest?

IAGO   Honest, my lord?

OTHELLO   Honest? ay, honest.

IAGO   My lord, for aught I know.

OTHELLO   What dost thou think?

IAGO   Think, my lord?

OTHELLO   Think, my lord?
By heaven, he echoes me,
As if there were some monster in his thought
Too hideous to be shown.—Thou didst mean
   something.
I heard thee say but now, thou lik'st not that,
When Cassio left my wife. What didst not
   like?
And when I told thee he was of my counsel[2]
In my whole course of wooing, thou criedst,
   'Indeed?'
And didst contract and purse thy brow
   together,
As if thou then hadst shut up in thy brain
Some horrible conceit[3]. If thou dost love me,
Show me thy thought.

IAGO   My lord, you know I love you.

OTHELLO   I think thou dost;
And, for I know thou'rt full of love and
   honesty,
And weigh'st thy words before thou give 'em
   breath,
Therefore these stops[4] of thine fright me the
   more;
For such things in a false disloyal knave
Are tricks of custom[5], but in a man that's just
They are close delations[6], working from the
   heart
That passion cannot rule.

IAGO   For Michael Cassio,
I dare be sworn I think that he is honest.

OTHELLO   I think so too.

IAGO   Men should be what they seem;
Or those that be not, would they might seem
   none!

OTHELLO   Certain, men should be what
   they seem.

IAGO   Why then, I think Cassio's an honest
   man.

OTHELLO   Nay, yet there's more in this.
I pray thee, speak to me as to thy thinkings,
As thou dost ruminate, and give thy worst of
   thoughts
The worst of words.

IAGO   Good my lord, pardon me;

Though I am bound to every act of duty,
I am not bound to that all slaves are free to.
Utter my thoughts? Why, say they are vile
   and false;
As where's that palace whereinto foul things
Sometimes intrude not? who has a breast so
   pure
But[7] some uncleanly apprehensions
Keep leets[8] and law-days, and in session sit
With meditations lawful?

OTHELLO   Thou dost conspire against thy
   friend, Iago,
If thou but think'st him wrong'd, and mak'st
   his ear
A stranger to thy thoughts.

IAGO   I do beseech you,
Though[9] I perchance am vicious in my guess
(As, I confess, it is my nature's plague
To spy into abuses, and oft my jealousy
Shapes faults that are not)—I entreat you
   then,
From one that so imperfectly conjects,[10]
You'ld take no notice, nor build yourself a
   trouble

Out of my scattering[11] and unsure obser-
vance.
It were not for your quiet nor your good,
Nor for my manhood, honesty, or wisdom,
To let you know my thoughts.

OTHELLO   Zounds! (What dost thou
mean?)

IAGO   Good name in man, and woman,
dear my lord,
Is the immediate jewel of our souls.
Who steals my purse steals trash. 'Tis some-
thing, nothing;
'Twas mine, 'tis his, and has been slave to
thousands;
But he that filches from me my good name
Robs me of that which not enriches him,
And makes me poor indeed.

OTHELLO   By heaven, I'll know thy
thought.

IAGO   You cannot, if my heart were in your
hand;
Nor shall not, whilst 'tis in my custody.

OTHELLO   Ha!

IAGO   O beware, my lord, of jealousy!
It is the green-ey'd monster which doth mock
The meat it feeds on.[12]

---

1 *wretch:* expression of utmost fondness
2 *of my counsel:* in my confidence
3 *conceit:* idea
4 *stops:* pauses, reticences
5 *tricks of custom:* habitual tricks

6 *close delations:* covert, involuntary accu-
sations
7 *But:* but therein
8 *leets:* synonymous with 'law-days' *(keep
leet:* hold court)
9 *Though:* supposing, granting that
10 *conjects:* imagines
11 *scattering:* random
12 *mock...feeds on:* tantalizes its victim

SCENES for Mixed Groups

The Diary of Anne Frank

dramatized by Frances Goodrich and Albert Hackett (1954) from the book *Anne Frank: Diary of a Young Girl*

Characters: ANNE FRANK—Anne is a fourteen-year-old. She is lively, polite, optimistic, and compassionate.
MR. FRANK—He is a gentle, cultured, middle-aged man with a trace of a German accent.
MARGOT FRANK—She is an eighteen-year-old who is quiet and shy.
MR. VAN DAAN—He is a tall, dignified man in his late forties.
MRS. VAN DAAN—She is a woman in her early forties.
MRS. FRANK—She is genteel and reserved. She has a slight German accent.
PETER VAN DAAN—He is a shy and awkward sixteen-year-old.

Situation: This play is based on historical fact and was inspired by Anne's diary, which was published after her death. It is the first night of the Jewish holiday of Hanukkah, the Festival of Lights. World War II is in progress, and the Frank and the Van Daan families are hiding from the Nazis on the top floor of a warehouse in Amsterdam, Holland. Mr. Frank is at the head of the table and has lit the shammes, or servant candle. All are dressed in their best; the men wear hats, and Peter wears his cap.

ANNE *(Singing)* "Oh, Hanukkah! Oh, Hanukkah! The sweet celebration."

MR. FRANK *(Rising)* I think we should first blow out the candle; then we'll have something for tomorrow night.

MARGOT But, Father, you're supposed to let it burn itself out.

MR. FRANK I'm sure that God understands shortages. *(Before blowing it out)* "Praised be Thou, oh Lord our God, who hath sustained us and permitted us to celebrate this joyous festival."

(He is about to blow out the candle when suddenly there is a crash of something falling below. They all freeze in horror, motionless. For a few seconds there is complete silence. MR. FRANK slips off his shoes. The others noiselessly follow his example. MR. FRANK turns out a light near him. He motions to PETER to turn off the center lamp. PETER tries to reach it, realizes he cannot and gets up on a chair. Just as he is touching the lamp he loses his balance. The chair goes out from under him. He falls. The iron lamp shade crashes to the floor. There is a sound of feet below, running down the stairs.)

MR. VAN DAAN *(Under his breath)* God Almighty! *(The only light left comes from the Hanukkah candle. . . . MR. FRANK creeps over to the stairwell and stands listening. The dog is heard barking excitedly.)* Do you hear anything?

MR. FRANK *(In a whisper)* No. I think they've gone.

MRS. VAN DAAN It's the Green Police. They've found us.

MR. FRANK   If they had, they wouldn't have left. They'd be up here by now.

MRS. VAN DAAN   I know it's the Green Police. They've gone to get help. That's all. They'll be back!

MR. VAN DAAN   Or it may have been the Gestapo, looking for papers.

MR. FRANK   *(Interrupting)* Or a thief, looking for money.

MRS. VAN DAAN   We've got to do something—Quick! Quick! Before they come back.

MR. VAN DAAN   There isn't anything to do. Just wait. *(MR. FRANK holds up his hand for them to be quiet. He is listening intently. There is complete silence as they all strain to hear any sound from below. Suddenly ANNE begins to sway. With a low cry she falls to the floor in a faint. MRS. FRANK goes to her quickly, sitting beside her on the floor and taking her in her arms.)*

MRS. FRANK   Get some water, please! Get some water! *(MARGOT starts for the sink.)*

MR. VAN DAAN   *(Grabbing MARGOT)* No! No! No one's going to run water!

MR. FRANK   If they've found us, they've found us. Get the water. *(MARGOT starts again for the sink. MR. FRANK, getting a flashlight)* I'm going down. *(MARGOT rushes to him, clinging to him. ANNE struggles to consciousness.)*

MARGOT   No, Father, no! There may be someone there waiting. It may be a trap!

MR. FRANK   This is Saturday. There is no way for us to know what has happened until Miep or Mr. Kraler comes on Monday morning. We cannot live with this uncertainty.

MARGOT   Don't go, Father!

MRS. FRANK   Hush, darling, hush. *(MR. FRANK slips quietly out, down the steps and out through the door below.)* Margot! Stay close to me. *(MARGOT goes to her mother.)*

MR. VAN DAAN   Shush! Shush! *(MRS. FRANK whispers to MARGOT to get the water. MARGOT goes for it.)*

MRS. VAN DAAN   Putti, where's our money? Get our money. I hear you can buy the Green Police off, so much a head. Go upstairs quick! Get the money!

MR. VAN DAAN   Keep still!

MRS. VAN DAAN   *(Kneeling before him, pleading)* Do you want to be dragged off to a concentration camp? Are you going to stand there and wait for them to come up and get you? Do something, I tell you!

MR. VAN DAAN   *(Pushing her aside)* Will you keep still? *(He goes over to the stairwell to listen. PETER goes to his mother, helping her up onto the sofa. There is a second of silence, then ANNE can stand it no longer.)*

ANNE   Someone go after Father! Make Father come back!

PETER   *(Starting for the door)* I'll go.

MR. VAN DAAN   Haven't you done enough? *(He pushes PETER roughly away. In his anger against his father PETER grabs a chair as if to hit him with it, then puts it down, burying his face in his hands. MRS. FRANK begins to pray softly.)*

ANNE   Please, please, Mr. Van Daan. Get Father.

MR. VAN DAAN   Quiet! Quiet! *(ANNE is shocked into silence. MRS. FRANK pulls her closer, holding her protectively in her arms.)*

MRS. FRANK   *(Softly, praying)* "I lift up mine eyes unto the mountains, from whence cometh my help. My help cometh from the Lord who made heaven and earth. He will not suffer thy foot to be moved. He that keepeth thee will not slumber . . ." *(She stops as she hears someone coming. They all watch the door tensely. MR. FRANK comes quietly in. ANNE rushes to him, holding him tight.)*

MR. FRANK   It was a thief. The noise must have scared him away.

MRS. VAN DAAN   Thank God.

A Raisin in the Sun
by Lorraine Hansberry (1959)

Characters: BENEATHA—She is about twenty years old, slim, intense, and educated. She is going to school to become a doctor at a time when women weren't encouraged or expected to pursue such a profession.
WALTER—Walter Lee Younger is a lean man in his mid-thirties. He is struggling to retain his self-esteem in the face of family and financial obstacles.
RUTH—She is Walter's wife, about thirty years old, a gentle, maternal woman who looks disappointed. She wants a happier household.

Situation: Written by an African American playwright, this play is set in Chicago's South Side, sometime after World War II. A cramped apartment is home to an African American family: Walter, his mother Lena, his sister Beneatha, his wife Ruth, and their son Travis.

WALTER   *(Senselessly)* How is school coming?

BENEATHA   *(In the same spirit)* Lovely. Lovely. And you know, Biology is the greatest. *(Looking up at him)* I dissected something that looked just like you yesterday.

WALTER   I just wondered if you've made up your mind and everything.

BENEATHA   *(Gaining in sharpness and impatience prematurely)* And what did I answer yesterday morning—and the day before that—?

RUTH   *(Crossing back to ironing board R., like someone disinterested and old)* Don't be so nasty, Bennie.

BENEATHA   *(Still to her brother)* And the day before that and the day before that!

WALTER   *(Defensively)* I'm interested in you. Something wrong with that? Ain't many girls who decide—

WALTER and BENEATHA   *(In unison)* — "to be a doctor." *(Silence)*

WALTER   Have we figured out yet just exactly how much medical school is going to cost?

BENEATHA   *(Rises, exits to bathroom. Knocks on the door)* Come on out of there, please! *(Re-enters)*

RUTH   Walter Lee, why don't you leave that girl alone and get out of here to work?

WALTER *(Looking at his sister intently)* You know the check is coming tomorrow.

BENEATHA *(Turning on him with a sharpness all her own. She crosses D.R. and sprawls on sofa.)* That money belongs to Mama, Walter, and it's for her to decide how she wants to use it. I don't care if she wants to buy a house or a rocket ship or just nail it up somewhere and look at it—it's hers. Not ours—hers.

WALTER *(Bitterly)* Now ain't that fine! You just got your mother's interests at heart, ain't you, girl? You such a nice girl—but if Mama got that money she can always take a few thousand and help you through school too—can't she?

BENEATHA I have never asked anyone around here to do anything for me!

WALTER No! But the line between asking and just accepting when the time comes is big and wide—ain't it!

BENEATHA *(With fury)* What do you want from me, Brother—that I quit school or just drop dead, which!

WALTER *(Rises, crosses down back of sofa)* I don't want nothing but for you to stop acting holy around here—me and Ruth done made some sacrifices for you—why can't you do something for the family?

RUTH Walter, don't be dragging me in it.

WALTER You are in it—Don't you get up and go work in somebody's kitchen for the last three years to help put clothes on her back—?

(BENEATHA rises, crosses, sits armchair D.R.)

RUTH Oh, Walter—that's not fair—

WALTER It ain't that nobody expects you to get on your knees and say thank you, Brother; thank you, Ruth; thank you, Mama—and thank you, Travis, for wearing the same pair of shoes for two semesters—

BENEATHA *(In front of sofa, falls on her knees)* WELL—I DO—ALL RIGHT? THANK EVERYBODY—AND FORGIVE ME FOR EVER WANTING TO BE ANYTHING AT ALL—FORGIVE ME, FORGIVE ME! *(She rises, crosses D.R. to armchair.)*

RUTH Please stop it! Your Mama'll hear you.

WALTER *(Crosses U.C. to kitchen table. Ties shoes at chair R. of table)*—Who . . . told you you had to be a doctor? If you so crazy 'bout messing around with sick people—then go be a nurse like other women—or just get married and be quiet—

BENEATHA *(Crossing toward L. end of sofa)* Well—you finally got it said—It took you three years but you finally got it said. Walter, give up; leave me alone—it's Mama's money.

WALTER HE WAS MY FATHER, TOO!

BENEATHA So what? He was mine, too—and Travis' grandfather—BUT the insurance money belongs to Mama. Picking on me is not going to make her give it to you to invest in any liquor stores—*(Sits armchair D.R. Under her breath)* And I for one say, God bless Mama for that!

(On BENEATHA'S line RUTH crosses U.L. to closet.)

WALTER *(To RUTH)* See—did you hear?— Did you hear!

RUTH *(Crosses D.C. to WALTER with WALTER's jacket from the closet)* Honey, please go to work.

WALTER *(Back of sofa, crosses U.C. to door)* Nobody in this house is ever going to understand me.

BENEATHA Because you're a nut.

WALTER *(Stops, turns D.C.)* Who's a nut?

BENEATHA You—You are a nut. Thee is mad, boy.

WALTER *(Looking at his wife and sister from the door, very sadly)* The world's most backward race of people, and that's a fact. *(Exits C.)*

BENEATHA *(Turning slowly in her chair)* And then there are all those prophets who would lead us out of the wilderness—*(Rises, crosses U.C. to chair R. of kitchen table. Sits. WALTER slams out of the house.)* Into the swamps!

RUTH Bennie, why you always gotta be pickin' on your brother? Can't you be a little sweeter sometimes?

(Door opens. WALTER walks in.)

WALTER *(To RUTH)* I need some money for carfare.

RUTH *(Looks at him, then warms, teasing, but tenderly)* Fifty cents? *(She crosses D.L. front of table, gets her purse from handbag.)* Here, take a taxi.

Letters to a Student Revolutionary
by Elizabeth Wong (1989)

Characters: KAREN—A modern young Chinese woman, Karen is not content with the choices she is offered by life in China. As a young girl, she had witnessed her mother being captured and executed.

BROTHER—Karen's brother, a devoted Communist soldier, believes that the individual is not important. He proved his loyalty to the state many years ago when he reported his mother for stealing food to feed her children and then witnessed her execution.

LU YAN—As married students, Lu Yan and Karen are active in the student movement for democracy.

Situation: In this play, Chinese American playwright Elizabeth Wong explores the choices that are open to women today in two very different cultures. Karen and Lu Yan optimistically take part in the student demonstrations for freedom in Tiananmen Square. Karen has been corresponding with Bibi, a Chinese American woman, who writes to her about democracy and freedom.

[Lights up on BROTHER, LU YAN, and KAREN who are lying on a plateau on a mountainside.]

KAREN Look at that sky. I see a dragon coiling ready to spring. I see a water buffalo. There's a big fat lumbering pig. That's you.

BROTHER I feel restless. It's funny to feel so restless.

LU YAN Ask Bibi to send us a copy of this Bill of Rights.

BROTHER What is this "pursuit of happiness"? Even if I were to have it, I would not know how to go about this "pursuit of happiness."

LU YAN I think to be on Lotus Mountain is what is meant by "life, liberty and the pursuit of happiness."

KAREN *(To* BROTHER*)* It means even *you* would count for something, you good for nothing.

BROTHER Oh? Who is lazy and who is not? I have written a novel.

LU YAN So why do you hide it?

BROTHER Because I am a bad novelist.

KAREN Well then, your book will be very popular.

LU YAN I think I will be a teacher in a great university. I have already applied for a transfer.

BROTHER Impossible.

LU YAN Maybe.

KAREN If only I could leave my job. I hate accounting.

LU YAN You do?

BROTHER I didn't know that.

KAREN Bibi sends me many fashion magazines. Only Bibi knows how I wish to be a designer of great fashion for very great ladies.

BROTHER Burlap sacks for old bags.

KAREN Lace, all lace and chiffon.

LU YAN You would look beautiful.

KAREN Not for me. For the people. I would be a dress designer and go to. . . .

LU YAN Paris?

BROTHER London?

KAREN America.

LU YAN People would clap and say, "Ahhh, of course, a Karen original."

BROTHER People will say, "How ugly. I will not wear this in a million years."

KAREN I would have a name. Then once I am famous as a clothes designer, I will quit and I would do something else. Maybe be a forest ranger.

BROTHER Or a fireman.

LU YAN Or an astronaut.

BROTHER Or a member of the central committee.

LU YAN Hah! You must be very old to be a member of the central committee.

KAREN Yes, a fossil. *(Beat)* Is it possible to be a somebody?

BROTHER Yes, I am a grain of sand!

KAREN A piece of lint.

LU YAN Those old men on the central committee. What do they know about us? Perhaps we should all take up our books and stone the committee with our new ideas.

BROTHER Lu Yan thinks he can change the world. But I'm telling you if we are patient, all things will come. *(Beat)* Things that die allow new things to grow and flourish.

KAREN Oh, my brother is a philosopher.

LU YAN No, he is right. They will die off and leave us with a nation of students. No politicians. Just you and me and Karen.

KAREN   Three wolves on the mountainside, sitting in the sun.

LU YAN   Change is sure to come.

KAREN   This is changing me.

(KAREN *indicates a small pile of books.*)

LU YAN   (*Looks at the titles*) Hemingway. Martin Luther King.

KAREN   Bibi sent them to me. And this.

(KAREN *turns on a tape recorder. The music is Karen Carpenter's "We've Only Just Begun." They listen.*)

The Dramatic Circle
by Adrienne Kennedy (1992)

Characters: SUZANNE ALEXANDER—Waiting in London for her husband to return from a dangerous mission in Africa, Suzanne Alexander is plagued with breathlessness, sleepwalking, and hysteria.
ALICE ALEXANDER—Helpless to comfort her sister-in-law, Alice Alexander can only accompany her to the American Embassy every day to inquire about her missing brother and to try to keep up her own optimism.
DR. FREUDENBERGER—A compassionate and perceptive physician, Dr. Freudenberger has a premonition that Professor Alexander might be enduring hardships and that his wife Suzanne might also be victimized. To prepare Suzanne for the darkness he knows she must face, the doctor introduces Suzanne and Alice to the classic novel *Dracula.* The group reads an excerpt from Dr. Stewart's diary in which he goes through bad times, and a woman, Lucy, is the victim of an unfair, tragic attack.

Situation: This radio play by African American playwright Adrienne Kennedy grew from a time in her own past when she waited in London for three weeks for her husband to return from Africa. In this scene, the two American women, desperate to escape their nerve-wracking and lonely waiting for even a little while, join a group that meets to read aloud from the classics.

DR. FREUDENBERGER   Your sister-in-law and I have had a good talk. I was thinking, since you're both here waiting for Professor Alexander, perhaps you'd welcome a little diversion. I'd like to invite you both to my home. My wife and I have a dramatic circle. We're currently reading Bram Stoker's *Dracula.* Readings will distract you both while you're waiting for Professor Alexander. Suzanne, you could read the role of Lucy, and Alice, you might read Mina. My house is in the Little Boltons.

ALICE ALEXANDER   Very well. Thank you, we are lonely. We know no one here. We're to see a West African writer, but he's in Paris. We will be happy to come to your dramatic circle.

DR. FREUDENBERGER   Lovely. Please come this evening, you're nearby. My wife, Heike, is a translator. She makes tea. We have sherry.

ALICE ALEXANDER   Thank you.

SUZANNE ALEXANDER   Thank you. Goodbye, Dr. Freudenberger.

ALICE ALEXANDER   Goodbye, Dr. Freudenberger.

DR. FREUDENBERGER   Oh no, please, please. I'm Sebastian.

(*Overlapping goodbyes*)

ALICE ALEXANDER   As we left I heard Dr. Freudenberger reading the paper I'd given him.

DR. FREUDENBERGER   "My life was transformed. Violence flared savagely when mobs appeared and the courtyards of the Tuileries ran with the blood of Swiss Guards. Danger struck everywhere."

(Music—Wagner chorus. Dramatic circle greetings)

ALICE ALEXANDER   We arrived at eight for the reading of *Dracula.* Dr. Freudenberger's parlor was small and dark with water-stained gold-and-white wallpaper. His tall wife, Heike, poured tea. Dr. Freudenberger sat behind a large desk, we read from crimson books. He had a giant handwritten script. We later discovered that all the participants were his patients. We read sitting in a circle.

(Music and voices in background)

DR. FREUDENBERGER   Ladies and gentlemen, please, everyone. We have two new actors tonight. They're both from America. I've invited them here to join us while they're here in England. In fact, both are writers themselves. Mrs. Alexander, Suzanne, writes essays and plays and Miss Alexander, Alice, writes poetry. So, let us begin.

Dracula, Chapter 15. Dr. Stewart's diary continued: "For a while sheer anger mastered me, it was as if he had, during her life, struck Lucy on the face. I smote the table hard and rose up as I said to him, 'Dr. Helsing, are you mad?' He raised his head and looked at me. And somehow the tenderness of his face calmed me at once. 'Would that I were. My madness were easy to bear compared with truth like this. Oh, my friend, why think you did I go so far round? Why take so long to tell you so simple a thing? Was it because I hate you and have hated you all my life? Was it because I wished to give you pain? Was it that I wanted now so late revenge for that time when you saved my life from a fearful death?'"

WOMAN   *(Reading)*: "'Oh, no. Forgive me,' said I. He went on."

WOMAN   *(Reading)*: "We found the child awake."

DR. FREUDENBERGER   "It had had a sleep and taken some food and altogether was going on well. Dr. Vincent took the bandage from its throat and showed us the punctures. There was no mistaking the similarity to those which had been on Lucy's throat. They were smaller and the edges looked fresher, that was all. We asked Vincent to what he attributed them and he replied that it must have been a bite of some animal, perhaps a rat, but for his own part he was inclined to think that it was one of the bats which are so numerous on the northern heights of London. 'Out of so many harmless ones,' he said, 'there may be some wild specimen from the south of a more malignant species. Some sailor may have brought one home and it managed to escape or even from the zoological gardens a young one may have got loose, or one he bred there from a vampire. These things do occur, you know. Only ten days ago a wolf got out, and was, I believe, traced up in this direction. For a week after the children were playing nothing but Red Ridinghood on the heath. And in every alley on the place until this bloofer lady scare came along. Since then it has been quite a gala time with them. Even this poor little mite when he woke up today asked the nurse if he might go away.'"

(Music. Voices)

ALICE ALEXANDER   After reading *Dracula* we had tea and sherry and listened to music. Dr. Freudenberger pulled his chair next to the divan.

(Piano music—Chopin)

DR. FREUDENBERGER   Tell me about your teaching in Ghana.

SUZANNE ALEXANDER   Oh, we teach Césaire, the plays of Wole Soyinka, Chinua Achebe and Richard Wright and many other writers.

DR. FREUDENBERGER   And do you write plays?

SUZANNE ALEXANDER   My most recent play is *She Talks to Beethoven*, a play set in Ghana about a time two years ago when David disappeared.

DR. FREUDENBERGER   He has disappeared before?

SUZANNE ALEXANDER   There were threats against his life, and he disappeared to protect me from danger.

DR. FREUDENBERGER   He must love you a great deal.

SUZANNE ALEXANDER   We went to school together as children. We won the state reading contest together.

ALICE ALEXANDER   After tea we read *Dracula* again. Then we started to say good night. Sebastian was once more at Suzanne's side.

DR. FREUDENBERGER   How do you spend your days in London?

ALICE ALEXANDER   Well, we walk all over, in Primrose Hill, Regent's Park, along Charing Cross Road. After we leave American Express we take tours of Trafalgar Square. Yesterday we went to Windsor in the rain.

SUZANNE ALEXANDER   Victoria grieved for Albert there.

ALICE ALEXANDER   In the evenings we return on the tour bus to Old Brompton Road and sit by the gas fire and write David.

SUZANNE ALEXANDER   Where is he? Where's my husband?

DR. FREUDENBERGER   Suzanne, you must rest. I'll walk you both home, you're just along the road. Perhaps I can help you. I know someone at the American Embassy, I'll ring there tomorrow. Also, another patient's daughter has lived in Ghana for years. I'll talk to her, but, Suzanne, you must not think of returning to Ghana. It might kill the baby. I forbid it.

SUZANNE ALEXANDER   I understand.

DR. FREUDENBERGER   I'll go with you to talk to the American ambassador tomorrow.

The Mask of Hiroshima
by Ernest Ferlita (1966)

Characters: CHORUS—The chorus is dressed in black and functions much like the choruses in Greek classics. The chorus recounts the human side of the dropping of the atomic bomb and recounts the details of the present.
OKUMA—He is a small Japanese man of sixty. His wife died seven years ago in the atomic

explosion. He is a tailor and wears a kimono. SHINJI—He is a Japanese man of twenty-nine who wears Western clothes. He is Okuma's son-in-law and a teacher. His wife, Hisa, is pregnant and has a fever.

Situation: The action of the play takes place in Hiroshima, Japan, in 1952, seven years after the city was destroyed by an atomic bomb. There is a bare platform at centerstage, and in front of the platform is the acting area of dream and memory. At the start of the play, the characters sit in full view of the audience. The chorus sits apart and then approaches the audience. In this scene, Okuma and Shinji discuss what is best for Hisa.

Chorus   Here we are in the city of seven
  rivers.
Seven years have passed, seven years
since that drift of elemental power
unleashed its light across our sky
to dim the rising sun.
(OKUMA *rises.*)
The man of many moons is Mister Okuma.
He is a tailor by trade.
His daughter Hisa is in bed with a fever,
and here he waits,
in the Hospital of the Red Cross.
(SHINJI *rises and paces. He walks with a slight limp.*)
Waiting with Okuma is Shinji Ishikawa.
Shinji is his son-in-law.
He is a teacher.
He remembers the last time his wife was sick.
But now there is more to fear,
for now she is with child.

OKUMA   I hope it is a boy.

SHINJI   I know that's what Hisa wants.

OKUMA   Everybody wants a boy. Some day it may be possible to decide ahead of time.

Then they will have to pass a law against
  boys.
(*Quickly*)
But I'll have you know I was very glad
when my little Hisa was born.
Yes, yes, that was a day
oversprinkled with flowers.
(*There is a rumble of thunder.*)
It is going to rain.
(SHINJI *moves a couple of paces to see if the doctor is on his way, limping slightly.* OKUMA *watches him.*)

OKUMA   I am ashamed.

SHINJI   Why?

OKUMA   I am ashamed that I alone, of
  all my family,
passed through that day unhurt.
On you, on Hisa, I see its marks so clearly;
on my wife it was the mark of death.
Why was I spared?
What god made me go alone the night before
to see my mother in Mukaihara?
"Come with me," I said to my wife.
"No," she said, "they will blow up the train."
And she begged me not to go.
When I got back and found her body,
the dark flowers of her kimono
had sucked in the sun
and left their shapes upon her skin.
(SHINJI *turns his face away. A clock strikes seven.*)

OKUMA   (*After the first stroke*)
Seven o'clock. Seven is a good number.
Nothing bad ever
happens at seven.

The Dining Room
by A. R. Gurney Jr. (1982)

Characters: FATHER—Father insists on proper speech and behavior from his children and on perfection from his maid.
ANNIE—Annie, the family maid, is hard-working and polite despite having such a perfectionist employer.
GIRL—Father's daughter, she absolutely adores him. He is affectionate toward her but is continually correcting and instructing her.
BOY—Like his sister, he adores his father; and like his sister, he is constantly being corrected or instructed.

Situation: This play has just one set, a dining room. In this play, Gurney portrays dining rooms as symbolic of the changing lifestyle of the American upper middle class. Here he portrays the dining room as it once was—the center of family life.

FATHER   Annie. . . .
(ANNIE *is almost to the kitchen door.*)

ANNIE   Yes, sir. . . .

FATHER   Did I find a seed in my orange juice yesterday morning?

ANNIE   I strained it, sir.

FATHER   I'm sure you did, Annie. Nonetheless I think I may have detected a small seed.

ANNIE   I'll strain it twice, sir.

FATHER   Seeds can wreak havoc with the digestion, Annie.

ANNIE   Yes, sir.

FATHER   They can take root. And grow.

ANNIE   Yes, sir. I'm sorry, sir.

(ANNIE *goes out.* FATHER *drinks his orange juice carefully, and reads his newspaper. A little* GIRL *sticks her head out through the dining room door.*)

GIRL   Daddy. . . .

FATHER   Yes, good morning, Lizzie Boo.

GIRL   Daddy, could Charlie and me—

FATHER   Charlie and I. . . .

GIRL   . . . Charlie and I come out and sit with you while you have breakfast?

FATHER   You certainly may, Lizzikins. I'd be delighted to have the pleasure of your company, provided—

GIRL   Yippee!

FATHER   I said, PROVIDED you sit quietly, without leaning back in your chairs, and don't fight or argue.

GIRL   (*Calling into kitchen*) He says we *can!*

FATHER   I said you *may*, sweetheart.
(*The* GIRL *comes out adoringly, followed by a little* BOY.)

GIRL   (*Kissing her* FATHER) Good morning, Daddy.

BOY   (*Kissing him too.*) Morning, Dad.
(*They settle into their seats.* ANNIE *brings out the* FATHER'S *"breakfast."*)

ANNIE   Here's your cream, sir.

FATHER   Thank you, Annie.

ANNIE   You're welcome, sir.
(ANNIE *goes out. The children watch their* FATHER.)

BOY   Dad. . . .

FATHER   Hmmm?

BOY   When do we get to have fresh cream on our shredded wheat?

GIRL   When you grow up, that's when.

FATHER   I'll tell you one thing. If there's a war, no one gets cream. If there's a war, we'll all have to settle for top of the bottle.

GIRL   Mother said she was thinking about having us eat dinner in here with you every night.

FATHER   Yes. Your mother and I are both thinking about that. And we're both looking forward to it. As soon as you children learn to sit up straight. . . . (*They quickly do.*) . . . then I see no reason why we shouldn't all have a pleasant meal together every evening.

BOY   Could we try it tonight, Dad? Could you give us a test?

FATHER   No, Charlie. Not tonight. Because tonight we're giving a small dinner party. But I hope very much you and Liz will come down and shake hands.

GIRL   I get so shy, Dad.

FATHER   Well you'll just have to learn, sweetie pie. Half of life is learning to meet people.

BOY   What's the other half, Dad?
(*Pause. The FATHER fixes him with a steely gaze.*)

FATHER   Was that a crack?

BOY   No, Dad. . . .

FATHER   That was a crack, wasn't it?

BOY   No, Dad. Really. . . .

FATHER   That sounded very much like a smart-guy wise-crack to me. And people who make cracks like that don't normally eat in dining rooms.

BOY   I didn't mean it as a crack, Dad.

FATHER   Then we'll ignore it. We'll go on with our breakfast.
(ANNIE *comes in.*)

ANNIE   (*To GIRL*) Your car's here, Lizzie. For school.

GIRL   (*Jumping up*) OK.

FATHER   (*To GIRL*) Thank you, Annie.

GIRL   Thank you, Annie. . . . (*Kisses FATHER*) Good-bye, Daddy.

FATHER   Good-bye, darling. Don't be late. Say good morning to the driver. Sit quietly in the car. Work hard. Run. Run. Good-bye.

(GIRL *goes off.* FATHER *returns to his paper. Pause.* BOY *sits watching his* FATHER.)

BOY   Dad, can I read the funnies?

FATHER   Certainly. Certainly you may.

(*He carefully extracts the second section and hands it to his son. Both read, the* BOY *trying to imitate the* FATHER *in how he does it. Finally—*)

FATHER   This won't mean much to you, but the government is systematically ruining this country.

BOY   Miss Kelly told us about the government.

FATHER   Oh, really. And who is Miss Kelly, pray tell?

BOY   She's my teacher.

FATHER   I don't remember any Miss Kelly.

BOY   She's new, Dad.

FATHER   I see. And what has she been

telling you?

BOY She said there's a depression going on.

FATHER I see.

BOY People all over the country are standing in line for bread.

FATHER I see.

BOY So the government has to step in and do something.
(*Long pause. Then—*)

FATHER Annie!

ANNIE (*Coming out of kitchen*) Yes, sir.

FATHER I'd very much like some more coffee, please.

ANNIE Yes, sir.
(ANNIE *goes out.*)

FATHER You tell Miss Kelly she's wrong.

BOY Why?

FATHER I'll tell you exactly why. If the government keeps on handing out money, no one will want to work. And if no one wants to work, there won't be anyone around to support such things as private schools. And if no one is supporting private schools, then Miss Kelly will be standing on the bread lines along with everyone else. You tell Miss Kelly that, if you please. Thank you, Annie.

(ANNIE *comes in and pours coffee.* FATHER *returns to his paper.* ANNIE *has retreated to the kitchen.* BOY *reads his funnies for a moment. Then—*)

BOY Dad. . . .

FATHER (*Reading*) Hmmm?

BOY Could we leave a little earlier today?

FATHER We'll leave when we always leave.

BOY But I'm always late, Dad.

FATHER Nonsense.

BOY I am, Dad. Yesterday I had to walk into assembly while they were still singing the hymn.

FATHER A minute or two late. . . .

BOY Everyone looked at me, Dad.

FATHER You tell everyone to concentrate on that hymn.

BOY I can't, Dad. . . .

FATHER It's that new stoplight on Richmond Avenue. It affects our timing.

BOY It's not just the new stoplight, Dad. Sometimes I come in when they're already doing arithmetic. Miss Kelly says I should learn to be punctual.

FATHER (*Putting down paper*) Miss Kelly again, eh?

BOY She said if everyone is late, no one would learn any mathematics.

FATHER Now you listen to me, Charlie. Miss Kelly may be an excellent teacher. Her factoring may be flawless, her geography beyond question. But Miss Kelly does not teach us politics. Nor does she teach us how to run our lives. She is not going to tell you, or me, to leave in the middle of a pleasant breakfast, and get caught in the bulk of the morning traffic, just so that you can arrive in time for a silly hymn. Long after you've forgotten that hymn, long after you've forgotten how to factor, long after you've forgotten Miss Kelly, you will remember these pleasant breakfasts around this dining room table.

SCENES
Monologues for Women

The Belle of Amherst
by William Luce (1978)

Character: EMILY—Emily is the historical character Emily Dickinson, a well-known nineteenth-century poet. In this scene she is fifty-three. She has auburn hair parted in the middle and drawn back to the nape of her neck. She is wearing a simple, white, full-length dress. She is a recluse who possesses tremendous inner strength.

Situation: This one-character play takes place in the Dickinson household in Amherst, Massachusetts. This monologue, set in 1883, opens the play. Emily has invited the audience to tea.

EMILY   (*She enters, carrying the teapot. She calls back over her shoulder.*) Yes, Vinnie, I have the tea, dear!

(*She places the tea on the tea cart, then looks up wide-eyed at the* AUDIENCE. *Slowly she picks up a plate with slices of dark cake on it, walks shyly downstage, and extends it to the* AUDIENCE.)

This is my introduction. Black cake. My own special recipe.

Forgive me if I'm frightened. I never see strangers and hardly know what I say. My sister, Lavinia—she's younger than I—she says I tend to wander back and forth in time. So you must bear with me. I was born December tenth, eighteen thirty, which

makes me—*fifty-three!*

Welcome to Amherst. My name is Emily Elizabeth Dickinson. Elizabeth is for my Aunt Elisabeth Currier. She's father's sister. Oh, how the trees stand up straight when they hear Aunt Libbie's little boots come thumping into Amherst! She's the only male relative on the female side.

Dear Aunt Libbie.

But I don't use my middle name anymore—since I became a *poet*.

Professor Higginson, the literary critic, doesn't think my poems are—no matter. I've had seven poems published—anonymously, to be sure. So you see why I prefer to introduce myself to you as a poet.

Here in Amherst, I'm known as Squire Edward Dickinson's half-cracked daughter. Well, I am! The neighbors can't figure me out. I don't cross my father's ground to any house or town. I haven't left the house for years.

The Soul selects her own Society—
Then—shuts the Door.
(EMILY *turns to the window, still holding the cake.*)

Why should I socialize with village gossips? There goes one of them now—Henrietta Sweetser—everyone knows Henny. She'd even intimidate the anti-Christ. Look at her! She's strolling by the house, trying to catch a glimpse of me. Would *you* like that?

So I give them something to talk about. I dress in white all year around, even in winter. "Bridal white," Henny calls it.

(*She mimics back-fence gossips.*)

"Dear, dear! Dresses in bridal white, she does, every day of the blessed year. Year in, year out. Disappointed in love as a girl, so I hear. Poor creature. All so very sad. And her sister Lavinia, a spinster too. Didn't you know? Oh, yes. Stayed unmarried just to be at home and take care of Miss Emily. Two old maids in that big house. What a lonely life, to shut yourself away from good people like us."

Indeed!

You should see them come to the door, bearing gifts, craning their necks, trying to see over Vinnie's shoulder. But I'm too fast for them. I've already run upstairs two steps at a time. And I hide there until they leave. You can imagine what they make of that!

One old lady came to the door the other day to get a peek inside. I surprised her by answering the door myself. She stammered something about looking for a house to buy.

(Mischievously)

To spare the expense of moving, I directed her to the cemetery.

A Raisin in the Sun
by Lorraine Hansberry (1959)

Character: MAMA—In her early sixties, Lena Younger is graceful, soft-spoken, and strong, both physically and emotionally. She wants her children, Walter and Beneatha, to be self-confident and well-respected, and she knows she must be the first one to make them feel that way.

Situation: Written by an African American playwright, this play is set in Chicago's South Side sometime after World War II. The apartment that the Youngers—an extended African American family—live in is cramped and shabby. In this scene, Mama finds a good use for a large share of the insurance money she received at her husband's death.

MAMA *(Crosses R. to WALTER)* Listen to me now. I say I been wrong, son. That I been doing to you what the rest of the world been doing to you. *(She turns off radio)* Walter— *(She stops and he looks up slowly at her and she meets his eyes evenly.)* what you ain't never understood is that I ain't got nothing, don't own nothing, ain't really wanted nothing that wasn't for you. There ain't nothing as precious to me—there ain't nothing worth holding on to, money, dreams, nothing else— if it means—if it means it's going to destroy my boy. *(Crosses U.R.C. to buffet for her pocketbook and money. He watches her without speaking or moving.)* I paid the man thirty-five hundred dollars down on the house. That leaves sixty-five hundred dollars. Monday morning I want you to take this money and take three thousand dollars and put it in a savings account for Beneatha's medical schooling.

(WALTER rises, crosses U.C.)

The rest you put in a checking account— with your name on it. And from now on any penny that comes out of it or that go in it is for you to look after. For you to decide. *(Puts money on coffee table and drops her hands a little helplessly)* It ain't much, but it's all I got in the world and I'm putting it in your hands. I'm telling you to be the head of this family from now on like you supposed to be.

The Effects of Gamma Rays on Man-in-the-Moon Marigolds

by Paul Zindel (1970)

Character: BEATRICE—Beatrice Hunsdorfer, a widow, is the anxious mother of two high school students, named Ruth and Matilda.

Situation: This scene takes place in the kitchen of Beatrice's house, which was converted from a vegetable store. She is calling her daughter's science teacher, Mr. Goodman, to question the safety of a project he has assigned.

BEATRICE   Mr. Goodman please. *(Pause)* How would I know if he's got a class? *(She finds a cigarette next to the hot plate.)* Hello, Mr. Goodman? Are you Mr. Goodman? Oh, I beg your pardon, Miss Torgersen. Yes, I'll wait. *(She lights her cigarette.)* Couldn't you find him, Miss Torgersen? *(Pause)* Oh! Excuse me, Mr. Goodman, how are you? I'll bet you'll never guess who this is . . . It's Mrs. Hunsdorfer—remember the frozen foods? You know, Ruth tells me she's your new secretary, and I certainly think that's a delight. *(She picks up the phone, crosses to U. of the kitchen table, puts the phone on the table, and sits.)* You were paying so much attention to Matilda that I'll bet Ruth just got jealous. She does things like that, you know. I hope she works hard for you, although I can't imagine what kind of work Ruth could be doing in that great big science office. She's a terrible snoop . . . *(Pause)* The attendance? Isn't that charming. And the cut cards! Imagine. You trust her with . . . Why I didn't know she could type *at all* . . . imagine. *(Pause)* Of course, too much work isn't good for anybody, either. No wonder she's failing everything. I mean, I never heard of a girl who failed absolutely everything regardless of what she was suffering from. I suppose I should say recovering from . . . *(Pause)* Oh, I'll tell you why I'm calling. It's about those seeds you gave Matilda. She's had them in the house for a while now and they're starting to grow. Now she tells me they had been exposed to radioactivity and I hear such terrible things about radioactivity that I naturally associate radioactivity with sterility, and it positively horrifies me to have those seeds in my living room. Couldn't she just grow plain marigolds like everyone else? *(Pause)* Oh . . . *(Pause)* It does sound like an interesting project . . . *(Pause)* No, I'm afraid that at this very moment I don't know what a *mutation* is. *(Pause)* Mr. Goodman . . . Mr. Goodman! I don't want you to think I'm not interested but please spare me definitions over the phone. I'll get down to the library next week and pick me out some little book on science and then I'll know all about mutations . . . *(Pause)*

No, you didn't insult me, but I just want you to know I'm not stupid . . . I just thought prevention was better than a tragedy, Mr. Goodman. I mean, Matilda has enough to worry about without sterility. *(She rises, picks up the phone, crosses R. and returns the phone to its shelf.)* Well, I was just concerned, but you've put my poor mother's heart at ease. You know, really, our high schools need more exciting young men like you, I really mean that. Really, I do. Goodbye, Mr. Goodman. *(She hangs up the phone, and then turns front.)*

I Remember Mama
by John van Druten (1944)

Character: KATRIN—Katrin is a petite blonde in her early twenties.

Situation: This monologue opens the play and functions as a prologue. The play takes place in and around San Francisco in 1910. Seated at a desk facing the audience, Katrin is writing a reminiscence of her childhood.

KATRIN *(Reading)* "For as long as I could remember, the house on Streiner Street had been home. Papa and Mama had both been born in Norway, but they came to San Francisco because Mama's sisters were here. All of us were born here. Nels, the oldest and the only boy—my sister Christine—and the littlest sister, Dagmar." *(She puts down her manuscript and looks out front.)* It's funny, but when I look back, I always see Nels and Christine and myself looking almost as we do today. I guess that's because the people you see all the time stay the same age in your head. Dagmar's different. She was always the baby— so I see her as a baby. Even Mama—it's funny, but I always see Mama as around forty. She couldn't *always* have been forty. *(She picks up her manuscript and starts to read again.)* "Besides us, there was our boarder, Mr. Hyde. Mr. Hyde was an Englishman who had once been an actor, and Mama was very impressed by his flowery talk and courtly manners. He used to read aloud to us in the evenings. But first and foremost, I remember Mama."

The Taming of the Shrew
by William Shakespeare (1592)

Character: KATHERINE—newly married

Situation: Katherine's husband has just instructed her to tell her headstrong women friends what they owe their husbands. Katherine (ironically?) does just that.

KATHERINE: Thy husband is thy lord, thy life, thy keeper,
Thy head, thy sovereign; one that cares for
   thee,
And for thy maintenance commits his body
To painful labour both by sea and land,
To watch the night in storms, the day in cold,
Whilst thou liest warm at home, secure and
   safe;
And craves no other tribute at thy hands
But love, fair looks and true obedience;
Too little payment for so great a debt.
Such duty as the subject owes the prince
Even such a woman oweth to her husband;
And when she is froward, peevish, sullen,
   sour,
And not obedient to his honest will,
What is she but a foul contending rebel
And graceless traitor to her loving lord?
I am ashamed that women are so simple
To offer war where they should kneel for
   peace,
Or seek for rule, supremacy and sway,
When they are bound to serve, love and obey.

. . . .

My mind hath been as big as one of yours,
My heart as great, my reason haply more,
To bandy word for word and frown for frown;
But now I see our lances are but straws,
Our strength as weak, our weakness past
   compare,

That seeming to be most which we indeed
    least are.
Then vail your stomachs, for it is no boot,
And place your hands below your husband's
    foot:
In token of which duty, if he please,
My hand is ready; may it do him ease.

I Love You, I Love You Not
by Wendy Kesselman (1988)

Character: DAISY—Daisy is a typical adolescent who is on a roller coaster of emotions. She feels that her parents are overbearing and that they do not understand her.

Situation: This play is set in the present in a country house, where Daisy is visiting her grandmother, Nana, for the weekend. Nana buys old classic books for Daisy. In this scene, Daisy's parents have called to make sure she is eating correctly and doing her homework.

[Light comes up on DAISY, *talking on the phone.]*

DAISY I hear. *(Long pause)* I hear you. *(Pause)* I hear you, Ma. *(Pause)* Okay. *(Pause)* Okay. *(Pause)* I said okay, didn't I? *(Pause)* O-KAY. *(Pause)* I'm sorry. *(Pause)* I said I was sorry. *(Pause)* I said it, didn't I? Didn't I? Didn't I just say it? *(Pause)* Well I did. *(Pause)* Well maybe you didn't hear me. *(Pause)* I'm not. *(Pause)* I'm not, Ma. *(Pause)* I'm not using a tone. *(Pause)* I am listening. *(Pause)* I—yes I am. *(Pause)* I am, I am. *(Pause)* Ma please. *(Pause)* Oh please don't. *(Pause)* Don't put him on. *(Pause)* Ma, do you have—Hi. *(Pause)* Fine. How are you? *(Pause)* Of course I heard her. I just talked to her. I am not

using a tone. Why do you two always say the exact same thing? I mean, always.

DAISY *(After a pause)* I'll practise, okay? *(Pause)* I'll eat. *(Pause)* I'm already eating. *(She grabs a piece of cake and stuffs it into her mouth.)* I'm eating, I'm eating. *(Pause)* No, I didn't. *(Pause)* Uh . . . *(Looking at Nana)* "ANNA KARENINA." *(Pause)* Just a few. Not many. *(Pause, looking at the books.)* About twenty. *(Pause)* They're not dirty. *(Pause)* They're not old. *(Pause, picking up an ancient book whose pages are falling out)* Well, maybe just a little old. *(Pause)* I have room. *(Pause)* On the top shelf. *(Pause)* The *very* top. *(Pause)* I know I can get them out of the library. *(Mumbling half to herself)* It's just not the same.

Fences
by August Wilson (1985)

Character: ROSE—She is a forty-three-year-old woman, devoted to her husband Troy and their son, Cory.

Situation: Written by an African American playwright, this play is set in 1957. It is the story of the Maxsons, who live in an ancient two-story brick house set off a small alley in a big-city neighborhood. Just before this monologue, Rose told her husband that she knows about his affair with another woman.

ROSE I been standing with you! I been right here with you, Troy. I got a life too. I gave eighteen years of my life to stand in the same spot with you. Don't you think I ever wanted other things? Don't you think I had dreams and hopes? What about my life? What about me. Don't you think it ever crossed my mind to want to know other men? That I wanted to lay up somewhere and forget about my responsibilities? That I wanted someone to make me laugh so I could feel good? You not the only one who's got wants and needs. But I held on to you, Troy. I took all my feelings, my wants and needs, my dreams . . . and I buried them inside you. I planted a seed and watched and prayed over it. I planted myself inside you and waited to bloom. And it didn't take me no eighteen years to find out the soil was hard and rocky and it wasn't never gonna bloom.

But I held on to you, Troy. I held you tighter. You was my husband. I owed you everything I had. Every part of me I could find to give you. And upstairs in that room . . . with the darkness falling in on me . . . I gave everything I had to try and erase the doubt that you wasn't the finest man in the world. And wherever you was going . . . I wanted to be there with you. Cause you was my husband. Cause that's the only way I was gonna survive as your wife. You always talking about what you give . . . and what you don't have to give. But you take too. You take . . . and don't even know nobody's giving!

The Search for Signs of Intelligent Life in the Universe
by Jane Wagner (1986)

Character: TRUDY—Insane is the first adjective that comes to mind when describing this bag lady. The truth is, Trudy is madly sane. She is brilliantly perceptive, very funny, and highly verbal. She is not intimidated by reality.

Situation: Set in modern-day Manhattan, this scene focuses on Trudy, a bag lady who wanders through the city's streets verbalizing her thoughts. This monologue opens the one-woman play.

TRUDY   Here we are, standing on the
    corner of
"Walk, Don't Walk."
You look away from me, tryin' not to catch
    my eye,
but you didn't turn fast enough, *did* you?

You don't like my *ras*py voice, do you?
I got this *ras*py voice
'cause I have to yell all the time
'cause nobody around here ever
LISTENS to me.

You don't like that I scratch so much; yes,
    and excuse me,
I scratch so much
'cause my neurons are
on *fire.*

And I admit my smile is not at its Pepsodent
    best
'cause I think my
caps must've somehow got
osteo*porosis.*

And if my eyes seem to be twirling around
    like fruit flies—
the better to see you with, my dears!

Look at me,
you mammalian-brained LUNKHEADS!
I'm not just talking to myself. I'm talking to
    you, too.
And to you
and you
and you
and you and you and you!

SCENES
Monologues for Men

Cyrano de Bergerac
by Edmond Rostand (1897)

Character: CYRANO DE BERGERAC—Captain of the Cadets of Gascoyne, Cyrano is the greatest swordsman in France, able to defeat a hundred enemies singlehandedly. He is also a wit, a poet, and a philosopher, generous and honorable. All of these impressive qualities, however, seem to be overshadowed by his astonishingly large nose.

Situation: This monologue is part of a scene in which Cyrano confesses to his friend, Le Bret, that he loves Roxanne. Le Bret tells Cyrano to reveal his love to Roxanne and assures Cyrano that he is a hero in her eyes. Cyrano responds with this speech.

CYRANO   My old friend—look at me,
And tell me how much hope remains for me
With this protuberance! Oh I have no more
Illusions! Now and then—bah! I may grow
Tender, walking alone in the blue cool
Of evening, through some garden fresh with
    flowers
After the benediction of the rain;
My poor big devil of a nose inhales
April . . . and so I follow with my eyes
Where some boy, with a girl upon his arm,
Passes a patch of silver . . . and I feel
Somehow, I wish I had a woman too,
Walking with little steps under the moon,
And holding my arm so, and smiling. Then
I dream—and I forget . . . And then I see
The shadow of my profile on the wall!

Julius Caesar
by William Shakespeare (1599)

Character: MARK ANTONY–A close friend and political ally of Julius Caesar's, Antony knows that Caesar did not want to be king of Rome.

Situation: Caesar has been assassinated for political reasons. His assassins, who include Brutus, have allowed Antony to speak at Caesar's funeral on the condition that he say nothing to make the crowd riot against the assassins, who control Rome now that Caesar is dead. Antony wants to see Caesar's assassins brought to justice.

MARK ANTONY Friends, Romans,
    countrymen, lend me your ears;
I come to bury Caesar, not to praise him.
The evil that men do lives after them;
The good is oft interred with their bones;
So let it be with Caesar. The noble Brutus
Hath told you Caesar was ambitious:
If it were so, it was a grievous fault,
And grievously hath Caesar answer'd it.
Here, under leave of Brutus and the rest—
For Brutus is an honourable man;
So are they all, all honourable men—
Come I to speak in Caesar's funeral.
He was my friend, faithful and just to me:
But Brutus says he was ambitious;
And Brutus is an honourable man.
He hath brought many captives home to
    Rome,

Whose ransoms did the general coffers fill:
Did this in Caesar seem ambitious?
When that the poor have cried, Caesar hath
    wept:
Ambition should be made of sterner stuff:
Yet Brutus says he was ambitious;
And Brutus is an honourable man.
You all did see that on the Lupercal
I thrice presented him a kingly crown,
Which he did thrice refuse: was this ambition?
Yet Brutus says he was ambitious;
And, sure, he is an honourable man.
I speak not to disprove what Brutus spoke,
But here I am to speak what I do know.
You all did love him once, not without cause:
What cause withholds you then, to mourn
    for him?
O judgement! thou art fled to brutish beasts,
And men have lost their reason. Bear with
    me:
My heart is in the coffin there with Caesar,
And I must pause till it come back to me.

[later in the same funeral oration]

If you have tears, prepare to shed them now.
You all do know this mantle: I remember
The first time ever Caesar put it on;
'Twas on a summer's evening, in his tent,
That day he overcame the Nervii:
Look, in this place ran Cassius' dagger
    through:
See what a rent the envious Casca made:
Through this the well-beloved Brutus stabb'd;
And as he pluck'd his cursed steel away,
Mark how the blood of Caesar follow'd it,
As rushing out of doors, to be resolved
If Brutus so unkindly knock'd, or no;
For Brutus, as you know, was Caesar's angel:
Judge, O you gods, how dearly Caesar loved
    him!

This was the most unkindest cut of all;
For when the noble Caesar saw him stab,
Ingratitude, more strong than traitors' arms,
Quite vanquish'd him: then burst his mighty
    heart;
And, in his mantle muffling up his face,
Even at the base of Pompey's statua,
Which all the while ran blood, great Caesar
    fell.
O, what a fall was there, my countrymen!
Then I, and you, and all of us fell down,
Whilst bloody treason flourish'd over us.
O, now you weep; and, I perceive, you feel
The dint of pity: these are gracious drops.
Kind souls, what, weep you when you but
    behold
Our Caesar's vesture wounded? Look you
    here,
Here is himself, marr'd, as you see, with trai-
    tors.

*[At the play's end, Antony stands over the
body of Brutus, who has fallen on his sword
in remorse for his part in Caesar's murder.]*

This was the noblest Roman of them all:
All the conspirators save only he
Did that they did in envy of great Caesar;
He only, in a general honest thought
And common good to all, made one of them.
His life was gentle, and the elements
So mix'd in him that Nature might stand up
And say to all the world 'This was a man!'

Wine in the Wilderness
by Alice Childress (1969)

Character: BILL—A confident artist, Bill Jameson is preparing for an exhibition.

Situation: This comedy-drama is set in a one-room apartment in a Harlem tenement building. The apartment is in a state of artistic disorder, decorated with pictures and ornaments from a variety of cultures. Bill is preparing a triptych (three paintings that combine to form one work) for an upcoming exhibition. In the following scene, Bill is about to start painting a woman named Tommy when a phone call from his agent delays him. Unbeknownst to her, Tommy represents Bill's image of a lost and abandoned African American woman.

BILL   . . . *(Phone rings. He finds an African throwcloth and hands it to her.)* Put this on. Relax, don't go way mad, and all the rest-a that jazz. Change, will you? I apologize. I'm sorry. *(He picks up the phone.)* Hello, survivor of a riot speaking. Who's calling? *(TOMMY retires behind the screen with the throw. During the conversation she undresses and wraps the throw around her. We see TOMMY and BILL, but they can't see each other.)* Sure, told you not to worry. I'll be ready for the exhibit. If you don't dig it, don't show it. Not time for you to see it yet. Yeah, yeah, next week. You just make sure your exhibition room is big enough to hold the crowds that's gonna congregate to see this fine chick I got here. *(This perks TOMMY's ears up.)* You ought to see her. The finest black woman in the world . . . No, . . . the finest *any* woman in the world . . . This gorgeous satin chick is . . . is . . . black velvet moonlight . . . an ebony queen of the universe . . . *(TOMMY can hardly believe her ears.)* One look at her and you go back to Spice Islands . . . She's Mother Africa . . . you flip, double flip. She has come through everything that has been put on her . . . *(He unveils the gorgeous woman he has painted . . . "Wine in the Wilderness." TOMMY believes he is talking about her.)* Regal . . . grand . . . magnificent, fantastic . . . You would vote her the woman you'd most like to meet on a desert island, or around the corner from anywhere. She's here with me now . . . and I don't know if I want to show her to you or anybody else . . . I'm beginnin' to have this deep attachment . . . She sparkles, man, Harriet Tubman, Queen of the Nile . . . sweetheart, wife, mother, sister, friend. . . .The night . . . a black diamond . . . A dark, beautiful dream . . . A cloud with a silvery lining . . . Her wrath is a storm over the Bahamas. "Wine in the Wilderness" . . . The memory of Africa . . . the *now* of things . . . but best of all and most important . . . She's tomorrow . . . she's my tomorrow . . .

You're a Good Man, Charlie Brown
by Clark Gesner, based on the comic strip
Peanuts by Charles M. Schulz (1968)

Character: CHARLIE BROWN—Although Charlie Brown is a bright young boy, he lacks self-confidence. He often feels lonely, depressed, and sorry for himself.

Situation: This monologue is set in a typical American school yard during lunchtime.

CHARLIE BROWN   I think lunchtime is about the worst time of the day for me. Always having to sit here alone. Of course, sometimes mornings aren't so pleasant, either—waking up and wondering if anyone would really miss me if I never got out of bed. Then there's the night, too—lying there and thinking about all the stupid things I've done during the day. And all those hours in between—when I do all those stupid things. Well, lunchtime is *among* the worst times of the day for me.

Well, I guess I'd better see what I've got. *(He opens the bag, unwraps a sandwich, and looks inside.)* Peanut butter. *(He bites and chews.)* Some psychiatrists say that people who eat peanut butter sandwiches are lonely. I guess they're right. And if you're really lonely, the peanut butter sticks to the roof of your mouth. *(He munches quietly, idly fingering the bench.)* Boy, the PTA sure did a good job of painting these benches. *(He looks off to one side.)* There's that cute little redheaded girl eating her lunch over there. I wonder what she'd do if I went over and asked her if I could sit and have lunch with her. She'd probably laugh right in my face. It's hard on a face when it gets laughed in.

There's an empty place next to her on the bench. There's no reason why I couldn't just go over and sit there. I could do that right now. All I have to do is stand up. *(He stands.)* I'm standing up. *(He sits.)* I'm sitting down. I'm a coward. I'm so much of a coward she wouldn't even think of looking at me. She hardly ever *does* look at me. In fact, I can't remember her ever looking at me. Why shouldn't she look at me? Is there any reason in the world why she shouldn't look at me? Is she so great and am I so small that she couldn't spare one little moment just to . . . *(He freezes.)* She's looking at me. *(In terror he looks one way, then another.)* She's *looking* at me.

(His head looks all around, frantically trying to find something else to notice. His teeth clench. Tension builds. Then, with one motion, he pops the paper bag over his head.)

A Thousand Clowns
by Herb Gardner (1961)

Character: MURRAY—Murray Burns is in his mid-thirties and used to write for a television situation comedy. He has been unemployed since he quit that job.

Situation: Murray has a one-room, second-floor apartment on the Lower West Side of Manhattan. Murray's older brother, Arnold, acts as Murray's agent. Here, Murray confronts his brother, whom he considers a prize example of a total conformist.

MURRAY   Oh, Arnie, you don't understand any more. You got that wide stare that people stick in their eyes so nobody'll know their head's asleep. You got to be a shuffler, a moaner. You want me to come sit and eat fruit with you and watch the clock run out. You start to drag and stumble with the rotten weight of all the people who should have been told off, all the things you should have said, all the specifications that aren't yours. The only thing you got left to reject is your food in a restaurant if they do it wrong and you can send it back and make a big fuss with the waiter. *(MURRAY turns away from ARNOLD, goes to window seat, sits down.)* Arnold, five months ago I forgot what *day* it was. I'm on the subway on my way to work and I didn't know what day it was and it scared the hell out of me. *(Quietly)* I was sitting in the express looking out the window same as every morning watching the local stops go by in the dark with an empty head and my arms folded, not feeling great and not feeling rotten, just not feeling, and for a minute I couldn't remember, I didn't know, unless I really concentrated, whether it was a Tuesday or a Thursday—or a—for a minute it could have been *any* day, Arnie—sitting in the train going through any day—in the dark through any year—Arnie, it scared the hell out of me. *(Stands up)* You got to know what day it is. You got to know what's the name of the game and what the rules are with nobody else telling you. You have to own your days and name them, each one of them, every one of them, or else the years go right by and none of them belong to you.

Man of La Mancha
The book for this musical was written by Dale Wasserman (1966).

Character: CERVANTES—A tall, thin man in his late forties, Cervantes displays a gentle courtliness. He is so honest that he is almost self-destructive. Cervantes's life is a catalog of catastrophe, and yet he never gives up hope or loses his sense of wonder at the world.

Situation: This musical play is an adaptation of *Don Quixote* by Cervantes. Born in 1547, Cervantes was a contemporary of Shakespeare. Cervantes's *Don Quixote*, set in Spain at the end of the sixteenth century, is about an idealistic knight whom everyone believes is insane. In this scene, set in a prison cell in the city of Seville, Cervantes muses about what madness actually is.

CERVANTES I have lived nearly fifty years, and I have seen life as it is. Pain, misery, hunger . . . cruelty beyond belief. I have heard the singing from taverns and the moans from bundles of filth on the streets. I have been a soldier and seen my comrades fall in battle . . . or die more slowly under the lash in Africa. I have held them in my arms at the final moment. These were men who saw life as it is, yet they died despairing. No glory, no gallant last words . . . only their eyes filled with confusion, whimpering the question: "Why?" I do not think they asked why they were dying, but why they had lived. *(He rises, and through the following speech moves into the character of DON QUIXOTE.)* When life itself seems lunatic, who knows where madness lies? Perhaps to be too practical is madness. To surrender dreams—this may be madness. To seek treasure where there is only trash. Too much sanity may be madness. And maddest of all, to see life as it is and not as it should be.

The Piano Lesson
by August Wilson (1990)

Character: BOY WILLIE—He is a thirty-year-old man who has an infectious grin and a boyishness that is apt for his name. He is brash, impulsive, talkative, and somewhat crude in speech and manner.

Situation: Boy Willie needs cash so that he can buy some land that has just been put on the market. After not having seen his sister for three years, he arrives at her house at five o'clock in the morning and tries to persuade her to sell her piano.

BOY WILLIE   Now, I'm gonna tell you the way I see it. The only thing that make that piano worth something is them carvings Papa Willie Boy put on there. That's what make it worth something. That was my great-grandaddy. Papa Boy Charles brought that piano into the house. Now, I'm supposed to build on what they left me. You can't do nothing with that piano sitting up here in the house. That's just like if I let them watermelons sit out there and rot. I'd be a fool. Alright now, if you say to me, Boy Willie, I'm using that piano. I give out lessons on it and that help me make my rent or whatever. Then that be something else. I'd have to go on and say, well, Berniece using that piano. She building on it. Let her go on and use it. I got to find another way to get Sutter's land. But Doaker say you ain't touched that piano the whole time it's been up here. So why you wanna stand in my way? See, you just looking at the sentimental value. See, that's good. That's alright. I take my hat off whenever somebody say my daddy's name. But I ain't gonna be no fool about no sentimental value. You can sit up here and look at the piano for the next hundred years and it's just gonna be a piano. You can't make more than that. Now I want to get Sutter's land with that piano. I get Sutter's land and I can go down and cash in the crop and get my seed. As long as I got the land and the seed then I'm alright. I can always get me a little something else. Cause that land give back to you. I can make me another crop and cash that in. I still got the land and the seed. But that piano don't put out nothing else. You ain't got nothing working for you. Now, the kind of man my daddy was he would have understood that. I'm sorry you can't see it that way. But that's why I'm gonna take that piano out of here and sell it.

A Few Good Men
by Aaron Sorkin (1990)

Character: JESSEP—In his forties, Jessep is a lieutenant colonel who is devoted to the Marine Corps.

Situation: Jessep is giving testimony at the court-martial of two marines charged with unofficially disciplining another marine so violently that the marine being disciplined died. This type of internal, unofficial discipline is known as a "Code Red." Jessep has just been told to tell the truth about "Code Red."

JESSEP   Captain, for the past month, this man has attempted to put the Marine Corps on trial. I think somebody . . . better address this question or people are liable to start listening to him.

[KAFFEE: Why is it impossible—?]

[JESSEP: Because you can't handle it, son. You can't handle the truth. You can't handle the sad but historic reality.]

[KAFFEE: What reality are you referring to, Colonel?]

JESSEP   We live in a world that has walls. And those walls have to be guarded by men with guns. Who's gonna do it? You? *(To Sam)* You, Lt. Weinberg? I have a greater responsibility than you can possibly fathom. You weep for Santiago, and you curse the Marines. You have that luxury. The luxury of the blind. The luxury of not knowing what I know: That Santiago's death, while tragic, probably saved lives. And my existence, while grotesque and incomprehensible to you . . . saves lives. You can't handle it. Because deep down, in places you don't talk about, you *want* me on that wall. You need me there. We use words like honor, code, loyalty. We use these words as a backbone to a life spent defending something. You use them as a punchline. I have neither the time nor the inclination to explain myself to a man who rises and sleeps under the blanket of the very freedom I provide, then questions the manner in which I provide it. I'd prefer you just said thank you and went on your way. Otherwise, I'd suggest you pick up a weapon and stand a post.

My Children! My Africa!
by Athol Fugard (1989)

Character: MR. M—A schoolteacher in a black township in South Africa, Mr. M is a truly inspiring teacher who helps young people navigate the treacherous waters of apartheid.

Situation: After learning that his brightest students have organized an illegal political action committee, Mr. M reports them to the police.

MR. M   We were on our way to a rugby match at Somerset East. The lorry stopped at the top of the mountain so that we could stretch our legs and relieve ourselves. It was a hard ride on the back of that lorry. The road hadn't been tarred yet. So there I was, ten years old and sighing with relief as I aimed for the little bush. It was a hot day. The sun right over our heads . . . not a cloud in the vast blue sky. I looked out . . it's very high up there at the top of the pass . . . and there it was, stretching away from the foot of the mountain, the great pan of the Karoo . . . stretching away forever, it seemed, into the purple haze and heat of the horizon. Something grabbed my heart at that moment, my soul, and squeezed it until there were tears in my eyes. I had never seen anything so big, so beautiful in all my life. I went to the teacher who was with us and asked him: "Teacher, where will I come to if I start walking that way" . . . and I pointed. He laughed. "Little man," he said, "that way is north. If you start walking that way and just keep on walking, and your legs don't give in, you will see all of Africa! Yes, Africa, little man! You will see the great rivers of the continent: the Vaal, the Zambesi, the Limpopo, the Congo and then the mighty Nile. You will see the mountains: the Drakensberg, Kilimanjaro, Kenya and the Ruwenzori. And you will meet all our brothers: the little Pygmies of the forests, the proud Masai, the Watusi . . . tallest of the tall and the Kikuyu standing on one leg like herons in a pond waiting for a frog." "Has teacher seen all that?" I asked. "No," he said. "Then how does teacher know it's there?" "Because it is all in the books and I have read the books and if you work hard in school, little man, you can do the same without worrying about your legs giving in."

He was right, Thami. *I* have seen it. It is all there in the books just as he said it was and I have made it mine. I can stand on the banks of all those great rivers, look up at the majesty of all those mountains, whenever I want to. It is a journey I have made many times. Whenever my spirit was low and I sat alone in my room, I said to myself: Walk, Anela! Walk! . . . and I imagined myself at the foot of the Wapadsberg setting off for that horizon that called me that day forty years ago. It always worked! When I left that little room, I walked back into the world a proud man, because I was an African and all the splendor was my birthright.

(Pause) I don't want to make that journey again, Thami. There is someone waiting for me now at the end of it who has made a mockery of all my visions of splendor. He has in his arms my real birthright. I saw him on the television in the Reverend Mbop's lounge. An Ethiopian tribesman, and he was carrying the body of a little child that had died of hunger in the famine . . . a small bundle carelessly wrapped in a few rags. I couldn't tell how old the man was. The lines of despair and starvation on his face made him look as old as Africa itself.

He held that little bundle very lightly as he shuffled along to a mass grave, and when he reached it, he didn't have the strength to kneel and lay it down gently . . . He just opened his arms and let it fall. I was very upset when the program ended. Nobody had thought to tell us his name and whether he was the child's father, or grandfather, or uncle. And the same for the baby! Didn't it have a name? How dare you show me one of our children being thrown away and not tell me its name! I demand to know who is in that bundle!

(Pause) Not knowing their names doesn't matter anymore. They are more than just themselves. The tribesmen and dead child do duty for all of us, Thami. Every African soul is either carrying that bundle or in it.

What is wrong with this world that it wants to waste you all like that . . . my children . . . my Africa! *(Holding out a hand as if he wanted to touch Thami's face)* My beautiful and proud young Africa!

Application
ACTIVITIES

Scenes

1. From "A Treasury of Scenes and Monologues," choose a scene for two people that you will direct. Review the entire play to better understand the characters and the subtext of the scene. Hold auditions for the parts (pp. 349–355) and issue critiques (p. 336). After you have cast the roles, review the different approaches to characterization as well as stage business and blocking found in Chapter 4. Hold several practices, and then present your scene to the class. After you have directed the short scene, try directing a short play or a longer scene.

2. The time and place in which a play is written often have a tremendous effect on the work. Select one of the scenes from "A Treasury of Scenes and Monologues" and research the history of its setting. Also, investigate the trends in theater at the time (see Chapter 7). After doing this, evaluate and analyze the historical and cultural influences on the play. Does the play directly reflect its time period? Does it follow the trends in the theater at that time? Describe the effects in an essay. Cite examples from the play.

3. Working in a group, choose a scene from "A Treasury of Scenes and Monologues" and focus on portraying the particular time period and culture that are represented in that selection. This may take some research. As you prepare the selection for presentation, pay close attention to dialect (see pages 147–150), costumes (see Chapter 12), and the characterization (see Chapter 4). Make sure your portrayal is a valid representation of the culture and the time.

Monologues

1. Choose a monologue from "A Treasury of Scenes and Monologues" and study it carefully in the context of the entire play. Present your interpretation of the monologue to the class. You might choose to rewrite or reword the selection, placing it in another time period or setting. It is important to simplify or intensify the meaning for your audience. Remember that this should not be a word-for-word presentation, but your interpretation of the work.

2. Choose a character from one of the monologues. Study the monologue within the context of the entire play. Either write a response to that monologue in the voice of the character who is addressed or rewrite the monologue in any voice you choose. Deliver your monologue to the class, emphasizing the emotions that the original monologue stimulated.

Readers Theater

*P*lays that might be difficult to stage can often be presented from scripts by a reader or a group of readers. Strictly speaking, **readers theater** is not acting, but it is most definitely theater. In readers theater, a reader serves as the medium to bring the drama and its characters before an audience. Through voice, facial expressions, and controlled but meaningful gestures and stances, the reader creates an imaginary stage peopled with interesting characters.

The appeal of readers theater depends on the interpreters' capacity, through vocal and facial expression, to involve the audience emotionally in the ideas of the author. Unlike conventional theater, the action in readers theater is imaginary rather than physical.

Readers theater takes many forms. The possibilities are limited only by the imagination. The subject matter can be any form of literature: poems, novels, short stories, or plays. It might involve many readers or a single reader. It can include an introduction, selected scenes, narrative connections, or summaries of certain portions of the action. Stage sets, lighting, and costumes are always simplified. Although by using simple movements a reader might provide a general impression of a character, the play is actually being read to the audience—there is no illusion of a fourth wall.

READINGS BY ONE PERSON

Platform readings of a play by one person usually take one of two different forms: a play review or a dramatic reading. In the former, the play is presented through selected scenes in conjunction with a well-prepared discussion of the author and the literary value of the play. In the latter, the

play, usually in condensed form, is read without comments or possibly with a short introduction and narrative connections between scenes. Some dramatic readings, called **monodramas,** involve "becoming" a single character or the author. Although these two forms of platform readings differ in their purposes and their degrees of formality, both require careful selection and editing of the play and any connecting or background material.

In selecting the literature for presentation, always consider the audience that will hear it. Your selection should not only suit your talents but should also be one you thoroughly enjoy. Your enthusiasm will be contagious.

Because both the play review and the dramatic reading involve interpretation, the principles that apply to all work in drama apply here. You must understand the play as a whole and how the specific selection you have chosen to read contributes to it. You must understand every character you present, including his or her relationship to other characters and to the theme of the entire play. You must be able to re-create their emotions in your presentation.

One-person readings require attention to the following elements:

A dramatic reading requires a simplification of the play, reducing descriptive and informative material and emphasizing compelling situations.

Play Reviews

- Choose passages for reading that are interesting in themselves. They should serve to exemplify the author's style as well as to bring out the personalities of the characters.
- Choose passages that lend themselves to effective reading. Occasionally it is wise to read one act in its entirety, but usually cuttings from a number of scenes are more interesting.
- Take particular care in condensing the plot. Read and study the play thoroughly; then consult any available sources for concise summary information.
- Avoid boring your audience with lengthy discourses on the author's philosophy and literary style.

- Before performing the scenes from the play, briefly describe the main characters. If possible, quote lines that characterize them, using either their own lines or those of other characters.

Dramatic Readings

- Choose passages with strong emotional appeal, preferably with an intermingling of humor and pathos.
- Reduce all descriptive and informative material to a minimum, leaving only compelling situations that lead up to a dramatic climax.
- Choose contrasting characters so they will be easily identified.
- Assume a suitable voice and move sufficiently to suggest the posture and location of each character when he or she speaks.
- Give necessary stage directions, and describe the set clearly. Although subordinate to the dialogue, these should never be presented casually.

GROUP READINGS

A play read by a cast demands careful planning and rehearsal. The play, of course, must be cut carefully to make the action flow properly. The main thrust of the plot must be clear; detailed subplots and lengthy speeches should be eliminated. The passages containing the best scenes of conflict and those essential to the theme should be retained.

In readings of this type, it is sometimes necessary to have a narrator read any introductory or descriptive material and summarize important parts that have been omitted. The narrator can affect the entire presentation, perhaps more than any other person. Situated outside the cast on a platform or behind a lectern, the narrator must have a voice that is clear and pleasing. An effective narrator must possess a strong sense of timing and climax.

Group readings offer unusual opportunities for creative presentations. If you have black or very dark drapes, the performers can wear black clothes and be lighted by spots so only their faces stand out. Spotlights or other individual lighting units work well against neutral curtains, screens, and walls. The performers might stand behind music stands or sit on stools. The stage might contain essential furniture, and the performers might dress in limited costumes to bring more reality to their roles. Settings and costumes, however, should help to create an illusion, so they should not be too striking or realistic. Group readings can take several popular forms.

Choral Reading In a choral reading, a number of actors serve as a chorus or as a narrator. They speak or chant lines individually, in small alternating groups, or in unison. Choral reading can be a powerful form of theater if the script is carefully designed.

Chamber Theater Chamber theater takes a non-dramatic literary work, such as a short story, a children's tale, or an essay, and turns it into a script. Stage directions and narrative phrases are often read. Lines are not necessarily limited to the one actor reading the part; they can even be broken into fragments and read by other actors.

Combination Reading and Performing This type of readers theater combines reading actors and performing actors. As the readers deliver the lines, the performing actors pantomime the action. This approach works well with children's theater and can be varied in many ways. For example, children might be invited to participate by furnishing sounds or by becoming objects, such as trees or doors.

BENEFITS OF READERS THEATER

One great advantage of readers theater is that it does not require memorization, so rehearsal time can be spent developing interpretation skills. Therefore, when a readers theater production is being cast, careful attention must be given to vocal effectiveness and facial flexibility.

Readers theater offers unique opportunities for actors. It is the only form of theater in which one person can take two or more parts without the help of makeup or costume. Because of its focus on the script, readers theater offers excellent opportunities for actors to perfect their interpretive skills while involving the audience in a genuine dramatic experience.

Group readings, such as *Love Letters,* by A. R. Gurney Jr., performed here by Kitty Carlisle Hart and Tony Randall, allow readers theater to be creative and flexible.

Part THREE

Appreciating the Drama

The history and development of drama mirrors human history and development. Today drama continues to be a universal means of expressing emotions and ideas. (Play: *Two Gentlemen of Verona*)

5 *The Structure of Drama*

In this scene early in Shakespeare's *Romeo and Juliet*, the two main characters, children from feuding families, meet and fall in love. The situations that arise from this initial incident provide the action in this classic tragedy.

Drama is life with the dull bits cut out.

—ALFRED HITCHCOCK, DIRECTOR

SETTING THE SCENE

Focus Questions

What are the narrative essentials of a written play?

What influence has Aristotle had on drama?

How does modern drama differ from traditional drama?

What does the exposition of a play reveal?

How is a plot divided into parts?

How do playwrights create characters?

What is the theme of a play?

How do playwrights use dialogue, action, and situation?

Vocabulary

protagonist	mood	plot	soliloquy	dialogue
exposition	preliminary	antagonist	theme	action
atmosphere	situation	denouement	moral	situation

The play is the central element of the art of theater. It is brought to life by the actors; expressed through the media of color, light, and movement against a background of stage and scenery; and unified by the creative vision of the director.

A play has four narrative essentials: exposition, plot, characters, and theme. These four elements are communicated through the dialogue and action of a drama. The way the playwright arranges and presents these four narrative essentials is the structure of the play.

Whatever the future structure of drama may be, the plays that will survive will be those that reveal the heights and depths of human experience and serve as an uplifting and creative force in civilization.

❦ Tradition and Innovation in Drama

An early attempt to identify the basic principles of playwriting came from the Greek philosopher Aristotle (384–322 B.C.) in the *Poetics*. As part of his discussion of tragedy, he describes what he considered to be the key elements of a successful play. He stresses that drama is an imitation of life, that we learn through imitation, and that learning something is the greatest pleasure in life. Aristotle also points out that human happiness or misery takes the form of action. He therefore identifies plot as the most important element of a play.

Aristotle's Key Elements of a Play

- Spectacle (the visible part of a play)
- Sound (the audible part of a play, especially a poetic play)
- Diction (language)
- Character (a person in a play)
- Reasoning (the way speech is used to present all aspects of the play, including the production of emotions such as pity, terror, and anger)
- Plot (the action and events of a play)

Aristotle maintained that the action must have unity: it must be complete in itself, with a beginning, a middle, and an end. Events must occur in logical order and must reach a plausible conclusion. The actions and speech of the main character, called the **protagonist**, must be believable. The protagonists should be "average or better" persons who experience happiness or misery as a result of their reactions to the situations of the plot. The resolution of the action in a tragedy should purge the emotions of the audience through pity and fear and reveal a universal truth.

Aristotle's theories gradually came to be considered rules, and these have been applied through the years by many dramatists. Although Aristotle calls only for unity of action and briefly mentions unity of time, the French and Italian neoclassicists of the sixteenth century set up rules requiring the use of three unities: time, action, and place. Their rules demanded that a play should consist of one action that occurs in one place within one twenty-four-hour period. The three unities became essential in French classical tragedy.

Later playwrights disregarded many of the traditional rules. There was a tradition, for example, for all plays to be divided into three or five acts. The climax came at the end of the second act in three-act plays and at the end of the third act in five-act plays. Now many plays consist of two parts or of several scenes with a single intermission or, occasionally, no intermission at all. This change affected what, for many years, had been accepted as the traditional plot structure.

Another trend in recent years is that playwrights' styles have been influenced by the type of stage for which a play is intended. Today the open stage is increasingly used. Unlike the **proscenium arch,** which strictly separates the audience from the actors, the open stages—the arena, and the thrust stage—eliminate the principle of aesthetic distance, the reminder that a play is a play and not reality. The resulting intimacy, along with the lack of realistic sets and stage curtains, affects the styles playwrights use for their plays.

Narrative Essentials

Despite modern innovations and experimentation, the traditional structure of drama still dominates the theatrical scene. Since you are studying the art of the theater, it is necessary for you to understand the four-part structure of the traditional drama.

EXPOSITION

As soon as possible after a play begins, the audience must know what kind of play is being presented, where and when it is taking place, who the leading characters are, and in what situations and conflicts they find themselves. These facts constitute the literary setting. The process of making them apparent to the audience is called the **exposition**. Playwrights know that exposition is necessary, but at the same time they realize that information without action is often uninteresting. A skillfully written exposition is brief and unobtrusive. It tells the *where, when, why*, and *who* in a subtle way. Today the time and the place in which the play is set are usually printed clearly in the program. Sometimes a playwright has a character state the facts. Shakespeare did this many times because he had no scenery to show the place and no programs to supply the information. In *Twelfth Night*, for example, the captain says to Viola, "This is Illyria, lady." The entire scene that follows (Act I, Scene 2) reveals information that the audience needs in order to understand the action of the play.

In this Broadway production of *Dracula* starring Frank Langella, lighting accentuates the coldness of Dracula's castle. The combination of lighting and scenery gives the play a foreboding atmosphere.

The exposition also establishes the atmosphere and the mood of the play. **Atmosphere** is the environment of the play, largely created by staging and lighting. The various tempos of speech and movement and the choice of language also contribute to the atmosphere. The atmosphere helps bring out the feelings that create the **mood**, or emotional feeling of the play. The characters, setting, lighting, and dialogue all help bring out the mood. The audience should be able to identify the mood at the start of the play. The mood of a play is subject to change or reversal as the play progresses. For example, Shakespeare's comedy *As You Like It* opens with a dark mood and ends on a lighter note.

The most important part of the exposition is the **preliminary situation,** sometimes called the **antecedent action.** This is a clearly defined explanation of events that have occurred in the lives of the leading characters *before* the action of the play begins. These events place them in the situation in which we find them at the beginning of the play.

Playwrights use various devices to handle the exposition of the preliminary situation. The most common technique is to have minor characters bring the audience up-to-date. More original methods are the use of prologues, telephone conversations, narrators, and ingenious scenic effects. In *The Caine Mutiny Court Martial*, a drama about a military court trial, front curtains are not used. The audience becomes a part of the action while clerks, attorneys, and attendants casually explain the case. In *The*

CUE ▼

Greek theater prohibited scenes of violence onstage. The audience learned about such events from speeches made by someone who witnessed them or by a **tableau** (tăb′ • lō′), a scene presented by silent and unmoving actors, showing the results of the violent act.

Diary of Anne Frank and *I Remember Mama,* the audience hears the young main characters as they write about themselves in their journals at the opening of the plays and between scenes.

The expert dramatist can convey a great deal of information very quickly. In *Romeo and Juliet,* Shakespeare, through the use of the chorus and the dialogue, supplies us with the following information about the preliminary situation:

- Romeo's and Juliet's families are bitterly feuding.

- Romeo thinks he is in love with Rosaline.

- Juliet has caught the interest of a man named Paris.

- Romeo and Juliet are doomed to death.

- The Prince of Verona decrees the death penalty for the next member of the feuding families to start a quarrel.

- Romeo hears of a party that Juliet's family is having and decides to attend in disguise.

Application
ACTIVITY

Read the first two scenes of any Shakespearean play. As you read, identify elements that reveal the *where, when, why,* and *who* of the play.

PLOT

The **plot** of the play is the series of related events that take place before the audience. It is the development and resolution of the major conflict. There is usually a problem facing the protagonist. From that problem a conflict arises between the protagonist and the **antagonist,** the person or force opposing the protagonist. It might be a clash of wills or wits. It might be a psychological struggle between phases of the protagonist's personality and the environment. It might be a battle between groups with ideological differences. Whether physical, mental, or emotional, the conflicting elements must give rise to suspense and then be resolved in some manner.

The plot usually unfolds in several stages. The chart that begins on the following page explains the stages in plot structure and the events in Shakespeare's *Romeo and Juliet* that conform to this structure.

Stages in the Plot Structure	How the Plot of a Play Develops	Plot Development in *Romeo and Juliet*
Preliminary Situation	This is the explanation of events that occurred before the action of the play begins.	We meet the protagonists, Romeo and Juliet, whose families are feuding.
Initial Incident	This is the first important event from which the rest of the plot develops. It makes the audience wonder what will happen next.	They meet, kiss, and fall in love.
Rising Action	This is the series of events following the initial incident. All or nearly all important characters are introduced, and the goals and obstacles facing the protagonists are revealed then. A series of situations develops from the conflict to lift the level of interest.	Romeo and Juliet profess their love and secretly marry. Romeo's friend Mercutio is killed by Tybalt, Juliet's cousin. Romeo kills Tybalt in retaliation and must flee. To avoid a forced marriage, Juliet takes a potion that makes her appear dead.
Climax	This is the turning point of the action. It is the moment of intense crisis that determines the outcome of the conflict.	Romeo fails to receive the message that Juliet took a potion but instead receives a message that Juliet is dead. Romeo rushes back to Verona, enters the tomb, and sees Juliet apparently dead. He takes poison. Juliet awakens to find Romeo dead and takes her own life with his dagger.
Falling Action	This is the series of events following the climax. It is usually shorter than the rising action. The incidents must be significant.	The deaths are discovered, and the friar explains Romeo and Juliet's marriage and how their deaths came about to the families.
Conclusion	This is the logical outcome of the preceding action: the success or failure, happiness or sorrow of the characters.	The Montagues and the Capulets come together, and the feud is dissolved.

PLOT STRUCTURE

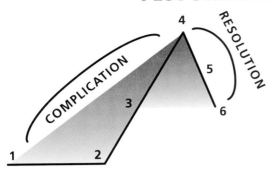

1. Preliminary Situation
2. Initial Incident
3. Rising Action
4. Climax
5. Falling Action
6. Conclusion

Another term for the resolution of a play is **denouement** (dā′ • nōō • mä^N′). The French for "untying the knot," it addresses the untangling of complications in a play and the resolution of these complications. In the *Poetics*, Aristotle explains, "By complication I mean everything from the beginning of the story up to the point where the hero suffers a change of fortune; by denouement, everything from the latter point to the end."

The sword fight between Tybalt and Mercutio in *Romeo and Juliet* stems from the conflict between the Capulets and the Montagues. The situations that arise from this conflict constitute the rising action that leads to the ultimate climax of the play.

The **situation** is the predicament or problem the plot revolves around. Georges Polti, in his book *The Thirty-Six Dramatic Situations,* proposes the following situations as the basis of all dramas.

The Thirty-Six Dramatic Situations

1. Supplication
2. Deliverance
3. Crime pursued by vengeance
4. Vengeance taken for kindred upon kindred
5. Pursuit
6. Disaster
7. Falling prey to cruelty or misfortune
8. Revolt
9. Daring enterprise
10. Abduction
11. The enigma
12. Obtaining
13. Enmity of kinsmen
14. Rivalry of kinsmen
15. Murderous adultery
16. Madness
17. Fatal imprudence
18. Involuntary crimes of love
19. Slaying of a kinsman unrecognized
20. Self-sacrificing for an ideal
21. Self-sacrifice for kindred
22. All sacrificed for a passion
23. Necessity of sacrificing loved ones
24. Rivalry of superior and inferior
25. Adultery
26. Crimes of love
27. Discovery of the dishonor of a loved one
28. Obstacles to love
29. An enemy loved
30. Ambition
31. Conflict with a god
32. Mistaken jealousy
33. Erroneous judgment
34. Remorse
35. Recovery of a lost one
36. Loss of loved ones

Although the phrasing is dated, no one has ever discovered any additional plot situations. In other words, it makes no difference whether a play is four hundred years old or will be written four hundred years from now, these are the conflicts on which all dramatic literature is based.

Application
ACTIVITIES

1. Choose a play or a story with which you are familiar. Outline the elements of the plot, using a chart similar to the one explaining the plot of *Romeo and Juliet*.

2. Test Georges Polti's assertion that all drama is based on just thirty-six situations. Recall several dramatic situations from plays or films. Do they fit one of Polti's categories?

CHARACTERS

There are few things in the world as interesting as people. The characters in a play should be people who can hold the audience's interest throughout the play. In a well-written play, even the most minor characters have interesting, unique personalities. Some plays, particularly in the twentieth century, use group protagonists, a number of people who together serve as the protagonist. In Thornton Wilder's *Our Town*, for example, it is the townspeople as a whole who are the main characters, even though Emily is the focal character and group representative.

In this production of *Whose Life Is It Anyway?*, Tom Conti plays the protagonist. Paralyzed after a traffic accident, he fights for the right to be allowed to die. Other actors who have also played this role include Mary Tyler Moore and Richard Dreyfuss. It is a challenging part—how would you show a well-rounded, believable character to the audience if you could move nothing below your neck?

Characters in a play must be vivid and varied in personality, with their dominant traits made evident through their speeches and actions. We often remember a well-developed characterization long after we have seen or read a play.

A playwright develops characters mostly through their words and actions. The characters' actions must suit their positions in life and their past experiences. The playwright also reveals characters by what they say to and about one another.

In writing the **dialogue**, or lines of the play, the dramatist must make a character speak as the audience would expect the women and men in the character's time, social class, community, and experience to speak. At the same time the playwright must advance the plot, motivate the actions of the characters, and place the characters in exciting or amusing situations. The playwright must often sacrifice beauty of language to naturalness of speech, yet the characters cannot talk aimlessly as people often do in reality; every word must serve a function in the development of the play.

Clever lines are valuable in comedy, but they should be consistent with the character of the person speaking them. Witty dialogue might actually hurt a play if it is not in harmony with the overall aim of the playwright.

In scenes where there is little action, the dialogue must be riveting enough to carry the scene.

In a soliloquy a character can disclose vital information to the audience without having to disclose it to other characters. The natural-sounding delivery of a soliloquy requires much practice.

Sometimes playwrights use soliloquies to reveal character. **Soliloquies** are speeches in which actors talk alone—think aloud—about themselves and their motives or about other people and situations. Soliloquies were accepted as a vital part of drama until realistic plays became popular. In life, people do not talk aloud to themselves very often. The soliloquy is such a simple way to reveal a character's inner thoughts, however, that modern playwrights still use it occasionally. Thornton Wilder uses the soliloquy in *Our Town*, as does Tennessee Williams in *The Glass Menagerie.*

The most important phase of characterization is understanding your character's motivation. Every action of a character must have a reason behind it, which in turn must be the result of both the character's

CUE

The best known of all soliloquies is Hamlet's famous "To be or not to be" speech, in which he thinks aloud about committing suicide.

At the conclusion of *Julius Caesar,* Mark Antony (played by Al Pacino) stands over the body of Brutus (played by Martin Sheen). As part of the falling action, Brutus has committed suicide by falling on his sword.

personality and the situation of the moment. To define the character's motivation and personality, a playwright must continually ask the following questions about each character.

- What does this character need or want?
- Who or what stands in the way of the character's needs or wants?
- What conditions affect the character's thoughts, words, and actions?
- Why does this character say or do certain things?

Application
ACTIVITY

Study a character in a play or a work of fiction. Use the questions above to define the character's motivation and personality. Then assume the part of that character as other members of your class ask you questions. Answer the questions as you think the character would answer them.

THEME

The **theme** is the basic idea of a play, which the author dramatizes through the conflicts of characters. Sometimes the playwright states the theme in words spoken by a character, but often it is left to the interpretation of the audience or the reader. There may be many ideas presented in a play, but do not mistake a minor truth for the main theme. The theme of a play is the specific idea that gives unity and purpose to everything that happens. Sometimes the writer states the theme in the title, as in *Whose Life Is It Anyway?*, *You Can't Take It with You*, and *She Stoops to Conquer*. At other times, the theme is actually stated in a key line, emphasized or expressed by the leading character as a personal philosophy of life, and then carried out in the situations resulting from this philosophy. For example, in *Man of La Mancha*, Cervantes writes, "Too much sanity may be madness, but the maddest of all is to see life as it is and not as it should be." The theme of *Romeo and Juliet* is left to the audience to infer. It might be stated as "The depth and beauty of pure love go beyond the barriers of prejudice and revenge."

A **moral**, on the other hand, is a lesson or a principle contained within a play or taught by a play. Although some plays make a moral statement, many plays have no particular moral. Instead, they are written to show how a certain type of individual would react under certain circumstances or simply to portray an interesting phase of life.

The theme of *Man of La Mancha*, the wistful longing for idealism and heroism, is expressed through the dialogue and situations of the play. One of the characters sums it up when he theorizes that real insanity is *not* allowing ourselves to dream of a better world.

5 REVIEW

Summary and Key Ideas

Summarize the chapter by answering the following questions.

1. Name and define the four narrative essentials of a play. How are these narrative essentials communicated by the dramatist?
2. Who first expressed the principles of traditional drama? What did he identify as the key elements of a play?
3. How does some modern drama differ from traditional drama?
4. How does mood differ from atmosphere?
5. What are the five major parts of plot structure that follow the preliminary situation?
6. Describe three methods of characterization available to playwrights.
7. How does a theme differ from a moral?

Discussing Ideas

1. Select a movie or a television play. Identify the four narrative essentials. Discuss how the dramatist presents each element.
2. Twentieth- and twenty-first-century playwrights often break the rules of traditional drama. Read either Samuel Beckett's *Waiting for Godot* or Eugène Ionesco's *The Chairs*. Describe some of the rules these dramatists break.
3. Describe a play or a movie that made you think about its theme.

FOCUS ON Community Theater

Would you like to give support to a resource that strengthens your community and lets people of all ages participate? Then community theater might be for you. Community theaters throughout the country provide a great venue for performing and viewing drama. Community theaters give burgeoning actors and directors the opportunity to practice and improve their skills.

Directing Community Theater The director is the link between the playwright and the actors. He or she must have strong skills in analyzing plays and working with people. Directors must also be familiar with all the arts and crafts that contribute to a production. With your teacher's permission, do some research using Internet sites such as the Community Theater Green Room (www.communitytheater.org) to find out more about what directing community theater involves. In a brief essay, summarize your findings.

Volunteering With a partner, work to find out more about community theaters in your town or state. Are they currently in need of volunteers? Share your volunteering information with the rest of the class.

THE STRUCTURE OF DRAMA

INDEPENDENT ACTIVITY

A Day in the Life   The first dramas people experience are in their own lives. Choose a day from your life and explain how you would use your day as the basis for a play. It can be an exciting or frustrating day or just a typical twenty-four-hour period—every day holds drama of one kind or another. As you construct the plan for your drama, incorporate the four narrative essentials.

Consider the following points:

- Decide whether you are the protagonist, the antagonist, or both.
- Make sure your exposition describes the *where, when, why,* and *who* of your drama and establishes the atmosphere and mood of your play.
- Plan your plot so that it follows the plot-structure diagram.
- Choose interesting characters, and plan to develop them well.
- Decide on a theme or a moral.

Cooperative Learning Activity

Analyzing a Nontraditional Play
With a group of classmates, read a modern play that has abandoned traditional dramatic structure, such as Edward Albee's *The Sandbox.* Use the plot-structure diagram on page 259 to trace the action. Then use the following questions to discuss why and how the playwright departed from traditional form.

- How does the playwright communicate the *where, when, why,* and *who* of the play?
- How does the playwright use dialogue, action, and situation to develop the characters?
- How does the plot depart from the plot-structure diagram?

- What is the theme or the moral of the play?
- Is the play more or less effective because it does not follow the traditional structure?

Compare your group's conclusions with those of other groups.

Across the CURRICULUM Activity

Literature   Choose a short story you like. How would you translate the story into a play? Identify the four narrative essentials. Analyze the plot according to the plot-structure diagram. Describe the characters, and evaluate their development in the story. Are they interesting? Do the dialogue, action, and situations adequately develop the characters? Can you infer a theme or moral from the story? How does a drama differ from a short story?

6 *Varieties of Drama*

In ancient Greece, actors wore masks. As drama has evolved through the ages, these two have come to symbolize the two major divisions of drama: tragedy and comedy.

The world is a comedy to those that think, a tragedy to those that feel.

—HORACE WALPOLE (1717–1797), AUTHOR

SETTING THE SCENE

Focus Questions

What are the differences between tragedy and comedy?

What are some of the devices playwrights use to make people laugh?

What are the types of comedy?

What dramatic styles have influenced the theater in the twentieth century?

Vocabulary

tragedy	farce	high comedy	melodrama
pathos	screen scene	comedy of manners	play of ideas
hamartia	aside	satire	theatrical conventions
catharsis	burlesque	fantasy	representational
comedy	parody	romantic comedy	presentational
low comedy	caricature	sentimental comedy	allegory

*Y*ou will need to be able to identify the varieties of drama in evaluating and studying plays. This knowledge will help you interpret roles and give you an overall understanding of the plays you watch and read.

The two most recognized varieties of drama are tragedy and comedy. Generally speaking, tragedies end in catastrophe—often the death of the tragic character. Comedies are usually lighthearted, with clever dialogue and amusing characters who are involved in funny situations. Plays that have qualities of both comedy and tragedy are called tragicomedies. Plays that do not fit the definition of tragedy but are serious in nature are simply called dramas.

Classification is further complicated by the many styles in which plays may be written. The most commonly recognized literary styles are romanticism, realism, naturalism, symbolism, and expressionism. In addition, there are period styles determined by theater conventions of historical eras, such as the ritualistic formalism of the Greek theater, the madcap antics of the commedia dell'arte, and the frenetic activity in plays of the Restoration period.

The following pages will provide you with ideas and terms you can use to analyze types and styles of plays from Greek tragedy to present-day performance pieces.

❧ *Tragedy*

CUE ▼

Five Characteristics Often Found in Tragic Characters

- They have a flaw or make an error that has serious consequences.

- They make no apology for their actions.

- They set goals based on unyielding beliefs.

- They know that almost everything worth having demands some sacrifice.

- They are willing to make the sacrifice themselves, never asking another to make sacrifices for them.

Many of the great plays throughout history have been tragedies. In fact, **tragedy** is considered by many to be humanity's highest literary achievement. Tragedies are sober, thoughtful plays that are based on profound human emotions and conflicts that do not change with time or place.

The focus of every tragedy is the **protagonist.** This character is a significant person who is engaged in a struggle but ultimately fails and is overcome by opposing forces. This struggle may be internal, that is, against forces within the tragic character. These forces may be virtues, such as a sense of duty, or weaknesses, such as too much pride. The struggle may be external, against forces outside the character. These forces may be divine or human authority or the pressures of society. Often the external forces are set into motion by a choice or error the character makes.

Whether the forces against which the tragic character struggles are internal or external, the tragic character has no control over them once the choice has been made or the action of the play has begun. The outcome appears to be predestined, and the audience sees that there is nothing the character can do to avoid it. This feature of tragedy is called inevitability: what will happen will happen. There is no way to prevent the protagonist's tragic fall. In *Romeo and Juliet,* for example, the prologue of the play tells us that Romeo and Juliet are "star-crossed lovers." Their fate is sealed, and there is nothing they can do to avoid the ultimate crisis.

The protagonist's struggle and the inevitability of the outcome elicit the audience's pity and compassion. The quality of the drama that arouses these feelings is called **pathos**. The audi-

In Shakespeare's *Julius Caesar*, the downfall of the protagonist, Marcus Brutus, is inevitable after he and the other conspirators have murdered Caesar. Shakespeare, a loyal subject of Queen Elizabeth, considered killing one's monarch to be worthy of the most severe consequences.

ence's emotions intensify the impact of the events leading to the outcome for the tragic character. By the time the tragedy ends, though, the pathos has been purged, and the audience feels a sense of release, known as **catharsis.**

The stature or significance of the protagonist changes with the times. When Shakespeare wrote his tragedies, monarchs were significant. Therefore, most of his protagonists were rulers, such as Macbeth, King Lear, and Julius Caesar. In more democratic times, a tragic character can be a seemingly common citizen. However common protagonists might seem, though, they possess something that either sets them apart from or elevates them above other people. Willy Loman in *Death of a Salesman* appears ordinary, but he is elevated by his dreams, just as Blanche DuBois in *A Streetcar Named Desire* is elevated by her hopes for a better life. Ken Harrison in *Whose Life Is It Anyway?* is set apart by his accident and resulting paralysis.

ARISTOTLE AND TRAGEDY

The most enduring description of tragedy is found in the *Poetics* by Greek critic-philosopher Aristotle. According to Aristotle, the tragic protagonist is an average or better person who, during the course of the play, is brought from happiness to misery. Through this suffering, the protagonist usually acquires a sense of awareness—of truth, of self, or of others. At the same time, the protagonist becomes alienated and isolated from society. The cause of the protagonist's difficulties is usually an action (or lack of action) brought about by **hamartia** (hä´ • mär • tē´ • ə), a character weakness or error in judgment. The most common form of hamartia is **hubris** (hyoo´ • brĭs), or excessive pride. The tragic character may be completely unable, however, to do anything about the hamartia.

While viewing a tragedy, the audience must be made to feel pity and fear. Aristotle felt that these audience reactions could be elicited in two ways: through spectacle or, preferably, through the structure and incidents of the play—the plot. In Aristotle's list of the elements of a play (see Chapter 5), plot was the most important; he felt that the plot was "the soul of a tragedy."

As the audience watches the tragic character progress toward his or her unhappy end, pity and fear increase. The pity, according to Aristotle, is for the protagonist, while the fear is for ourselves. We the audience know that we could easily have made the same error in judgment, and we would then have been forced to pay the same price. When a person of significance or stature, struggling against dynamic forces, finally falls, the resulting effect on the audience brings about a purging or cleansing that results in an emotional release called **catharsis** (kə • thär´ • sĭs).

Tragedy includes scenes of recognition and of reversal. Recognition usually occurs in one of two ways. The protagonist achieves an inner awareness or an insight into truth as a result of great personal suffering. Shakespeare's characters King Lear and Othello both come to understand how tragically wrong they have been only after the deaths of Lear's daughter and Othello's wife. In another kind of recognition, the protagonist identifies a loved one, a relative, or a friend from a birthmark or scar or by some other means. Reversal takes the form of an ironic twist in which an action produces an effect opposite to what would at first seem likely.

CUE ▼

- Tragedy is based on strong human emotions felt and understood by all people regardless of time and circumstances.

- Comedy often depends on situations unique to a particular time or circumstance.

A MODERN DESCRIPTION OF TRAGEDY

One of the most interesting descriptions of tragedy since Aristotle's is found in the following speech by the Chorus in Jean Anouilh's *Antigone*.

> Tragedy is clean, it is firm, it is flawless. It has nothing to do with melodrama—with wicked villains, persecuted maidens, avengers, gleams of hope, and eleventh-hour repentances. Death, in a melodrama, is really horrible because it is never inevitable. The dear old

father might so easily have been saved; the honest young man might so easily have brought in the police five minutes earlier.

In a tragedy, nothing is in doubt and everyone's destiny is known. That makes for tranquility. Tragedy is restful; and the reason is that *hope*, that foul, deceitful thing, has no part in it. There isn't any hope. You're trapped. The whole sky has fallen on you, and all you can do about it is to shout. Now don't mistake me: I said "shout": I did not say groan, whimper, complain. *That*, you cannot do. But you can *shout* aloud; you can get all those things said that you never thought you'd be able to say—or never even knew you had it in you to say. And you don't say these things because it will do any good to say them: you know better than that. You say them for their own sake; you say them because you learn a lot from them.

In melodrama, you argue and struggle in the hope of escape. That is vulgar; it's practical. But in tragedy, where there is no temptation to try to escape, argument is gratuitous: it's kingly.

Pictured here is the chorus from Jean Anouilh's *Antigone*. In Anouilh's version of Sophocles' classic play, Creon and his niece Antigone clash over which has priority: duty to family or duty to obey one's king.

Application
ACTIVITIES

1. Watch Arthur Miller's *Death of a Salesman,* one of Shakespeare's tragedies, such as *Hamlet, Julius Caesar,* or *Macbeth,* or another tragedy. Then, answer the following questions:

   - Against what forces is the protagonist struggling?
   - What is the protagonist's main weakness?
   - Does the play communicate a sense of inevitability? Explain.

2. After viewing the tragedy, read Anouilh's description of tragedy again. Explain why you agree or disagree with his views.

3. How is the tragedy you watched a representation of the time in which it was written? Research its historical period, and evaluate the influence of time and place on the work. Regardless of the time period, does the tragedy have the sense of emotional timelessness? Explain.

❧ *Comedy*

The word ***comedy*** is derived from the Greek words, *komos* and *ode,* meaning "revel song." Comedies are usually societal and conciliatory: all the characters come together at the end of the play. Even the villains usually rejoin the group. While comedy often depends on circumstances unique to a particular time and place, the greatest and most enduring comedies have taken situations and characters with which most audiences can easily identify. These plays have had lasting appeal because audiences recognize the people and understand their predicaments.

There are many types of comedy. Some cause great belly laughs; some bring laughter to the point of tears; and some cause only inner smiles or chuckles. Comedy does not always make you laugh out loud, but most comedy will amuse, delight, or at least please you.

In comedy, the protagonist overcomes opposing forces or achieves desired goals or both. The protagonist is often a less-than-average person in some way. The comic protagonist may be an idealist, a romantic, an extreme pragmatist, a blunderer, a dreamer, or even a rogue.

Comedy, like all drama, is built around character, situations, and dialogue. A strange character bumbling along through life, like Elwood Dowd

CUE ▼

Shakespeare (1564–1616) of England, Molière (1622–1673) of France, and Bernard Shaw (1856–1950) of Ireland are considered three of the world's great writers of comedy.

in *Harvey*, provokes laughter. The pleasure-loving but cowardly Falstaff in Shakespeare's *Henry IV* and *The Merry Wives of Windsor* and the linguistically confused Mrs. Malaprop in Sheridan's *The Rivals* become funny in themselves. Comic situations consist of predicaments that seem insurmountable or improbable. Mistaken identities, rash promises, or a series of events in which everything seems to go wrong are typical comic situations. Trying to live one life in town and a different one in the country makes the situation in Wilde's *The Importance of Being Earnest* amusing.

TRAGEDY VERSUS COMEDY	
Tragedy	**Comedy**
Inevitable—there is no way to change or to stop the outcome	Predictably unpredictable—you can expect the unlikely
Universal theme and appeal	Often time and place oriented
Emotional	Intellectual, mental
Protagonist fails to achieve goals	Protagonist achieves goals
Protagonist alienated from society	Protagonist often becomes leader of new society; even villain is usually accepted
Protagonist average or better	Protagonist less than average
Protagonist falls from leadership, losing respect, dreams, position	Protagonist achieves success, often as a result of own mistakes or shortcomings

Application
ACTIVITIES

1. Read or watch a comic play or film. Explain how it fulfills the seven parts of the definition of comedy given in the chart above.

2. Does the historical period have more influence on the comedy in question 1 above or on the tragedy in question 3 from page 274? Why? Did you feel it was a specific portrayal of the place and time in which it was written? Write a report comparing and analyzing the effects that historical period and culture have on the comedy and tragedy you studied.

It is difficult to determine what makes people laugh. Sometimes we laugh at very strange things—the exaggerated, the grotesque, even the horrifying. Other times we laugh out of embarrassment, to save ourselves from tears, or sometimes, it seems, for no reason at all. Partly because of this unpredictable response, comic plays are more difficult to perform successfully than serious plays. What is funny today may not be funny tomorrow. What is humorous in New York City might not be amusing in London or St. Louis. It is possible, however, to identify seven common causes of laughter: exaggeration, incongruity, anticipation, ambiguity, recognition, protection, and relief.

Exaggeration   The most noticeable characteristic of comedy is probably exaggeration. Exaggeration can take several forms. It might take the form of overstatement. In *The Teahouse of the August Moon*, when Sakini takes a piece of gum from his mouth, carefully wraps it in a piece of paper, puts it away in a matchbook, and says, "Tootie-fruitie. . . . Most generous gift of American sergeant," he is overstating the importance of the gift. Exaggeration can also be an understatement. When Sherlock Holmes says, "Elementary, my dear Watson," he is understating the amount of effort required to solve the mystery in question.

Exaggeration may include physical characteristics—a bulbous nose or large teeth—and mannerisms—a strange walk or a twitching eye. It may also include mental characteristics, such as the almost-too-brilliant child prodigy or the incredibly dense person.

Another form of exaggeration stems from the "humors" of Shakespeare's time. The humors (blood, black bile, yellow bile, and phlegm) were considered personality determiners that make people giggly, carefree, happy-go-lucky (blood); moody, philosophical, love-sick

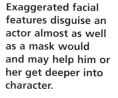

Exaggerated facial features disguise an actor almost as well as a mask would and may help him or her get deeper into character.

(black bile); impatient, hotheaded, passionate (yellow bile); and dull, lazy, sluggish (phlegm). These personality types are such exaggerations of the normal that when they are well acted, audiences respond with laughter or tears.

Incongruity Anything that seems out of place, out of time, or out of character is an example of **incongruity.** For example, a modern reference in a play that is obviously set in the past often provokes laughter.

In this scene from *Fool Moon*, the actors lounge incongruously on the crescent moon as if it were a park bench.

In theater, incongruity comes in many forms. It may be an unnatural action, such as a soldier who walks like a wind-up toy or actors who behave like cats. It is present in Gogol's *The Inspector General* when government officials mistake a penniless traveler for a government inspector and treat him accordingly. Incongruity may be an unnatural sound—a piercing, brayish laugh, severely trilled *r*'s, or an undulating pitch that soars up and down—that makes an audience laugh. The incongruity might be a twist, a turn of events that changes the logical completion of a pattern, or it might be a reversal, when the tables are turned and the weak overcome the strong or the underdog triumphs. The irrelevant, often in the form of dialogue about an unimportant detail when something critical is at stake, is still another form of humorous incongruity.

Anticipation The key to many laughs is **anticipation,** or looking forward to a potential laugh. The old gag of the banana peel on the sidewalk is an excellent example of anticipation. The observer will start to laugh even before the clown takes the disastrous step.

Anticipation also plays a role in comedies of mistaken identity such as *She Stoops to Conquer.* Young Marlow has been told that the Hardcastle estate is an inn. When he arrives, he is greeted by Mr. Hardcastle, the father of the woman he is on his way to court. Marlow, however, assumes that Mr. Hardcastle is the innkeeper, and so Marlow orders him around as if he were a servant. This reversal of roles, along with the anticipation that the truth will eventually be known, is a source of laughter.

A character who eavesdrops, as the background character is doing in this scene from Shakespeare's *Much Ado About Nothing,* creates pleased anticipation in the audience. The audience knows that the unauthorized information will sooner or later get the eavesdropper into trouble.

Several techniques are used to create anticipation. A common one is the **plant**—an idea, a line, or an action emphasized early in the play, sometimes called **foreshadowing,** and used later for a laugh. In order for the idea to provoke laughter, however, at least three exposures are required: one to plant, one to establish, and one to clinch. This is often called a **running gag.**

Incompletion is another technique that causes anticipation. A line or bit of action is started but never finished. The audience completes the thought with laughter.

The **anticlimax**, or letdown, is also based on anticipation. Excitement about something is built up to great proportions, and then, like a bursting bubble, there is nothing.

Ambiguity Double meaning, or **ambiguity,** is the heart of many humorous lines. Puns and word play depend on the audience's recognizing the possible interpretations and almost always selecting the least likely one. Even names like Lydia Languish, Lady Teazle, and Sir Benjamin Backbite have a humorous ambiguity. Are they the names of people, descriptions of characters, or both?

Recognition Discovering hidden or obscure meanings is called **recognition.** An audience is often amused to recognize the difference between a character's inner motivation and the apparent motivation. For example, in *Fiddler on the Roof,* Lazer Wolf approaches Tevya with the intent of buying a cow. Tevya, however, thinks that Lazer Wolf wants to marry his oldest daughter. The audience finds the misunderstanding very funny; when Tevya recognizes his mistake, the audience is again amused.

We are also amused when we discover what is going to happen just before it actually does. The take—the mouth-agape freeze of farce—often brings down the house. The character sees or hears something that apparently does not sink in, takes a step or two, and then suddenly the meaning hits. Sometimes the meaning hits on several levels, causing double or even triple takes.

Protection One of the most important elements of comedy is the **protection** factor. Cruel, violent, grotesque, and abusive actions and events often cause laughter because the audience is protected by knowing that these things are not really happening or that they are not as damaging as they seem. The secret of humor in the cartoon in which the character runs off a cliff is the protection factor. The character falls a hundred feet to apparent doom but amazingly reappears in the next frame. The old slapstick of a pie in the face is another example; this causes considerable commotion but hurts no one. We can be truly amused when we are certain no one will really be injured and it is safe to accept the illusion as real.

Relief A good comedy builds up pressure and then releases it. This **relief** of pressure is humorous when the pent-up emotions are allowed to explode in a laugh.

A typical comic sequence might unfold like this: a comic character lights the fuse on a powder keg and places it in the path of an adversary (the plant). The fuse goes out at the last moment and the adversary passes by unharmed (anticlimax or letdown). The character approaches the powder keg to see what went wrong (anticipation). The powder keg blows up in the comic character's face (incongruity). The comic character emerges ragged and soot-covered, but unharmed (protection and relief).

Application
ACTIVITY

Read or watch a comic play or film. As you watch, note which of these seven techniques the playwright uses to create humor. Which technique is the most effective?

❧ *Types of Comedy*

From the study of comedy in ancient Greece come the classifications of Old, Middle, and New Comedy. Old Comedy was characterized by its scathing satirical attack on political events and figures. Middle Comedy evolved to focus more on social occurrences, which called for the incorporation of everyday speech. This classification still contained a satirical edge that differentiates it from New Comedy. Menander, the man credited with the origination of New Comedy, presented a sentimental view of life and tried to appeal to audiences' intellect rather than base sense of humor.

The Old, Middle, and New Comedy classifications are used only for the comedies of ancient Greece. The general terms used to classify comedy from that time forward are *low* and *high*. Understanding the classification of a play will help you with the portrayal of your character or help you direct a play and remain true to the author's intentions.

CUE ▼

The term *slapstick* is derived from an old stage prop consisting of two thin boards hinged together. The slapstick made a loud but harmless sound when applied to the backside of a performer.

LOW COMEDY

The term *low comedy* is not intended to belittle this type of drama. **Low comedy** focuses on physical antics, such as appear in *The Three Stooges.* Silent films had to rely on visual physical humor to generate laughter. The situations and characters in low comedy are usually outlandish, and the play is usually exaggerated in style and performance.

In *A Funny Thing Happened on the Way to the Forum,* Mickey Rooney leads Roman soldiers on a merry chase.

Farce   A comic technique often present in other types of plays, farce is one of the main types of low comedy. A **farce** is based on improbable characters and implausible coincidences and events.

Farces include practical jokes, clowning, and many physical indignities, such as ear pulling, shin kicking, and pie throwing. Farces usually include chase scenes—through gardens or houses, around furniture, or in and out of doors. *Charley's Aunt*, written in 1892 by Brandon Thomas, is an example of a full-length farce. It includes a hilarious chase scene through the Oxford Botanical Gardens.

Farces may also have screen scenes. In a **screen scene,** some of the actors hide—behind doors, inside closets, or behind bushes—from the other actors onstage. The concealed characters always overhear the onstage dialogue and may pop out to say something, talk to each other, or make **asides**—lines spoken directly to the audience.

Many comedies that are not classified as full-length farce still have elements of farce in them. Since the end of World War II, many authors have used farcical techniques to enhance the serious themes in their works. Examples of these plays include Samuel Beckett's *Waiting for Godot* and Eugène Ionesco's *The Chairs.*

Burlesque   Like farce, **burlesque** relies on physical comedy and exaggeration. They are usually less coherent than farces and much more exaggerated. Burlesque is a mockery of a broad topic, such as a style, societal view, or literary form, and the audience should have previous knowledge of the play's subject, or they will not understand the entirety of its humor. For example, to fully understand the well-known burlesque *The Boyfriend* (1954), a viewer must know that the boy-meets-girl scenario was predominant in the musical theater of the 1920s. When burlesque came to the United States, it evolved into the bawdy variety show that the word *burlesque* often connotes. However, there is a marked difference between European burlesque, addressed here, and American burlesque.

Parody   This type of comedy is a mockery of a certain person or work, incorporating a **caricature,** or exaggerated feature, of the subject. Parody, like burlesque, requires prior knowledge of the subject being ridiculed. It, too, includes physical comedy, but relies less on it than burlesque does. It is unusual to find an entire play that is a parody since the topic of ridicule is so limited. However, these works do exist; for example, the Mel Brooks' movie *Spaceballs* is a parody of *Star Wars.* More commonly, parody is incorporated into a specific scene of a work.

▼ **CUE**

The word *farce* comes from the Latin word *farcire*, meaning "to stuff." When first used in the theater, it referred to any sort of impromptu addition "stuffed" into a play, especially jokes or gags.

Intellectual humor constitutes **high comedy.** When viewing high comedy, it is essential to pay close attention to the dialogue, because high comedy relies almost exclusively on witty dialogue, not physical action. As in parody and burlesque, there is a particular subject being ridiculed. The only difference is the way in which this ridicule is presented.

Comedy of Manners   Also called drawing room comedy because the main action of these plays take place in the drawing rooms of upper-class citizens, a **comedy of manners** usually mocks the pretenses of the upper class. Built on clever use of language, the wit of a comedy of manners includes puns, paradoxes, epigrams, and ironies. The dialogue is clever, often attacking socially-accepted standards of the day.

Comedy of manners was extremely popular during the Restoration period. Wycherly, Congreve, and Sheridan were all creators of this genre. Their plays are still produced today in theaters across the country.

Satire   Like parody or burlesque, satire ridicules human folly, societal views, or individuals. Unlike a writer of parody or burlesque, a satirist usually has the goal of changing something for the better by ridiculing it. **Satire** is intellectual in its attack. You will find in satirical works a mockery using language rather than physical antics.

One of the foremost authors of this style was Ben Jonson, but satire has been around since the Old Comedy of Aristophanes. Oscar Wilde and Bernard Shaw are well-known satirists, as are Noël Coward and Tom Stoppard.

CUE

One of the most famous comic protagonists is the swashbuckling Cyrano de Bergerac. His protruding nose is the source of both uproarious laughter and profound pity as he secretly endures his hopeless love for the beautiful Roxanne. The movie *Roxanne*, starring Steve Martin, is a modern version of this classic.

Application
ACTIVITY

Read one of the comedies mentioned in this section. If the play is available on video, you may prefer to watch it. Consider how the play fits the category. Make a list of the characteristics that identify it as low or high comedy. Note any examples of the following: slapstick, chase scene, screen scene, parody, caricature, witty dialogue, satire.

🌿 Other Types of Drama

Many plays cannot be categorized as tragedy or comedy since they have elements of both pathos and humor in them. This type of play is more abundant than either pure tragedy or pure comedy. Examples include fantasy, romantic comedy, and melodrama, to name a few. The types have developed and changed throughout history, sometimes evolving into a style of writing in theater *and* fiction and sometimes evolving from literature. Some of these types of drama are still written today, but others were simply reactions to previous styles, and their popularity has not withstood the test of time. As you read about these different types of theater, you will realize that not all works can be categorized because many include elements from several genres.

Fantasy   Dealing with unreal characters, with dreams, and with imaginary times and places, **fantasy** usually occurs in a land of make-believe that is often inhabited by spirits who have supernatural powers, gods from another world, witches, and flawless heroes. Fantastical works often have a basis in reality, such as the movie *The Never-Ending Story* in which a boy is picked on and beaten by bullies but finds his escape in a story that features him as the hero. The use of fantasy within plays is not a new trend; even Shakespeare incorporated it in *A Midsummer Night's Dream* and *The Tempest*, supplying his audience with both frightening and humorous characters. Some modern plays are also based on fantasy, such as *Peter Pan* and *The Wizard of Oz*. The legend of King Arthur is another popular topic in fantasy fiction.

The fantasy play *The Wiz* contains human characters, animal characters, and unreal characters, including witches and fairy godmothers.

Romantic Comedy Written in the style of **romanticism,** which originated in the eighteenth century, **romantic comedies** feature plots focusing on love affairs between flawless heroes and virtuous heroines. These two characters are ideally suited for each other, and they are presented as too good to be true. Their love affair has its ups and downs but always ends happily. Romantic comedies, such as Shakespeare's *The Merchant of Venice* and Lerner and Loewe's *Brigadoon,* are still presented today; however, very few are authored in this era.

Sentimental Comedy Although classified as a comedy, this genre lacks humor. As a reaction to Restoration drama and the immorality present in it, **sentimental comedy** is marked by an emotional and ideal presentation of material, to the point of being **schmaltz.** In this type of play, the hero and heroine are so virtuous they seem to be caricatures, and the villain shows no redeeming values. The characters are flat, and the plot contrived, with virtue always prevailing. Richard Steele is the best-known writer of the sentimental comedy with his plays *The Tender Husband* and *The Conscious Lovers.* Due to their lack of substance, the popularity of sentimental comedies was short lived.

Melodrama Originating in nineteenth-century England, **melodrama** is marked by its use of stock characters and implausible plots. Like sentimental comedy, melodrama presents a trite storyline where a virtuous maiden is threatened by an evil villain, but is rescued by a flawless hero. Every act of a melodrama concludes with a climax, leaving the audience, which was usually the illiterate commoners of nineteenth-century England, hanging on for the resolution. The sets were spectacular, and the staging of events such as earthquakes and shipwrecks was nearly always present.

Although melodrama is based on the structure of tragedy, it focuses more on the actions of the characters rather than on their motivations. It also lacks the sense of inevitability that is so necessary in tragedy. Melodrama presents a clear-cut view of morality, leaving no room to question the motivations of the villainous character, who must be motivated by evil intent, or the virtuous character, who in turn must be motivated by the search for right. It does, however, include the suffering of innocent, virtuous characters, as in tragedy, but these good characters always triumph in the end. The true form of melodrama exists only in nineteenth-century classics, such as *Marie Martin* and *The Streets of London,* but many melodramatic elements are present in the modern plays of O'Neill and many popular movies.

Play of Ideas Sometimes called a problem play or a social drama, a **play of ideas** deals with a social problem, such as racism, classism, or sexism. This genre might also deal with questions of wrong and right, or numerous other philosophical arguments. The playwright usually presents a solution to the problem covered, or at least guides the characters in the right direction. For example, Athol Fugard, a white South African, voices in his plays a strong opposition to the South African government's policy of racial segregation called *apartheid.* Many feel that his work was important in focusing opposition to apartheid, which was finally repealed in 1991. For example, in his play *My Children! My Africa!* he emphasizes the importance of love for and loyalty to Africa by pointing out the atrocities that famine and war have wrought. Fugard has also authored *Blood Knot* and *Sizwe Banzi Is Dead.*

Some other famous plays of ideas include Henrik Ibsen's *An Enemy of the People,* which demonstrates how a man from a small town stands for

David Mamet's two-character play *Oleanna* uses personal relationships in a university setting as a forum for exploring current social issues.

civic integrity against all other citizens; Bertolt Brecht's *The Caucasian Chalk Circle,* which attacks the selfishness of the elite; and Lorraine Hansberry's *A Raisin in the Sun,* which shows an African American family struggling to escape poverty.

CUE ▼

Agatha Christie's *The Mousetrap,* a melodrama of the "whodunit" variety, holds the all-time record for continuous performances of a play.

Psychological Drama   As serious plays, **psychological dramas** are often penetrating and sometimes painful; the playwright battles the complexities of the human psyche and personal relationships. Eugene O'Neill wrote psychological as well as social drama. *Long Day's Journey into Night* was a very personal play, in which O'Neill explores some of the difficulties of his own early life. Tennessee Williams was one of America's great psychological dramatists. With *The Glass Menagerie, The Rose Tattoo,* and many other plays, he shows family and personal struggles. Marsha Norman in *'Night, Mother* deals with a troubled woman and her relationship with her mother; in *Who's Afraid of Virginia Woolf?* Edward Albee explores human weakness and the torment people create when they are unable to accept weakness in those around them.

The "Whodunit"   The suspense in a **"whodunit"** of solving a crime or of a courtroom drama tremendously heightens dramatic effects and hooks audiences. Some popular "whodunits" are *Ten Little Indians,* and *The Mousetrap.*

Allegory   A play that teaches moral concepts through characters who personify abstract qualities and concepts, such as truth, justice, love, death, and humanity, can be considered an **allegory.** Allegory has been a popular form of storytelling throughout history. The classic example is *Everyman.* In this medieval play, Everyman is suddenly summoned to meet Death. He must appear before God for judgment on his life. In his desperate need, all his friends—Five Wits, Fellowship, Kindred, Discretion, Beauty, Strength, and Knowledge—fail him. Only his Good Deeds will go with him.

SOME SPECIAL FORMS OF DRAMA

Children's Theater   A large part of contemporary theater is devoted to **children's theater**—drama written, designed, and performed for children. Many high school drama groups produce at least one children's play each season. Regional, civic, and professional theater groups often include children's theater as part of their seasons. Some even run a separate children's theater schedule. Many original scripts and new adaptations are available for production.

Puppet Theater   Puppets have long been a part of theater the world over. In recent years, however, children's television programs have prompted a new interest in puppets. Enormous puppets combined with masked actors in the American Repertory Theater production of Andrei Serban's *King Stag* create powerful adult theater. For a special section on **puppet theater,** see page 328.

Monodrama   A **monodrama** is a play written to be performed by a single actor. In *Before Breakfast,* an O'Neill tragedy, a nagging wife drives her husband into committing suicide offstage. In *The Search for Signs of Intelligent Life in the Universe,* Lily Tomlin created an enormous variety of characters in a series of monologues that were part comedy and part social criticism.

A popular form of monodrama is the impersonation of historical figures: Hal Holbrook as Mark Twain, Cornelia Otis Skinner as the wives of Henry VIII, Robert Morse as Truman Capote, among many.

In the last part of the twentieth century, **performance art** became increasingly popular. This form of monodrama often involves juxtaposing many different elements of theater in a novel way. Performance artists such as Laurie Anderson use video, multiple screens, megaphones, and music to create full-length, loosely constructed theater pieces.

Monodrama requires an actor who can single-handedly command the attention of an audience. Here, Ben Kingsley portrays Irish poet William Butler Yeats.

Application
ACTIVITY

Using the following situation or one that you create, explain what would be emphasized if it were produced as a social drama or as a psychological drama. How might it be turned into a monodrama? How could it be adapted as a "whodunit" or suspense drama?

Dramatic situation: A couple has adopted and raised a baby. Now the child is ready to start the first grade. Suddenly the birth parents come forward with a legal reason for the child to be given back to them.

🌊 Styles of Drama

The term **style** refers to the way in which a play is written, produced, and acted. Dramatists choose the style of language and action they feel best expresses their ideas. Directors and scenic artists present plays in a style they feel suits the script. Classifying plays by style is sometimes difficult because playwrights and directors combine styles to create the effects they want.

Style relies heavily on **theatrical conventions,** such as setting and other visual elements, to convey particular interpretation. The director and designer may blend costume, scenery, and lighting to create an effect that is more abstract than realistic. Highly stylized productions have included characters dressed like the animals they resemble in spirit, characters wearing masks, and Shakespearean characters dressed in simple, uniform garments that are not tied to a particular time or place.

Most plays are **representational**, a style sometimes called "fourth-wall" theater. The play is performed as if the audience were watching the action through an imaginary fourth wall, one of the most common theatrical conventions. The **presentational** style, on the other hand, acknowledges that an audience is present. Characters may address the audience, and some action may even take place in the seating area, as in Wilder's *Our Town.*

The term **avant-garde** applies to new and experimental styles of any art form. Many techniques accepted today as common theater practices were once considered avant-garde. In the United States, much of the new experimentation takes place off-Broadway and off-off-Broadway. While many avant-garde movements quickly disappear, a few become part of the continuing theater. Once a style is accepted, of course, it is no longer considered avant-garde.

THEATER STYLES AND TRENDS

The styles described below have all been a part of twentieth-century theater, even though some of them began hundreds of years before.

Romanticism   A literary and artistic movement that began in the eighteenth century, **romanticism** focuses on emotions and imagination. Romanticism became popular in the theater as a reaction to the strict neoclassicism that predominated in French theater in the seventeenth and eighteenth centuries. Romantic plays were elaborately staged and featured ideal characters. With love as the primary theme, **romantic comedies** became one of the favorite forms of romanticism. In fact, romantic comedies are one of the few works of this style that are still presented. Of course, many modern plays and movies contain elements of romanticism.

In the romantic play *Beauty and the Beast,* the beast symbolizes the human desire to be loved in spite of savage behaviors that from time to time make every human unlovable.

Realism   This dominant style of the twentieth century takes an opposite approach. **Realism** in plays presents life as it actually is—often unpleasant and unhappy, but not necessarily so. The characters talk and act as people in ordinary life do. The outcome of the play makes sense in the real world. Sets and scenery contribute to the real-life atmosphere. The Norwegian playwright Henrik Ibsen has been called the father of realism as well as the father of modern drama. He introduced realism in *A Doll's House* in 1879.

Naturalism   The style called naturalism grew out of realism and out of the idea that human beings have little self-determination but act in response to forces of nature and society that are beyond their control. **Naturalism** is often sordid and shocking as it depicts life as it is with no holds barred.

Symbolism   In theater, symbolism is the use of one element—a character, a prop, or a piece of scenery—to represent something else. However, the dramatic movement **symbolism** began in the late nineteenth century in France as a reaction against realism. Dramatists began to use symbolic elements to represent emotions, ideals, and values. Early twentieth-century Belgian playwright Maurice Maeterlinck is best known for his symbolist dramas. Other plays that display elements of symbolism include Ibsen's later plays, such as *The Wild Duck*, Chekhov's *The Cherry Orchard* and *The Sea Gull*, and the early plays of Yeats.

Expressionism   The characters and sets of **expressionism** tend to be distorted, oversimplified, and symbolic rather than realistic. The message of expressionism is often the uselessness of human hopes and dreams in the face of mechanistic forces. The movement began in Germany, and most of the notable expressionistic playwrights are German. The two best-known expressionists in Germany were Georg Kaiser (*From Morn to Midnight*) and Ernst Toller (*The Machine Wreckers*). American playwright Eugene O'Neill's *The Hairy Ape* and *The Emperor Jones* are also examples of expressionism.

Epic Theater   First developed by Bertolt Brecht, **epic theater** is a journalistic, nonemotional style. It uses signs, projections, films, and loudspeakers to present events in an episodic form. The epic theater is a reaction against emotionalism and naturalism. Brecht's plays, for example, do not necessarily involve the spectators in the problems and feelings of the characters, and entertaining is a secondary goal. Brecht's plays set forth events in an objective episodic form, using broad aspects of human experience rather than individual relationships. Some of his best-known plays are *Mother Courage*, *The Caucasian Chalk Circle*, and *The Threepenny Opera*.

This production of *Metamorphosis*, a stage adaptation of Franz Kafka's famous short story, used constructivism to suggest an inhuman atmosphere. Here ballet star Mikhail Baryshnikov portrays the protagonist, a victim of bourgeois society, who woke up one morning to find himself transformed into a cockroach.

Constructivism One trend of the early twentieth century produced the style known as constructivism, or Socialist Realism. Originated by Russian playwright Vsevolod Meyerhold, **constructivism** was in direct contrast to realism. Productions in the constructivist style were not based on real life and were not staged on traditional picture-frame stages. Instead, backgrounds of mechanical skeletons on various levels were connected by arches, ramps, ladders, and platforms. On these, actors were trained to move with precise symbolic movements designed to take the place of spoken language. Although the acting style associated with constructivism is fading, similar sets and skeletal frameworks are still used occasionally to suggest location and feeling.

Theater of the Absurd The phrase *theater of the absurd* was coined by twentieth-century drama critic, Martin Esslin, to describe the playwrights of the 1950s and 1960s whose drama presented the belief in the absurdity of human life. French writer Albert Camus influenced the development of the theater of the absurd with his philosophical essay "The Myth of Sisyphus." In this essay Camus suggests that human hopes and plans are ridiculous because the universe is a random place where things happen for no reason.

An absurdist world view leads playwrights to explore the theme of chaos. In **theater of the absurd,** language, a tool typically used to establish meaning, is proven unreliable. In absurdist plays, dialogue is usually meaningless or illogical, and, in some cases, absent altogether. *Waiting for Godot* by Samuel Beckett is one of the best-known plays in the absurdist style. Other important absurdist playwrights include Eugène Ionesco, Edward Albee, and Arthur Adamov.

Waiting for Godot, by Samuel Beckett, is one of the masterpieces of the theater of the absurd. The two main protagonists wait for a mysterious character who never arrives.

The school of philosophy known as existentialism is closely linked with the theater of the absurd. According to existentialism, we begin our lives in a random world that only offers us possibilities. Faced with free choice, we define our existence through our decisions, our actions, and our relations with other beings. In *No Exit* by Jean-Paul Sartre, three characters who have never met are put into a room and told they cannot leave. With no one to interact with but one another, the characters slowly begin to discover who they are.

Tom Stoppard's *Rosencrantz and Guildenstern Are Dead* is a lesson in existential frustration. Rosencrantz and Guildenstern have no information outside of the fact that they were sent for. They spend the entire play trying to find out what they are supposed to do, but before they discover the answer, their time onstage is over.

Theater of Involvement The participation of members of the audience in the action of the performance characterizes the **theater of involvement,** also called participatory theater. *Paradise Now* was one of the first productions staged as an involvement play. Involvement has been successful in such productions as *Cats,* in which performers go into the audience and play directly to individuals, and in *Tony n' Tina's Wedding*, in which the audience is called on to participate as wedding guests.

Theatricalism The style known as **theatricalism** simply says, "This is the theater. Accept it for what is, as it is." Theatricalism makes no pretense of reality because dramatic situations are *not* real situations. The cardboard moon, wooden-dowel swords, and the mute wall of *The Fantasticks* are illustrations of theatricalism.

Total Theater **Total theater** involves a fusion of all the performing arts into one presentation. Dance, mime, atmospheric music, and creative costuming and staging are combined with high-tech audiovisual special effects. Robert Wilson's *Einstein on the Beach* is an example.

Application
ACTIVITY

Choose one of the styles of theater mentioned in the previous pages, and trace its history from the beginning to the present. Include a thorough description of the style, cultural origins, and names of famous playwrights and philosophers associated with it. It would be helpful to view a play or a film written in that particular style. You might want to organize your information in the form of a time line, or you may find it more useful to trace the development on a map.

6 REVIEW

Summary and Key Ideas

Summarize the chapter by answering the following questions.

1. Compare the protagonist in a tragedy to the protagonist in a comedy.
2. What should an audience feel at the end of a tragedy?
3. List and describe seven causes of laughter.
4. Describe four types of drama that have characteristics of both comedy and tragedy.
5. Describe three styles of twentieth-century theater.

Discussing Ideas

1. What is the appeal of tragedy for an audience? What is meant by the "inevitability" of tragedy?
2. Discuss this statement: "Tragedy is universal; comedy is rooted in a particular time or place." Cite examples of plays or movies you have seen that support this statement.
3. Would you classify most of the comedy shows that appear on television as high comedy, low comedy, or something else? Give examples.
4. What is the principal difference between representational and presentational drama?
5. What risks do playwrights take when they create experimental drama? What risks might the audience take when they attend an experimental drama?

FOCUS ON Dramatic Texts

When you read a dramatic text, take time to think about the work's overall structure.
Then, think about the writer's style, noting his or her expressive qualities and characteristic language. Finally, decide what genre, or category of literary work—such as comedy or tragedy—the work belongs to. Analyzing these features of text will help you learn the playwright's purpose for writing.

Analyzing Structure All drama, whether live theater, film, or television, has the same basic structure. Choose a film or a television show that you've seen recently. In a one-page essay, outline the elements of the work's dramatic structure—the presentation of the exposition, plot, characters, and theme. To gain a deeper appreciation of the work, figure out what genre the work belongs to and do some research to learn more about the genre's history.

Evaluating Texts With a small group, select a play to read. After reading, get together to evaluate one of the following elements of the text: theme, setting, style, genre, or characterization. On your own, take time to reflect on the discussion. If your school was performing the play, how would such a discussion affect the play's staging?

VARIETIES OF DRAMA

INDEPENDENT ACTIVITY

Performance Art   Choose a poem that you consider to have a special message for your peers, and use it as the basis for an experiment with this innovative style of drama. Begin by practicing reading the poem aloud in different ways, and consider singing, shouting, or whispering as part of your interpretation. Then add accompaniments to your reading, such as music and dance. You might even consider supplementing your performance art with elements of epic theater. For example, slides flashed on a screen behind you might help reinforce your words and theme. Present your drama to the class.

Cooperative Learning Activity

Stylization

With a group of classmates, choose a scene from a drama that is set in the past. The drama you choose should be something that most of the class will recognize, such as *Julius Caesar* or *Cyrano de Bergerac*. Rewrite the scene using modern language. Present your scene in stylized form, wearing jeans and T-shirts, formal wear, leotards, choir robes, or costumes of your choice, as long as they are not authentic to the period of the original play. Discuss with the class how this adaptation differs from the original. Which does the class prefer? Why?

Across the CURRICULUM Activity

History   Working alone, with a partner, or with a group, choose a theme from history, such as war, progress, intolerance, or great leadership, and create a show featuring readings and short scenes from a variety of sources. Aim for a mixture of drama, short story, essay, and poetry from different historical periods. As an alternative, choose an interesting person and create a one-person show that focuses on his or her life and what he or she achieved. Readings from *Anne Frank: The Diary of a Young Girl* by Anne Frank; *Growing Up Puerto Rican* edited by Paulette Cooper; *My Lord What a Morning* by Marian Anderson; *Manchild in the Promised Land* by Claude Brown; *Native Son* by Richard Wright; or *Portrait of Myself* by Margaret Bourke-White might provide inspiration.

7 *History of Drama*

This scene depicts costumes and masks similar to those used in the commedia dell'arte. The painting, by Claude Gillot, is entitled *The Two Coaches*.

All the world's a stage and all the men and women merely players.

—WILLIAM SHAKESPEARE, *As You Like It*

SETTING THE SCENE

Focus Questions

How did the drama begin?

What characterized the drama of ancient Greece?

How did drama change during the Middle Ages and the Renaissance?

Who were the great Elizabethan playwrights?

How has American drama developed?

Vocabulary

trilogy	Passion Play	Morality play	Peking Opera
closet dramas	mansions	Moral Interludes	No (Noh)
Saint plays	cycle	commedia dell'arte	Bunraku
Mystery plays	folk drama	raked	Kabuki

The history of drama is closely related to the history of humanity. When the first hunters recounted their adventures using pantomime, when the first storytellers told their tales in rhythmic chants, and when the first organized groups of people found expression in the pantomime of war and fertility dances, the dramatic impulse demonstrated itself. Later, primitive actors used masks to portray gods or animals.

As civilization developed in different cultures, drama took definite forms. People worshiped gods and glorified earthly rulers with elaborate pageantry. Tales were told of the epic adventures of noble characters engaged in mighty conflicts or of humorous characters bumbling through their comic paces. These tales led to dramatic presentations, ultimately to be written and acted out again and again as societal ritual.

🎭 *Origins of Western Drama*

The earliest record of something very much like a theatrical performance comes from Egypt. Carved on a stone tablet about four thousand years ago, this account tells how Ikhernofret of Abydos arranged and played the leading role in a three-day pageant made up of actual battles, boat processions, and intricate ceremonies that told the story of the murder, dismemberment, and resurrection of the god Osiris.

GREEK DRAMA

CUE ▼

Greek tradition holds that Thespis, an actor-playwright, introduced masks into Greek plays.

Western drama started to develop in Greece in the sixth century B.C. as part of the worship of the Greek god Dionysus. To commemorate the god's death, a group of chanters, called the chorus, danced around an altar on which a goat was sacrificed. Therefore, this chorus was called the goat-singers, and their ritualistic chant was called the goat-song, or *tragos*. From *tragos* the word *tragedy* was derived. These ceremonies in honor of Dionysus evolved into dramatic contests. According to Greek folklore, Thespis won the first competition. Legend says that when Thespis stepped from the chorus and engaged in a dialogue with the other members, he became the first actor. The term *thespian* has been given to actors ever since.

The dramatic contests became part of a festival that lasted five or six days. On each of the last three days, a different playwright would present four plays. The first three plays were tragedies, often forming a **trilogy**— three plays related by theme, myth, or characters. The fourth play was customarily an irreverent, bawdy burlesque called a satyr play. Playwrights competed fiercely to win the laurel wreath at these dramatic contests.

Production in the Greek theater was a highly complex art form that used many clever mechanical devices. At first, performances were held in the open on hillsides surrounding a circular area called the orchestra, where the chorus danced. Wooden (later stone) seats were added to form the theater. It is believed that some theaters seated more than seventeen thousand patrons.

At the rear of the acting area was a small hut called the *skene,* where the actors changed masks and costumes. Later, the *skene* was enlarged into a stone building. A second story and wings were added, and scenery was painted on the front. On the roof of the *skene* was the god walk, from which the actors portraying the gods delivered their monologues.

Another device used in Greek plays was the *machina*, a cranelike hoist that permitted actors to appear above the stage as if flying. The *machina* could also lower actors from the roof of the *skene* to the orchestra. The *machina* was sturdy enough to carry a chariot and horses or sev-

This is the Theater of Dionysus as it looks today. You can still see the stone seats that at one time seated up to 17,000 spectators.

eral persons. Usually the character lowered by the *machina* represented a god from Mount Olympus who came to earth to settle the affairs of human beings, including the dilemma of the playwright who could not resolve the conflict satisfactorily without intervention from the gods. From the use of this contrivance came the term *deus ex machina* (god from the machine). This term is still used today to indicate an artificial plot device an author introduces late in a play to resolve difficulties. An unknown relative who leaves a legacy, a long-lost letter, and the discovery of a relative assumed dead are typical of *deus ex machina*. (Usually such a plot resolution weakens the play and works out acceptably only in farce, melodrama, or fantasy.)

Originally the theater was for men only, both as performers and spectators. Women did not attend the theater until the fourth century B.C.

The chorus was an integral part of early Greek plays. The chorus served to explain the situation, to bring the audience up-to-date, to make a commentary on the action from the point of view of established ideas, and to engage in dialogue with the actors. Over time, the responsibilities of the chorus diminished as the scope of the actors' roles expanded. Still, vestiges of the Greek chorus are found in theater today. The chorus in Anouilh's *Antigone,* the stage manager in *Our Town,* and El Gallo in *The Fantasticks* are three well-known examples of a modern chorus.

To ensure audience recognition, Greek tragic actors customarily wore masks, padded costumes, and boots with thick soles, called *cothurni* or *buskins.* Comic actors typically wore rather grotesque masks, costumes with exaggerated padding, and a type of sandal called a *sock.*

Any discussion of Greek theater must begin with tragedy. The Greek tragedies, considered classics of Western literature, involve conflicts that evolve from the clash between the will of the gods and the ambitions and desires of humanity. The plays show how useless human efforts are in the face of fate. The greatest writers of Greek tragedy are Aeschylus, Sophocles, and Euripides, who wrote in the fourth and fifth centuries B.C.

Aeschylus expanded the number of actors and reduced the size of the chorus. He is noted for the elevation and majesty of his language, which many feel has never been surpassed. Many critics refer to him as the father of tragedy. Of his ninety plays, only seven have been preserved. Aeschylus left us the only surviving Greek trilogy, the *Oresteia*. It tells the story of the murder of Agamemnon, the revenge taken by his children, and the punishment and final acquittal of his son.

One of the greatest Greek tragedians, ranked with Shakespeare as one of the great playwrights of all time, is Sophocles. A writer of exquisitely crafted plays, he refined plot structure to create beautifully unified works. Believing that human beings have divine qualities that elevate their struggles against fate, he achieved an amazing balance between the power of the gods and the importance of humanity. Inquisitive, yet reverent, Sophocles allows his characters to question fate and the wills of the gods. As a result, his characters are among the strongest ever to walk on a stage. He wrote more than one hundred plays, of which only seven have survived.

In Sophocles' tragedies, such as *Antigone*, pictured here, characters attain deep insights into the human condition. This wisdom, though, is only attained through suffering and loss.

Sophocles' *Oedipus Rex* stands as one of the world's most powerful examples of dramatic irony. Aristotle described it as the ideal tragedy. It is the story of a man who, through a combination of fate and his own character, unwittingly kills his own father and marries his mother. When he realizes the truth of his situation, he puts out his eyes in horror.

Sophocles' *Antigone* is also one of the world's great tragedies. Antigone is Oedipus's daughter. Her two brothers, Eteocles and Polynices, having disagreed about who should rule, have killed each other. Their uncle, Creon, having taken over the throne, has decreed that Polynices was in the wrong and, consequently, must remain unburied. The Greeks believed that desecration of the dead was offensive to the gods and that the soul of a body not given proper burial was doomed to wander eternally. Antigone defies Creon's decree in order to fulfill her higher loyalties to her family and the gods. She attempts to bury Polynices, is caught, and is placed in a cave to die. It is not until his own world crumbles around him that Creon realizes that human laws cannot supplant the laws of the gods.

CUE

A modern version of *Antigone*, by Jean Anouilh, has been widely performed in colleges and high schools.

The playwright Euripides became more interested in people's lives than in the religious views of his day. He emphasized human relationships and became the master of **pathos**, human sorrow and compassion. Of the ninety-two plays written by Euripides, seventeen tragedies and one satyr play exist in their entirety. *The Trojan Women* is one of literature's strongest indictments of war. *Medea* is the tragedy of a woman who seeks revenge on her husband to the extent of killing her own sons in order to grieve him. *Medea*, as well as *Antigone*, still ranks among the most poignant portrayals of women in dramatic literature.

One of the outstanding authors of Greek comedy is Aristophanes, who contributed forty plays, eleven of which have been preserved. Aristophanes, who considered nothing sacred, was a skilled **satirist** and a keen observer of humanity. His barbed wit mocked the leaders of Athens and the gods themselves. Three of his best-known plays are *The Frogs*, a writers' contest between Aeschylus and Euripides in Hades, judged by Dionysus himself; *The Clouds*, a travesty on Socrates and Greek education; and *Lysistrata*, a scathing attack on war.

Aristophanes' first nine plays represent what has come to be known as Old Comedy, which is noted for its wild comic fantasy. His last two plays are classified as Middle Comedy, being quieter and more coherent. Roman and, later, Renaissance writers were more influenced by the gentle treatment of everyday life in the New Comedy of Menander. Menander was a Greek playwright who wrote approximately one hundred years after Aristophanes. Although Menander wrote more than one hundred comedies, only one of his scripts—*Dyskolos*—has survived in its entirety.

ROMAN DRAMA

CUE ▼

As the Roman Empire grew, the cultural life of Rome began to decay. To gain the favor of the Roman mob, the emperors knew they must continue to amuse them with such spectacles as gladiatorial fights, wild-beast shows, and chariot races.

Roman drama was largely an imitation of Greek drama. In fact, the first work of Roman drama was commissioned to Andronicus, an author from a Greek colony. This first Roman tragedy was most likely a translation from a Greek play, and most Roman dramas that followed were adaptations of Greek plays. There were, however, a few plays written about the history of Rome. The majority of original Roman plays were comic representations of daily life, focusing on comical business rather than the development of plot or character. Plautus and Terence were two notable writers of Roman comedy. Only Terence's plays, however, showed appreciable improvement on their Greek counterparts.

At the time Terence and Plautus were writing, there were no permanent theaters. The stage was erected only when needed for a presentation. Over the next two hundred years interest in entertainment evolved, and theaters expanded into **amphitheaters,** large circular arenas that were surrounded by tiers of seats. At this time, the beginning of the first century A.D., Seneca, a writer of bombastic tragedies, was the only author to attempt anything like a play. Ironically, his plays, called **closet dramas,** were intended to be read rather than performed.

MEDIEVAL DRAMA

During the Middle Ages, drama developed along different lines throughout Europe. It is impossible to positively track this development because few records exist. The earliest evidence of drama in the Middle Ages is a partial manuscript from a western European liturgical drama dating to the tenth century. However, the prohibitions established by the Roman Catholic church against secular drama suggest the existence of other performances: acrobats, mimes, and dancers. The liturgical drama of this time was definitely influential in the development of drama, but did not direct the course of later secular plays.

The liturgical drama first came into existence as a question-and-answer song performed by monks on Easter. These "plays" were sung in Latin, and the performers eventually included priests, choirboys, and, later, nuns. Soon after the rise in popularity of the Easter service, liturgical dramas became a Christmas tradition also. As the occasions for performances grew, the dramas were translated from the Latin into the vernacular of the region and members of the congregation were allowed to perform in the plays. Saint and Mystery plays became popular forms of church drama.

Saint plays are based on legends of saints, and **Mystery plays** are based on biblical history. **The Passion Play,** which addresses the last week of Christ's life, is a well-known liturgical drama performed for the Easter service.

The early Saint and Mystery plays were staged in the churches on platforms called **mansions.** These mansions represented biblical settings such as Heaven, Hell, and the Sea of Galilee. As the popularity of these dramas increased, they were moved out of the church to the town square where the mansions were placed in a straight line. Some of these stages were permanent, but evidence exists that the players toured from city to city using these settings.

By the late fourteenth century, the medieval craft guilds had taken over the presentation of the Saint and Mystery plays in England. Most were performed during the festival of Corpus Christi, which had been officially instituted in A.D. 1311. Even though these guilds were secular, the members were associated with the church. Each guild presented one part of the story; for example the shipwrights presented the *Noah* pageant.

The craft guilds would tour through the country and present the liturgical plays on pageant wagons, which were stages on wheels. The **pageant wagons** were divided into two levels: the upper level was a platform stage, the lower level was a dressing room. Each guild had its pageant wagon decorated according to which play in the **cycle**—a series of short plays depict-

▼ **CUE**

The Passion Play, written in the medieval mystery play tradition, is still performed in Europe at Oberammergau, Germany, by the citizens of the Bavarian village where it was first performed in 1634. It has been produced every ten years since 1760.

Shown here is a scene from the Passion Play performed every ten years at Oberammergau, Germany.

ing religious history from creation through doomsday—they presented. The guilds moved through town as they presented their plays.

While the liturgical dramas were developing, the secular dramas, called **folk dramas,** were developing simultaneously. The first record of a folk play comes from twelfth-century England. Folk plays usually took place during planting time, harvest time, and Christmas and were staged outdoors. These plays were presented for folk festivals, which often coincided with Christian holidays. Out of these performances arose the famous Robin Hood plays (c. 1300), with the hero stealing from the rich and giving to the poor. An increasing amount of secular material, especially humorous incidents, made it into the liturgical performances. Also, the secular actors began presenting the popular liturgical dramas.

Since the popularity of drama was increasing by the fifteenth century, the church began presenting plays that were not for a specific holiday celebration. These **Morality plays** were didactic in nature, teaching the difference between right and wrong in the context of the devil and God battling for souls. These plays usually took the form of allegories dramatized by symbolic characters who represented abstract qualities, such as the title character who represents humankind in *Everyman*, the only Morality play that is still performed.

Since the church did not approve of the secular presentations of the traditional liturgical drama, the secular dramatists began presenting Morality plays, which evolved into Moral Interludes by the early sixteenth century. **Moral Interludes** were shorter than the traditional Morality play, and they included more humorous characters and incidents.

These secular dramatists became the first acting companies, and eventually came under the patronage of the nobility. Under the influence of the nobility, forms of drama evolved even further to include chronicle plays, productions based on historical events, and masques, highly artistic spectacles glorifying the nobility for which they were written and performed.

Application
ACTIVITY

Choose one of the historical cultures covered in the previous pages and research the trends in drama at that time. Prepare a presentation for the class in which you tell how the time period and the culture influenced the theater. You should note the effects the government, as well as the popular religion of the period, had on drama.

🪶 *The Renaissance and Drama*

Renaissance (meaning "rebirth") is the term commonly used to describe the transition from the medieval to the modern world in western Europe. Beginning in Italy in the early fourteenth century, the Renaissance eventually reached all of Europe and England. This rebirth of interest in the classics and belief in the potential for human perfection touched almost every aspect of life. Painting, sculpture, and architecture flourished, but drama did not—at least not for many years.

THE RENAISSANCE IN ITALY

Although the early offerings of Italian playwrights featured weak imitations of classical plays, cheap obscenities, or poorly constructed scripts, some advances in the dramatic arts were made in Italy during the Renaissance. Theater architecture was developed, as was stage equipment. Sets with perspective and colored lighting were introduced.

Another contribution to drama made by Italy during the Renaissance was the opera, an attempt to revive the simplicity and humanism of ancient Greek drama. Originally opera was an attempt by a group of

Opera is still a popular form of drama, regularly performed in most major American cities. Because opera originated in Italy, Italian remains the international language of opera.

scholars in Florence to imagine how the music of ancient Greek drama sounded. Opera introduced to theater music that emphasized the words with a solo vocal line and simple instrumental accompaniment. By the early seventeenth century, this form of Italian drama was being imitated in England and France.

Commedia dell'arte ("comedy of the profession") was performed by professional troupes specializing in comic improvisation that provided much of the new interest in theater from the sixteenth through eighteenth centuries. Commedia dell'arte troupes had mastered the art of playing out their comic **scenarios**, plot outlines posted backstage before each performance. There were no fully composed play scripts. Instead, the scenarios were detailed plot outlines that included *lazzi* and certain memorized lines. The *lazzi* were special humorous bits of stage business, usually set apart from the main action. A well-known *lazzi* was one in which the stage action continued while a comic actor laboriously caught a fly. Actors memorized set speeches, such as declarations of love, hate, and madness. The troupes also learned stock jokes, proverbs, songs, exit speeches, and comments on extraneous matters that could be used whenever convenient.

A manager led each troupe and usually wrote the scripts for it. Most plots were based on comic intrigue involving fathers who put obstacles in the way of their children's romances. Servants were very important characters, often successfully completing the matchmaking.

All the characters of the commedia dell'arte were stock types representing two social classes: the upper class and the servant class. The characters were identified by their costumes and, generally, by their masks; the **innamorati** and **innamoratae**, however, did not wear masks. The chart on the opposite page describes the most common characters in the commedia dell'arte.

Stock Characters of Commedia Dell'Arte

Upper-class characters	
Innamorati/ Innamoratae	Beautifully dressed young lovers; speak a refined language
Pantalone	A middle-aged or elderly man • a father who competes romantically with his son • a husband deceived by a young wife • an overly protective father guarding his young daughter from suitors
Dottore	Elderly gentleman; friend, sometimes rival of Pantalone; originally a law professor, later a medical man lacking common sense; ancestor of absent-minded professor; master of doubletalk and jargon

Male servant characters	
Arlecchino/Harlequin (zanni)	Usually clever persuaders and schemers; excellent at ad-libbing and acrobatics; clever pranksters, agile in mind and body
Brighella	A thief and bully; street-wise; later becomes lackey
Scapino	Crafty and unprincipled; runs away from danger
Pulcinella	A hump-backed, doltish male character
Pedrolino	A simple, awkward male character
Capitano	A boastful, cowardly Spaniard who brags of battles never fought and romances never experienced
Scaramuccia	A mustached servant; sometimes clever, sometimes cruel

Female servant character	
Fontesca	A serving maid; appears in many plays as Columbina, a clever and high-spirited flirt

Many stock characters of the commedia dell'arte have evolved into characters we recognize today. Pulcinella was a sometimes foolish, sometimes malicious character with a hooked nose and high-peaked hat. He was the ancestor of Punch of the Punch and Judy shows, puppet shows popular on the streets of cities in Great Britain in the eighteenth and nineteenth centuries. Still another of the male servants was Pedrolino, who later became known as Pierrot, the moonstruck eternal lover—melancholy and gentle, but always too romantic and too sad. Later, a sincerely devoted sweetheart, Pierrette, was paired with him, and they became the eternal lovers. To this duo, the temptress Columbina was added to form the eternal triangle. Another variation of the servant character, Pagliacci, was the man who must make others laugh while his own heart breaks. Scaramuccia later became the French character Scaramouche, who is considered to be the ancestor of the wicked mustached villain common in Victorian melodramas.

THE RENAISSANCE ELSEWHERE IN EUROPE

Written drama evolved in Spain, where Cervantes (1547–1616), Lope de Vega (1562–1635), and Calderón (1600–1681) contributed to the mounting interest in theater. One of Spain's foremost the-

TRAGÉDIES CÉLÈBRES
La vie est un songe
Calderon de la Barca. 1601 1682

Acte III, Scène 3.
Le roi : Regarde-moi me jeter à tes pieds!
Sigismond Roi, Père
Relève-toi et tends-moi la main

Véritable Extrait de viande LIEBIG.

Voir l'explication au verso.

atrical contributions is Don Juan, a character derived from a Spanish legend. This sensual character recurs in dramas from the fifteenth to twentieth centuries.

France developed professional theater under the patronage of the state with such great plays as *The Cid* by Corneille (1606–1684); *The Miser, The Misanthrope,* and *The Imaginary Invalid* by Molière (1622–1673); and *Phaedra* by Racine (1639–1699).

Strolling players kept the drama alive during this period by appearing before the public in village squares and before the nobility in their castles. They created melodramatic history plays, rowdy comedies, and romantic love stories that were the origins of the great dramas of later generations.

THE RENAISSANCE IN ENGLAND

The climax of Renaissance drama came during the Elizabethan Age in England. This was a period in which drama was the expression of the soul of a nation, and theater became a vital force in the lives of the people.

One of the first English comedies, *Ralph Roister Doister*, was produced in 1552. The author, Nicholas Udall (1504–1556), modeled his comedy on Plautus's plays. The first true English tragedy was *Gorboduc*, which was performed in 1562. Many other notable plays were written in England during this period.

Famous Elizabethan Plays	
Author	**Play**
John Webster (c.1580–1634) Thomas Heywood (c.1570–1641) Thomas Kyd (1558–1594) Francis Beaumont (1584–1616) Beaumont and John Fletcher (1579–1625)	*The Duchess of Malfi* *A Woman Killed with Kindness* *The Spanish Tragedy* *The Knight of the Burning Pestle* *The Maid's Tragedy*

THREE ELIZABETHAN DRAMATISTS

Towering above all the brilliant actor-playwrights responsible for the glory of the Elizabethan period, three produced plays that have never lost their appeal. The plays of Marlowe, Jonson, and Shakespeare continue to be produced today.

Christopher Marlowe   Christopher Marlowe (1564–1593) introduced the first important use of blank (unrhymed) verse, the

CUE

In the Elizabethan theater, specially trained boys played all female roles.

"mighty line" of English poetic drama. Combining an extraordinary use of language and the excitement of melodramatic plots, he wrote *Tamburlaine the Great, The Jew of Malta,* and *Edward II.* These plays present the glory and the horror of the age. It is his *Doctor Faustus,* the story of a man who sells his soul, however, that brilliantly bridges the gap between the medieval age and the Renaissance.

Ben Jonson Ben Jonson (1572–1637) was a master of English comedy. He wrote *Volpone, The Alchemist,* and *Every Man in His Humour.*

To the Elizabethans, the word *humor* (or *humour,* as the British spell it) referred not to an attitude of amusement, but to a personality trait. The Renaissance was a period in which anatomical study, as well as the arts, was developing. Scholars believed that all matter was made of four elements—air, earth, fire, and water—and that the human body was composed of these same four elements, each having its own effect on the personality. The balance of the four in each person's body decided his or her type.

The Humors		
Element	Body Fluid	Personality
air fire water earth	blood yellow bile phlegm black bile	sanguine—light-hearted, happy-go-lucky choleric—angry, hot-tempered phlegmatic—dull, listless melancholy

The humor of most interest in Elizabethan plays is that of black bile, represented by earth and the melancholy personality. The melancholy character fell into three main types: the lover, the malcontent, and the intellectual. Hamlet is an excellent example of the intellectual melancholy humor. Although most stage figures had a predominating humor, a balanced personality was the most desired. This is evidenced by Mark Antony's tribute to Brutus in *Julius Caesar:* " . . . the elements [were] so mixed in him that Nature might stand up and say to all the world, this was a man."

Jonson widened the scope of the humors to include any strong personality trait, especially a weakness, a foible, or a folly that could make a character laughable.

William Shakespeare William Shakespeare (1564–1616) is considered by many people to be not only the greatest Elizabethan dramatist but perhaps the greatest dramatist of all time. He is a towering literary figure whose characterizations, beautiful poetry, and never-to-be-forgotten lines echo a majesty best expressed by his friendly rival, Ben Jonson, who said that Shakespeare "was not of an age but for all time."

The ideal way to become acquainted with Shakespeare is to see his plays, not merely to read them or read about them. The plays were written by a practical man of the theater who intended them to be seen—not read—by a loud, boisterous audience accustomed to shouting its approval or hissing its displeasure. A play had to be exciting, moving, and violent, filled with fury, humor, and truth, in order to keep such an audience interested. Shakespeare's characters felt emotions— love, jealousy, ambition, joy, and grief— that are as universal today as they were four hundred years ago.

The characters form the center of interest in Shakespeare's plays. Note exactly how each is introduced and how well defined the personality immediately becomes. Because in his day theatergoers did not receive programs to provide explanations, Shakespeare used the soliloquy and accurate descriptions by other actors to delineate his characters. A **soliloquy** is a speech delivered by an actor alone on the stage that reveals the character's innermost thoughts.

THE GREATS
★ ★ ★ ★ ★
Elizabethan playwright William Shakespeare produced some of the world's most enduring plays.

Application
ACTIVITY

Read any of Shakespeare's plays and find examples of dialogues apparently intended for the people who viewed his productions from the area surrounding the pit (the groundlings). Look especially for remarks identified as asides.

Built in 1576 by James Burbage, the first English public playhouse, the Theatre, was located outside London. His son Cuthbert Burbage was the manager of the company later housed in the famous Globe theater, with which Shakespeare was associated as actor-playwright.

THE ELIZABETHAN PLAYHOUSE

The design of Elizabethan theaters was inspired by inn yards, where the audience stood around a platform stage or watched the onstage action from rooms surrounding a courtyard. These playhouses were many-sided buildings with two levels for acting and three for seating. The acting platform, usually five to six feet above ground level, has been called an unlocalized platform stage because little or no scenery was used to indicate locale. A line from the play, or possibly a symbolic object, was usually enough to inform the audience of the play's geographical setting.

Behind the stage was the **tiring house,** a room that functioned as the actors' dressing room. In the center rear of the stage

ELIZABETHAN THEATER

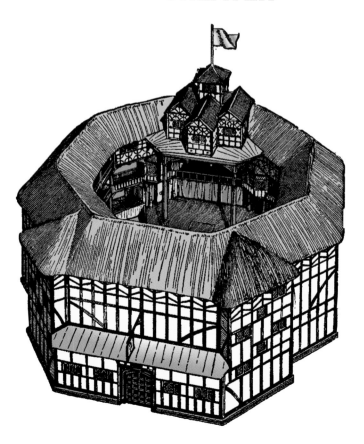

was a curtained recess called the **study,** or inner below. This area was used to reveal particular settings, such as a bedroom or the tent of Antony in *Antony and Cleopatra.* In the center of the second-level acting area was a shallow balcony, the **tarras,** behind which a curtain called the **arras** was often hung to conceal another recess called the **chamber.** This area might have been used by musicians, or even members of the audience. Under the stage was a cellar that held the devices used to project ghosts and demons through trapdoors in the floor of the stage. These trapdoors were used in scenes like that of the gravediggers in *Hamlet.*

The **Heavens,** a roof supported by two ornate columns, was above the stage. The sun, moon, stars, clouds, and the signs of the zodiac were painted on the underside of the roof. An actor who spoke of the heavens and earth had only to point to the roof over-

▼ CUE

In some of his plays, Shakespeare commented sharply on the lack of discernment of the people standing in the pit, who reeked of garlic and body odor, ate and drank during the performances, and reacted loudly to what they liked and disliked.

The original Globe theater opened in 1599 but burned in 1613. It was immediately rebuilt and operated until 1642. In 1989 excavation began to find the original foundation—five percent of which was uncovered. Historians used that portion of foundation along with other archaeological evidence to rebuild the twenty-sided theater. Its opening season was the summer of 1997.

head and the stage floor beneath to create the illusion of a microcosmic universe. The back wall of the stage looked like the outside of a multistoried Elizabethan house.

Above the Heavens was what appeared to be a small house, which was appropriately called the **scenery hut.** This structure housed the machinery that raised and lowered actors to the stage, often implying these actors were ghosts or supernatural creatures. When a play was to be performed, a trumpeter played in the tower above the scenery hut. A flag was flown from the tower on the days of performances, too.

Because there was no electricity at this time, the area surrounding the stage, known as the pit, was open to the sky to supply sunlight. Since these structures were not protected from the elements, the floor was sloped toward a central drain to carry off rainfall. The members of the audience who paid a penny to stand in the pit were called **groundlings.** The groundlings were typically apprentices, soldiers, sailors, country folk, and "cut purses," the Elizabethan equivalent of present-day pickpockets. The surface of the pit consisted of a mixture of ash, sand, silt, and hazelnut shells, partially because the audience amused itself during the play by eating nuts and apples. The more refined audience occupied the gallery seats, for which an additional fee was charged. The most expensive seats were next to, above, or even on the stage.

The stage of the reconstructed Globe features an ornate back wall that has three openings. The pillars on each side of the stage are made of oak and painted to look like marble. They support the Heavens, the name given to the painted ceiling of the stage.

🦋 *Later Drama in England*

Following the Elizabethan era, England experienced a period of civil war, beginning in 1642, that ended with the formation of a republican government controlled by the Puritans. For eighteen years, all theater was banned. It was not until the Restoration in 1660, when the monarchy was restored and Charles II became king, that theater became legal again.

RESTORATION DRAMA

Important innovations were made in drama during the Restoration. (Most of them, however, were incorporations of developments in Europe.) With the English Royal Patent of 1662, which awarded a theater monopoly to two entrepreneurs, women appeared as players for the first time. The patent said that "all women's parts should be performed by women" and that plays and acting should be considered "not only harmless delights but useful and instructive representations of human life."

Theater buildings influenced by Italian theater practice and closed to the sky were built during this period. Audiences were seated on level floors. So that they could all see the performance, the stage floor was **raked**, that is, sloped upward away from the viewers. The actors, therefore, moved "up" and "down" the stage. This is how the terms *upstage* and *downstage* came into existence. It was also during the Restoration that elaborate scenery and mechanical equipment came into use in England.

Among the Restoration dramatists are a few whose plays are still performed today. William Wycherley (1640–1716), with *The Country Wife,* started the fashionable trend in comedies. William Congreve's (1670–1729) *Love for Love* and *The Way of the World* set a standard for later comedies of manners. George Farquhar (1678–1707), with *The Beaux' Stratagem,* brought a refreshing breath of the country into the dissolute city life depicted on the stage.

> ### ▼ CUE
>
> During the Restoration, only two playhouses had official sanction. Their names are still famous: the Drury Lane Theater and Lincoln's Inn Fields. From these two theaters came the term *legitimate theater,* which we now use to refer to professional stage plays.

ENGLISH DRAMA SINCE 1700

The eighteenth century produced only two outstanding playwrights. Richard Brinsley Sheridan (1751–1816) wrote two social comedies: *The School for Scandal* and *The Rivals,* which features the immortal Mrs. Malaprop, the world's greatest misuser of words. Oliver Goldsmith (1730–1774) was a dramatist whose fame in the theater rests on one play, *She Stoops to Conquer.*

This is a nineteenth century playbill from Gilbert and Sullivan's comic opera *The Mikado.* Comedy saw a revival in popularity during the eighteenth and nineteenth centuries.

The London stage of the nineteenth century established the trends that have given it the prestige it holds today. Gilbert and Sullivan created their clever comic operas, among them *The Mikado, H.M.S. Pinafore,* and *The Pirates of Penzance.* Oscar Wilde, with his genius for epigrams and brilliant dialogue, wrote *The Importance of Being Earnest* at the end of the century.

Of all English dramatists, many people feel that Irish-born Bernard Shaw (1856–1950) ranks as the greatest playwright next to Shakespeare. Shaw was a playwright dedicated to the exploration of ideas through drama. His satiric humor and fascinating characters keep alive such plays as *Saint Joan, Candida, Man and Superman, Caesar and Cleopatra, Pygmalion, Androcles and the Lion,* and *Arms and the Man.*

Shaw stresses two concepts in his plays. The first of these was what he called the "Life Force"—the belief that humanity will improve and strengthen in spite of itself. Shaw states this philosophy strongly in the third act of *Man and Superman* in a dream sequence often presented alone as "Don Juan in Hell." The second idea is called the "Thinking Person's Society." Shaw said that of every group of 1,000 people, there are 700 who do not think, 299 idealists, and 1 thinking person. Shaw hoped to turn the idealists into thinkers through engagement with his dramas.

England is still a center for theater lovers today. They flock to London to the National Theatre, the Barbican, and the West End, where they can choose from any number of productions of all types. They are assured versatile and superlative acting at reasonable prices.

Summer theater festivals flourish throughout Great Britain. Of these, the Royal Shakespeare Memorial Theatre at Stratford-upon-Avon, the Edinburgh International Festival, and the Malvern Festival offer the most varied and exciting fare.

You may be familiar with the works of such modern British playwrights as John Osborne, who introduced the "angry young men" in *Look Back in Anger*; J. B. Priestley *(An Inspector Calls)*; T. S. Eliot *(Murder in the Cathedral)*; Harold Pinter *(The Caretaker)*; Tom Stoppard *(Rosencrantz and Guildenstern Are Dead)*; Caryl Churchill *(Top Girls)*; Peter Shaffer *(Amadeus)*; and Alan Aychbourn *(Absurd Person Singular)*.

🐚 *Later Drama Elsewhere in Europe*

Drama has flourished throughout Europe for three centuries. European dramatists have initiated trends that have been followed in other parts of the world.

Czechoslovakia The Čapek brothers in the former Czechoslovakia achieved fame in the 1920s and 1930s with expressionistic plays that deal with social issues. The theme of *R. U. R. (Rossum's Universal Robots)*, for example, is robots taking over humanity.

Germany Goethe (gœ´•tə), who wrote from the 1770s to the early 1800s, towers above all other German writers. His poetic drama *Faust* tells the tragedy of a man who sold his soul to the devil to attain all his worldly desires and regain his youth. It is written in verse and has inspired three operas as well as literary works in languages other than German. Goethe and Friedrich von Schiller developed an approach to theater and acting that influenced actors and playwrights far beyond their geographical sphere.

In the 1890s, Gerhart Hauptmann began the new era of realism, called naturalism, in the German theater. His most noted work is *The Weavers*, a great drama that sets forth a social issue built around a group protagonist.

Henrik Ibsen, a nineteenth-century Norwegian playwright, is sometimes referred to as the father of modern drama. The scene shown is from one of his masterpieces, *Hedda Gabler.*

From the 1920s through the 1950s, Bertolt Brecht developed epic theater. *Mother Courage, The Caucasian Chalk Circle,* and *The Good Woman of Setzuan* are among his plays most often produced in the United States.

France   Molière, Voltaire, Victor Hugo, and Alexandre Dumas in the seventeenth, eighteenth, and nineteenth centuries, produced important drama in France. In the late nineteenth century, Edmond Rostand wrote *Cyrano de Bergerac,* the romance of a poet-swordsman with a huge nose. The story is world-famous, and several movies have retold the tale. Many French writers found success in the last half of the twentieth century. Among them are Jean Giraudoux *(Tiger at the Gates, The Madwoman of Chaillot)* and Jean Anouilh *(The Lark, Antigone, Becket),* who have been popular in the United States. Jean-Paul Sartre's *No Exit* and *The Flies* reflect an existential outlook. Although he was born in Ireland, Samuel Beckett's plays were written in France. He is especially known for *Waiting for Godot.* The musicals *Les Misérables* and *Miss Saigon* by Alain Boublil and Claude-Michel Schonberg have made a major impression on theater audiences in recent years.

Ireland   Drama in Ireland has a brief but brilliant history, starting at the turn of the twentieth century with the plays of William Butler Yeats and Lady Gregory. Yeats was dedicated to retelling the ancient tales of Ireland through poetic drama. *At the Hawk's Well* beautifully combines myth, dance, and poetry. Augusta (Lady) Gregory was mainly responsible, along with Yeats, for establishing theater in Ireland. Her own plays include *Spreading the News* and *Hyacinth Halvey,* and she collaborated with Yeats on several others. John Millington Synge, who wrote in the early 1900s, is considered by many to be one of the finest Irish dramatists. *The Playboy of the Western World* and *Riders to the Sea* are frequently produced today. Sean O'Casey, with *Juno and the Paycock* and *The Plough and the Stars,* was the prominent mid-century voice of Irish theater. Late twentieth-century Irish playwrights include Brian Friel *(Dancing at Lughnasa)* and Brendan Behan *(The Hostage).*

Italy   Luigi Pirandello, who wrote in the early 1900's, held the conviction that people are not what they appear. This is central to the themes of his plays. His works are complicated and intriguing. *Six Characters in Search of an Author* and *Henry IV* are the most frequently produced of his works.

Norway   During the last half of the nineteenth century, Henrik Ibsen of Norway, sometimes called the father of modern drama and the father of realism, introduced realism in dialogue and characterization. His chief theme—that society must protect and develop the individual rights of each person—had a special appeal for Americans. Ibsen wrote two magnificent dramas in the Romantic style, *Peer Gynt* and *Brand*, but it is his realistic dramas—*A Doll's House, Ghosts, Hedda Gabler, An Enemy of the People,* and *The Master Builder*—that account for his widespread popularity.

Russia Two Russians are especially influential in their contributions to the theater. The early realist playwright Anton Chekhov was perhaps the greatest Russian dramatist. Written primarily in the late 1890s, his plays include *The Sea Gull, The Three Sisters, Uncle Vanya,* and *The Cherry Orchard.* Konstantin Stanislavski, Chekhov's greatest interpreter, had a tremendous influence on acting. Portions of his writings are used as the basis for defining Method acting, the acting theory centered on the inner understanding of a role plus the perfecting of the physical response. (More can be found about Stanislavski in Chapter 4.) The Moscow Art Theater, which Stanislavski founded and directed, became the finest in the world from the viewpoint of ensemble and realistic production.

Spain José Echegaray employed the verse form and the imagery of the Romantics, but his plays often deal with controversial social issues of the late 1800s and early 1900s. He was the only Spanish dramatist whose plays were acted abroad until Jacinto Benavente won the Nobel Prize for literature in 1922 for *The Passion Flower.* Symbolist playwright Federico García Lorca's *Blood Wedding,* written in the 1930s, is frequently seen in university theaters.

Drama in Asia

China Drama in China dates to A.D. 200, beginning with rituals that combined song, dance, gestures, and costumes. When theater captured the interest of the ruling dynasties, drama based on traditional Chinese myths and legends became an important art form.

Chinese drama has traditionally been linked to the government and the country's political situation. Translated Western dramas of the early twentieth century, such as the stage adaptation of *Uncle Tom's Cabin,* were brought to China from Europe and the United States. When the Japanese invaded China in 1937, playwrights wrote new plays and reworked old plays to include patriotic propaganda. With the establishment of the People's Republic in 1949 came more government involvement in the arts, but this time it was in the form of censorship. At the end of the Cultural Revolution in 1972, the regulation of theater ended and a strong dramatic tradition that had been suppressed for twenty-three years emerged.

Peking Opera, developed early in the nineteenth century, incorporates aspects of historical drama, spoken drama, song drama, dance drama, and ballet—the five main types of drama in China today. Despite the history of governmental regulation, many traditional aspects have remained intact in the various types of Chinese drama. The stage settings are scarce and symbolic; for example, a desk might symbolize a mountain if an actor stands on it, or it might symbolize an altar if the actor kneels. Costumes are often stylized, representing traditional characters and social classes throughout Chinese history. Symbolic colors and designs that represent different human qualities are used in makeup. Even though these traditions prevail, the tradition of exclusively using male actors has not, and today both women and men appear onstage.

Japan   Three forms of drama that are uniquely Japanese—*No, Bunraku,* or doll theater; and *Kabuki*—have been introduced to the rest of the world.

No   In an attempt to create a form of drama suitable for the Japanese nobility, fourteenth-century actor Zeami Motokiyo fused and refined two earlier, rougher forms of entertainment. The result was **No** drama. Zeami looked to classical Japanese literature for the subject matter of *No,* bringing to life brave warriors, honorable young women, and revered gods and demons. *No* combines words, dance, and music that are rhythmically coordinated to the events of the story.

These traditional forms of *No* have been passed down from generation to generation by actors who dedicate their lives to the art form. There are generally three parts in a *No* production: *jo-ha-kyu.* To understand these parts, think of the *jo* as the introduction, the *ha* as the body, and the *kyu* as the conclusion. However, the *ha* of a *No* production is also broken down into the *jo, ha,* and *kyu.* This highly-structured form of drama usually starts with a story about a god and progresses to include a warrior play, a love story with a beautiful woman, and a frenzied closing dance by a god or demon.

No is still performed in Japan much as it was performed almost six hundred years ago. In keeping with tradition, only men are players in *No.* However, due to the changing tastes of audiences, the tempo of *No* has slowed over the centuries.

Actors of Kabuki theater devote their entire lives to their art. As a result, Kabuki productions are characterized by extraordinary richness.

Bunraku   In the late 1600s, puppets, chanting, and music were combined in **Bunraku,** or Japanese doll theater. *Bunraku* puppets are four-foot tall marionettes carved from wood in intricate detail— including realistic, moveable eyes, eyebrows, and mouths. Each puppet is manipulated by three puppeteers dressed in black who hold the puppet close to their bodies as they move around the stage. Dialogue is assigned to specialized chanters who appear onstage to perform each scene. As in *No,* only men are players in *Bunraku.*

Kabuki   In the seventeenth century, **Kabuki** developed as a form of entertainment for the general population. Striving to be fashionable and up-to-date, *Kabuki* borrows the popular aspects of many Japanese drama styles, including *No* and *Bunraku.* Like these two forms of drama, *Kabuki* permits only male performers; however, *Kabuki* distinguishes itself through characteristic makeup and costuming, assorted musical styles, demanding vocal displays, and production-enhancing stage settings. Today *Kabuki* is enjoying a revival with Japanese youth as it continues to be an innovative art form.

▼ **CUE**

The special *No* theater is like a temple, with an eighteen-foot square extending into the audience. The square is supported by four wooden pillars that form part of the action.

🪷 *Drama in the United States*

The American Company, managed by David Douglass, was the first professional company to produce plays in the American colonies. The first play was *The Prince of Parthia,* by Thomas Godfrey, presented on April 24, 1767, in Philadelphia. It was strictly an imitation of British blank-verse tragedies and had only one performance. *The Contrast,* by Royall Tyler, which opened at the John Street Theater in New York City on April 16, 1787, was the first comedy to achieve professional success in the United States. It introduced Jonathon, the original typical Yankee—shrewd, wholesome, and humorous—who has appeared in many guises since. *Fashion,* by Anna Cora Mowatt, produced in 1845, however, is considered to be the first uniquely American comedy. It, like *The Contrast,* satirizes social pretenders.

Actors   The first actors on American stages were English professional troupes who presented popular London plays. The legendary family that links the early American stage with the modern is the Barrymores. John Drew was an Irish actor who came to America in 1846; he married Louise Lane, the first female American actor-manager. They had three children: John Drew; Sidney; and Georgiana, who married Maurice Barrymore, a dashing Irish actor. The Barrymores were the parents of Lionel, Ethel, and John, who were America's leading actors for years.

▼ **CUE**

The first theater in America was built in Williamsburg, Virginia, in 1716, but there was no trace of it left by the time the city was restored in the 1920s.

Two noteworthy American actors broke new ground when they found success abroad. Ira Aldridge (1804–1867) was the first great African American actor to achieve international fame when he appeared as Othello in London. He was also critically acclaimed for his portrayal of King Lear in Russia. Charlotte Cushman (1816–1876) became the first American woman to find success on the stage abroad. She popularized the nineteenth-century practice of women playing male roles with her portrayals of such Shakespearean characters as Hamlet and Romeo.

Edwin Booth (1833–1893) is one of the greatest romantic actors America has produced. His illustrious career suffered an eclipse when his brother, John Wilkes Booth, also a well-known actor, assassinated Abraham Lincoln. Edwin Booth retired temporarily after the assassination and never appeared again in Washington, D.C.

Playwrights Well into the early part of the twentieth century, American playwrights continued to follow prevailing conventions. Beginning in the 1920s, however, American theater became more innovative, sometimes even experimental. The social problems of the twentieth century have

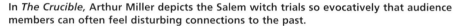

In *The Crucible,* Arthur Miller depicts the Salem witch trials so evocatively that audience members can often feel disturbing connections to the past.

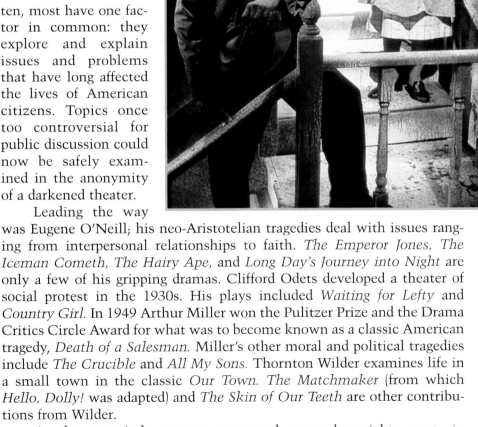

In *A Raisin in the Sun*, playwright Lorraine Hansberry explores the stresses that pull at and the ties that bind family members.

been explained and dramatized in the plays of many American playwrights. Whatever the type of play or the style in which it was written, most have one factor in common: they explore and explain issues and problems that have long affected the lives of American citizens. Topics once too controversial for public discussion could now be safely examined in the anonymity of a darkened theater.

Leading the way was Eugene O'Neill; his neo-Aristotelian tragedies deal with issues ranging from interpersonal relationships to faith. *The Emperor Jones, The Iceman Cometh, The Hairy Ape,* and *Long Day's Journey into Night* are only a few of his gripping dramas. Clifford Odets developed a theater of social protest in the 1930s. His plays included *Waiting for Lefty* and *Country Girl.* In 1949 Arthur Miller won the Pulitzer Prize and the Drama Critics Circle Award for what was to become known as a classic American tragedy, *Death of a Salesman.* Miller's other moral and political tragedies include *The Crucible* and *All My Sons.* Thornton Wilder examines life in a small town in the classic *Our Town. The Matchmaker* (from which *Hello, Dolly!* was adapted) and *The Skin of Our Teeth* are other contributions from Wilder.

As the twentieth century progressed, new playwrights wrote in earnest about problems of American society. Although James Baldwin was best known for other forms of literature, his plays *Blues for Mister Charlie* and *Amen Corner* were important influences on the civil rights movement of the 1960s. Lillian Hellman explores the moral landscape of the South in her plays *The Children's Hour* and *Little Foxes*. Lorraine Hansberry wrote about a variety of social issues, such as equality for women and family solidarity. She was the first African American and the youngest person to win the New York Drama Critics Circle Award when she won in 1959 for *A Raisin in the Sun*. Known as the "playwright of woman's selfhood," Susan Glaspell wrote plays that were influences in the feminist movement in the early twentieth century. Her most critically acclaimed works include *Alison's House*, for which she won a Pulitzer Prize, and *Trifles*.

Charles Fuller won the Pulitzer Prize in 1982 for his play about problems in the military, *A Soldier's Play*. Alice Childress deals forthrightly with racism in her plays *Wine in the Wilderness* and *Trouble in Mind*. The first African American to win the Pulitzer Prize for drama, Charles Gordone won in 1970 for *No Place to Be Somebody*, in which he explored what motivates people to survive against fantastic odds. Neil Simon, one of the most prolific writers of the twentieth century, writes comedies that are both personal and universal. *Barefoot in the Park*, *The Odd Couple*, *Brighton Beach Memoirs*, and *Biloxi Blues* are just a few of his many successful efforts.

David Henry Hwang skillfully blends Eastern and Western cultures in his plays *M. Butterfly* and *FOB*. Loneliness, gender conflict, and the paradox of reality and myth are presented in terse, pointed dialogue in the plays of David Mamet. *Glengarry Glen Ross*, which won the Pulitzer in

This scene is from *FOB* by David Henry Hwang, who also wrote *M. Butterfly*.

1984, and *Oleanna* are two of his best-known efforts. August Wilson's plays examine African Americans throughout the twentieth century. Wilson's goal is to ask one question for each decade of the century and to answer it in a play. *Fences* won the Pulitzer Prize in 1987, and *The Piano Lesson* won in 1990. Wendy Wasserstein has been dubbed the "voice of her generation" for her comedies dealing with how bright, well-educated women cope with the often-conflicting demands of career and family in the age of feminism. The *Heidi Chronicles* is her best-known play. Music, dance, and poetry are combined in Ntozake Shange's *for colored girls who have considered suicide/when the rainbow is enuf.* This coming-of-age play probes the experiences of women who feel isolated from the rest of society. Beth Henley, whose best-known plays are *Crimes of the Heart* and *The Miss Firecracker Contest,* examines the emotional struggles of Southern women and their families. Henley's offbeat humor and intimate tone shed a unique light on the conflict between freedom and responsibility. John Guare uses farcical comedy to look at domestic relations, society, politics, and religion. His most popular plays are *The House of Blue Leaves* and *Six Degrees of Separation.* Known mostly for his off-Broadway successes, Sam Shepard employs a unique blend of styles to expose the myths of the American culture. His *Buried Child* won the Pulitzer Prize in 1979.

Henley's *Crimes of the Heart* provides the actors with a challenging opportunity to portray roles of depth and humor. The actors playing the three sisters must portray their feelings toward each other with an understanding of their past life together.

Summary and Key Ideas

Summarize the chapter by answering the following questions.

1. How did drama probably originate?
2. What was the function of the Greek chorus?
3. Name three authors of Greek tragedies and some of their works.
4. How did the Saint and Mystery plays change drama?
5. What is the Renaissance? How did it affect drama?
6. Describe some of the characters of the commedia dell'arte.
7. Who were the great Elizabethan dramatists?
8. What is the essence of the *No* theater?
9. Identify the following playwrights: Shaw, Cervantes, O'Neill, Goethe, Ibsen, Marlowe, Miller.

Discussing Ideas

1. If you could choose one period in the history of the theater in which to be an actor, which would it be? Why?
2. Shakespeare was an actor as well as a playwright. How do you think his stage experience affected his writing?
3. Shakespeare said, "All the world's a stage. . . ." What do you think this means?

FOCUS ON Theater and American Society

What do medieval craft guilds and the playwrights of recent times have in common?
In their style and subject matter, both show the influence of the social concerns of the people of their day.

Analyzing Theater and Society In *A Raisin in the Sun*, playwright Lorraine Hansberry explored the relationships in an African American family struggling to overcome poverty. Her topic matter was so fresh that writer James Baldwin commented, "Never before, in the entire history of the American theater, had so much of the truth about black people's lives been seen on stage." Hansberry was continuing a tradition of playwrights interested in social change. Do research to help you find two American playwrights who were influenced by the civil rights movement of the 1950s and 1960s. After learning about their work, write a one-page paper analyzing how the playwrights were influenced by events in American society.

Exploring Criticism Comparing the views of different critics can help you understand a work better. Find two pieces of dramatic criticism—or critical writing—about the work of one of the playwrights you found in your research. Give the class a short presentation comparing and contrasting the pieces of criticism.

HISTORY OF DRAMA

INDEPENDENT ACTIVITIES

Modern Morality Play   Choose one of Aesop's fables, such as "The Fox and the Hare" or "The Boy Who Cried 'Wolf'," and use it as the basis of a short morality play. Keep in mind that your goal is to illustrate and teach a lesson about right and wrong behavior. The characters should personify virtues or qualities. Sketch out the conflict and its resolution and have a classmate help you present your play. Ask the class to identify what the characters represent.

Shakespearean Interpretation   Choose a particularly moving or meaningful monologue from a Shakespearean play. Use the role-scoring questions in Chapter 4 to analyze your character; then present your monologue to the class. Discuss why this character, and so many of Shakespeare's characters, are still recognizable today. What might explain the survival of Shakespeare's work?

Cooperative Learning Activity

Tragic Greek Myths   Greek tragedy and some myths have in common the theme of conflict between the gods and a mortal who fights to be in control of his or her destiny. In fighting for such a goal, however, a person is guilty of hubris, or overwhelming pride, and there are consequences. With a group of classmates, choose a myth that embodies this theme and turn it into a Greek tragedy, complete with chorus. Have the class suggest alternative ways of resolving the conflict.

Across the CURRICULUM Activity

History   Drama has evolved from rough pantomimes of wars and hunts to the more refined productions of the Renaissance through drama today. To better understand the importance of drama, research the historical and cultural developments in theatrical styles and genres. Perhaps you will find it easier to narrow your search to a certain century or a certain culture. Look for some reflection of the life of the times in the theatrical trends. Use your findings to argue in favor of one of the following:

- Drama is a mere form of entertainment.
- Drama is a reflection of the lives and times of cultures.

Discuss your research in a group and see if anyone has found evidence to support or refute your argument.

Puppet Theater

Puppets have long been a part of theater throughout the world. From the earliest forms of Asian drama to the most recent American television programs, puppet theater has engaged and delighted both sophisticated adults and naive children. Skilled puppeteers can generate a drama as intense and powerful as any found on the traditional stage or as whimsical and imaginative as *The Muppets* or *Sesame Street*. In fact, it is this versatility that affords the student of drama great challenges and great opportunities.

KINDS OF PUPPETS

Puppets are as diverse as the art of puppetry itself, ranging from elaborate, costumed characters to a few dabs of paint on a puppeteer's hand. In American theater and television three types of puppets are most frequently used.

Hand Puppets

The most common type of puppet is the glove or hand puppet. In its simplest form, this puppet consists of a cloth tube into which the puppeteer inserts his or her hand. By manipulating the fingers and thumb, a face and mouth are formed and contorted into various expressions. Eyes, nose, ears, and whiskers can be suggested by attaching

Bunraku, ancient Japanese puppet theater, is still performed today. The puppeteers dress in black, and all but the master puppeteer wear black gauze hoods.

buttons or similar items. Some hand puppets incorporate rigid material around the mouth to form movable jaws. By opening and closing the jaws, the puppeteer can create the illusion of speech. The three-finger puppet allows the puppeteer to insert the fingers or the thumb into both arms and the head.

When using any of the hand puppets, the puppeteer must exercise care to conceal the junction of his or her arm and the puppet. This is accomplished by covering his or her wrist and arm with a black sleeve or a material that matches the skirt of the puppet.

Rod Puppets

A second type of puppet is the rod puppet. Rod puppets are controlled from below by rods made of wire or thin strips of wood. Usually a main rod supports the weight of the puppet while smaller rods operate individual parts of the puppet's body. Like most puppets, rod puppets can be constructed either from simple materials like tongue depressors and plastic spoons or from highly crafted synthetic materials, using swivel

The Muppets, shown in both photos, are popular examples of rod puppets.

connections at various body joints. Some of the familiar puppets seen on television are complex combinations of hand puppets and rod puppets that require several puppeteers to operate.

Marionettes

Marionettes, a third type of puppet, are controlled by strings from above. As with rod puppets, the strings are attached to various parts of a jointed body. These strings are operated from a wooden control bar. Black or clear nylon strings are used because they cannot easily be seen by the audience.

THE CHALLENGE OF PUPPETRY

The challenge lies in merging oneself with a lifeless bundle of cloth, Styrofoam™, string, and similar materials to create a single performer. With the challenge, however, comes opportunity; puppets provide a mask behind which an inexperienced actor can feel safe to experiment with imaginative characterizations. Through the medium of the puppet, it is possible for an actor truly to "let go."

The manipulation of a puppet, especially the marionette or rod types, requires practice and experimentation. Once you have become skillful at handling the puppet, however, the possibilities for puppet theater are virtually limitless. Some puppet theater is entirely visual, using only the actions of the puppet to tell the story. Others use adaptations of existing scripts. Still others rely on entirely original material. Before deciding on a script, however, you must determine a purpose for the puppet show and identify the audience. Is the performance intended to entertain, to teach, or to attain some special goal? Will the audience be familiar with the story? What are the ages and interests of the people in the audience?

It is usually a good idea to write a scenario or a walk-through for the puppets to determine the sequence of action, puppet and voice changes, and similar requirements. This might be followed with a reading or a performance before a trial audience.

It is particularly important to know the size of the puppet theater and the audience's view of the stage. One good strategy is to videotape a rehearsal to be certain that the audience is seeing what you intend and not what you wish to conceal.

Producing the Drama

Taking a drama from the playwright's script to its final presentation requires many people. The contributions made by these people include planning and directing the drama as well as designing and creating scenery, lighting, costumes, and makeup.

8 Producing the Play

Many kinds of rehearsals go into a successful production. Until you have memorized your lines, you will rehearse with the script in hand.

good audition is one in which the performer . . . reveals who and what he [she] is as a human being while at the same time giving the auditors an idea of the extent of his [her] talents.

—FRED SILVER, MUSICAL AUDITION COACH

SETTING THE SCENE

Focus Questions

Who are the key members of a production staff, and what are their responsibilities?

What items are included in a master production schedule checklist?

How do you prepare a budget?

How do you make a promptbook?

How do you conduct and/or participate in an audition?

How do you prepare a résumé?

What are the different types of rehearsals?

What are dress rehearsals?

How do you create a rehearsal schedule?

What are curtain calls?

Vocabulary

producer	technical director	publicity manager	blocking rehearsal
director	stage manager	house manager	working rehearsal
assistant director	grip	promptbook	polishing rehearsal
prompter	properties chief	audition	technical rehearsal
scenic designer	business manager	reading rehearsal	dress rehearsal

*P*roducing a play can offer opportunities that you may find as stimulating and exciting as acting in a play. Design and construction of sets and costumes, handling lighting equipment, and managing backstage, onstage, and publicity matters can provide challenges and satisfaction.

School stages may range from simple ones in classrooms to theaters having computerized lighting consoles, sophisticated recording and sound equipment, fine dressing rooms, and ample work and storage space. If your school does not have all of these facilities, do not be dismayed. A small stage, a crowded backstage area, and the minimum of stage lights are limitations that may challenge your imagination and ingenuity. As a result, your productions may well be equal to those presented more easily with extensive physical equipment. Whatever the size and equipment of your theater, having a share in a full-length public production is a rewarding experience.

The Production Staff

Without the group of responsible, hard-working, and talented people that make up the production staff, producing a play would be impossible. After the preliminary planning and preparation are complete, the production staff must work intensively for several weeks to make the play or musical a reality. The size of the staff is determined by the size of the production, the specific technical demands of the production, and the availability of capable and enthusiastic people.

THE ARTISTIC STAFF

CUE ▼

Many actors seek the opportunity to work with successful directors, both for the learning experience and for the association with an exceptional director or production.

Every venture needs a person who can envision the end product and be actively involved with the production as it takes place. In the world of dramatic presentations, the **producer** is that person. In professional theater, the producer finds investors willing to provide the money to fund a show. The producer hires the director and the production staff, establishes a budget, and sees that the bills are paid. In a high school production, the producer may also be the director.

The **director** is responsible for creating a team that will work cooperatively toward a common goal. The drama teacher is usually the director of the public productions in high school. Some high schools today have a trained, and professionally experienced, teacher-director.

In the professional theater, the director is usually credited with the play's overall success or failure. The ideal director inspires actors to have confidence in their abilities and to use intelligence in building their roles. In an effort to mold all phases of production into a unified whole, the

As he works with these actors in *Much Ado About Nothing,* the director must have an eye for detail in order to see how each character relates to the play as a whole.

CUE ▼

Although each person on the production staff may be creative, the director's final word must be "law."

director must be someone who can coordinate a multitude of details and, at the same time, delegate responsibilities. During most production schedules there are distractions and conflicts that require the director to possess a reserved but commanding demeanor that gives the team a feeling of assurance. The director is responsible for onstage empathies and backstage morale. He or she should be a person who can see the areas of needed improvement and who has the ability and personality to communicate the means by which improvement can be made. This communication is accomplished in rehearsal and through oral, written, or taped notes called **critiques**.

The director is responsible for producing the playwright's intentions as faithfully as possible. He or she accomplishes this by studying the script, the author's style, the play's theme, and the characters' relationships. The professional director is also responsible for auditions, casting, blocking, preparation of a promptbook, and the opening of the show. In both professional and high school productions, the director and the staff can have a delightful experience working together as a team to produce a play.

In the school theater, a student is usually the **assistant director**. This student is preferably someone who is interested in the "big picture" of theater and is capable, dependable, and willing to take on many of the director's responsibilities. The assistant director serves as a liaison between the director and the cast and crew; sometimes the assistant director takes charge of rehearsals at the request of the director. This position allows a student to see the rehearsals, the actors, and the overall production from a unique perspective.

One of the most important positions in the production of a play is that of the **prompter.** It is a job that requires both reliability and intelligence. Some directors do not use a prompter during the performance, preferring to have the actors know they are on their own, while other directors feel that a skilled prompter is essential. It is critical that this person attend every rehearsal. During rehearsals the prompter writes notes from the director in the promptbook. These notes should include information on interpretation, movement, and positions. Color-coded light and sound cues are often included in the promptbook, also. By including a floor-plan sketch, the prompter can clarify any questions concerning stage groupings, crosses, and changes.

Every pause should be marked so that an unnecessary prompt will not be given. If emergencies arise during the performance, the prompter can often save the show by giving correct cues and lines. If the cast starts to skip passages, the prompter can feed the vital lines to bring the actors back on track. This position

CUE ▼

Responsibilities of the Assistant Director

- Take attendance
- Set up rehearsal room
- Take charge of rehearsals
- Read lines for absent actors
- Write down blocking
- Assemble program

is a difficult one because the prompter must follow the script word by word in both rehearsals and performances. If an actor hesitates in rehearsal or calls out "line," the prompter must be ready to immediately give the necessary assistance. Most prompters whisper the first word of the line. Then, if the actor does not pick up the line, the prompter gives the first three words of the line a little louder. If that is unsuccessful, the prompter responds according to the director's instructions. In rehearsal, the scene is usually stopped, the prompter gives the line to the actor, and the cast backs up a line or two and proceeds. In a performance, it is up to the other actors onstage to pick up the scene and proceed.

Settings, costumes, makeup, and lighting are the responsibilities of the **scenic designer.** Whether simple or complex, the design of these elements works best when it gives the play visual dimensions that are in harmony with the aims of the director. Sometimes the **technical director** will oversee the design of costumes and lighting instead of the scenic designer. The technical director executes the designs of the scenic designer. With the assistance of a crew, the technical director is responsible for building sets, painting drops, creating costumes, and hanging lights. Both the scenic designer and the technical director must serve the director's intentions effectively, simply, and beautifully to achieve a unified production.

A high school drama director gives instructions to student actors. Directors of high school productions are usually responsible for coordinating all aspects of the productions.

The crew members who manage the technical details play a big part in determining how the audience will perceive the performance.

Application
ACTIVITIES

1. Make a chart of the positions on the artistic staff. Then list the responsibilities that accompany each position. Compare the responsibilities of the staff members, noting which of these responsibilities overlap. After analyzing the jobs, note the one for which you feel most qualified. Even though you probably do not have the experience, you should have an idea of the talents and personality traits needed for the particular position. List your qualifications.

2. After your analysis, write Help Wanted ads for two of the artistic staff positions. Describe the responsibilities of each position and the qualifications applicants should possess.

THE BEHIND-THE-SCENES STAFF

Although often unseen by the audience, all the people working behind the scenes are absolutely crucial to a successful production. Aided by the stage crew, the **stage manager** takes charge backstage during rehearsals. A good stage manager is essential to a smooth production. In some cases, the stage manager and the crew act as both the stage carpenters who build the sets and the **grips** who move the scenery. The stage manager keeps track of all cues and effects and makes cue sheets for the stage crew that contain cues for lights, sound, curtains, and set and prop changes.

During the performance, the stage manager usually sits at a prompt table in the stage-right wing just upstage of the proscenium and calls all cues to the technical crew. In addition, the stage manager must handle all emergencies that arise during the performance. The stage manager times each full rehearsal and each performance. Occasionally during a production with many performances, the stage manager will turn over the backstage supervision to the assistant stage manager and go out "front" to watch the performance from the audience's perspective, taking notes on projection, timing, and cues.

In the professional theater, the stage manager has to be versatile and experienced in all phases of theater production, including acting and directing. In addition to running the show backstage, the stage manager directs brush-up rehearsals, trains new cast members, and keeps the production fresh and sharp.

Also necessary for a successful production are the **properties chief** and the **properties assistants.** Their responsibilities include acquiring the

▼ CUE

As behind-the-scenes staff, you may do a lot of computer work for various business tasks (for example, creating publicity materials). If you spend long periods on the computer, take short breaks frequently to avoid muscle cramping and eyestrain.

The person working the ticket window should be responsible and enthusiastic. It is a good job for someone interested in the financial aspects of play production.

furniture and props that fit the designer's plan, storing them, preparing a prop table, and giving hand props to the actors backstage just before entrances. These positions require hard work, dependability, and ingenuity.

Hand props should be kept on the side of the stage from which the actors who use the props will make their entrances. Props are returned to the prop table after use and should never be touched by anyone other than the props crew and the actor by whom they are used. The prop table should have a list of the props posted over it and should be marked with the location and identification of each prop. After each rehearsal and performance, the props crew should store the props in a secure storage area.

The responsibility of financial arrangements for the production belongs partially to the producer but mostly to the **business manager.** Both should monitor production and publicity expenses in an effort to achieve a reasonable profit. In addition to financial issues, the business manager is also responsible for accurately listing in the programs names of cast members, all production staff, committee chairpersons, and acknowledgments for favors and assistance from businesses and individuals. Although guided by school policy, business managers usually

- handle funds and pay bills
- handle the printing and selling of tickets
- issue tickets to salespersons
- monitor sales
- supervise the ticket booth
- order the printing of programs
- supervise advertisement sales (if applicable)

CUE ▼

If your school provides an office for theater management and publicity planning, maintain an efficient workspace and avoid clutter hazards, such as those that can cause tripping, by keeping supplies neat and organized.

SAMPLE BUDGET WORKSHEET

John Adams High School Drama

Production: _____

Dates: _____

Projected Income:

Tickets sold _____ @ $ _____ = $ _____

_____ @ $ _____ = $ _____

Other income:

  Concessions $ _____

  Program ads   _____

Total Projected Income: $ _____

Projected Expenses

  Royalty $ _____

  Play books   _____

  Tickets   _____

  Programs   _____

  Advertising   _____

  Scenery   _____

  Properties   _____

  Costumes   _____

  Makeup   _____

Miscellaneous:

  Custodial fees $ _____

  Police department   _____

  Fire department   _____

  Ushers   _____

  Box-office staff   _____

Total Projected Production Costs $ _____

Projected Net Income (Total income

less total production costs) $ _____

The publicity for a production can be just as important as the staff and the finances. The person who promotes the show in the school and the community is the **publicity manager.** The public press, other schools' newspapers, local radio and television stations, and closed-circuit television stations may give space or time to notices about school productions. There are almost limitless possibilities for promoting a play. The publicity manager and assistants have an opportunity to make original and artistic contributions to the success of a production. The school's art department can be an excellent source for contributions.

CUE

If you plan to post flyers to publicize a performance, find out whether you need permission from a property owner or operator. Unauthorized areas should be avoided.

Advertising should be consistent with the spirit and style of the play. For example, when promoting comedies, cartoons of the cast and humorous items about the funniest rehearsal situations can be featured, possibly with comic quotations from the play. The title of the play itself, the playwright, the skill or prominence of the performers, the past achievements of the director, and the striking scenic effects can also furnish material for publicity.

An important part of planning a successful production is considering the needs of the audience. The **house manager** must juggle a variety of duties to ensure both the physical comfort of the audience and smooth admission and intermission periods. The responsibilities will probably resemble these shown here.

Responsibilities of the House Manager

To the audience
- Repair damaged seats.
- Check ventilation.
- Maintain comfortable temperature.
- Provide competent ushers.

To the ushers
- Provide training.
- Specify dress code.
- Provide programs for the audience.
- Assign equipment such as flashlights.

To the playhouse
- Collect ticket stubs for the business manager.
- Signal the end of intermission.

School productions frequently involve still more people. Firefighters and police officers are often required. In some communities, they will be on hand if they are notified that a production is scheduled; otherwise, they must be hired. In some schools, members of the faculty are in attendance for supervision, and they often collect and sell tickets out front.

A crew member may be in charge of furnishing recorded music for the curtain raiser or intermissions. If so, the selections should be approved by the director far in advance, and they should be properly rehearsed. Music should be in keeping with the production but subordinate to it, not added as a special feature. Be sure that any permissions required for the use of music are secured well in advance.

Productions need many people who are not directly involved with the drama. Crowd control, traffic management, ticket sales and collection, and program production and distribution require willing workers.

Application
ACTIVITIES

1. Discuss difficulties that might arise during a performance. How might the stage manager avoid or overcome them?

2. Choose one mode of publicizing a particular play. Make an oral or visual presentation of your promotion.

▼ CUE

To create publicity for a show, actors might go out in public in full costume to perform a short scene. This may be a good attention-getting strategy, but actors should be careful to choose safe areas and times.

※ *Prerehearsal Activities*

An abundance of planning and scheduling must be done before the actual rehearsals can begin. How well these prerehearsal steps are taken often makes the difference between a smoothly run production and a chaotic one. The first step is the selection of a play. Before or immediately after play selection, a tentative budget should be prepared. If production costs will be a determining factor, the budget should be established first. Work toward resolving each step to ensure success from the outset.

FIRST STEPS

Choosing the right play is one of the first decisions to be made. The right choice has much to do with the success of the production. Before the choice can be made, several plays should be read. This may be done by the director, the director and the staff, or the director and a play-reading committee. It is important that those making the decision know the purpose of the proposed production. Is it primarily a school project, or is it to raise funds for a specific cause or organization? Whatever the purpose, it is important to select the best play possible as far as script quality, strength of parts, and entertainment value are concerned.

Things to Consider When Choosing a Play

1. Does it fulfill its designated purpose?
2. Does it appeal to a particular audience?
3. Has your audience recently seen it?
4. Does it provide variety in your annual productions?
5. Is it adaptable to your actors' abilities?
6. Is it adaptable to the size and equipment of your stage?
7. Does it fit your budget?

Rather than compromise the quality of a script, it is better to present classics (most of which require no royalty) or cut production expenses sufficiently to pay the royalty of a first-class contemporary play. Remember that there are many classics that most people will thoroughly enjoy. There are also many entertaining plays of the nineteenth century that have been released from royalty charges.

Before a play is finally selected, the director or some authorized person should contact the publisher controlling the acting rights of the play. The director should state the dates, the number of performances planned, and the various ticket prices and should request authorization to present the play. Many regulations restrict the presentation of plays by amateurs, especially in larger cities where stock and road companies appear. Therefore, full permission should be obtained for a public performance before preparations start.

If the budget has not been established, it must be set before proceeding further. The director must estimate the probable size of the audience and take into account sets and props that can be obtained without expense. Because scheduling is crucial for a smooth production, the director should set up a master production schedule containing the items found on the checklist shown on the opposite page.

CUE ▼

The size of the cast requires attention in the choice of a play. When the cast is large, more students receive the benefits of training and experience.

Master Production Schedule Checklist

1. Production budget established
2. Play-reading committee selected
3. Committee reports given
4. Play selected
5. Staff organized
6. Production meetings held with director, stage manager, technical director, scenic designer, lighting designer, and costumer
7. Production rights obtained
8. Research started
9. Scripts ordered
10. Promptbook prepared
11. Floor plan designed
12. Designs for scenery, lights, and costumes made
13. Tryouts held
14. Cast selected
15. Stage and costume crews recruited
16. Publicity committee organized
17. Costume measurements taken
18. Costumes rented or purchased
19. Light plot prepared
20. Floor plan on rehearsal floor
21. Blocking rehearsals begun
22. Tickets ordered
23. First publicity release written
24. Scenery begun
25. Program prepared and printed
26. Working rehearsals started
27. Costumes fitted for first time
28. Publicity photos arranged
29. Props secured
30. Second publicity release written
31. Tickets placed on sale
32. Scenery construction completed
33. Special effects secured
34. Lighting, cue sheets, and prop plots completed
35. Tickets distributed
36. Costumes fitted for second time
37. Lighting checked for first time
38. Polishing rehearsal timed
39. Set or sets completed
40. Major press releases written
41. Technical rehearsals held
42. Final set touches completed
43. Dress rehearsals held
44. Performances given

After-Production Schedule

1. Costumes/props checked in
2. Bills paid and tickets audited
3. Scenery struck and stored
4. Props put away
5. Borrowed items returned
6. Rented costumes returned
7. Owned costumes cleaned, stored
8. Dressing rooms cleaned
9. Thank-you letters sent
10. Final financial statement drawn

The director must study the play from every angle to determine the style and atmosphere to be carried out in the sets and costumes. Then she or he must decide how best to express the theme, how to emphasize the conflict, the suspense, and the climax of the plot, and how the characters and their relationships with one another should be portrayed. For a

Before constructing the full-scale set, it can be useful to make a scale model from the floor plans. This way, you get an idea of what your set will actually look like before you go to all the trouble of constructing the real thing.

period play, the director must also study the historical background, the social conditions, and the attitudes of the people represented, as well as the clothing, furnishings, and manner of speech and movement of the period.

After studying the play, the director must make a floor plan. This is an overhead view of the set that helps the director plan the action that will take place on the stage. During this early period, the director should have frequent conferences with the scenic designer and the stage manager concerning many aspects of the production.

After the director, the scenic designer, and the stage manager have made overall plans, the director must visualize important scenes carefully and plan for effective grouping and movement. Entrances and exits must be logical and orderly. The location and the size of furniture should be planned carefully to create balanced and effective stage pictures. Light sources, such as windows, lamps, and fireplaces, should be marked on the floor plan. Even backstage storage areas for furniture, props, and sets must be diagrammed.

The backbone of a production is the **promptbook**, started by the director during the planning period and containing the entire play script. Into this book go the director's plans and eventually the telephone numbers and addresses of everyone involved in the production. The easiest way to make a promptbook is to paste the pages of the play in a large loose-leaf notebook. This system requires two copies of the play. If there is only one copy available for this purpose, page-sized windows can be cut in the sheets of the notebook, and each page of the script can be fastened into these windows with cellophane tape or glue.

Large margins around the script are essential for sketches, cues, and notes. These are first made by the director in the preliminary planning and then added to and changed during rehearsals. Marginal notes show script cuttings, stage directions,

CUE ▼

When your play is finished, save the promptbook and a copy of the program and photographs of the production. You may want to use them for future reference.

Sample Promptbook Page

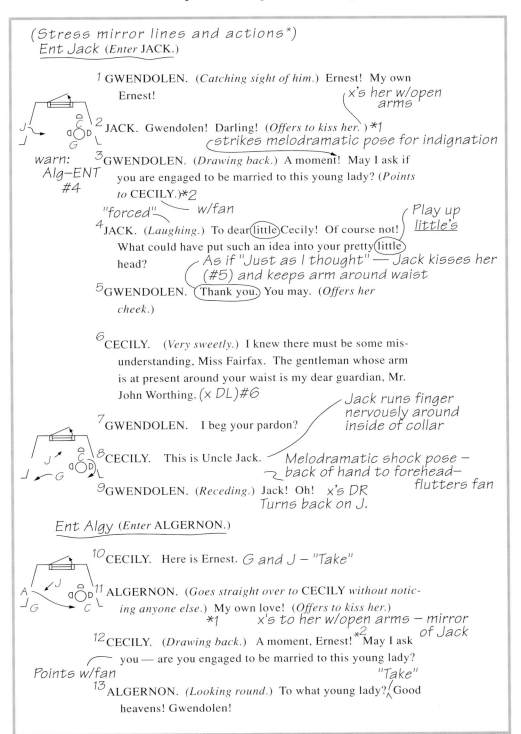

(Stress mirror lines and actions*)
Ent Jack (*Enter* JACK.)

1 GWENDOLEN. (*Catching sight of him.*) Ernest! My own
Ernest!

x's her w/open arms

2 JACK. Gwendolen! Darling! (*Offers to kiss her.*) *1

strikes melodramatic pose for indignation

warn:
Alg—ENT
#4

3 GWENDOLEN. (*Drawing back.*) A moment! May I ask if
you are engaged to be married to this young lady? (*Points
to* CECILY.)*2

"forced" — w/fan

Play up little's

4 JACK. (*Laughing.*) To dear (little) Cecily! Of course not!
What could have put such an idea into your pretty (little)
head?

As if "Just as I thought" — Jack kisses her
(#5) and keeps arm around waist

5 GWENDOLEN. (Thank you.) You may. (*Offers her
cheek.*)

6 CECILY. (*Very sweetly.*) I knew there must be some misunderstanding, Miss Fairfax. The gentleman whose arm
is at present around your waist is my dear guardian, Mr.
John Worthing. (x DL)#6

Jack runs finger
nervously around
inside of collar

7 GWENDOLEN. I beg your pardon?

8 CECILY. This is Uncle Jack.

Melodramatic shock pose —
back of hand to forehead—
flutters fan

9 GWENDOLEN. (*Receding.*) Jack! Oh! x's DR
Turns back on J.

Ent Algy (*Enter* ALGERNON.)

10 CECILY. Here is Ernest. G and J — "Take"

11 ALGERNON. (*Goes straight over to* CECILY *without notic-
ing anyone else.*) My own love! (*Offers to kiss her.*)
*1   x's to her w/open arms — mirror of Jack

12 CECILY. (*Drawing back.*) A moment, Ernest! *2 May I ask
you — are you engaged to be married to this young lady?

Points w/fan

"Take"

13 ALGERNON. (*Looking round.*) To what young lady? Good
heavens! Gwendolen!

and markings of difficult passages for pauses, phrasing, and emphasis. The sketches or diagrams of floor plans and sets show positions of furniture and actors as they move in every scene. Stage groupings of actors can be drawn with the initials of the characters' names marked in little circles. Most directors like to sketch important crosses and countercrosses and mark actors' movements with symbols.

The stage manager adds to the promptbook cues for lights, sound effects, curtains, and other effects both on and off the stage. As rehearsals progress, individual cue sheets are made from the book by the stage manager and are given to the following: electrical technician, wardrobe staff, props committee, sound technician, and anyone whose tasks require written directions.

When marking the promptbook, pencils should be used so that changes may be made when necessary. Use different colors for particular types of cues and warning signals, such as red for lights, blue for curtain, and green for entrances and exits. Most directors and stage managers want warn cues marked in the promptbook. A **warn cue** advises the stage manager of an entrance, a sound effect, or a lighting change before it is to take place. For example, "WARN: phone 1: 2 rings" means that the phone is to ring twice, one page from that point in the script. Most stage managers give a "Warn" from one-half page to one page before the execution of a cue. They give a "Stand By" about ten seconds before a cue, and they give "Go" at the moment of execution. Refer to the example on the upper left-hand corner of the sample promptbook page shown on page 347.

Application
ACTIVITIES

1. Work in groups to evaluate plays for possible production in your school. Each group should review a play from a different time period, such as a Greek tragedy, a twentieth-century musical, and an eighteenth-century comedy. First answer the questions on page 344. Then analyze the production needs for each play, considering settings, costumes, actors required, and royalty costs. After each group has presented its findings to the class and made a recommendation, the class should decide which play would be the best choice.
2. After choosing a play, research its cultural, social, and political aspects. Write notes that would help the designers as they plan the play's technical and visual elements (lights, sound, scenery, costumes, and makeup).

CASTING THE PLAY

Few phases of production are more important to the ultimate success or failure of a play than the choice of the cast. Casting demands tact, sincerity, fairness, and sound judgment. Those planning to audition should fill out an audition form similar to the one shown on the following page. The director must cast not solely on the basis of the tryout but also from past experience with the individual and especially from a projection of what that actor will be able to do after weeks of rehearsal and direction. This ability to look ahead goes hand in hand with a director's ability to visualize the final production even before the first rehearsal. A successful production demands that actors be equipped physically, mentally, and temperamentally to give convincing interpretations of the roles assigned to them.

One of the most important experiences for an actor is the **audition**. Some of the most talented actors fail to get parts because they give poor auditions. In some public schools, auditions are limited to drama and speech students. In others, they are open to all students. This is a matter to be decided by the director or by the individual school. Perhaps the director will want to use a point system based on stage experience and service to help determine eligibility for roles. In some schools, scholastic standing in other departments and good citizenship are considered before an applicant is allowed to audition.

Every possible means of publicizing the roles to be filled should be used prior to the tryouts. Posters, articles in the school newspaper, and

A Chorus Line is a play about the drama and anxiety that accompany an audition and the necessity to relax and just be yourself.

TRYOUT INFORMATION FORM

NAME (LAST NAME FIRST)	CLASS	AGE	PHONE
ADDRESS	SEX	HEIGHT	WEIGHT

PREVIOUS ACTING EXPERIENCE

WHAT VOCAL PART DO YOU SING?   WHAT MUSICAL INSTRUMENT DO YOU PLAY?
  S   A   T   B   EXPERIENCE:

WHAT DANCE TRAINING HAVE YOU HAD?

LIST YOUR CLASS SCHEDULE

1	4	7
2	5	8
3	6	9

WILL YOU BE ABLE TO ATTEND ALL REHEARSALS?   YES_____   NO_____
IF NOT, WHAT CONFLICTS ARE THERE?

ARE YOU INTERESTED IN WORKING ON ANY OF THE FOLLOWING COMMITTEES?

MAKEUP	PROPERTIES	SCENERY CONST.
PUBLICITY	COSTUMES	STAGE CREW

ARE YOU INTERESTED IN BEING STUDENT DIRECTOR?

PROMPTER?   TECHNICAL DIRECTOR?   STAGE MANAGER?

DIRECTOR'S COMMENTS
    VOICE (QUALITY):   IMAGINATION: STAGE PRESENCE:

    VOICE (PITCH):   ANIMATION: PHYSICAL APPEARANCE:

    VOICE (VARIETY):

PARTS CONSIDERED FOR:

posted descriptions of the characters are all good ways of circulating the information. If possible, the director might place a copy of the play on reserve in the school library for all applicants to read or might make the play available in some other way.

The audition arrangements must be determined by the number of people who wish to read for the play, the length of time that can be devoted to casting, and the kind of play to be presented. When possible, it is usually preferable to hold tryouts in the auditorium or theater in which the play is to be performed.

When the applicants have assembled, the director can explain all details of the tryouts, discuss the play briefly, and describe the characters. Each applicant should be asked to fill out a form giving name, address, phone number, height, weight, past experience in school plays, and any previous commitments that might interfere with attendance at rehearsals. Applicants should complete *all* requested information.

Methods of conducting auditions vary with directors. Some directors combine audition formats. This is especially true of tryouts for musicals because actors very often have to be able to act, sing, and dance.

▼ **CUE**

When auditioning, it sometimes pays to know something about the director. What shows has that director done? What are his or her favorites? Be careful in your choice of material. You may strike a responsive chord, or you might find yourself competing with "ghosts of the past."

Types of Auditions, Tryouts, or Readings	
Open audition	For professional nonunion actors For entire school student body
Closed audition	For professional union actors only For certain school students only, such as drama club members
Prepared audition	May use rehearsed material, including memorized lines and actions
Textual tryout	Material from manuscript or printed play, may be either monologue or scene Same as prepared audition
Cold reading	Uses unfamiliar material. Must read with imagination, feeling, and confidence Not penalized for errors in interpretation if director does not summarize material May be textual or improvisational
Improvisational audition	Must improvise scene around assigned character and situation

If the cold reading uses a scene, the actor might have the disadvantage of playing with another actor with whom he or she is unfamiliar. On the other hand, the actor has the advantage of playing against someone.

After preliminary auditions, the director will make a list of those considered for parts. These individuals will be invited to **callbacks**, auditions to read again from the script, sometimes with candidates for other roles. Occasionally, there may need to be further callbacks until final casting can be determined. By this time, any problems concerning rehearsal attendance, dependability, responsiveness to suggestions, and general attitudes should be solved as completely as possible.

Perhaps the most important aspect of auditions is that they be conducted in a friendly and relaxed atmosphere. Each student who tries out must know that she or he is being given a fair chance. Good auditions can set morale at a high level for the rest of the production.

Application ACTIVITIES

1. Pretend that you are preparing your own material for an upcoming prepared audition. Choose the text, either monologue or scene, and then plan your actions and memorize your part. Ask a classmate to take the role of the casting director and give you friendly feedback.

2. Look at the sample Tryout Information Form. Write a brief description of the committee on which you would like to work or the particular position you would like to fill in the production of the play.

YOU AND YOUR AUDITION

Planning for your audition will take time and careful preparation, especially if the production is professional. Those of you wanting to pursue acting as a professional career should have a **résumé,** such as the one shown on the opposite page, and a portfolio. Your résumé should include an eight-by-ten-inch black and white headshot photograph of you as you appear offstage, not as a character in costume. The résumé should also include all the important information a casting director wants to know: name, address, phone number, type of voice (if you sing), vital statistics, experience, education and professional training, and special skills. Since all actors are typed by class of performer, include at the top of the résumé your type classification. For example, if acting is your strongest skill, then dancing, then singing, your classification would be actor-dancer-singer. Similarly, there are dancer-singer-actors and many other classifications.

The portfolio you present at an audition should include other photographs of you as you appeared in specific roles. If possible, select roles that show your range of abilities from drama to comedy to musical theater. If available, include reviews of your performances and sample programs of the plays in which you have appeared.

JOYCE JACKSON ACTRESS-SINGER-DANCER HOME PHONE: (121) 555-1317
4950 Cove Road OTHER PHONE: (121) 555-6071
Stamford, CT 06904 Soprano: low G–high C

Age Range: 16–30   Height: 5'6   Weight: 108   Hair: Blonde, long   Eyes: Blue   Dress: 7/8

EXPERIENCE:

HANSEL AND GRETEL	Wicked Witch	Courtyard Playhouse, N.Y.C.
GUYS AND DOLLS	Sarah Brown	Rochester, Minn., Civic Theatre
THE FANTASTICKS	Luisa	Highland Summer Theatre, Minn.
DARK AT THE TOP OF THE STAIRS	Flirt Conroy	Highland Summer Theatre, Minn.
DIRTY WORK AT THE CROSSROADS	Nellie Lovelace	Ohio Valley Summer Theatre
NAUGHTY MARIETTA	Marietta	Ohio Valley Summer Theatre
THE SOUND OF MUSIC	Maria	Mosby Dinner Theatre, Virginia
OKLAHOMA!	Understudy for Laurey and Dancing Laurey (played by Kathleen Conry of Broadway's NO, NO NANETTE)	Mosby Dinner Theatre, Virginia
ANYTHING GOES	Hope Harcourt	Club Bone Dinner Theatre, N.J.
MARY POPPINS	Mary Poppins	Club Bone Dinner Theatre, N.J.
LAUGHING GAS (original musical)	Mrs. Krause	Cavalier Productions, Virginia
HAPPY BIRTHDAY, AMERICA!	Voice-overs	Library Theatre, Washington, D.C.
AMAHL AND THE NIGHT VISITORS	Mother	Kenyon, Minnesota
MAN OF LA MANCHA	Antonia & Housekeeper	Boulder, Colorado

EDUCATION AND TRAINING

DEGREE: Bachelor of Music Ed. in Voice, University of Colorado
GRADUATE: Acting—Mankato State College, Minn., under Dr. C. Ron Olauson
STUDY: Ohio University under Robert Winters
Private study with Richard G. Holmes (Senator Dawes in Broadway's INDIANS), Washington, D.C.
DANCE: Ballet—6 years   Modern—2 years   Tap—1 year
SINGING: 8 years classical and musical comedy training, some belting
MODELING: J. C. PENNEY CO., 3 years floor modeling and fashion shows—Denver, Colorado
Print and promotional work in Colorado for Wells, Rich, Green Inc. of N.Y.C.
OTHER: Play piano; Teach piano and voice; Sing in Italian, German, Spanish, French
SKILLS: Accents: Norwegian, Swedish, Cockney, Irish, Southern
Own and drive a car
Public elementary school teacher

In order to have the best audition possible, you must know your own abilities well. You must be honest in your self-appraisal, neither conceited nor overly modest. Know what kind of actor you are and what kinds of roles you can play. You may aspire to play every great role ever written, but if you are objective, you know that you are best suited for certain roles. The director will be looking for certain vocal and physical attributes. Know how you sound to an audience by listening to a recording of your voice. Look in the mirror, and be objective about what you see. Bear in mind that auditioning is a selling job that begins when the director first sees you.

Dress appropriately for the audition. Line, color, and style are important. Avoid wearing anything that might be distracting or might draw attention away from you and your talent. If you know the play, you can help the director visualize you in a part if your clothes suggest the part you desire. Take care not to overdo the suggestion, however.

If you have a prepared audition, there are many points to consider as you prepare. Do not try to read dialogue between two or more characters. Monologues long enough for an audition are few and hard to find. That is why the same material is often found in monologue and scene books. Those same few books of monologues are available to everyone, every show, every year. Directors might become tired of repeatedly hearing the same audition material. One effective solution is to turn a dialogue into a monologue. This requires skill and practice, but the result is an audition selection that is fresh.

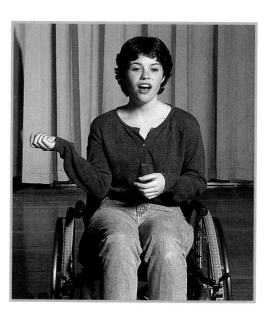

An audition may involve memorizing a monologue. Practice until you are comfortable with the material, and then relax and be yourself.

Many of the long speeches found in plays are expository, or informational. Information is important but does not provide exciting or moving audition material. Look for something that expresses emotions, conflict, and action. Avoid selections that were intended to be delivered in dialect if (a) the part you are seeking is not in that dialect, (b) you are not really proficient in that dialect, or (c) you want to do that selection without the dialect, but the selection is so well known that it probably would not "sound right." Also, avoid speeches that have been associated with particular actors. You might find yourself competing with a star rather than with your peers.

Preparing for Your Audition

Consider the following:

1. Whenever possible, know the play for which you are auditioning.
2. Know the character or characters you believe you can play.
3. Select a monologue or single-character scene that suits the character or play for which you are auditioning.
4. Prepare a series of short monologues rather than one long one, such as ten to twelve auditioning pieces that last from a few seconds to a minute each.
5. Be certain that each piece is just long enough to show what you can do.
6. Show the director your range of acting abilities in five minutes. This is especially important if auditioning for a whole season or a repertory group.
7. If you have a vocal audition, use the accompanist provided or bring an accompanist. Do not accompany yourself.
8. Sing appropriate music.

During Your Audition

Remember the following:

1. Play to the director.
2. Neither avert your eyes from nor stare at the person evaluating you.
3. Walk to your auditioning position showing confidence, even if you are nervous.
4. Pause for a moment when finished.
5. Leave the stage with poise.
6. Smile, even if you are cut off or interrupted.
7. Do not appear hurt or flustered.
8. Show the director your positive side.

▼ CUE

Develop a good audition attitude. Look forward to auditioning. Shake off the nervousness. Show a little hunger for the part. Be ready, willing, and eager to take a part, whatever part is offered to you. Also learn how to handle rejection.

🕸 *Rehearsals*

The best way to become part of the play as a whole and to appreciate the director's motivation for movements and tempos is to faithfully attend rehearsals. There are different kinds of rehearsals, all of them important. You can profit from the director's suggestions to the other actors and thus avoid their mistakes and profit from their achievements. If a rehearsal is set for specific roles, however, be sure you obtain the director's permission to sit in.

REHEARSAL SCHEDULES

When making a rehearsal schedule, the director considers the time allotted for preparing the production, the length and difficulty of the play, and the availability of the cast. For instance, if the audition-rehearsal-performance period of a full-length straight play has been set at seven weeks, after-school rehearsals should probably be two to three hours a day, five days a week.

A schedule for the entire rehearsal period should be finalized, and copies should be made for participants. This procedure helps parents understand how much time will be involved in the production.

Sample Seven-Week Audition-Rehearsal Schedule

Week 1:	Auditions and first rehearsal (3 hours)
Monday	Auditions
Tuesday	Auditions
Wednesday	Callbacks (if necessary)
Thursday	Cast posted
Friday	Reading rehearsal
Week 2:	Blocking and line-check rehearsals (2 1/2 hours)
Monday	Blocking Act I
Tuesday	Rehearsal Act I
Wednesday	Line-check Act I
Thursday	Blocking Act II
Friday	Rehearsal Act II
Week 3:	Blocking and line-check rehearsals (2 1/2 hours)
Monday	Line-check Act II
Tuesday	Run-through Acts I and II
Wednesday	Blocking Act III
Thursday	Line-check Act III
Friday	First run-through Act III

Week 4:	Working rehearsals (2 1/2–3 hours)
Monday ⎤	Special scenes—chases, fights, and so on—private
Tuesday ⎦	rehearsals
Wednesday	Act I concentrated
Thursday	Act II concentrated
Friday	Act III concentrated

Week 5:	Working rehearsals (full stage crew, 3 hours)
Monday	Acts I, II, III in sequence
Tuesday	Acts II, III, I—in that order
Wednesday	Acts III, I, II—in that order
Thursday	Problem scenes only
Friday	Final working run-through

Week 6:	Polishing rehearsals (all crews, 3–3 1/2 hours)
Monday	Run-through and dress parade
Tuesday	First technical rehearsal
Wednesday	Second technical rehearsal
Thursday	Problem scenes and changes
Friday	First complete run-through

Week 7:	Polishing rehearsals and performances (4–5 hours)
Monday	Second complete run-through
Tuesday	Final run-through
Wednesday	First dress rehearsal
Thursday	Final dress rehearsal
Friday	Performance
Saturday	Performance

There is a lull in the rehearsal as one of the actors checks his lines. As the production develops, the director will designate a person to supply the actors with lines when needed.

The seventh week is important and should be carefully scheduled in an effort to accomplish many last-minute tasks. On Monday of this last week, the staff should hold its last rehearsal in which interruptions can be made, problems discussed, final costumes and props checked, and all details settled.

At least two dress rehearsals are recommended. However, if there is only one dress rehearsal, it should come on the Wednesday or Thursday before a Friday-night performance. Tuesday may be spent in a final run-through. It is wise to invite a few people to a dress rehearsal to accustom the cast to playing before an audience. Some directors leave the night before the performance free for final adjustments. Others feel that a continuous flow right up to opening night is desirable. The auditorium should probably be closed to all other activities during the last three weeks, and enough time must be given to the technical director and the crew to "hang the set." Consider the sample rehearsal schedule when planning for your next production.

READING REHEARSALS

The first rehearsal, called the **reading rehearsal,** is crucial in setting the tone and establishing expectations for the entire rehearsal and production process. The director should expect all members of the production team and the chairpersons of committees involved in the backstage activities to be present. This is an appropriate time for the director to discuss the value of working together toward the objectives of presenting the best production possible and the importance of maintaining the spirit of the play. The director might want to point out some factors that make a fine performance, such as perfect timing, excellent individual characterizations, and coordination of onstage and backstage activities.

At a reading rehearsal, some directors prefer to read the play themselves, suggesting the interpretation of the entire play and of the individual roles. Others prefer to give the cast the opportunity to suggest their own characterizations by reading the assigned parts, while the director merely points out important details of phrasing, timing, and inflections. Whatever the method, the reading rehearsal should build a clear conception of the play and of conduct during rehearsals. Everyone should take careful notes.

Usually, several reading rehearsals make actors feel more secure about interpretation when rehearsing onstage. In the first hours of work on the play, the director can sense actors' abilities to understand lines and project personality. The director can also judge the actors' willingness to respond to direction and the extent to which they pay attention. If there is ample time, a number of reading rehearsals can "set" the characters and the lines. More reading rehearsals are necessary when dialects or stage diction is required.

BLOCKING REHEARSALS

Rehearsals in which the movement and the stage business are worked out are called **blocking rehearsals.** The major blocking areas of the traditional stage are shown on the following page. Movement and stage groupings should be established before work on the interpretation of lines begins.

  The director will already have worked out plans for using the stage area, emphasizing important groupings and keeping effective stage pictures. However, in early rehearsals, most directors are willing to discuss possible changes and to incorporate spontaneous reactions of the actors. When the fundamental blocking of the first act has been set, the blocking of the second act should follow. The two acts can then be brought together at a combined blocking rehearsal. Following this, the third act should be set, and the first and second reviewed. As soon as the business of the first act is clarified, the lines and blocking may be memorized.

Reading rehearsals help a cast develop good timing and a unified understanding of the play.

The Acting Areas—Nine-area

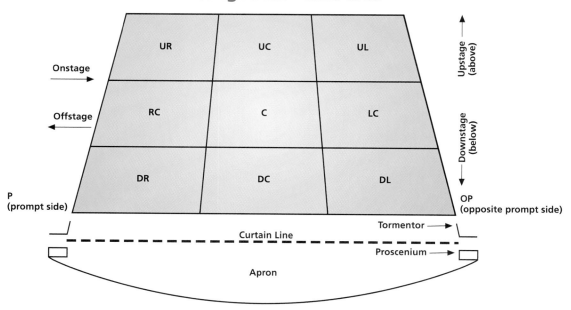

The Acting Areas—Fifteen-area

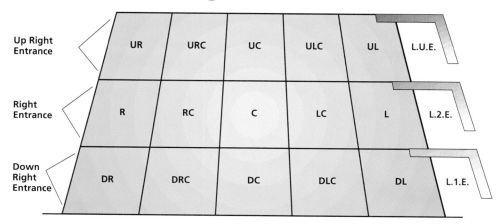

Both diagrams indicate directions from the actor's point of view. The lower diagram shows entrance positions used with the old wing setting—L.1.E. (left first entrance), etc.—and early box sets—down right entrance, etc. These symbols are still used with many musical plays.

When planning stage business, the director must be sure that all gestures and movements are meaningful. In order to avoid later delay, the director should try in early rehearsals to eliminate tendencies of actors to fidget, shift weight, and gesture ineffectively. Actors should understand that every gesture and cross must be motivated and definite and that the center of interest should be accentuated at all times. The director must adhere to fundamental directions when dealing with inexperienced people.

If blocking rehearsals cannot be held in the auditorium, the assistant director should arrange a rehearsal area that has exactly the same dimensions as the stage. She or he should then indicate the entrances and exits with chalk or tape and obtain furniture that resembles the pieces that will eventually be used. If rehearsal furniture cannot be obtained or is not of the same size or shape, the floor should be marked with the correct dimensions to facilitate proper blocking.

During this period a feeling of camaraderie will probably develop, and the actors and crew members should feel free to approach the director with their problems and suggestions. They should receive considerate attention and advice. The director is largely responsible for establishing morale because his or her methods will be copied subconsciously by the cast and the crew.

It is sometimes difficult for actors to make the necessary movements an intrinsic part of their dialogue, especially when the real setting may be difficult to visualize. Directors can assist them in understanding their movements by explaining how character groupings, movements, and setting fit into the big picture, giving the production unity, proportion, and balance.

A set's foundation is made of platforms and ramps. These structures should be put in place as soon as possible so that the actors can get used to them.

WORKING REHEARSALS

After all the action has been blocked, the most creative part of rehearsing begins. At the **working rehearsal** interpretation is developed, and words and action are put together. All the acting techniques previously discussed are coordinated with the director's carefully thought-out plans. Some directors use the terms *essential* and *accessory* to describe actions. The former are set by the director; the latter are worked out as a means of character delineation by the actor.

CUE ▼

Remember, practice and rehearsal are not synonymous. Practice, for the most part, is what you do on your own time; rehearsal is what you do in the presence of the director and the other members of the cast.

The interpretations of the roles are fine-tuned during the working rehearsals. The director should have absolute control of the production, for the director alone has planned the stage settings, the action, the tempo, and the rhythm to create an artistic whole of which the actors are only one part. The director is also privileged to change his or her mind without question. However, individual and group discussions where ideas can be exchanged and questions answered should be arranged or encouraged informally offstage. Actors might find that writing character sketches of their roles before such discussions helps clarify their thinking about defining their characters.

By the time working rehearsals begin, memorization should be almost completed. Real characterization can begin only after the actors are "offbook," meaning that no scripts can appear onstage. At this point, actors should be left relatively free to move and speak, because spontaneous physical and vocal responses frequently improve a scene. Actors should not, however, be permitted to fix a false inflection or swallow important words and phrases. Having an actor write a paraphrase of a passage may help her or him appreciate the exact meaning of the lines. It is sometimes helpful if the director stops an actor suddenly and asks a pointed question, such as "What is happening to your character in this scene?" Only as a last resort should the director read the lines.

Speeding up or slowing down words and action to attain a certain mood or meaning is often difficult for inexperienced actors. It is during the working rehearsals that the director helps the actors develop tempo by offering suggestions such as the following:

- Pick up cues rapidly.
- Listen effectively.
- Hold for a laugh or pause.
- Point lines.
- Break up long speeches with action.
- Use appropriate body movement.

Producing a play is a collaborative process. During working rehearsals, the director, prompter, and actor work together to develop a good tempo and mood.

This phase of interpretation is especially critical. Actors tend to return to early rehearsal practices under the pressure of performance, so no false inflections or moves, especially gestures, must become set. With troublesome lines, sometimes bridging is helpful. **Bridging** is adding words before or after the difficult ones. Beginners must help each other by feeding cues properly, by listening effectively but not conspicuously, and by taking themselves out of a scene when necessary. Most inexperienced actors have trouble giving sufficient time on pauses. Here it is frequently helpful to have them count from one-half to two beats for a desired effect. Restraining movement in order to give a meaningful gesture or a glance a chance to register is very important.

The location of the director is crucial during working rehearsals. Most directors sit onstage beside the prompter during early rehearsals and quietly interrupt to ask questions and to give directions. Other directors place the prompter on one side of the stage and seat themselves about halfway back in the auditorium in order to check the entire stage area. Usually a combination of methods is preferable. When sitting too near the actors, the director does not get a good perspective of the stage picture, the sense of unity of the action as a whole, or the clear and harmonious blending of the voices. On the other hand, if the director is near, the intimate question-and-answer procedure can be used to inspire an actor to think through a problem. A good procedure is to begin working intimately with a scene, bringing out details and correcting mistakes. Then the director can retire to a distance and watch the entire action from different vantage points while checking the clarity of key lines and words, the spacing of the actors, and the continuing effect of stage pictures.

Projection of lines is the means by which the play is heard and understood and is an absolute necessity. If you have been practicing regularly, you should understand the fundamental principles. Your work now is to correlate the physical processes of correct breathing and articulation with the psychological consciousness of speaking to everyone in the audience. You should by this time be breathing correctly and relaxing your inner throat muscles, while at the same time clarifying the important words with flexible lips and tongue.

Speaking intelligibly, not necessarily loudly, is necessary to convey the exact meaning of your lines. From the first rehearsal, you should have begun marking the pauses, the words, and the phrases that must be stressed to emphasize meanings. The most common fault of inexperienced actors is to drop the last words of every sentence instead of breathing between thought groups. Often the most vital words are at the end of the sentence and must be heard. Unless you are specifically told by the director to speak upstage, it is wise to speak front or diagonally front (three-quarter front), turning your head toward the person you are addressing on sentences of little consequence.

Mock costumes and props should be used as soon as possible in the rehearsal schedule, especially in period and stylized plays. The assistant director coordinates the crews that obtain whatever the play requires, such as hand props, costumes, and furniture. The assistant director is also responsible for checking that props are stored properly after rehearsals.

In addition to the general rehearsal schedule, a second, specialized schedule should be worked out for actors who are together in a number of scenes. These scenes or fragments of scenes can be rehearsed separately under the direction of the assistant director. Important roles can often be rehearsed separately, also. This schedule of simultaneous rehearsals avoids long periods of waiting for actors. In addition, intensely emotional scenes should always be directed privately until the action is crystallized and the responses are natural and convincing.

POLISHING REHEARSALS

The real joys of directing and acting are experienced in the **polishing rehearsals.** With lines memorized and action set, all phases of the production can be brought together in an artistic whole. From the standpoint of the actor, these rehearsals should bring the creative satisfaction of developing the subtle shades of vocal inflection and non-verbal communication that make the character truly alive.

Special effects, such as these seen in *Cats*, require many technical rehearsals. Come opening night, this scene must feel as routine as the play's simpler scenes.

Polishing rehearsals provide satisfaction not only among actors but also among stage crews. All exits and entrances, props, sets, and basic furniture should be onstage and in position. Sound effects necessary for cues should also be set. Only then can the actors find themselves in the environment of the play and become a part of it. Once the mechanics of fitting themselves into the sets have been mastered, the actors can complete their search for identity with their roles in relation to the play as a whole.

To a director, the most important element in play production is **rhythm.** The rhythm of a play is the overall blending of all the elements of the production with particular stress on tempo, action, and dialogue. It is during the polishing rehearsals that the rhythm of the play is set and maintained. The entire production staff must work as a team to synchronize all aspects of the production—voices, sound effects, actions, lighting, and even the music between acts—into the rhythm established by the director. Sound, light cues, and sound effects must be carefully timed. A single extraneous sound, a slight motion, an unmotivated gesture, or a poorly timed sound cue can destroy the effect of a scene. The director must scrutinize every stage picture from all parts of the auditorium. The director is responsible for the tempo of the production. Some ways of adjusting and maintaining the tempo of a production include the following:

- Speed up cues.
- Eliminate irrelevant action.
- Clarify speech.
- Assist cast to point their lines.
- Assist cast to hold their pauses.

If the play is dragging because of pauses between sentences, it is helpful to have a rapid-fire line rehearsal, with the actors conversationally running through the play without any action or dramatic effects. To pace the timing and to make sure of clarity, some directors listen to difficult scenes without watching them.

It is only when the pieces are brought together that the director can see exactly what is still needed to make the play a success. The complete play should be put together in rehearsal about ten days before the first performance. From that time forward, remembering the following things might be helpful.

1. Rehearsals should be by acts, with as little interruption as possible.
2. Schedule separate rehearsals for difficult scenes.
3. Prop committee should have all props ready.
4. Curtain calls can be rehearsed.
5. Intermission can be timed.
6. Costume changes should be timed (now or after dress rehearsal) and worked into the overall rhythm of the play.

Application
ACTIVITY

Memorize a short monologue, and pretend you are in a polishing rehearsal. Combine any vocal inflections and actions that bring the part to life. Ask your classmates for critiques.

TECHNICAL REHEARSALS

Settling as many matters as possible before dress rehearsals is always preferable. The best way to ensure that actors and stage crew members are ready to work together is to schedule **technical rehearsals.** During technical rehearsals, every crew member and actor must get his or her materials organized and performance duties clearly in mind. If there is no time for technical rehearsals, the group must go directly from the polishing to the dress rehearsals.

The first time the cast and the technical crew work together with the set, there will probably be confusion and delays in getting lamps to work, doors to open, curtains to come down exactly on time, and props to be in the right place at the right time. Basic scenery units should be onstage as soon as possible so that necessary adjustments can be made. Ideally, the stage should be completely ready three weeks before the performance. The cast and backstage crews should be working together so that costumes, makeup, scenery, props, and furniture can be considered simultaneously from the standpoint of color, light, and form.

A technical run-through is necessary to work out the kinks in the production. In *Noises Off*, one actor helps situate another actor's costume.

Bringing It Together	
Director	Move through the auditorium, checking sight lines, acoustics, and total effects. Take notes to share with cast after final curtain. Involved persons should record director's suggestions.
Stage Manager	Make stage plot for each scene, showing exact positions of flats and furniture. Number all pieces, and appoint stagehands to place, remove, and store them backstage.
Crews	Rehearse to establish the sequence of action so that changes can be made in seconds. Specific crew members should always handle the curtain, lights, and props in order to ensure exact timing.
Lighting	Rehearsals are imperative. Experimentation yields effective results. Use lighting for rapidly changing effects. Use lighting to establish mood and time of day. Light should not leak, reflect, or splash. Use backstage floodlights to kill shadows. Make sure no circuits are overloaded.
Props	Arrange pictures, props, and household effects to present a "lived-in" look. Curtains should be the right color and should drape well.

CUE ▼

"Eventually? Why not *now*?" is an excellent motto for everyone involved with a play.

Not all details of setting, costume, and makeup will be ready, but the essentials should be. A technical run-through of the whole play with changing of available costumes, coordination of all effects, and possibly curtain calls will help make the dress rehearsals run like performances.

It is easier to attend to the inevitable details before, rather than on the day of, the performance. As many matters as possible should be settled before the dress rehearsals. The planning is worth the effort if it avoids hectic dress rehearsals and a slipshod performance.

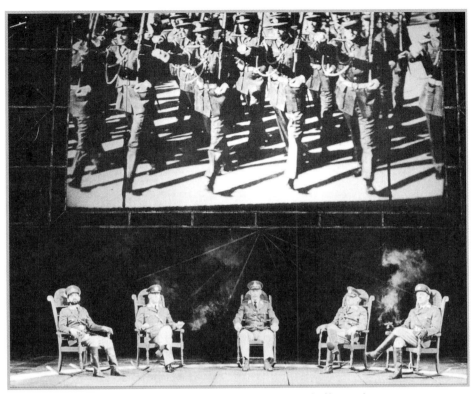

The award-winning rock opera *Evita* relies heavily on special effects. The screen must lower and the film must begin at precisely the right moment.

DRESS REHEARSALS

The final preparations for a performance conclude in a **dress rehearsal,** an uninterrupted rehearsal with costumes and props. A dress rehearsal will feel like a real performance. It is the last chance to smooth out the wrinkles of past rehearsals. If possible, two dress rehearsals for a straight play and three or four for a musical should be held. Sometimes it is beneficial to invite a small audience to the final dress rehearsal so that the cast can learn to point lines and hold the action for laughter and applause.

Usually photographs of the cast in various scenes are taken at a dress rehearsal. The pictures should be taken either before or after the rehearsal so that the timing of the production and the establishment of moods are not interrupted.

The final dress rehearsal should begin on time and go straight to the end without interruption. The cast and crew should be instructed to adjust whatever is seriously wrong as well as possible while the action continues. The main consideration is to avoid awkward pauses and the repetition of lines or action.

Backstage organization must be efficient. Each person has specific responsibilities. The chain of command might resemble the following:

Director	Final authority—check makeup, costumes, props, lights, and stage before going out front
Stage Manager	Full responsibility for the backstage—check lights and stage before curtain goes up; see that cast is ready; get crew members in places; give signals for lights, curtain, sound effects
Prompter	Responsibility for actors' lines—should not be interrupted once the curtain is up, must remain alert every instant the play is in progress and must be inaudible and invisible to the audience

When the final dress rehearsal is finished, the actors should put away their makeup, hang their costumes, and leave the dressing rooms in order. It is the responsibility of each actor to inform the wardrobe crew if costumes need pressing or mending.

During final rehearsals, some directors sit at the back of the auditorium and dictate notes, which are written on separate sheets of paper for each performer. As these are given out, the director explains the correction and might ask the actor to run through the line or business. Other directors prefer to give critiques orally and to have the cast record the comments. Both the cast and the crew should feel encouraged and confident after a dress rehearsal. If there is continued cooperation, a good dress rehearsal should ensure a satisfactory performance.

Application
ACTIVITY

Do you think a dress rehearsal is really necessary if the other rehearsals have gone well? Explain your reasons.

CURTAIN CALLS

Curtain calls—the appearance of a play's cast in response to the audience's applause—should be rehearsed and should never be considered as an add-on. The last impression that an audience has of a play is of its curtain call. Therefore, the finishing touch of a good production is a polished curtain call.

The form of a curtain call is determined by the director and by the style of the show. There are simple curtain calls in which the actors take bows in reverse order according to importance of role. There are "frozen" curtain calls in which the actors pose in suspended animation. There are also curtain calls in which the actors line up side by side, take hands and bow as a group. Thrust and arena productions usually require some type of moving or shifting curtain call that allows the actors to take their bows to the different sections of the audience.

The director will prepare the cast for a definite number of curtain calls, but the stage manager will determine how many will be taken at each performance. It is important to keep in mind that curtain calls are largely a matter of time. An audience will applaud for a certain length of time, depending on the quality of the production and the number of characters. A curtain call should be executed quickly and efficiently. Do not expect or desire standing ovations. The "everybody on their feet" attitude seen in so many high schools has robbed many students of the rare thrill of a true standing ovation.

▼ CUE

Every actor, no matter how small the part, should participate in the curtain call in costume and makeup. This is really the final scene of the performance.

THE GREATS
★ ★ ★ ★ ★
Nathan Lane and Matthew Broderick take curtain calls after a performance of *The Producers.* Lane and Broderick won acclaim for their roles in the Mel Brooks musical.

Summary and Key Ideas

Summarize the chapter by answering the following questions.

1. Briefly explain the responsibilities of the following: prompter, technical director, stage manager, property chief, business manager, publicity manager, house manager.
2. What is the purpose of a master production schedule?
3. Why is the promptbook "the backbone of a production"?
4. Define the following terms: open audition, closed audition, prepared audition, cold reading, improvisational audition, and textual tryout.
5. What information should be included in a résumé? in a budget?
6. Explain the purposes of each type of rehearsal: blocking, working, polishing, technical, and dress.
7. Why should curtain calls be rehearsed?

Discussing Ideas

1. Considering the production facilities available at your school, discuss the kinds of productions that would be most successful for you.
2. Discuss the effect that limited facilities might have on a production. How can such limitations actually lead to a more successful play?
3. Discuss the role of the director in casting. Why is the director's ability to look ahead of crucial importance?

FOCUS ON Collaboration

As a student of drama, you will learn about your own strengths and weaknesses and about your effect on others. You will also become a more communicative person. Here are some tips that will help you get the most out of your collaboration with others:

- An actor or technician who wishes to improve accepts and seeks constructive criticism. The intent of any critical comments should be to improve the performance, not to belittle the actors or crew.
- When you are given the opportunity to evaluate a fellow actor's performance, first try to find something that deserves praise, such as the voice, animation, or interpretation. Then comment on the things that can be improved.

Evaluating Performances Practice your critiquing skills with a group of six classmates. Each of you should prepare and perform a short monologue. Then each group member should critique one other group member's performance. Make sure to be polite, fair, and impersonal, to begin with what you liked, and to include helpful suggestions about what to improve.

Reflecting After reflecting on the comments you heard, make a list of ways that actors might benefit from critiques.

PRODUCING THE PLAY

INDEPENDENT ACTIVITY

Writing a Résumé   Suppose that in this weekend's newspaper you read an article about your community playhouse doing a production for children. The play is *Cinderella*. Choose a character from the play and write a résumé that someone who is interested in playing that part might submit. Based on what you think the requirements of the part are, make up the facts about this potential actor.

Follow the sample résumé shown on page 353. If you wish, the résumé may be about yourself.

Help Wanted Ad   Your drama club wants to present Arthur Miller's *Death of a Salesman*. Unfortunately, your faculty adviser, who would normally act as the director, cannot direct this production. Brainstorm a list of characteristics you would like to find in a director and make a list of qualifications for the job. Use the lists to write a Help Wanted advertisement for the newspaper aimed at attracting the ideal person for the position.

Cooperative Learning Activity

Promptbook
As a class, choose a play in the public domain (one no longer under copyright). Working in small groups, create a promptbook for the first scene or two. Photocopy the first five pages of the play, and paste them onto larger pieces of paper (to provide wide margins). One person should be in charge of markings for stage directions; another for pauses, phrasing, and emphasis; another for actors' movements across the stage; and another for lighting, sound effects, and curtain notations. Compare your completed promptbook with that of another group, and add any kinds of notations you may have missed.

Across the CURRICULUM Activity

Math   Using the planning form on page 341, prepare a budget for the production of a play that is in the public domain and therefore has no royalty payments. Consider the anticipated income from all sources, such as ticket sales, patrons or sponsors, program advertising, and special school funds, against all anticipated expenses, including advertising, printing, and purchase or rental of equipment, costumes, and properties. Present your budget to the class. If the anticipated income falls short of the anticipated expenses, what adjustments can you and your classmates make to balance the budget without impairing the production?

9 Producing the Musical Play

This is a high school production of *A Chorus Line*, one of the longest running Broadway productions of all time.

*D*eciding what is to be sung and what is not to be sung is really what writing a musical is about.

—STEPHEN SONDHEIM, COMPOSER

SETTING THE SCENE

Focus Questions

What are the types of musical theater?

What are the special concerns in planning and directing a musical play?

What techniques work well for performers in a musical play?

What are the special staging requirements of a musical play?

Vocabulary

opera	musical play	satire	backlighting
operetta	crossover	concept musical	reversibles
comic opera	change music	hanging plot	coordinates
musical revue	spoof	storage plot	combo
musical comedy			

*T*he musical is a special type of theatrical performance that has become quite popular both in and out of the school. Theatergoers in the United States have long been attracted to the sound, color, and pageantry that go along with musical theater. Just as *The King and I, Oklahoma!,* and *South Pacific* thrilled audiences in years past, many of the current best-attended productions around the country are musicals. *Cats, Les Misérables,* and *The Phantom of the Opera,* for example, consistently sell out as their traveling companies play across the United States. Musical theater comes in many types and styles. Some musicals are lavish, extravagant productions with spectacular scenery and costumes. Others are entertaining on a smaller scale. All have one thing in common, though—music.

In a musical revue, music is the focus of the production. The scenes from *Ain't Misbehavin'* consist of production numbers tied together with almost no plot to slow the pace.

🎵 *Types of Musical Theater*

Originating as an attempt to re-create ancient Greek theater, **opera** is one of the oldest forms of musical theater. Since in opera the voice and the orchestra are the only media of performance, opera is "total music." Even conversations are sung, not spoken as in other forms of musical theater. The **operetta** includes lighter music and the singer/actor speaks lines rather than sings them. Operettas are usually built on light plots that serve only to connect one song to another. Plot, characters, and acting are secondary to the music. Some popular operettas are *The Student Prince, Babes in Toyland*, and *The Merry Widow.* An offshoot of the straight operetta is the humorous and satirical **comic opera.** For many years, the comic operas of Gilbert and Sullivan have been very popular as high school shows. Among the favorites are *The Mikado, H.M.S. Pinafore*, and *The Pirates of Penzance.*

The **musical revue,** another form of musical theater, usually consists of a loosely connected series of sometimes lavish production numbers with virtually no plot. The Ziegfield Follies is the most famous example of this form of musical theater. *Ain't Misbehavin'* is a more recent musical revue.

As the name implies, a **musical comedy** combines music and humor. Music remains the most important element, and the plot still tends to be secondary. Musical comedy differs from comic opera in that the characters are more believable and the dialogue is clever. Some of the musical comedies popular with high schools are *Anything Goes; No, No, Nanette; Annie Get Your Gun; Guys and Dolls*; and *The Pajama Game.*

Oklahoma! is the production that introduced the **musical play,** a form of musical theater characterized by an increased emphasis on real people in real situations. In the musical play, acting and choreography are an integral part of the production. A well-written musical play contains a good story, clever dialogue, interesting characters, well-designed choreography, bouncy tunes, and meaningful ballads woven into an entertaining package of color and spectacle. Because it provides excellent opportunities for showmanship and talent, it has replaced many operettas and variety shows in high school theater.

The musical play has become a major part of high school theater for several reasons. The sophistication of contemporary audiences demands more than a stage full of people in a simple musical revue. In addition to having greater audience appeal, a musical play involves many students onstage, in the orchestra pit, and behind the scenes.

Musical Play Terminology

book: the script of a musical

cabaret style: a show produced in a small space with limited seating

change music: the music played between scenes while sets are being changed

choreographer: a person who designs dance for the stage

choreography: the dances designed for a production

chorus: the singers other than the principals

combo: a small group of instrumentalists

composer: a person who writes music

conductor: a person who directs an orchestra

crossover: a short scene played in front of a shallow drop or curtain while scenery is being changed

entr'acte: music that precedes the second-act curtain

lead-in line: the line or lines of dialogue immediately preceding a song

librettist: a person who writes the book (script)

libretto: the book, including lines of dialogue and lyrics

lyricist: a person who writes words to music

lyrics: the words to a song

overture: the music, usually a medley of the show's songs, played at the beginning of the show

principals: the named characters in a musical play

production number: a large-scale musical number involving many performers in lavish costumes; frequently a dance number *recitative*: singing style that is closer to speaking than to singing

score: the music of a show as composed

segue (sĕ´•gwā): the continuation of music from one number to the next without stopping; a transition

sidekick: a secondary male lead, often a comic role and a friend to the lead; counterpart to the soubrette.

sides: booklets containing half sheets of paper on which the cues and lines for one character are written

soubrette: a secondary female lead, usually a comic role

underscore: music played to accompany dialogue

vamp: to repeat measures of music until a singer or scene is ready

🌾 *Planning for the Musical Play*

Staffing a musical play is considerably more difficult than staffing a straight play. A musical play usually needs a vocal director, an instrumental director, and a choreographer in addition to a play director, a costumer, a business manager, a technical director, and a publicity director. The play director, however, is in charge of the entire production.

The director of a musical play must know all aspects of musical theater: acting, singing, dancing, orchestrating, and set designing. This does not mean that the director needs to be an expert in all of these areas. She or he, however, must be sufficiently knowledgeable in each of these areas to visualize how they work together to produce a unified performance.

When selecting a musical play for production, careful consideration must be given to costs as well as to acting, technical, and musical requirements. Discovering midway through rehearsals that costs are running over budget or that the abilities of the performers are not suited to the musical demands can be quite discouraging.

Questions to Ask When Selecting a Musical

- Are the production costs within our budget limits?
- Do we have the staff to direct this show?
- Do we have the acting, scenery, musical, and lighting capabilities this show requires?
- Do we have the time required to prepare this show?
- Will this musical play please the performers *and* the audience?
- Is this musical play suitable for high school production?

Once the director and the staff have been chosen, a budget must be prepared. The total expenses for a musical are considerably more than for a straight play (two to ten times more). These expenses include costs not associated with the production elements of the play. For instance, royalty and script costs are significantly more complicated. Before producing a musical play, you must contact the publisher of the work to request permission to hold public performances of that play. Every publisher has a different formula for calculating royalty costs, which may include or exclude certain rehearsal materials, such as scripts, in the fee quoted.

A royalty fee is normally based on the number of seats available for sale and the ticket prices charged. For example, if your auditorium seats 1,500, but you plan to use only the front section seating 500, report your capacity as 500. Have tickets for only 500 seats. Do not sell more than those 500 seats unless you contact the publisher of the play and make the necessary royalty adjustments for the additional seats you intend to sell. Some royalty fees include music rental for one month; some publishers charge music rental separately. An additional fee is charged for a longer rehearsal time. Most schools need the music for at least two months.

As the types of musicals have increased, directors have had to weigh an expanding number of factors in choosing a musical play that is appropriate for high school. Few directors can handle every type of musical available to them, and fewer still can satisfy the many technical demands that are critical to certain musical plays. Many recent musicals depend greatly on elaborate sets, lavish costumes, and high-tech equipment that is difficult to acquire or duplicate on a small scale. These technical demands must be considered as a director chooses a musical for production.

Peter Pan, **with all its technical demands, might be too complex to produce on the high school stage.**

West Side Story requires only simple sets and costumes, making it quite easy to stage if able and energetic dancers and singers can be cast.

Under the best of circumstances, a musical play is much more difficult to cast than a straight play. Singing and dancing abilities as well as acting skill must be considered. Some shows require that the leads be skilled in all three of these areas; other shows require skills in only one or two of these areas. Very often the musical play chosen is too complex for a particular school to do well. It may require more strong characters than can be cast, or the vocal requirements may be too demanding. Some shows call for instruments, such as bassoons and harps, that most schools do not own. There may not be sufficient time to train students in the special skills the show requires, such as tap dancing. Perhaps the best actor has "two left feet," or the individual with the finest voice cannot act. Another often-forgotten factor in producing a musical is the effect interpersonal relationships can have on a production. Since there are usually more cast members in a musical than in a straight play, there are more interpersonal relationships to consider when casting. Be aware of the personality mixture. Many potentially fine shows have been marred by squabbling among cast members.

Once the casting is completed, a rehearsal schedule must be planned. The size and scope of a musical play are greater than those of a straight play and, therefore, require more rehearsal time. Most directors want a minimum of eight weeks of rehearsal. For the first few weeks, it is more efficient to rehearse several groups simultaneously. The orchestra can rehearse by itself. The dancers can rehearse with the choreographer to piano accompaniment or a rehearsal tape of the orchestra. The chorus can rehearse with the vocal director. If possible, it is best to stagger rehearsal schedules so that the chorus members do not have to sit through an entire rehearsal just to sing one or two songs. The principals can rehearse with the play's director. Step by step, the separate elements are combined. Rehearsals of the vocal and dance numbers begin with the orchestra, then the vocal numbers are rehearsed in the context of entire scenes, and finally, all the groups join to rehearse the entire show. Because a musical play has so many elements, allow at least two weeks for rehearsal with the entire cast and four days for dress rehearsals.

Application
ACTIVITY

Work with two or more classmates to analyze the nonproduction costs of a musical play. Choose a musical play and find out what the script and royalty charges would be. Compare your findings with the findings of groups investigating other musical plays.

Directing the Musical Play

Directing a musical play is a very complex task. The director must understand the structure of the play and the role music plays within that structure. Because lyrics are important to the development of action, theme, and character, they must be clearly understood.

Lyrics are more easily understood when sung directly to the audience, as shown here in *How to Succeed in Business Without Really Trying.*

SPECIAL CONSIDERATIONS

Musical plays usually have many scenes (ten to thirty or more). This means that some scenes must be played in front of a curtain or a **drop,** scenery painted on a piece of fabric that can be dropped like a curtain, on an eight- to ten-foot segment of the stage while scenery is being changed behind the curtain. This is called playing a scene "in one." Musical theater stages are usually divided into three depths, each eight to ten feet deep. Performers may enter one, two, or three, depending on how deep, or upstage, the entry is made. Some "in one" scenes consist of characters walking across the stage together or entering from opposite sides and meeting onstage. Such scenes are called **crossovers.** Crossovers may also be played on the apron of the stage in front of the act curtain.

CUE ▼

In professional theater, scene changes occur in a matter of seconds due to the use of turntables, moving belts, tracks in the floor, and other scenic equipment.

The director must work with the technical director to determine the exact scenery shift time so that the smoothness and rhythm of the production are not lost. Some contemporary musicals actually feature the changing of scenery and do not attempt to conceal it. Well-choreographed set changes can heighten an audience's appreciation of the artistry of the theater. In more traditional productions the conductor may vamp the **change music**—the music played to cover the sound of scenery changes—if it becomes apparent that a shift cannot be completed quickly.

Stage positions are extremely important in directing a musical play. Center, down center, and down right are the locations for most solos. Since we are a left-to-right-oriented society, an audience always turns to its left (stage right) when there is a large open stage, as there usually is in musical plays. As a result, down right is a very strong solo position. The chorus must be blocked in groups to avoid solid lines that look like a school chorus onstage. Groups should consist of one, two, three, four, five, or seven people. Odd-number groupings are preferable, however. The asymmetrical look of odd-number groups provides a dynamic sight line, while the symmetrical look of even-number groups provides a static sight line. There is a tendency for the downstage end of a large chorus to "creep" too far downstage, shutting off the view for parts of the audience. Choruses must guard against this and maintain their groupings and positions. Otherwise, they will drift together into one large mass.

Getting these groups of chorus members on and off the stage presents a real traffic problem. The director must rehearse extensively on chorus entrances and exits to make them smooth and inconspicuous.

Another difficulty in directing a musical play is teaching the performers to project over the underscore. Actors sometimes feel overwhelmed by the orchestra. If the actors cannot project over the orchestra,

A mask of any kind, even if it doesn't fully cover the mouth, hinders projection and makes it harder to be heard over the underscore. The title character from *The Phantom of the Opera* delivers melody and lyrics to the audience despite a fully orchestrated underscore, a half mask, and his own bent-backed posture.

the director may have to ask the orchestra to play more softly. Other options are to cut back on the number of instruments playing the underscore, to omit the underscore entirely, or to supply soloists with individual cordless microphones.

Certain circumstances may cause a director to have a performer recite lyrics rather than sing them. In some cases, the director may seek to produce a desired effect. In others, a performer may have trouble reaching certain notes. Although some performers may feel embarrassed reciting lyrics, personal feelings must be secondary to doing what is best for the show. Reciting with strength and character is preferable to singing without these qualities. Some of the best-known numbers in musicals have been performed in the recitative style.

The cast should know which musical numbers are melodic and which are rhythmic. Melodic songs are those with pleasing sound combinations combined with moving lyrics, such as ballads and "theme" songs. "Memory" in *Cats* and "The Music of the Night" in *The Phantom of the Opera* are examples of melodic numbers. Rhythmic numbers, such as "Summer Nights" in *Grease,* focus on tempo, musical style, beat, and orchestration.

PERFORMANCE PRINCIPLES

Experienced directors have learned to remind the cast over and over again of certain simple but important principles for performing a musical play.

1. Stress the first beat of each measure.
2. Make the words intelligible.
3. Sing "through the eyes."
4. Play out to the audience.
5. Keep the scene focused.
6. Be alive in character.
7. Play in a state of action.
8. Enjoy yourself—and look it!

Let's examine each principle closely.

1. One of the secrets for putting life into a musical play is vocally attacking the first beat of each measure. Most show tunes are either lively, bouncy, driving numbers or emotional, heartfelt songs, and the key words come on the first beat. Melodic numbers in particular gain power and emotional impact through emphasis on the first beat. For crispness and strength, singers should attack each initial consonant instead of sliding into the vowels.

2. Lyrics can be difficult to understand, especially when they are sung as high notes. Trained singers are taught to substitute "more singable" vowel sounds for certain vowels. Do not allow this substitution to make words unintelligible or strange to the audience.

3. "Singing through the eyes" adds life to a musical number. By imagining that the singing is being projected through the eyes rather than through the mouth, the singer lifts the sound, making it stronger.

4. It is especially important for the performers in a musical play to include the audience. Unlike a straight play in which the characters interact primarily with other characters, the musical play's strength lies mainly in songs and dances that are played directly to the audience.

5. Musicals usually require more stage space and more people than straight plays do. Therefore, the attention of the audience must be directed to the key characters in a scene. In a musical play, the key character is usually the soloist. This focus can be accomplished by the members of the chorus in several ways: shoulders that are closest

FROM THE PROS

"Lyrics reflect character through diction, grammar, and rhetorical patterns. An audience must assume that the words a character is given to sing reflect something about the character."

—RICHARD KISLAN, AUTHOR OF *The Musical*

To prevent a production from becoming static and uninteresting, chorus members should be involved in the action as they sing.

to the soloist can be turned upstage; downstage shoulders can drop slightly. Chorus members can also kneel on their downstage knees or even recline on the floor with their heads toward the soloist.

6. Members of the chorus often do not realize their importance to the total production. The director must stress the need for each chorus member to develop a well-defined character with a function in every scene. The "I'm just a chorus member" attitude must become "I'm Sam Tilsbury, owner of the corner drugstore in River City, whose wife, Martha Mae, just bought our son Freddie a double-belled euphonium from that fast-talking swindler, Harold Hill." Remember, the audience sweeps its eyes over the entire cast looking for someone really "alive" or really "dead." One "dead" chorus member can spoil an entire scene.

7. Standing erect and motionless may be appropriate for a choir or some opera choruses, but it is usually boring in a musical. Singing while moving or doing something is always stronger. Principals can learn to deliver their lines in an even more active state than they would in a straight play. They "set" their actions by momentarily freezing a gesture, pose, or movement before continuing on the line or business. This is particularly effective when the lead-in line is delivered just before the song is to be sung. Chorus members rarely stand straight and tall; they lean, crouch, bend their knees, gesture, move, and dance.

8. The final technique that the director should teach to the cast is to enjoy, enjoy, enjoy. Excitement, pleasure, and energy are contagious. An audience is eager to be drawn into the spirit of a play. When a cast appears to have fun, the audience shares the enthusiasm.

DIFFERENT TYPES OF MUSICAL PLAYS

Some types of plays are particularly difficult to direct, especially when presented as a musical play. A spoof is such a play. **Spoofs,** or light parodies, are farcical and poke fun at certain subjects or eras. For example, *Little Mary Sunshine* pokes fun at a style of musical film; *Once upon a Mattress* laughs at fairy tales; *The Boy Friend* ridicules the musicals of the 1920s and the mechanical style of acting that was popular at that time.

Satires are also difficult to produce successfully, especially in musical form. Satires criticize certain aspects of human behavior or society. For example, *How to Succeed in Business Without Really Trying* satirizes the shenanigans that often accompany getting ahead in the business world. To direct a satire effectively, the director must make sure that the audience clearly understands what is being criticized. The director must also pace a musical satire expertly so that the comic moments and the serious moments stand out at the appropriate times.

Concept musicals are built around a single theatrical idea. Plot, if any, is secondary to situation. The production is usually a series of independent scenes loosely tied together. The director's main concern is how the show is handled, not what it has to say. It is sometimes difficult to break away from the traditions of the musical play to make the "concept" of a production the focus. *Cats, A Chorus Line,* and *Starlight Express* are concept musicals.

In *Cats* the obvious concept is that the characters are cats. Not only must the performers look like cats, but they also must move like cats and think like cats. In *A Chorus Line* the concept is that of dance auditions. The actors play actors auditioning for a musical. *Starlight Express* features different types of train engines. Using costumes, makeup, and roller skates, the actors mimic trains competing with one another.

Some musical plays are controversial, and unless the director interprets such a work carefully, the audience may not be prepared for some of the disturbing elements portrayed through character, plot, song, and dance. *Cabaret* is such a play. There is a temptation to stress the surface aspects of the play, which are depicted quite vividly in the cabaret scenes. By overemphasizing the frivolous, titillating, and bawdy side of *Cabaret,* however, the director might fail to communicate the play's serious commentary on the destruction of human lives and values and on the social structure during the time just prior to the rise of Nazi Germany.

CUE

In the jargon of the theater, a "pace show" is a show with a brisk tempo, like *George M;* a "heart show" is a show that requires special sensitivity, like *Man of La Mancha;* and a "splash" is a musical with large production numbers, like *Hello, Dolly!*

In the concept musical *Starlight Express*, the performers portray trains, and the setting is an elaborate system of ramps and runways that simulate a locomotive roundhouse.

Application ACTIVITY

Choose a musical play to compare with one of the straight plays you have studied. Pay attention to how the use of music and dance affects the treatment of theme, character, setting, and action in the two plays. Do you think it makes a play richer to incorporate more than one art form, or do you think multiple art forms distract the audience's attention from the play's message? Explain your conclusions in a short written report.

❧ Staging the Musical Play

Stage settings are discussed in detail in Chapter 10, but there are many unique staging decisions associated with musical plays. (Refer to Chapter 10 for the definitions of unfamiliar terms.) Scenery, lighting, and costumes require special consideration in musical plays. Moreover, the music adds an entirely new dimension to the staging. Not only must it be performed well, it must also be coordinated with the action onstage.

SCENERY AND LIGHTING

One of the director's first decisions is to determine the number of sets needed for the production. Few high schools can build as many sets as the script calls for; therefore it may be necessary to combine, eliminate, or reuse some scenery. Often the only choice is to play a scene in front of a traveler or the act curtain. After determining the number of scenes and set changes required, the director must decide which scenes will use drops, which will use wagons, which will use set pieces, and which scenes will be played in front of a curtain. (See Chapter 10 for information on sets.)

Professional theaters often have sixty or more counterweight lines on which to hang scenery. Few high schools have that many, and some schools have no fly system at all for hanging drops. Of those schools that have some kind of system for hanging drops, some do not have counter-weighted or electric winch systems and must raise and lower scenery manually. However, the lack of such professional equipment should not be discouraging. Drops can be rented from stage scenery firms, and raising and lowering scenery manually can prove to be as quick and smooth as using winch or counterweighted systems.

CUE ▼

If your school's stage has limited fly space and wing areas, consider putting different scenes on opposite sides of a set and reversing them for various scenes. See the explanation of prism sets in Chapter 10.

Another way to handle scenery is by using revolving and jackknife wagon stages. These are especially effective when a scene calls for a lot of furniture or set pieces; with scenery mounted on them, these stages allow for quick scene changes. Wagons can also be mounted with walls that are hinged so that the flats can be flipped over, revealing the other side. Unfortunately, wagons take up considerable wing space, and many schools have limited side stage areas.

There are often special scenic demands that are difficult to handle on any stage: fog or mist, flying apparatus, carousels, Wells Fargo wagons, automobiles, and surreys, for example. Sometimes it is better to work around such problems if you cannot treat them adequately on your stage. Rather than try inadequate substitutes, it may ultimately be better to choose another show.

Once all the scenery decisions are made, the technical director or the stage manager makes a hanging plot and a storage plot for the play. A **hanging plot** shows all the fly lines and what is on each. A **storage plot** shows the wing areas and how the scenic units are to be stored during the show.

Because a musical play typically uses more stage space than a straight play does, a musical usually requires more lighting. Limited lighting equipment and range increase the likelihood of shadows appearing onstage. If the instruments are available, backlighting soloists and one- or two-character scenes is quite effective. **Backlighting** throws light on the performer from above and slightly upstage. This causes a glow, or halo effect, that makes the actor stand out from the background or chorus.

A **follow spot**—a spotlight that can be moved so that it follows a performer as he or she moves—can create another lighting effect. These spotlights make soloists stand out. However, follow spots can do strange things to the drop behind the performer; if the chorus is behind the soloist, the spot may cut off the heads of the chorus members. Also, some high school stage floors have a shiny surface that reflects a glare onto the scenery and chorus members behind the illuminated performer. Most directors dim the stage lights during a solo if a follow spot is used, then bring them back up after the applause. The audience recognizes this dimming as an acceptable theatrical convention.

▼ **CUE**

White or flesh pink follow spots work best. Amber, red, blue, and green turn costumes and makeup purplish or black.

The lighting in this scene from *How to Succeed in Business Without Really Trying* emphasizes the soloist, center.

HANGING PLOT FOR WILD SONG

LINE NO.		USE	DISTANCE FROM CURTAIN LINE
16	～	Cyc	24'
15	～	Countryside drop	22'6"
14	～	Gymnasium interior	21'8"
13	—	Ballet drop	20'
12	E	4th electric (3rd border)	18'6"
11	～	Leg #2 (strike) garden drop	17'
10	～	Teaser #3	16'
9	～	Scrim	14'6"
8	～	Traveler	13'
7	E	3rd electric (2nd border)	11'6"
6	～	Teaser #2	10'
5	～	Garden portal	9'3"
4	～	Leg #1 (strike) town hall exterior	8'
3	E	2nd electric (1st border)	6'
2	～	Teaser #1 (strike) show curtain	4'6"
1	E	1st electric — X-ray—500 watt fresnels	1'6"
0	～	Act curtain	0

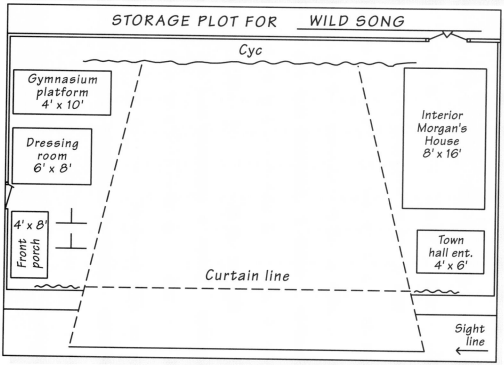

STORAGE PLOT FOR WILD SONG

Cyc

Gymnasium platform 4' x 10'

Dressing room 6' x 8'

Interior Morgan's House 8' x 16'

4' x 8'

Front porch

Town hall ent. 4' x 6'

Curtain line

Sight line

COSTUMES AND MUSIC

Costumes for musical plays should be bolder and more exaggerated than those used in straight plays, since the many lights used in a musical play can deaden an actor's appearance. Costumes are more colorful and more highly stylized. Most musicals are bright, lively productions, and costume colors that would appear gaudy and unbelievable in a straight play are acceptable in a musical play. Costumes for a musical can be quite elaborate, so it might be wise to consider renting them.

Dance costumes, especially for shows with several large production numbers, should be reversibles and coordinates. **Reversibles** are garments such as vests, scarves, belts, and skirts that are made double-faced so that reversing one or more of these articles of clothing creates the illusion of a different costume. **Coordinates,** which can also be reversible, are separates or interchangeables. Costume coordinates such as hats, scarves, ties, vests, jackets, blouses, shirts, skirts, gloves, belts, spats, and shoes can be used in varied combinations.

The director and costumer should select or approve all costumes. This will prevent embarrassing situations that can occur when costumes are not in balance or when similar costumes end up side by side. A chorus member in a wonderful homemade costume may outshine the other people onstage, or a principal's costume may be too drab for the role.

▼ **CUE**

Do not try to imitate a Broadway show where a character appears in a new outfit in every scene. This is too costly in time and money. One well-made, well-designed costume is far better than several mediocre ones.

The costumes in this production of *The Wiz* are colorful, flowing, and intricate, giving the stage picture extra interest.

Although musical plays can be presented with piano accompaniment alone, an orchestra can greatly enhance the quality and impact of a production. A full orchestra, however, is not always possible. There is a trend in high school productions to replace full orchestras with **combos** (smaller groups of musicians) or with electronic instruments that can replicate the sounds of a complete orchestra.

Most musical plays open with an overture that features a medley of the show's total score. A similar but briefer orchestral piece, the *entr'acte,* precedes the second-act curtain. Unfortunately, orchestras often play too loudly during acts, drowning out lines and lyrics, since few high school voices are strong enough to be heard over a "full pit." Good rapport must exist between the conductor and the director so that the priorities of the production can be met without creating animosity or sacrificing the quality of sound.

One of the most critical problems facing a high school musical production is the limited vocal range of young voices. Rewriting the music or transposing it used to be a last resort. However, there are now computer discs available for many shows that will transpose the music, print out copies for all vocal and instrumental parts, and prepare rehearsal tapes for vocal and dance numbers. When this service is unavailable, the best way to allow for any vocal limitations of high school singers is to choose a musical that requires a limited vocal range. Using only a piano or a keyboard for one particular number rewritten in a transposed key weakens that number when the rest of the show is fully orchestrated.

CUE ▼

Choose a musical play that suits your budget, your stage, and your community's taste and values.

Poor acoustics is another common problem in high school musical productions. Many schools do not have a recessed orchestra pit, so sound tends to attack the audience. Other schools have tile, brick, or masonry on the auditorium floor and the apron of the stage. Such hard surfaces act as reflectors, and sound cannonades into the audience with deafening loudness. Sometimes the sound can be balanced by carpeting the floor of the orchestra pit, if there is one, and draping sheets of acoustical material or old stage curtains over the front rows of seats. Some high schools solve their sound problems by building a shell around the orchestra so that the sound is slightly contained. Microphones for the actors can help if they are of high quality and are properly placed. Individual cordless microphones are often the best solution.

Communication between the pit and the stage is important. The conductor of the show, usually the instrumental director, must give clear signals to the performers onstage. These signals must not be confused with those meant for the orchestra. Most conductors lead the orchestra with

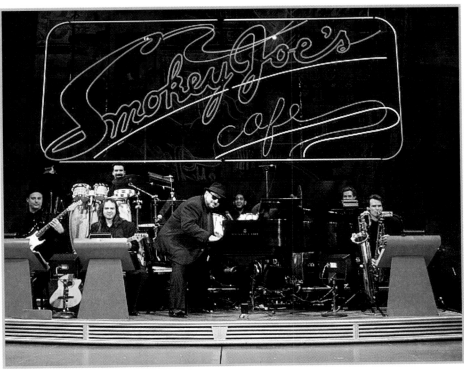

Sometimes the musicians are actually part of the play, as in this scene from *Smokey Joe's Cafe.*

their right hands and cue the stage with their left. The cuing system the conductor wishes to use should be made clear to the cast in early rehearsals. Giving the pitch to stage performers is also quite vital in pit-to-stage communication. Remember, the conductor is in charge of the pit *and* the performers onstage once he or she raises the baton.

Application
ACTIVITY

Read the script or view a performance or movie version of a musical play. Choose one aspect to analyze: lighting, scenery, costumes, or music. Analyze this element in terms of its appropriateness for performing in your school and community. Make a recommendation regarding the musical's possible performance. Be prepared to defend your recommendation.

9 REVIEW

Summary and Key Ideas

Summarize the chapter by answering the following questions.

1. Describe the following forms of musical theater: opera, operetta, comic opera, and musical comedy.
2. Why is staffing more difficult for a musical play than for a straight play?
3. What questions should be addressed when selecting a musical for production?
4. Name and describe three types of musical plays.
5. Identify and explain some key performance principles for musicals.
6. What unique staging problems do musicals present?

Discussing Ideas

1. Why does a musical play demand a good working relationship among these participants: actor, conductor, choreographer, and director?
2. Why are stage positions and movements so important in musical plays?
3. Listen to a recording or watch a video performance of a musical. Discuss several numbers and scenes in which you think the performers demonstrate one or more of the principles listed on pages 384–385.
4. Discuss some of the pitfalls of producing a musical play. What effect can each have on the production?

FOCUS ON Music

Once you get a taste of musical theater, you may find yourself wanting more. Expressing yourself through music is a great, fun way to learn about yourself, explore your talents, and connect with the people around you.

Performing Musical Theater With a small group, choose a musical play to read. Make sure the musical is available on video so you can watch it, too. Then select a scene containing a song that your group can perform without accompaniment. Work together to present the scene informally to your class. For help with presenting the scene, see the Reference Section.

Exploring Careers Your involvement with music doesn't have to stop with high school. You may want to study music further—or even consider it as a career. Do some research on one of the following career options for professional musicians: music teacher, instrumentalist, vocalist, composer, or recording engineer. Then write a one-page report describing the training, skills, and discipline needed to become a professional musician. In your opinion, how should a person decide whether music is a good career option? Include your answer in your report.

PRODUCING THE MUSICAL PLAY

INDEPENDENT ACTIVITY

Comparing Adaptations   Read a play from which a musical has been adapted, and then watch a video of the musical. Some possibilities include *Romeo and Juliet/West Side Story, Pygmalion/My Fair Lady,* and *The Matchmaker/Hello, Dolly!* In an oral report for your class, make some comparisons between the structure and length of the play and the musical. Which important plot ideas are conveyed through lyrics? Which form tells the better story? Which would make a better production?

As an alternative, make the same sort of comparison between a work of literature and a musical such as *The Once and Future King/Camelot, Tales of Sholem Aleichem/Fiddler on the Roof, Don Quixote/Man of La Mancha, Oliver Twist/Oliver, Les Misérables/Les Misérables,* or *Old Possum's Book of Practical Cats/Cats.*

Cooperative Learning Activity

Rock Opera
Since *Hair* was produced in the 1960s, rock operas, such as *Godspell, Joseph and the Amazing Technicolor Dreamcoat,* and *Tommy,* have been popular musicals on and off Broadway. With a group of classmates, select five or six songs by a favorite performing artist or group. Devise a simple plot that connects the songs. Together, plan the staging of one scene of your rock opera. Decide what the set will look like, what lighting you will need, and what makeup and costuming will be necessary. Block the action of the central character and any chorus members. Present your ideas to the class in the form of diagrams and pictures.

Across the CURRICULUM Activity

The Living Arts
Theater, music, art, dance—all these arts, as they have each developed throughout history, have overlapped each other. The elements of which they are comprised, their components, the ways they communicate to their audiences, and their natures can all be compared.

Choose a specific culture or historical period and research the movements and trends in the arts. Also examine the broad scope of these trends, noting how and when they appear in the different art forms. You might want to choose a particular movement to investigate, such as realism, tracing its history from culture to culture and art form to art form. In your report, you should include examples of the different trends you find. If possible, supply photographs or books on your topic for the class to view as you give your presentation.

10 *Stage Settings*

Stage settings establish a play's atmosphere. In Andrew Lloyd Webber's *Sunset Boulevard,* shown here, the characters are dwarfed by the imposing paneled room that includes a sweeping staircase.

he theater, for all its artifices, depicts life in a sense more truly than history.

—GEORGE SANTAYANA, POET AND PHILOSOPHER

SETTING THE SCENE

Focus Questions

What are the purposes of scenery in a play?

What are the effects of scenery in a play?

How has scenic design developed from the Renaissance through modern times?

What are some types of sets?

What are some of the basic principles and considerations of set design?

How do you construct and erect a set?

How do you paint and build scenery?

How do you shift and set scenery?

What are some tips for backstage safety?

Vocabulary

box set	curtain set	value
unit set	unity	tints
permanent set	emphasis	shades
screens	proportion	intensity
profile set	balance	saturation
prisms or *periaktoi*	hue	

A thorough study of the theater must include developing appreciation of stage settings and knowledge of how they are designed and constructed. Through the years, audiences have come to expect scenery that not only presents a specific locale effectively but also adds an essential dimension to the production in terms of detail, mood, and atmosphere. Scenery and lighting definitely have become an integral part of contemporary play writing and production.

All drama students should have a basic knowledge of stagecraft and design. You will find there are many things backstage to be done by those with enthusiasm and a willingness to learn. Backstage theater experience can bring you the satisfaction of knowing that you have played a part in making a successful show possible and can help you discover talents and acquire skills that will be useful beyond your theater experiences.

NOTE: Many traditional theater terms are used in this chapter. If you are uncertain about the meaning of a term, check the Glossary at the back of this book.

Purposes of Scenery

Sets, also called scenery, serve numerous purposes, some basic and others quite complicated and even psychological. The most important purpose of scenery is to provide a place to act. The set should define the time and the setting of the play.

Time	Historical period
	Season of year
	Time of day
	Changes in time during the play
Setting	Climate and geographical conditions
	Socioeconomic situation
	Cultural background
	Political-governmental system of area
	Interior or exterior
	Rural or urban
	Real or imaginary

A set should also help inform the audience about the effects of the environment on the characters, and how, in turn, the characters' personality traits affect their surroundings. For example, in *You Can't Take It with You*, the strange conglomeration of mismatched objects found in the living room indicates the let-one-do-as-one-pleases attitude of the Sycamore family.

Minimal scenery focuses attention on the characters. In this production of *M. Butterfly* by David Henry Hwang, John Lithgow's character controls center stage even though he is seated.

Another important function of a set is to reveal the interrelationships between people as well as their ranks, stations, influence, or positions in their families, offices, or communities. Scenery can provide a means of focusing audience attention on the actor. Elevating an actor on a stairway or a platform provides a strong stage position. Furniture and actors can be arranged to facilitate triangular blocking with the key actor at the center upstage point of the triangle. Well-placed doorways can dramatically frame the actor.

Some plays call for the simplest scenery possible. *Our Town* has been a popular play for high school productions not just because of the power of its drama but because it does not require any scenery. In *Our Town*, Thornton Wilder uses the most effective designer: the audience's imagination. This play has inaccurately been called "the play without scenery"; there *is* scenery, however—the scenery that Wilder felt was necessary for the universality he sought. Many directors and their casts have failed to recognize that such a stage design demands an even stronger interpretation of the roles by the actors than do productions with conventional scenery.

Scenery should also indicate the style of the production. For example, sets for plays done in the romantic style are very different from sets for plays in the epic style. (See Chapter 6 for a discussion of styles of drama.) Of course, stage settings are not totally realistic, especially when presented on a proscenium stage. Theater **conventions**—practices generally accepted

Compare the sketch of a set for *Porgy and Bess* with the photograph of the actual set. The scenic designer's sketch of a crowded, old-fashioned neighborhood comes to life after the set is constructed.

in lieu of realistic depiction—determine general positions for set pieces and entrance areas. Following are a few of the staging conventions used in the theater:

- Almost all furniture faces the audience.
- Exterior doors are usually offstage right.
- Interior doors are usually stage left or upstage.
- Fireplaces tend to be placed on stage-right walls.
- French doors are usually stage left.
- Living-room and dining-room furniture often appear in the same area.

Another important function of scenery is to create mood and atmosphere. The reaction of the audience to the actors and the script may be determined to a great extent by the mental framework a set creates. For example, if the set is painted in bright yellows, oranges, and pinks, the audience will expect the play to be correspondingly light and cheery. On the other hand, if a set is painted in violets, dark blues and greens, grays, and black, the audience will expect the play to be heavy and serious. The scenic designer utilizes the known psychological effects of color and design to arouse a subconscious emotional reaction from the audience. Sets should be aesthetically satisfying, however, even when an atmosphere of fear, chaos, or mystery is intended.

CUE

"Use the least to say the most" is a basic rule for all aspects of theater—from acting to stagecraft.

Scenic Design

Set designers must always remember that a scenic design can be only as elaborate or difficult as the crew and budget can handle. Effective design adds to a production color and life that can make theater an exciting experience. Even costumes seem more appropriate and attractive against an appropriate background. In addition, a careful selection of stage furnishings can make the set and its people seem complete and correct.

SCENIC DESIGN AND THE DRAMA STUDENT

The basic high school drama course is concerned more with the principles of scenic design and construction than with the actual building of sets. However, some knowledge of scenic design is valuable whether or not you plan to take a course in stagecraft. Every performer needs to know the role of the director, the scenic designer, the technical director, the stage manager, and the stage crew in order to appreciate the contribution each makes and to achieve the spirit of cooperation essential to successful productions.

The lighting and scenery combine to give the setting of *Frankenstein* a gloomy, ominous atmosphere.

In bringing a play to life, the scenic designer is next to the director in importance. The aim of both is to create an atmosphere that expresses the meaning of the play. Scenic designers do not build real rooms, houses, or mountaintops; instead, they use painted canvas, creative lighting, and special effects to stir the imagination of the audience so that the playwright's dream seems a reality. The scenic designer works with scenery, lighting, makeup, and costumes to create illusions. The more convincing the illusions, the better the production.

Effective scenery and design should . . .

- match the author's intent and the director's interpretation
- always serve the actor, never dominate him or her
- complement the costumes, never clash with them
- never become an obstacle course for blocking
- work toward consistency, avoiding distractions
- aid the action of the play, not hinder it
- fit the needs of the play
- be simple in design, construction, and shifting

Application
ACTIVITY

Select a scene from a familiar play or from A Treasury of Scenes and Monologues. Write a short description of the amount and type of scenery you would use to fulfill the basic purposes of scenery discussed on pages 398–401.

DEVELOPMENT OF SCENIC DESIGN

From the Renaissance to contemporary times, devoted theater technicians and designers have striven to improve scenery and light design in an effort to more intensely convey meanings through visual sensations.

Renaissance   Stage design as we know it came into being in Italy in the mid-fifteenth century. The oldest structure still remaining is the solidly built and heavily decorated Teatro Olimpico, still perfectly preserved in Vicenza. It was modeled after the ancient Roman theaters and opened on March 3, 1585. Behind the entrances appeared painted stucco walls showing city streets in perspective. Lining those streets are buildings covered with statues of diminishing size. This technique produced the amazing effect of a city stretching into the distance.

The large central entrance of the Teatro Olimpico was the forerunner of the proscenium arch. The first real proscenium was an elaborate structure surrounding a frame with a curtain. Behind this frame, actors performed against painted scenes. To facilitate scenery changes, ***periaktoi,*** prism sets modeled after the revolving prisms of the Greek theater, were sometimes used.

The proscenium arch evolved from the arched entrance of the Teatro Olimpico in Italy. The columns and statues shown in this model resemble those in ancient Roman theaters.

The raked stage, another Renaissance invention, became popular in England and was still used in London early in the twentieth century. In an attempt to create perspective, the stage floor was slanted upward toward the back of the stage. The terms *upstage* and *downstage* came into being; actors actually walked up or down the stage.

Both the beautifully elaborate scenery used in performances of dramatic allegories and the simple house facades of the Elizabethan playhouse were representative of the Renaissance. Dramatists experimented with backdrops, wing settings, revolving stages, and **shutters**—movable flats on tracks used for quick scene changes.

Restoration   In England during the Restoration period, most of the acting took place on raked aprons, with little action in the scenery behind the proscenium. At this time, the proscenium was a very thick wall with one or two doors in each side wall to enable the actors to enter on the apron rather than in back of the frame.

Nineteenth Century   In the nineteenth century, more efforts were made to suit the scenery to the individual play. Certain scenes, however, remained typical:

- interior sets—canvas drops and wings painted to represent a room
- exterior scenes—painted trees, fountains, gates, and pathways
- entrances—wings parallel to the back wall
- street scenes—painted buildings, store windows, signs, and street lamps

By the middle of the nineteenth century, designers were seeking greater accuracy in historical and realistic representation. The beginnings of realism took root with these notable changes:

- the gradual shrinking of the apron
- the addition of orchestra seats
- the elimination of painted backdrops
- the closing of the wings, which gave the illusion of left and right walls onstage

Twentieth Century   The cry for realism was answered in the twentieth century by André Antoine in France and David Belasco in the United States. Their stage sets were so photographically accurate that their style of design was called **naturalism.** Belasco was so concerned with exact detail that his scenery sometimes distracted the audiences from the action of the play. The naturalists were important because their ultrarealistic sets worked toward making the drama more realistic.

Most realistic stage sets today are designed with selective realism. This modified form of realism, developed because the many details of naturalism confused the audience, stems from a belief that an impression of

This realistic set for *"MASTER HAROLD"* . . . *and the boys* by Athol Fugard shows the St. George's Park Tea Room in Port Elizabeth, South Africa. Actor Danny Glover, gesturing broadly, dominates the simple setting.

actuality is better theatrically and artistically. The designer selects scenic elements that convey the idea of the locale rather than attempting to create an exact replica of it.

The modern realistic interior set in a proscenium theater has all essential entrances, doorways, windows, and so on placed in a two-sided or three-sided room. The room is usually placed off-center and at an angle instead of squarely on the stage in the old-fashioned manner. The proscenium stage has been called "fourth wall theater." The fourth wall is imaginary, of course, and its presence is only suggested. Furniture usually faces that fourth invisible wall, through which the audience observes the action. There have been attempts to treat the fourth wall as an actual wall by placing a sofa with its back to the audience or by having an actor look out an imaginary window while facing the fourth wall. Lighting has helped establish this illusion of reality.

Twentieth-century exterior sets are quite often only suggestive. **Plastics**—three-dimensional structures—and **cut-outs**—two-dimensional profiles—are placed against a drop or sky cyc. A **ground row,** a type of low cut-out, is used to break the line between the floor and the drop and to give the illusion of distance.

The twentieth century has seen many experiments in scenic design. Two important designers were Adolphe Appia and Gordon Craig. Both experimented in symbolic scenic design. Adolphe Appia concentrated on three-dimensional forms, which he contended were essential for the performance of the three-dimensional actor. He emphasized the importance of the actor and used dramatic lighting innovations to focus attention on the performer. Gordon Craig, on the other hand, believed the essential message of a play could be conveyed most effectively by the scenic designer. He even suggested eliminating the actors and replacing them with super-marionettes.

TRADITIONAL SETS

Stage sets are as varied as plays and the characters that appear in them. Selectivity, simplicity, and consistency are important to a stage designer. Sets should be planned so that they may be built firmly, handled easily, and packed efficiently. Most of all, actors should be able to move about easily and safely and should feel that the set provides an appropriate atmosphere for the characters they are portraying.

The most common type of interior set has been the **box set,** which replaced the old wings and drops of the nineteenth century, but it, too, has been replaced by other forms in recent years. The box set consists of two or three walls built of flats and often covered by a ceiling.

Another common type of set, the **unit set,** is made up of several scenic units that can be moved about the stage, turned, and interchanged to create several settings. A unit might be a building placed down left with a ground-level wooden door and a second-level balcony window. The appearance of the unit can be completely altered by moving it up right, changing its angle, and removing the wooden door and the balcony rail. Unit sets are quite practical for schools that wish to present multiset plays, to present a program of one-act plays, or to build units that can be arranged to fit the needs of almost any play in a small theater.

This setting from *Philadelphia Story* uses a box set with three sides and a ceiling to give the impression of a room. Box sets give a set depth and naturalness.

Perspective of a Box Set

Elevation of a Set Built with Flats

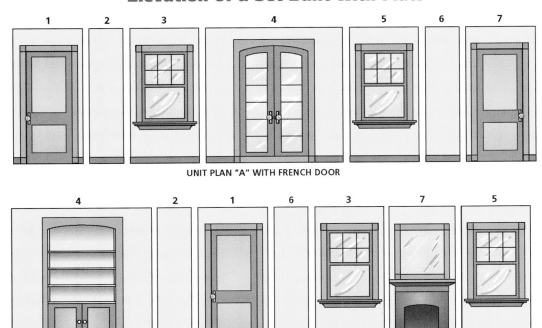

1   2   3   4   5   6   7

UNIT PLAN "A" WITH FRENCH DOOR

4   2   1   6   3   7   5

UNIT PLAN "B" WITH BOOKCASE AND FIREPLACE

Permanent Set

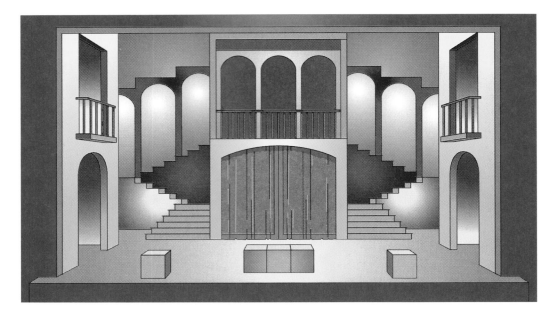

The **permanent set,** yet another type of staging, rarely changes during the play. There are basically three kinds of permanent sets. Most high schools use a single permanent set for straight plays. A simple doorway can be either an interior or an exterior entrance, a gate, or a passageway. The platform is equally versatile. Controlled lights help determine the locale. A second important type of permanent set consists of many openings, some of which are large. Doors, windows, arches, curtains, and backing units are placed within or behind the openings to simulate scene changes. The third type is a modification of the permanent set, called the multiple set, which has several distinct acting areas separated with dividers, such as platforms or railings. Flexible, controlled lighting is necessary.

Further opportunities for scenic variations are provided by using screens and profile sets. **Screens** consist of two-fold and three-fold flats, which are used either to form walls against a drapery background or to cover openings or furnishings as a quick means of changing scenes. Screens can be almost any height and width and are usually freestanding.

Profile sets, sometimes called cut-down or minimum sets, can be constructed of screens, but the chief difference between profile sets and screens is that the profile set, like the box set, forms the entire perimeter of the setting. Colors and patterns from gobos that suggest changing moods and emotions may be aimed against the background cyclorama to bring about a strong identification with the action.

Screen Set

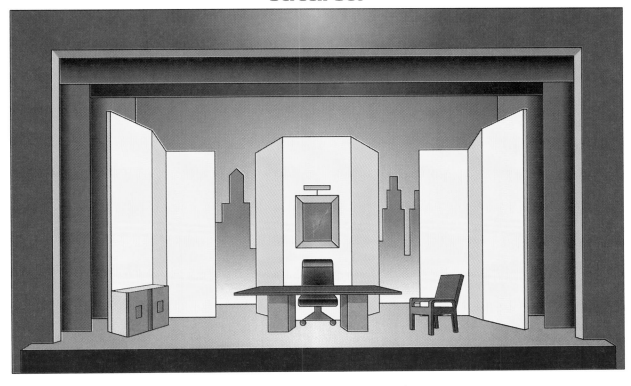

When fast changes with a minimum of equipment and space are needed, **prisms**, also called ***periaktoi***, can be used. These are usually equilateral or isosceles triangles mounted to a wheeled carriage, which can be pivoted. Each *periaktos* is made up of either three six-foot flats or two four-foot flats and one six-foot flat. At least four *periaktoi* are needed, but for more variety in combination and position and for more set possibilities, six or eight can be used. Doorways can be created in the following ways:

- Use a space between two *periaktoi*. This is the simplest method.
- Hook a normal floor flat between two *periaktoi*.
- Hang inserts, or plugs, between two *periaktoi*. The shape of the plugs can either resemble ordinary doors or match a stylistic design.

Window, bookcase, and fireplace flats can also be used as one side of a *periaktos*. The *periaktoi* are especially valuable for schools that lack fly space, have trouble masking the sides of the stage, or need quick changes with limited equipment.

Set designers have frequently used curtain sets as substitutes for constructed scenery. A **curtain set** simply uses curtains as a backdrop for a play. The typical school cyclorama rarely provides an

Periaktoi Set—Rotating Eight *Periaktoi* to Create Three Different Sets

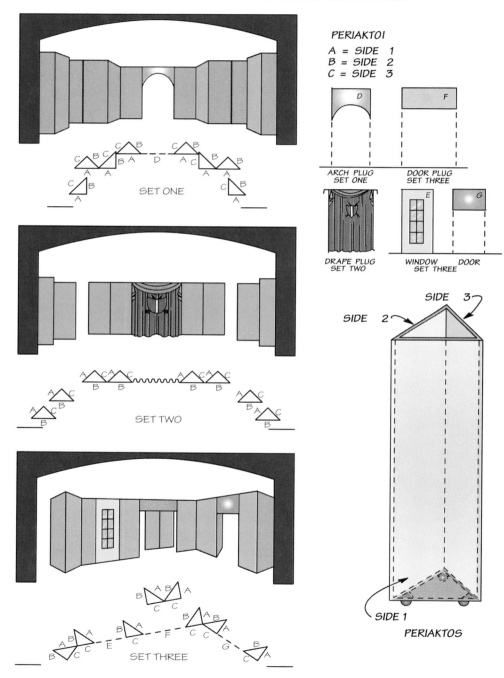

PERIAKTOI
A = SIDE 1
B = SIDE 2
C = SIDE 3

D

F

ARCH PLUG
SET ONE

DOOR PLUG
SET THREE

DRAPE PLUG
SET TWO

E

G

WINDOW
SET THREE

DOOR

SET ONE

SET TWO

SET THREE

SIDE 2

SIDE 3

SIDE 1

PERIAKTOS

Curtain Set

adequate background for a play, but sometimes limitations of space, equipment, and budget force the director to use a modified curtain set. There are, however, many effective ways to use curtains. A formalistic set with ramps, platforms, columns, and so on might look best against a curtain set. The placing of a few flats, such as doorways, windows, and fireplaces, between curtains can often turn a plain curtain set into an acceptable theatrical set. Stage drapes can be gathered or pulled back much like huge window curtains. Nevertheless, curtains can never be transposed into convincing realistic sets. One of the disadvantages of a curtain set is that the acting area is always the same size and shape. Therefore, many designers who have had to use curtain backgrounds have used freestanding set pieces and furniture to "shape" their sets within the frame of the cyclorama.

The use of a black cyclorama can be quite impressive. Controlled lighting can be used to make the actors and furnishings stand out sharply against the black space. White furniture and white makeup are also especially striking against a black background.

Another kind of set that is very effective is the **skeleton set**. This kind of set consists simply of frames and openings that can be left empty or filled by draperies, backings, and doors.

OPEN-SPACE TECHNIQUES

Scenic artists have had to develop new techniques of set design for the **thrust stage,** a low platform stage that projects into the audience. Since the audience surrounds the thrust stage on three sides, conventional scenery should be placed deep on the stage to avoid blocking the audience's view. Designers have used cut-down sets and screens quite successfully, but one of the most effective innovations is the **floating-screen**, or **multiple-plane set**. This technique employs single flats or narrow drops that are placed or hung at various depths parallel to the front of the stage to provide concealed entrances for actors and suggest a locale.

Arena stages (theater-in-the-round) use a different approach. Since the audience completely surrounds the stage, scenery will undoubtedly block the view of at least some of the spectators. Objects normally placed on walls, such as pictures, are often casually laid on tables or suspended from thin wires. For example, a mirror may be simply an open frame suspended from above. A window may be represented by only a partial frame. The furniture must allow the actors to move constantly in *S* and circular patterns.

🌿 *Procedures in Scenic Design*

The basic goal of scenic design is to create a functional background for the action without intruding on that action. A set may have aesthetic appeal, establish tone and atmosphere, convey symbolism, and even aid in the expression of the theme. If it does not provide the actors with a workable environment, however, it has failed in its primary function.

Although the designer has overall responsibility for the scenic design, both the designer and the director must work together during different phases of the planning. The sequence of a designer's tasks during the early planning is important.

Designer's Preliminary Tasks
1. Read the play several times.
2. Discuss the play and production style with the director, who provides the foundation for design, including the basic floor plan.
3. Make a sketch, called a **rendering,** that scenically expresses the meaning and spirit of the play.
4. Consider available equipment, funds, and materials.
5. Enlarge the sketch into a perspective drawing.
6. Work out a detailed floor plan showing positions and sizes of entrances, windows, and all props.
7. Build a three-dimensional model of the set design.
8. Draft elevations and working drawings (detailed construction illustrations or blueprints).

FLOOR PLAN—BOX SET

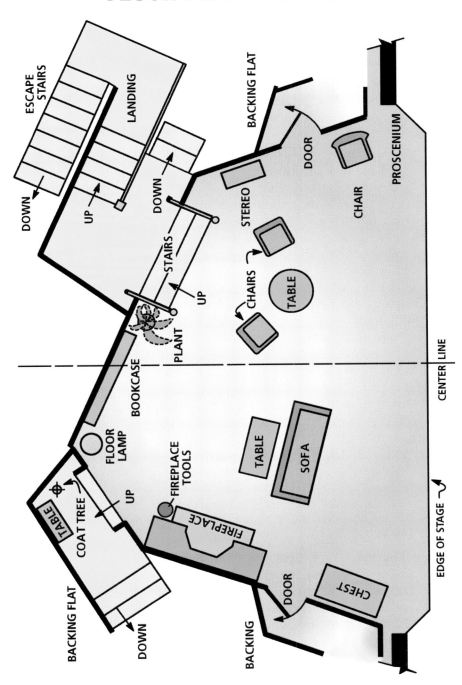

ESCAPE STAIRS

LANDING

BACKING FLAT

DOWN

UP

DOWN

DOOR

STEREO

STAIRS

UP

CHAIRS

PLANT

BOOKCASE

FLOOR LAMP

FIREPLACE TOOLS

UP

COAT TREE

TABLE

BACKING FLAT

DOWN

FIREPLACE

DOOR

BACKING

CHEST

TABLE

SOFA

CHAIR

TABLE

PROSCENIUM

CENTER LINE

EDGE OF STAGE

PREDESIGN CONSIDERATIONS

Numerous factors must be considered before a production can be designed. Although the budget of the production is important, the stage, the equipment, and the number and kinds of sets to be used also affect the design. When several sets are required, the designer must always plan for the weight and mobility of scenic units and for the available fly space, among countless other factors. Before designing a set, the scenic designer should answer certain important questions.

PREDESIGN CHECKLIST

Size and shape of auditorium

Is the floor raked? What type of seating arrangement is being used? (This is important in gymnasium-auditorium combinations and in small theaters.)

Space

How much storage space is available? What are the dimensions of the apron and wings? What equipment is available? How deep is the fly space? Are flies high enough to handle a drop without tripping? Is the system manual, electrically winched, or counterweighted?

Flats, drops, and scrims

How many flats, drops, and scrims are there? What are the heights and the widths of flats?

Special units

How many constructed platforms, ramps, and staircases are there?

Lighting

What kind of lighting equipment is available? How flexible is this equipment?

A scenic designer should also be aware of two other basic considerations when planning a scenic design: the play and the audience.

The Play The first consideration of scenic design is the play itself—its theme, type, and style. The designer must be aware of important scenes and of special effects essential to the play, including lighting needs. The functional aspects of the set—the location of doors, windows, fireplaces, elevated areas, essential props, and so on—provide the information necessary for a preliminary design. Since a set is the background for actors, their experience, ages, sizes, costumes, and makeup must be considered. A scenic designer must plan a set with and without people

CUE

Time and sound are two important factors to consider when scenery is shifted. During a scenery change, a long wait and an excessive amount of noise coming from the stage can be disconcerting for an audience.

Even from this distance and angle, the simple set for *Les Liaisons Danger- euses* is fully visible to the audience.

to produce one that looks appropriate with both the maximum and the minimum number of performers who will occupy it.

The Audience   Naturally, the designer must also consider the audience. Because the spectators must see all important action, the designer must take sight lines from the front corner seats and the highest balcony seats. This means that the side walls must be raked (set at an angle) so that every person in the audience can see each entrance. Likewise, the designer must position elevated upstage platforms so that the upper balcony audience will not see "headless" actors. Second-story levels are often slightly raked toward the audience. The designer might have to "cheat down" the height of a second story and even lower the heights of doors and banister rails to accommodate the highest seats.

Application
ACTIVITY

Make a survey of your theater or auditorium using the Predesign Checklist on the opposite page. Add any additional information that might be helpful if you were planning a production. Be prepared to discuss the information you gather.

ARTISTIC CONSIDERATIONS

Because stage design is a specialized art, a scenic designer should keep in mind several artistic principles. One of the most important principles is **unity**. This principle demands that all elements of the set form a whole that centers around the theme of the play. All furniture and properties must coordinate with the background and, if possible, should be a part of the stage design in period and composition.

Another important principle is **emphasis**, or focusing the audience's attention on a particular object, area of the stage, or piece of furniture. Everything else on the stage should be subordinate to this center of interest. A good set design can emphasize a point of interest in several ways.

- Place it in a prominent position.
- Paint it a color that makes it stand out from the rest of the set.
- Make it the focus of all lines of interest.
- Play light upon it.

Proportion and balance are also important artistic principles. **Proportion** uses the human being as the unit of measurement. In realistic plays, all scenic elements are scaled to a person six feet tall. Nonrealistic sets may make people appear dwarfed or engulfed by rocks or towering buildings.

This stage picture from *Hello, Dolly!* is balanced; the performers are evenly distributed over the stage with the "Yonkers" sign as a central axis.

Balance requires an equal distribution of emphasis from one side of the stage to the other. This may be achieved through line, mass, and shape. For example, an archway might be balanced by a large upright chest, or a staircase might be balanced by a dominant portrait. Except in stylized settings, asymmetrical or informal balance is preferable to perfect symmetry.

The **central axis** is the focal point in the design, usually the deepest point just off-center. The halves of the stage on either side of this axis should be balanced but not exactly alike. The director and the scenic designer must work closely together because the position, number, and importance of people onstage influence the balance of the scenic pattern. For example, a strong character who is to exemplify spiritual leadership and is the center of interest in a scene might be placed on a higher level against tall columns, a high arched doorway, or long drapes, with the other characters, perhaps a large crowd, below. The emphasis of the strong character's influence in the minds of the audience will offset the size of the crowd, and the stage picture will balance.

Equally important is the artistic principle of **line.** The lines in draperies, columns, or costumes alter the sense of proportion and may even have a psychological effect on the observer. For example, consider the potential psychological connotations of the following:

Long vertical lines	dignity, elevation, hope, or spirituality
Horizontal lines	emotional stability, calmness, or tranquility
Diagonal lines	driving force, strife, uncertainty, or concentration
Curved Lines	ease, comfort, wealth, or expanse
Curves and angles	intense excitement (if combined with contrasting colors)
Crooked/jagged lines	chaos, shattered dreams, injustice, or pain

The final two artistic values of importance to scenic designers are mass and shape. **Mass** takes into consideration the concepts of bulk and weight, both of which are difficult to determine unless tested under the lights. Dark-colored objects usually appear heavier than light-colored objects. **Shape** often influences both the concept of mass and the psychological reaction to objects on the stage. Remember that shape is outline, while mass is three-dimensional. Shapes may be geometric or free-form, natural or stylized, realistic or impressionistic. A circle may seem infinite or eternal; a square or cube may appear staid or unimaginative; a triangle may seem uplifting or securely founded; a diamond may seem calming and restful. Both mass and shape influence the balance of a set.

The rising diagonal lines of stretched fabric in this scene from Čapek's *R.U.R.* (*Rossum's Universal Robots*) give it a sense of otherworldly strangeness appropriate for a futuristic drama. The bareness of the set, combined with white scenery and costumes, makes everything seem clean and simple.

USE OF COLOR

Color is one of the most important elements of staging because various colors and their combinations produce very different emotional effects. The relationship between characters or scenes and the colors used might be important factors in a play's success. Onstage, color effects are achieved by playing colored lights on the pigments used in sets, costumes, stage furnishings, and even makeup. Because colored light makes very definite and often surprising changes in the appearance of pigment, it is necessary to experiment with both light and pigment to get the desired result. Although this may be a long and involved process, it is fascinating to see what happens to fabrics and painted surfaces under different lighting.

The primary pigment colors are red, yellow, and blue. The secondary colors are orange, green, and violet. The primary colors of light are red, green, and blue, and the secondary colors are yellow, cyan (a light blue-green), and magenta.

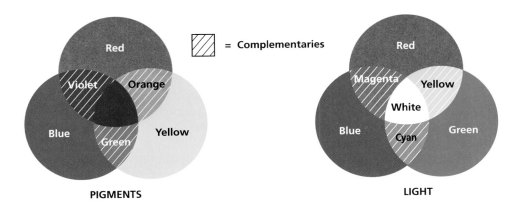

= Complementaries

PIGMENTS

LIGHT

Sets and costumes are sometimes color coded for both identification and emotional response. **Color coding** means identifying the emotional tone of a scene by its color dominance; for example, a "pink scene" may be one of romantic fantasy; a "red scene" may be one of anger or passion. Characters, too, may be color-coded in stylized productions.

Colors differ from each other in hue, value, and intensity. **Hue** indicates the purity of color—the redness, the blueness, and so on. The various colors seen in the spectrum of a beam of light passing through a prism are called hues. As light falls on different surfaces, the colors are absorbed or reflected. A surface that absorbs all the hues except green appears to be green because it reflects only that color.

If the emphasis of a costume or prop is important, the value of the color is a consideration. The **value** of a color is its lightness or darkness and is determined by the amount of black or white mixed with it. Each color is said to have a value scale, running from white at one end to black at the other. Consider the differences between light or pastel colors, **tints**, and dark or deep colors, **shades**.

▼ CUE

Black is the absence of light and therefore is the absence of color. White is the fusion of all the spectral colors.

Tints	Shades
contain more white suggest youth, comedy, informality	contain more black suggest dignity, seriousness, repose

Color can also differ in its intensity. **Intensity**, often referred to as **saturation,** is the brightness or dullness of a color. To add intensity to a color, illuminate it with a light of the same color. To lessen the intensity of a color, add gray to the pigment or place the color by its complementary color. The complementary color for any one of the three primary colors (red, blue, yellow) can be achieved by mixing together the two other primaries. For example, if you wish to get the complementary color of red, mix together the other two primary colors, blue and yellow, and you get green. (Refer to the illustration on the previous page.)

A color wheel is an invaluable aid in designing because it shows the relationships of the various hues. The colors next to each other on the wheel are analogous, or contain the same hue. For example, yellow, yellow-orange, and orange are analogous, since they all contain yellow. When analogous colors are used, a dash of complementary color provides balance.

Since neither pigments nor materials for coloring lights are likely to have pure color, endless experiments are required to get a desired effect. You can experiment with the effect of light on the pigments on actual sets as they are built. Run through the color cycle of night to day—black, pale gray, light yellow, light red, deep red, orange, and full daylight. Then reverse this cycle to run from daylight through the sunset hues to darkness, ending with the green-blue conventionally used to simulate moonlight on the stage.

CUE ▼

A point to remember: green-blue and blue-green are not the same color. The color named second is the dominant hue. Therefore, green-blue is blue with a tinge of green in it, and blue-green is green with a tinge of blue.

In *Roseleaf Tea,* the stage lighting creates beams of weak sunlight that make natural shadows.

In any stage set there should be a controlling color scheme that carries out the predominant mood and atmosphere of the production. The most effective color schemes are those that give a single, unifying impression. Remembering that colors are referred to as warm or cool might be helpful when striving for a single impression to give continuity to a play. Red, orange, and yellow are warm colors. You see them in sunlight and fire. Blue, green, and violet are cool colors. You see them in deep pools and in shadows under leafy trees. Warm hues seem to advance, or move forward in space, because they attract attention quickly. Cool colors appear to recede, or move back in space, because they are less noticeable. However, a stage background or set piece painted in warm colors looks smaller because it seems nearer, while one painted in cool colors looks larger. A warm-colored costume or object generally catches the eye at once and looks important. Objects or persons dressed in cool colors are generally less noticeable to the audience. The warm colors are stimulating and exciting, appropriate for highly emotional scenes and for comedies. Cool colors give a sense of tranquility and are usually the predominant colors in serious comedies and in tragedies. One should bear in mind that too much stress on warm colors can be very irritating and too many cool colors depressing.

Certain stage traditions are based on known reactions to color. Following these traditions is an important means of getting satisfactory empathetic responses from the audience. Colors are used in stage design to communicate the following qualities:

blue	calm, cold, formal, spiritual, pure, truthful, depressing
orange	exhilarating, cheerful, lively
red	aggressive, passionate, bloody, angry, strong
yellow	cheerful, happy, youthful, cowardly
pink	fanciful, romantic
green	youthful, eternal, reborn, jealous
soft green	restful, soothing, tranquil
purple	mournful, mystic, regal
gray	neutral, depressing, negative, somber
brown	earthy, common, poverty-stricken
black	melancholic, tragic, gloomy, deathlike
white	truthful, pure, chaste, innocent, peaceful

CUE ▼

To emphasize a costume or prop, place it against a background of a different value or hue. To make the costume or prop inconspicuous, show it against a background of its own value or hue.

Numerous other design aspects contribute to a balanced production. If a design is to be interesting, it must have variety through contrast and subordination. Too often high school stage settings give every scenic element equal strength and dominance. This is not to say that a single motif carried through an entire scene of a production will not effectively underscore the unity and harmony of design. The key to good design is simplicity. Cluttered sets, overly designed walls, or too many colors should be avoided in artistic stage sets.

Application
ACTIVITY

Decide on a color scheme for a scene from a play that you have seen or read. Remember to consider the personalities and roles of the characters in that scene.

🌿 *Constructing the Set*

Selectivity, simplicity, and consistency should be remembered when planning, designing, and constructing the set for a production. Sets should be planned so that they can be built firmly, set up steadily, struck rapidly, carried easily, and packed away efficiently. Above all, they must blend with the actors and with the theme of the play. The most common sets involve draperies, flats, or drops, most of which must be bought or rented; or designed, assembled, and painted.

CONSTRUCTING THE FLAT

The basic unit of construction for box sets, screens, *periaktoi*, and cut-down scenery is the flat; therefore, learning as much as possible about flats is to your advantage as a scenic designer or stage crew member. Also, since most plays require an interior set, you should learn the procedures for flat building, assembling, and painting.

The most satisfactory height for flats for the high school stage is twelve feet, although ten- and fourteen-foot flats are not uncommon. Large university and professional stages with high prosceniums may accommodate flats up to twenty-four feet high. On the following page is a list of the basic flats needed.

By painting the pieces of a set in neutral colors, you can plan to use the pieces interchangeably to create more than one scene.

Plain Flats		Special Flats		
Width	*Number Needed*	*Type*	*Width*	*Number Needed*
1 ft.	2–4	Door flat	5–6 ft.	2–3
1 1/2 ft.	2	Window-bookcase flats	5–6 ft.	2
2 ft.	2–4	Fireplace flat	5–6 ft.	1
3 ft.	6–8	Arch flat (booked)	8 ft.	1
4 ft.	6–8	French door, sliding door	8 ft.	1
5 or 6 ft.	6–8	(booked)		
	24–32			7–8

This system requires about thirty to forty flats, depending on the size of the stage. One of the advantages of this system is that there are matching flats for alcoves, bay windows, *periaktoi*, and columns. Another advantage is that it is easy to plan wall dimensions and designate flats accordingly. Care must be taken to keep the design from turning out nearly symmetrical, however.

CUE

The best fabric for covering flats is canvas, but its cost makes it prohibitive for most groups. The next best choice is unbleached muslin.

To construct a flat, you will need some basic materials: lumber, fabric, hardware, rope, and glue. Most flats are built of #2 grade 1″ × 4″ pine. The boards used for stiles and rails should be absolutely straight and free of any loose knots. The corner braces are made from 1″ × 2″ stock. The corner blocks, keystones, and mending plates are cut from 1/4″ plywood. Refer to page 426 for a detailed illustration of a flat.

Another kind of flat is the rigid flat, which can be built from plywood instead of cloth. These flats are strong, require little frame bracing, and last longer than those made of cloth, but they are much heavier than cloth flats.

The special stage hardware needed for a well-made flat includes three lash-line cleats, two tie-off cleats, and a stage brace cleat. Clout nails (1 1/4″ soft nails that clinch themselves when a piece of heavy metal is placed under the stile or rail before hammering), threepenny box nails, or screws are used to attach plywood to the frame. Staples and diluted white glue are used to fasten cloth to the finished frame.

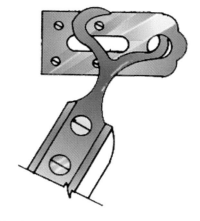

**STAGE BRACE CLEAT
W/ BRACE HOOKED**

Framing is the first step in the construction of a flat. The most common joint used is the **butt joint,** a joint formed by fastening pieces together end to end. However, **miter joints**—joints formed by cutting the ends of the pieces at an angle and fitting them together—are better, since they are stronger and do not chip or split as easily. When using butt joints, cut the top and bottom rails to the exact width the finished flat is to be. This allows the flat to slide without splitting the stiles. This also means that the boards used for the stiles must be cut to the desired height of the flat minus the width of the two rails. Check exact lumber sizes with a lumber salesperson and always measure carefully. Common names for lumber sizes do not reflect actual sizes. For example, 1″ × 4″ lumber is always less than one inch by four inches. Check your measurements again before cutting. A good rule to remember is "Measure twice; cut once."

After cutting the top and bottom rails and the two stiles, assemble the frame. If you do not have a template, you can use an adjustable framework as a mold, or you can nail two boards at a ninety-degree angle to serve as a square. Framing is easier when one person can hold the square while another person does the nailing. Then, keeping the square in place, nail on the corner blocks. A butt joint requires eleven nails; a miter joint needs only ten nails. If you use a butt joint, the grain of the corner block must run across the joint.

Whenever you attach anything to the back of a flat, it must be set back three-fourths of an inch from the edge. A scrap piece of 1″ × 4″ wood on edge will serve as a guide. This allows two flats to be joined at a right angle without a crack appearing between the flats.

Next, put in one or two **toggle rails,** or bars. Toggle rails should be set at the same height so that keeper hooks may hold a stiffener board when the set is erected. Usually eight- to ten-foot flats require one toggle, while flats twelve feet and taller require two toggles. The toggles should be cut the width of the flat less the width of the two stiles. *Do not measure the toggle by the space between the stiles.* If necessary, force the stiles in or out so the total width is exactly the same as the top and bottom rails. Cover the joint with keystones.

You can now install the corner braces. Notice that both are on the left side of the flat. If they were on opposite corners, the flat would torque (twist) diagonally. Corner braces do not need to be exact but are approximately the length of a rail. A forty- to sixty-degree angle is created if the corner braces are placed properly. Use mending plates to secure the joint, and your flat is fully framed. (Mending plates are 1 1/2″ × 5″ pieces of 1/4″ plywood cut lengthwise with the grain.) At this point your flat is fully formed. Now screw on the hardware.

> **CUE**
>
> The most important tool for scenery building is probably the framing square. Usually made of metal, this tool has at least one ninety-degree angle and at least two straight edges. It is used to check right angles.

THE FLAT

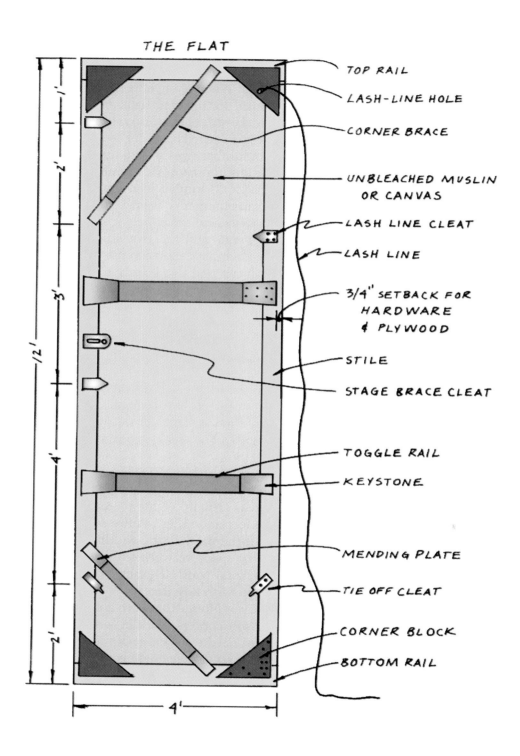

- TOP RAIL
- LASH-LINE HOLE
- CORNER BRACE
- UNBLEACHED MUSLIN OR CANVAS
- LASH LINE CLEAT
- LASH LINE
- 3/4" SETBACK FOR HARDWARE & PLYWOOD
- STILE
- STAGE BRACE CLEAT
- TOGGLE RAIL
- KEYSTONE
- MENDING PLATE
- TIE OFF CLEAT
- CORNER BLOCK
- BOTTOM RAIL

12'
1'
2'
3'
4'
2'
4'

Make the frame flameproof by washing it with a solution of two pounds of borax, two pounds of sal ammoniac, and two gallons of water. Then turn the flat face side up and cover it with muslin. The muslin should overlap all sides unless there is a finished edge, which can be placed one-quarter inch from the outer edge of one stile. Place staples every four inches, one-quarter inch from the inner edge of one stile or rail. Many set builders prefer to drive the staples only partway and remove them after the glue dries. Others drive staples all the way and leave them.

Once the cloth is stapled in place on one stile, following these steps may simplify the next task.

1. Fold the cloth back over the staples.
2. Spread glue onto the stile.
3. Fold the cloth back down onto the glue.
4. Smooth the cloth down with a wood block.
5. Carefully stretch the cloth across the frame.
6. Allow it to "belly" to the floor in the center.
7. Be careful at the corners. There will be extra material because of the bellying of the cloth. Be sure the fabric does not pull or wrinkle.
8. Repeat the stapling-gluing process on the other stile and on both rails.
9. *Do not place any glue on toggles or corner braces.*
10. Now staple one-half inch in from the outer edge of the frame around all four sides.
11. Flameproof the cloth with the same solution that was used on the frame.

You are now ready to **size**, or paint on a glue-water mixture, a process that prepares the cloth in the following ways:

- It seals the pores.
- It provides a good painting surface.
- It stretches the cloth like an artist's canvas.

The easiest sizing to use is made from a commercial cold-water sizing to which a little whiting has been added. Some brands of sizing need a little more water than the directions on the box indicate. To see whether sizing is properly thinned, dip your fingers into the mixture. They should tend to just stick together. After the sized muslin dries, use a razor knife to trim the selvage (waste) off one-quarter inch from the outer edges of the stiles and rails. Do not trim the cloth flush with the outside edge of the flat, or the cloth will be pulled loose when the flat is handled.

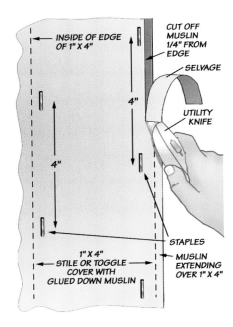

INSIDE OF EDGE OF 1" X 4"

CUT OFF MUSLIN 1/4" FROM EDGE

SELVAGE

4"

UTILITY KNIFE

4"

4"

STAPLES

MUSLIN EXTENDING OVER 1" X 4"

1" X 4" STILE OR TOGGLE COVER WITH GLUED DOWN MUSLIN

A crew puts the finishing touches on a large backdrop.

To finish the flat, put a length of rope, called a lash line, through the hole drilled in the upper right corner block, knot the end, and pull it back tightly. Cut the rope six inches longer than the flat.

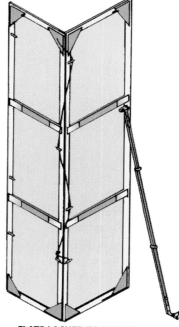

FLATS LASHED TOGETHER
STAGE BRACE SECURED
WITH STAGE SCREW

ERECTING THE SET

Flats can be either lashed or hinged together. If you plan to hinge all scenery, every hinge should be matched using loose pin (backflap) hinges. Tight pin hinges are good only if the hinges are to be removed after the production. If only one set is required for the play and if it is permissible to nail into the stage floor, it is usually advisable to **floor block**—to tack a small block of wood to the floor on both sides or each union where two flats meet. This keeps the walls straight and strengthens them. Stop cleats or stop blocks may be placed on the back of flats to prevent one flat from being pushed behind the other, especially at sharp angle junctions. Walls that shake and rattle when a door is slammed have been identified with amateur theater far too often. Proper bracing will eliminate nearly all such distractions.

Adjustable stage braces provide support for an individual flat. One brace is used for each flat except for door flats and occasionally for window flats, which need two braces. The hook of the brace is inserted upside down and turned over firmly against the stile as shown. It is very important that the brace be correctly installed; a hole in the muslin and a wobbly flat might be the price of incorrect installation. The brace can be anchored to the floor by stage screws or by a floor plate. If stage screws can be used, drill a hole before inserting the screw. If the wood forming the stage floor is reasonably close-grained, the same hole can be used over and over for many years. (The dust from the stage will fill the hole sufficiently to secure the brace time after time.) If holes cannot be drilled in the floor, a wood block may be lightly tacked to the floor and the stage screw anchored into the block.

ADJUSTABLE STAGE BRACE

When there are restrictions against the use of any nails or screws in the floor or when the wood is too soft to hold such hardware, a floor plate is an easy solution. A floor plate is simply a piece of plywood with a nonslip rubber pad on its underside and a special hardware adapter, which any school shop can make, bolted to the brace. Stage weights or concrete blocks are placed on top of the floor plate to hold it in place. Pieces of two-inch lumber will work satisfactorily if there is not enough time to make floor plates.

FLOOR PLATE WITH ADAPTED LEG ON STAGE BRACE

PLYWOOD WITH RUBBER ON BOTTOM

Another type of bracing is the **jack**. A jack is a triangular wooden brace hinged to fold out of the way or placed on wheels to allow large units to be moved more easily. Jacks are often used with set pieces and ground rows. Similar in function to the jack is the **foot iron,** an L-shaped piece of strap iron attached to the back of the flat and anchored to the floor with a stage screw. Foot irons are most often used when there is insufficient space for jacks or braces.

The use of keeper hooks is another means of strengthening walls. Wherever there are two or more flats in a straight line, these handy pieces of hardware can be hooked over the top and toggle rails of each flat, and a stiffener board can be dropped into the notches, making the entire wall section one solid unit. Some technicians prefer hinged stiffeners, but keeper hooks are convenient, quick, and effective and can be made by any metal shop.

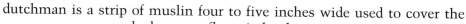

Once the set is assembled, apply the dutchman. A dutchman is a strip of muslin four to five inches wide used to cover the cracks between flats. A dutchman is never used on a set that is to be shifted, except booked flats or screens. The dutchman is dipped in sizing, placed over the crack, and brushed down smoothly. If flats are perfectly matched, a strip of masking tape can be substituted for a dutchman.

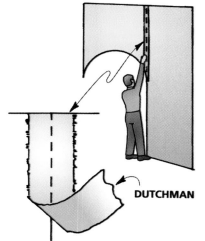

DUTCHMAN

Novice grips can have a difficult time trying to move flats, but there are some simple techniques that make the task far less awkward.

Edging   One grip lifts a flat from the floor to a position for moving by edging, or getting the flat up on one side. Another grip grasps the stile and pulls the flat up.

Walking   Walking a flat requires two or three grips. One grip puts a foot against the bottom rail to steady the flat, and one or two others lift the top rail, gradually raising the flat to an upright position by moving hand-over-hand on the stiles. With two grips, the one with his or her foot against the bottom of the flat should also hold onto a stile to guide and steady the flat.

Floating   The best and safest way to lower a flat is by floating. One grip simply places a foot against the back of the bottom rail, pushes the flat over, and allows it to fall or float to the floor face down.

Running   Moving a flat is called running it. A grip grasps an upright flat with both hands on the stile on the side toward which the flat is to go, lifts that edge slightly, and slides the flat along without actually lifting or carrying it. A grip should not try to grasp both stiles and move the flat because the flat will act like a sail, pulling the grip forward or falling backward on him or her.

Application

Using a large piece of cardboard or a similar object, practice methods of handling a flat that are discussed on the previous page.

PAINTING SCENERY

Painting the set is certainly one of the important steps in the completion of a set, but it does not need to be the chore it often seems to be. One of the problems faced by a less-experienced production staff is choosing and handling scenic paints. There are certain paint qualities that are worth considering, as well as a few approaches that can be taken.

1. **vinyl, acrylic-base scenic paints**   Colors are pure, and costs are fairly reasonable. These are generally recommended for stage settings. At least one manufacturer features a line of paint in a form designed for high school use.
2. **ready-to-use casein paints**   Their cost is higher than that of vinyl acrylics, and fewer colors are available. Casein is more water repellent than dry color and can be used for scenery placed outside or in damp locations.
3. **latex paint**   Readily available and inexpensive, latex covers well, will not bleed through, and cleans up easily with soap and water. A good paint or hardware store can mix almost any desired color. It might be less expensive, however, to start with a base, either an existing paint or a pastel base from a paint store, and add universal tinting colors, also available at paint stores. A disadvantage of latex, however, is that when it is painted heavily on muslin, the cloth absorbs the paint, causing the life of the cloth to be shortened and the paint to crack.

After the paint has been chosen, the next step is to apply the base coat. For best results, apply paint in random strokes or in figure eights. An uneven base coat is better than a smooth finish, which has a flat appearance and emphasizes all the flaws in the set. Some scenic painters **scumble** the base coat, which requires two or more brushes and two or more tones of the base color. Paint each tone on a small area and blend the tones together. The paint will set unless you work quickly.

After applying the base coat, highlight and shadow the set and then texture it. Highlights and shadows are essential if the scenery is to be convincing and alive. Before applying these realistic dimensional touches, the painter must consider the primary light source, that is, the direction and cause of the predominant light. Moldings, paneling, wainscoting, shingles, siding, bricks, and rocks must be carefully painted, even when they are built in three dimensions. You can create realistic bricks by applying a base coat of mortar color and using a rubber sponge block cut to brick size. Press the sponge, dipped in paint, onto the scenery. Use from two to four colors such as red, gray, dark yellow, and green. You can also cut three-dimensional bricks and rocks from Styrofoam™ and glue them to plywood. Cardboard works well for making shingles.

A painter here works on a flat. Even though he is just a few feet away from the flat, he must imagine what his paint strokes will look like to an audience member in the last row.

There are several methods of texturing, any one of which may work well for your particular sets.

Spattering is the most common method of texturing. Use at least two colors, one a shade darker and the other a tint lighter than the base color. You may also use the complementary color to blend and harmonize the colors in the set. Dip a four-inch brush into paint that has been diluted one-third to one-half, wipe it "dry" on the side of the pail, and shake the brush once onto an old flat or dropcloth. Then stand a short distance from the set and strike the handle of the brush against a board held by the other hand, causing drops of paint to spatter the flats. This is a difficult technique to master, so practice on an old flat first. The dark spattering coat should normally be heavier at the top of the walls to make them appear shadowed. Spattering can also be done by using a very thin paint in a plastic spray bottle.

SPATTERING

Rag rolling is a second method of texturing. Dip a rag or rolled-up piece of frayed burlap in paint, then roll it over the walls to make them look like rough plaster.

RAG ROLLING

Stippling is a texturing method that involves gently touching the flat with a sponge, a crumpled rag, or the tip of a dry brush which leaves clusters of paint drops. Be sure to rotate the tool you are using to avoid creating an obvious pattern.

SPONGING

Featherdusting is another popular and quick texturing technique. Dip an inexpensive featherduster into the paint, shake it off over an old flat or dropcloth, and gently press it against the flat. By turning the handle slightly, you will get a different pattern each time the duster is applied. Featherdusting is especially good for foliage effects.

Dry brushing may be used for wall texturing or for simulating wood grain. For walls use a dry brush, stroke in one direction with a light color, and repeat with a dark color. For a woodgrain effect, use long, straight strokes with a dark color, and then repeat the process with a lighter color.

DRY BRUSHING

Scenery painting is an art that develops with time, experience, and experimentation. Watch what happens to colors and textures under various lighting effects, and then consider how you would represent them scenically.

Profile scenery and drops are challenges to stage painters because such scenery almost always represents a three-dimensional object or a perspective scene. **Gridding** is the process used to make the enlarging from a sketch to a drop. Mark off the drop into one- or two-foot squares and scale the sketch proportionally, as shown. You may also transfer a drawing by using a projector. Most copy machines can copy the drawing onto a piece of clear plastic to produce a transparency. This can then be projected onto the drop and outlined. It is important, for either of these methods, that the drawing be a simple outline with clean lines.

One of the most challenging painting tasks for the inexperienced scenery painter is the painting of rock walls. These often end up looking like strange masses randomly placed in a large amount of gray mortar. On a real wall the rocks are laid in a layer of mortar, light causes highlights and shadows, and the texture and the color of the rocks give the viewer the feeling of bulk and weight. Such scenery should be painted using at least four colors with a wet-brush technique, which involves blending the colors while the paint is wet.

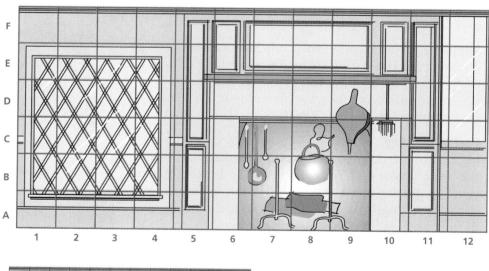

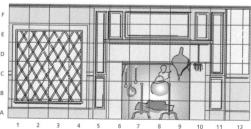

TRANSFERRING A BACKDROP DESIGN FROM THE SKETCH TO THE DROP THROUGH THE USE OF A SCALED GRID

Painted wallpaper patterns can be applied using stencils, carved blocks of rubber sponge or carpet padding, pattern rollers, and old paint rollers. Stencils can be cut out of plywood or out of stencil paper that is strengthened by a coat of acrylic, placed in a wooden frame, and reinforced with wires.

Application
ACTIVITY

Try your skill at one of the methods of texturing, or design a wallpaper pattern by first making your own stencils. For the wallpaper you can use manila paper or any other paper to which paint will adhere.

SOLVING PROBLEMS

Because many plays and musicals require different scenery effects as well as scenery and set changes, ingenuity can be helpful when trying to achieve these effects and changes efficiently.

In addition to various methods of painting to achieve different scenery effects, there is also a repertory of materials that can be used to create three-dimensional props and scenery. Two materials seem to be the most frequently used: plastics and papier-mâché.

1. Plastics have many uses on the stage. Expandable plastics can be formed into rocks or almost anything for which a mold can be formed. Because Styrofoam™ can be cut, shaped, glued, or pressed so easily, it can be made into bricks, molding, statues, and trim. It can also be painted to replicate a variety of different textures.
2. Papier-mâché has long been a special-effects material for the stage. You need wheat paste or stage sizing, strips of newspaper or paper towels, and chicken wire, wire cloth, or cardboard. With these supplies, you can create small and large objects for the set.

▼ CUE

Safety rules for handling plastics: Have adequate ventilation. Wear protective clothing and masks.

Many problems might be encountered onstage. The complexity of the production might determine their number or severity. Proper planning should curtail many of them, however. Some common problems and their solutions appear on the following page.

Insufficient stage space
- If the stage is shallow or lacks wing space, it can be extended out into the pit area or over the front center seats.
- A runway can be built out from the center or can enclose the pit and the orchestra.
- Acting areas can often be added to the side of the apron with platforms.

Inadequate fly space
- Double, or trip, drops for storage.
- Use short drops that can be raised as high as possible and concealed with low-hung borders.

Overly large stage opening
- Lower the grand drape to change the height of the opening.
- Add a false beam or ceiling to replace the first border.
- Add a false proscenium, a teaser, or tormentors to decrease height and width.

Side areas that need masking
- Use portals or tabs similar to false prosceniums.
- Use screens, wings, hanging banners, and backs of double-walled wagons.

Surfaces unsuitable for acting
- If floors are rough, sticky, or noisy, use a reversible canvas floor cloth—brown on one side and green for grass on other side.
- Use carpets to reduce noise and provide a realistic appearance to a room (carpets should lie flat or be tacked down).
- Pad stairs, wagons, and platforms to lessen noise.

Application
ACTIVITY

Choose a scene from a play and identify any problems that might exist in staging that scene on your school stage. Suggest solutions.

CUTAWAY OF A STAGE

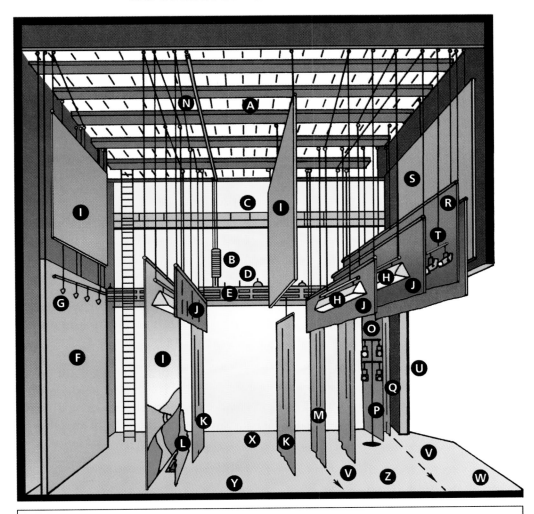

A	Gridiron	**N**	Spare batten
B	Counterweight system	**O**	Tormentor
C	Weight floor	**P**	Tormentor "tree" or boomerang
D	Pin rail	**Q**	Act curtain
E	Fly deck (gallery)	**R**	Grand drape (valance)
F	Sky drop or cyc	**S**	Fire curtain
G	Cyclorama floods	**T**	Spotlight batten (bridge)
H	Border lights	**U**	Proscenium arch
I	Drop	**V**	Curtain line
J	Teaser (border curtain)	**W**	Apron
K	Leg	**X**	Wings
L	Ground row	**Y**	Acting area
M	Traveler	**Z**	"In one"

SHIFTING THE SETTING

Shifting the scenery requires well-trained crew members who know what their jobs are and how to get them done efficiently.

The stage manager "runs the show" backstage.

Grips move flats, *periaktoi,* and set pieces.

The flycrew raise and lower flown scenery and draperies.

The prop crew check properties in and out as they are set or struck.

The set dressers set and strike a set's finishing touches.

There are many ways to change scenery in addition to those discussed earlier in this chapter. A booked set may be dropped inside an existing set. Screens can also be used for a set within a set. Drops are the most frequently used type of flown scenery. Ground rows are usually brought in to mask the junction where the drop meets the floor, and portals and false prosceniums are used to mask the sides of the stage. The masking of the wing areas, a problem associated with all exterior sets and now quite regularly associated with the musical play, is a challenge to the designer—the solution to which is often an even greater challenge to the crew. Once again, a black cyclorama can help simplify the problems. Even a full curved sky cyc will close off the audience's view of the backstage areas. But a sky cyc might make entrances and exits difficult.

CUE ▼

It might be necessary to make changes in full view of the audience. The "invisible" stagehand—clothed in black—might be your only recourse.

Wagon sets are another means of executing scene changes. A set is placed on a wheeled platform that can be rolled out onto the stage. A type of wagon arrangement that often works quite well is the jackknife. The jackknife wagon, shown on the next page, is stored perpendicular to the curtain line on the side of the stage, usually behind the tormentor or false proscenium, and is pivoted out when needed. A second wall can be attached back-to-back to the wagon, making two sets possible for each wagon. Wagons require storage space in the wings, which may be lacking, but they are often the best solution when fly space is not available.

Some directors have complained that the elevation of the wagon destroys the illusion they desire and eliminates the use of the apron unless the actor steps down from the wagon. This problem may be corrected in one of two ways.

1. Treat the wagon as a natural elevation, such as a hallway above a sunken living room or a porch with the apron as the lawn.
2. Build up the apron with platforms that are flush with the front edge of the wagon. Treat the apron as an extension of the wagon set. Add hinged returns to the side walls of the set to frame the apron acting area. This method takes more work but is worth the effort.

A circular revolving stage can be used if you have the budget, equipment, time, and skill. As many as three sets may be placed on a revolving platform. However, revolving stages are expensive to build and take special mechanical equipment to rotate smoothly. It is possible to build stages that can be moved manually. If this is to be done, however, it would

TWO WAYS OF CHANGING COMPLETE SETS

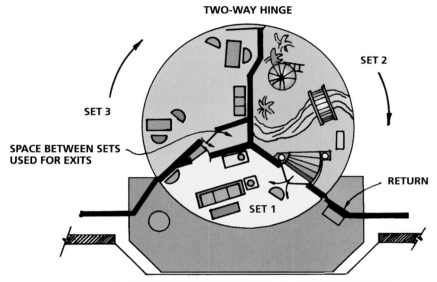

TWO-WAY HINGE

SET 2

SET 3

SPACE BETWEEN SETS USED FOR EXITS

RETURN

SET 1

A 3-SET REVOLVING STAGE WITH AN APRON EXTENSION

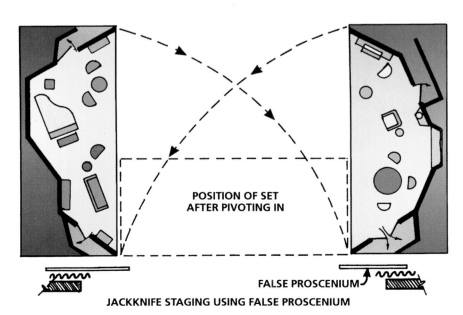

POSITION OF SET AFTER PIVOTING IN

FALSE PROSCENIUM

JACKKNIFE STAGING USING FALSE PROSCENIUM

probably be simpler and certainly more economical to bolt wagons together to make a revolving square with two sets back to back. Of course, once a set is out of view of the audience, it can be redressed for a new setting.

On many stages, the counterweight systems have been replaced by electric winches. This has often caused more problems than it has solved. The winches are slow, and the number that can be operated at one time is often limited.

Scenery that can be carried or rolled onto the stage, such as benches, lampposts, rocks, and trees, are called set pieces. Before designing and building set pieces, the scenic designer must decide how the unit will be used. Is it only for show, or must it support weight or operate in some manner? Those pieces that operate, such as windows that can open, lamps that can light, or a tree that can support an actor sitting on a branch, are called practical or practical-usable. Because theater is illusion, and time and expense are always to be considered, few set pieces are built to be practical unless the script requires it. Columns, trees (both shown below), and rocks may be plastic, that is, three-dimensional, or simply two-dimensional cut-outs. Three-dimensional pieces allow for more light and shadow effects, but cut-outs might better convey a stylization and the feeling of illusion.

SET PIECES: COLUMNS AND TREES

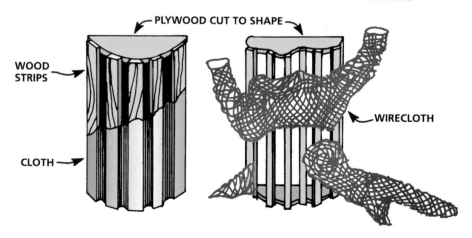

PLYWOOD CUT TO SHAPE

WOOD STRIPS

CLOTH

WIRECLOTH

🎭 *Stage Safety*

The safety of actors, crew members, and the audience is always of great concern. Power equipment, stage weights, electric winch systems, paints, plastics, and protruding nails are just a few of the materials that might lead to physical injury.

The fire curtain and the fire doors should be checked on a regular basis to make sure that they are operating properly. The deluge systems that replaced asbestos curtains have many design and operation problems that often make them a threat more than a safety feature. The emergency controls should not be situated so that they can be activated accidentally. The shut-off crank must be accessible and never be chained off. The water should not drain into the orchestra pit. If it does, there should be several drains to carry off the water, and the electric outlets in the pit should be at least a foot from the floor. Despite these precautions, a pit-draining deluge system poses a real threat to musicians in the pit because of the electric cords that are attached to music-stand lights and musical instruments.

General Stage-Safety Rules

1. Know the location and operation of all fire extinguishers and fire alarms.
2. Know what to do if the sprinklers, the fire curtain, or the deluge system is set off.
3. When you hear "Heads!" move quickly out of the way. Scenery is coming down.
4. When you are above the stage and using a tool such as a wrench to adjust lights or tighten bolts, always tie the tool to a line attached to your belt so that it will not fall.
5. When you remove a weight from a batten, be certain that an equal amount of weight is removed from the counterweight system.
6. If an imbalanced counterweighted line takes off, do not try to stop it by hand.
7. Always wear goggles when operating power equipment and floating flats.
8. Do not wear loose-fitting or fringed clothing or dangling jewelry when operating power equipment or when moving around gears or winches.
9. Always wear shoes, preferably safety shoes.
10. Remove all protruding nails in boards, and keep nails swept off the floor.
11. Be sure there is adequate ventilation when using materials that emit toxic fumes.
12. Know the number and wattage of instruments plugged into a circuit before turning it on.
13. Do not smoke or allow anyone else to smoke backstage.
14. Be alert and concerned about your safety and the safety of others.

Neon lights against the dark background emphasize the colorful costumes in *Crazy for You*. The lights and colors complement the play and add to its impact.

Scenery and the Performance

The drama student should recognize that scenery is an integral part of modern play production. However, scenic design has developed as a complement to the play and might lose its impact if looked upon as an end in itself. If scenery swallows up the performer, the costume, the makeup, or the acting; if the scenery is in poor taste or is not aesthetically satisfying; if inappropriate sets cause the mood of the play to be lost; or if the set is a showpiece for a talented designer or for exuberant art students and does not serve the play—then the purposes and intent of the playwright and the director become distorted and meaningless.

Scenery should add to and never detract from the overall merit of a production. A little imagination, some inexpensive materials and equipment, and the enthusiasm and talents of high school students can easily bring to the audience a setting that enhances the total production by making it an "everything-seemed-to-go-together" performance.

In order to accomplish this goal, high school directors, designers, and production committees should work together to carefully select scenic elements, emphasizing those they wish to convey to the audience and minimizing or eliminating those that would not make a positive contribution. It is often the frequently overlooked little things that may make a realistic set look complete—the right number and kinds of pictures on the wall; the knickknacks on the shelf; the flowers in the vases around the room; the choice of carpets, drapes, lamps, and furnishings; a flickering fire in the hearth; the shadow lines and texturing on the walls. It is usually the smallest number of elements with the greatest impact of identification and meaning that make a set the most satisfying.

▼ **CUE**

Selecting a few perfect elements can create an atmosphere more efficiently than filling a stage with scenery and furniture that is not quite appropriate for the production.

By using realistic tile flooring and props, the set designer for *FOB*, by David Henry Hwang, created a set that gives the production a realistic atmosphere.

10 REVIEW

Summary and Key Ideas

Summarize the chapter by answering the following questions.

1. Why should drama students study stagecraft?
2. What is the purpose of scenery? How can it enhance a performance?
3. How has scenic design evolved over time?
4. Name and describe three types of sets.
5. What things must a designer know before designing a set?
6. What are four artistic considerations in building a set?
7. Describe the steps in constructing a flat.
8. What is the best fabric for flats? What is the next best choice?
9. Which crew members are responsible for shifting scenery?
10. List at least ten safety rules for staging a play.

Discussing Ideas

1. How does "using the least to say the most" apply to stagecraft?
2. After watching a play, analyze the work of the set designer. How many sets were there? What types of sets were used? What colors dominated? What did the set contribute to or take away from the play?
3. Describe a realistic set for the balcony scene of *Romeo and Juliet*.

FOCUS ON Safety

Constructing another world on the stage can mean real-world dangers. That's why it's best to make safety a priority for all of the people involved in a production, right from the start. Preparation and attitude are key. All cast members should be aware of hazards and should be prepared to deal calmly and effectively with problems that arise.

Compiling Safety Guidelines Find books, magazines, or Internet sites that give safety information and guidelines for theaters or theater companies. Some companies and theater schools post their guidelines online. (Always check with your teacher before using the Internet for research.) Compile a list of information or tips that are new to you or that seem especially relevant to your venue. Share your research with the class.

Practicing Safety Measures Devise a situation that would test another student's knowledge of appropriate safety measures. Then get together with a partner to exchange situations and discuss solutions. Do this several times to make sure that both of you have a good handle on the guidelines. You might want to perform this exercise every time your class puts on a theatrical production.

STAGE SETTINGS

INDEPENDENT ACTIVITIES

A Play Without Scenery   Because of budget considerations, scenery has been eliminated for this year's play. With this in mind, choose a play in which ideas are more important than locale. You might consider plays like *Whose Life Is It Anyway?* or *The Diary of Anne Frank.* Using only objects such as platforms, boxes, and ramps, sketch what the stage would look like for at least two scenes of the play. Include a written explanation of how this bare-bones set will intensify and reflect the meaning of the play.

Visual Metaphor   Sometimes a central visual metaphor can be very effective in a set design. Read over a play that you know well and select a visual metaphor for it. For example, you might choose the fragile unicorn in *The Glass Menagerie* or a tombstone for *Death of a Salesman.* Then decide how you will use the metaphor. How many set pieces might resemble it? How could it be enlarged and used in all the settings? Create a perspective drawing of your metaphorical set.

Cooperative Learning Activity

Troubleshooting   Imagine that your drama class wants to present a play such as *Barnum* or *Bye Bye Birdie* that demands more physical space than your stage and auditorium can accommodate. With a group of your classmates, brainstorm ways that you might make better use of the available space or compromise on the scope of your presentation. For example, you might build a thrust stage or add platforms to the sides of the stage. Brainstorm ways to make the staging possible, come up with some specific suggestions and drawings, and present your ideas to the class. Discuss with them whether your design will make an effective production or interfere with the integrity of the play.

Across the CURRICULUM Activities

Woodworking   Choose a play that has several different locales, such as *The Miracle Worker* or *The Matchmaker.* Build a three-dimensional model of a multiple set with distinct acting areas. Decide how you will separate one area from another.

Art   Choose a scene from a favorite play and design the setting in several rough sketches. Then demonstrate for your classmates how to paint scenery. You may want to concentrate on one very specific task, such as different ways to create texture, or you may want to illustrate a more general procedure, such as the way gridding is done. As an alternative, show your classmates how to make stylized plants, trees, and flowers out of papier-mâché for a children's play.

11 Lighting and Sound

Lighting can be used to divide the stage and to give depth to the space, as in this set from *Beehive*.

With the light I state my vision, my version of the universe.

—JENNIFER TIPTON, TONY AWARD-WINNING LIGHTING DESIGNER

SETTING THE SCENE

Focus Questions

How does lighting affect a play?

What basic equipment should be available for a performance?

How are lighting plans and cue sheets prepared?

What is basic sound equipment for the theater?

How are sound effects made?

Vocabulary

spotlight	floodlight	backlight	tweeters
dimmer	Fresnel	scrim	midrange
light panel	portable striplight	light plot	woofers
cable	roundels	lighting cue sheet	feedback
connector	gelatin	acoustics	intercom systems
ellipsoidal reflector spotlight	key light	microphone	sound-effects board
follow spot	fill light	amplifier	sound plot
	sidelight	speakers	sound cue sheet

*S*tage technology, including lighting and sound, is a rapidly expanding phase of the theater arts. Lighting is taking the place of paint in many productions because it instantly transforms backgrounds, indicating changes in mood, action, and location. Sound effects, in addition to music played between scenes, also affect mood, action, and location.

Designing effective and imaginative lighting and sound can be intriguing and challenging, whether you are working with the simplest or the most sophisticated equipment.

🎭 *Stage Lighting Effects*

Imagine that as the curtain opens we look in on an antiquated English manor house. The room is dark except for a flickering glow from the fireplace. A dim figure appears in the archway, silhouetted against the diffused light of the entrance hall. The room instantly comes to life as the young woman presses the wall switch and the chandelier and the two sconces over the fireplace illuminate the right half of the stage. She presses another switch, and the lamp by the chair at stage left brightens the rest of the room. The actor swiftly crosses upstage to the high window and pulls the drapery cord. Immediately the stage is flooded by bright sunlight reflected off the snow-covered terrain outside. She crosses down right to the fireplace and places two more logs on the dying fire. As she stirs the coals, a reddish glow warms her face. She turns, takes two steps toward the table, center, looks at her watch and utters the first line of the play: "I *do* wish Martin would hurry. It's been nearly three hours since he called."

Dramatic backlighting creates a mysterious atmosphere in this scene from the Agatha Christie melodrama *The Unexpected Guest*.

The audience probably did not notice that after the initial flash broke the darkness, the room continued to brighten. It is unlikely, too, that they noticed the "sunlight" dimming slightly after the first rays struck the actor's face. Nor would we expect the viewers to question whether the fire glowed as brightly after she turned toward the middle of the room to deliver her first line. Certainly, the audience never wondered what lighting equipment was used for that effect. Audiences accept the illusions created by modern stage lighting.

For hundreds of years, plays were performed almost exclusively in the daytime out of doors or in buildings open to the sky. The use of many candles and torches eventually made it possible to present plays in a completely enclosed structure. It was not until gaslight replaced candles in 1803, however, that artificial light aroused much interest. By the 1820s, Thomas Drummond, of England, had developed one of the earliest spotlights, an oxyhydrogen flame directed against a block of calcium oxide, or lime. Actors soon learned how to play in the "limelight."

With the greater use of artificial lighting, however, came the increased danger of fire. The history of theater has been blackened by the ashen shells of once-active playhouses. By the end of the nineteenth century, electricity had revolutionized home and theater lighting. Today we present well-lighted plays with the aid of modern computerized equipment.

All students of drama—actors, directors, and crew—should understand the basic principles of light, its peculiarities, qualities, and effects on actors, audiences, costumes, makeup, and pigments.

🎋 Lighting Equipment

▼ **CUE**

The versatile **spotlight** meets flexibility needs most effectively. It is mobile and easy to control; it also provides multiple services and the best control of light distribution.

The ideal lighting equipment for the school stage is flexible, efficient, and economical. Of these, flexibility is the most important consideration. Flexibility is determined by (1) mobility: how easily you can move an instrument about the auditorium according to the needs of various productions; (2) control: how easily you can control the amount of light, usually by a dimmer panel; and (3) multiple service: how many different areas you can light with the instrument.

When determining the lighting equipment needed, you must consider the availability and number of **dimmers**, the size of the stage (especially the depth of the acting area and of the apron), the height of the theater ceiling or the distance to the balcony rail, the availability of mounting locations, and, of course, the budget. Every high school, however, should try to have the minimum equipment described in the chart on the following page.

Common Equipment

Light Panel

a console from which the brightness of light is controlled

- The operator can choose which dimmer on this console will control the brightness of the light of any given instrument.
- The most common type has plugs connected to each outlet or instrument in the auditorium. These can be inserted into a "patchboard."
- A modern option is a computerized solid state relay system (SCR) with memory and monitor. Set-ups with one dimmer per circuit are also available. These electronic consoles cannot be overloaded because the electrical load does not pass through the console. Schools purchasing an SCR should always obtain one that allows for manual control as well as program capabilities.

Cable

heavily insulated wire for joining instruments to electrical outlets or to a switchboard

Connector

device for joining cables to each other or for joining cables to instruments

- Stage cables and conductors are essential to the safe conduction of electricity. The danger of overloads, shorts, and fires is still great on most high school stages. It is easy to be careless about completing an electrical circuit safely.

Common Equipment

Ellipsoidal Reflector Spotlight 	**a highly efficient light with an ellipsoid-shaped reflector; used in pairs** • For front lighting, one pair of 500 to 1,000 watts each is needed for every eight to ten feet of proscenium opening. • For washes, sidelighting, and backlighting, ten to twelve more are required. • These spots are often mounted in the ceiling, on balcony rails, or on electric battens.
Follow Spot 	**a long-range, high-wattage light capable of following an actor's movements on stage; essential for every stage**
Floodlight 	**a high-wattage light, open at one end, containing a metal shell and a highly reflective inner surface** • Floodlights are used for special effects such as sunlight and moonlight. • A minimum of four is needed; additional ones are required to light cycloramas.
Fresnel 	**a spotlight with a stepped lens, used to project a clear, strong light with a soft edge** • At least fourteen 500-watt instruments are needed. • They are mounted on a pipe just behind the grand drape and on pipes located one-third to two-thirds upstage.
Striplights and Portable Striplights 	**lamps arranged in metal troughs, usually with three or four circuits; sometimes called borderlights when hung from pipe battens above the stage** • Three to four of each are required for general stage use and scenic color blending. • They are used for side lighting, backing or entrance lighting, or cyclorama lighting.

Other desirable equipment includes the following:

- ellipsoidal reflectors for mounting on side walls of the auditorium
- additional Fresnels for the first batten
- one or two automated lighting fixtures
- a second follow spot
- blacklight units and special-effects projector
- pipe clamps for hanging instruments
- color frames for each spotlight and floodlight

In addition, it is desirable to have some color media, such as **roundels** for striplights or **gelatin** for the spots and floods. The best colors for the color media in the striplights are red, blue, and yellow because a combination of these three colors will make all the colors in the spectrum. Amber is sometimes substituted for the yellow; this choice is wise only if the light panel is one of toggle switches rather than dimmers or if a stronger overhead light is desired.

You will find that new types of lighting equipment are constantly appearing. The tungsten-halogen lamps provide much more efficient light at far less cost than incandescent bulbs. Many T-H bulbs will last four times as long as conventional bulbs. The T-H bulbs run very hot and require gels that will not fade quickly or warp from the heat. The T-H lamp will crack or bulge if exposed to perspiration from fingers. Therefore, the lamps must be carefully installed with the protective covers in place. If the lamp is later removed, it should be cleaned with isopropyl alcohol.

Application
ACTIVITY

Suppose that you are in charge of purchasing lighting equipment for a new theater at your school. Obtain catalogs from lighting companies. Create the following three purchase lists: one for a school that can purchase only the minimum equipment, a second for a school with more resources, and the third for a school with unlimited resources. (*Resources*, in this case, refers to money, a theater facility, people, and time.)

⚛ *Basic Lighting Principles*

Without a doubt, lighting is the most important element in scenic design because it affects the creation of mood and atmosphere. The exuberant nature of a musical is enhanced by the cheerfulness of a brightly illuminated stage. A mystery takes on a spine-tingling quality when the high walls and deep recesses of a deserted mansion are lost in the depths of shadows. An eerie fog, an iridescent liquid in a witch's cauldron, the ghostly whiteness of a full moon, the aura of intrigue and death in the shadowy alleys of counterespionage—you can create each of these on stage by the right choice of color, gobos, and proper distribution and brightness of light from carefully selected instruments. Effective stage lighting is based on three qualities of light: intensity, or brightness; color; and distribution, or area covered.

INTENSITY

The lighting designer should never allow actors to be lost in unintentional pockets of dark shadows. Nor should the lighting designer try to eliminate all shadows with generalized bright light. This results in one huge flat glow of light, which is the most common lighting error on the high school stage. This problem stems from the incorrect notion that lighting a set means turning all available instruments on full. This garish amber-white light makes actors "dead" on the stage or makes them disappear into the set. Many of the most successful designers today use only spotlights and floods. Others add borders and foots for blending only. In any case, strong lights should be kept off the walls of a set. Most designers suggest keeping the upper walls in shadow.

Intense lighting can be used to emphasize certain aspects of a scene. This character in *The Crucifer of Blood*, a Sherlock Holmes mystery, is unobtrusively lit from the front, but the overall effect of the lighting is to make the audience think the scene is illuminated by only the "moonlight" streaming in through the latticed windows.

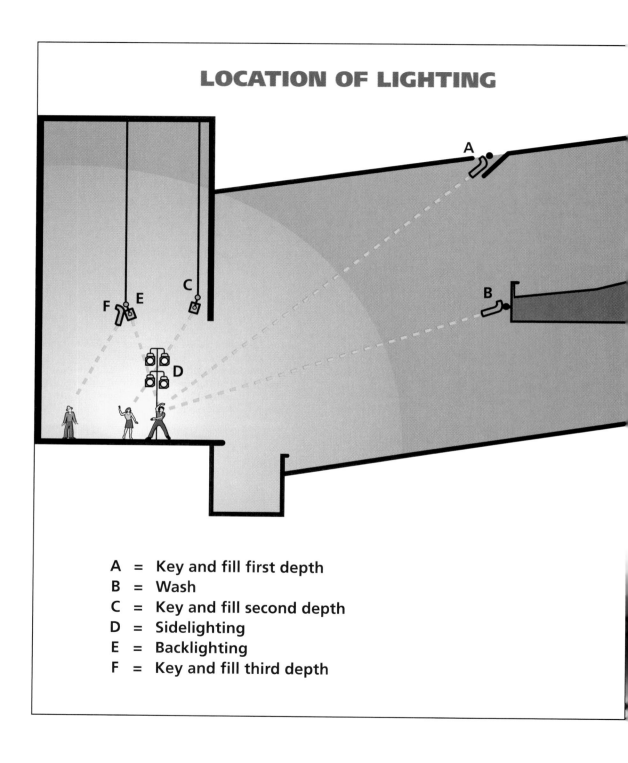

LOCATION OF LIGHTING

A = Key and fill first depth
B = Wash
C = Key and fill second depth
D = Sidelighting
E = Backlighting
F = Key and fill third depth

Diagram of a general lighting plan for downstage areas

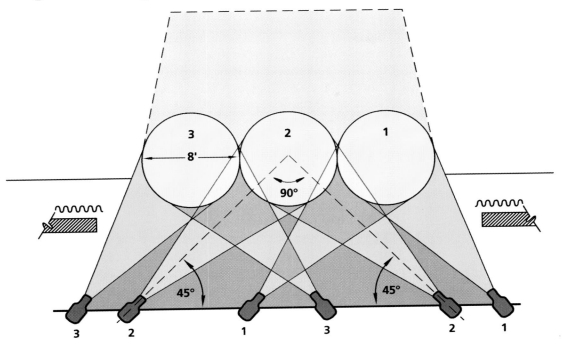

Diagram of a general lighting plan for upstage areas

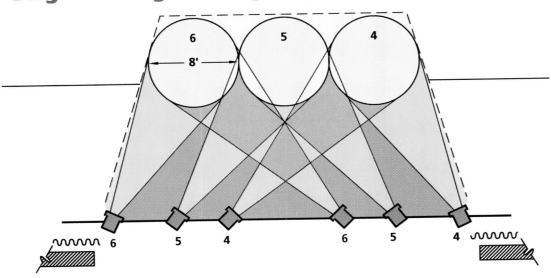

Most lighting changes should happen gradually by **dimming up** or **dimming down.** Lights rarely pop on or off except when a light switch is flipped onstage. Even then, not all instruments come on at once. Within a scene, lights normally change with a **crossfade:** some lights come up at the same time others dim down. The audience should not consciously notice that a change is taking place. Technicians must therefore begin light changes far in advance in order to accomplish them smoothly.

There are some general considerations to remember when working with stage lights. Brightly lighted scenes, especially of the type frequently found in musical plays, can cause changes in the appearance of makeup and costumes. Strong amber can turn colorful fabrics into a drab brown; too much red may wash the rouge out of the actors' faces.

Night scenes are always difficult to light without having costumes and makeup turn black under a green-blue light. Therefore, the colors used in most night scenes will make rouge and lipstick look grotesque. When scenes are to be played in the dark, it is always best to have some light even if no attempt is made to represent natural light sources. An unlighted stage is dead. Figures outlined against a moonlit window, a shaft of light through a window or skylight, a crack of light from under a door, or the glow of an old-fashioned streetlight can provide a realistic source for the stage light. However, if no other choice is left, a beam or two of colored light that is there solely for the reason that the actors must be seen will meet the requirements for light. The audience should never be left completely in the dark for more than a few seconds.

Sharply contrasting colored lights give this scene from *Blood Wedding* a high level of energy. The blue light conveys serenity, while the red light conveys power and movement.

COLOR

The effect of light on color is difficult to predict accurately because of the relationship between light, pigments, and dyes. Some generalizations, however, can be made:

red light on red	= red
red light on blue	= violet
red light on green	= gray
red light on yellow	= orange
red light on purple	= red
blue light on red	= violet-black
blue light on blue	= blue
blue light on green	= blue-green
blue light on yellow	= green
blue light on orange	= brown
amber light on red	= brown
amber light on blue	= greenish-orange
amber light on green	= greenish-orange
amber light on violet	= red
green light on red	= black
green light on green	= green
yellow light on blue	= blue-green
yellow light on green	= green
yellow light on violet	= brown

▼ **CUE**

As a general rule, tragedies and serious dramas emphasize cool colors, whereas comedies stress warm colors.

The only way to produce green light is by using green color media. The delicate colors are the most preferred gelatins in use today. No-color pink, flesh pink, straws, and ambers—especially bastard amber, a light scarlet—are some of the warm colors used. And special lavender, surprise pink, no-color blue, and medium and daylight blue are some of the best cool color gelatins. Sometimes designers use frost and chocolate for special effects. Green-blue makes a better night scene than blues or violets. Many lighting designers prefer white light from an ungelled instrument as a cool light source.

Curtains, costumes, and furnishings are affected by light. Smooth, shiny fabrics reveal light and shadows. Heavy, coarse materials, no matter how inexpensive, absorb much light and often appear quite expensive to the audience; outing flannel can look like expensive velour. The important consideration is the brilliance of the color of the material and the color of the stage lighting for the scene in which the material is to be used. Patterns and prints cause many problems, as do several colors in the same costume. Lighting period plays is always difficult, for the mixture of lace, silk, velvet, wigs, and makeup is a lighting technician's nightmare.

DISTRIBUTION

The most effective lighting considers the natural light sources on the set—the sun or moon, a streetlight, lamps, fireplaces, televisions, candles, or lanterns. To avoid a pasteboard-figure effect, designers usually pair spotlights. One uses warm colors and comes from the same side of the stage as the sources of natural light. The other comes from the opposite direction, the direction of diffused or reflected light, and uses cool colors. Each spotlight is aimed in and down at a forty-five-degree angle toward the area to be lighted (see illustration on page 454). This results in the most dramatic effect of highlight and shadow. Designers usually avoid straight-on lighting from centrally located instruments because it serves as a general wash. (A **wash** eliminates shadows and brings a strength of light to the central acting area.) Instead, spotlights used for the wash are best located on the balcony or on the sides of the auditorium and aimed diagonally across the stage.

The most important acting areas need the most light. Bringing a greater quantity of light into a given acting area makes the actor playing in that area stand out. In any lighting plan there is always **key light,** the strongest light aimed at each acting area, and **fill light,** light that fills in the shadows. **Sidelighting** from upstage of the tormentor, using a different color from the front lighting, can help model actors' features and accent costumes. It also adds a touch of life to the production. **Backlighting** comes from above and behind the actor, setting the performer off from the background. The lighting designer may help shift the focus of attention back and forth with the smooth flow of light from one actor or area to another throughout the play.

For this scene from *Les Liaisons Dangereuses*, key light emphasizes the character, while fill light points up the chaise longue behind him.

Assemble a variety of fabrics of different colors and textures. Then using a series of colored lights, observe the effect of the various colored lights on the fabrics. Share your findings.

❋ *Special Lighting Effects*

Lighting is probably the designer's most versatile source of special effects, accomplishing such feats as pinpointing a face in a crowd, changing the stage into a blazing inferno, suspending animation, or creating the illusion of a silent movie by the use of a flicker wheel or strobe.

Using a **scrim**, or gauze drop, creates some of the most striking scenic-lighting combinations. Lighting a scrim from the front makes it nearly opaque, and lighting it from behind makes it semitransparent. Scrims, properly lighted, help create fog, mist, and dream scenes. Actors and cut-out scenery may be silhouetted against the scrim by backlighting.

The setting for this scene from the Sherlock Holmes mystery *The Crucifer of Blood* is the River Thames in London. A smoke machine and overhead lighting produce the illusion of the dense fog that often covers the Thames late at night. The lighting also isolates the characters against the dark background.

FUNCTION	INSTRUMENT NUMBER	INSTRUMENT TYPE	LOCATION	LOAD WATTS	COLOR	DIMMER WATTS	NOTES
AREA 1 KEY	1	8" ELLIPSOIDAL	BEAM- L	750	34		FRAME OFF RETURN
AREA 2 KEY	2	" "	BEAM- L	750	34		
AREA 3 KEY	3	" "	BEAM- L	750	34		
AREA 1 FILL	4	" "	BEAM- R	750	54		
AREA 2 FILL	5	" "	BEAM- R	750	54		
AREA 3 FILL	6	" "	BEAM- R	750	54		FRAME OFF RETURN
L. CENTER WASH	7	" "	BALCONY R	1000	33		
R. CENTER WASH	8	" "	BALCONY R	1000	33		
L. CENTER WASH	9	" "	BALCONY L	1000	60		
R. CENTER WASH	10	" "	BALCONY L	1000	60		
AREA 4 KEY	11	6" FRESNEL	1ST ELEC L	500	33		
AREA 5 KEY	12	" "	1ST ELEC L	500	33		
AREA 6 KEY	13	" "	1ST ELEC LC	500	33		
AREA 4 FILL	14	" "	1ST ELEC RR	500	54		FRAME TO ENTRANCE
AREA 5 FILL	15	" "	1ST ELEC R	500	54		
AREA 6 FILL	16	" "	1ST ELEC R	500	54		
STAIRCASE & LANDING	17	" "	2ND ELEC L	500	34		
STAIRCASE & LANDING	18	" "	2ND ELEC LC	500	54		
BOOKCASE AREA 5	19	" "	2ND ELEC C	500	34		FRAME OFF WALL
FOYER LANDING	20	" "	2ND ELEC RC	500	34		
BOOKCASE	21	" "	2ND ELEC R	500	54		FRAME OFF WALL
FOYER LANDING	22	" "	2ND ELEC R	500	54		
LEFT BACKLIGHT	23	6" ELLIPSOIDAL	2ND ELEC LC	500	33		
RIGHT BACKLIGHT	24	" "	2ND ELEC RC	500	33		
STAIRCASE SPECIAL	25	" "	BOOM UL	500	08		AT TOP OF BOOM
FOYER SPECIAL	26	" "	BOOM UR	500	08		AT TOP OF BOOM
FIREPLACE SPECIAL	27	ROLL LOG	FIREPLACE	200	14		
SL. EXIT SPECIAL	28	6" ELLIPSOIDAL	1ST ELEC L	500	12		
SR. EXIT SPECIAL	29	" "	1ST ELEC R	500	06		

LIGHTING PLAN FOR *ONCE IN A LIFETIME*

Painting or dyeing a scrim makes an impressive traverse curtain, which provides a fine background for short scenes, especially in musical plays. Such a painted scrim can also create the illusion of "passing through." In *The Music Man,* for example, a scrim could be painted to represent the outside of the Madison Public Library. With front lighting, the scrim looks like any ordinary drop, but when the lights come up in the library (behind the scrim), the watchers feel as if they have passed directly through the library's walls.

LIGHTING PLOT
ONCE IN A LIFETIME

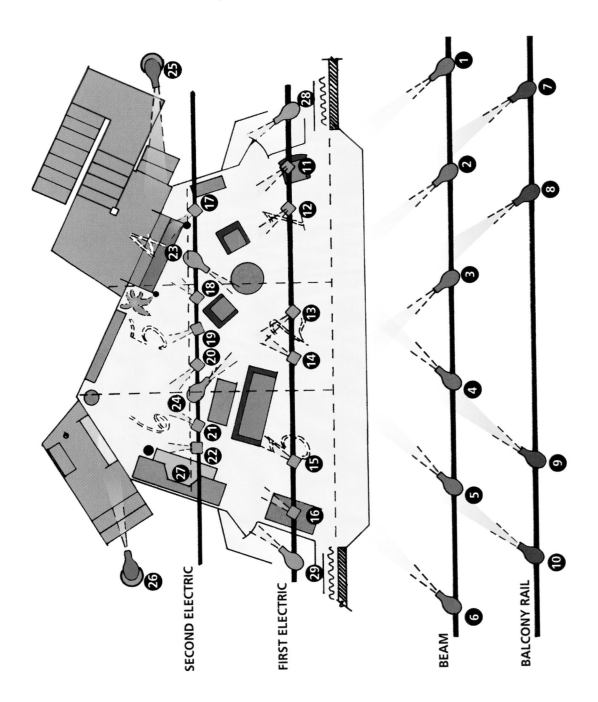

SECOND ELECTRIC

FIRST ELECTRIC

BEAM

BALCONY RAIL

What is normally considered a negative effect of light can create one of the more unusual lighting effects. Makeup using colors that wash out under normal stage light is applied over standard makeup. Makeup the same color as the lights has a tendency to disappear. By changing the dominant lighting colors or by having the character move into the beam of a special spot, the actor may suddenly assume the mask of death, the features of an angel, or the ugliness of a Mr. Hyde as the "invisible" makeup is seen.

Few techniques match the possibilities for unique special effects that can be attained by using black light. Many new colors of luminous paint, paper, and fabrics have been developed that increase the flexibility of black light.

Lighting is used to simulate theater marquees in this scene from *42nd Street*. Notice that the marquees vary in size and that the bulbs making up the show titles vary in size and distance from one another. These effects, along with the staggered rows of performers, give the scene depth.

✵ Planning the Lighting

As soon as the director and crew have worked out the needs for costumes, makeup, scenery, and furnishings, it is time to begin work on the lighting. Using the information provided by the director and the scenic designer, the lighting technician must create the light plot and the lighting cue sheet. The **light plot** shows the location of each lighting instrument and the area or object each illuminates. Almost all important acting areas need paired spotlights. However, some locations, such as doorways and windows, can be adequately lighted by one spotlight.

Once the light plot is prepared, the lighting technician can work out the cue sheet. The light plot indicates how the light board is to be set up for each scene. The **cue sheet** shows what changes are to take place: which controls, which instruments, what setting to use, and the length of time each change will take. These are listed chronologically as they appear in the play, including warning cues, execution cues, and timing cues (how to count the time during a change). The matter of timing is of great importance. Electronic systems can be programmed so that they are on timed settings. If the production gets off schedule, the lighting cues will not synchronize with the production and the lighting technician can override the system.

LIGHTING CUE SHEET FOR:

CUE NO.	PAGE	CONTROL NO.	AREA	START CUE	RDG.	COMPLETE CUE	RDG.
1	3	M₁ M₂ M₃	1,2,3	FOGHORN	O	BOATSWAINS WHISTLE	8
2	3	12,14	6,8	FRANK: "DO YOU THINK..."	O	PHIL: "I DON'T BELIEVE IT"	10
3	5	M₁ M₂ M₃ 12,14	1,2,3 6,8,	SCREAM (KILL)	8 10	(IMMEDIATE BLACKOUT)	O
4	8	M₁ M₂ M₃ M₄ M₅	1,2,3 4,5	CAR COMING UP DRIVE	O	CAR STOP	10

Lighting can be preplanned, but since the effects of light on any particular surface or color are unpredictable, the only way to properly light a production is to actually try the costumes, makeup, and scenery under the lights.

All lighting cues need to be worked out in rehearsals, although it saves the time and the patience of the director and cast if most preliminary run-throughs and experimentations can be done in technical rehearsals held separately from cast rehearsals.

The lighting technicians need to see that all equipment is in working order, that cables are not laid where they may be tripped over, and that exposed cables are taped down. Square knots or twist lock connectors should secure each connection, faded gels must be replaced, and any instruments that might have been accidentally moved by actors or crew during scene shifts must be realigned. The lighting crew needs to be alert to the dangers of reflective surfaces—mirrors, highly polished furniture, glass-fronted cabinets, sequins, jewels, or anything else that might throw a blinding light into the eyes of the audience or reveal backstage areas.

All of the action in the play *The Woods* takes place on an outdoor front porch setting. Lighting is used to indicate the time of day that differentiates the scenes.

Three Common Problems in Lighting

Problem	Cause	Solution
The actor "turns on the lights" and the audience waits five seconds before lights change.	The light booth is at floor level or on an elevated platform, stage right so the technician cannot see the actors.	• Wire onstage lights directly into the power source so they really work, as in a home. • Wire onstage switch to a cue light that technicians can see. This reduces the delay to one that is imperceptible.
All or most stage lights can be only on or off.	Available equipment does not include a dimmer, or dimmers are linked directly to border or footlights only.	• Invest in a small portable console and do necessary wiring.
Inadequate or no lighting equipment is available.	Budget limitations may be the problem.	• Purchase small, inexpensive spotlights and floods. • Solicit gifts from parents' groups, drama club boosters, or other groups.

Application
ACTIVITY

Determine what the lighting resources are in the theater used for your school's productions. Select a scene from a play and prepare a light plot and cue sheet for the scene.

🐚 Sound

From theater's beginnings, sound has been a key element in presentation. In fact, the word *audience* is derived from the Latin word *audire,* meaning "to hear." Combined with realistic gestures and expressions, the projection of an actor's voice, including inflections and proper diction, results in artistic expression.

Volume, or loudness, was not an issue when theatrical audiences were small. However, as theater evolved and attendance increased, the need for voice projection and volume also increased. Actors had to pay attention not only to raising the volume of their voices but also to retaining voice quality, for the more loudly an actor speaks, the more he or she must focus on proper diction and projecting inflection.

The structure of theater buildings and auditoriums plays an important part in the projection of sound. A theater's **acoustics,** or qualities that determine the audibility and trueness of the sound of the actors' voices, must be considered when presenting a production.

🐚 Sound Equipment

Sound equipment is used in theater for various purposes, including amplification, sound effects, and music. There are several basic pieces of sound equipment, which can be divided into two categories: amplification equipment and recording equipment. Amplification equipment is used to increase the volume of the actors' voices, allowing the entire audience, no matter how large, to hear the onstage dialogue. Recording equipment is used to add music and sound effects.

AMPLIFICATION EQUIPMENT

An amplification system consists of microphones (mikes), amplifiers, and speakers. Cables, cords that deliver the electrical sound impulses from one device to another, connect these. The accuracy of the sound depends in part on the quality of the system but even more on the skill of the sound technician. An amplification system should not be viewed as a tool to improve an actor's voice. Rather, it should be used simply to increase its volume, enabling the audience to hear.

Microphones Electronic amplification of the voice begins with the **microphone,** a device that receives sound waves and changes them into electronic impulses. There are several types of mikes, each designed for a specific use. The general-purpose microphone, most commonly used for speeches, functions best for backstage lines or announcements in play productions. Usually unidirectional—that is, picking up sounds from only one direction—a general-purpose mike works best when a person speaks into it from a distance of one to two feet.

Another type of microphone, often used by singers, is designed for close-up use (approximately two to ten inches from the mouth). This type of mike is ideal for musical productions. Close-up mikes are often cordless, allowing the user to move freely about the stage. However, if the mike has a cord, the scene must be carefully blocked so that other actors and props do not become entangled in the cord as the user moves about the stage.

In contrast to the close-up mike, the apron mike picks up sound from a distance of ten to fifteen feet. This type of mike is useful for choral numbers in musicals and also for straight plays. With a reception range of forty-five degrees left and right of center (both horizontally and vertically), apron microphones can amplify an entire production. Placed on the apron of the stage, these mikes must be cushioned in a "mouse," a specially designed foam rubber holder, to avoid picking up stage traffic. For an alternative to a mouse, the technician can place the shaft of the mike on a thin nest of foam with the mike head extended and almost touching the floor. This "nest" can be carved out of the foam that spotlight lamps are usually packed in. A normal-sized stage requires four apron mikes. For strong reception downstage center, place the two center mikes on the floor at a forty-five-degree angle facing each other with the heads nearly touching. Place the other two apron mikes at the sides of the apron. This setup is particularly effective for musical productions because it allows for movement by a soloist or for an equal pick-up of two or more performers in the center-stage area. Actors using an apron mike must stand no closer than three to four feet upstage of the mike. If they are any closer, their voices will not be amplified.

A rifle microphone, also called a shotgun mike or a gun mike, has a long, sensitive range but a narrow pickup pattern. If acoustics are poor and a performer cannot be picked up with other miking, a rifle mike can be the best solution. Placed on the apron down center and down right for soloists, or suspended overhead and aimed upstage at a point of critical action, rifle mikes can fill a critical gap.

A skillful sound technician can greatly affect the mood of a production.

Overhead miking, whether with rifle mikes or with other types of mikes, generally fits a single-set show best. The constant movement of scenery in musical productions means that any overhead mikes must either be continually raised out of the way and then lowered again or be hung so high they are useless.

The microphone most commonly used in professional productions is the radio mike. Sometimes called a lapel mike or a body mike, it can be clipped to an actor's collar, placed in the hair, or hidden in the costume. This mike is powered by a battery pack belted or taped to the actor. Each radio mike requires its own receiver, and a technician must control each mike independently. When radio mikes are being used in a production, every battery pack should be checked before every performance. Also, special attention should be paid to the placement of these microphones; they will amplify the movement or rubbing of costume materials, and if two performers are close to each other, both mikes might pick up one performer and give double amplification. Performers must make a habit of turning off their radio mikes when they leave the stage, to avoid amplifying backstage conversations.

Amplifiers and Mixers   An **amplifier** receives a small sound signal from a mike or other source, increases the strength of the signal, and outputs it to a speaker or other destination. To judge the strength of amplification required, the basic formula is one watt per audience member; therefore, most high-school auditoriums need 250 to 1200 watts. A sound specialist can evaluate an auditorium and advise on the necessary equipment.

Ideally, the amplifiers should have at least twelve inputs, or connector receptacles that accept cables from a source, such as a mike. There should be at least eight inputs for mikes, one for each other accessory, and at least one spare input. If the amplifiers do not have enough inputs, a mixer can be added to the system. A mixer can control several mikes individually while it requires only one amplifier input. The amplifiers should also have a sufficient number of outputs leading to the auditorium speakers, to all the monitors—backstage, light and sound technicians, projection booth, pit, greenroom, waiting room—and, for special effects, at least one output located on each side of the stage.

A mixer enables the sound operator to listen to the incoming signal; to adjust each input for volume, tone, and timing; and to send the mixed sound to the speakers. A mixer equipped with foldback lets the mixed sound go to specified speakers placed so the people making the sound can hear themselves with no time delay. Mixers can also supply sound outputs to echo machines, noise gates, samplers, and delay machines to alter the sound further. Today many school productions find that a combination of several mixer-amplifiers meets their needs best.

A Simplified Sound System

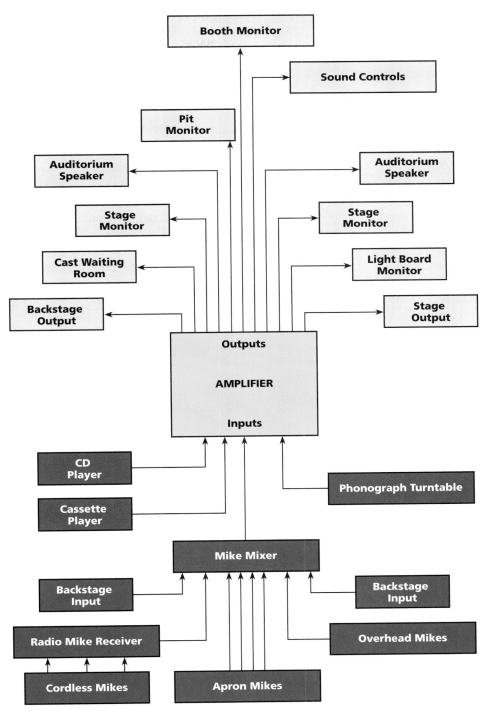

Too much amplification can damage hearing. Adjust volume not only for sound quality but also for safety.

Speakers   Cone-shaped devices driven by electromagnets that convert electrical impulses into sound are called **speakers,** which project sound. There are three major types of speaker cones: **tweeters,** which reproduce high-pitched sounds; **midrange,** which reproduce sounds occurring in the middle range; and **woofers,** which reproduce low-pitched sounds. Speaker cones are usually housed in boxes with fabric covering the large end of the cones. Speaker positions must vary with the size and shape of the auditorium, but generally speakers are positioned on both sides of the audience. Often speakers are placed above the stage or even above the audience as well.

Two frequent problems that occur with the projection of sound are ringing and feedback. **Ringing,** which does not originate with the speaker, is a high-pitched sound usually caused by mike volume that is too high. **Feedback** is loud, ear-piercing sound caused by the amplified sound being fed back into the mikes that are picking up the original sound. Dropping a microphone, placing speakers so they face each other, or moving a microphone downstage of the speakers can all result in feedback. Fairly inexpensive solutions to these problems include **antifeedback units** that locate feedback and eliminate it and **compressors** that sense loud sounds and compress them, lowering the volume. However, a sound technician should pay close attention to the placement of the speakers and the volume levels of the mikes. She or he should work closely with the director to avoid stage movements that require actors to move out of areas of proper reception.

Intercom Systems   These systems are separate from the general amplification system. Consisting of a base amplifier, headsets, and either battery packs or permanent stations into which the headset connectors can be plugged, **intercom systems** allow communication between the stage manager and members of the stage crew. A two-channel system allows the stage manager to talk to a specific crew member or to the entire crew.

RECORDING EQUIPMENT

Cassette players, reel-to-reel tape players, compact disc players, and turntables allow for the addition of sound effects and pre-show and intermission music. Using cassette or reel-to-reel tape players gives the production staff the opportunity to produce their own sound effects, which can then be played through the general amplification system during the performance.

For more basic sound effects, a sound-effects board, sometimes called a bell board, can be used. A **sound-effects board** consists of several appliances—a doorbell, a door chime, a buzzer, an old-fashioned phone bell, and an electronic phone-tone maker—attached to a piece of plywood. If possible, add a phone ringer, a device that makes a phone ring onstage.

GENERAL SOUND PRINCIPLES

1. The human ear is the best judge of sound quality and volume. If possible, place the sound controls in the auditorium, perhaps centered behind the last row of seats. At least, there should always be someone from the sound crew in the audience checking the sound without a headset (although this crew member may have access to a headset for communications).

2. Each night's show will be unique. At a comedy, for instance, audiences will laugh at different lines from night to night. Performers may alter their positions near microphones and may even alter their delivery. The sound crew must always be ready to adjust to the changes to produce the best possible sound for each show.

3. Professional sound and acoustics experts should equalize the sound system—that is, balance it to the room (auditorium)—and then seal it so the main equalizer cannot be tampered with.

4. Sound levels for mikes, monitors, and accessories must be determined before a performance. Speakers, singers, and actors must arrive early for sound testing. Then everyone can be assured that the equipment is ready; no one will be tempted to tap a mike head (which can damage it badly) or say "Testing, testing" or "Is this thing on?" in the audience's hearing.

5. Sound needs may vary for the same auditorium at different times of the year. Heavy clothing worn by audience members will absorb surprising amounts of sound; in winter, therefore, mikes can be turned up a little. Adjustments may have to be made even after a performance starts if there is considerable coughing in the audience.

6. A microphone should "precede" the user—that is, it should be turned up a bit before the user speaks and then be brought up to its full level as the speaker begins. This technique prevents two common distractions: one is an "explosion" of sound that happens when the mike is turned up to full the moment the speaker begins; the second is the embarrassing "silence with moving lips" that happens when the mike is turned up too late.

7. Caution speakers about "swallowing the mike"—that is, standing too close to it. This can cause plosive sounds (such as *bŭh* and *pŭh*) to "pop" distractingly.

8. SAFETY: Use duct tape to secure all cables in traffic areas.

❄ Sound Effects

Sound effects are essential for most productions. A ringing telephone, a barking dog, and a thunderstorm are examples of sound effects often required in stage productions.

There are two main types of sound effects used for stage productions: live and recorded effects. Live sound effects are sounds made at the time they are heard by using special props. For example, if a telephone is necessary for a production, a real telephone onstage can be wired to the sound-effects board. Because the phone rings on cue and stops ringing when the actor picks it up, real effects like these help to ensure that the timing of the sound effect coincides with the action in the play. In the same way, building real doors and installing real doorbells also add to the believability of a production. If a script calls for a slamming door offstage, but a door is not needed as scenery, miniature (scale) doors can be built to produce the sound effect backstage.

Many live sound effects are made by special machines. For example, a thunder machine uses a large sheet of galvanized iron that hangs from a bar. When struck, the iron sheet rumbles and makes the sound of thunder. In addition to conventional machines, using everyday objects imaginatively provides an inexpensive way to produce sound effects. For example, to make the sound of raindrops falling, drop dry sand or uncooked rice onto a tambourine; crumple a large sheet of cellophane to produce the sound of fire. For a safe and tidy way to make the sound of glass breaking, shake a tightly sealed box of broken glass.

Recorded sound effects are being used more and more in stage productions today. For much of the twentieth century, sound effects were recorded onto vinyl phonograph records and cued for stage productions, but trying to place the needle on the precise groove of the record at the precise moment often led to errors. Fortunately, tape players and, more recently, compact disc players have made recorded sound effects easier to cue. Any sound can be professionally recorded on tape or compact disc for reproduction during a play. Some popular recorded effects include traffic noises, sirens approaching or departing, the audio portion of a television program, and the sounds of natural disasters (for example, earthquakes or tornadoes). Recorded effects are especially successful when used with real props. For example, a radio used as an onstage prop can be wired to backstage sound equipment. When the actor turns the prop on, the recorded radio show sounds as if the prop produced it. For greater authenticity, place the speaker onstage near the prop.

There are many ways to obtain recorded sound effects for a production. Various theater supply companies sell previously recorded sound-effects tapes and compact discs at a small cost. Sound-effects recordings are also available for specific productions, but always be certain to obtain permission to use prerecorded sound effects that fall under copyright laws. The fee for permission to use these effects is often very low.

It is also possible to record your own sound effects. A synthesizer or a keyboard can produce a variety of interesting sound effects. Many computers are equipped with programs that make, record, and store original sound effects. When making your own sound effects, be sure to record them in the order in which they will be played. If you have a reel-to-reel tape recorder, splice in white or colored leader tape (tape that does not record) between sound effects and label each effect on the leader tape.

🌿 *Planning Sound*

▼ CUE

To produce high-quality sound, set the volume level low on the tape player or record player, and control the volume of the sound on the amplifier.

Pre-show music and intermission music add a professional touch to a production. Select the music carefully to match the style and mood of the show. Monitor the volume level carefully because the noise from a talking audience may call for an adjustment of the music level downward for comfort. Unless you have chosen works in the public domain, be sure to obtain permission and pay any fee required to use the music.

A **sound plot** shows the pieces of equipment and their settings for each sound in the show, including music, actors' dialogue, and sound effects. If a show has much live sound or live mixing of music, it is wise to schedule separate sound-plotting sessions to make the technical rehearsal go more smoothly.

A **sound cue sheet** includes each sound effect, its cue number, the script page number, the name of the effect, the volume level, and the length in seconds of the effect. The stage manager should have all sound cues marked in the promptbook and should call all sound cues, including microphone warm-up cues. The stage manager should decide how to alter the sound levels and timing for each performance's specific conditions.

Application
ACTIVITY

With a partner, choose a scene, perhaps from "A Treasury of Scenes and Monologues," and plan the sound and sound effects. Design a sound plot and a sound cue sheet. Refer to the lighting plot and lighting cue sheet on pages 461 and 463.

Summary and Key Ideas

Summarize the chapter by answering the following questions.

1. Describe several ways in which lighting enhances a performance.
2. Identify the lighting equipment necessary for a musical production in your high school.
3. Describe Fresnels, floodlights, and striplights.
4. What is the most common error in the lighting of high school plays?
5. What information is included in a lighting plan and cue sheet? In a sound cue sheet?
6. Describe the use of four kinds of microphones.

Discussing Ideas

1. If you were lighting a single figure in a simple white costume standing against a white background on a fairly small stage, describe how you could produce the following atmospheres: (a) supernatural—the figure is an angel or a friendly alien; (b) eerie—the figure is evil, a murderer, perhaps; (c) comic—the figure is a happy clown.
2. Why do people working on costumes, makeup, and set painting need to communicate with the lighting crew?
3. How might natural light sources such as sunlight affect the light plot?
4. Why is speaker placement important?

FOCUS ON ▶ Stage Technicians

If you love science, computers, or working with your hands, good news. Your skills are much needed in the theater. The people who build the sets, handle the props, and run the equipment are vital to the success of any professional production.

Exploring Careers Learn more about how to turn mechanical or technical skills into a career in the arts. Choose one of the following to research: lighting technician, sound board operator, carpenter, or stage manager. Besides finding information in books and on the Internet, you may want to write a letter to your local theater company requesting an interview with one of their stage technicians. Share what you learn with the class.

Comparing Careers Choose an arts career that you learned about in a different chapter, such as musician or radio announcer. Then make a chart comparing and contrasting that career with the technical career you researched. Your chart should show the training, skills, and discipline each career path requires. Which career would suit you better? Write a paragraph explaining your answer.

LIGHTING AND SOUND

INDEPENDENT
ACTIVITIES

Supporting Pantomime   Imagine that you have been asked to do the sound and lighting for a pantomime. The performer will be dressed in mostly white (with only a few touches of black) and will wear white makeup. How will you highlight the subtlety of gesture and expression? What sound effects and music will add to the performance? Create a detailed light plot for the pantomime presentation. Explain to your classmates the rationale for your decisions, and demonstrate, if possible, how this performance will look under the lights. Describe and demonstrate your sound effects and music.

Music and Sound Effects   Select several poetry excerpts from the Application Activities in Chapter 3, and plan a poetry reading. Devise music and sound effects that will enhance the poems. If possible, produce a recording of your sound track for the class and have someone read the poetry in time with your sound cues.

Cooperative Learning Activity

Creating Mood and Atmosphere

Color, light, and sound add emotional overtones that can either support or detract from the overall effect of a dramatic presentation. With a group of your classmates, discuss the colors, lighting effects, music, and sound effects that you would use to create the following atmospheres or moods.

- A reunion between a pair of long-separated lovers
- An enchanted forest
- A secret attic room that has not been entered for twenty-five years
- A family gathering with a typical mixture of affection and conflict
- The office of an executive who is about to be fired

Across the CURRICULUM *Activities*

Science   In a play, lighting has the capacity to establish important background information about the time of day, the weather, and even the season during which the action takes place. Based on what you know about the positions of the sun and the moon and weather in general, how might you show changing time and weather conditions onstage? Write a brief report as part of your planning.

History   During the Middle Ages there were distinct differences between the ways in which nobility and serfs lived. Imagine that your drama club is doing a production with a medieval setting and you have been asked to design the lighting. How will you show the differences between the classes? Create a light plot that illustrates your solution.

12 *Costuming*

In addition to establishing a time period, a costume reveals much about the personality of its wearer. Captain Hook's costume in *Peter Pan* indicates that Hook is proud, authoritarian, and vain.

*T*he thing about performance, even if it's only an illusion, is that it is a celebration of the fact that we do contain within ourselves infinite possibilities.

—DANIEL DAY LEWIS, ACTOR

SETTING THE SCENE

Focus Questions

Why is effective costuming important to a good production?

What is color coding?

What is a costume parade?

What is the most important consideration in a period costume?

What is the key to believable period costuming?

How do you determine whether to rent, borrow, or make costumes?

How do you measure for costumes?

Vocabulary

color coding	costume silhouette	wardrobe manager
swatch	costume plot	dressers
costume parade	building	

Costuming is one of the integral parts of play production. The costume is not merely a means of characterizing a role as effectively as possible. In its color and silhouette, it is also a vital part of the total stage design. If the color of a costume is not in harmony with other colors on the stage or if it is not appropriate to the historical period of the play, it can destroy the atmosphere of the production, no matter how beautiful it may be in itself or how flattering it is to the actor. A wise director will therefore work very early in the planning stages of the production with the designer and the person in charge of costumes to be sure that each costume is appropriate in all respects.

❧ *Effective Costuming*

A costume should express the personality of the character. It should reveal social status, tastes, and idiosyncrasies. It should aid the audience's understanding of the actor's relationship to the other characters and to the play itself. The costume may be in harmony with others onstage or in strong contrast to them. **Color coding**—matching characters by color or pattern—can provide a subtle means of identifying members of the same family, the same group, or pairs of lovers.

In any production, the effect of a costume on both the actor and the audience is what counts onstage. Since costuming is a part of the total design of a production, actors usually have little to do with the design of their costumes. The taste of the director and designer, not the actor, must govern the choice of material and color. Ultimately, the meaning of the play must control all costume decisions.

Often, in high school productions, which almost always have limited budgets, costumes are designed or rented only for period or stylized plays. For contemporary plays, student actors

These ancient Greek costumes are historically accurate, yet simple to make.

Medieval garb for both men and women of the upper class often included an elaborate headdress. These costumes are typical of 15th-century dress in Burgundy, now part of France.

are frequently asked to find something from their own wardrobes. This works if the student is portraying someone of the same age, personality type, social position, and so on, but this is rarely the case. For most plays, the actors' personal wardrobes cannot provide suitable costumes without some modifications. Ideally, then, all costumes should be designed or provided for all actors in all plays.

Inexperienced actors are usually reluctant to appear as anything but attractive on the stage, forgetting that the audience should react to the characters within the context of the play, not to the individuals playing the parts. No director will ever deliberately insist on unbecoming or ludicrous lines or colors unless they are necessary to the correct interpretation of the play. The psychological effect of being comfortably costumed, however, greatly assists an actor's work. Understanding the theories of costuming helps actors cooperate intelligently in wearing whatever is designed for them in their roles.

COSTUME DESIGN

The first step in costume design, as in all phases of theater production, is to study the play carefully. The costume designer should then meet with the director, scenic designer, and technical director to discuss costumes that will fit the theme, style, period, colors, scenery, lighting, and budget. Together they can then choose materials for costumes. Measurements of the cast should be taken and preliminary sketches should be made.

▼ CUE

Long and flowing costumes can be a safety hazard. Designers should avoid them unless the play requires them. When such costumes are essential, actors should practice walking in clothing of the style.

The stripes, rigid shoulders, and detailed collars make these costumes identifiable as English Tudor dress from around 1530.

CUE ▼

Ask the designer to modify your costume if you have any safety concerns. Make sure that your costume will not make you fall or overheat under hot lights. Masks should allow you to breathe easily and see clearly.

Before costumes are sewn, fabric samples, or **swatches**, should be tried under the lighting planned for the show. The lighting might be changed, however, and it is almost always the costumer who must make adjustments. Once the fabrics are selected, the costumes can be sewn and fitted. A wise costumer will have actors wear the costumes under the lights again before making the final fitting and adding the trim. This is called a **costume parade** and is part of the production schedule. Once each costume is completed, it should be checked one last time under the lights before the dress rehearsal.

When designing costumes for a historical or period play, keep in mind that a historically accurate costume is not always

Familiar details can subtly make period costumes seem less foreign to a modern audience. These actors' contemporary hairdos will add a familiar touch to their Restoration costumes from around 1660.

essential; it might even have a negative effect on the production. Authentic costumes, especially those that expose parts of the body, such as Egyptian, Greek, or Roman costumes, might make a particular actor uncomfortable. It is better to adapt the costume to the actor than to insist on historical correctness. Every historical or national costume has two or three identifying characteristics that are enough to give the impression of the era or geographical region. A collar, cape, belt, or hat may be all the audience needs to accept the costume as being of a given time and place. The addition of a few accessories such as jewelry, handkerchiefs, or gloves will make the costume seem complete.

These Colonial American costumes are complete right down to the buckles on the man's shoes. They date from around 1775, or the late eighteenth century.

Attention to the complete effect is essential to a production. Inappropriateness in details such as shoes, hats, purses, fans, jewelry, and parasols can ruin the harmony of the design and mood of the play. Any masks, wigs, and hairpieces must also contribute to the total effect.

All accessories should be obtained as early as possible so that the actors can use them during rehearsals. If the real accessories are not readily available, actors should have appropriate substitutes. Several weeks of rehearsals are necessary for an actor to appear natural when using accessories such as opera glasses, a monocle, a sword, or a cane. When such accessories are added at the last minute, actors might look and feel awkward. They might also discover that their well-rehearsed stage movements no longer work. For example, an actor who will be wearing a costume with a wide hoop skirt might not be able to maneuver through narrow passages; nor will she be able to get close to another person or object without the back of the hoop tipping up embarrassingly. If the hoop skirt is not available during rehearsals, a hoop alone might be used to create the same effect.

The time period from the late eighteenth century through the mid-nineteenth century (about 1850) is characterized by a wide range of clothing, from the formal attire shown in the two photos here to the fur hats and buckskins worn by traders.

Simplicity of both design and color characterize these 1890s costumes.

These costumes from 1905 feature a straw boater and a cane for the man, a hat and short cape for the woman.

 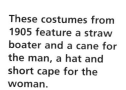

When designing costumes for a cast of characters, costumers should remember that not everyone follows the dictates of fashion. While some people dress in the height of fashion, others continue to dress in styles from previous years or choose classic styles that change very little over a period of years. There are those who wear offbeat, unusual, or bizarre clothing that suits their nonconformist personalities. There are still others whose economic status does not allow for a new wardrobe every time the styles change. Accordingly, play characters who are old-fashioned, conservative, offbeat, or eccentric should be dressed in costumes that reflect their characteristics.

COSTUMERS' CONSIDERATIONS

- the kind of action that will take place
- the comfort of the actors
- the ease with which a costume can be put on and taken off, especially when costume changes are necessary
- the durability of the design and fabric
- the historical period of the play
- the total design of the production
- the director's conceptualization of the play

By 1910 women's dress had begun to reflect the influence of the automobile; silhouettes were much simpler and skirts shorter, to facilitate gracefully entering and exiting a car.

The total design of the play determines whether the costumes should be stylized. Some period plays adapt well to modern dress. Formal attire (tuxedos and evening gowns) can be worn for many plays, particularly classical tragedies. Flowing robes, mosaic patterns, or variations in black and white fabrics may also be used for certain stylized plays.

Application ACTIVITY

You are the costumer of an American play set in the present. In this play, two young people from totally different backgrounds meet and become friends. For each of the following characters, draw or describe a complete costume that would help the audience recognize the character's personality traits. If you choose to draw the costumes, label the different elements of your design. Assume the teenage characters are your age.

- teenage girl
- teenage boy
- the girl's grandmother
- the boy's father

CUE

A costume may become more comfortable as you develop a better understanding of how the costume contributes to your character's personality. However, if a costume still feels uncomfortable after several rehearsals, speak to the director about modifying the costume so that you feel more at ease onstage.

APPROPRIATENESS

Each historic period has its own distinctive line and form in dress, which is called the **costume silhouette.** Look carefully at the silhouettes in this chapter, and notice that each period has its own characteristics. If a costume does not recreate the basic silhouette of the period, it is not effective, no matter how beautiful or elaborate it might be. The cut along with the style and material must be appropriate to the social background and period of the play. This is a very important principle.

Small details become important onstage. For example, long skirts are more graceful than short ones, especially when the actor is seated. Draped scarves and stoles are very effective if they are skillfully handled. Trimming, to be noticed, must be somewhat conspicuous. Lapels and pockets may be outlined with trim so that they can be distinguished from the jacket.

The 1920s marked a drastic change in fashion. Women's hemlines now displayed not only ankles but also calves for the first time, and hip-level sashes were often worn.

Compare this woman's costume from the 1930s and the woman's costume from the 1920s. The 1930s dress is much more conservative.

By the 1940s, women had begun to enter the workplace in greater numbers, and their clothes reflected that fact.

On the stage, certain problems of dress are also intensified. To avoid problems, an actor should check his or her appearance in a full-length mirror at a distance to get a proper perception of how he or she will appear onstage. The director should observe every costume from various parts of the auditorium. Costumes should fit well and bring out the best physical characteristics of the actor—unless a particular role dictates otherwise. It takes time in rehearsal to make a different style of clothing feel natural. The actor must not be self-conscious in the costume if it is to look authentic. Sometimes high school performers "pull back" in their roles because they feel ill at ease in their costumes. A director must be sensitive to the feelings of the actors and not ask that they wear costumes that might make them feel embarrassed or uncomfortable.

No matter how appropriate the costume, the actor must learn to wear the costume properly. He or she must seem natural and at ease, knowing the maximum stretch or reach allowable, how to turn and sit, and how to remove scarves and gloves or snap a fan.

COLOR, LINE, AND MATERIAL

Costume designers must treat every character in a play as an individual. Each character's costume must somehow reflect that character's station in life, personality, idiosyncrasies, or philosophy. At the same time, all the costumes in a play must go with each other in basic design. The color, line, and material of the costumes all contribute to this basic design.

In *Beauty and the Beast,* the color, line, and material of the Beast's costume suggests that there is more to this character than one might have expected of an animal—such qualities as style, elegance, wealth, and taste.

Costumes for contemporary comedies, farces, children's plays, and fantasies are normally made of light material in bright or pastel colors. Restoration comedy calls for costumes made of satins, laces, and brocades, and the costumes usually exemplify an overemphasis on style as much as the characters themselves do. High comedy often deals with characters of taste and social grace; costumes for these fashionable characters require careful selection of color and material and also special attention to line.

In realistic plays, designers can use almost any material that will create costumes suitable for the characters' personalities and for the overall stage picture. In symbolic and allegorical plays, audiences tend to assume that the costumes are part of the symbolic meaning of the play. Therefore, extra thought should be given to the fabric, texture, and pattern of costumes for these types of plays.

The color of a costume has a lot to do with how the audience responds to a character. A pale yellow will make an actor appear young and light in spirit. Maroon suggests martyrdom and suffering. Refer to the list on page 422 for additional emotional values of colors.

▼ CUE

Costumes for tragedies are usually made from heavy materials in muted or dark colors in order to convey the desired somber effect to the audience.

The costumes for *Starlight Express* utilize a variety of materials that include padding and roller skates.

In general, blondes should wear cool colors, with touches of warm color contrast, and delicate designs and materials. Dark-haired performers should wear warm colors; they can risk brilliant fabrics and stronger color contrasts. Ordinarily redheads should emphasize their coloring by wearing yellow, orange, green, and golden brown.

Designers must keep the individual actor's body shape in mind when creating a costume. Garment lines should harmonize with those of the body without constriction or exaggeration. The following chart shows costume features that can affect the appearance of a character onstage.

Costume features that slenderize	Costume features that add weight
• long, vertical lines in costumes, hair styles, and hats • black, dark, muted colors • subtle patterns • non-lustrous materials • dark velvet (absorbs light; takes off pounds)	• horizontal lines in costumes (especially at the shoulder), hair styles, and hats • white or light colors • bold patterns • light, glossy materials such as satin • long clinging skirts, high hats, and V-necks

Stage lighting is another important consideration when selecting costume fabrics. Prints must be carefully tested; stage lights turn small or pale patterns into an undefined mass of color, which may create a grotesque effect. Texture not only determines the outline of the costume but also

COSTUME PLOT FOR:			MEAS. CARD	1ST FITTING	COMPLETE	OUT	IN
CHARACTER	SCENE	COSTUME DESCRIPTION					
JULIE (CINDY PHELPS)	I,i	BLUE CHECKED GINGHAM PINAFORE W/WHITE BLOUSE AND WHITE APRON. WIDE BRIMMED STRAW HAT. WHITE PARASOL	✓	✓	✓	✓	
"	I,ii	LT. GREEN COTTON BLOUSE WITH PUFFED SLEEVES. PINK SKIRT W/BUSTLE. BLACK PURSE		✓	✓	✓	

This form can be expanded to include columns for type, amount, and cost of materials.

contributes to the effects of a material under the lights. Heavy or soft materials, such as velvet, burlap, cheesecloth, and flannel, react well under stage lighting; these more inexpensive materials often appear richer than many costly fabrics. Drapery material and even carpeting have been used for costumes for this very reason. Knitted materials drape beautifully and cling to the figure, emphasizing lines.

Oilcloth, cardboard, plastics, rubber sheeting, felt, and other similar materials, including the special plastic molding materials now available, can be used for trim, accent features, and appliqués. All sorts of familiar materials can be utilized in creating bizarre or unusual outfits.

A **costume plot** should include every costume in the production. It should describe the colors, fabrics, and accessories for each design. Ruled columns placed next to the items in the costume description can be used to check off each listed task as it is completed. Such plots help assure that the costumes are ready before dress rehearsals.

Application
ACTIVITY

Working in groups of three or four, select a familiar play. It might be a contemporary comedy, a Shakespearean tragedy, a farce, or any other play. Decide on the personality traits of the main characters in the play. Then create a fabric book containing swatches of cloth that show the colors, patterns, and textures you would choose for each character's costume. The swatches can be glued or stapled to the pages of the fabric book.

❧ *Obtaining the Costumes*

One of the first problems a costume manager faces is deciding whether the costumes are to be rented, borrowed, adapted from thrift store clothing, or made. This decision must be made in time for the costumes to be collected with a minimum of effort and expense.

RENTING OR BORROWING COSTUMES

If you decide to rent costumes, be careful. Rented costumes are very expensive. Many costume companies will not have what you want or all that you need when you need it. Be particularly cautious when suppliers say they do not have quite what you requested but will fix you up with something just as appropriate.

Modern productions such as *Godspell* often do not require intricate costuming. In fact, many of the costumes for this production can be created by the actors themselves, using simple leotards as a base and adding details from thrift stores such as collars, suspenders, and hats.

If you send out of town for costumes, be prepared for a few surprises when the costumes arrive. The first surprise may be that the costumes do not fit properly. This is usually due to inaccurate measurements. The costume manager needs to know what measurements to take and how to take them. The diagram on page 497 provides instructions on how to measure for proper costume fit. Some costume houses will send costumes that are in poor condition. Substitutions are common; accessories may not be what you expect; and the use of interchangeables—such as using the same hat for several purposes simply by changing the identifying trim or badge—can result in a sameness you did not anticipate. Period boots and shoes should be part of the complete costume. Many costume houses send boot covers to be worn over regular shoes. Boot covers make poor substitutions for boots because they do not look natural when an actor walks. Also, boot covers make dancing almost impossible. Wigs are usually considered part of a rented period costume. "Perforated" wigs made of human or animal hair are much preferred to cloth-based synthetic wigs. Only when you deal with very large firms can you hope to get the footwear, wigs, colors, or patterns that you need. Otherwise, you take what they have.

One of the chief drawbacks of rented costumes is that they might be available for only one dress rehearsal or at most for only forty-eight hours prior to the first performance without additional charge. Most costume houses charge an additional fee for each performance day after the opening night. Some, however, will quote a flat rate per week including dress rehearsals and performances. Rental costumes are never available for publicity photos unless you rent them for that purpose. This can be done only if you are dealing with a local company. In general, all costume orders should be placed well in advance of dress rehearsal and performance dates. This means that measurements must be taken shortly after casting. Before committing yourself to a costume house, check to find out how far in advance orders must be placed. Your schedule might not allow for ordering from costumers too far away.

With so many reasons against renting, does renting make sense? It frequently does because appropriate costumes can enhance the overall quality of a production. Formal evening dress (especially in period styles), military or ceremonial uniforms, unusual national costumes, medieval armor, and certain special properties such as muskets, raccoon coats, tiaras, and top hats are often unobtainable from any other source.

If you do rent, often it is best to deal with a large firm or, better still, two reliable companies. The choice of costumes of an individual company for certain historical periods is usually limited, and you do not want your

CUE

Some leading costume houses can provide you with costumes actually worn in the Broadway production of a play. Such elaborate, expensive costumes are normally far beyond the budget of most high school productions, however.

Preliminary sketches of costumes should suit the play's theme, style, period, colors, scenery, lighting, and budget.

audiences to tire of seeing the same costume over and over again. If at all possible, the director, designer, and costume manager should go to the costume company personally to select the costumes to be used. If you do not rent, there is always the temptation to take the easiest, cheapest route, which usually means making numerous substitutions or using apparel completely unsuitable for the play.

Having the members of the cast buy or borrow their own costumes might seem to be the simplest method of costuming a production, but it seldom is. It is very difficult to obtain garments that will achieve the planned and desired effect, even those that at first seem easy to get. In period plays, suitable costumes lent by generous friends are apt to be valuable and fragile, and no assurance can be offered that they will not be soiled or torn. Makeup stains that will not come out, delicate lace that is snagged, and materials that disintegrate under the strain of a performance are hard to explain to the owner of such treasured heirlooms. If a play calls for modern costumes, borrowing might be a possibility. If you must borrow costumes, treat them carefully.

On the positive side, when actors borrow or buy their own costumes, there is little or no cost other than the cleaning of the borrowed costumes. As previously mentioned, it is not easy for students to look older in their own clothes, and seldom do the wardrobes of character and actor match. Also, the actor might be especially careful with a purchased costume or one that belongs to a friend or relative.

Application
ACTIVITY

Look through the phone book, and make a list of costume houses. Then call two or three places to find the following information:

- types of costumes available
- rental fees for a full production
- how the company rents (by day, week, month)
- how far in advance an order must be placed
- if the company will deliver and pick up the costumes
- charges for damaged or lost articles

MAKING YOUR OWN COSTUMES

Building is the term that costumers use for making costumes. It almost always is preferable to renting and borrowing. The cost of making costumes might be about the same as, and sometimes a little more than, the rental fee; however, the major difference is that in the end you have exactly what you want and welcome additions to the costume wardrobe, rather than just a high bill for costumes that must be returned.

There are other good reasons for building. Those students who design and make the costumes gain valuable experience and have the pride and satisfaction of seeing the part a good costume plays in creating an effective stage picture. A more uniform pattern for the play in both color and line is possible, and the costumes are made to fit individual actors. Both the costumer and the actor take a personal interest in this facet of production, and can develop a mutual respect for each other's contribution to the play. It is exciting for the designer, as well as a relief to the publicity director, to have the actual costumes available for publicity photos. It means that the publicity director can set up a poster featuring real scenes from the play.

When you are ready to make costumes, individual sketches and costume plots should include notes on the kind, amount, and cost of materials. Dyeing material creates a more satisfactory and unified costume scheme. However, it requires skill in a complex activity, a place for dyeing, and people willing to work until the job is completed. Before the dyeing is done, patterns should be cut to the exact measurements of the actors and be approved by the director, scenic designer, and actors. When all material has been dyed and checked under the lights, it may be cut from the patterns and sewn together.

CUE ▼

A wardrobe room is essential for making, storing, and caring for costumes. If your school does not already have a wardrobe room, work with classmates to establish one. Stock the wardrobe room with costumes, accessories, materials, and other necessary supplies. Spread the word around the school and community for items you could use to establish a well-stocked wardrobe room.

IMPORTANT MEASUREMENTS

- For women
  height, bust, waist, hips (approximately seven inches below natural waistline), back of neck to waist, waist to shoe tops, across back from shoulder to shoulder, and arm length from top of shoulder to wrist

- For men
  height, chest, waist, inseam, back of neck to waist, across back from shoulder to shoulder, collar size, and arm length from top of shoulder to wrist

TAKING MEASUREMENTS

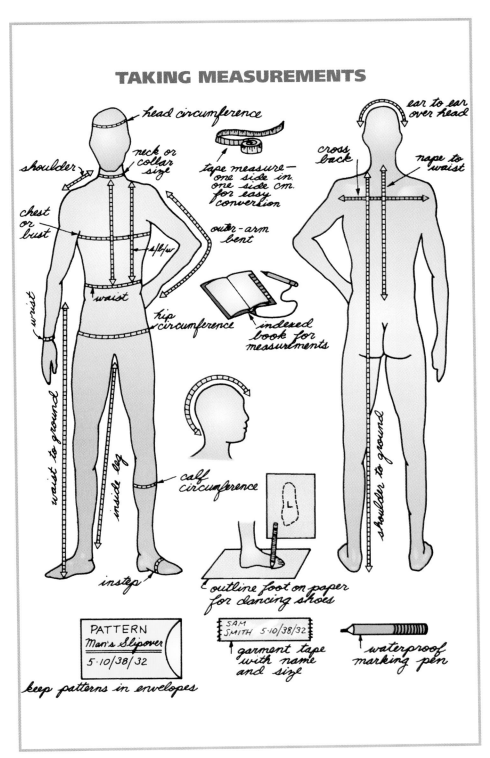

head circumference

neck or collar size

shoulder

tape measure — one side in. one side cm. for easy conversion

chest or bust

s/b/w

outer-arm bent

wrist

waist

hip circumference

indexed book for measurements

ear to ear over head

cross back

nape to waist

waist to ground

inside leg

calf circumference

instep

outline foot on paper for dancing shoes

shoulder to ground

PATTERN
Man's Slipover
5·10/38/32

keep patterns in envelopes

SAM SMITH 5·10/38/32

garment tape with name and size

waterproof marking pen

The costumes of the quintet that make up the chorus in *A Little Night Music* work with the scenery to project the desired effect: one of blending together while still maintaining each person's individuality.

The completed garments must be strong enough to stand the strain of rehearsals and performances, but they do not necessarily require elaborate, ornamental sewing. Pinking edges and basting rather than stitching are quite acceptable for much of costume making. Details, such as a row of buttons, are usually nonfunctional or "dumped" in order to save sewing time and facilitate quick changes. **Velcro**™, strips of material that adhere to each other instantly when pressure is applied, can replace unreliable zippers and can allow for the fast removal of costumes. Costumes for dancers need extra material or stretch material under the arms for greater freedom of movement. For that matter, all costumes should be built with extra material in seams, darts, and hems so that the costume can be altered for another actor in the future. Do not build a costume that will fit only one person if you plan to use it again.

Never overlook the possibility of making over old clothes or revamping old costumes. Thrift stores are often gold mines for old clothes that can be altered into costumes. It is a good practice to save fabric remnants for trim or accessories or for additions to a costume of the same material at a later date. Men's old suits can be cut and remade into cutaways without a great amount of work. Even beautiful hats can be made from a few materials, a little imagination, ten minutes in the library, and considerable patience.

The main emphasis in costume planning should be on the total effect as seen from the auditorium. A costume cannot be judged by its design alone. The costume must be observed in action onstage with the correct scenery and lighting. Costume design and construction are challenging, but the effort is rewarded by the achievement of an artistic production.

CUE ▼

When old clothes are used for costumes, make sure that they have been thoroughly washed or dry cleaned, for safety's sake.

🌿 Caring for Costumes

After the costumes have been obtained, they must be cared for during rehearsals and performances. A competent **wardrobe manager** should be chosen. The wardrobe manager will keep a costume plot as shown on page 491 and will choose responsible assistants in all the dressing rooms. Assistants, called **dressers**, help the actors with their changes, hang up clothes, keep all accessories close at hand, and see that everything is returned in good condition after the performance. The wardrobe manager sees that every costume is complete, in good repair, and identified by character and actor. Actors should have a designated place for their costumes, such as costume racks marked by tags or dividers. The wardrobe manager checks with the cast for problems that might have developed with zippers, rips, and the like, keeping needle and thread and a few handy supplies like hooks and eyes, buttons, Velcro™, and elastic on hand during all performances. An ironing board, steam iron, spray starch, and a glue gun should also be readily available.

CUE

Dressing rooms should be covered with paper if long trains or fine materials are worn. Protruding nails, unexpected steps, low ceilings, and other backstage hazards should be eliminated or clearly identified.

After the performance all borrowed clothing should be dry-cleaned or washed before being returned to the owner. Also, the wardrobe manager should see that all school costumes are cleaned and stored. However, before any costume is returned or stored, it should be checked carefully for any needed repairs. After almost every production, some costumes will need to be repaired or, in extreme cases, replaced. Some makeup, powder, spirit gum, and nail polish are almost impossible to remove. Torn fabrics can seldom be mended satisfactorily. The cost of any repairs or replacements should be included in the budget. Each actor and the costume director must personally see that every costume, accessory, and all property is returned in the condition in which it was received.

Application
ACTIVITIES

1. Work with a partner to compare the costs of renting, buying, or building costumes. First select a play; then, using a chart, list the main characters, their costumes, and the cost of each option for obtaining the costumes.

2. Make a checklist of a wardrobe manager's and an actor's costume responsibilities. Display the poster in your wardrobe room.

CHAPTER 12 REVIEW

Summary and Key Ideas

Summarize the chapter by answering the following questions.

1. What can a costume reveal about a character?
2. What is color coding? How is it used for character identification?
3. When in the production schedule should a costume parade take place?
4. When could the attempt to create historically accurate costumes have a negative effect on a production?
5. What is a costume silhouette? Why must it be accurate for costumes to be effective?
6. List the important measurements for men and women.
7. What are the positive and negative aspects of renting costumes?
8. What are the major benefits of building your own costumes?

Discussing Ideas

1. Costume designers recognize that styles change over time. Discuss styles that have been popular during the last five years.
2. Discuss the problems you might encounter in your own school if you chose to rent costumes. Decide if renting would be practical.
3. Discuss the feasibility of building your own costumes for a production. How would you proceed? Whose help could you seek?

FOCUS ON — Period Clothing

Learning about period clothing can give you insight into the lives of people in different cultures and eras. Clothing reveals much about an era's material conditions, social divisions, and values.

Evaluating Costumes Using the Internet as a launching point, do research into the clothing people wore in the United States at the time of the Civil War. Then watch at least two movies, television shows, or live plays set during that time. With a partner, discuss the role that costumes played in each production. Were the costumes historically accurate? Did the costumes make the productions more believable? Did the costumes enhance other elements of the productions, such as the acting? Write a brief summary of your discussion.

Exploring Careers From what you've learned, how important do you think it is for a costume designer to understand the history of clothing? What else might designers need to understand? Do research to learn about the training that costume professionals typically receive. Share your discoveries in a short presentation to the class.

COSTUMING

INDEPENDENT ACTIVITY

Show, Don't Tell Costuming serves multiple purposes in a play. In addition to indicating the historical period, the clothing that a character wears can illustrate his or her age, social status, occupation, and state of mind. Costuming may also indicate a character's relationships with others and may reinforce the dramatic tension in the play. Keeping these things in mind, choose a period play and imagine that you are the costume designer. Decide what costumes the cast will need and how the costumes should look. You might want to make sketches of some or all of the costumes. Suggest colors, fabrics, and accessories for the costumes you design. Then create a costume plot for the cast. Some of the plays that you may want to consider include *The Tempest, Tartuffe, The Octoroon, The Three Sisters,* and *The Importance of Being Earnest.*

Cooperative Learning Activity

Representational Costuming

With a group of your classmates, choose a modern play that interests you, such as Eugene O'Neill's *Long Day's Journey into Night,* Bertolt Brecht's *The Good Woman of Setzuan,* Eugène Ionesco's *The Bald Soprano,* or Harold Pinter's *The Homecoming.* Read the play aloud together and discuss the conflict, characters, atmosphere, and theme. The group should choose a specific scene to dramatize, and each person should choose a character to portray. Without discussing costuming, group members should bring to class several articles of clothing and accessories that represent their characters and aid in their characterization. Discuss each article's suitability, and present a "dress rehearsal" for the rest of the class.

Across the CURRICULUM Activities

Sewing/Tailoring Your drama class is planning to do a production of *My Fair Lady* for the local elementary schools. Because some actors will have to play dual roles, as both Cockney men and women and ladies and gentlemen at Ascot, the director has asked you to come up with some ways in which costume changes can be accomplished with a minimum of effort and expense. Design a basic costume that can be used for these two different roles with only minor additions or subtractions.

History Building authentic-looking yet practical and comfortable historical costumes is a goal of costume designers. Do some research into the clothing styles of your favorite period in history. Then make some suggestions on how to achieve authenticity as well as practicality. Accompany your suggestions with sketches or a model.

CHAPTER 13 Makeup

In China, theater makeup is stylized. The eyes are emphasized and the mouth stands out against the foundation color of the cheeks. With this makeup, even a tiny change in an actor's expression can be read by all audience members.

cting deals with very delicate emotions. It is not putting up a mask. Each time an actor acts he [she] does not hide; he [she] expresses himself [herself].

—JEANNE MOREAU, ACTOR

SETTING THE SCENE

Focus Questions

Why use stage makeup?

What belongs in a makeup kit?

How do you create highlights and shadows?

What wigs and beards work best?

What effect does stage lighting have on makeup?

Vocabulary

chiaroscuro	highlighting	facial mask
foundation	shadowing	blender
matte	blocked out	prosthetics

*M*akeup should be one of the most rewarding phases of your dramatic experience. Most stage actors design and apply their own makeup. To help acquire the makeup skills essential to every performer, you should study faces to see how they show the effects of age and emotion. Take special note of differences in skin color and texture, places where wrinkles occur, prominent bone structure, folds in the flesh, as well as the direction and patterns of hair growth. You will find that the changes that take place in facial expression are closely related to the changes in personality, stature, and voice that occur when an actor develops an effective characterization. Bone structure is key to facial makeup. Every student needs to know the bone-muscle relationship and how it alters with age and differs with ethnicity. It is essential that you study your own bone structure carefully before designing makeup for a role.

❦ *The Basics*

The techniques of makeup application are closely related to the portrait artist's approach: the face is made a blank mask and then the principles of **chiaroscuro**—the use of highlight and shadow—are applied to model the features into the desired effect. Makeup should be designed on a makeup worksheet similar to the one on the next page.

Before completing the worksheet, you will need to carefully consider the stage setting and its impact on the actors' makeup. On the school stage, makeup must be handled with special care. Youthful faces do not always lend themselves readily to older roles, and heavy makeup inexpertly applied looks "tacked on." Only a slight amount of foundation should be used. It is much better to use too little than to use too much. For classwork, a little makeup and an appropriate hairstyle can suggest age and ethnicity effectively.

When you design makeup for a large production, however, the makeup requirements change considerably. The larger the auditorium or the more dramatic the lighting, the more makeup is needed. Stage lights can wash the color from an actor's face until the face has a pasteboard effect. Too much light from above results in deep shadows under all the bony prominences. In addition, there must be proper lighting from the sides. Otherwise shadows distort the actor's face; the eyes can appear lost in deep sockets, and the nose may take on strange shapes. Unfortunately, few high school productions use side lighting.

Be sure to set aside enough time to apply your makeup without hurrying. Your appearance will be the first thing the audience notices about you. These two photos show Joel Grey applying makeup for his role as the master of ceremonies in *Cabaret*.

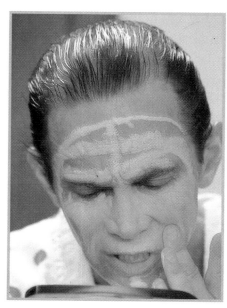

MAKEUP WORKSHEET

PLAY:_____

CHARACTER:_____

ACTOR:_____

Foundation:_____
Eye shadow:_____
Eyeliner:_____
Moist Rouge:_____
Dry Rouge:_____
Shadow:_____
Highlight:_____
Powder:_____

Hair:_____
         Style:_____
         Color:_____
Beard/mustache:_____
Forehead:_____
Eyes:_____
Cheeks:_____
Nose:_____
Mouth:_____
Prosthetics:_____
Special:_____

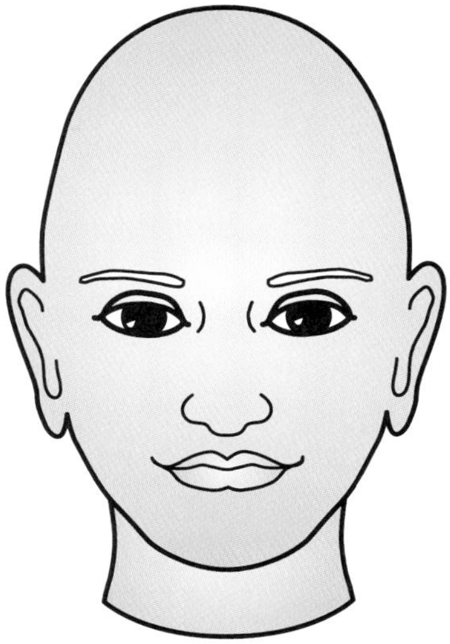

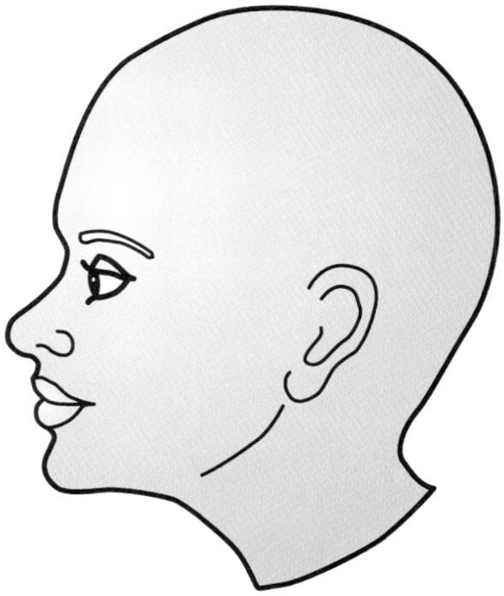

Proper care of makeup supplies, the kit, and the makeup room is essential. Designate a makeup crew to handle all supplies and always have a complete makeup kit available for emergencies.

Makeup plays an integral part in the development of any character, and most high schools keep a well-stocked makeup kit as a backup to the actors' own kits. Makeup is a very personal thing, and many amateurs and all stage professionals have their own personal kits. This is a matter not just of individual makeup requirements but also of hygiene. The dangers of passing bacteria, viruses, and skin ailments from one person to another have caused many high school directors to require students to furnish their own makeup supplies. If you are really interested in drama, you should begin assembling your own personal makeup kit. Excellent starter kits are available from leading makeup manufacturers.

MAKEUP KIT ESSENTIALS

foundation: Foundation, or base, makeup comes in creme, stick, or pancake. Shades range from light pink to dark sunburn to very dark brown. For older character parts, you may need to mix various tones.

clown white: This is a special foundation color used for stylized makeup and highlighting. It comes in greasepaint or pancake form.

face powders: They come in translucent or in shades that harmonize with the foundation.

moist rouge: This comes in light, medium, and dark shades.

liners: These are greasepaints in such colors as blue, brown, green, violet, maroon, yellow, and white.

lipsticks: Women use moist rouge or stage lipstick; men use brownish rouge, if anything.

lipstick brush: This brush should only be found in personal makeup kits.

makeup pencils: Brown, maroon, red, and black pencils are needed.

dry rouge: This is available in many shades.

mascara: This cosmetic for coloring the eyelashes and eyebrows comes in black, brown, and white.

cold cream, Albolene™, mineral oil, baby oil, or *makeup remover:* These are used for dissolving and removing makeup.

powder puffs: Keep both the large and small sizes.

absorbent cotton: This has many uses.

powder brush: This is used for removing excess powder.

hair whitener: White mascara, liquid white shoe polish, clown white, or washout hair colorants can be used.

hair colorants: These are used to change hair color temporarily.

liquid body makeup: This is used in a shade that matches the foundation.

sable or *camel hair brushes* and *round toothpicks* or *lining pencils:* Use for lining eyes, highlighting, and shadowing.

A makeup kit is one of an actor's most important tools.

crepe hair: This is available in shades to match most natural hair colors.

spirit gum and spirit gum remover (or alcohol): Spirit gum can be used to attach mustache, etc.

liquid latex: Use to attach beards and build up features.

nose putty or derma wax, black tooth enamel, white tooth enamel, and artificial blood: Use these to build up features and make scars and wounds.

collodion: Material used for building up the flesh or texturing the skin.

miscellaneous supplies: large mirrors, cleansing tissues, hand mirror, comb, brush, scissors, needles, black and white thread, straight pins, hairpins, bobby pins, safety pins, paper towels, and soap

For group makeup, individual portions of base, soft liners, and moist rouge may be placed on a piece of wax paper—much like an artist's palette. This will allow each performer to have her or his own makeup supply. Care must be taken by the crew not to mix the individual portions into one another. Sanitation and sterilization are extremely important! Crew members should wash their hands frequently with an antibacterial soap and rinse with rubbing alcohol. Personal makeup kits, including combs and brushes, should never be shared!

Application
ACTIVITY

Assemble a portfolio of pictures showing close-ups of interesting faces that you might want to use as models. Accumulate pictures from sources such as cartoons, magazines, and photographs. What makes each face unique? What makes it interesting to you?

🌿 *Straight Makeup: The Six Steps*

Straight makeup is used when the character to be played is very similar in age and characteristics to the actor. These principles apply for high school students playing roles from the early teens through the mid-twenties. Procedures for older roles are discussed later in the chapter.

Make preparations for makeup well in advance—at least half an hour for a straight role and an hour for a character part. Men should be clean-shaven but should never shave less than half an hour before applying makeup. Actors, male and female, should always check with the director before getting a haircut or changing hairstyles.

Before applying makeup, cleanse your face thoroughly. Then moisten the fingertips with cold water and cool the surface of your face. Actors with oily skin may need to use an astringent to assure a dry surface before applying makeup. The use of a non-greasy moisturizer under a clown white or other full foundation will create a uniform facial texture and will help later during makeup removal.

STEP ONE: THE FOUNDATION

The first step in the makeup process is the application of the correct **foundation** base color. The foundation turns the face into a blank mask upon which facial features are accentuated and shaped with makeup. The

Powder is used to remove the shininess caused by creme foundation. Be sure to apply only a light coat of powder, though, or your face will appear too dry and your features will be hidden.

foundation also provides pigment to replace that which is washed out by stage lights and gives a character color to help create a visual impression. Even dark skin may appear ashen without foundation, since the lights can drain away much of the natural pigment color.

There are two types of foundation that actors usually wear for the stage today: creme makeup and cake (pancake) makeup. Creme is preferred because of its ease of blending, and it works well with soft liners. The foundation base color should be selected according to the character's age, ethnicity, health, occupation, and experiences. Generally speaking, men use darker foundations than women.

Creme base is usually applied directly with the fingers after a few spots have been dabbed on the face and neck. However, it may also be applied with a rubber or synthetic sponge. Although a creme base is not overly greasy, it does require powdering because it reacts to body heat and has a tendency to become shiny when moist. Consequently, some actors like to powder a creme foundation with translucent powder, pat the surface with a moist sponge, and then apply more makeup. A thin coat should be spread over the face and all exposed parts of the head and neck areas, including the ears. The foundation should be worked gently into the hairline to avoid a halo effect around the face. Creme base should also be spread into the collar line, the back of the neck, and as far down the chest as is exposed or where body makeup will be applied. If the upper torso will be seen, move about, stretch, gesture, or reach as you would in a performance. This will help you determine how much of the chest and shoulders needs to be covered with makeup.

Cake (pancake) foundation was originally designed for motion picture makeup but has become quite popular with many stage actors, particularly actors in school groups. Cake makeup goes on easily with a damp sponge or brush—a natural silk sponge works best. If cake highlights, shadows, and rouge are used, there is no need to powder. In fact, a light final coat of cake foundation sets and softens the total makeup effect. Since it is water-soluble, pancake makeup washes off easily after the performance. In spite of its easy application and cleanup, however, the disadvantages of pancake makeup often outweigh the advantages. Pancake makeup melts under heat and runs under perspiration. In addition, pancake makeup is very difficult to mix and does not blend well with soft liners. Most high school makeup kits have only grease liners, which are not compatible with the **matte** (flat) finish of cake foundation. Therefore, most makeup experts do not recommend pancake makeup for use by young, inexperienced actors.

▼ **CUE**

Certain foundation colors are typically used for particular characters or character types.

Pinks blonds and children
Yellows ill or anemic characters
Tans healthy, active characters
Reds blustery, robust, or weather-worn characters

STEP TWO: SHADOWS AND HIGHLIGHTS

The application of shadow and highlight is really the most important aspect of modeling the face. **Highlighting** and **shadowing** are used for three purposes:

1. to bring out features
2. to correct features
3. to change features to indicate age, character, or physical impairments

For shadowing, use a base at least five shades darker than the foundation color, or use brown, reddish-brown, or maroon lining color. Never use gray except for extreme makeup, for it makes the face look skull-like or dirty.

Every shadow has a highlight. For highlighting, use a base at least five shades lighter than the foundation, or use yellow or white liner. White is usually best to use for actors with light complexions. For more olive skin tones, light tan or yellow is preferred. For darker skinned actors a light brown or yellow will give the desired results. If your chin, nose, or brows are too prominent, blend a shadow over that part of the face. If, on the other hand, some part of your face is not emphasized enough, apply a highlight to that area. It is almost always necessary to shadow the sides of the nose and highlight the bridge in order for the nose to be seen under bright stage lights.

The highlights and deep shadows in Richard Kavanaugh's makeup enhance his portrayal of a deranged follower of Count Dracula.

Dark skinned performers need to highlight the outer edge of their nostrils in order to maintain the nose's three-dimensional quality.

Next, lightly shadow the "laugh wrinkle"—the wrinkle that runs from the nostril to the outer corner of the mouth. Begin by applying shadow to the crease of the wrinkle and blend toward the cheek. Then, smile and apply the highlight to the rounded ridge of the cheek that is formed. Finally, gently blend the highlight and shadow together. A camel hair brush is the most satisfactory tool for lining, but a round toothpick may work quite well if you are careful to make the lines thin and sharp before blending them out. Also, a makeup pencil may be used if the point is kept wedge-shaped and sharp.

STEP THREE: ROUGE AND LIPSTICK

Apply moist rouge to cheeks and lips next. For a feminine straight part, select a color that blends with your hair color, the foundation, and your costume. Place the moist rouge where it will help shape your face to that of your character. Dark skinned actors should use an orange-red or copper tone. The manner in which you apply the rouge will vary according to the shape of your face.

Oval Face	Apply in a crescent shape to the cheekbone and blend up and out.
Round Face	Blend along the cheekbone and downward closer to the nose.
Long Face	Place high on the cheekbone and blend out toward the temples.

Blending is always important in makeup, but especially when applying moist rouge. You should never see where the rouge ends unless your character is a person who is obviously overly made up. Men should use moist rouge sparingly—just enough for a healthy glow. Although rouge may be washed out under strong light, it often gives the same effect as shadowing. Use very little, if any, rouge for night scenes, since both blue and green lights will turn red into a dark brown or purplish black.

Female actors should use moist rouge or stage lipstick for the lips, because with the many pigments found in commercial lipsticks, it is impossible to predict how they will react under modern lighting. Male actors, if they use lip makeup, should use brown or reddish-brown lining color.

Lipstick may be applied with the little finger if the natural lip line is followed. If the shape of the lips is to be altered or emphasized, however, a lipstick brush should be used. The lips should be **blocked out** by covering the outer edges with the foundation when it is applied, and the new shape should be drawn on. Outlining the newly shaped lips with a darker red, brown, or black helps to define the new shape. The lower lip should receive a slightly lighter shade or should be highlighted a little, since the lower lip naturally catches more light.

For female actors the shape of the lips is determined by the role. The lipstick should be blended on the inside so that a definite line is not

▼ **CUE**

Always be certain that your makeup is safe for your skin type. There are special makeups for sensitive skins or for people with allergies. Some makeups, such as glitter, should never be used near the eyes.

visible when the mouth is open. It is important that the corners of the mouth receive just enough rouge to define the mouth against the foundation. This is particularly important for musicals because the mouth is opened very wide when singing. It is usually inadvisable to "roll" the lips to distribute the color as is often done for everyday makeup. Rolling the lips can make the lip shape lose definition and therefore not project well to the audience. Blotting should be done gently for the same reason.

STEP FOUR: EYES AND EYEBROWS

Applying makeup to the eyes and brows is the next step. The eyes and the mouth are the most expressive features of the face, and the brows give the greatest character to the eyes. The purpose of eye shadow is to beautify the eyes, to make them seem larger, and to indicate character. Apply eye shadow to the upper lids only, beginning with a heavy application in the crease and fading out, blending the color over the eyelid. The choice of color is determined by the color of hair and costume, the personality of the character, and the degree of stylization desired. Blue, blue-gray, violet, or brown may be used, with brown being the safest and most flattering color.

CUE ▼

Prevent skin problems by softening makeup with cold cream or makeup remover. Wipe the makeup off with a cleansing tissue before washing your face. Then wash your face with soap and warm water.

Another technique that enlarges and accents the eyes is eye lining. Brown or black lining color may be used, but black is acceptable only for dark-complexioned actors or characters who would use heavy eye makeup. If false lashes or heavy mascara will be applied later, the upper line is omitted by many actors. Otherwise, you should use a sable brush or round toothpick to draw a line close to the lashes, starting about two thirds of the way in towards the nose and extending beyond the outer corner of the eye about one-fourth inch and curving slightly upward. The lower line is drawn starting about one third of the way from the outer corner out to the upper line, curving downward slightly, without meeting the upper line. Both lines should be softened by running the finger gently over them. If an eyebrow pencil is used, it must be sharp, or the lines will be too heavy. A thin white line under the center of the eye inside the eyeliner makes the eyes appear even larger.

In straight parts, the eyebrows should frame the eyes rather than attract attention. Brown or black pencil may be used to shape the brows. Most natural eyebrows do not have identical arches; by matching them, makeup can improve their appearance. In character makeup, many different effects can be achieved by changing the eyebrows. Close, heavily drawn brows appear villainous. Lifting the brows into a round, thin arch gives an amazed or stupid expression. Twisted brows or brows dropped at contrasting angles make a face seem plaintive, menacing, or leering.

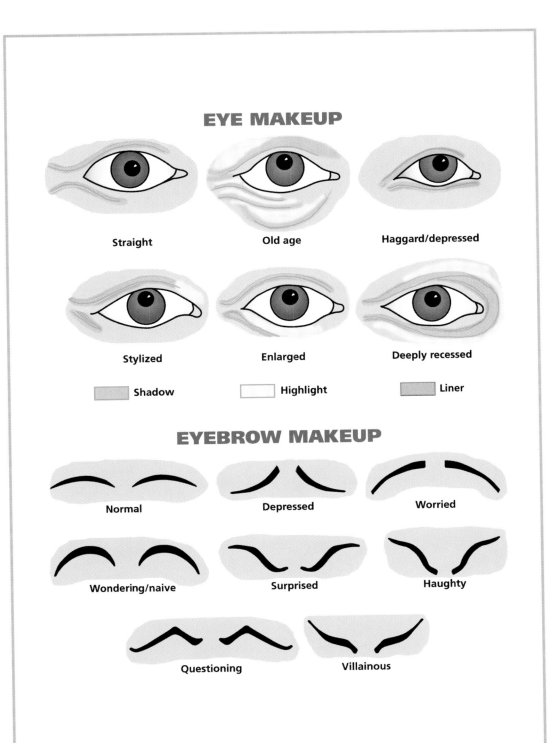

EYE MAKEUP

Straight

Old age

Haggard/depressed

Stylized

Enlarged

Deeply recessed

Shadow   Highlight   Liner

EYEBROW MAKEUP

Normal

Depressed

Worried

Wondering/naive

Surprised

Haughty

Questioning

Villainous

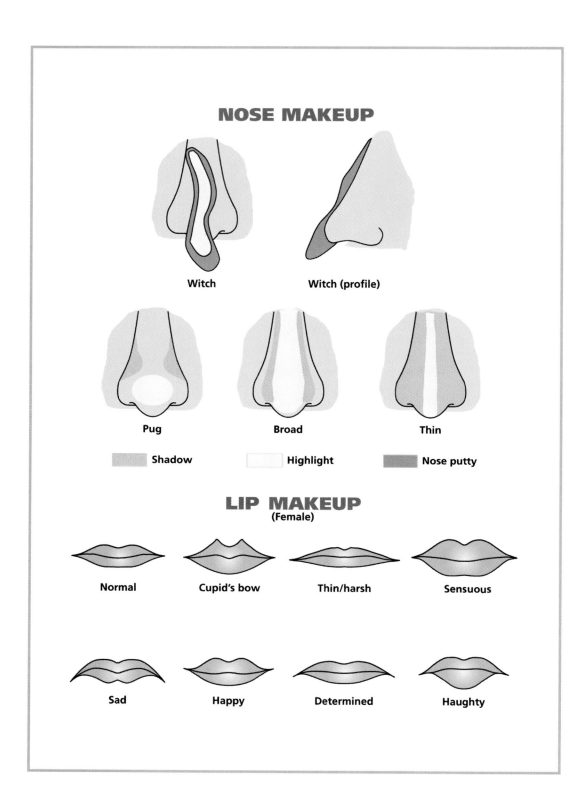

NOSE MAKEUP

Witch

Witch (profile)

Pug

Broad

Thin

Shadow   Highlight   Nose putty

LIP MAKEUP
(Female)

Normal

Cupid's bow

Thin/harsh

Sensuous

Sad

Happy

Determined

Haughty

STEP FIVE: POWDERING

The most important step in the application of creme makeup is applying powder. Use powder that is translucent or a shade that is one tone lighter than the foundation. Powder, when properly applied, sets the makeup, softens the lines and colors, and gives a matte finish, which removes the shine of the makeup under lights. Powder must be squeezed into the puff and the excess shaken off. Then it should be pressed into the makeup thoroughly but gently. Be very careful not to rub or smear the makeup. An even coat of powder holds the makeup in place and prevents it from running under lights.

Some makeup authorities suggest patting the powder on, but actors who are inexperienced with makeup often find that by patting they can get spots of heavy powder that are difficult to remove, or they pick up globs of lining color on the puffs and transfer that color to other parts of the face. Be certain that you have powdered all of the exposed skin areas, including the eyelids, ears, neck, and lips. Brush off the extra powder very lightly with a powder brush, but do not disturb the lines or leave any streaks or powder spots.

STEP SIX: FINISHING TOUCHES

After the powder, you may apply the finishing touches. If the powder dulled the cheeks, dry rouge may be used to restore the color, but be sure no lines or spots of rouge are visible.

Female actors should now apply mascara or false eyelashes. Use brown mascara instead of black unless you are a real brunette. False eyelashes, attached with liquid adhesive and carefully trimmed to suit the character and lighting, are often very effective and in many ways preferable to mascara.

Application
ACTIVITY

Practice designing makeup using the makeup worksheet on page 505. Create a sketch of your own face as a model. Then complete the worksheet for a particular character. Work with a partner to test your skills as a makeup artist. Use the completed makeup worksheets and follow the six steps for applying makeup to create the characters you have designed.

❧ *Special Makeup Problems*

Sometimes an actor's appearance needs to be altered drastically. Anyone playing a character with facial scars, blemishes, or baldness or a young actor playing an elderly character presents special makeup problems. When skillfully applied, however, makeup can transform an actor into a convincing character.

AGING

Of all the makeup problems commonly encountered by high school actors, the most difficult to handle effectively is aging. Young faces do not lend themselves well to the illusion of age. It is even more challenging to demonstrate the toll of many years of mental anguish or physical exposure to conditions such as severe weather. Consequently, the methods suggested by some makeup authorities work well with older actors but do not result in a convincing appearance of middle or old age with most high school students.

The key to all makeup is bone structure. The actor needs to know her or his own bone structure before designing makeup for a role. Most serious acting students have facial masks made of their faces. A **facial mask** is a plaster casting taken of the face. The basic bone structure that the mask preserves does not alter much with time although the face may change considerably in appearance with age. These changes are due primarily to a pulling away of the muscles of the face, resulting in the sagging effect seen in old faces.

CUE ▼

To emphasize the sagging jowls that often characterize age, place cotton, sponges, or tissues in your cheeks.

Aging with makeup begins with the choice of foundation color. With age, the skin color tends to pale. Therefore, use light foundation colors, such as yellow, tan, or pale pink. However, it is through the modeling of the face that the real effects of aging are portrayed. This modeling involves paying attention to three basic characteristics: lines, highlights, and shadows. Lines create wrinkles; highlights and shadows create folds of the skin, which deepen the wrinkles. It is the contrast in highlights and shadows that creates the illusion of old age. The older the character, the greater the contrast.

There are two basic methods for applying wrinkles. The first assumes you have already applied the highlights and shadows. If you have natural wrinkles, you can usually mark them in the foundation by raising the brows, squinting the eyes, smiling, and pulling the chin in. Then, while the lines are still visible, draw the wrinkles on with brown or reddish-brown liner. If you do not have natural wrinkles yet, you will have to follow the same procedure, but draw the lines while the muscles are still contracted.

OLD-AGE MAKEUP

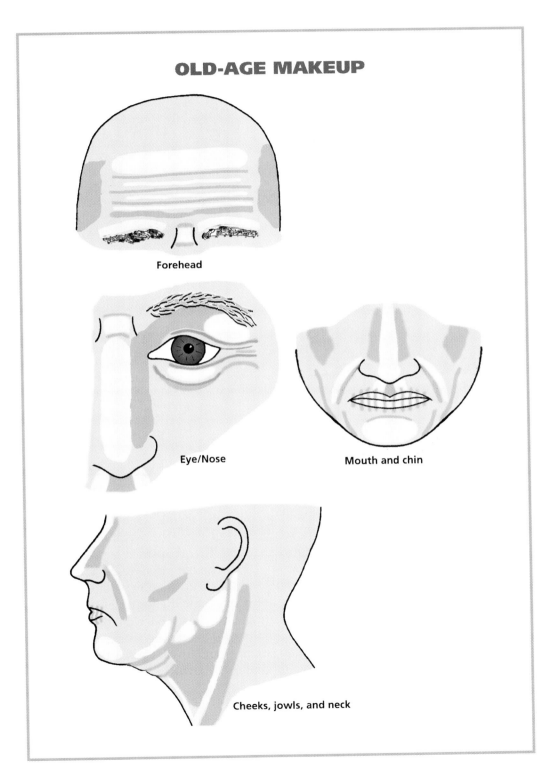

Forehead

Eye/Nose

Mouth and chin

Cheeks, jowls, and neck

In *Tru,* Robert Morse gave a one-man performance that portrayed a lonely Truman Capote reviewing his eventful life. Aging makeup applied to Morse's face follows the natural wrinkle lines.

CUE ▼

When roughening skin texture, keep latex out of the hair. If you don't, when the latex is removed, the hair will be pulled.

The second method requires you to draw the wrinkles before applying the foundation. To use this method, spread brown liner over the areas where you plan to draw wrinkles. Form the wrinkles carefully, and wipe off the visible liner before relaxing the face. When you relax the muscles, the wrinkles should be clearly marked by the remaining liner. Form the wrinkles again, and apply the foundation. After this step, highlight the folds of skin, relax, and blend the wrinkles into shadows.

The most common locations for aging wrinkles are the forehead, between the brows, beneath the eyes (bags), the nasolabial folds (the smile wrinkle—from the nostrils extending to the outside corners of the mouth), vertically on the upper and lower lips, at the corners of the mouth, beneath the lower lip, under the jaw (the jowls), and horizontally on the neck.

Never draw too many lines on the forehead. Follow your natural wrinkle lines. Be especially careful when drawing age lines at the outer corner of the eye and below the eye, for if they are too heavy they will appear as smudges rather than wrinkles.

When highlighting a wrinkle to make the wrinkle deep and sharply defined, a thin line of highlighter is drawn above the wrinkle line and blended outward until the highlight gradually fades into the foundation color.

For aging, the areas of the face to highlight include these:
- frontal crest (the top of the forehead just below the hairline)
- arch (the area above and below the eyebrows)
- outer third of the eyelid
- lower curve of the eye pouches (See the drawing on page 517.)
- bridge of the nose
- cheekbones
- nasolabial folds
- chin
- jowls
- Adam's apple (men only)
- wrinkles of the forehead and the eyes
- tendon stretching from behind the ear to the breastbone

For aging, the areas of the face to shadow include these:
- depression in the forehead
- between the frontal crest and the arch
- inner half of the eyelid next to the nose
- pouch (the soft area below the eyes)
- sides of the nose
- temporal depression (the side of the skull just beyond and between the frontal crest and the arch)
- inside edge of the nasolabial folds
- depression between the ridges above the upper lip
- depression beneath the lower lip
- hollows of the cheeks
- lower edges of the jowls
- depressions of the neck

There are additional factors to consider when using makeup that conveys aging. As people age, their lips tend to become paler and thinner. To produce this effect with makeup, spread the foundation color to block out the edges of the mouth. Draw new lip contours by using a lighter foundation color, a reddish brown or maroon liner, or a light covering of white liner. Use darker rouge in old-age makeups. Apply the rouge lightly for a natural effect or more heavily if a made-up look is desirable. Hair also changes with age. Use gray, silver, or white color on the hair at the temples, in streaks, or overall. Brows may also be grayed or whitened and brushed gently inward toward the nose if a shaggy appearance is desired.

Skin tone changes with age. Stippling with a plastic stipple sponge helps give skin the appearance of age and is particularly effective for aging the smooth skin of young actors. To stipple the skin, use two or three colors. Place a dab of each color in the palm of the hand. Take the sponge and dip it into each color. Then lightly touch the sponge to the face so that the little holes in the sponge leave tiny dots on the face.

Another technique uses liquid latex to roughen skin texture. Liquid latex comes in tan, flesh, and white. Stipple the latex over a stretched section of skin and allow it to dry. When the skin relaxes, a wrinkled-textured face is the result, which is ready to be covered with foundation. However, this rough surface is more difficult to cover smoothly.

Another clue to age that is often forgotten by actors is the appearance of hands and legs. The hands clearly reveal age and should always be made up for the portrayal of an older person. The tendons, knuckles, and other bones need to be highlighted. The sides, depressions, and wrinkles of the fingers need to be shadowed. To portray extreme old age, strongly pronounced blood vessels should appear on the backs of the hands. Similarly, the legs can either be covered or aged by the stippling technique used on the face.

WIGS AND BEARDS

Hair is an integral part of both makeup and costume. Well-planned and carefully dressed hair styles can help transform actors into characters who fit more effectively into specific times and locales. The use of easily removed hair tints can change an actor's stage persona. Hair whitener, white mascara, liquid white shoe polish, clown white, or wash-out colorants are used to gray or whiten the hair. The use of ordinary cornstarch or white powder is not wise. Cornstarch has a tendency to deaden the highlights of the hair, and a cloud of white powder arises if anyone touches it.

Wigs, hairpieces, and falls are quite helpful in changing hairstyles to fit character types and historic periods. However, only expensive wigs appear natural and effective. They should be individually fitted, if the budget permits, and they should be adjusted and handled with great care. Wigs are put on from the front and fitted back over the head. The real hair, if it shows, must be tinted to match the wig. A bald wig must fit perfectly, and the places where it meets the forehead and neck must be cleverly concealed by makeup. One way to do this is to place adhesive tape over the edge of the **blender**, the edge of the wig, and work the foundation up over the tape onto the foundation material of the wig. If inexpensive cloth wigs

CUE ▼

If a costume change is required, cover the hair with a protective scarf.

are to be used, the forehead edge of the blender can be cut unevenly and then glued down with spirit gum.

For men, eccentric haircuts and hairdos are often more realistic than wigs. Male actors can easily change the color of their hair with wash-out colorants. The hair should be freshly washed so that there is no natural oil on it. The colorant may then be sprayed or applied in a rinse with a wet toothbrush, brushing it back from the forehead.

Beards, mustaches, and sideburns require time and practice to apply realistically. Too many beards seem to be merely tacked to the point of the chin—probably because they were. Although professionally prepared beards and hairpieces are available, most are too expensive for school use. Professional pieces are made by a process called perforating, in which strands of real hair are tied into a net material. Another material used to create beards for the stage is wool crepe. Crepe hair comes in many colors, including grays, salt-and-pepper blends, blondes, light and dark browns, and black. Crepe hair comes braided and is sold by the yard. It is curly when unbraided and must be straightened for most use. Either dampen the crepe hair and tie it across the arms or back of a chair to dry overnight, or

Makeup design considerations must balance the character traits of a role, the features of the actor, the style of the production, and the size of the theater. In this production of *King Lear*, the actors use makeup to enhance their characterizations without drawing the audience's attention away from the tragic nature of the play.

iron the damp hair dry. Then the hair may be cut into lengths somewhat longer than the trimmed beard or mustache is to be. Colors may be blended together for a more realistic appearance. Fan the hair between the fingers and thumb, and apply to the adhesive-coated area.

Spirit gum is a popular adhesive, although liquid latex is also used. One disadvantage of latex is that it must never get into the actor's natural hair or brows, but it is preferable if you must wear beards and sideburns for several performances. A piece of nylon stocking cut approximately the shape of the beard can be glued to the face with latex; the hair is then applied to the nylon. The beard and nylon are trimmed to shape, but instead of discarding the beard at the end of the performance, you can peel off the nylon-backed hairpiece to be used for future performances.

When making a beard, always consider the patterns and directions of natural hair growth. Before applying the hair, be certain that the face is clean-shaven. If spirit gum is to be used, make sure all skin areas to which hair is to be attached are free of makeup. Apply only a small amount of hair at a time, starting at the point of the chin and shingling upwards. In a similar fashion, apply the hair beneath the chin. However, the shingling in this case is from the point of the chin downwards. When all the hair is in place, press it to the face with a towel. It can then be combed and trimmed to shape.

An unshaven effect can be created by stippling gray-blue or lining color that matches the hair color on the foundation with a stipple sponge just before powdering. An even more realistic effect can be achieved by cutting crepe hair into tiny bits, spreading the shredded hair over the surface of a smooth towel, and transferring the hair to the face, which has been sparingly coated with spirit gum or latex.

Application
ACTIVITY

Prepare a full beard or mustache on a nylon backing for yourself or for a classmate.

FACIAL FEATURES

There is a wide variety of materials and techniques available for altering facial features. Liquid latex can be used for molding eyelids, cheeks, noses, and other built-up features attached to the skin with additional latex. These molded pieces are called **prosthetics.** Prosthetics are best made on a facial mask by taking a plaster casting of the entire face, including the closed eyes. After the plaster has set, you have an exact replica of the face. Shape the desired prosthetic piece in clay on the facial mask. Make a plaster casting of this clay model to provide a mold for the liquid latex. Pour the latex into the mold and allow it to set. When the hardened latex is removed, you have a prosthetic piece ready to be attached to the face.

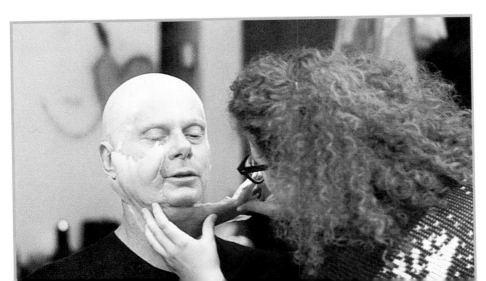

A prosthetic chin is applied to Robert Morse for his portrayal of Truman Capote in *Tru.*

Nose putty can also be used to change facial features. It is used to build up noses, chins, cheekbones, and ears and for creating warts, scars, and other blemishes. When you use nose putty, be sure the putty is kneaded into a pliable mass before it is placed on the face. Add a little cold cream to make it more workable and a little spirit gum for better adhesion. Afterward, use alcohol or acetone to dissolve the nose putty.

Another useful material is collodion. There are two types of collodion—flexible and nonflexible. Flexible collodion is used for building up the flesh or texturing the skin. For example, a double chin may be built up with layers of cotton that have been coated with spirit gum. When the "chin" is as large as desired, coat the cotton with diluted collodion (thinned with an equal amount of acetone), brushing outwards and extending the collodion about half an inch beyond the cotton. Nonflexible collodion is used for making indentations and scars and for drawing up the flesh. To form a skin depression, apply the nonflexible collodion with a brush and allow each layer to dry until the indentation is deep enough. To draw up the flesh, stretch the skin in the area to be painted and allow the collodion to dry. Then relax the skin. Collodion may be peeled off or removed with acetone.

Adhesive tape and tooth enamel can also be very effective for character makeup. Tape can be used to lift up or pull down eyelids and eyebrows. Tape may be used to pull parts of the face to suggest the effects of scars or paralysis. Tooth enamel comes in black, white, ivory, or cream. The black enamel is used to block out teeth, to make teeth appear pointed or chipped, and to make large teeth seem smaller. The white enamels are used to cover discolored, filled, or capped teeth and braces. The teeth must be dry before the enamel is applied.

Notice the raised scars on the forehead of Frankenstein's monster. Such scars can be created with liquid latex, nose putty, nonflexible collodion, or adhesive tape.

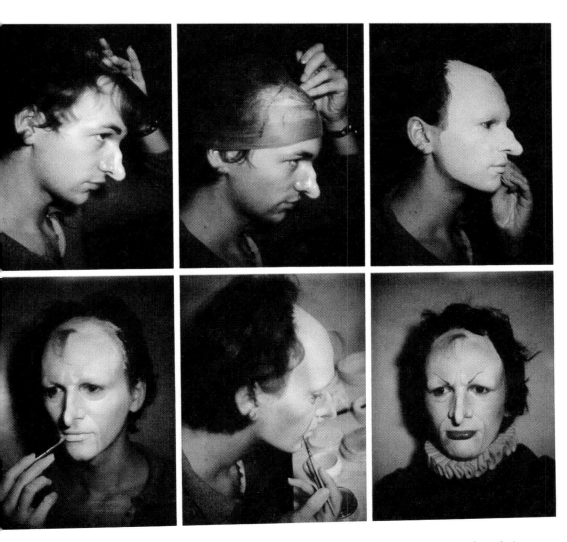

Nonrealistic makeup is an example of theatricalism. (upper left) Soaping out the front hair. Nose built up with nose putty. (upper center) Making outline of bald area on nylon stocking, which will cover soaped-out hair. (upper right) Applying the foundation with a sponge. Eyebrows have been blocked out. (lower left) Modeling the face with highlights. (lower center) Applying shadows. (lower right) Completed makeup, with painted eyebrows, rouge, and full lower lip. Makeup by student Lee Austin.

In addition, derma wax and liquid latex may be used to form cuts, scars, and other skin blemishes. Derma wax should only be applied to areas of the skin that will remain untouched during the performance because it will remain soft and can be ruined by contact.

Application ACTIVITY

Draw a mask of your own face. Indicate the bone structure and features. Then choose a character from a play and indicate the types and colors of makeup you would use if you were to play that part, and show where you would apply the makeup.

BIZARRE MAKEUP

Bizarre makeup may be tried if it is in keeping with the type of play and style of production. Stylized makeup—including "white masks," clown-like faces, and mosaics—can be quite effective onstage. Special makeup has been developed for use with ultraviolet light. Changeable makeup really involves two makeup designs, one visible under ordinary light and the other visible under special lighting. For example, place a character wearing red makeup under red light, and that character will appear to be without makeup. Change to blue or green light, and the red will appear to be black.

Makeup this complex, involving not only the face but the hands as well, takes even a skilled makeup artist hours to apply. This Beast from *Beauty and the Beast* has a unique mixture of animal and human features.

Animal makeup is fun and challenging. Most animal makeup can be suggestive rather than realistic. This allows the makeup designer to be creative in selecting makeup materials. For example, the designer can work with crepe hair, feathers, construction paper, foam rubber, Styrofoam™, pipe cleaners, drinking straws, patches of cloth, and so on. Plastic bottles can be shaped into teeth. Liquid latex, nose putty, and derma wax can build up facial features or be molded into beaks, snouts, and horns.

Nonhuman illusions can be created with hoods and half masks. Upper head pieces constructed of foam rubber, Styrofoam™, or paper can be worn like a hat or can be attached to a cap that will fit snugly.

The first step in creating animal makeup is to develop a workable design that considers the identifying features of the animal and the actor.

Begin with a photograph or sketch of the actor. Next, make a drawing of the animal's face that is the same size as the drawing of the actor's face. Outline the prominent features of the animal onto the drawing of the actor's face. Finally, fill out a makeup worksheet similar to that shown on page 505.

Application
ACTIVITY

Work with a partner to demonstrate creating animal or nonhuman faces. First use only makeup; then use latex nose putty or other materials.

MAKEUP AND LIGHTING

Always be aware of the effects of light on makeup. Amber light, which is too frequently used on the high school stage, causes the complexion to yellow, the rouge to fade, and blue eye shadow to look gray. Green-blue, the gel most frequently used for night scenes, will turn rouge purplish-black. Be certain that you know the lighting that will be used while you are onstage so that pigments can be selected or mixed in order for the light to reflect the proper colors. Finally, it is wise to plan a costume-makeup rehearsal to check the effects of light and costume on makeup.

Remember that in both class and school plays it is the actor, not the makeup and costume, who creates the real illusion. The care spent on a first-class ensemble of correct costume, makeup, hairdress, and accessories, however, will give you an assurance that will help you create a convincing characterization. Makeup is an integral part of the actor's appearance. It is to be used and enjoyed as another tool in the actor's craft.

FROM THE PROS

"No makeup is complete without an actor underneath, for makeup does not in itself create character—it only helps to reveal it."

—RICHARD CORSON,
MAKEUP ARTIST

Summary and Key Ideas

Summarize the chapter by answering the following questions.

1. Define *chiaroscuro*.
2. What are the most expressive features of the face?
3. How does makeup support effective characterization?
4. What is the first thing that must be done before any makeup can be applied?
5. Identify the six steps in applying makeup.
6. What are the purposes of highlighting and shadowing?
7. What is the most difficult makeup problem for the high school stage?
8. What kinds of beards and wigs work best for actors?

Discussing Ideas

1. Discuss the effect that lighting has on stage makeup. What characteristics of lighting must you take into consideration when planning effective makeup?
2. Consider the problem of making up a teenage actor as a seventy-year-old man or woman. Discuss the kinds of things you could do with makeup so that the young actor would appear convincing.

FOCUS ON ▸ Audience Behavior

Whether you're at the movies or you're watching a live musical or theatrical performance, it's important to demonstrate responsible audience behavior. That includes being polite and respectful, maintaining quiet when quiet is called for, and applauding or laughing when and if appropriate. See page 160 for more on proper audience behavior.

Behaving with Courtesy Whenever your classmates are performing and you're the audience—or whenever you view any live production—be sure to apply appropriate behavior. Also be sure to behave responsibly when you go to the movies. You may want to get together with a partner to compare audience behavior at movie showings and live theater. Is it basically the same, or are there some things one audience does that the other audience doesn't? Does the "right" behavior depend on the genre of the production?

Music versus Drama Think of musical performances you've attended in the past. What kind or kinds of music have you heard live? How did the audience behave? Draw up a list of guidelines that you would give fifth graders who are about to attend a musical performance. Be careful to show which guidelines apply to all music and which apply only to one kind of music, such as rock or classical. Share your guidelines with a small group.

MAKEUP

INDEPENDENT ACTIVITY

Mime   Although many mimes wear white-face to draw attention to themselves, this type of makeup is certainly not a requirement. Devise a makeup routine for yourself that will highlight your features and facial expressions as well as communicate that you have a unique type of performance. Don't try to cover up or hide your face, but use the lines and muscles that are there. Experiment with variations—make one eyebrow different from the other, or use red or black shapes such as a tear, a flower, or a circle that can become your facial trademark. Then make faces at yourself in the mirror. Try to discover the effect your makeup has on your expressions. How does the makeup cause you to feel? Once you have created the makeup that fits with your image of yourself as a mime, display it for your classmates.

Cooperative Learning Activities

Creating Special Effects   Using a classmate as a model, demonstrate for the class special makeup effects such as a black eye, freckles, an open wound, a missing tooth, and a bald head.

Bizarre Makeup   Using a classmate as a model, demonstrate for the class nonrealistic makeup for such characters as a witch, an animal, and a clown. Experiment with novel color combinations and the use of unusual materials, such as foam rubber, Styrofoam™, feathers, drinking straws, cloth, plastic bottles, and so forth.

Across the CURRICULUM Activities

History   Study photographs of the same person from youth to old age. You'll find a wealth of material in the biographies of famous people. Pay particular attention to what time does to the person's face. Then create a makeup demonstration for your class that shows how the face changed as it aged.

Art   Choose a portrait, such as Rembrandt's *Self-Portrait*, John Singleton Copley's *Mrs. Thomas Boylston*, Leonardo da Vinci's *Mona Lisa*, Hans Holbein the Younger's *Henry VIII*, or Edouard Manet's *A Bar at the Folies-Bergère*, from an art history textbook. Create a reproduction of the portrait with makeup on your own face or on a partner's face. Display the original and discuss with your classmates how the original and your copy are both similar and different.

How to Judge a Play

*L*earning to judge good theater will enhance your enjoyment of what theater has to offer. A specialist in judging plays is called a **critic.** A critic reviews new productions on television or radio or in newspapers or magazines. A good critic, however, does not go to a play looking for things to criticize. The most highly trained and enthusiastic theatergoers free their imaginations and emotions and at the same time use their intelligence and discrimination to heighten their appreciation of what they are seeing. You can learn to evaluate drama by training yourself to notice certain aspects of the play and the performance.

THE PLAY ITSELF

To judge a play fairly, allow your attitude to be colored by the type of play you are seeing. You cannot judge a light social satire by the same standards as you would a romantic drama in blank verse. You cannot judge a tragedy and a farce by the same standards, nor can an experimental production be judged by the standards of a traditional production. Keep the following considerations in mind when you evaluate a play.

The Theme

Your first consideration in evaluating a play should be the theme. Determine for yourself the playwright's purpose. Consider the following questions:

1. What did the author try to do, and was it accomplished?
2. Was it worthwhile?
3. Is the fundamental idea underlying the play true or false in its concept of life?
4. Is the theme consistent with the setting, the plot, and the characters presented in the play?

The Plot

Another consideration is the plot, which is the backbone of the play. The plot should hold your intense interest and arouse your sense of curiosity. If the play is good, you may be wondering what is going to happen next. Evaluate whether the events are plausible and the situations are interesting in themselves. Decide if the plot stirs you emotionally and satisfies you intellectually. Ask yourself these questions:

1. Does the play have a clear-cut sequence of events?
2. Does it rise to a strong and convincing climax?
3. Does the suspense hold until the end?
4. Is the play emotionally stirring?
5. Does it have a logical conclusion?
6. Are you satisfied by the final outcome?

The Dialogue

Your appreciation of dialogue will increase as you see more plays. A dramatist's style is revealed through dialogue. There are numerous aspects of good, believable dialogue. One aspect is the witty repartee, or swift give-and-take of conversation, among characters. As you evaluate, also listen for clever figures of speech that are natural to the characters. Then ask yourself these questions:

1. Is the dialogue brilliant and entertaining in itself?
2. Is it consistent with the characters and setting?
3. Is the dialogue an end in itself?
4. Is it an adequate means of plot advancement and characterization?
5. After seeing the play, do you remember the lines because of their significance or their beauty?

The Characterization

A final consideration when evaluating a play is characterization, which is enhanced by dialogue. Characterization is an element that reveals the playwright's skill. When evaluating a play's characterization, ask yourself these questions:

1. Are the characters true to life?
2. Do they fit into the social and geographical background of the play?
3. Do they arouse strong feelings, such as sympathy, affection, amusement, disgust, admiration, or hatred?

4. Are the characters' actions in keeping with their motives?
5. Does the protagonist evoke empathy?
6. How is each character unique, and what function does each serve?
7. Are the relationships between characters clear and believable?
8. Are the situations at the climax and the conclusion a result of the characters' inherent natures?

THE PRODUCTION

Since the days of ancient Greece, people have enjoyed watching plays. Audiences today, however, are more knowledgeable about the details of play production than ever before. Your study of drama coupled with a few guidelines will help you understand a play and appreciate the methods of its presentation.

The Set Design

That which first meets the eye—the setting—is an important factor. The setting helps determine the atmosphere of the play and serves as the environment in which the characters live. The scenic designer works closely with the director, stage manager, and backstage crew to create the proper effects with sets and lighting. Most scenic designers strive toward these common major goals of scenic art:

A colorful, creative set helps create an energetic, upbeat atmosphere for a production.

- To create atmosphere
- To establish a center of interest
- To help carry out the fundamental purpose of the play

Modern lighting and mechanical and electronic effects also play a vital part in attaining an effective set design. As you evaluate what you see onstage, consider these questions:

1. Is the setting in keeping with the play itself?
2. Is the setting pleasing and artistic?
3. Does it help evoke the desired emotional reaction to the play?
4. Are the costumes and properties in harmony with the background?
5. Does the setting add to or detract from enjoyment of the play?
6. Is the interest centered on the total effect or on the details?
7. Does the set overpower the actors?

The Direction

The most important factor in the ultimate success of a production is the director, because the director is personally responsible for every phase of the play. In evaluating the direction of a play, you should note how the director develops contrast in casting, costuming, and interpretation; how he or she composes stage pictures that emphasize the center of interest; and how the actors, lighting, setting, and costumes create the proper atmosphere. As you consider the following questions, keep in mind that the director is responsible not only for the style in which the play is presented but also for the interpretation of the theme.

1. Is the theme clearly expressed?
2. Are the stage pictures focused and strong without seeming contrived?
3. Does the blocking seem natural yet motivated?
4. Is the center of interest established in each sequence?
5. Is the pace appropriate for this particular play?
6. Do the actors, settings, costumes, lighting, and style present a clear sense of unity?
7. Do all elements of the play appear to be effective and appropriate for the message of the play?
8. Is the overall production creative, entertaining, and satisfying?

The Acting

Of all the aspects of a play, the acting generally arouses the keenest response from the audience. A good actor, remaining true to his or her

character, creates a role that is constantly convincing. Remaining true to the period and spirit of the play, yet maintaining a natural spontaneity, is also crucial to fine acting. Remember, good actors avoid attracting attention to themselves. Further, the spectators in the very last row of the theater should be able to hear each actor clearly. In addition, ask yourself these questions when you evaluate acting:

1. Is the interpretation of any given role consistent with the play as a whole?
2. Is the character as created by the actor believable?
3. Are you aware of the actor's use of practiced techniques to influence the audience?
4. Does the actor appeal to your emotions? Do you laugh, suffer, or rejoice?
5. Is the actor's voice pleasing and appropriate for the role?
6. Is the use of dialect convincing yet intelligible?
7. Does the actor remain in character every moment?
8. Do you think of the actor as becoming one with the role, or are you aware of the person playing the role?
9. Does the actor become an acceptable part of the style of the production?

The Audience Reaction

Judging the ultimate success of a performance can be tricky. The reaction of the audience might or might not be a fair criterion. However, if the play does not satisfy playgoers, then something must be off course. The fault may lie with the play or with its production, for the average audience is usually eager to be pleased.

Of course, not all plays are suitable for all audiences. Local politics or religious views, for example, may affect an audience's response to a play. Nevertheless, if a drama deals with fundamental human reactions, presents a definite aspect of a universal theme, and is produced in an appropriate manner, it should hold the interest of the audience. Think about these factors as you observe the audience:

1. Is the audience attentive, involved, or restless during the performance?
2. Does the audience show emotional responses or applaud?
3. Is there an immediate show of appreciation for clever lines, dramatic situations, and skillful acting?
4. Does the applause seem spontaneous and wholehearted or merely polite?

Adapting and Interpreting Drama

As movie and television technology developed, the essentials of drama were adapted to fit these new forms of entertainment.

Television drama brings theater into the home. Shown here are Andre Braugher (standing) and Kyle Secor (left) with a guest on *Homicide: Life on the Street.*

Wherever there's magic and make believe and an audience—there's theater. . . . It may not be YOUR theater, but it's theater for somebody somewhere.

—CHARACTER IN ALL ABOUT EVE *(1950)*
WRITTEN BY JOSEPH MANKIEWICZ

SETTING THE SCENE

Focus Questions

How did moviemaking develop?

What is unique about movie production and acting?

How did television develop?

What is unique about television production and acting?

What roles do critics play in the success of productions?

How does the audience affect the success of productions?

Vocabulary

animation	dissolve	storyboard	review
live-action film	crosscut shot	film editing	analysis
close-up	story idea	three-camera system	receipts
zoom	the treatment	criticism	ratings

Films, televisions, videos, laserdiscs, cable, satellite dishes, CD-ROMs, and digital imagery have become part of our vocabulary and our daily lives. They have the power to bring the theater into every living room, but not without some adjustments. In making the transformation from stage to screen, the basics of theater have been modified, rearranged, compressed, stretched, and adapted to fit these new media. In the process, however, certain fundamental principles have endured and remained true to their origins. While new technologies have brought theater to millions of people throughout the world, one simple fact remains: the mission of the media, whatever its form, is to entertain, to amuse, and to educate.

❧ *From the Stage to the Big Screen*

Up to this point, you have primarily studied the live theater, the skills it requires, and its history and development. Many of you, though, are familiar with drama in other forms. Most, if not all, of you have been to a movie theater or watched television. These vehicles for dramatic presentation are very similar to, but also somewhat different from, the live theater.

Film began its development prior to the invention of television, and provided much of the technology necessary for the evolution of television programming. If we were to look at the development of dramatic entertainment on a time line, then, film would follow live theater and come before television.

THE HISTORY OF FILM

In 1824, Peter Mark Roget, best known for his thesaurus, wrote a paper entitled "Persistence of Vision with Regard to Moving Objects." In it he proposed that an image briefly perceived by the eye remains in sight for a fraction of a second even after the image is no longer present. This phenomenon, he reasoned, would allow the eye to blend a series of sequential images if they were presented quickly enough. If each image in the sequence were changed slightly from the one before, the illusion of movement could be achieved. The moving picture was born. Inventors raced to find a practical way to produce moving pictures, conceiving such devices as the exotically named zoetrope, a wheel that spun hand-drawn images in front of the viewer, and the kinetograph, an early forerunner of the motion-picture projector.

The development of moving pictures advanced further when, in 1885, George Eastman invented a paper film that could be used to create a set of sequential pictures in so-called "flip books." He later developed an improved photographic film stock that consisted of a celluloid strip that substantially simplified the filmmaking process. Eastman called his new film "Kodak" because he liked the letter K and wanted the name both to start and end with it.

In 1891, Thomas Edison, along with W. K. L. Dickson, combined the technology of the photograph and Roget's discovery of the persistence of vision to invent the first motion picture camera. He relied on popular theater acts of the time—jugglers, acrobats, and other vaudeville performers—to provide the subject matter for his new invention. One such performer was magician J. Stewart Blackton. After becoming interested in the notion of moviemaking, Blackton rented Edison's equipment and started making movies under the name Vitagraph Film Company.

Blackton experimented extensively with the equipment and with the concept of **animation,** or making drawn or inanimate objects appear to live and move. He produced the first drawn animation, *Humorous Phases of Funny Faces,* in 1906. It involved drawing and photographing a series of chalk figures on a blackboard. He also experimented with the first stop-motion animation, which resulted in *Humpty Dumpty Circus* in 1906. In this experiment, he moved children's toys around, stopping them at various intervals and photographing each slight change in position. These films laid the foundation for the art of animation and eventually led to the sophisticated animation we now find in films such as Twentieth Century Fox's *Anastasia* (1997) and the first entirely computer-generated film, *Toy Story* (1995).

Not all early films were animated, though. **Live-action films,** those in which the action is provided by living creatures, were also developing. The earliest films in the United States were not intended to be projected at all. Short features such as *Kiss* (1896) were simply pieces of unedited film made to be viewed on a Kinetoscope—a hand-held device consisting of a light and a lens.

The craft of moviemaking continued to evolve through the early part of the twentieth century. A former projectionist for Edison, Edwin S. Porter, brought film closer to its modern style in *The Great Train Robbery* (1903). His innovations included the use of camera movements and the continuity of editing, which involves cutting pieces of film together to produce a smooth, straightforward story. Soviet filmmaker Sergei Eisenstein set the standard for other silent films when he produced *Battleship Potemkin* (1925), which remains a classic.

Sound was always important to both theater and film. The old silent movies were anything but silent for the audience. A theater pianist would play music to accompany the film. Sometimes there was even a drummer to provide sound effects needed to enhance comedies. Charlie Chaplin went so far as to compose complete musical scores for his work. A full symphonic orchestra accompanied *Battleship Potemkin.*

▼ **CUE**

When Blackton became disenchanted with filmmaking, he sold his studio to Jack, Harry, Sam, and Albert Warner, who renamed the studio Warner Brothers.

Walt Disney was a pioneer in animated films. Walt Disney Studio's 1940 release of the innovative *Fantasia* marked a new era in animated feature films.

While sound was a major step forward in the evolution of film, it was disastrous for some established actors whose careers had grown out of film, which up to that point had been silent, rather than theater. Their voices lacked the character and quality theater-going audiences had come to expect. Consequently, many silent-film actors could not make the transition to "talkies."

One of the most successful stories of transition from the stage to the screen is that of a family that was destined to become an acting dynasty—the Barrymores. John, Ethel, and Lionel Barrymore, a respected stage family, became a distinguished film family as well. Ethel and Lionel's stage-trained voices allowed them to move from silent films into the talkies. John, one of the brightest stars on Broadway, easily made the jump to films. Because of his classically handsome side-view, he became known as the "great profile," a tribute that would not have been possible in a theatrical setting because close-up views of stage actors were rarely possible. Despite their many successes, the trio starred in only one film together, *Rasputin and the Empress* (1932). The Barrymore tradition, however, continues to this day with Drew Barrymore, who has starred in films ranging from Steven Spielberg's hit *E.T.: The Extra-Terrestrial* (1982) to Wes Craven's *Scream* (1996).

With the advent of sound on film, movies had all of the capabilities of the theater and few of its physical limitations. The first sound film, *The Jazz Singer* (1927), seemed to predict the future when Al Jolson uttered the now-famous words, "You ain't heard nothin' yet."

CUE ▼

Mickey Mouse made history in Walt Disney's *Steamboat Willie* (1928) by becoming the first cartoon character to speak. Today, when sound is being added to a film, it is referred to as "Mickey Mousing."

DIFFERENCES BETWEEN THE STAGE AND FILM

Early filmmakers naturally borrowed heavily from the conventions of the theater. Webster defines a convention as "an established technique, practice, or device." Setting, for example, is a theatrical convention. We know that the trees and flowers we see in the scenery are not real, but we accept them as being trees and flowers. We know that we are not actually looking into someone's living room from which one wall has been removed, but we accept the set as a living room. Because of the differences between the stage and film, though, many theatrical conventions changed as they became conventions of moviemaking.

Early films were no more than theatrical works performed before a camera. In a sense, the movie camera simply assumed the position of a member of the audience in a theater. Like a member of the audience, the camera remained in a fixed position, sometimes turning left or right as one might move the head. In imitation of a theater environment, actors were placed thirty feet from the camera.

Key Events in the History of the Movies

1824   Peter Mark Roget advances the theory of persistence of vision.

1872   Eadweard Muybridge begins experiments on sequential photography.

1885   George Eastman invents paper film, replacing the cumbersome and fragile glass film.

1887   Thomas Edison and W. K. L. Dickson use a perforated film to capture sequential movement.

1891   Edison and Dickson invent the first movie camera.

1895   The Lumière Brothers publicly show a projected film in Paris—the birth of movies.

1920s   The number of movie palaces skyrockets. The Roxy in New York seats 6,200 people and employs a staff of 300.

1927   Sound comes to the movies in Warner Brothers' *The Jazz Singer*. Movie admissions in Europe rise from 60 million a week in 1927 to 110 million a week in 1929.

1930   Of 122 million people living in the United States, 95 million attend a movie each week.

1932   Technicolor™ is invented and begins to appear in movies.

1953   Wide screen CinemaScope™, stereo, and 3D challenge television's growing audience.

1982   The first totally computer generated sequence appears in a feature film, *Star Trek II*.

1993   Computer generated life forms are used to create special effects in *Jurassic Park*.

The famous director D. W. Griffith, however, changed all of that. One of the greatest innovators in film history, Griffith guided movies from the stage-proscenium style of filmmaking that was standard for the day to a style that used a variety of shots, light and shade composition, and film editing. He started to use the **close-up,** a shot taken at a very close distance, and the **zoom,** using a zoom lens to shoot the subject from a distance that makes the subject appear to be very close, in addition to other techniques that greatly advanced the art of moviemaking. In terms of both style and content, his 1915 film, *The Birth of a Nation,* became one of the most influential pictures in film history.

As the camera began to move around, no longer acting as a member of the audience, scenery had to become more three-dimensional, more real. The movie camera could go into a real room or outside beneath a real tree, so stage scenery could no longer give movie audiences the effects they demanded.

Because the audience is usually fairly distant from a stage actor, the stage acting style is usually a bit exaggerated or overly dramatic. This is necessary in order for the audience in the balcony to appreciate the action as much as those sitting in the first rows. A movie camera, though, can zoom in on the actor and record the slightest movement, expression, or word. Thus the stage style of acting does not appear natural to the film audience.

Another convention of the theater that changes with film is the ability to communicate time and place. On the stage, with some exceptions, time is fairly one-dimensional—it moves forward. To depict several actions occurring at once onstage, each action must be staged and spotlighted separately. Unfortunately, it is difficult for all members of the audience to focus on multiple sections of the stage at the same time. Filmmakers, however, can use camera shots, camera angles, and film editing to show jumps in place and time. Such radical techniques as the **dissolve,** which shows the passage of time by superimposing one shot onto another as the first fades away, and the close-up greatly improved the art of storytelling. Another technique, called the **crosscut shot,** switches abruptly from one scene to another to show events happening at the same time but in different places.

Application
ACTIVITY

Describe how you would stage four familiar kinds of scenes—for example, a scene in a mall or in a kitchen—for a stage production and for a movie. Focus on the differences in the theatrical conventions.

Innovative use of a variety of camera shots made D. W. Griffith's *Birth of a Nation* a classic in moviemaking. In this scene, John Wilkes Booth, played by Raoul Walsh, jumps from the theater box after shooting Abraham Lincoln, played by Joseph Henabery, as Mrs. Lincoln (Alberta Lee) attends to her injured husband.

❧ *From Movies to Television*

When moving pictures first appeared, audiences were amazed that they could walk into a familiar building in their hometown and through their imaginations go places and see things they had never thought possible. As movies became an accepted part of our culture, more and more people took advantage of the entertainment opportunity movies provided.

As Mickey Mouse was making history by speaking his first words in 1928, another entertainment breakthrough was on the horizon. When the Radio Corporation of America (RCA) began testing something called television, they were on the brink of discovering a medium that would forever change the way we live.

The development of television from moving pictures was somewhat less radical than that from the stage to movies because by that time, audiences were accustomed to recorded entertainment. Television, however, was a breakthrough because it made entertainment cheaper, more accessible, and more convenient. It brought tragedy, comedy, and information right into the living room.

Unlike the movies, which by their nature require time to film, edit, produce, and distribute to their audiences, electronic television signals (electromagnetic waves) are sent through transmitters and picked up by antennas that feed them to television sets, allowing for almost instantaneous transmission of programs. That is why early television specialized in live events such as sports, disasters, and important speeches.

Technological progress was slowed during World War II because technicians were focused on the war effort, but interest in

▼ CUE

In 1939 the British Broadcasting Company (BBC) was showing a Disney cartoon, *Mickey's Gala Premiere.* When war was declared, the screen went dark. When the war ended six years later, the station signed back on and picked up the cartoon exactly where it had left off.

Twelve Angry Men, written by Reginald Rose, was presented on live television in 1954, winning three Emmy awards. Rose's teleplay was adapted to the screen for the 1957 film, shown here, starring Henry Fonda, E. G. Marshall, Martin Balsam, and Lee J. Cobb.

developing television came back stronger than ever after the war to begin what we now know as the Golden Age of Television. The concept of the television show as we know it appeared after World War II when programming expanded to include news, comedy, drama, and sports. Early television had two major drawbacks: it was black and white, and the screen was extremely small. These initial limitations, however, were no problem for vaudeville-style variety acts and nightclub performers who were accustomed to the small stage. The popularity of Milton Berle, Phil Silvers, Red Skelton, and Jackie Gleason caused sales of television sets to soar.

Often performed live, early teleplays such as *Marty, Twelve Angry Men, Requiem for a Heavyweight,* and *The Miracle Worker* benefited from the experiences and experiments of moviemakers. Close-ups and movable camera shots were employed from the start. Even so, when these teleplays were redone for the big screen, the moviemakers' advantages of unlimited settings, multiple takes, and crosscutting enhanced the production.

Andy Griffith and Ron Howard starred in *The Andy Griffith Show,* which ran for 249 episodes starting in 1960. Still in reruns, the program is representative of the type of wholesome family entertainment made popular on television.

In the last fifteen years, television has experienced what some critics refer to as the Second Golden Age. The one-hour drama format suddenly made leaps forward in tone and quality. The writing on such shows as *Hill Street Blues, MASH, Seinfeld,* and *E.R.* seemed to adopt the issue- and character-driven style of playwrights such as Arthur Miller. In fact, many distinguished writers who have written in other media,

Recent dramatic offerings on television are receiving critical acclaim for their quality and creativity. Pictured left to right are Jerry Orbach, Carey Lowell, and Benjamin Bratt in *Law and Order*.

including Woody Allen, Neil Simon, Rod Serling, Paddy Chayefsky, and Gore Vidal, have written dramatic works for television. Television has become the new home for the kind of thought-provoking, issue-centered material usually reserved for serious live theater.

Highly innovative form-stretching shows and unusual hybrids of absurdity and drama such as *Picket Fences* and *The X-Files* illustrate future possibilities for increased complexity of tone in television writing. None of these shows were content to stick to a single format. The story might be based in a law office, hospital, or police station, but the problems and relationships at their core are reflections of contemporary life. Shakespeare might say these programs are indeed "holding the mirror up to nature."

Application
ACTIVITIES

1. Find out more about television history. Choose a television program or a star and find out all you can. Share what you find with the class.

2. Do you prefer watching productions made for film or productions made for television? Explain your answer. What are the differences and the similarities?

❦ Dramatic Structure and the Screen

Whether for live theater, film, or television, all drama has the same basic structure. First the characters and their situation are introduced to the audience (exposition). Then an incident or problem arises that drives the plot. The conflict is then played out through a series of incidents. Finally, the conflict or problem is resolved in some manner (see Chapter 5 for an explanation of the development of plot).

WRITING AND FILMING MOVIES

Movies and television productions are generally written in several stages. In the first stage the **story idea** itself is expressed, usually in a few sentences. For example, the story idea for *Jurassic Park* might have been expressed in the following way:

> An island becomes a computerized theme park that uses cloned dinosaurs. A storm hits the island and allows the dinosaurs to escape. These dinosaurs threaten visitors. Some visitors are killed, and others eventually escape from the island on a helicopter.

The second stage, known as the **treatment,** involves telling the story in narrative form without the use of dialogue. The amount of detail included in the treatment varies, but an average treatment for a two-hour film can run anywhere from four to twelve pages in length. Because film executives are bombarded with film ideas, treatments allow them to view ideas quickly and to choose ideas worth pursuing without reading entire scripts.

Next is the script stage, where the treatment is fleshed out and the narrative is converted to dialogue. There are two basic script formats: a film format used for movies and a tape format used for many television shows. One major difference between film and television is that filming for a movie usually takes place on location while taping for most TV programs takes place in a studio. This is, however, not as universally true as it once was. Many television programs now occasionally shoot some of their scenes on location as well as on a set in a studio. Generally, though, writers like to think that "film goes anywhere, tape stays in the studio." Film scripts are normally about 120 pages long. The assumption is that if each page represents one minute of the performance, the film will run about two hours.

To help the filmmaker visualize the screenplay, a useful tool called the storyboard was developed in the 1920s by Webb Smith of the Walt Disney Studio. The **storyboard** is simply the depiction of the script in comic-book form. Disney used it to help artists make short cartoons and eventually to develop feature-length animated films. The storyboard was later employed for the development of live-action as well as animated films. Today its use is commonplace among filmmakers. Steven Spielberg, George Lucas, James Cameron, and Robert Zamekis all use storyboards to help them stage stunts, develop special effects, and combine different techniques on film.

The storyboard for a special-effects film becomes a blueprint for each scene. Each drawing lists what effects will be used in the shot. *The Empire Strikes Back* had almost five hundred panels in its storyboard, while *The Return of the Jedi* had almost one thousand. Dennis Muren and the other special-effects wizards at George Lucas's special-effects company, Industrial Light & Magic, took the storyboard process one step further in *The Return of the Jedi* by filming three-dimensional storyboards called animatics.

Unlike live drama, in which action and dialogue proceed from beginning to end in sequence with no chance of a retake, a film is rarely shot in sequence, and multiple takes are commonplace. Which elements of the script are filmed may depend on the locations, the weather, and the availability of the actors. In the 1939 film *The Wizard of Oz*, Judy Garland's singing of "Somewhere Over the Rainbow" was the last scene to be filmed, yet it appears early in the final version of the film.

Film editing, done by the editor in conjunction with the director, involves choosing and sequencing the various pieces of film so that the end

In 1980, George Lucas released the second part of the *Star Wars* trilogy, *The Empire Strikes Back.* Among its stars were Billy Dee Williams who plays Lando Calrissian. He is shown here with Darth Vader (David Paows) and Bobba Fett (Jeremy Bullock). Lucas used storyboards to plan the special effects in the movie.

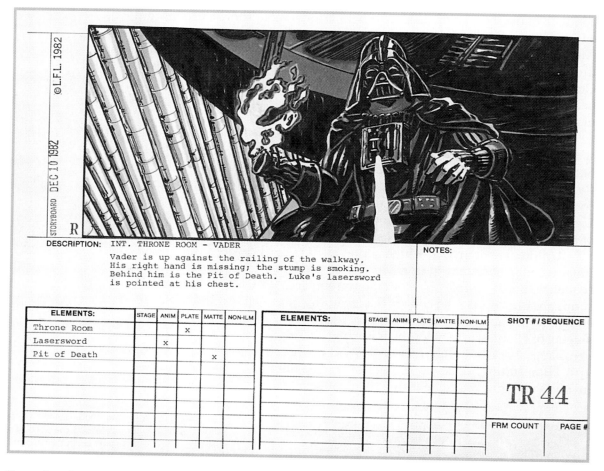

DESCRIPTION: INT. THRONE ROOM - VADER

Vader is up against the railing of the walkway.
His right hand is missing; the stump is smoking.
Behind him is the Pit of Death. Luke's lasersword
is pointed at his chest.

NOTES:

ELEMENTS:	STAGE	ANIM	PLATE	MATTE	NON-ILM
Throne Room			x		
Lasersword		x			
Pit of Death				x	

ELEMENTS:	STAGE	ANIM	PLATE	MATTE	NON-ILM

SHOT # / SEQUENCE

TR 44

FRM COUNT   PAGE #

© L.F.L. 1982
STORYBOARD DEC 10 1982
R

Shown here is a storyboard used in the production of George Lucas's *The Return of the Jedi*.

FROM THE PROS

"Special effects are a means, a tool for telling a story. A special effect without a story is a pretty boring thing."

—GEORGE LUCAS
WRITER, PRODUCER, DIRECTOR

product tells a coherent story. Editing can make two people filmed at different times appear to be in the same room. Many an aspiring new actor has labored through take after take of his or her scene only to find the film on the proverbial "cutting room floor."

In an animated film, the various voices of the animated characters are recorded separately and then edited together. The sound editor makes it seem as if the characters are carrying on a conversation, even though the actors might have recorded the dialogue weeks, months, or even years apart. Similarly, the graphic elements are "layered." The characters and the settings in which they appear are created separately and later merged to create what the audience sees.

Working in a small group or with a partner, choose a scene from a movie, a television program, or a play. You might want to choose a scene from "A Treasury of Scenes and Monologues." Assume that the scene will be part of a movie, and draw a series of storyboards for that scene. Using the storyboard from *The Return of the Jedi* as a model, include the description of the setting and action directly below the picture.

SPECIAL CIRCUMSTANCES OF TELEVISION

Television has some special dramatic considerations. Much television programming is made up of comic or dramatic series. The same characters with the same personal traits appear in the same basic setting week after week. A television situation comedy (called a sitcom, for short) or a drama normally requires a writer to address only the development and resolution of the plot. Since the exposition (the characters and their situations) is already established, the writer can advance quickly to the problem faced in the episode.

Writing a television script presents one obstacle not found in film: commercials. Writers must make sure the program is written in segments that can be broken up by commercial advertisements. He or she must make interest in the show so compelling that the viewer will sit through the almost eight minutes of commercials aired in a half-hour program. Ideally, a point of high interest will come just prior to each commercial break so viewers will want to return to the program. Integrating these breaks into the dramatic structure is not an easy task. Remote-control channel changers have made it easier for viewers to check, and become interested in, other programming during commercial breaks, adding to the challenge of the script writer's task.

The introduction and the common use of taped programming in television allows television producers to do retakes of scenes much as moviemakers do. Television programs, however, tend to occur on a tighter schedule than movies do, so timesaving tactics are sometimes employed. For example, when taping a television show, some production companies tape the dress rehearsal before a live audience and then edit the dress rehearsal into the final tape. Some directors prefer to keep the live audience's reaction in the final version. Because of multiple retakes

▼ CUE

At a cost of $200 million, the 1997 film *Titanic* became one of the costliest films of all time. However, it had already grossed that amount by its twenty-fifth day of release. The high cost was due in part to its spectacular special effects.

The Miracle Worker is an example of a script that has been adapted for theater, film, and television. Patty Duke played Helen Keller in the 1962 movie. She is shown here as Annie Sullivan with Melissa Gilbert as Helen Keller in the 1979 television presentation.

resulting from actors' miscues, prop or technical problems, and the many other situations associated with a performance, a thirty-minute taped show may take two or three hours to tape.

Most television shows are taped using a **three-camera system** that was developed by Desi Arnaz and cameraman Karl Freund while taping *I Love Lucy*. This use of multiple cameras allows the director to switch from close-ups to wide-angle shots and to get various camera angles on the same actor during just one take. This form of taping offers greater coverage of shots and remains an industry standard to this day. Although this system now usually includes more than three cameras, the term *three-camera system* is still used.

Application
ACTIVITIES

1. Choose three of your favorite movies and write the story ideas that might have been presented (see the story idea for *Jurassic Park* on page 546).

2. Watch a television sitcom or drama. What techniques does the writer use to get audience members to continue watching after the commerical break?

❧ *Performing Before the Camera*

The success of all acting, whether it is on the stage, in film, or on television, depends on preparation. Even a brilliant improviser must be familiar with the character and the situation he or she is portraying. It is safe to say no actor can be too familiar with the text. Rehearsing thoroughly and diligently is crucial. Nevertheless, preparing and performing before a live audience is not the same as preparing and performing before a camera. Although some aspects remain the same, such as moment-to-moment truthfulness, full investment, focus and relaxation, acting for the stage requires different skills than those required for film or TV. The challenges are related but distinctly different.

DIFFERENCES BETWEEN STAGE AND FILM ACTING

Perhaps the fundamental differences arise because the performer onstage has a live audience. The playwright, actor, and audience have a more personal relationship. Audience reaction is immediate, and the actor is able to make adjustments as the play unfolds. Before a major new play or musical is performed before New York critics and audiences, for example, it is often tried out and refined in places like Boston, St. Louis, or Cincinnati and adjusted according to audience response. Plays that run for weeks, months, and even years are constantly evolving. Lines may be rewritten and interpretations refined. Unlike actors before a camera, actors onstage can reach out to and win over their audiences during the course of the play. Constantly making adjustments based on the individual audience means that a stage play for an actor and a director is never really finished or "in the can" in the sense that a movie is.

ℱROM THE PROS

"Theater is a writer's medium, television is a producer's medium, and film is a director's medium."

—JAMES LIPTON
HOST OF BRAVO NETWORK'S *INSIDE THE ACTOR'S STUDIO*

Dustin Hoffman is known as a film actor, having been nominated for an Oscar six times and winning Best Actor twice. In 1985 he turned his acting skill toward television, appearing in *Death of a Salesman*, written by Arthur Miller, which also starred John Malkovich.

Moviemakers face a somewhat different challenge. While they may also try out a film on test audiences, their options are somewhat limited by costs and the patchwork manner in which movies are put together. Test audiences prompted Warner Brothers to revise the ending of *Little Shop of Horrors* (1986) and turned a potential box office flop into a success. Such examples are fairly rare, however. While an actor may be asked to repeat a scene again and again, fundamental changes rarely occur once production has begun.

The audience's physical perception is also an important distinction between acting onstage and acting onscreen. A person viewing a stage play always has a wide-angle view of the action. There are no close-ups to focus attention on one actor, a detail of the setting, a twitch of the lip, or a nervous movement of a hand. This challenges key performers in the theater to fill the stage with their voices and their presence at appropriate times and requires minor performers to be mindful of their important but supporting roles. Any member of the audience might focus on any character at any time.

Film actors must be constantly aware that the camera records everything they do—no matter how small or subtle the action. The actor's every muscle twitch, hesitation, breath, and gesture is exactly recorded. The lens of a camera is a much finer point of focus than a theater audience is. A blink, the flare of a nostril, or the curl of a lip can speak volumes in a close-up. Film acting requires subtleties that would be lost onstage.

Physical acting onstage must be energized and fully driven, involving voice, body, and gesture. The audience agrees to make believe that the story told in front of them, live, in the same room, is wherever and whenever they are being told. The playwright paints with words, but the filmmaker paints with visual images. Film and television have the capacity to present real locations, properties, and even weather. The accompanying acting must therefore be equally real.

With time and experience, a film actor can become quite skillful at playing for the single eye of the camera. The stage actor, on the other hand, must strive to open up his or her performance to all of the eyes filling the theater.

Film acting calls for control and understatement. Morgan Freeman's quiet style won an Oscar nomination for Best Actor in 1989 for *Driving Miss Daisy*. He is shown here with his co-star in that movie, Jessica Tandy.

Like the camera, the presence of highly sensitive recording equipment and microphones on the sets of films and in television studios requires some adjustments on the part of the performers. Because members of a live stage audience might be in the last row or balcony two hundred feet away, strongly projected voices are sometimes necessary to the stage actor's technique. This is not true in film.

Stage acting has become far less theatrical and more naturalistic over the last fifty years. This change may be due in part to changing expectations because of long-term exposure to the realistic acting in film and television. Another factor of the change in style is modern microphones that are virtually undetectable but allow voices to be projected and amplified. Consequently, the distinction between film acting and stage acting has diminished. Even so, the crucial differences in voice projection, physical acting, size and openness of the performance, and the relationship between actor and audience remain.

FILMING OUT OF SEQUENCE

In addition to audience, performers on the stage or the screen are profoundly affected by the manner in which the final performance is put together. The stage play is presented to a live audience from beginning to end. Even though individual scenes and acts may be rehearsed time and time again in isolation, there is always a strong context for the scene, a continuity provided by an ongoing and healthy collaboration with the director and other members of the cast. Preparation proceeds strongly from the whole to the parts and back to the whole. The stage actor has rehearsal time to build a character scene by scene over a four-week period of eight-hour days and six-day weeks.

Film or television dramas, on the other hand, are shot wildly out of sequence, often in random snippets. Actors read scripts in isolation without the benefit of discussion with the director or the other actors. Sometimes only in the first take of a scene, called the "master shot," are all the actors present with the full set. Future takes of close-ups and specifically chosen set-ups are filmed later and edited in. Scenes planned for filming on a given day may be shuffled due to weather or schedule changes with little notice. Performing in such piecemeal fashion requires an actor to work hard to keep the order of the story and the development of character in mind. He or she must be familiar with the entirety of an assigned role from the first day of shooting, drawing on what stage actors call the "emotional memory" of the master shot.

All acting requires imagination and focus, but in film special demands are made on an actor. He or she may be called on to address a rolling camera as though speaking to another actor, but, of course, no one

▼ CUE

During the making of *Jurassic Park*, sound designer Gary Rydstrom had to make sounds for a creature that no human being had ever heard—the dinosaur. Rydstrom looked to nature for a solution. The frightening sounds of the raptors in the film are actually a combination of sounds made by a dolphin and a walrus. Rydstrom fed the sounds into a computer and created the combination on a keyboard.

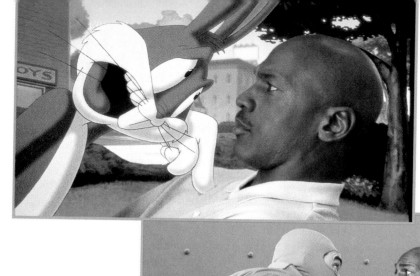

In 1996 Michael Jordan appeared with a cast of animated characters in Warner Brothers' *Space Jam*. In order to appear to be interacting with cartoon characters, Jordan was first filmed in a scene with a person acting in place of the cartoon character. Later a computer was used to substitute the animated character, in this case Bugs Bunny, for the actor.

is there except the camera operator, director, and a crew of technicians. In many recent, big-budget, state-of-the-art special-effects films, the other actor will be added in later by computer or other technical means. The actor filming his or her "half" of the scene must rely purely on concentration, instinct, and imagination. Moreover, attention to the details of the actions and tasks being performed is vital in film since a scene might be filmed over and over. Each shot and take must match precisely, down to the placement of a drinking glass or the fold of an actor's clothing.

Application
ACTIVITIES

1. Explain how acting on the screen differs from stage acting. Think of some actions that can be done on-screen that are impossible onstage.

2. Choose a famous actor, male or female, and find out what kind of training or experience he or she had before becoming successful. How did he or she get the first "big break"?

Assessing the Success of a Production

The art and craft of drama have always been subject to review and analysis, called **criticism.** When drama moved onto the movie and TV screen, critics continued to offer their reviews and analyses. Modern media present us daily with critical reviews. Newspapers, magazines, the Internet, and even television itself provide us with critics' opinions and recommendations concerning new movies and upcoming television programs. These criticisms can affect the audience's response to a production and therefore the ultimate success of that production.

TWO TYPES OF CRITICISM

Although individual critics may approach a work from widely varying perspectives, their criticisms can be roughly divided into two types: reviews and analyses. Critics whose **reviews** appear in newspapers and popular magazines and on TV or the Internet might include some analysis of the works to support their opinions, but their primary function is to recommend or not recommend a movie or television program to their audience. Some would prefer to call such people reviewers rather than critics. The review type of criticism is probably the type that is most familiar to the viewing public.

The growth of criticism in the media has been accompanied by a change in the role of the critic. Some critics today have become personalities in their own right. Roger Ebert and the late Gene Siskel are thought by many to have influenced this trend. Both began by writing movie reviews for different newspapers. They were later paired in a syndicated television show on which they reviewed and discussed current movies. Their insights and frequently sharp differences of opinion made them immensely popular. Their well-known mark of a good movie, "two thumbs up," has found its way into the vocabulary of film.

Positive reviews can help boost ticket sales. Caution should be exercised, however, when considering the advice or opinion of a reviewer as a factor in deciding to attend a movie or watch a TV show. Many a moviegoer has been disappointed by a movie that critics and reviewers have raved about.

Consider that, as all people do, reviewers have individual tastes. Rarely is it possible to find a reviewer whose taste exactly matches yours. Moreover, a popular critic or reviewer may be more interested in advancing his or her own career and celebrity status than in offering a carefully weighed assessment of a film or a TV program. There might be many

Many people consider the opinions of professional critics when deciding whether to see a movie. Critics such as Roger Ebert (left) and the late Gene Siskel (right) have accustomed viewers to "thumbs up" or "thumbs down" reviews.

reasons, but questions concerning the fairness and impartiality of reviews offered in such contexts are reasonable. You must decide.

Critics who write for journals and film industry publications tend to be analytical in their approach. They are less interested in a production's popular appeal than in its literary value or artistic appeal. A person writing this type of review would carefully look at individual aspects of both the script and the production and how they work together.

A detailed **analysis** of a production might include describing and evaluating these aspects of the script: theme, plot, dialogue, and characterization. The production, which is the result of combining the script with the creative efforts of the participants, can be examined by looking at the set design, direction, acting, and audience reaction. When analyzing a given movie or program, you might find the need to evaluate other aspects of the production, but those listed provide a basis for a comprehensive analysis. An additional category for film and television analysis might be the editing—are there unexplained or illogical jumps in the action? For more information about each of the categories, see "How to Judge a Play" on pages 530–534.

THE AUDIENCE AND THE PRODUCTION

Producers of stage plays must be very sensitive to critical reviews and to audience response, rewriting shows if necessary to please audiences. Movies that are not well received can be released to television or the video market. By doing so, a filmmaker can save the enormous costs associated with distributing and promoting a film. Some movies, like Disney's *Honey, We Shrunk Ourselves,* bypass the theaters entirely and are released straight to video. By acting quickly, it is sometimes possible for a movie studio to recover its costs and turn a profit on a poor movie.

A stage production, however, has nowhere else to go. The huge investment in a play must be recovered through ticket sales. Therefore, the producer is more inclined to refine, revise, and do whatever is necessary to turn a weak play into a successful one.

Just how much a critical review affects the success or failure of a film is difficult to say. Numerous factors come into play. *The Lost World*, Steven Spielberg's sequel to the highly successful *Jurassic Park*, received some terrible reviews but went on to earn more than 200 million dollars. Perhaps the success of the earlier *Jurassic Park*, provided it with a built-in audience. Maybe by opening in some six thousand theaters at once, the film became "critic proof." By the time the critics had their say, tens of thousands of people had already seen the movie.

MEASURING SUCCESS

Measuring the commercial success of stage plays and movies is not necessarily a simple matter. In the case of the traditional stage play, the **receipts,** or money taken in from ticket sales, by and large tell the story. The same is more or less true of movies. Some movies, such as *Star Wars* and *The Lion King* spawn a secondary source of income from the sale of toys, games, T-shirts, and a host of related items.

For commercial television, the process of measuring success becomes more complex. With no ticket sales to calculate, television networks rely on outside firms to assess the size of the viewing audience. These **ratings,** as they are typically called, are determined by monitoring a relatively small number of homes that are theoretically representative of national viewership. Based on the findings, these ratings services project the size of each show's audience and rank shows competing in the same time slot accordingly. Using these rankings, television networks set the prices for commercials. The higher the rating, the more costly a minute of commercial time.

The ratings process is not without controversy. Critics of the process argue that the sample is too small and by its nature unrepresentative, since

The movie *The Lion King* increased its profits substantially when the production company authorized sales of merchandise carrying the movie logo and pictures from the movie. Many other movies have likewise profited through merchandising.

it ignores the thousands of people who do not watch television because of the lack of quality programming. The critics point to dozens of programs that enjoyed superb critical reviews but were canceled because they lost the ratings wars.

The competition for audience has become quite fierce in recent years. The person searching for entertainment today has many options. With the advent of the rental video, pay-per-view movies, and the multiplex theater, film lovers can choose among several current movies or elect to wait for the video or television showing. A TV viewer has scores of channels to choose from and can exercise that choice with the touch of the handy remote control. When satellite dishes, direct TV, and cable television are added to the entertainment mix, today's audience faces an almost unlimited number of choices but has only a limited amount of money to spend on them.

THE CHANGING AUDIENCE

Perhaps because of so many options, the attention span of the public has steadily declined since the turn of the century. In response, movies have become more quickly paced. Television programs are more action packed than ever. TV news shows have replaced the single reporter with a succession of cuts from the anchor desk, to the field, to a co-anchor, always punctuated with a liberal sprinkling of visuals. The audience of the nineties, for example, who are accustomed to quick cuts and fast-moving cameras, have a difficult time sitting through a film like Stanley Kubrick's *2001: A Space Odyssey* because its pace is slow and its shots are relatively long.

Whether television and the movies influence society or reflect it is an age-old argument, but it is one that still applies to today's audiences. Depending on their point of view, critics either blame or praise networks like MTV and Nickelodeon for the quick editing and bold images that have found their way into the general media. Whether networks are to blame for the audience's decreased attention span or are just capitalizing on it is an issue that continues to be debated. One thing is certain, however: people want fast-paced, instant entertainment, and they are getting it.

The modern audience has changed in another way, too. Thanks to large-screen televisions, theater-style sound systems, and videotapes, people have become accustomed to enjoying the theater experience in their living rooms. Talking may be acceptable in the privacy of one's home, but it is not appreciated in a crowded theater. The on-screen requests to remain silent and clean up any trash serve as reminders to observe proper theater etiquette.

The audience, however, need not take all the blame. The theaters themselves are at least partly responsible for audiences' seeming indifference

Stanley Kubrick's *2001: A Space Odyssey,* released in 1968, is a classic science-fiction production. Shown in this scene are Gary Lockwood (left) and Keir Dullea (right).

to their surroundings. The early movie houses were referred to as "palaces" because of their grand scale and lavish interiors. The elaborate curtains, lushly carpeted lobbies, large restrooms, and uniformed ushers all transported the audience to a special place to watch a special event. Audience members dressed up as if they were going to watch a live performance, and they were on their best behavior.

The movie palaces of the past have been torn down, converted to other uses, or remodeled to contain numerous small-screen theaters. These multi-picture complexes, or multiplex theaters, are austere in contrast to the elegant surroundings, amenities, and large staffs of the old palaces. The smaller screens, fewer seats, and stark atmosphere of today's theaters contribute to the lack of spectacle and awe. Because many of the new theater complexes are very large, crowds and parking can be a problem, which might even work to keep more people watching films at home.

Even though luxury and atmosphere in theaters might have been sacrificed to progress, films and television continue to improve the quality and quantity of entertainment available to all of us. Technology and the creativity of moviemakers and television producers make the entertainment business one of the most dynamic areas of our modern culture. Advancements in film and television affect not only critics and audiences, but also influence the traditional stage drama from which they sprang.

Application
ACTIVITIES

1. Find two or more reviews of a current movie in newspapers or magazines. Identify points of agreement and disagreement between two of the reviewers. Then view the movie yourself and decide which reviewer most closely reflects your assessment of the movie.

2. Using the information found on pages 530–534, write an analysis of any movie or television program you choose.

CHAPTER

14 REVIEW

Summary and Key Ideas

Summarize the chapter by answering the following questions.

1. What was Mark Peter Roget's contribution to the invention of the moving picture?
2. Explain how the camera was first used in filmmaking; then describe the changes made by D. W. Griffith.
3. What were the limitations of early television?
4. What is a storyboard and what purpose does it serve?
5. What special problems do commercials pose for the TV writer?
6. How is the success of productions assessed in theater? Film? Television?

Discussing Ideas

1. How do the acting skills required of a movie actor differ from those required of an actor on the stage?
2. Discuss the following statement: "Unlike the film actor, the stage actor can reach out and win over an audience."
3. What is meant by the expression "Less is more" as it applies to the film actor?
4. Discuss what factors affect your decision to see a movie.

FOCUS ON ▶ Criticism

Critics play an important role in the culture of theater and film. To strengthen your own critical abilities, read dramatic criticism—and write your own. Using your own experiences and understanding to analyze theater will help you build closer connections to drama that you see and read.

Exploring Criticism Some critics—known as literary critics—take a literary approach to drama, examining the scripts of plays primarily as literary works. Critics referred to as drama critics generally choose an approach that pays equal or nearly equal attention to the script and the production. Choose two published critics, either literary or dramatic,

to investigate. The critics may write about live theater, film, or television. Find out if the critics belong to any particular schools of criticism. Read several pieces by each critic to help you get a sense of their style. Then compare and contrast the work of the two critics in a short presentation to the class.

Be the Critic Write a two-page critical analysis of a movie, play, television program, or other dramatic production of your choice. Be sure that your analysis evaluates aspects of the script as well as the creative effort involved in the production. See pages 530 to 534 for more information on how to evaluate drama.

THEATER AND OTHER MEDIA

INDEPENDENT ACTIVITIES

Situation Comedy Select two or more situation comedies currently appearing on television. Watch several performances of each; then write a description of the "situation" and the character types that repeatedly occur in each episode. Decide which situation is more successful in generating comedy. Create a plan for a new situation comedy by describing a situation and several character types that have the potential for multiple comic plots. Provide one example of such a plot.

Film Adaptation A scene from a play must ordinarily undergo some adaptation before being brought to the screen. A director must decide when to use close-ups or wide-angle shots. He or she must decide which actor, action, or object to focus the camera on. Music might also be used to underscore a scene.

Choose one of the scenes provided in Part Two of this book, and adapt it for a screen presentation. Write directions for the camera crew and decide on any music you wish to add. You may choose to make several rough sketches to show how you imagine the screen appearing during particular parts of the dialogue.

Cooperative Learning Activity

Demonstration
Work with a partner to create a simple demonstration of the persistence of vision theory proposed by Roget. This can be accomplished by drawing two images on either side of a card, attaching the card to a pencil or similar long, narrow stick, and spinning the card rapidly. The two images will appear as a single image to a viewer. For example, if a drawing of a bird appears on one side and a bird cage on the other, the bird will appear to be in the cage.

Across the CURRICULUM Activity

Language Arts
Attend a showing of a new movie, preferably on the day of its first showing. If possible, sit through several showings of the film. Then write a review of the film assessing its strengths and weaknesses and decide whether you would recommend the film to others. Summarize your review by awarding it from zero to four stars, with four stars being the highest rating. Compare your rating with those of professional reviewers.

15 *Theater and Other Art Forms*

This version of *Cinderella*, starring Whitney Houston, Bernadette Peters, Jason Alexander, and Brandy, effectively combines music, dance, and costumes to create a dazzling production.

Theater is a potpourri. It can contain anything that [a person] offers to others. . . .

—BERNARD BECKERMAN, CRITIC

SETTING THE SCENE

Focus Questions

How does each art form communicate theme, mood, action, character, and setting?

What elements and communication methods do different art forms share?

How are art forms affected by society and historical events?

What part do music, art, and dance play in drama?

Vocabulary

composer	ballet	Broadway musical
melody	modern dance	art director
lyrics	tap dance	opera-buffa
troubadours	synthesis	
choreographer	performance art	

Many art forms, including dance, music, and fine art, are combined in theatrical productions to support and enhance theme, mood, character, action, and setting. Because each art form provides a unique sensory experience, the appeal of the drama is broadened and enriched. As you study art forms in relation to theater, keep in mind that each art form also exists independently of theater. Dance has a history of its own, for example, as do music, fine art, and other art forms. In order to understand the contributions of each art form to theater, you must be familiar with the features of the art form itself.

🎵 *Music*

CUE ▼

Modern scientists have discovered that the Greeks were partially right in assigning emotional powers to music. In fact music is used today in treating pain, relieving tension, and stimulating brain activity.

Music can only be fully expressed through performance because it is an auditory means of communication—it must be heard. The **composer,** or author, depends on musicians and conductors to interpret the work. The listeners must then translate sounds they hear into emotions and imagery. The ancient Greeks believed that musical scales had moral value because of the emotional responses they produced. They believed music could move a person to action or even make a listener lose consciousness. They also believed music could help bring about spiritual and physical well-being.

The **melody,** or main musical phrase, expresses the general feeling of a composition. The tools a composer works with to shape the melody are tempo, rhythm, volume, key, and harmony. Through the combinations and variations of tempo and rhythm, a composer can write a slow, lulling song or a fast, exciting song, thereby expressing different moods. Volume also affects mood, setting, character, and theme. If a composer chooses a high volume, he or she could be presenting an angry or an exuberant mood or character. When the volume is low, the mood might be relaxing or suspenseful. With the variations of volume in a composition come changes in mood and the development of theme. The choice of key and harmony can determine whether a composition is melancholy or joyful. The choice of musical instruments is another factor in expression; every instrument contributes a different sound to a composition. Whether a composition is written for a single instrument, for a symphony including violins and tympanis, or for a band using a drum set and electric guitars, each composition combines elements of tempo, rhythm, volume, key, and harmony to express mood, setting, character, and theme. A musical composition tells a story, and the imagination of each person involved—composer, conductor, musician, audience member—builds a slightly different story. Often, the addition of words, called **lyrics,** helps the listeners interpret the music. Like poetry, lyrics express themes, moods, and settings and sometimes describe characters. Because the rhythm and tempo of the melody can limit word choice, the meaning of the lyrics is often metaphorical or abstract. Thus a musical composition becomes a story that is different for each listener.

Another factor that adds to the versatility of music is the abundance of opportunities for hearing it. From the concertos heard while waiting on hold on the telephone to a song heard on the radio, music plays a part in everyday life. You don't always have to listen intently to a song or a composition to enjoy it. In fact you probably find yourself humming along without paying attention. The frequent opportunities for listening allow

music to reach people that other art forms do not reach.

Early humans, it is believed, made the first music by banging hollow logs with rocks and sticks, clapping their hands, stomping their feet, and imitating animal sounds. This primitive music aided in storytelling. The first historical traces of visual and written records of music come from Egypt. *Feast at the Home of Nakht,* an ancient Egyptian mural dating from c. 1360 B.C., shows basic string instruments. Written records tell of choral groups that performed for Egyptian kings. Unfortunately, no musical scores from ancient Egypt were written down, so we don't know what Egyptian music sounded like.

The ancient Greeks were the first to write down their music, allowing musicians to play a piece of music they had never heard. Most Greek music of the time was used to set the mood for poetry. Music was also a part of drama; the chorus would chant its lines. In Rome, music was considered one of the four essential areas of knowledge. Vitruvius, a Roman philosopher, included in his essay on architecture a description of how *hydraulis,* or hydraulic (water-powered) organs, were built. Like the Egyptians, the Romans did not write down their music, but we do know that Roman music was played in processions, in theatrical productions, and in gladiatorial contests.

During the Middle Ages, music became a staple of the Christian church. Church music enabled the members of the congregation to pay homage to God. As the Gothic Age began in the tenth century, trends in composition changed from religious music to music that communicated the composer's emotional struggles to the audience. Thus Gothic music was more personal and expressive than the music that preceded it. Most of the existing history of Gothic music comes from performers called **troubadours,** strolling musicians who set popular poetry to music they wrote. The Gothic era also gave us the first record of a female composer, Abbess Hildegard von Bingen, who wrote music that used either religious verses or her own poetry for lyrics.

Since the Gothic Age, music has gone through many changes. In the Renaissance, music expanded from the church into the households of the aristocracy. At festive dinners and dances, a small group of musicians secluded in an alcove or balcony would play background music. From this time on, musical history is full of geniuses whose works have survived to

CUE ▼

Another way that music has reached a broad audience is through MTV, Music Television, which broadcasts popular songs that are illustrated with videos.

this day. The baroque era gave us such composers as Vivaldi, Handel, and Bach; classicism gave us Haydn and Mozart; romanticism gave us Beethoven and Brahms; and realism gave us Wagner (väg′ • nər) and Tchaikovsky (chī • kôf′ • skē). Although each era had its own set of musical standards, the communication of theme became the main objective of composers. They also branched out, writing music for operas and for professional dance performances, such as ballets. Ballets and operas gave composers scope to describe characters and create a concrete setting in their music as the story was acted out onstage. Mozart was commissioned to write the music for *The Magic Flute,* a story of two sets of lovers and the trials they endured. With his ethereal music, he conveys the mystical, romantic world in which the lovers live.

At the beginning of the twentieth century came the modern era, when people loved to listen to such popular music as ragtime, blues, jazz, and swing. From these types of music came rock and roll, a musical movement that expressed rebellion and defiance of traditional values. The song "Rock Around the Clock" by Bill Haley and The Comets marked the beginning of this movement. The Beatles, one of the most influential rock bands, focused on social issues and Eastern religions in much of their music. On the other hand, bands such as the Rolling Stones mainly addressed emotional issues and youthful revolt. By late in the twentieth century, rock and roll encompassed many genres that had their own sounds and purposes. U2 rose to popularity through the bold social and political statements made in such songs as "Sunday Bloody Sunday"; whereas Bruce Springsteen often uses his songs to tell stories, such as in "Born to Run." REM, in the song "Man on the Moon," challenges the information that the media circulate, and Rap musician Puff Daddy makes a social statement about the conditions of America's inner cities. Many bands, such as the Orb, focus on rhythm and dance beat to emphasize the mood of their music.

Application
ACTIVITY

Choose a song approved by your teacher to analyze. Give your interpretation of the theme of the composition. Explain what leads you to this interpretation. What, do you think, was the writer's purpose in composing this work? If the song has lyrics, how do they affect the communication of theme, mood, character, and setting? Present a report to your class, and, if possible, play a recording of the music you chose.

🌿 *Dance*

Dance is primarily a kinesthetic and a visual medium; however, most dance performances are accompanied by music, making dance both a visual and an auditory experience. Dancers use body language to communicate the theme, mood, and plot of a work to their audience. Their movements are designed by a **choreographer,** who combines a series of steps to produce a unique work. Choreographers may picture the mood, theme, tone, and plot they wish to portray, but they can't relate these elements directly to the audience. When the choreography is complete, the choreographer must instead depend on the dancers to interpret meaning and then translate this meaning to the audience, just as a composer must depend on musicians and a conductor to interpret and communicate his or her musical composition. Unlike the painter and the sculptor, whose canvas and sculpture are completed once for all time, the choreographer and the composer produce works that are open to the interpretation of the performers and of the audience members afresh at each performance.

Many classical **ballets,** such as *Swan Lake* and *The Nutcracker*, have plots with characters and action the dancers must present to the audience. Many other dances do not have plots, but they do have themes or moods for the dancers to portray. Dancers communicate the elements of plot, character, theme, mood, and action to the audience by executing the steps choreographed for the performance. They also rely on the accompanying music to enhance these elements. Often the intent of a choreographer is to produce movements and poses that portray universal emotions. Even audience members who know nothing of dance technique can find both meaning and satisfaction in a good dance production.

Dance, of course, is an ancient art form. In early human history, warriors and hunters celebrated their victories with ritual dances. Later, folk dances were handed down through generations, and nearly everyone joined in. Members of royal courts and the poor were equally likely to dance. Dancing was intended for participation, not observation. In fact, professional dance performances did not exist until the eighteenth century.

In 1993, Macaulay Culkin starred as the Nutcracker Prince in a motion-picture production of George Balanchine's *The Nutcracker.*

King Louis XIV of France is generally credited with having originated professional dance. Louis XIV loved to dance, but as he aged, his love for food proved stronger than his love of dance, and he was no longer able to participate in the elaborate dances he held at Versailles. Unwilling to be the only person not dancing, he built a balcony over a ballroom, from which he and other members of his court could watch the dancers below. Suddenly, the purpose of dancing changed: dancing was no longer thought of as primarily entertainment for the participants, but rather as a spectacle for the observers. Louis XIV later started the first dance school in Paris, and France became a leader in developing ballet technique. Ballet steps today are still named in French.

The first ballet performances were nothing like those of today. At first, only men performed. When women began appearing onstage, they were forced to wear the costumes of the times. Cumbersome corsets and long gowns of the eighteenth century made movement difficult. Any kind of vigorous dancing was impossible for the female dancers, so the men surpassed them in technique, developing sophisticated, daring routines. Slowly, the styles of the costumes worn by women became more accommodating. By the middle of the nineteenth century, female ballet dancers were wearing tutus and tights and were often upstaging men with such techniques as dancing on the tips of their toes. Toe dancing was made possible by the invention of *pointe* shoes, which were designed to support the ballerina's feet. Some men's roles even began to be played by women. Russian dancers and choreographers, who dominated the field in the late nineteenth century, changed the course of ballet and introduced many of the most famous ballets, including *Swan Lake, The Nutcracker,* and *Sleeping Beauty.* Russia provided the twentieth century with some of the superstars of ballet. Rudolf Nureyev (no͞or´ • ĭ • yĕv) and Mikhail Baryshnikov (bə • rĭsh´ • nĭ • kôf´) were both born in the former Soviet Union.

Out of classical ballet came many other forms of **modern dance.** Isadora Duncan (who danced from 1899 to 1927) is often considered the founder of modern dance. She believed that the structured techniques of ballet were too confining; she let her hair fall naturally over loose-fitting robes, and she ignored structure in favor of communicating soul and emotion to her enraptured audiences. Fred Astaire, another twentieth-century dancer, delighted his large audiences. His **tap dances,** included in famous movie routines with equally talented partners like Ginger Rogers, changed dance. His dances, like all dances, were a visual product, but the sound of his shoes clicking against the dance floor produced rhythm and music, making his dances an auditory experience as well. Multiculturalism also changed dance. Choreographer Alvin

CUE ▼

Mikhail Baryshnikov broke new ground in the synthesis of dance and music when he danced to the beat of his own heart. Artist Christopher Janney attached a device to the dancer that captured the electrical impulses passing through his body as he danced. These impulses then regulated the accompanying music.

Ailey, for example, set his dances to African American spirituals and southern blues songs. He formed the Alvin Ailey American Dance Theater, a multiracial troupe. Another choreographer, Arthur Mitchell, composed a Creole version of the classic ballet *Giselle.* Mitchell started the Dance Theater of Harlem and incorporated ballet, jazz, and modern dance into his performances. Other modern dance choreographers, such as Twyla Tharp, have blended several types of dance, like ballet, jazz, and tap, into their dance routines. Contemporary dances often have themes different from traditional ballets. Modern-dance choreographers generally portray universal emotions, but in the twentieth century, they have also added social commentary to their dances, using dance as a medium to explore the social problems of the day.

Alvin Ailey choreographed dances for African American spirituals in his most popular production, *Revelations.* The Alvin Ailey American Dance Company has performed in many countries around the globe.

Application
ACTIVITIES

1. Working with a partner, choose a brief scene—either one from a play or one that you invent—and interpret it through dance movements. If you want, choreograph your scene to music of your choosing. Keep in mind that even everyday movements can be incorporated into dance. The key is to portray interactions without dialogue. Perform your dance for the class; then discuss what was most and least successful about your performance.

2. Nations and cultures often develop special styles of dance that employ traditional costumes and specific movements. Investigate the traditional dances and costumes associated with a culture of your choosing; then report your findings to the class.

Jackson Pollock uses line and color to create mood in his painting *Number 8.* Pollock's innovative technique included squirting, drizzling, and dripping ordinary house paint onto huge canvases.

🌺 *Fine Art*

Fine art is a visual art form produced through many mediums. Paintings, sketches, sculptures, and even some crafts are considered fine art. Sometimes it is difficult to understand the message or main idea of a particular artwork. Like drama, fine art forms communicate mood, characters, setting, and theme in many ways. In order to understand a work of art, it is helpful to learn about some of the basic elements that make up fine art—color, line, texture, shape, form, and space.

Each of these elements is present to some extent in every work of art—no matter what art medium is used. Through the blending, contrasting, and placement of color, an artist can express the overall emotion, or mood, of a work. Color is also used to symbolize ideas or other nonvisual concepts. Lines are used in art to form images, emphasize or de-emphasize the outlines of objects, form borders, and define spaces. Lines may also convey setting and express action in a work of art. Texture, through the use of fine, delicate brushstrokes or thick, heavy brushstrokes, may affect the mood and, therefore, the interpretation of a painting. In sculpture, texture defines and separates forms and space. Shapes, which are two-dimensional, and forms, which are three-dimensional, define objects in a work of art and are made up of any or all of the other elements. Space, the distance or area between, around, or within objects, can be either two- or three-dimensional. Space is often used to emphasize or de-emphasize certain parts of a painting or sculpture. For example, by leaving empty space around an object, an artist forces an observer's eye to focus on that object.

Character, setting, and mood all contribute to interpretation. Sometimes an artist might make a statement by portraying characters in new and surprising ways. A kind, gentle historical character might be portrayed as villainous, or a villainous character might be portrayed as kind and gentle. This type of role reversal often served as political propaganda. Jacques-Louis David, a court painter for Napoleon, portrayed Napoleon as a benevolent ruler who sacrificed his spare time for his subjects' benefit.

David conveyed this theme through details in the portrait's setting. Setting also affects the interpretation of mood and is sometimes used to identify and place characters in context. In landscape paintings, often the setting itself is the character.

Some modern artists don't use objects, people, or landscapes in their works; instead, these artists include only colors, lines, textures, or abstract shapes to convey theme or mood. Twentieth-century American painter Jackson Pollock produced paintings with no apparent characters or setting. Instead he expressed mood through his technique of spattering colors on large canvases.

To fully understand a piece of fine art, you must try to identify its theme, or main idea. The basic elements of art are used to convey theme, but other factors also affect interpretation. For example, consider the work's historical background and the purpose it served. The Native Americans of the western United States used cave and rock paintings to express ideas, actions, and emotions. A drawing of a buffalo might identify an area where buffalo gathered or might mark a warrior's first successful hunt.

Many paintings and sculptures throughout history have illustrated important historical events or people, while more recent artists have used their work to comment on social issues. Francisco Goya, an early nineteenth-century Spanish painter, illustrated the consequences of war in his painting *The Third of May, 1808.* Knowing the history of the French invasions of Spain will aid your understanding of this painting by Goya.

Artists are also influenced by the various artistic movements that have shaped art forms throughout history. In the mid-nineteenth century, artists became interested in representing a true depiction of everyday life, giving birth to **realism.** Playwright Henrik Ibsen, known as the father of realism, began the realistic movement in drama with his play *A Doll's House.* Gustave Courbet and Édouard Manet are painters known for their realist styles, while in literature, Gustave Flaubert's *Madame Bovary* epitomized the realist movement. Many artists, dramatists, and composers are categorized according to the artistic movement with which their style is associated.

This painting, *The Third of May, 1808,* is part of Francisco Goya's *Disasters of War*, a series of paintings that chronicles the French invasion of Spain in 1808.

Application

Look at a painting or a sculpture. Identify the artist's use of the basic elements of art—color, line, texture, shape, form, and space. Then write your interpretation of the work, explaining how each of these elements contributes to mood, character, setting, and theme.

Common Elements and Influences

As you learn more about different art forms, you'll find that most share similar communication methods and elements. A comparison can be made among the art forms of music, dance, and fine art. Even though visual interpretation and auditory interpretation differ, the main elements of theme, mood, character, and setting may be conveyed in similar fashions. For example, mood is often created by color and line in fine art. In music, mood is also created by color and line if you imagine the harmonies and keys as the color and the melody as the line. Dance, which usually combines the visual and auditory senses, portrays color with the accompanying music, the costumes, and the scenery; it portrays line with the movement and placement of the dancers. Not only do these art forms share communication methods, they also share many of the same influences, including the historical context and the artistic movement of the period in which the works appeared.

The art forms of dance, music, fine art, and literature have always been influenced by social and philosophical movements of the day. Consider, for example, the romantic period, which began in the late eighteenth century and continued through the first half of the nineteenth century. Romantics had similar, although not identical, views about life and art. They were primarily striving for freedom and free expression of their personal feelings. Unlike the classicists who preceded them, romantics did not seek perfection of form and design. If classicism was the age of reason, then romanticism was the age of individuality, nature, and emotion, which flowered in the "cult of feeling." In literature, the famous romantic poet William Wordsworth wrote that ". . . all good poetry is the spontaneous overflow of powerful feelings."

Authors expressed romantic moods and themes through descriptions of beauty, and their works were often set in nature. In fine art, painters ignored the strict forms of past years and gave voice to their personal feelings. Eugène Delacroix, one of the leading painters of the romantic movement, painted a scene of people's search for freedom

in his famous work *Liberty Leading the People.* Other romantic painters joined their literary counterparts in using nature as a setting. Such painters as J. M. W. Turner and Jean-Baptiste-Camille Corot (kô • rō′) are famous for their landscapes.

As a result of the romantic movement, composers began listening to their own needs, primarily composing works for the general public instead of works commissioned by the aristocracy. Although the music of the romantic period is as diverse as the art and literature of the time, the composers of this era shared a desire to achieve an emotional response from the audience. They called forth emotions by producing "musical tension," although each composer had a different idea about how to do so. Many renowned composers such as Beethoven, Schubert, Chopin, and Verdi (vâr′ • dē) were romantic composers.

The romantic era also had a profound impact on the world of dance. Romantic ballets, such as *Giselle* and *Les Sylphides,* demanded that ballerinas be fairy-like creatures with pale skin, pink tights, and pink satin *pointe* shoes. Performances often had supernatural settings and ghostly mists. As women of the time were rejecting the previous age's tight corsets in favor of softer, flowing garments, so too did ballerinas, gaining more freedom of expression. The romantic period's tutu had a stiff white bodice, but the skirt (falling anywhere from just below the knee to just above the ankle) was made of many layers of soft fabric, which flowed gently about the dancer as she moved.

Romanticism influenced all of the art forms, sometimes resulting in similar themes, moods, and characters. Other periods throughout history have also given rise to an expression common to the art forms. A search for realism in literature and drama, for example, paralleled a search for realism in fine art and music. Artists from each art form work to communicate the ideas, themes, and moods that are widespread in their era.

CUE

At an early age, Beethoven had to give up performing due to the onset of deafness. Despite this handicap, he continued composing until his death. The movie *Immortal Beloved* tells his life story.

Application

1. Choose two art forms and compare and contrast their means of communicating theme, mood, setting, and character. Compare the elements used, but be sure to explain how the art forms are different. Investigate the ways these art forms reach their audience. Discuss your findings with the class.

2. Investigate a historical period, focusing on a particular artistic movement. In a report, include the social and political occurrences of the day, along with the many art forms affected by the movement.

Synthesis of Art Forms in Theater

The **synthesis,** or combination of elements to form a whole, of art forms in theater produces a comprehensive visual and auditory performance. Because drama is a type of literature, movements in drama have closely followed movements in literature. Philosophy has also had an impact on drama. In ancient Greece, the philosopher Plato wrote about mimesis (imitation) and Aristotle wrote an essay on the elements of tragedy. More recently, philosopher Jean-Paul Sartre crossed over from philosophical writing to write the play *No Exit,* which portrayed his existentialist ideas.

Playwrights express their artistic ideas and interests, as well as comment on life as they perceive it, through the synthesis of dialogue, fine art, music, and dance. In fact some of the most imaginative art combines aspects of different art forms.

Performance art blends a wide variety of art forms and is always unique and unprecedented. These performances include a combination of some or all of the following art forms: music, dance, fine art, poetry, improvisation, comedy, and acting. Some performance artists begin their shows with only an idea and improvise the entire performance. Spalding Gray, for example, takes the stage with only a list of key words and tells stories of his life, always adding a comic twist. Performance art began in the 1960s as an **avant-garde** art form—a term that still applies to performance art today. In the 1980s, Laurie Anderson brought performance art to mainstream culture. In her performances, she focused on difficult social issues and human emotions, enhancing the performances with synthesized music, innovative lighting, and striking gestures and poses. At the end of the 1990s, performance artists like Anderson, Gray, and Eric Bogosian were drawing large audiences around the world. Like performance art, theater also incorporates many art forms.

Performance artist Laurie Anderson communicates her message through the inventive use of music, monologue, gesture, lighting, and special effects.

MUSIC AND THEATER

Music has accompanied theater since the beginning of Western drama. The ancient Greek dramas began as a chorus that chanted dialogue. As drama evolved, individuals began to step out of the chorus to speak their lines, but the role of the chorus remained intact. The chorus has even been used in modern plays, such as Jean Anouilh's *Antigone*. The use of music by the chorus sets the mood and establishes setting and character.

Perhaps the kind of theater that depends the most on music is the **opera.** In the seventeenth century, opera was born in an attempt to reproduce ancient Greek performances. Opera changed the role of music—both instrumental and vocal—from accompaniment to the focus of the production. Many composers have written operatic works, including Handel, who composed the *Messiah,* and Mozart, who wrote music for *The Marriage of Figaro.* Opera communicates largely through music, which is responsible for establishing mood and theme. Opera is usually performed in Italian or German; unless subtitles are provided, audiences that speak other languages must rely on the music and stage performance to interpret the play.

As time passed, opera evolved into several different genres, and one of them gave us the musicals we have today. Music plays a tremendous role in setting mood and illustrating character in musical theater. For example, in Prokofiev's (prō • kō′ • fē • əf) musical fairy tale *Peter and the Wolf,* a different musical instrument is introduced when each character is introduced. The instrument and its particular melody remain associated with that character. The high-pitched, fluttering sounds of the flute represent birds. The invigorating sounds of rhythmical violins represent Peter, and the ominous sounds of kettledrums represent the hunters.

In the twentieth century, adding popular music to theater resulted in **Broadway musicals.** In the middle of the century, Rodgers and

Hammerstein, George and Ira Gershwin, and Lerner and Loewe popularized this form of theater with productions like *Oklahoma!* More recently, works like *Hair, Jesus Christ Superstar, Tommy,* and *Bring in da Noise, Bring in da Funk* successfully used contemporary music to convey plot, character, mood, and setting.

Music is important in film, too. Obviously, films like *Evita* rely heavily on music, but other films that don't have music as the main focus rely on it as well. The theme music of a film sets the mood. For example, the opening music for *Star Wars* sets an exciting, adventurous mood. Background music also conveys mood and has become more important since the rise in popularity of soundtracks. The addition of music to film has given writers and directors more to work with: now they can rely on music to enhance or even convey mood, theme, character, action, and setting.

DANCE AND THEATER

Dance, like literature and fine art, has evolved over the centuries. During the twentieth century, the philosophy of the modernists influenced literature, fine art, and dance. In literature ordinary speech replaced "poetic," or literary, speech. In the world of fine art, such artists as Picasso and Cézanne began to present objects subjectively instead of simply copying an object's appearance. Dance, too, has seen a modern era. Revolutionary dancer Isadora Duncan replaced traditional, rigid dance steps with freer movements that expressed her emotions. Another choreographer, David Gordon, constructed pieces in which the dancers appeared not to be dancing at all. Instead, they moved around the stage performing ordinary movements.

German-born modern dancer Hanya Holm ran a dance school in the United States, where she taught students to use dramatic movements. Holm was also a choreographer, providing dance routines for such musical productions as *My Fair Lady, Camelot,* and *Kiss Me Kate.* Musicals frequently include dance routines in their productions, aiding in the communication of mood, character, theme, and plot. The style of dance chosen for a performance affects the interpretation of tone, as do the styles of music, costume, and stage direction.

Modern dance, jazz, and tap were not the only dance styles included in musical theater productions. George Balanchine was a famous Russian ballet choreographer who founded the New York City Ballet. In the 1930s, he choreographed *Ziegfeld Follies,* a Broadway musical starring Josephine Baker and Bob Hope. With this production, ballet became part of the popular musical. Richard Rodgers and Lorenz Hart soon wrote *On Your Toes,* a musical about ballet and jazz that was also choreographed by Balanchine. Rodgers and Hart went on to write three more musicals for which Balanchine provided the choreography. Another famous ballet choreographer, Agnes de Mille, provided the dance routines for *Oklahoma!*, a musical by Richard Rodgers and Oscar Hammerstein II.

Just as the composers of musical theater have used dance to aid communication, so, too, have dance choreographers seen the benefits of adding other elements to their performances to relay mood, theme, and plot to their audiences. Many modern dance routines, especially, rely on other art forms to enhance communication. Some choreographers have added dialogue to their performances in an effort to communicate their themes and ideas to the audience. The addition of dialogue to dance routines narrows the gap between theater and dance performances. Acts like those of Stomp, a contemporary performance group that blends auditory and visual effects, also narrow the gap between the theater and dance. Instead of using an orchestra or a band to provide music to accompany their dance routines, the members of Stomp provide their own percussion as they dance. Their performance is even more revolutionary because of the "instruments" they use. They make music with such everyday items as brooms, dustbins, hubcaps, plastic bags, and lighters.

FINE ART AND THEATER

Fine art in theater takes many forms, including stage design, costumes, makeup, and lighting. All of these forms combine in theater to help convey theme, character, setting, and mood in stage productions. Therefore, it is important to view the stage in a theater production as if it were a painting or a sculpture. In that way, one can fully appreciate theater as a complete art form.

As drama developed over time, the importance of art in the theater grew, as did the role of the art director. The **art director** determines the overall "look" of the play. He or she must work closely with the director and the makeup, costuming, and lighting designers to achieve the desired effect in a production. The first thing the audience sees when the curtain goes up or the lights go on is the set. This first impression can establish the mood of the entire production before a single line is spoken. The extravagant staircase in *Sunset Boulevard*, for example, conveys an entirely different mood from the stark, barren bench and dead tree in *Waiting for Godot*. The art director can suggest a variety of moods by creatively using lines and space. To convey a sense of confinement, the art director might place the ceiling and walls close to the actor. By spreading elements of the set far apart and leaving the ceiling open, the art director can suggest freedom and openness.

Theater has always reflected the artistic styles and tastes of the time. In fact many art directors have borrowed from great artists, popular genres, and great works of art in designing their shows. The scenery of Steven Sondheim's *Sunday in the Park with George* was based on the paintings of the French artist Georges Seurat (sə • rä´). Seurat was the first painter to use a technique called pointillism. Rather than presenting a realistic image, Seurat used small dots of paint in contrasting colors to form images. His most famous pointillist work, *A Sunday Afternoon on the Island of La Grande Jatte,* illustrates a Parisian park bustling with people.

The expressionist movement came to the stage in the early twentieth century through the works of the Norwegian artist Edvard Munch (mo͝ongk). Munch is best known for his work *The Scream,* which illustrates this expressionist idea: artists should produce art that explores how human emotions affect one's view of the world. In 1906 Munch was asked to incorporate his dark, eerie style into a design for Henrik Ibsen's play *Ghosts.* Theater critics praised Munch's design for successfully conveying the mood of the play.

Another artist who influenced theater is Marc Chagall. One of nine children from a poor Jewish family living in Russia, Chagall studied art and developed an artistic style unlike anyone else's at the time. After the Communist Revolution in Russia, Chagall designed stage sets at the Jewish Theater in Moscow. It is no surprise that the art direction for *Fiddler on the Roof* was based on Marc Chagall's paintings. The play and many of Chagall's paintings share the same theme—the trials of being Jewish in Russia.

Filmmakers, like theater directors, often look to fine artists for artistic direction in motion-picture productions. Artists are often consulted during the preliminary stages of film production and asked to draw a series of concept illustrations. For example, George Lucas contacted artist Ralph McQuarrie to create production drawings that would establish the look for Lucas's *Star Wars* trilogy of films. Lucas's perception of the future included dented machines, robots with makeshift parts, and faulty equipment. McQuarrie's drawings brought to life Lucas's original vision of a world that had a "lived-in" look—a radical departure from the white, sanitized vision of earlier science fiction films like *2001: A Space Odyssey.* Some modern directors, such as Ridley Scott (*Alien,* 1979; *Blade Runner,* 1982), are known for their distinctive settings. In the setting for *Alien,* with its eerie smoke, dark images, and unique structures, Scott effectively uses color, texture, shape, and space to convey the mood of a frightening futuristic world.

FROM THE PROS

"There are certain moments in movies where the background can be as important as the actor."

—RIDLEY SCOTT, DIRECTOR

This setting from *Alien* uses neutral colors, rough textures, unfamiliar shapes, and empty space to create the image of a frightening, hostile world.

Application ACTIVITY

Choose a scene from "A Treasury of Scenes and Monologues." Then choose a specific work of art or an artistic style that might effectively convey the mood and theme of the scene. Summarize your choice in a report or a class demonstration.

THEATER AND MUSICAL THEATER

Drama is set apart from other forms of literature by the way it communicates meaning, theme, mood, setting, and plot. Instead of simply writing text down and relying on readers to interpret the written word, dramatists write dialogue that is meant to be spoken by actors. Therefore, the work of a dramatist is interpreted several times: by the director, who interprets and communicates meaning to the actors; by the actors, who interpret and communicate meaning to the audience; and by the audience members, who form their own interpretations, using both the original words provided by the dramatist and the expressions, gestures, and intonations provided by the actors.

Theater In straight plays, the use of fine art often sets the scene. Many famous artists have crossed over to work on set design, giving the production an additional flavor. For example, David Hockney's stage design,

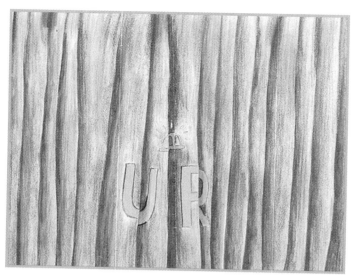

This drawing by David Hockney was used as a set design in Alfred Jarry's absurdist play *Ubu Roi*. Even Hockney's eraser marks and corrections were transposed to the final set design.

with his crudely drawn lettering to denote location, illustrated the cartoonish quality of Alfred Jarry's absurdist depiction of life in *Ubu Roi*. Costumes and stage lighting are also art forms that help convey the mood and setting of a play. Whether the work is a period piece or a stylized production, costumes and stage lighting contribute to communicating the theme to the audience. The introductory music, whether light and melodious or dark and dramatic, prepares the audience for the mood of the production, while background and change music sustain it.

Musical Theater   Like theater, musical theater integrates elements of art, dance, music, and drama in one performance. In musical theater, however, music is the key element, not simply an accompaniment. Its origin is opera, a staged musical production introduced in Florence, Italy, in the seventeenth century. Operas include elaborate costumes, which are often considered artworks in themselves. Dance is often included in the production. Lighting, elaborate scenery, and costumes help establish the mood and the setting. Mozart, one of the most renowned composers of opera, advanced the form by blending accomplished classical music with "real" characters, whose emotions and situations would have been familiar to his audiences. Many other composers based their operas on famous works of literature, such as *Faust*. Not all operas are written in classical music: George Gershwin combined elements of jazz, blues, spirituals, and folk music in his folk opera, *Porgy and Bess.*

Until the nineteenth century, musical productions other than opera were mostly farcical plays that featured popular musical numbers occurring randomly within them. In Italy a performance called **opera-buffa,** which incorporated dialogue and light music, began to appear. In France this kind of lighter performance became known as opéra-comique and later opéra-bouffe. Instead of the serious plots and heavy music of the opera, opéra-bouffe offered a series of comical, satirical sketches. This allowed for the addition of creative costuming and more relaxed set design. One of the hits of the time, *Don Quichotte and Sancho Panza*, borrowed heavily from literature. The characters were taken directly from Cervantes's early seventeenth-century work *Don Quixote.* The gifted composer Hervé set Cervantes's story to music and produced a successful blend of literature and popular music.

With the rise of such superstar composers as Irving Berlin, Cole Porter, Jerome Kern, and George Gershwin, musical comedies became very popular in the 1920s. They featured elaborate costumes and sets that portrayed the light-hearted mood of the productions. These musical comedies also included popular dance, which energized the performance. Broadway musicals still blend various art forms to achieve mood. Whether presenting a musical tragedy such as *West Side Story* or a spoof such as *How to Succeed in Business Without Really Trying,* the combination of various art forms in theater always helps to communicate theme, mood, action, character, and setting.

Application
ACTIVITY

Choose a movie or a videotape of a play to watch. As you view it, pay particular attention to the different art forms that are blended into the work. Make notes of how the music, set design, and choreography affect the representation of theme, mood, character, and action. You may need to view the work more than once to pay attention to all of the art forms used. Compile your observations in a report and present it to your class.

Musical theater incorporates many art forms in a single production. In *Fiddler on the Roof,* folk dancing, traditional music, and realistic costuming and stage design combine to portray Jewish life in a small Russian village.

Summary and Key Ideas

Summarize the chapter by answering the following questions.

1. How do melodies and lyrics affect interpretation of music?
2. How has ballet affected dance?
3. What are the main elements used in fine art to convey mood, theme, character, action, and setting?
4. What are the responsibilities of the art director?
5. How do time period and historical events affect different forms of art?
6. How does the synthesis of many art forms in theater help convey theme?

Discussing Ideas

1. Which current movies or television shows use music effectively to establish mood? Explain why you think so.
2. Discuss the following statement: "Movement is the heart of ballet." Do you agree or disagree with this statement? Explain your reasons.
3. Analyze the elements of a piece of fine art pictured in this chapter. Discuss how the artist's use of line, color, texture, and any other element clarifies the theme or mood.
4. How much impact do you think society and history have on art forms? Discuss your opinions with the class. Cite examples to back up your point.

FOCUS ON The Arts

Other art forms have had a powerful impact on the theater. The stage is a place where many disciplines blend to give us challenging artistic experiences.

Analyzing the Arts Use what you learned in this chapter to write an essay comparing and contrasting the methods of communication of fine art, music, dance, and theater. Also describe the reciprocal relationships between the theater and the other arts. Include examples to support your ideas.

Viewing and Doing Watch a piece of theater that combines more than one art form. You might view performance art, an opera, a musical, a Gene Kelly or Fred Astaire movie, or a movie or play with a striking appearance. Evaluate how all the elements of the production worked together. Then, keeping in mind what you've learned, get together with a small group to plan and present an informal performance that synthesizes two or more art forms—such as a scene with a musical or dance number. For help with constructing the performance, see the Reference Section.

THEATER AND OTHER ART FORMS

INDEPENDENT ACTIVITIES

Children's Musical   Make a plan for adapting a children's story to the musical theater. Begin by choosing a story you think would make a good musical. It might be a familiar children's story like *Hansel and Gretel* or a lesser-known story from a children's book. Decide on the actors you would want in the starring roles. Identify places where a song on a particular subject might be appropriate. Finally, choose well-known children's songs, like "Old MacDonald Had a Farm," or any other appropriate songs to use in the musical.

You Are the Art Director   Plan the stage design for a play with which you are familiar. Begin by reading the play and interpreting its mood and theme. Next, create sketches or gather pictures to coordinate an overall "look" for the setting. Be sure to include an appropriate use of color, space, and props. Prepare a short presentation for the class in which you explain the play and how your design effectively conveys its mood and theme.

Cooperative Learning Activity

Music Video   Work with several classmates to create a music video using a video camera and a recording of a song that has your teacher's approval. It might be a rock song or a ballad. Listen to the recording several times and discuss what kinds of images would enhance the musical experience. Calculate when and how long each image should appear on-screen. Finally, film the sequences you have decided on and present your music video to the class.

Across the CURRICULUM Activity

History   Create a time line that illustrates a limited time period. Investigate that time period, including the period's important artistic movements. Report the effects these movements had on literature, philosophy, theater, fine art, music, and dance. On your time line, list several of the influential writers, composers, choreographers, and artists of the movement and their popular works. To make your time line more interesting, you might want to include pictures of the authors or of their works.

Media and Culture

Culture: shared information, beliefs, and values

In the United States until the opening of the twentieth century, families could largely control the culture their children were exposed to. Now young people have access to electronic media—film, television, and computer technology—that deliver huge amounts of information and entertainment. How does this flood of cultural input affect us—that is, how do the media shape society? On the other hand, how does society shape the media?

THEATER AND CULTURE

A social conscience has always been evident in theater. The earliest Greek tragedies dramatized the retribution of the gods for human arrogance and pride. From medieval dramas, through Restoration comedies, and up to the present, English theater has often ridiculed human weaknesses and society's foolish ways. In the 1850s in the United States, dramatizations of Harriet Beecher Stowe's novel *Uncle Tom's Cabin* brought the horrors of slavery to audience after audience and contributed to the cause of the abolitionist movement. Even musicals have been a force for cultural and social change. *Showboat* (1927), for example, caused audiences to think about family and how we treat one another. More recently, the threat of AIDS was powerfully addressed in the musical drama *Rent* (1996).

Even though theater is live while other media are transmitted, theater affects people's attitudes much less than today's electronic media (film, television, and information technology) do. There are two main reasons for theater's relatively weaker cultural influence. First, a play cannot reach many people at a time. Even *A Chorus Line*, whose fifteen-year Broadway run set a record of 6,137 performances, was seen by only 6.5 million people over fifteen years. In comparison, the television miniseries *Roots* was watched, wholly or partly, by 130 million people in just eight days the first time it was broadcast in the late 1970s. Second, what the audience sees on the stage is only suggestive of reality. A theatergoer must use imagination to supply the details. By bringing an active mental process to the presentation, the theatergoer becomes involved with the message and shapes it with his or her own sense of reality. As a result, theater lacks the immediacy that is possible with other media; therefore, theater does not make the immediate impression that films, television, and information technology can make.

FILM, TELEVISION, AND CULTURE

Movies were one of the first media to expose young people to new cultural influences. In the early 1900s, movies and newsreels were weekly fare for many, especially children, who saw on the big screen people, places, and events they might otherwise never have heard of. Influence of the media increased after World War II as television sets were found in more and more homes. Actor and producer Shelley Duvall talks about television's effect on children:

> It opened up my eyes to other countries, other cultures. This is *very* important for a child. American kids, in either an urban or a rural location, have generally never been outside their cities. They don't have a clue about what people are like in other cities and countries. The only culture they're exposed to without television is the local one. I think television helps open their eyes to other worlds, and to the possibilities that lie ahead for them as they grow up.

Not only are today's viewers seeing many more hours of television and movies than any previous generation saw, but the experience is more intense now than ever before. Improvements in the arts of makeup,

Instructional television, including documentaries, can turn the entire world into a classroom. This type of programming brings viewers sights and sounds that they might never have the opportunity to experience in person.

costuming, special effects, cinematography, and editing, among others, have made sure that what we see and hear strikes us as real. We respond emotionally. Bright colors, rapid camera cuts, close-up shots, and advanced special effects and computer-generated images seize our attention and keep it. In fact, we use our experiences with the media—along with our other experiences, of course—to build our knowledge of the world and life. In a way, the media are shaping a world that becomes reality for the viewers, who may have thought they were simply being entertained.

That television can inform and educate is no new discovery. Horace Newcomb, a professor at the University of Texas, said on *60 Minutes* that he judged *Gunsmoke* (1955–1975) to have been "one of the important shows in the history of television." He went on to explain that "*Gunsmoke* was teaching us about race relations and showing us how to defend human rights, at a time when nobody was doing that overtly." Television makes possible a more unified society by showing—in both news and entertainment—social change as it occurs and by helping us become familiar with the unfamiliar. When families watch together, they can experience together the educational and informative as well as the entertaining qualities of the medium. Matt Groening, creator of *The Simpsons*, said in a 1990 interview, "[T]hat's one of the goals of *The Simpsons*: to do a show that each member of the family can get into on his or her own level."

The exaggerated realism of *The Simpsons* represents a reaction to idealized television families popularized on television in the fifties and sixties.

The more channels there are, however, the more likely it is that something on television will displease someone. How can a person affect the media? Letters, phone calls, and e-mail complaining to the producers or to the governing bodies (such as the Federal Trade Commission) have often resulted in objectionable materials being changed or withdrawn. No television network, sponsor, or movie studio wants to become known for being inaccurate or deceptive, for offending community standards, or for treating any segment of the population unfairly. Individuals can also join advocacy groups, which have a greater ability to support and publish research than individuals have. Petitions and even boycotts have often succeeded in effecting change in the media. On a smaller scale, families can discuss what they see on a television show, advertisement, or movie. By talking about it, families can help young viewers distinguish between the media's message and real life.

INFORMATION TECHNOLOGY AND CULTURE

Today anyone with a computer, a modem, a telephone line, and an access provider can post a question or a response on a bulletin board, partake in a real-time typed conversation, play an interactive game, write to a government official, make a purchase, or look up information. Unlike other media, the online computer is interactive—that is, one can both receive and send, enabling an exchange of ideas. Information technology is changing education, leisure, business, medicine, government, and almost everything else in our culture. Information has become wealth. The role of this electronic medium in United States society is to remove boundaries—physical isolation, lack of access to libraries, lack of education—to allow the user to participate in worldwide events that will build the future.

The real benefit will come for the next generation, those people born into the twenty-first century. Their education will be supplemented by interactive multimedia—television, computers, videodiscs, and more—supplying knowledge from the biggest and most easily accessible information bank ever imagined.

Reference Section

❦ How to Produce a Play

The Production Process

The following guide will take you and your class stage-by-stage through the production process—your key to building an effective public performance. To aid your understanding, you will begin by producing a specific work, *The Importance of Being Earnest,* First Act. However, you can adapt the process outlined here to any script that you and your classmates select.

During your preparation time, maintain an encouraging, positive spirit with your classmates and work together to accomplish your best with each stage of the process. The rewards will be tremendous.

Objectives

- To collaborate to present unified productions for public performance
- To practice and master acting, stagecraft, and directing skills
- To analyze dramatic texts for structure, genre, and historical context

The Stages of the Process

The most essential stages of the production process are shown below.

Select and read the script
⇩
Analyze and evaluate the script
⇩
Find a place to stage the play
⇩
Cast the play
⇩
Conduct rehearsals
⇩
Create set designs, props, and costumes
⇩
Present a public performance

The stages of production often overlap, and their order can vary according to your needs and goals. There will be times when you and your classmates will need to work on several stages simultaneously. At each stage, you should consider how your decisions will affect other areas of production. As you proceed, use what you've learned about the production process in earlier chapters. **Review Part Four, pages 332–529, for detailed descriptions of job responsibilities and production procedures.**

Starting the Process

Imagine that you and your classmates have just formed a new theater company. Each of you is a member of a team working together to achieve a common goal—to create a unified production of a long scene for public performances at your school and in your community. Your company will debut with the First Act from *The Importance of Being Earnest*, a comic play by Oscar Wilde. Like many newly founded theater companies, you are operating on a shoestring budget. You will aim to keep your production costs low. Your biggest concern, though, will be to practice and master basic production procedures to incorporate in future productions.

Reading the Scene
BUILDING BACKGROUND

Oscar Wilde's last and greatest play, *The Importance of Being Earnest*, opened on February 14, 1895, and still dazzles readers with its hilarious wit and satiric vision. Set in England during Wilde's time—the late Victorian period—the play portrays members of the English upper class, a small percentage of the population that controlled most of the nation's land, money, and politics. London, the setting for much of the play, was at that time a smoky, congested city of nearly five million people. It was the center of politics, culture, and commerce. It was also a playground for the wealthy.

In *Earnest*'s First Act, the reader is introduced to Algernon Moncrieff and his friend Jack Worthing. These wealthy young men are charming and lovable but frivolous to the extreme. Both have a gift for stretching the truth to help themselves maintain their easy, pleasurable lives. Their little deceptions create a series of crises that nearly ruin their chances for true romance.

Terms to Know

ensemble acting a type of acting in which a group of cast members collaborate to produce a unified effect

farce a type of comedy characterized by clowning, practical jokes, and improbable characters and situations

genre a category of literary work, such as poetry, fiction, and drama. The two most recognized genres of drama are tragedy and comedy.

style the way in which a play is written, acted, and produced

---

THE IMPORTANCE OF BEING EARNEST
CAST OF CHARACTERS

Jack Worthing a wealthy young man whose engagement to Gwendolen Fairfax is stalled because of unanswered questions about his family background

Algernon Moncrieff Jack's upper-class friend, who wants to marry 18-year-old Cecily Cardew

Lane Algernon's servant

Gwendolen Fairfax Algernon's cousin, whose romance with Jack is thwarted by her snobbish mother, Lady Bracknell

Cecily Cardew a romantic young woman under Jack's care, who falls in love with Algernon even before she meets him

Lady Bracknell Gwendolen's mother and Algernon's Aunt Augusta, an overbearing woman with strong ideas about social class

Miss Prism Cecily's strict governess, who accidentally misplaced Jack when he was a baby

Rev. Chasuble a minister in love with Miss Prism

The characters who appear in the First Act are Algernon Moncrieff, Lane, Jack Worthing, Lady Bracknell, and Gwendolen Fairfax.

THE IMPORTANCE OF BEING EARNEST

First Act

> ### Key for color coding
>
> = set and props
> = entrances and exits
> = stage movements and gestures
> = tone of voice (delivery of lines)

SCENE

Morning-room in ALGERNON'S flat in Half-Moon Street.

The room is luxuriously and artistically furnished. The sound of a piano is heard in the adjoining room.

[LANE *is arranging afternoon tea on the table and, after the music has ceased,* ALGERNON *enters.*]

ALGERNON. Did you hear what I was playing, Lane?

LANE. I didn't think it polite to listen, sir.

ALGERNON. I'm sorry for that, for your sake. I don't play accurately—anyone can play accurately—but I play with wonderful expression. As far as the piano is concerned, sentiment is my forte. I keep science for Life.

LANE. Yes, sir.

ALGERNON. And, speaking of the science of Life, have you got the cucumber sandwiches cut for Lady Bracknell?

LANE. Yes, sir. [*Hands them on a salver.*]

ALGERNON [*Inspects them, takes two and sits down on the sofa*]. Oh! . . . by the way, Lane, I see from your book that on Thursday night, when Lord Shoreman and Mr Worthing were dining with me, eight bottles of champagne are entered as having been consumed.

LANE. Yes, sir; eight bottles and a pint.

ALGERNON. Why is it that at a bachelor's establishment the servants invariably drink the champagne? I ask merely for information.

LANE. I attribute it to the superior quality of the wine, sir. I have often observed that in married households the champagne is rarely of a first-rate brand.

ALGERNON.   Good heavens! Is marriage so demoralizing as that?

LANE.   I believe it *is* a very pleasant state, sir. I have had very little experience of it myself up to the present. I have only been married once. That was in consequence of a misunderstanding between myself and a young person.

ALGERNON [*languidly*].   I don't know that I am much interested in your family life, Lane.

LANE.   No, sir; it is not a very interesting subject. I never think of it myself.

ALGERNON.   Very natural, I am sure. That will do, Lane, thank you.

LANE.   Thank you, sir.

[LANE *goes out.*]

ALGERNON.   Lane's views on marriage seem somewhat lax. Really, if the lower orders don't set us a good example, what on earth is the use of them? They seem, as a class, to have absolutely no sense of moral responsibility.

[*Enter* LANE.]

LANE.   Mr Ernest Worthing.

[*Enter* JACK. LANE *goes out.*]

ALGERNON.   How are you, my dear Ernest? What brings you up to town?

JACK.   Oh, pleasure, pleasure! What else should bring one anywhere? Eating as usual, I see, Algy!

ALGERNON [*stiffly*].   I believe it is customary in good society to take some slight refreshment at five o'clock. Where have you been since last Thursday?

JACK [*sitting down on the sofa*].   In the country.

ALGERNON.   What on earth do you do there?

JACK [*pulling off his gloves*].   When one is in town one amuses oneself. When one is in the country one amuses other people. It is excessively boring.

ALGERNON.   And who are the people you amuse?

JACK [*airily*].   Oh, neighbours, neighbours.

ALGERNON.   Got nice neighbours in your part of Shropshire?

JACK.   Perfectly horrrid! Never speak to one of them.

ALGERNON.   How immensely you must amuse them! [*Goes over and takes sandwich.*] By the way, Shropshire is your county, is it not?

JACK.   Eh? Shropshire? Yes, of course. Hallo! Why all these cups? Why cucumber sandwiches? Why such reckless extravagance in one so young? Who is coming to tea?

ALGERNON.   Oh! merely Anut Augusta and Gwendolen.

JACK.   How perfectly delightful!

ALGERNON.   Yes, that is all very well; but I am afraid Aunt Augusta won't quite approve of your being here.

JACK.   May I ask why?

ALGERNON.   My dear fellow, the way you flirt with Gwendolen is perfecly disgraceful. It is almost as bad as the way Gwendolen flirts with you.

JACK.   I am in love with Gwendolen. I have come up to town expressly to propose to her.

ALGERNON.   I thought you had come up for pleasure? . . . I call that business.

JACK.   How utterly unromantic you are!

ALGERNON.   I really don't see anything romantic in proposing. It is very romantic to be in love. But there is nothing romantic about a definite proposal. Why, one may be accepted. One usually is, I believe. Then the excitement is all over. The very essence of romance is uncertainty. If ever I get married, I'll certainly try to forget the fact.

JACK.   I have no doubt about that, dear Algy. The Divorce Court was specially invented for people whose memories are so curiously constituted.

ALGERNON.   Oh, there is no use speculating on that subject. Divorces are made in Heaven—[JACK *puts out his hand to take a sandwich.* ALGERNON *at once interferes.*] Please don't touch the cucumber sandwiches. They are ordered specially for Aunt Augusta. [*Takes one and eats it.*]

JACK.   Well, you have been eating them all the time.

ALGERNON.   That is quite a different matter. She is my aunt. [*Takes plate from below.*] Have some bread and butter. The bread and butter is for Gwendolen. Gwendolen is devoted to bread and butter.

JACK [*advancing to table and helping himself*].   And very good bread and butter it is too.

ALGERNON.   Well, my dear fellow, you need not eat as if you were going to eat it all. You behave as if you were married to her already. You are not married to her already, and I don't think you ever will be.

JACK.   Why on earth do you say that?

ALGERNON. Well, in the first place, girls never marry the men they flirt with. Girls don't think it right.

JACK. Oh, that is nonsense!

ALGERNON. It isn't. It is a great truth. It accounts for the extraordinary number of bachelors that one sees all over the place. In the second place, I don't give my consent.

JACK. Your consent!

ALGERNON. My dear fellow, Gwendolen is my first cousin. And before I allow you to marry her, you will have to clear up the whole question of Cecily. [*Rings bell.*]

JACK. Cecily! What on earth do you mean? What do you mean, Algy, by Cecily! I don't know anyone of the name of Cecily.

[*Enter* LANE.]

ALGERNON. Bring me that cigarette case Mr Worthing left in the smoking-room the last time he dined here.

LANE. Yes, sir.

[LANE *goes out.*]

JACK. Do you mean to say you have had my cigarette case all this time? I wish to goodness you had let me know. I have been writing frantic letters to Scotland Yard about it. I was very nearly offering a large reward.

ALGERNON. Well, I wish you would offer one. I happen to be more than usually hard up.

JACK. There is no good offering a large reward now that the thing is found.

[*Enter* LANE *with the cigarette case on a salver.* ALGERNON *takes it at once.* LANE *goes out.*]

ALGERNON. I think that is rather mean of you, Ernest, I must say. [*Opens case and examines it.*] However, it makes no matter, for, now that I look at the inscription inside, I find that the thing isn't yours after all.

JACK. Of course it's mine. [*Moving to him.*] You have seen me with it a hundred times, and you have no right whatsoever to read what is written inside. It is a very ungentlemanly thing to read a private cigarette case.

ALGERNON. Oh! it is absurd to have a hard and fast rule about what one should read and what one shouldn't. More than half of modern culture depends on what one shouldn't read.

JACK.   I am quite aware of the fact, and I don't propose to discuss modern culture. It isn't the sort of thing one should talk of in private. I simply want my cigarette case back.

ALGERNON.   Yes; but this isn't your cigarette case. This cigarette case is a present from someone of the name of Cecily, and you said you didn't know anyone of that name.

JACK.   Well, if you want to know, Cecily happens to be my aunt.

ALGERNON.   Your aunt!

JACK.   Yes. Charming old lady she is, too. Lives at Tunbridge Wells. Just give it back to me, Algy.

ALGERNON [*retreating to back of sofa*].   But why does she call herself little Cecily if she is your aunt and lives at Tunbridge Wells? [*Reading.*] 'From little Cecily with her fondest love'.

JACK [*moving to sofa and kneeling upon it*].   My dear fellow, what on earth is there in that? Some aunts are tall, some aunts are not tall. That is a matter that surely an aunt may be allowed to decide for herself. You seem to think that every aunt should be exactly like your aunt! That is absurd. For Heaven's sake give me back my cigarette case. [*Follows* ALGERNON *round the room.*]

ALGERNON.   Yes. But why does your aunt call you her uncle? 'From little Cecily, with her fondest love to her dear Uncle Jack.' There is no objection, I admit, to an aunt being a small aunt, but why an aunt, no matter what her size may be, should call her own nephew her uncle, I can't quite make out. Besides, your name isn't Jack at all; it is Ernest.

JACK.   It isn't Ernest; it's Jack.

ALGERNON.   You have always told me it was Ernest. I have introduced you to every one as Ernest. You answer to the name of Ernest. You look as if your name was Ernest. You are the most earnest-looking person I ever saw in my life. It is perfectly absurd your saying that your name isn't Ernest. It's on your cards. Here is one of them. [*Taking it from case.*] 'Mr Ernest Worthing, B.4, The Albany.' I'll keep this as a proof that your name is Ernest if ever you attempt to deny it to me, or to Gwendolen, or to anyone else. [*Puts the card in his pocket.*]

JACK.   Well, my name is Ernest in town and Jack in the country, and the cigarette case was given to me in the country.

ALGERNON.   Yes, but that does not account for the fact that your small Aunt Cecily, who lives at Tunbridge Wells, calls you her dear uncle. Come, old boy, you had much better have the thing out at once.

JACK. My dear Algy, you talk exactly as if you were a dentist. It is very vulgar to talk like a dentist when one isn't a dentist. It produces a false impression.

ALGERNON. Well, that is exactly what dentists always do. Now, go on! Tell me the whole thing. I may mention that I have always suspected you of being a confirmed and secret Bunburyist; and I am quite sure of it now.

JACK. Bunburyist? What on earth do you mean by a Bunburyist?

ALGERNON. I'll reveal to you the meaning of that incomparable expression as soon as you are kind enough to inform me why you are Ernest in town and Jack in the country.

JACK. Well, produce my cigarette case first.

ALGERNON. Here it is. [*Hands cigarette case.*] Now produce your explanation, and pray make it improbable. [*Sits on sofa.*]

JACK. My dear fellow, there is nothing improbable about my explanation at all. In fact it's perfectly ordinary. Old Mr Thomas Cardew, who adopted me when I was a little boy, made me in his will guardian to his granddaughter, Miss Cecily Cardew. Cecily, who addresses me as her uncle from motives of respect that you could not possibly appreciate, lives at my place in the country under the charge of her admirable governess, Miss Prism.

ALGERNON. Where is that place in the country, by the way?

JACK. That is nothing to you, dear boy. You are not going to be invited . . . I may tell you candidly that the place is not in Shropshire.

ALGERNON. I suspected that, my dear fellow! I have Bunburyed all over Shropshire on two separate occasions. Now, go on. Why are you Ernest in town and Jack in the country?

JACK. My dear Algy, I don't know whether you will be able to understand my real motives. You are hardly serious enough. When one is placed in the position of guardian, one has to adopt a very high moral tone on all subjects. It's one's duty to do so. And as a high moral tone can hardly be said to conduce very much to either one's health or one's happiness, in order to get up to town I have always pretended to have a younger brother of the name of Ernest, who lives in the Albany, and gets into the most dreadful scrapes. That, my dear Algy, is the whole truth pure and simple.

ALGERNON. The truth is rarely pure and never simple. Modern life would be very tedious if it were either, and modern literature a complete impossibility!

JACK. That wouldn't be at all a bad thing.

ALGERNON. Literary criticism is not your forte, my dear fellow. Don't try it. You should leave that to people who haven't been at a University. They do it so well in the daily papers. What you really are is a Bunburyist. I was quite right in saying you were a Bunburyist. You are one of the most advanced Bunburyists I know.

JACK. What on earth do you mean?

ALGERNON. You have invented a very useful younger brother called Ernest, in order that you may be able to come up to town as often as you like. I have invented an invaluable permanent invalid called Bunbury, in order that I may be able to go down into the country whenever I choose. Bunbury is perfectly invaluable. If it wasn't for Bunbury's extraordinary bad health, for instance, I wouldn't be able to dine with you at Willis's tonight, for I have been really engaged to Aunt Augusta for more than a week.

JACK. I haven't asked you to dine with me anywhere tonight.

ALGERNON. I know. You are absurdly careless about sending out invitations. It is very foolish of you. Nothing annoys people so much as not receiving invitations.

JACK. You had much better dine with your Aunt Augusta.

ALGERNON. I haven't the smallest intention of doing anything of the kind. To begin with, I dined there on Monday, and once a week is quite enough to dine with one's own relations. In the second place, whenever I do dine there I am always treated as a member of the family, and sent down with either no woman at all, or two. In the third place, I know perfectly well whom she will place me next to, tonight. She will place me next Mary Farquhar, who always flirts with her own husband across the dinner-table. That is not very pleasant. Indeed, it is not even decent—and that sort of thing is enormously on the increase. The amount of women in London who flirt with their own husbands is perfectly scandalous. It looks so bad. It is simply washing one's clean linen in public. Besides, now that I know you to be a confirmed Bunburyist I naturally want to talk to you about Bunburying. I want to tell you the rules.

JACK. I'm not a Bunburyist at all. If Gwendolen accepts me, I am going to kill my brother, indeed I think I'll kill him in any case. Cecily is a little too much interested in him. It is rather a bore. So I am going to get rid of Ernest. And I strongly advise you to do the same with Mr . . . with your invalid friend who has the absurd name.

ALGERNON. Nothing will induce me to part with Bunbury, and if you ever get married, which seems to me extremely problematic, you will be very glad to know Bunbury. A man who marries without knowing Bunbury has a very tedious time of it.

JACK.   That is nonsense. If I marry a charming girl like Gwendolen, and she is the only girl I ever saw in my life that I would marry, I certainly won't want to know Bunbury.

ALGERNON.   Then your wife will. You don't seem to realize, that in married life three is company and two is none.

JACK [*sententiously*].   That, my dear young friend, is the theory that the corrupt French Drama has been propounding for the last fifty years.

ALGERNON.   Yes; and that the happy English home has proved in half the time.

JACK.   For heaven's sake, don't try to be cynical. It's perfectly easy to be cynical.

ALGERNON.   My dear fellow, it isn't easy to be anything nowadays. There's such a lot of beastly competition about. [*The sound of an electric bell is heard.*] Ah! that must be Aunt Augusta. Only relatives, or creditors, ever ring in that Wagnerian manner. Now, if I get her out of the way for ten minutes, so that you can have an opportunity for proposing to Gwendolen, may I dine with you tonight at Willis's?

JACK.   I suppose so, if you want to.

ALGERNON.   Yes, but you must be serious about it. I hate people who are not serious about meals. It is so shallow of them.

[*Enter* LANE.]

LANE.   Lady Bracknell and Miss Fairfax.

[ALGERNON *goes forward to meet them. Enter* LADY BRACKNELL *and* GWENDOLEN.]

LADY BRACKNELL.   Good afternoon, dear Algernon, I hope you are behaving very well.

ALGERNON.   I'm feeling very well, Aunt Augusta.

LADY BRACKNELL.   That's not quite the same thing. In fact the two things rarely go together. [*Sees* JACK *and bows to him with icy coldness.*]

ALGERNON [*to* GWENDOLEN].   Dear me, you are smart!

GWENDOLEN.   I am always smart! Am I not, Mr Worthing?

JACK.   You're quite perfect, Miss Fairfax.

GWENDOLEN.   Oh! I hope I am not that. It would leave no room for developments, and I intend to develop in many directions.

[GWENDOLEN *and* JACK *sit down together in the corner.*]

LADY BRACKNELL.   I'm sorry if we are a little late, Algernon, but I was obliged to call on dear Lady Harbury. I hadn't been there since her poor husband's death. I never saw a woman so altered; she looks quite twenty years younger. And now I'll have a cup of tea, and one of those nice cucumber sandwiches you promised me.

ALGERNON.   Certainly, Aunt Augusta. [*Goes over to tea-table.*]

LADY BRACKNELL.   Won't you come and sit here, Gwendolen?

GWENDOLEN.   Thanks, mamma, I'm quite comfortable where I am.

ALGERNON [*picking up empty plate in horror*].   Good heavens! Lane! Why are there no cucumber sandwiches? I ordered them specially.

LANE [*gravely*].   There were no cucumbers in the market this morning, sir. I went down twice.

ALGERNON.   No cucumbers!

LANE.   No, sir. Not even for ready money.

ALGERNON.   That will do, Lane, thank you.

LANE.   Thank you, sir. [*Goes out.*]

ALGERNON.   I am greatly distressed, Aunt Augusta, about there being no cucumbers, not even for ready money.

LADY BRACKNELL.   It really makes no matter, Algernon. I had some crumpets with Lady Harbury, who seems to me to be living entirely for pleasure now.

ALGERNON.   I hear her hair has turned quite gold from grief.

LADY BRACKNELL.   It certainly has changed its colour. From what cause I, of course, cannot say. [ALGERNON *crosses and hands tea.*] Thank you. I've quite a treat for you tonight, Algernon. I am going to send you down with Mary Farquhar. She is such a nice woman, and so attentive to her husband. It's delightful to watch them.

ALGERNON.   I am afraid, Aunt Augusta, I shall have to give up the pleasure of dining with you tonight after all.

LADY BRACKNELL [*frowning*].   I hope not, Algernon. It would put my table completely out. Your uncle would have to dine upstairs. Fortunately he is accustomed to that.

ALGERNON.   It is a great bore, and, I need hardly say, a terrible disappointment to me, but the fact is I have just had a telegram to say that my poor friend Bunbury is very ill again. [*Exchanges glances with* JACK.] They seem to think I should be with him.

LADY BRACKNELL.   It is very strange. This Mr Bunbury seems to suffer from curiously bad health.

ALGERNON.   Yes; poor Bunbury is a dreadful invalid.

LADY BRACKNELL.   Well, I must say, Algernon, that I think it is high time that Mr Bunbury made up his mind whether he was going to live or to die. This shilly-shallying with the question is absurd. Nor do I in any way approve of the modern sympathy with invalids. I consider it morbid. Illness of any kind is hardly a thing to be encouraged in others. Health is the primary duty of life. I am always telling that to your poor uncle, but he never seems to take much notice . . . as far as any improvement in his ailment goes. I should be much obliged if you would ask Mr Bunbury, from me, to be kind enough not to have a relapse on Saturday, for I rely on you to arrange my music for me. It is my last reception, and one wants something that will encourage conversation, particularly at the end of the season when everyone has practically said whatever they had to say, which, in most cases, was probably not much.

ALGERNON.   I'll speak to Bunbury, Aunt Augusta, if he is still conscious, and I think I can promise you he'll be all right by Saturday. Of course the music is a great difficulty. You see, if one plays good music, people don't listen, and if one plays bad music people don't talk. But I'll run over the programme I've drawn out, if you will kindly come into the next room for a moment.

LADY BRACKNELL.   Thank you, Algernon. It is very thoughtful of you. [*Rising, and following* ALGERNON.] I'm sure the programme will be delightful, after a few expurgations. French songs I cannot possibly allow. People always seem to think that they are improper, and either look shocked, which is vulgar, or laugh, which is worse. But German sounds a thoroughly respectable language, and, indeed I believe is so. Gwendolen, you will accompany me.

GWENDOLEN.   Certainly, mamma.

[LADY BRACKNELL *and* ALGERNON *go into the music-room,* GWENDOLEN *remains behind.*]

JACK.   Charming day it has been, Miss Fairfax.

GWENDOLEN.   Pray don't talk to me about the weather, Mr Worthing. Whenever people talk to me about the weather, I always feel quite certain that they mean something else. And that makes me so nervous.

JACK.   I do mean something else.

GWENDOLEN.   I thought so. In fact, I am never wrong.

JACK.   And I would like to be allowed to take advantage of Lady Bracknell's temporary absence . . .

GWENDOLEN.   I would certainly advise you to do so. Mamma has a way of coming back suddenly into a room that I have often had to speak to her about.

JACK [*nervously*].   Miss Fairfax, ever since I met you I have admired you more than any girl . . . I have ever met since . . . I met you.

GWENDOLEN.   Yes, I am quite well aware of the fact. And I often wish that in public, at any rate, you had been more demonstrative. For me you have always had an irresistible fascination. Even before I met you I was far from indifferent to you. [JACK *looks at her in amazement.*] We live, as I hope you know, Mr Worthing, in an age of ideals. The fact is constantly mentioned in the more expensive monthly magazines, and has reached the provincial pulpits, I am told; and my ideal has always been to love someone of the name of Ernest. There is something in that name that inspires absolute confidence. The moment Algernon first mentioned to me that he had a friend called Ernest, I knew I was destined to love you.

JACK.   You really love me, Gwendolen?

GWENDOLEN.   Passionately!

JACK.   Darling! You don't know how happy you've made me.

GWENDOLEN.   My own Ernest!

JACK.   But you don't really mean to say that you couldn't love me if my name wasn't Ernest?

GWENDOLEN.   But your name is Ernest.

JACK.   Yes, I know it is. But supposing it was something else? Do you mean to say you couldn't love me then?

GWENDOLEN [*glibly*].   Ah! that is clearly a metaphysical speculation, and like most metaphysical speculations has very little reference at all to the actual facts of real life, as we know them.

JACK.   Personally, darling, to speak quite candidly, I don't much care about the name of Ernest . . . I don't think the name suits me at all.

GWENDOLEN.   It suits you perfectly. It is a divine name. It has a music of its own. It produces vibrations.

JACK.   Well, really, Gwendolen, I must say that I think there are lots of other much nicer names. I think Jack, for instance, a charming name.

GWENDOLEN.   Jack? . . . No, there is very little music in the name Jack, if any at all, indeed. It does not thrill. It produces absolutely no vibrations . . . I have known several Jacks, and they all, without exception, were more than usually plain. Besides, Jack is a notorious domesticity for John! And I pity any woman who is married to a man called John. She would probably never be allowed to know the entrancing pleasure of a single moment's solitude. The only really safe name is Ernest.

JACK.   Gwendolen, I must get christened at once—I mean we must get married at once. There is no time to be lost.

GWENDOLEN.   Married, Mr Worthing?

JACK [*astounded*].   Well . . . surely. You know that I love you, and you led me to believe, Miss Fairfax, that you were not absolutely indifferent to me.

GWENDOLEN.   I adore you. But you haven't proposed to me yet. Nothing has been said at all about marriage. The subject has not even been touched on.

JACK.   Well . . . may I propose to you now?

GWENDOLEN.   I think it would be an admirable opportunity. And to spare you any possible disappointment, Mr Worthing, I think it only fair to tell you quite frankly beforehand that I am fully determined to accept you.

JACK.   Gwendolen!

GWENDOLEN.   Yes, Mr Worthing, what have you got to say to me?

JACK.   You know what I have got to say to you.

GWENDOLEN.   Yes, but you don't say it.

JACK.   Gwendolen, will you marry me? [*Goes on his knees.*]

GWENDOLEN.   Of course I will, darling. How long you have been about it! I am afraid you have had very little experience in how to propose.

JACK.   My own one, I have never loved anyone in the world but you.

GWENDOLEN.   Yes, but men often propose for practice. I know my brother Gerald does. All my girl-friends tell me so. What wonderfully blue eyes you have, Ernest! They are quite, quite blue. I hope you will always look at me just like that, especially when there are other people present.

[*Enter* LADY BRACKNELL.]

LADY BRACKNELL.   Mr Worthing! Rise, sir, from this semi-recumbent posture. It is most indecorous.

GWENDOLEN.   Mamma! [*He tries to rise; she restrains him.*] I must beg you to retire. This is no place for you. Besides, Mr Worthing has not quite finished yet.

LADY BRACKNELL.   Finished what, may I ask?

GWENDOLEN.   I am engaged to Mr Worthing, mamma.
     [*They rise together.*]

LADY BRACKNELL.   Pardon me, you are not engaged to anyone. When you do become engaged to someone, I, or your father, should his health permit him, will inform you of the fact. An engagement should come on a young girl as a surprise, pleasant or unpleasant, as the case may be. It is hardly a matter that she could be allowed to arrange for herself . . . And now I have a few questions to put to you, Mr Worthing. While I am making these inquiries, you, Gwendolen, will wait for me below in the carriage.

GWENDOLEN [*reproachfully*].   Mamma!

LADY BRACKNELL.   In the carriage, Gwendolen! [GWENDOLEN *goes to the door. She and* JACK *blow kisses to each other behind* LADY BRACKNELL'S *back.* LADY BRACKNELL *looks vaguely about as if she could not understand what the noise was. Finally turns round.*] Gwendolen, the carriage!

GWENDOLEN.   Yes, mamma. [*Goes out, looking back at* JACK.]

LADY BRACKNELL [*sitting down*].   You can take a seat, Mr Worthing.

[*Looks in her pocket for notebook and pencil.*]

JACK.   Thank you, Lady Bracknell, I prefer standing.

LADY BRACKNELL [*pencil and notebook in hand*].   I feel bound to tell you that you are not down on my list of eligible young men, although I have the same list as the dear Duchess of Bolton has. We work together, in fact. However, I am quite ready to enter your name, should your answers be what a really affectionate mother requires. Do you smoke?

JACK.   Well, yes, I must admit I smoke.

LADY BRACKNELL.   I am glad to hear it. A man should always have an occupation of some kind. There are far too many idle men in London as it is. How old are you?

JACK.   Twenty-nine.

LADY BRACKNELL.   A very good age to be married at. I have always been of opinion that a man who desires to get married should know either everything or nothing. Which do you know?

JACK [*after some hesitation*].   I know nothing, Lady Bracknell.

LADY BRACKNELL.   I am pleased to hear it. I do not approve of anything that tampers with natural ignorance. Ignorance is like a delicate exotic fruit; touch it and the bloom is gone. The whole theory of modern education is radically unsound. Fortunately in England, at any rate, education produces no effect whatsoever. If it did, it would prove a serious danger to the upper classes, and probably lead to acts of violence in Grosvenor Square. What is your income?

JACK.   Between seven and eight thousand a year.

LADY BRACKNELL [*makes a note in her book*].   In land, or in investments?

JACK.   In investments, chiefly.

LADY BRACKNELL. That is satisfactory. What between the duties expected of one during one's lifetime, and the duties exacted from one after one's death, land has ceased to be either a profit or a pleasure. It gives one position, and prevents one from keeping it up. That's all that can be said about land.

JACK. I have a country house with some land, of course, attached to it, about fifteen hundred acres, I believe; but I don't depend on that for my real income. In fact, as far as I can make out, the poachers are the only people who make anything out of it.

LADY BRACKNELL. A country house! How many bedrooms? Well, that point can be cleared up afterwards. You have a town house, I hope? A girl with a simple, unspoiled nature, like Gwendolen, could hardly be expected to reside in the country.

JACK. Well, I own a house in Belgrave Square, but it is let by the year to Lady Bloxham. Of course, I can get it back whenever I like, at six months' notice.

LADY BRACKNELL. Lady Bloxham? I don't know her.

JACK. Oh, she goes about very little. She is a lady considerably advanced in years.

LADY BRACKNELL. Ah, nowadays that is no guarantee of respectability of character. What number in Belgrave Square?

JACK. 149.

LADY BRACKNELL [*shaking her head*]. The unfashionable side. I thought there was something. However, that could easily be altered.

JACK. Do you mean the fashion, or the side?

LADY BRACKNELL [*sternly*]. Both, if necessary, I presume. What are your politics?

JACK. Well, I am afraid I really have none. I am a Liberal Unionist.

LADY BRACKNELL. Oh, they count as Tories. They dine with us. Or come in the evening, at any rate. Now to minor matters. Are your parents living?

JACK. I have lost both my parents.

LADY BRACKNELL. Both? To lose one parent may be regarded as a misfortune; to lose *both* looks like carelessness. Who was your father? He was evidently a man of some wealth. Was he born in what the Radical papers call the purple of commerce, or did he rise from the ranks of the aristocracy?

JACK. I am afraid I really don't know. The fact is, Lady Bracknell, I said I had lost my parents. It would be nearer the truth to say that my parents seem to have lost me . . . I don't actually know who I am by birth. I was . . . well, I was found.

LADY BRACKNELL.   Found!

JACK.   The late Mr Thomas Cardew, an old gentleman of a very charitable and kindly disposition, found me, and gave me the name of Worthing, because he happened to have a first-class ticket for Worthing in his pocket at the time. Worthing is a place in Sussex. It is a seaside resort.

LADY BRACKNELL.   Where did the charitable gentleman who had a first-class ticket for this seaside resort find you?

JACK [*gravely*].   In a hand-bag.

LADY BRACKNELL.   A hand-bag?

JACK [*very seriously*].   Yes, Lady Bracknell. I was in a hand-bag—a somewhat large, black leather hand-bag, with handles to it—an ordinary hand-bag in fact.

LADY BRACKNELL.   In what locality did this Mr James, or Thomas, Cardew come across this ordinary hand-bag?

JACK.   In the cloak-room at Victoria Station. It was given to him in mistake for his own.

LADY BRACKNELL.   The cloak-room at Victoria Station?

JACK.   Yes. The Brighton line.

LADY BRACKNELL.   The line is immaterial. Mr Worthing, I confess I feel somewhat bewildered by what you have just told me. To be born, or at any rate bred, in a hand-bag, whether it had handles or not, seems to me to display a contempt for the ordinary decencies of family life that reminds one of the worst excesses of the French Revolution. And I presume you know what that unfortunate movement led to? As for the particular locality in which the hand-bag was found, a cloak-room at a railway station might serve to conceal a social indiscretion—has probably, indeed, been used for that purpose before now—but it could hardly be regarded as an assured basis for a recognized position in good society.

JACK.   May I ask you then what you would advise me to do? I need hardly say I would do anything in the world to ensure Gwendolen's happiness.

LADY BRACKNELL.   I would strongly advise you, Mr Worthing, to try and acquire some relations as soon as possible, and to make a definite effort to produce at any rate one parent, of either sex, before the season is quite over.

JACK. Well, I don't see how I could possibly manage to do that. I can produce the hand-bag at any moment. It is in my dressing-room at home. I really think that should satisfy you, Lady Bracknell.

LADY BRACKNELL. Me, sir! What has it to do with me? You can hardly imagine that I and Lord Bracknell would dream of allowing our only daughter—a girl brought up with the utmost care—to marry into a cloak-room, and form an alliance with a parcel. Good morning, Mr Worthing!

[LADY BRACKNELL *sweeps out in majestic indignation.*]

JACK. Good morning! [ALGERNON, *from the other room, strikes up the Wedding March.* JACK *looks perfectly furious, and goes to the door.*] For goodness' sake don't play that ghastly tune, Algy! How idiotic you are!

[*The music stops and* ALGERNON *enters cheerily.*]

ALGERNON. Didn't it go off all right, old boy? You don't mean to say Gwendolen refused you? I know it is a way she has. She is always refusing people. I think it is most ill-natured of her.

JACK. Oh, Gwendolen is as right as a trivet. As far as she is concerned, we are engaged. Her mother is perfectly unbearable. Never met such a Gorgon . . . I don't really know what a Gorgon is like, but I am quite sure that Lady Bracknell is one. In any case, she is a monster, without being a myth, which is rather unfair . . . I beg your pardon, Algy, I suppose I shouldn't talk about your own aunt in that way before you.

ALGERNON. My dear boy, I love hearing my relations abused. It is the only thing that makes me put up with them at all. Relations are simply a tedious pack of people, who haven't got the remotest knowledge of how to live, nor the smallest instinct about when to die.

JACK. Oh, that is nonsense!

ALGERNON. It isn't!

JACK. Well, I won't argue about the matter. You always want to argue about things.

ALGERNON. That is exactly what things were originally made for.

JACK. Upon my word, if I thought that, I'd shoot myself . . . [*A pause.*] You don't think there is any chance of Gwendolen becoming like her mother in about a hundred and fifty years, do you, Algy?

ALGERNON. All women become like their mothers. That is their tragedy. No man does. That's his.

JACK. Is that clever?

ALGERNON. It is perfectly phrased! and quite as true as any observation in civilized life should be.

JACK. I am sick to death of cleverness. Everybody is clever nowadays. You can't go anywhere without meeting clever people. The thing has become an absolute public nuisance. I wish to goodness we had a few fools left.

ALGERNON. We have.

JACK. I should extremely like to meet them. What do they talk about?

ALGERNON. The fools? Oh! about the clever people, of course.

JACK. What fools!

ALGERNON. By the way, did you tell Gwendolen the truth about your being Ernest in town, and Jack in the country?

JACK [in a very patronizing manner]. My dear fellow, the truth isn't quite the sort of thing one tells to a nice, sweet, refined girl. What extraordinary ideas you have about the way to behave to a woman!

ALGERNON. The only way to behave to a woman is to make love to her, if she is pretty, and to someone else if she is plain.

JACK. Oh, that is nonsense.

ALGERNON. What about your brother? What about the profligate Ernest?

JACK. Oh, before the end of the week I shall have got rid of him. I'll say he died in Paris of apoplexy. Lots of people die of apoplexy, quite suddenly, don't they?

ALGERNON. Yes, but it's hereditary, my dear fellow. It's a sort of thing that runs in families. You had much better say a severe chill.

JACK. You are sure a severe chill isn't hereditary, or anything of that kind?

ALGERNON. Of course it isn't!

JACK. Very well, then. My poor brother Ernest is carried off suddenly in Paris, by a severe chill. That gets rid of him.

ALGERNON. But I thought you said that . . . Miss Cardew was a little too much interested in your poor brother Ernest? Won't she feel his loss a good deal?

JACK. Oh, that is all right. Cecily is not a silly romantic girl, I am glad to say. She has got a capital appetite, goes on long walks and pays no attention at all to her lessons.

ALGERNON. I would rather like to see Cecily.

JACK. I will take very good care you never do. She is excessively pretty, and she is only just eighteen.

ALGERNON.   Have you told Gwendolen yet that you have an excessively
pretty ward who is only just eighteen?

JACK.   Oh! one doesn't blurt these things out to people. Cecily and
Gwendolen are perfectly certain to be extremely great friends. I'll
bet you anything you like that half an hour after they have met, they
will be calling each other sister.

ALGERNON.   Women only do that when they have called each other a lot
of other things first. Now, my dear boy, if we want to get a good table
at Willis's, we really must go and dress. Do you know it is nearly
seven?

JACK [*irritably*].   Oh! it always is nearly seven.

ALGERNON.   Well, I'm hungry.

JACK.   I never knew you when you weren't . . .

ALGERNON.   What shall we do after dinner? Go to a theatre?

JACK.   Oh, no! I loathe listening.

ALGERNON.   Well, let us go to the Club?

JACK.   Oh, no! I hate talking.

ALGERNON.   Well, we might trot round to the Empire at ten?

JACK.   Oh, no! I can't bear looking at things. It is so silly.

ALGERNON.   Well, what shall we do?

JACK.   Nothing!

ALGERNON.   It is awfully hard work doing nothing. However, I don't
mind hard work where there is no definite object of any kind.

[*Enter* LANE.]

LANE.   Miss Fairfax.

[*Enter* GWENDOLEN. LANE *goes out.*]

ALGERNON.   Gwendolen, upon my word!

GWENDOLEN.   Algy, kindly turn your back. I have something very
particular to say to Mr Worthing.

ALGERNON.   Really, Gwendolen, I don't think I can allow this at all.

GWENDOLEN.   Algy, you always adopt a strictly immoral attitude
towards life. You are not quite old enough to do that. [ALGERNON
retires to the fireplace.]

JACK.   My own darling!

GWENDOLEN.   Ernest, we may never be married. From the expression on
mamma's face I fear we never shall. Few parents nowadays pay any
regard to what their children say to them. The old-fashioned respect

for the young is fast dying out. Whatever influence I ever had over mamma, I lost at the age of three. But although she may prevent us from becoming man and wife, and I may marry someone else, and marry often, nothing that she can possibly do can alter my eternal devotion to you.

JACK. Dear Gwendolen!

GWENDOLEN. The story of your romantic origin, as related to me by mamma, with unpleasing comments, has naturally stirred the deeper fibres of my nature. Your Christian name has an irresistible fascination. The simplicity of your character makes you exquisitely incomprehensible to me. Your town address at the Albany I have. What is your address in the country?

JACK. The Manor House, Woolton, Hertfordshire.

[ALGERNON, *who has been carefully listening, smiles to himself, and writes the address on his shirt-cuff. Then picks up the Railway Guide.*]

GWENDOLEN. There is a good postal service, I suppose? It may be necessary to do something desperate. That of course will require serious consideration. I will communicate with you daily.

JACK. My own one!

GWENDOLEN. How long do you remain in town?

JACK. Till Monday.

GWENDOLEN. Good! Algy, you may turn round now.

ALGERNON. Thanks, I've turned round already.

GWENDOLEN. You may also ring the bell.

JACK. You will let me see you to your carriage, my own darling?

GWENDOLEN. Certainly.

JACK [*to* LANE, *who now enters*]. I will see Miss Fairfax out.

LANE. Yes, sir. [JACK *and* GWENDOLEN *go off.*]

[LANE *presents several letters on a salver to* ALGERNON. *It is to be surmised that they are bills, as* ALGERNON, *after looking at the envelopes, tears them up.*]

ALGERNON. A glass of sherry, Lane.

LANE. Yes, sir.

ALGERNON. Tomorrow, Lane, I'm going Bunburying.

LANE. Yes, sir.

ALGERNON. I shall probably not be back till Monday. You can put up my dress clothes, my smoking jacket, and all the Bunbury suits . . .

LANE.   Yes, sir. [*Handing sherry.*]

ALGERNON.   I hope tomorrow will be a fine day, Lane.

LANE.   It never is, sir.

ALGERNON.   Lane, you're a perfect pessimist.

LANE.   I do my best to give satisfaction, sir.

[*Enter* JACK. LANE *goes off.*]

JACK.   There's a sensible, intellectual girl! the only girl I ever cared for in my life. [ALGERNON *is laughing immoderately.*] What on earth are you so amused at?

ALGERNON.   Oh, I'm a little anxious about poor Bunbury, that is all.

JACK.   If you don't take care, your friend Bunbury will get you into a serious scrape some day.

ALGERNON.   I love scrapes. They are the only things that are never serious.

JACK.   Oh, that's nonsense, Algy. You never talk anything but nonsense.

ALGERNON.   Nobody ever does.

[JACK *looks indignantly at him, and leaves the room.* ALGERNON *lights a cigarette, reads his shirt-cuff and smiles.*]

ACT DROP

- Who are Jack's real parents?

- Will Jack marry Gwendolen?

- Why is it so important to be named Ernest?

- Will Algernon meet Cecily? Will they get along?

Read the rest of the play to find out the answers to these questions.

Analyzing and Evaluating the Script

Before producing a play, consider the play's key elements (dramatic structure, theme, setting, historical context, literary style, genre, and characters) and how those elements will influence the production. All cast and crew members should have a detailed understanding of the play to use as a basis for future decisions.

After everyone in your class has had a chance to do a first reading, schedule a time to analyze and evaluate the script in small groups. Use the topics below as jumping-off points for your analysis. Also see Chapter 8, pages 332–373, to review job responsibilities and to get more information about how to begin production.

EXAMINING WILDE'S PLAY

1. One important theme of Wilde's play is "the importance of style and appearance." Another important theme is "deception as a way of life." Together, make a chart listing actions, events, or dialogue that relate to each of these themes.

2. Find dialogue and events that show that Wilde's play is a farce. Why do you suppose Wilde chose comedy as the vehicle for his message and not some other genre?

3. What ideas do you have about the appearance and personality of Jack, Algernon, Gwendolen, and Lady Bracknell? Use evidence from the play to support your answers.

A Note on Cast and Crew Assignments

The process and order of stages described here may be adjusted to suit the needs of your class. Before you begin exploratory discussions, you and your class may want to work with your teacher to assign job duties and roles. You may then arrange your discussions on the basis of the assignments. (See "Casting the Play" on page R25 for more on how to assign roles.)

EXAMINING THEATER AND SOCIETY Outside of class, work individually to do historical research about the play. What was the moral climate of late nineteenth-century Britain? Which serious social issues are reflected in the farcical world of Wilde's play? What clothing and furnishings characterized the period? What historical aspects of the play do you consider the most important for you and your classmates to communicate to your audience? Write your answers to these questions in a short report to share with your classmates.

MAKING A PROMPTBOOK

Under the guidance of your director and teacher, create a promptbook—a script marked with notations and cues—to use during rehearsals of the First Act. Follow these steps:

- Buy an inexpensive or used paperback of the play. Break the spine of the book and separate the pages.

- Paste each page on hole-punched notebook paper and place all the pages in a three-ring binder.

- Make up a color coding key (like the one shown on page R4), a symbol system, stick-figure drawings, a numbering system, or any other notations that would help the director to coach actors.

For more on creating promptbooks, see Chapter 8, pages 346–348.

Finding a Place to Stage the Play

For your first public performances, consider staging the scene for other classes at your school. To keep operating expenses down, consider converting the front of a large classroom into a stage. Some small professional theater companies with very limited budgets present excellent performances in storefronts to as little as twenty audience members seated in folding chairs.

You might also find places to stage public performances in your neighborhood. Ask your teacher for help in staging such a performance. You may find a new audience in one of the following venues: a seniors center or nursing home; a hospital; a middle school class; a shopping mall; a park district field house; or a local library.

Casting the Play

Your director (a student) and the managing director (your teacher) should set up auditions for the production. For this class project, you may prefer to conduct a closed rather than an open audition. If possible, students may audition in pairs to give the director a chance to see how various members of the ensemble cast interact with one another. For more on casting and auditioning, see Chapter 8, pages 349–355.

Production Checklist
A play director usually keeps a checklist to track completion of important production tasks. Use the lists on pages 345 and 368 for help with tracking tasks.

Conducting Rehearsals

With the cast in place, your group is now ready to begin the exciting work of rehearsals. Refer to the chart on the following page while planning and scheduling your rehearsals.

Type of Rehearsal	Description	Goal
Reading Rehearsals	Director and cast members practice reading the play aloud.	To help actors develop good timing and a unified understanding of the play
Blocking Rehearsals	Director refers to the play's stage directions and guides the actors' movements.	To help actors practice how, when, and where to move onstage
Working Rehearsals	Director fine-tunes the actors' performances and stage presence.	To help actors practice their memorized lines, expand their character interpretations, and coordinate their words and movements.
Dress Rehearsals	Director leads uninterrupted rehearsals that include costumes and props.	To help actors and entire production team undergo the dynamics of a real performance

Creating Set Designs, Props, and Costumes

Your class should have a team of designers to develop the mechanical and visual aspects of the production. Have the team brainstorm cost-cutting and time-saving ideas for stage scenery, props, and costumes, based on analysis of the script. Here are a few ideas to get you started:

- Create a makeshift sofa for the opening scene—Algernon's apartment. Tie the legs of three or four folding chairs together to build the frame of the sofa. Drape a large decorative throw over the chairs and pin the back of the fabric to make it look more fitted.
- Make a tea table by covering a small folding table, such as a TV tray table, with a tablecloth.
- Research clothing of the Victorian upper class. Since costumes are very costly to rent, consider other options to traditional costuming. For example, use modern costumes that show a "touch of class." Jack and Algernon might wear white shirts with ascots or ties.
- Use local thrift stores as a source for costumes and props.
- Instead of painting a backdrop, use a slide projector to project an image resembling Victorian wallpaper on a blank wall.

All involved with the production should review and apply the safety rules on page 441.

Presenting and Evaluating Your Public Performance

After making any final improvements, present your performance to your chosen audience, using the information in this Reference Section and in Part Four, pages 332–529, as your guide. Afterwards, write an essay evaluating the experience. Give your answers to the following questions:

- Which aspect of collaborating in production decision making did you enjoy the most? Which aspect did you find most challenging? How did you handle the challenge, and what was the result? Tell what you learned from the most challenging aspects of the production.
- Describe how it felt to see your unified production go public. What aspect of that experience stood out for you?
- What effect did your preplanning have on the ultimate production? In particular, how did your analysis and evaluation of the dramatic text—the script—impact the production?

EXTENSION ACTIVITIES

1. **Cast and direct duet scenes from the play.** To give everyone in your class a chance to perform different duties, mount a public performance titled *A Festival of Duet Scenes*, using scenes from *The Importance of Being Earnest.* You might include the duet scenes on pages 163–165 and 206–208 of the textbook, as well as a variety of other duet scenes from the play.

2. **Videotape the live theater production.** Have students in your class interested in filmmaking techniques use a video camera to shoot one of your public performances. Show your completed video to another class and get their responses.

3. **Explore the arts.** Research developments in fine art, theater, music, literature, and dance during the late Victorian era. Summarize what you learn in a report. Then use your report to create a chart comparing and contrasting characteristics of each art form during that time. This activity may inspire you to explore how you might incorporate music, dance, or fine art into future performances.

Rubric for Play Production

Your play production should

- present a unified production to a chosen audience
- include well-rehearsed and directed performances
- demonstrate an understanding of stagecraft
- reflect analysis of the dramatic text for structure, genre, and historical context

How to Write a Dramatic Script

Many playwrights express their views on social issues through their plays. Because theater scenarios can grab an audience's attention, drama is often used to communicate a message. In this guide to scriptwriting, you will write a dramatic scene focusing on an issue you feel strongly about. By doing so, you may move others to feel as you do. You may also create work for production by your class.

Writing a scene will give you insight into the discipline of a playwright. Whether they write as a career or as an avocation, most successful playwrights have their own method of artistic discipline. Some may need to set aside a place and time to write. Some may feel more inspired to write somewhere outside their homes. After you complete your scene, think about and describe the habits of artistic discipline you developed in completing your assignment.

THE WRITING PROCESS

Prewriting

LOOK FOR A STORY

A dramatic scene has the elements of any good story—such as characters, setting, conflict, and plot—but the telling is done through actions, dialogue, and stage directions. One way to find story ideas is to choose an issue that matters to you and imagine how that issue might affect specific people. Ask yourself questions like these:

- What news story has stayed in my mind?
- What human condition makes me sad or angry?
- What traits do I admire most in people?

To brainstorm for ideas about the people, or characters, who would be involved, ask:

- Who would be affected by this issue?
- What people or groups of people might conflict over this issue?
- How could someone overcome the problems created by this issue?

CONSIDER YOUR AUDIENCE

Who is most likely to see your scene performed? These people will be your audience. As you plan your scene, consider what kinds of material will grab their attention and keep them interested.

CONSIDER YOUR PURPOSE

You want to entertain your audience, but your main purpose is to communicate a particular message. Consider which format has the best chance of getting your message across—a stage drama, a radio drama, a TV sitcom, or a commercial.

MAKE A PLAN

After you've chosen an issue to dramatize, work out the story details, just as if you were writing a short story. What conflict will drive the plot? What characters will deal with the conflict? Where will the action take place? To begin, you might fill out a chart like the one shown.

Student Model	
Theme	Class differences can't disguise our common humanity; we all suffer equally when disasters strike.
Setting	The interior of a spacious suburban home
Conflict/Problem	A wealthy and fashionable employer has no understanding of or sympathy for her cleaning person and that person's problems.
Main Character(s)	Abigail Suarez, a wealthy and fashionable suburbanite; and Elizabeth, her cleaning person.
Complications/Climax	Abigail's lack of understanding and sympathy make her impatient with Elizabeth's tardiness and obligations, but a sudden crisis creates a bond and mutual concern.
Resolution	The two women, connected by their motherhood, set off to see if their children have been harmed. Abigail suddenly sees Elizabeth as a human being, not just an employee.

A graphic like this can help you plan the plot of your scene.

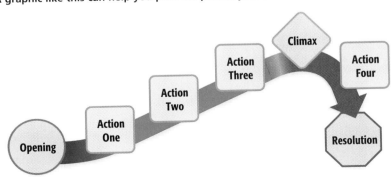

Drafting

WRITE YOUR DRAFT

Get your ideas down in script format, but don't worry if everything doesn't flow smoothly yet. You'll have time later to perfect each character's dialogue.

Student Model
ABIGAIL: *[angry and perturbed]* I don't care about your excuses, Elizabeth; your job is to show up here at 10 sharp every Thursday to clean the house, and that's that. I'm too busy to be waiting around all morning to let you in.
ELIZABETH: I know, Mrs. Suarez. I won't be late again. *[Pauses; then adds meekly]* Is there anything extra to do today, or just the usual?
ABIGAIL: The usual . . . oh . . . except my book group's meeting here tomorrow to discuss *The Pilot's Wife,* and we'll use the solarium, so make sure that looks extra good.

Revising

SET THE SCENE

Check to make sure your stage directions in the opening scene describe the set, the mood, the location, and the characters present.

EVALUATE YOUR SCRIPT

Let your draft sit for at least a few hours. Then read the scene and try to picture each detail as you read. Mark places that need improvement, using the Rubric for Revising. Then ask classmates to read the scene aloud while you listen. Request feedback and make the changes that you think will improve your scene.

Rubric for Revising
Your revised dramatic scene should have
- dialogue and action that catch the audience's attention
- stage directions that make the action clear
- a setting appropriate for the action
- a message that emerges from the action and dialogue

Student Model
spacious, even oversized
[Interior of a suburban home. Seated at a desk in the writing area of the large, modern kitchen is Abigail Suarez, dressed as if she just ^glassed-in ^thirty-three-year-old walked out of a mall window showing the latest fashions. The in fashionable casual attire ⊙ kitchen window looks out onto a large formal garden. Abigail is busy marking pages in a catalog. getting ready to place ^her next order⊙]
[The doorbell rings. Abigail heads for the side entrance to the kitchen.]
ABIGAIL: Well, Elizabeth, late again, I see. you're ⊙
ELIZABETH: [She enters and takes off jacket.] I'm sorry, Abigail. We hurriedly a worn and faded So ⊙ Mrs. Suarez ⊙ overslept and I had a difficult time getting Thomas to the school bus. the hardest

Editing/Proofreading

When you feel satisfied with your scene, proofread for errors in grammar, usage, mechanics, and spelling.

Proofreading Tip
Decide how you are going to indicate stage directions and then check to make sure that you do so consistently.

Student Model

ELIZABETH: There's no time for this, Abigail—*[hurriedly putting on jacket]* Don't make me . . . Don't make me—

ABIGAIL: *[cutting her off, with nastiness]* I don't know why I've put up with this for—

ELIZABETH: For heavens' sake, Abigail. That was the school. It's the bus—

Publishing/Presenting

Before you perform your scene, choose a cast, a director, and a stage manager. You may decide to direct, act, or do both. On a copy machine or computer printer, make a copy of your script for each person involved in the scene. Then start rehearsing and building the set and props. If you are presenting a radio production or readers theater, plan and rehearse sound effects. Consider audiotaping or videotaping your scene for presentation later. See pages R1–R27 for more information on presenting scenes.

Reflecting

Reflect about whether your scene effectively communicated a message about a particular issue. If so, what made the scene effective? If not, did the scene succeed in other ways? Make a note of what you have learned by writing this dramatic scene. How might this knowledge help you in other kinds of writing?

A

acoustics: theater's qualities that determine the audibility and trueness of sound

act curtain: the curtain hung just upstage of the proscenium that opens and closes at each act or scene

acting area: the portion of the stage used by the actors during the play

action: that which happens onstage to hold the audience's attention

ad-lib: to improvise stage business or conversation, especially when an actor has missed or forgotten lines and other actors must supply the missing information

allegory: a form of storytelling that teaches moral concepts by using symbolic characters, events, or objects

ambiguity: an unclear or double meaning

amperage: the strength of an electrical current flowing through a wire

amphitheater: an oval or round structure with no roof that has tiers of seats rising from the center, used for public performances of plays and other productions

amplifier: a simple piece of sound equipment that receives a small sound signal from a microphone or other source, increases the strength of the signal, and outputs it to a speaker or other destination

analysis: critique of a production that might include considering, describing, and evaluating various aspects such as theme, plot, dialogue, and characterization

animation: concept of making drawn or inanimate objects appear to live and move

antagonist: the person or the force working against the protagonist in a play

antecedent action: a clearly defined explanation of the events in the lives of the leading characters before the start of a play's action; also called the preliminary situation

anticipation: a device used in comedy in which the audience is looking forward to something, such as an actor slipping on a banana peel that has been dropped

anticlimax: a result much less important than what preceded it; often used to provoke laughter by building something up in great proportions and then plummeting into a letdown

antifeedback units: inexpensive solution to the problem of feedback

apron: the section of the stage in front of the curtain ➤

arc spotlight: a very powerful spotlight with carbon rods as electrical conductors, used as a long-distance follow spot or for effects; also called a carbon arc spotlight

APRON

arena stage: a stage without a proscenium arch and with seats on four sides, allowing close association between actors and spectators

arras: in the Elizabethan playhouse, a curtain hung behind the tarras, a shallow balcony, to conceal another recess called the chamber

art director: person who determines the overall "look" of the play by working closely with the director and the makeup, costuming, and lighting designers to achieve the desired effect in a production

aside: a line spoken directly to the audience

assistant director: the person who acts as the liaison between the director and the cast and crew and who takes charge of the rehearsal when the director is absent

at rise: who and what are on the stage when the curtain opens

atmosphere: the environment of the play created by staging and lighting

audition: a tryout for a position in a play

auditorium: the place in the theater where the audience sits

automated light fixture: a spotlight that can follow a target or a pattern and change gels or gobos as programmed by a computer

avant-garde: word describing new or experimental styles of an art form

B

backdrop: a large piece of cloth, on which scenery is painted, that is fastened to battens and hung at the back of the stage setting; also called drop

backing: flats or drops behind the scenery openings to mask the backstage area; also called masking

backlighting: the use of lighting instruments above and behind performers to accent the performers and set them apart from the background

backstage: the area behind the set that is not visible to the audience, including dressing rooms, the greenroom, prop rooms, shops, offices, and storage areas

balance: the visual symmetry of the stage

ballet: dance in which the dancers communicate a storyline or a mood to the audience

barn doors: a metal frame with two or four flaps used to shape the light pattern of a spotlight

batten: a long piece of wood or pipe from which scenery, lights, and curtains are suspended; also used at top and bottom of a drop

bit part: an acting role with very few lines

blackout: stage direction to turn off all stage lights suddenly

blender: the edge of a bald wig that must be made to blend with an actor's skin

blocked out: a natural facial feature obscured with neutral makeup; also planned or roughly sketched, as the movement during a scene

blocking rehearsal: a rehearsal at which the movement and groupings on the stage are practiced

blocking yourself: getting behind furniture or other actors so that you cannot be seen by the audience

body language: communication that uses gestures, posture, and facial expressions instead of words

book (noun): the script of a musical

book (verb): to hinge two or three flats together so they will stand free or fold up ➤

boomerang: a polelike stand having horizontal arms (pipes) for hanging lighting instruments, usually located just upstage of the proscenium or tormentor; also called a tree or a boom

border: a short curtain hung across the stage above the acting area to mask the overhead lights from the audience; also refers to overhead striplights

border light: a type of striplight hung from pipe battens above the stage; also called borders

box set: a two-wall or three-wall set representing an interior of a room, often covered by a ceiling

brace: an adjustable, polelike support for flats

breaker: an electrical device that cuts off the electrical current when a circuit is overloaded; may be reset once the problem has been corrected

bridge: the first electrical pipe just upstage of the proscenium from which spotlights may be hung; also called X ray

bridging: words the director adds to the script before or after difficult ones to help an actor present lines

Broadway musical: production that incorporates contemporary music to convey plot, character, mood, and setting

building: the term used by costumers for making a costume

building a scene: using dramatic devices, such as increased tempo, volume, and emphasis, to bring a scene to a climax

bump up: to increase light intensity quickly

Bunraku: Japanese drama that features wooden, elaborately costumed marionettes that are about four feet tall; also called Doll Theater

burlesque: a form of low comedy that mocks a broad topic

business: any specific action, other than a change of location, performed on the stage, such as picking up a book or pouring tea; used to establish atmosphere, reveal character, or explain a situation

business manager: the person responsible for the financial arrangements of a production

butt joint: a joint that brings together two surfaces by fastening them end to end

C

cabaret: a show produced in a small space with limited seating, such as a restaurant or a nightclub

cable: heavily insulated wire for joining lighting instruments to electrical outlets or to a switchboard

callbacks: the cast-selection process by which actors return for a second or third tryout

caricature: an exaggeration of a certain feature of a character or a literary work

cast by type: actor cast in a straight part in which the character physically resembles the actor

catastrophe: in a story, an unlucky event that may strike the leading character or one of the major characters

catharsis: the emotional release an audience feels after the downfall of a tragic character

catwalk: a narrow bridge in the flies near the ceiling that provides access to stage scenery and lighting units

central axis: the deepest point onstage that is just off center

chamber: in an Elizabethan playhouse, a recess behind the second-level acting area which might have been used by musicians, or as seating members of the audience

change music: the music played between scenes while sets are being changed

character-centered approach: an approach to telling a story that focuses on a character or a group of characters who experience different situations

character part: role in which an actor portrays traits that differ from his or her own to produce a desired character

characterization: putting together all facets of a character to bring life and interest to that character

cheat out: a stage technique in which an actor who is facing sideways pivots the torso and turns the face toward the audience

chiaroscuro: treatment of light and shade; the use of makeup to highlight and shadow the face

children's theater: theater written, designed, and performed for children

choreographer: a person who designs dance for the stage

choreography: the dances designed for a production

chorus: a group of actors in Greek drama who commented on the main action of the play; in Elizabethan drama, actors who presented the prologue; in present-day theater, the singers in a musical, other than the principals

circuit: the complete path of an electrical current

circumflex inflection: the use of the voice to blend two or three sounds for a vowel that normally has a single sound, allowing the actor to stress or to change a word's meaning

cleat: a piece of wood or metal attached to a surface to strengthen it

climax: the turning point in a play

clock reference: the manner in which an arena stage may be divided, starting with the twelve o'clock position assignment

close-up: a shot taken at a very close distance, first used by famous director, D. W. Griffith

closed audition: a tryout open to only union members

closet drama: a play meant to be read rather than acted

clout nail: a malleable, self-clinching nail used in flat construction

cold reading: a tryout during which an actor uses material never seen before

color coding: matching characters by color or pattern

color frame: a metal holder that fits into a lighting instrument to keep a color filter in place

combination: the putting together of inclinations, rotations, and isolations

combo: a small group of instrumentalists

comedy: a play that treats characters and situations in a humorous way and has a happy ending

comedy of manners: a play that shows the humorous traits of a particular segment of society, usually the upper class

comic opera: a humorous or satirical operetta

commedia dell'arte: professional improvised comedy that developed in Italy during the Renaissance

complication: an incident that complicates the plot; Aristotle's term for the combination of the preliminary situation, the initial incident, and the rising action

composer: a person who writes music

compressors: devices that sense loud sounds and compress them; inexpensive solution to feedback

concentration: the ability to direct all thoughts, energies, and skills toward a given goal

concept musical: a series of loosely connected scenes that focus on a theatrical concept

conclusion: the final outcome of the preceding action of a play

conductor: the person who directs an orchestra and cues onstage performers

conflict: a struggle between two opposing forces

connector: a device for joining cables to each other or to instruments

consistent inconsistency: trait of a character an actor chooses to emphasize, such as a dialect

constructivism: an abstract style of stage setting that employs skeletal structures instead of realistic props; also called Socialist Realism

control console: an electronic light control board, usually with a key pad, a programmed memory system, and a monitor

convention: a special or traditional way of doing things

coordinates: costumes that are separates, which are interchangeable, or sometimes reversible, such as ties, vests, and so on

corner block: a triangle nailed to the corners of a flat to strengthen and stabilize the joints

corner brace: a cleat nailed across the corner of a flat to strengthen it

costume parade: a procession during which actors wear their costumes under the lights to ensure the compatibility of the colors

costume plot: an outline that describes the colors, fabrics, and accessories for each costume design; kept by wardrobe manager

costume silhouette: each historic period's own distinctive line and form in dress

countercross: movement in opposite directions by two or more actors to balance the stage picture

counterweight system: a system of lines and weights that gives mechanical advantage to the raising and lowering of scenery

cover: to obstruct the audience's view of something onstage

crash box: a box offstage into which something can be thrown to create the sound of breakage

crisis: a moment of decision for the leading character; the highest point of conflict

critic: a specialist in evaluating plays

criticism: review and analysis of drama

critique: a positive or negative evaluation

cross: to move from one position to another onstage

crosscut shot: technique used by filmmakers that switches abruptly from one scene to another to show events happening at the same time in different places

crossfade: the dimming of one set of lighting instruments as another set comes up

crossover scene: a short scene played in front of a shallow drop or curtain while scenery is being changed

crossovers: a term that describes characters walking across the stage together or entering from opposite sides and meeting on the stage

cue: the last words, action, or technical effect that immediately precedes any line or business; a stage signal

cue sheet: a document prepared after the light plot; indicates what lighting changes are to take place and when; see light cue sheet

curtain: the curtain or drapery that shuts off the stage from the audience; when written in all capital letters in a script, it indicates that the curtain is to be closed

curtain calls: the appearance of a play's cast in response to an audience's applause

curtain line: the imaginary floor line the curtain touches when closed

curtain set: the use of curtains as a backdrop for a play

cut: to stop action; to omit

cut-down set: like the box set, forms the entire perimeter of the setting; can be constructed of screens; also called the profile set or minimum set

cut in: to break into the speech of another character

cut-off lines: lines interrupted by another speaker and indicated in the script by dashes

cut-out: two-dimensional pieces of scenery used to represent three-dimensional objects such as rocks or bushes; also called a profile

cycle: a series of short plays depicting religious history from creation through doomsday, performed by medieval guilds in the late fourteenth century

cyclorama: a background curtain hung around the three sides of the stage; also called a cyc

D

dance pre-done: ritualistic drama, such as traditional tribal dances

deluge system: a fire-safety system that provides a fan-shaped water curtain between the stage and the audience

denouement: an element of plot that refers to the untangling and resolution of complications

deus ex machina: a Greek term meaning "god from the machine"; in Greek theater, an actor playing a god was often lowered onto the stage by a crane to settle worldly affairs. The term is now used to describe any device an author introduces late in a play to resolve plot difficulties.

dialogue: the lines of a play spoken by characters

diction: the selection and pronunciation of words and their combinations in speech

dimmer: an electrical device that controls the amount of current flowing into a lighting instrument, thus increasing or decreasing the intensity of the light

dimming down: reducing light gradually

dimming up: increasing light gradually

director: the person in charge of molding all aspects of production—acting, scenery, costumes, makeup, lighting, and so on—into a unified whole

dissolve: radical technique used by filmmakers that shows the passage of time by superimposing one camera shot over another as the first fades away

down: the part of the stage toward the audience; also called downstage

drama: a literary composition performed onstage

dress rehearsal: an uninterrupted rehearsal with costumes and props; the final rehearsal before the first performance

dressers: assistants who help actors with costume changes and who help care for costumes

dressing the stage: keeping the stage picture balanced during the action; as a technical term, the placing of furnishings, pictures, and similar items to complete and balance a set

drop: see backdrop

dry brushing: a technique using a dry paintbrush to add texture to painted flats

dutchman: a muslin strip four to five inches wide that covers the gap between flats

E

electric winch system: a mechanical means of raising and lowering battens using an electric motor to turn a winch

elevation: an eye-level-view drawing showing the flats arranged in a continuous row to be used in a set, or any front or rear head-on two-dimensional drawing

ellipsoidal reflector spotlight: a highly efficient lighting instrument with a reflector shaped like an ellipsoid ➤

emotional acting: the playing of a role in such a way that the actor weeps, suffers, or struggles emotionally; also called subjective acting

emotional memory: the recalling of specific emotions, such as fear, joy, or anger; technique used by actors in developing characterization

empathy: emotional identification with someone or something outside oneself; ideally, the audience develops empathy with the characters in a play.

emphasis: the focus of the audience's attention on some part of the stage

energy: the fuel that drives acting, enlivens performances, creates empathy, and makes powerful characters

entr'acte: music that takes place between acts in a play

epic theater: a learning theater developed in Germany by Bertolt Brecht between the two world wars that causes the audience to think deeply about important social problems in order to correct them

etiquette: proper behavior

exaggeration: an overstatement; an enlargement of the truth

existentialism: school of philosophy that teaches that we define ourselves through our choices and actions; closely linked to theater of the absurd

exit: to leave the stage; also called exeunt when plural

exposition: the information put before an audience that gives the where, when, why, and who facts of a play

expressionism: a highly symbolic and poetic style of drama that features distorted, oversimplified, and symbolic rather than realistic characters

externalization: the process by which an actor shows the audience a character's true personality through interpretation, nonverbal expression, voice quality, pitch, rate, and physical action

F

facial mask: those parts of the face that vibrate when a person hums; a plaster casting taken of the face

fade-off lines: lines that actors trail off rather than finishing

falling action: the series of events following the climax

falling inflection: the use of the voice to signal the end of a statement or to express depression, finality, or firmness

false proscenium: a frame built inside the proscenium to reduce the size of the stage opening

fantasy: a play that deals with unrealistic and fantastic characters

farce: a kind of comedy characterized by clowning, practical jokes, and improbable characters and situations

featherdusting: a method of texturing using a featherduster dipped in paint to create a different pattern each time, such as foliage

feedback: a frequent problem that occurs with the projection of sound; a loud, ear-piercing scream that happens when the amplified sound is fed back into the microphones that are picking up the original sound

feeding: giving lines and action in such a way that another actor can make a point or get a laugh

fill light: the light that fills shadows, aimed opposite a key light

film editing: involves choosing and sequencing the various pieces of film so that the story is coherent; done by the editor in conjunction with the director of a film

fire curtain: a fireproof curtain closing off the stage from the auditorium

flat: a wooden frame covered with cloth used as the basic unit of structure of a box set

floating screen: a set made of single flats or narrow drops placed at various depths parallel to the front of the stage

floodlight: a high wattage (500 to 1,500 watts) lighting instrument with a metal shell open at one end, the inner surface of which is painted white, is polished metal, or has a mirror to reflect the nonfocused light; also called a flood ➤

floor block: a small block of wood tacked to the floor on both sides of a flat or at each union where two flats meet

floor plan: a drawing of the overhead view of a set showing the exact location of all entrances, walls, and furniture

floor pocket: a receptacle for stage plugs mounted in the floor

fly (noun): system for hanging drops

fly (verb): to raise or lower scenery

fly space: area above the stage where scenery is hung when not in use; also called a loft

flycrew: stagehands who raise and lower flown scenery and draperies

focus: the direction of an actor's attention, action, emotion, or line delivery to a definite target

foil: an acting role that is used for personality comparison, usually with the main character

folk drama: plays originating during the Middle Ages that were presented outdoors during planting time, harvest time, and other secular holidays

follow spot: a long-range, high-wattage (1,000 to 2,600 watts) lighting instrument capable of picking up or following a person moving on the stage, with a beam strong enough to stand out against normal stage lighting; may be xenon, carbon arc, quartz, or incandescent type ➤

foot iron: an L-shaped piece of strap iron attached to the back of a flat and anchored to the floor with a stage screw; often used when there is insufficient space for jacks or braces

footlights: striplights along the front of the apron that throw light up and back toward the acting area; seldom used today; also called foots

foreshadowing: a line, an action, or an idea emphasized early in a play that gives the audience clues to the conclusion

foundation: a base color in makeup

fourth wall: used in representational theater; the imaginary wall through which the audience watches the action of the play

Fresnel: a spotlight featuring a Fresnel or stepped lens, which projects a clear, strong light with a soft edge ➤

funnel: a metal cylinder that can be placed in a gel holder to control the spread of light; also called a top hat, high hat, or snoot

fuse: a protective device set in an electrical circuit that is destroyed by the passage of excessive current

G

gauze: a drop made of fabric that seems almost opaque when lit from the front and semitransparent when lit from behind; also called a scrim

gelatin: a transparent color medium placed on lighting instruments to produce different colors; also called gel

genre: a category characterized by a particular style or form of artistic, dramatic, literary, or musical composition

gesture: a movement of any part of the body to help express an idea

giving the scene: shifting audience attention from one actor to another

gobo: a stencil placed in the gel holder of a spotlight to project a pattern ➤

grand drape: a curtain at the top of the proscenium, usually made of the same material as the act curtain, used to lower the height of the proscenium opening

greenroom: a waiting area offstage used by actors

gridding: the process used to enlarge a sketch to a drop

gridiron: a series of heavy beams or a metal framework just under the roof of the stage to which are attached the pulleys or blocks through which lines pass to raise or lower scenery; also called a grid

grip: a stagehand who moves scenery

ground cloth: a canvas covering for the floor of the acting area; also called a floor cloth

ground row: a low profile of scenery that can stand by itself, used to mask the bottom of the cyc or backdrop and to give the illusion of distance

groundlings: in an Elizabethan playhouse, the members of the audience who each paid a penny to stand in the pit

H

hamartia: an error in judgment or a shortcoming on the part of a tragic protagonist

hand props: properties, such as tools, weapons, or luggage, carried onstage by an individual player

hanging plot: a listing of all the flying scenery and what is on each piece, prepared by the technical director or the stage manager

Heavens: in an Elizabethan playhouse, a roof supported by two ornate columns above the stage with the sun, moon, stars, clouds, and the signs of the zodiac painted on the underside

high comedy: a type of comedy that includes comedy of manners and satire and that is characterized by clever lines, word plays, and allusions

highlighting: the term used for applying make-up to bring out facial features

hit: to emphasize a word or a line with extra force

holding for laughs: waiting for an audience to quiet down after a humorous line or scene

house manager: the person responsible for distribution of programs, seating of the audience, and training of the ushers

hubris: an act of excessive pride; a form of hamartia

hue: the purity of color

hues: various colors seen in the spectrum of a beam of light that passes through a prism

humanities: branches of learning that seek to understand the human experience and have primarily a cultural character, such as drama, music, literature, and art

humor: an appeal to the heart, in which the audience feels amusement, tenderness, compassion, love, or pity

humors (or humours): the personality traits explored in Elizabethan drama

I

illusion of the first time: a situation in which an audience is led to believe that each performance is the first

illusory walk: a mime convention in which the mime "walks" without moving through space

impressionism: a type of play that seeks to make the audience react and see as a character does when stirred by intense emotion

improvisation: the impromptu portrayal of a character or a scene without any rehearsal or preparation

improvisational audition: a tryout at which the actor is assigned a character and given a brief description of a situation to perform with no preparation

inclination: the bending of the body to the front, the side, or the rear

incompletion: a line or a bit of action that is started and not finished and is used to provoke laughter

incongruity: that which seems out of place, out of time, or out of character

inflection: modulation, variety in pitch

ingenue: a female lead between the ages of sixteen and thirty

initial incident: the first event in a play from which the rest of the plot develops

***innamoratae* and *innamorati*:** stock characters in commedia dell'arte; young lovers who speak a refined language

intensity: the brightness or dimness of color or light

intent: the inner force driving a character's behavior

intercom system: system separate from the general amplification system that allows communication between the stage manager and members of the stage crew

internalization: the process an actor uses to get within a character to learn what the character is like

iris: a shutter device used to change the diameter of a beam of light

isolation: the process of separating parts of the body for individual development and expression

J

jack: a triangular brace for supporting scenery ➤

jackknife: a two-part stage set that can be stored in the wings perpendicular to the proscenium and pivoted into place to form a continuous line across the back of the stage

JACK

jigger: a board used as a spacer in three-fold booked flats

jog: a narrow flat, usually less than two feet in width, used to form such things as corners, alcoves, and bay windows

juvenile: a male lead between the ages of sixteen and thirty

K

***Kabuki*:** Japanese drama from the seventeenth century that combines aspects of both *No* and *Bunraku* forms of drama

key light: the strong source of light aimed at an acting area

keystone: a wedge-shaped block placed over the joints of the toggle rail and the stiles of a flat

kill: command to turn off a light

kinesthesis: sometimes called "muscle memory"; the neuromuscular sense the body has in a particular physical position

knap: the second sound after landing a blow—a sliding, slapping sound or clap

L

lash line: a rope used for lashing flats together

laugh curve: the audience's reaction that actors listen for in order to anticipate the length of time the audience will laugh

leading center: the part of the body that appears to lead gestures, such as the chest as a leading center for a brave character

leading roles: the main characters in a play

left (L) and right (R): terms used to refer to the stage from the actor's point of view, not that of the audience

legitimate theater: originally, officially sanctioned stage plays; now the term is applied to regional and community theater, movies, and television as well

legs: narrow drapes, usually hung in pairs, stage left and stage right, to mask the backstage area

librettist: the person who writes the book (script) of a musical

libretto: the book for a musical, including lines and lyrics; also the text of an opera

light cue sheet: the lighting technician's guide for all dimmer readings and settings at act or scene openings and for all lighting changes; also called cue sheet

light panel: a console from which the brightness of light is controlled ➤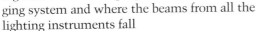

light plot: a diagram showing the placement of the lighting instruments and plugging system and where the beams from all the lighting instruments fall

line: an artistic value in staging that alters proportion and affects the observer psychologically, such as the use of vertical lines in drapes to suggest dignity

Linnebach projector: a lantern for projecting images from a slide onto a backdrop from the rear of the backdrop

live-action films: films in which the action is provided by living creatures

load: the wattage of lights and electrical pieces of equipment supplied by one circuit; an overload will burn out a fuse or trip a breaker

low comedy: a type of comedy that is quite physical, sometimes vulgar, and highly exaggerated in style and performance

lyricist: a person who writes words to music

lyrics: the words to a song

M

mansions: a series of acting stations that represented biblical settings; the Saint plays and Mystery plays were performed with mansions.

masking: see backing

mass: an artistic value in staging that takes bulk and weight into consideration

master gesture: a distinctive action that is repeated and serves as a clue to a character's personality, such as a peculiar laugh or walk

matte: flat or dull makeup that is achieved by powdering

melodrama: originally considered serious plays, now usually plays based on romantic plots that have little regard for convincing motivation or detailed characterization and that have the primary goal of keeping an audience involved using any means

melody: main musical phrase expressing the general feeling of a composition

memorizing: committing the lines of a script to memory

mending plate: a piece of plywood used to strengthen scenery at cracks or joints

microphone: a device that receives sound waves and changes them into electronic impulses thereby amplifying the voice; also called a mike

midrange: type of speaker cone that reproduces sounds occurring in the middle range

milk: to draw the maximum response from the audience through the use of comic lines or action

mime: an offspring of pantomime that conveys abstract ideas; also refers to the person performing a mime

miter joint: a joint used in flat construction that brings together two surfaces by angling the edge of each surface to be joined

mixer: a device that adds outputs to an amplifier

mock heroic: the form of low comedy in which a character who is not of heroic proportions is humorously elevated; also called an epic

modern dance: form of dance that ignores structure in favor of communicating soul and emotion; founded by Isadora Duncan

monodrama: a play written to be performed by a single actor

monologue: a speech by a single actor

monotone: an unvaried speaking tone; lack of inflection throughout a speech

mood: the emotional feeling of a play

moral: the lesson or the principle contained within or taught by a play

Moral Interlude: a short version of a Morality play that usually includes more humorous incidents

Morality play: a play dealing with right and wrong, usually in the form of an allegory

motivated sequence: the natural way in which a person responds to a stimulus—the brain registers, the body responds and then reacts—as mirrored by an actor in an improvisation

motivation: the reason behind a character's behavior

multiple-plane set: a set with several distinct acting areas separated with dividers such as platforms or railings

musical comedy: a form of musical theater; a combination of operetta and musical revue; loosely connected production numbers

musical play: a form of musical theater in which the emphasis is on real people in real situations

musical revue: a production consisting of a series of independent song-and-dance scenes tied loosely together; often satirical

Mystery play: a form of religious drama based on biblical history

N

nasality: the quality of sound produced through nasal passages

naturalism: a style of theater that assumes humans have little self-determination but act in response to forces of nature and society that are out of their control

No: a six-hundred-year-old Japanese form of drama employing standard characters, simple plots, and intricate language; the oldest form of drama to be preserved in its exact form; also called *Noh*

nonverbal communication: communicating without words, using facial expressions, gestures, and body language

O

objective acting: see technical acting

observation: the careful noting of people's emotions, physical characteristics, and voice and diction patterns from which characters are modeled

offbook: rehearsal without scripts

offstage: off the visible stage; also called off

onbook: rehearsal with scripts

onstage: on the visible stage; also called on

open audition: tryout open to nonunion actors

opera: a form of musical theater in which all conversations are sung

operetta: a form of musical theater in which the music is lighter than opera and conversation is spoken

optimum pitch: the ideal highness or lowness of the voice

originality: freshness of acting style

overlap: to move or speak before another actor has finished speaking

overture: the music, usually a medley of the show's songs, played at the beginning of a musical

P

pace: the movement or tempo of the play as it progresses

pageant wagon: a stage on wheels, on which the medieval guilds of the late fourteenth century performed Saint or Mystery plays

pantomime: acting without words

parabolic reflector: an economical lamp with a built-in reflector available in narrow, medium, or wide widths; also called a par

paraphrasing: restating lines in one's own words

parody: a type of low comedy that mocks a certain work by imitating the author's style for comic effect

part-whole memorization: studying cues or lines of script line-by-line until they are committed to memory

Passion Play: a play concerned with the last week in the life of Christ

pathos: an element in drama that arouses feelings of pity and compassion in an audience

pause: a lull or a stop in dialogue or action in order to sustain emotion

Peking Opera: a form of Chinese drama that originated in the nineteenth century

performance art: a type of monodrama that combines many different elements of theater in a novel way

periaktoi: see prisms

permanent set: a set that remains the same throughout a play, regardless of change of locale

personal props: small props that are usually carried in an actor's costume, such as money or a pen

perspective: a head-on view of a set having the illusion of depth

picking up cues: speaking immediately on the last word of the previous speaker for rapid speech; attaching a line to the previous speech with no time interval between

pin connector: a special stage connector used for joining cables or instruments; also called a slip pin connector ➤

pit: the front part of the auditorium where the orchestra might be located—often below stage level

pitch: the relative highness or lowness of the voice

places: the stage command for actors to take their positions at the opening of an act or a scene

plant: a device, such as an idea, a line, or an action, emphasized early in a play; used to create anticipation

plastic: a three-dimensional article or structure that is part of a stage set

play of ideas: a play that deals with a social problem or ethical issue, sometimes presenting a solution

playing the conditions: interpreting characters with the help of the elements of time, place, weather, objects, and the state of the individual

playing the moment: responding to each line, action, and character in the permanent present; for example, an actor who does not open a door before the knock

playing the object: using objects, such as a phone or a fork, to project character

playing the objectives: using all the methods, including physical or mental acts or objects, to reach the goals of characters

playing the obstacles: facing each crisis or obstacle that stands in the way of an objective of the character

plot (noun): the series of related events that take place in a play

plot (verb): to plan stage business, as to plot the action; to plan a speech by working out the phrasing, emphasis, and inflections

pointing lines: emphasizing a particular idea through the presentation of lines

polishing rehearsal: the final rehearsal at which all parts of the play are brought together so that flaws can be worked out

portable striplight: a light used for sidelighting, backing, entrance lighting, or cyclorama lighting requiring three circuits

portal: a drop that has its lower middle section removed so that it will mask only the top and sides of the stage; may be built with flats

practical: a term applied to props that are not only decorative but also functional, such as lamps that can be turned on

preliminary situation: a clearly defined explanation of the events in the lives of the leading characters before the start of a play's action

prepared audition: a tryout in which the actor uses material that has been memorized and thoroughly worked out

presentational: a play in which the audience is recognized as an audience and the play as a play; consequently, the actors may speak directly to the audience

preset dimmer: a type of dimmer board that allows two or more lighting patterns to be set in advance

primary source: an individual whose posture, movements, habits, voice inflections, and mannerisms are observed in order to build character

principals: the main characters in a play or the named characters in a musical play

prisms: sets made up of three six-foot flats or two four-foot flats and one six-foot flat, shaped as equilateral or isosceles triangles mounted on a wheeled carriage that can be pivoted; also called *periaktoi*

producer: the person who finds the financial investors, hires the director and production staff, sets the budget, and pays the bills for a theatrical production

production number: a large-scale musical sequence involving many performers in lavish costumes; frequently a dance number

profile: two-dimensional pieces of scenery used to represent three-dimensional objects such as rocks or bushes; also called a cut-out ▼

profile set: like the box set, forms the entire perimeter of the setting; can be constructed of screens; also called a cut-down set or minimum set

PROFILE

projection: the control of the volume and quality of the voice so that it can be heard clearly by everyone in an audience

promptbook: a script marked with directions and cues for use by the prompter

prompter: the person who keeps the director's promptbook and makes notes on cues, signals, and so on

pronunciation: the manner of saying words using the correct sounds and placing the accents on the stressed syllables

prop crew: stagehands who check properties in and out as they are set or struck

properties: all the stage furnishings, including furniture and those things brought onstage by the actors; also called props

properties assistant: assistant to the properties chief

properties chief: the person who is in charge of acquiring the props, storing them, arranging them on the set, preparing the prop table, and giving the actors the props they need

proportion: a principle of stage design that uses the human being as the unit of measurement

proportional dimming: a feature of some older lightboards; allows several instruments to dim simultaneously at different intensities

proscenium arch: the arch opening between the stage and the auditorium

prosthetics: molded latex pieces of eyelids, cheeks, noses, and other features that are attached to the skin with additional latex

protagonist: the main character in a play

protection: a situation in which the audience laughs because it knows violent actions are not realistic; for example, a character in a cartoon who falls off a cliff and reappears in the next frame without a scratch

psychological drama: a play that addresses the complexities of the human psyche and personal relationships

publicity manager: the person who handles the advertising and promotion of a play in the press, on the radio, and in other media

puppet theater: a type of theater in which the actors operate puppets

Q

quadrants: the four sections into which an arena stage might be divided

quality: the individual sound of a particular voice

R

rag rolling: a method of texturing by using a rag or rolled-up piece of burlap that is dipped in paint and rolled on flats to give the painted flat the appearance of rough plaster

rail: the horizontal element in flat construction

rake: to slant or set at an angle; a raked stage inclines from the area closest to the audience upward to the rear of the stage.

ramp: a sloping platform connecting the stage floor to a higher level

rate: the speed at which words are spoken

ratings: the process used to measure the success of commercial television in which television networks rely on outside firms to assess the size of the viewing audience

readers theater: form of theater in which plays are read to an audience from a script and brought to life by the readers' voices, facial expressions, and controlled movements

reading rehearsal: a rehearsal at which the play is read by the director or by members of the cast

realism: a style of theater that presents life as it actually is

receipts: the money earned from ticket sales of a movie or a play

recitative: a singing style that is closer to speaking than to melodic singing

recognition: in tragedy, a scene in which the protagonist either achieves an inner awareness as a result of great personal suffering or identifies a lost loved one or friend; the discovery of hidden or obscure meanings

regional theaters: theaters that present any type of play for as long as they wish, repeating plays when and if it is profitable to do so

relief: an easing of pressure that results in laughter

rendering: the initial pencil sketch or watercolor for a stage setting

repertoire: the parts or songs an actor knows; all the plays a theater group has produced

repertory theaters: theaters that, at regular intervals, present plays that are familiar to actors

representational: a play performed as if the audience is watching the action through an imaginary fourth wall

resonance: the vibrant tone produced when sound waves strike the chambers of the throat, head, nose, and mouth

résumé: a short account of a person's career and qualifications prepared by the applicant for a position; In the theater, an 8" x 10" headshot photograph is part of the résumé.

reversal: an ironic twist in a tragedy in which an action produces an effect opposite to what at first would seem likely; when the "tables are turned"

reversible: a costume that is double-faced so that by reversing it the illusion of a different costume is created

reviews: type of criticism with the primary function of recommending or not recommending a movie or television program to an audience

rhythm: the overall blending of all the elements of a production with particular stress on tempo, action, and dialogue

right (R) and left (L): terms used to refer to the stage from the actor's point of view, not that of the audience

ringing: a frequent problem that occurs with the projection of sound, usually caused by the microphone volume being too high

ring up: to raise the curtain

rising action: the series of events following the initial incident in a play

rising inflection: the use of the voice to indicate questioning, surprise, or shock

role scoring: the process of analyzing a character

romantic comedy: a play that presents an idealized love affair; written in the style of romanticism

romanticism: eighteenth-century literary and artistic movement that focused on emotions and ideals

rotation: turning or pivoting a body part in smooth circles

roundel: a transparent color medium placed on striplights to produce different colors

running gag: device of comic anticipation that requires three exposures to provoke laughter: the plant, the establisher, and the clincher

S

Saint play: a religious play based on the lives and legends of saints

satire: a style of comedy that presents humorous attacks on accepted conventions of society, holding up human vices and follies to ridicule

saturation: the brightness or dullness of a color

scenarios: plot outlines for the commedia dell'arte

scenery hut: in an Elizabethan playhouse, what appeared to be a small house above the Heavens; housed the machinery that lowered and raised actors to and from the stage, often implying these actors were ghosts or supernatural creatures

scene-stealing: calling attention to one's presence onstage and diverting attention away from the main actors

scenic artist: a person who designs settings, costumes, makeup, and lighting; also called a designer

schmaltz: extreme sentimentality

schwa (ə): a pronunciation symbol with the sound of "uh," as in about; often the vowel sound in an unstressed syllable

score: the music of a show as composed

screen scenes: farcical scenes in which some of the actors hide from the other actors onstage yet are still able to hear and comment on the onstage dialogue

screens: two-fold and three-fold flats used either as walls against a drapery background or to cover openings or furnishings when changing scenes

scrim: a drop made of fabric that seems almost opaque when lit from the front and semitransparent when lit from behind; also called a gauze

script: the written text of a play

script scoring: the marking of a script for one character, indicating interpretation, pauses, phrasing, stress, and so on; also called scripting

scumble: to use two or more brushes and two or more tones of a base color to make an uneven base coat of paint on a flat

secondary sources: books that help in developing characterization

segue: a music term that means the music continues on to the next number without stopping

sentimental comedy: eighteenth-century genre that was a reaction to the immorality in Restoration drama; presents life as ideal

set: the scenery for an act or a scene

set dressers: stagehands responsible for setting and striking the finishing touches on a set

set pieces: scenery, such as trees, rocks, and walls, that can be carried or rolled onto the stage and that stand by themselves

set props: properties placed onstage for the use of actors

shades: dark or deep colors

shadowing: the term used for applying makeup to bring out, to change, or to correct facial features

shape: an artistic value that influences both mass and the psychological reaction to objects onstage by using geometric forms or free-forms; for example, a circle to symbolize the infinite

share a scene: situation in which two actors stand or sit parallel to each other

showmanship: a sense of theater and the ability to present oneself effectively to an audience; stage charisma

shutters: movable flats on tracks used for quick scene changes

sidekick: a secondary male lead, often a comic role and a friend to the lead; counterpart to the soubrette

sidelighting: the placing of lighting instruments behind the tormentor position for facial modeling and costume accent

sides: booklets containing half sheets of paper on which the cues and lines for one character are written

sight line: a line for the side walls and elevation of the set established by taking a sighting from the front corner seats and upper balcony seats

silicon-controlled rectifier (SCR): an electrical device that controls power flow; used in most modern dimmers

situation: a problem or challenge a character or characters must face

situation-centered approach: an approach to telling a story that takes a single situation or a series of situations and puts characters in them to show how different personalities respond to the same event

size: a glue-water mixture that seals the pores in the muslin that covers a flat

skeleton set: a set consisting of frames and openings; usually used on an open stage

sky cyc: a smooth cloth hung at the back and sides of the stage and painted to give the illusion of the sky

Socialist Realism: constructivism

soliloquy: a speech delivered by an actor alone onstage that reveals the character's innermost thoughts

soubrette: a secondary female lead, often a comic role and a friend to the lead; counterpart to the sidekick

sound cue sheet: a chart that includes each sound effect, its cue number, the script page number, the name of the effect, the volume level, and the length in seconds of the effect

sound-effects board: sometimes called a bell board, consists of several appliances—a doorbell, a door chime, a buzzer, an old fashioned phone bell, and an electronic phone-tone maker—attached to a piece of plywood

sound plot: plot showing the pieces of equipment and their settings for each sound in the show

spattering: a method of texturing in which paint is scattered onto a flat in droplets

speakers: cone-shaped devices driven by electromagnets that convert electrical impulses into sound

splash: light that strikes outside the intended area, as on the grand drape, the proscenium, or the upper walls; also called spill

spoof: a farcical literary work that pokes fun at certain subjects or time periods

spotlight: a metal-encased lighting instrument that can be focused, having a lens and a mirror that give out a concentrated light that can be directed specifically; used to light acting areas; also called a spot

stage business: the part of acting that involves the use of hand props, costume props, stage props, other actors, and parts of the set (doors, windows, lighting fixtures)

stage directions: notes in the script of a play indicating stage business and blocking, including directions right (R), left (L), downstage (D), upstage (U), center (C), and combinations of these

stage fright: the nervous anticipation some actors feel before going onstage to perform

stage manager: the person who is completely in charge backstage during the rehearsals and performances

stagecraft: techniques and devices of the theater

stealing a scene: attracting attention from the person to whom the center of interest legitimately belongs

stile: a vertical part of a panel or frame

stippling: a method of texturing using a sponge, a crumpled rag, or the tips of a dry brush, leaving clusters of paint drops

stock character: common in commedia dell'arte, a character who displays the same character traits in many different productions; for example, the maiden, the flirt, the braggart soldier, and so on

stop cleat: a piece of metal or wood attached to the back or corner of a flat to keep an adjacent flat flush

storage plot: a diagram showing how scenic units are to be stored in the wing areas during a show

storyboard: the depiction of the script in comic-book form to help the filmmaker visualize the screenplay; was first developed by Webb Smith of the Walt Disney Studio

story idea: first stage in writing for film and television, usually expressed in a sentence or two

straight part: a role in which the actor and the character portrayed are similar in appearance and personality

stretching a character: making a role unique, individual, and interesting

strike: to remove an object or objects from the stage; to take down the set

striplights: lamps arranged in metal troughs, usually with three or four circuits; also called strips ➤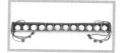

study: in the Elizabethan playhouse, a curtained recess in the center rear of the stage, also known as the inner below

style: the way in which a play is written, acted, and produced

subjective acting: see emotional acting

substitution: the use by an actor of a personal experience to relate to the experience of a character within a play

subtext: the meaning "between the lines" that an actor must draw from the script

supporting roles: those characters who act as contrasts to others; characters with whom other characters, usually the protagonist, are compared

sustained inflection: the use of the voice to suggest calmness, decisiveness, or steadiness of purpose by staying on the same note

swatch: a fabric sample

switchboard: the panel that holds the dimmers, switches, and breakers; ideally, all stage circuits are united in this one board so they can be controlled at one location. A portable switchboard is often the most satisfactory type for a school theater.

symbolism: the use of characters, props, and sets to exemplify ideas; for example, a bluebird may symbolize happiness; a late nineteenth-century artistic movement that began as a reaction against realism

synthesis: a combination of elements to form a whole

T

tab: a narrow drop

tableau: a scene presented by silent, unmoving actors showing the results of a violent act; used in Greek theater, which prohibited violence

tag line: a final line in a play, especially one that serves to clarify a point or to create a dramatic effect

taking oneself out of a scene: the actor's turning away from the audience into a three-quarter-back or full-back position

taking the stage: using the entire stage, usually during a lengthy speech

tarras: in the Elizabethan playhouse, a shallow balcony in the center of the second-level acting area

teaser: a curtain or a set of flats hung just upstage of the act curtain, used to adjust the height of the stage opening ➤

technical acting: use of learned skills of acting, movement, speech, and interpretation to create roles; no emotional response is used; also called objective acting

technical director: a person who executes the designs of the scenic artist with the help of a crew

technical rehearsal: rehearsal at which lighting, scenery, and props are used so that changes go smoothly

tempo: the speed at which the action of a play moves along

textual tryout: a tryout in which an actor uses material from a manuscript or a printed play; may be a monologue or a scene

theater: a building used for the presentation of plays

theater of involvement: theater in which members of the audience participate in the action of the play

theater of the absurd: a form of theater based on the assumption that human hopes and plans are ridiculous; employs unconventional language

theatricalism: a style of theater that does not try to imitate reality and presents drama as drama, not real life

theme: the basic idea of a play

thespian: an actor; relating to the theater

three-camera system: system used in most television shows in which the multiple use of cameras allows the director to switch from close-ups to wide-angle shots and to get various camera angles on the same actor during one take

throw: the distance from a lighting instrument to the area to be lit

thrust stage: a low platform stage that projects into the audience

timing: the execution of a line or a piece of business at a specific moment to achieve the most telling effect

tints: light or pastel colors

tiring house: in the Elizabethan playhouse, a room that functioned as the actors' dressing room

toggle rail: a rail placed across the back of a flat for strength

top: to make a line stronger than the line or lines preceding it by speaking at a higher pitch, at a faster rate, or with greater volume and emphasis

tormentors: side pieces, such as flats or drapes, placed just upstage of the proscenium to narrow the opening

total theater: theater in which all the performing arts are fused into one presentation

tower: a platform on which lights can be hung

tragedy: a play in which the protagonist fails to achieve desired goals or is overcome by opposing forces

traveler: a stage curtain upstage of the act curtain that opens to the right and left rather than moving up and down

treatment: the second stage in writing for film and television which involves telling the story in narrative form without the use of dialogue

trilogy: a set of three related plays

trip: to double a drop for raising when there is insufficient fly space

troubadours: strolling musicians that set poems to popular melodies during the Gothic era

tungsten-halogen (T-H): a type of lamp that is more efficient than incandescent bulbs; now used in spotlights, floodlights, and follow spots

turning the scene in: focusing audience attention on the actor who is the real center of the dramatic action by having the other actors shift their bodies and look at this key character

tweeters: type of speaker cone that reproduces high-pitched sounds

twist: an unexpected event or outcome in a plot

twist lock connector: a type of electrical stage connector that will not pull apart when inserted and twisted ➤

typecasting: identifying and casting an actor in the same kind of role over and over

U

underscore: music played to accompany dialogue

understudy: a person who learns a role and who can perform it in the absence of the actor

uniqueness: an actor's ability to shape a character's personality without making it a copy of someone else's portrayal

unit set: a basic stage setting from which several settings can be created

unity: a situation in which all elements of the set form a perfect whole, centering on the main idea of the play

unnatural: machinelike or puppetlike

unnatural sounds: sounds, such as undulating pitches, that soar up and down like a slide trombone, drawing laughter from an audience

upstage: the area of the stage away from the audience toward the rear of the stage; also called up

upstaging: improperly taking attention from an actor who should be the focus of interest

V

value: the lightness or darkness of a color

vamp: to repeat music until a singer or scene is ready to begin

Velcro™:   strips of material that adhere to each other when pressure is applied

versatility: the ability to change style or character with ease

villain: a character who functions as the antagonist in a play

voiced: referring to consonants, such as *b, d,* and *v,* that cause vibration of the vocal folds when sounded

voiceless: referring to consonants, such as *p, t,* and *f,* that do not cause vibration of the vocal folds when sounded

volume: the strength, force, or intensity with which sound is made

W

wagon sets: sets placed on a wheeled platform that can be rolled onto the stage

walk-on: a small acting part without spoken lines

wardrobe manager: the person responsible for creating the costume plot and for caring for costumes during rehearsals and performances

warn cue: notification of an upcoming action; usually an indication in the promptbook that such things as an entrance, a lighting change, or a sound effect will soon take place

wash: a low-level fill light, usually aimed from the balcony rails

wash out: the drain (absorption) of color by light that leaves the actor, costume, or scenery lifeless in appearance

wattage: the measurement of electric power; all lighting instruments, lamps, dimmers, and fuses are given wattage ratings to identify their electrical capacities.

whodunit: a crime-solving or courtroom drama

whole-part memorization: the committing to memory of individual lines of a script after whole units of the play have been read several times

wing setting: a set made with pairs of wings on both sides of the stage, used with a matching backdrop

wings: the offstage areas to the right and left of the set; also one or more flats, usually hinged at an angle but sometimes parallel to the curtain line, used as entrances but concealing backstage areas

woofers: type of speaker cone that reproduces low-pitched sounds

working backwards: a technique in which an actor prepares the audience for what a character will do later

working drawing: a detailed drawing showing how a piece of scenery is to be constructed

working rehearsal: a rehearsal at which interpretation of the play is developed and words and actions are put together

Z

zoom: style of camera shot, using a zoom lens to shoot the subject from a distance that makes the subject appear to be very close; first used by famous director D. W. Griffith

S

Acknowledgments

Grateful acknowledgment is given playwrights, publishers, and agents for permission to reprint the copyrighted material in this book. Every effort has been made to determine and contact copyright owners. In the case of any omissions, the Publisher will be pleased to make suitable acknowledgments in future editions.

Georges Borchardt, Inc. for the excerpt from *Man with Bags* by Eugene Ionesco. Copyright © 1975 by Editions Gallimard. Reprinted by permission of Georges Borchardt, Inc.

Matthew Calhoun for the excerpt from *The Breakfast Special* by Matthew Calhoun. Reprinted by permission of the author.

Brian Clark for the excerpt from *Whose Life Is It Anyway?* by Brian Clark. Copyright © 1978 by Brian Clark. First published in the United Kingdom by Amber Lane Press in 1978. First published in the United States of America in 1979 by Dodd Mead & Company.

Creative Artists for the excerpt from *A Few Good Men* by Aaron Sorkin. Copyright © 1990.

Dramatists Play Service, Inc. for the following: excerpts from *Wine in the Wilderness*[1] by Alice Childress. Copyright © 1969, by Alice Childress. Excerpt from *Harvey*[2] by Mary Chase. Copyright © 1943, by Mary Chase (under the title *The White Rabbit.*) Copyright renewed, 1970, by Mary Chase. Copyright © 1944, by Mary Chase. (under the title *Harvey*). Copyright renewed, 1971, by Mary Chase. Excerpts from *The Dining Room*[3] by A. R. Gurney Jr. Copyright © 1982, by A. R. Gurney Jr. Coypright © 1981 as an unpublished dramatic composition. Excerpt from *How I Got That Story*[4] by Amlin Gray. Copyright © 1981, by Amlin Gray. Copyright © 1979, as an unpublished dramatic composition. All excerpts reprinted by permission of the authors and Dramatists Play Service, Inc.

Ernest Ferlita for the excerpt from *The Mask of Hiroshima* by Ernest Ferlita. Copyright © 1966 by Ernest Ferlita. Reprinted by permission of the author.

Samuel French, Inc. for the following: excerpt from *Butterflies Are Free*[5] by Leonard Gershe. Copyright © 1969 by Leonard Gershe. Excerpt from *Green Grow the Lilacs*[5] by Lynn Riggs. Copyright © 1930 by Lynn Riggs. Copyright renewed 1957 by Howard E. Reinheimer. Copyright © 1931 by Lynn Riggs. Copyright renewed 1958 by Howard E. Reinheimer. Excerpt from *Haiku*[5] by Katherine Snodgrass. Copyright © 1988, 1989 by Katherine Snodgrass. Excerpts from *I Love You, I Love You Not* by Wendy Kesselman. Copyright © 1988 by Wendy Kesselman. Excerpt from *Prologue to Glory* by E. P. Conkle. Copyright © 1936, 1938 by E. P. Conkle. Copyright renewed 1963, 1966 by E. P. Conkle. All excerpts reprinted by permission of Samuel French, Inc.

Graham Agency for the excerpt from *On Golden Pond* by Ernest Thompson. Copyright © 1979.

Harcourt Brace & Company for the excerpt from *I Remember Mama—A Play in Two Acts* by John van Druten. Copyright © 1945 by John van Druten and renewed 1972 by Carter Lodge. Reprinted by permission of Harcourt Brace & Company.

Henry Holt and Company, Inc. for the excerpt from *Cyrano de Bergerac* by Edmond Rostand, translated by Brian Hooker. Copyright © 1923, 1937 by Henry Holt and Company, Inc. Copyright renewed 1951 by Doris C. Hooker.

Cover Michael Shay/FPG; **xi** Martha Swope/Time, Inc.; **xiv** F. Darmigny/Sygma; **6** Aaron Haupt; **8** Martha Swope/Time, Inc.; **9** Joseph Schuyler/Stock Boston; **11** J.P. Laffont/Sygma; **12** P. Guerrini/Gamma Liaison; **15** Ted Rice; **17** Gamma Liaison; **18** Jerome Lawrence & Robert E. Lee Theatre Research Institute, The Ohio State University; **22** Richard Hackett; **24** F. Darmigny/Sygma; **26** Jack Vartoogian; **29** Aaron Haupt; **32** (tl tr)Jerome Lawrence & Robert E. Lee Theatre Research Institute, The Ohio State University, (c)Joan Marcus, (bl)Martha Swope, Time,Inc., (br)Corky Lee; **33** B. Willougby/Sygma; **35** Carol Rosegg; **38** Martha Swope; **39** Daniel Simon/Gamma Liaison; **40** Jerome Lawrence & Robert E. Lee Theatre Research Institute, The Ohio State University; **42** UPI/Corbis-Bettmann; **45** D. Fineman/Sygma; **47** Martha Swope; **48** Lauren Kurki/Ann Mantel/Clark University; **53** R. Knowles/Gamma Liaison; **57** Martha Swope; **58** Christian Altorfer; **60** Martha Swope/Time, Inc.; **62** Stuart Davis/Gamma Liaison; **64** Frank Siteman/The Picture Cube; **66** Aaron Haupt; **68** Martha Swope/Time, Inc.; **69** Aaron Haupt; **70** Bob Daemmrich/Stock Boston; **73** Jerome Lawrence & Robert E. Lee Theatre Research Institute, The Ohio State University; **74** Aaron Haupt; **76, 77, 79, 81** Martha Swope/Time, Inc.; **89** Doug Martin; **94** Mark Burnett; **96, 98** Martha Swope/Time, Inc.; **100** Charlie Erickson; **102** TASS/Sovfoto; **103** Aaron Haupt; **104** Martha Swope/Time, Inc.; **106** Joseph Schuyler/Stock Boston; **108** Jerome Lawrence & Robert E. Lee Theatre Research Institute, The Ohio State University; **110, 113, 114** Martha Swope/Time, Inc.; **115** Corky Lee; **118** Martha Swope/Time, Inc.; **120** Joseph Schuyler/Stock Boston; **122** Martha Swope/Time, Inc.; **123** Blair Seitz/Photo Researchers; **126** Martha Swope/Time, Inc.;**129** Pamela Price/The Picture Cube; **131** Doug Martin; **132, 135, 137, 138** Martha Swope/Time, Inc.;

139 Jerome Lawrence & Robert E. Lee Theatre Research Institute, The Ohio State University; **141** Martha Swope/Time, Inc.; **144** Joan Marcus; **145, 147** Martha Swope; **151** Aaron Haupt; **153, 155** Martha Swope/Time, Inc.; **156** Joan Marcus; **159** (t)Richard Feldman/American Repertory Theatre, (b)P. Guerrini/Gamma Liaison; **161** Jerome Lawrence & Robert E. Lee Theatre Research Institute, The Ohio State University; **248** Clive Barda/Performing Arts Library; **250** Joseph Schuyler/Stock Boston; **251** Martha Swope/Time, Inc.; **252** Jennifer W. Lester; **256** Martha Swope/Time, Inc.; **259** Jennifer W. Lester; **261** Martha Swope/Time, Inc.; **262** Joan Marcus; **263** MAK-I; **264** Martha Swope/Time, Inc.; **265** Carol Rosegg; **266** Bill Miles/The Stock Market; **268** Uniphoto; **271, 273** Martha Swope/Time, Inc.; **276** Ted Rice; **277** Joan Marcus; **278, 280** Martha Swope/Time, Inc.; **283** Martha Swope/Time, Inc.; **285** William Macy/Sygma; **287** Sygma; **289** Joan Marcus/Marc Bryan Brown; **291, 292, 294** Martha Swope/Time, Inc.; **296** Erich Lessing/Art Resource, NY; **299** Art Resource, NY; **300** Martha Swope/Time, Inc.; **303** Uli Weyland/Gamma Liaison; **305** Clive Barda/Performing Arts Library; **306** The Bridgeman Art Library; **308** Mander & Mitchenson; **311** National Portrait Gallery, London; **316** Mary Evans Picture Library; **318** Yoram Kahana/Shooting Star; **320** Paola Koch/Photo Researchers; **322** Joan Marcus; **323** Jerome Lawrence & Robert E. Lee Theatre Research Institute, The Ohio State University; **324** Corky Lee; **326** Scott Cunningham; **329** Henson Productions/J. Barrett/The Kobal Collection; **331** Charlie Westerman/Gamma Liaison; **332** Brian Smith/Gamma Liaison; **335** Martha Swope/Time, Inc.; **337** Bill Bachmann/Stock Boston; **338** (t)Cathlyn Mellon/Tony Stone Images, (b)Jeff Greenberg/The Picture Cube; **340** MAK-I; **343** Doug Martin;

346 Novosti-R.I.A./Gamma Liaison; 349 Martha Swope; 354 Doug Martin; 357 Sygma; 359 Blair Seitz/Photo Researchers; 361 Liamute E. Druskis; 363 Martha Swope/Time, Inc.; 365 369 Martha Swope/Time, Inc.; 371 Reuters NewMedia Inc./Corbis; 372 Matt Meadows; 374 Plymouth Theater; 377, 378 Martha Swope/Time, Inc.; 379 Joan Marcus; 381 W & D McIntyre/Photo Researchers; 385 Martha Swope/Time, Inc.; 387 Joan Marcus; 389 Martha Swope/Time, Inc.; 391 Joan Marcus; 392 Tim Courlas; 396 Morgan-Spooner/Gamma Liaison; 399, 400, 402 Martha Swope/Time, Inc.; 403 Joe Viesti/Viesti Associates; 405 Martha Swope/Time, Inc.; 406 Jerome Lawrence & Robert E. Lee Theatre Research Institute, The Ohio State University; 415 Martha Swope/Time, Inc.; 416 Joan Marcus; 419 Robert Capese/McGraw-Hill; 420, 421 Jerome Lawrence & Robert E. Lee Theatre Research Institute, The Ohio State University; 423 Bob Daemmrich/Stock Boston; 428 Novosti-R.I.A./Gamma Liaison; 432 Gamma Liaison; 442 Joan Marcus; 443 Corky Lee; 444 Novosti-R.I.A./Gamma Liaisom; 446 Jerome Lawrence & Robert E. Lee Theatre Research Institute, The Ohio State University; 448 Coleman Photography; 450, 451 Aaron Haupt; 453 Martha Swope; 456 Jerome Lawrence & Robert E. Lee Theatre Research Institute, The Ohio State University; 458, 459 Martha Swope/Time, Inc.; 462 Pozarik/Gamma Liaison; 464 Lauren Kurki; 466 Charlie Westerman/Gamma Liaison; 467 Larry Hamill; 476 Martha Swope/Time, Inc.; 477, 479 Aaron Haupt; 480 Matt Meadows; 481 Aaron Haupt; 482, 483, 484, 485, 486 Matt Meadows; 487 (t)Matt Meadows, (b) Aaron Haupt; 488 Aaron Haupt; 489 Gamma Liaison; 490 Martha Swope; 492 Cary Wolinsky/Stock Boston; 494, 498, 500 Martha Swope/Time, Inc.; 502 Raymond Piat/Gamma-Liaison; 504, 507 Douglas Kirkland/Sygma; 508 Ted Rice; 510 Martha Swope, Time, Inc.; 518 Martha Swope/Time, Inc.; 521 Carol Rosegg; 522 Spencer Grant/The Picture Cube; 523, 524 Martha Swope/Time, Inc.; 525 Richard Corson; 526 Gamma Liaison; 528 Martha Swope/Time, Inc.; 544 The Everett Collection; 545 The Everett Collection; 547 Walt Disney Collection/The Everett Collection; 551 MPTV; 552 The Kobal Collection; 553 PhotoFest; 555 The Everett Collection; 556 Lucasfilm, Ltd.; 558 Photofest; 559, 560 The Kobal Collection; 562 Photofest; 564 Everett Collection; 565 Mark Steinmetz; 567 Larry Hamill; 568 MPTV; 570 Photofest; 573 Erich Lessing/Art Resources; 575 Corbis Bettmann; 577 Photofest; 578 Centre Georges Pompidou/Art Resources, NY; 579 Museo del Prado, Madrid, Spain/Giraudon, Paris/SuperStock; 573 Erich Lessing/Art Resources; 574 Corbis/Bettmann; 578 Everett Collection; 580 "Ur Curtain", drawing for Ubu Roi, 1966 crayon, pencil on paper 15 X 20; 581 Everett Collection; 582 PhotoFest; 585 Tim Courlas; 586 Everett Collection; 532 through 542 Aaron Haupt.